Teaching the Trivium

Christian Homeschooling in a Classical Style

Also by Harvey Bluedorn:

Books

A Greek Alphabetarion, 1993
Handy English Encoder & Decoder, 1994
Vocabulary Bridges from English to Latin & Greek, 1994
Homeschool Greek, A Thorough Self-teaching Grammar of Biblical Greek, 1996
The Covenantal Allegory, A Study of the Covenant Promises Made to Abraham, 1997

Pamphlets

The Biblical Evidence for House Assemblies, 1993
Observations on the Order of the Assembly, 1994
An Acceptable Sacrifice of Praise, 1995
Woman's Role in the Gathered Assembly, 1995
On Family Worship, 1997
The Sabbath Syllogism, 1998
The Logical Defense of the Faith, 1998

Teaching the Trivium

Christian Homeschooling in a Classical Style

For the Lord giveth wisdom:
out of His mouth cometh knowledge
and understanding.
— Proverbs 2:6.

by Harvey & Laurie Bluedorn

May 2001
TRIVIUM PURSUIT

Teaching The Trivium
by Harvey & Laurie Bluedorn

Library of Congress Control Number: 2001117112

Trivium Pursuit
PMB 168, 139 Colorado Street
Muscatine, Iowa 52761
309-537-3641
www.triviumpursuit.com

"Thou shalt not muzzle the ox that treadeth out the corn. And, The labourer *is* worthy of his reward." — First Timothy 5:18 (First Corinthians 9:9; Deuteronomy 25:4; and Luke 10:7; Matthew 10:10; Deuteronomy 24:15)

"Therefore, behold, I *am* against the prophets, saith the LORD, that steal my words every one from his neighbour." —Jeremiah 23:30

". . . Thou shalt not steal, . . . Thou shalt love thy neighbour as thyself." — Romans 13:9 (Matthew 19:18; Mark 10:19; Luke 18:20; First Corinthians 6:8,10; Ephesians 4:28; Exodus 20:15; Leviticus 19:11,13; Deuteronomy 5:19 and Leviticus 19:18; Matthew 5:43; 7:12; 19:19; 22:39; Mark 12:31; Luke 10:27; Galatians 5:14; James 2:8)

"Render therefore to all their dues: . . . honour to whom honour." — Romans 13:7

"That no *man* go beyond and defraud his brother in *any* matter: because that the Lord *is* the avenger of all such, as we also have forewarned you and testified." — First Thessalonians 4:6 (Leviticus 19:13; Deuteronomy 32:35; Proverbs 22:22,23)

Biblical quotations are either from the King James Version, common 1769 edition of Dr. Benjamin Blayney, or else they are our own very literal translation, abbreviated v.l.t.. Occasional corrections of the KJV are enclosed in brackets. Alternate translations follow a forward slash [/abc], more literal translations follow a backward slash [\xyz].

Authors' Preface

When we were married in 1973, the term "Homeschooling" had not been coined. Nevertheless, the Lord impressed upon our consciences at that time the commitment to homeschool what children He might give us. The Lord blessed us with our first child in 1975. In 1980, we taught him how to read, and we have since homeschooled all five children with whom the Lord has blessed us.

In 1989, we were asked by an Iowa Homeschool convention to give a seminar on teaching Latin, Greek, and Logic. We have now given seminars in forty-four states. We would never have chosen this role for ourselves. Others have called us to it.

In 1993, we began a small magazine, called *Teaching the Trivium*, which forced us to write down some of what we had learned – and were learning. After much and varied experience in homeschooling, in applying a classical model and method for education, in speaking, and in writing, we concluded that it was finally an appropriate time for us to put together in an orderly manner those things about which we had learned. In the spring of 2000, we published a series of eight booklets called, *The Teaching the Trivium Booklet Series*. Within the Lord's providence, we have now transformed and expanded those booklets into a complete book.

We have subjected all of what we have written to criticism. Parts of this book have gone through twelve years of correction. We invite your further criticism for the improvement of any subsequent editions. We ask the Lord to make use of our labors, despite their faults.

In this book, we lay down a spiritual and philosophical foundation and a practical program for Christian Homeschooling in a classical style. We can't fill in all of the details to satisfy every situation. Instead, we give our principles and suggestions, and we guide you to other sources. Our emphasis is communicating the picture and encouraging the practice. May it please the Lord to use this work to further His kingdom.

The book design and typography was by Nathaniel Bluedorn. The scene in oils on the cover and the chapter title illustrations are by Johannah Bluedorn. The illustrations at the end of Chapter One are by Helena Bluedorn. This book would never have been completed without the help of all our children.

Harvey & Laurie Bluedorn
April, 2001

Contents

Chapter Six 149

Teaching Logic

Chapter Seven 175

Teaching Rhetoric

Chapter Eleven 301

The Early Knowledge Level: Ten Things to Do Before Age Ten

Chapter Twelve 343

The Later Knowledge Level: Ten Things to Do With Children Ages Ten Through Twelve

Chapter Thirteen 393

The Understanding Level:
Ten Things to Do With Children Ages Thirteen Through Fifteen

Chapter Fourteen 413

The Wisdom Level:
Ten Things to Do With Children Ages Sixteen Through Eighteen

Part One

Chapter One

The Transformation of Classical Education: A Biblical Vision for Homeschooling

And be not conformed to this world:
but be ye transformed by the renewing of your mind,
that ye may prove what *is* that good, and acceptable, and perfect, will of God.
— Romans 12:2

BREAKING OUT OF THE MOLD

Have you ever experienced the frustration of trying to make things fit – but they just won't go together? Something is the wrong shape, or size, or color, so the pieces just won't match. That's just what we've found with trying to fit Homeschooling into a classroom mold, and trying to match traditional classical education with Biblical Christianity. Things just don't go together. Something must be changed. This book is an attempt to make that change.

Our Lord speaks a parable which addresses these very issues. He begins with a story about old garments and new patches.

> And he spake also a parable unto them; No man putteth a piece of a new garment upon an old; if otherwise, then both the new maketh a rent, and the piece that was *taken* out of the new agreeth not with the old. — Luke 5:36

The shrinkage rate is different for various fabrics and between new unwashed cloth and old pre-washed cloth. From these observations, we derive the principle that we cannot just try to patch together two things of dissimilar fabrics or natures. If we do, then things may look fine at first, but when the patched garment comes out of the wash, we will see that the problem has actually become worse. The old garment is more torn than before, and the new patch doesn't match. Of course, our Lord was talking about how the things of the Gospel could not be patched onto the things of the Law, but this principle applies to other things as well. What this parable describes is precisely what we found when we tried to homeschool by a classroom model. Things fell apart in the wash. Chapters Two and Three will cover some of the reasons why the two just won't fit together.

Our Lord continues His parable with a story about new wine and old wineskins.

> And no man putteth new wine into old bottles [/wineskins]; else the new wine will burst the bottles [/wineskins], and be spilled, and the bottles shall perish. But new wine must be put into new bottles [/wineskins]; and both are preserved. — Luke 5:37,38

When fresh wine is stored in fresh wineskins, the wineskins bulge and stretch. But once the wineskins have been stretched, their stretching quality is lost. Filling them with fresh wine only makes them bulge until they break. From these observations, we derive the principle that we must not put new and living spiritual things into old and dead carnal containers which will not stretch. If we try, then we end up losing both the new and the old. But if we put the old aside, and we put the new things in new containers, then both are preserved. Of course, our Lord was talking about how the spiritual things of the New Covenant could not be contained within the administration of the Old Covenant, but the principle fits with other situations as well. We have found that when we tried to fit Biblical Christianity within the old and dead carnal container of classical education and the Greek Academy, that the latter was burst and the former was spilled. Chapters Four through Ten will touch on many of these bursts and spills.

Our Lord concludes His parable with a word about old and new tastes.

> No man also having drunk old *wine* straightway desireth new: for he saith, The old is better. — Luke 5:39

If you're satisfied with one thing, then you're reluctant to change to another. Ain't it the truth! Jesus was, of course, referring to how those who had lived their whole lives under the Law of Moses were reluctant to embrace the Law of Christ. There is something good about this predisposition toward conservatism. It keeps us from making rash changes and it preserves continuity. But when the situation truly demands a change, conservatism becomes a difficult obstacle which must be overcome. The conservatives are actually afraid of the unfamiliar. They'll give you a grocery list for why they shouldn't change. It'll upset things. Yes. It'll require new work. Yes. It'll force us to rethink things. Yes. Then they will require an argument from you for everything. Well, this whole book is an argument. We are attempting to write a different charter for classical education. Let's begin with some definitions.

WHAT IS CLASSICAL EDUCATION?

Classical Humanism

Is "Classical Education" reading Homer and Plato, or Caesar and Cicero? There are some who declare that reading such ancient classical authors is the very essence of any education which could be styled *classical*. But we believe a more accurate name for this would be a "Classical *Humanist* Education." A humanist in the classical sense is one who studies what are called the "humanities," primarily classical Greek and Roman literature.

The Renaissance – the rebirth of learning (1350-1650) – involved a rebirth of the humanist philosophy and culture of ancient Greece and Rome. There was nothing Christian about this ancient philosophy and culture. If we defined *classical* by this humanist standard, then we could not avoid the influence of its philosophy and culture. Indeed, an unbound and unbalanced focus upon classical Greek and Roman literature would drive us in every direction except toward Christ. So, do we want to be identified with Classical Humanist Education?

A Classical Model and Method

We define "Classical Education" more narrowly. We pursue and apply a classical model and a classical method for education – the Trivium. (Chapter Four explains the Trivium model and method.) In other words, we happen to fit into a classical form and frame – a classical style, but we have only incidental interest in the ancient classical materials – the humanist literature. We do not want to learn language and logic and elocution so that we can really read *Homer* and *Virgil*, and really think like *Aristotle* and *Seneca*, and really speak like *Demosthenes* and *Cicero*. We want to learn language, logic, and elocution so that we can really *read*, and *think*, and *speak* – period! We want to acquire these useful tools. But we do not want to use these tools the same way in which the ancient Greeks and Romans used them. They used these tools to serve everything except the true and living God. We want to use these tools to serve nothing but the true and living God.

"Classical" is the term which men apply to this style of education, and we said earlier that we happen to fit into this classical style. We want to make it clear, however, that the reason we happen to fit into this classical Greek and Roman style is because we Christians had it before they did. No, we are not spouting an anachronism. The fact is, they stole our tools and used them for their own pagan purposes. We're just taking back what is rightfully ours. As you follow our argument throughout this book, you will understand what we mean.

Christian Limits to Classical Uses

Because we are Christians, we want to be careful not to pursue non-Christian goals. Non-Christian goals are, in fact, anti-Christian goals. There is no neutral ground lying between Christian and non-Christian – as if both sides could agree to some things. We do not deny that some things appear neutral on the surface – to the lazy-minded, who look no deeper than the surface. There are many things which, if they were somehow considered by themselves, then they could be used in a Christian or in a non-Christian way. But that's just it – they are never by themselves. They are always being used in some way. Anything which fails to confess that Jesus Christ is Lord necessarily denies Him, even if it says nothing – no, especially if it says nothing.

> And every spirit that confesseth not that Jesus Christ is come in the flesh is not of God: and this is that *spirit* of antichrist . . . . — First John 4:3

> For many deceivers are entered into the world, who confess not that Jesus Christ is come in the flesh. This is a deceiver and an antichrist. — Second John 1:7

> He that is not with me is against me; and he that gathereth not with me scattereth abroad. — Matthew 12:30

The non-Christian takes advantage of the Christian by manipulating him into thinking that some things are neutral. Any territory which Christians acknowledge as neutral is territory which has been inattentively conceded to the devil as a playground for him to practice his hidden mischief. We are the rightful owners of this world.

> . . . For all things are yours; Whether . . . the world, or life, or death, or things present, or things to come; all are yours; And ye are Christ's; and Christ *is* God's. — First Corinthians 3:21-23

> He that overcometh shall inherit all things; and I will be his God, and he shall be my son. — Revelation 21:7

Here's the point: we must reclaim territory for our Lord. We need to take it back, clean it up, and return it to its rightful use in service to our Lord. Before we can use anything – including classical authors – we must sift it through the critical screen of the Scriptures. The Scriptures contain all that we need in order to test the usefulness of anything.

What We Mean by "Classical"

We choose to limit our meaning of *classical* to include only *what is of good form and lasting value* (classical), *and which conforms to a Biblical standard within a Biblical worldview* (Christian). We must carefully sift everything which is classical in the *humanist* sense through the critical screen of the Scriptures, and we must give whatever passes that screening a new meaning within the Biblical worldview. So, by *classical*, we do not mean all culture and literature of Ancient and Mediaeval times, or of Renaissance and Reformation times, or even of Colonial and early American times. Our focus is instead upon – out of all of these cultures and times – what is redeemable for Christ. We do not want to baptize these cultures, in whole or in part, and call that "Christian." We want to sort through the rubble and save only what can be brought into conformity to the obedience of Christ and thereby be made useful for His Kingdom. And there are things which can be made useful. We follow a *classical* model and a *classical* method, but we are not bound to follow the ancient *classical* materials. We will be revisiting these same issues throughout this book.

TRANSFORMATION FROM THE INSIDE OUT

This world is not in proper order. Things are out of place. Things are used for wrong purposes. Things are valued for the wrong reasons. It is our job, as Christians, to put things back into their proper order – beginning with our own minds.

> And fashion not yourselves to this age: rather, be transformed by the renewing of your mind, in order for you to test and prove what *is* the will of God: what *is* good, and acceptable, and fully-formed — Romans 12:2 (v.l.t.)

We encounter, from every direction, this pressure to conform ourselves to the age. We are to resist it to the opposite extreme. We are to allow ourselves to be transformed by renovating the structures in our mind, bringing them into conformity to the mind of God as revealed in Scripture. When we arrange our minds by God's standards, we will then see the world differently, and we will be able to discern the will of God for every area of our life – what is good in principle before God's eyes, what is acceptable in value to His tastes, and what is fully-formed in purpose toward His goals.

Once we see things from God's perspective – God's worldview – then we can begin to make sense out of the world and its ways. Then we can discern the disorder and we can put things back where they belong, give them their proper value, and use them for their correct purposes.

All true transformations begin on the inside, and work their way outward. The first transformation is our regeneration, where the inward man is renewed in the image of Christ.

> And be renewed in the spirit of your mind; And that ye put on the new man, which after God is created in righteousness and true holiness. — Ephesians 4:23,24

> And have put on the new *man*, which is renewed in knowledge after the image of him that created him: — Colossians 3:10

The image of God is in truth, holiness, and righteousness. Every man has the image in a formal sense – he is made with a capacity to act in truth, holiness, and righteousness, but the only true way to do these things is toward God. Natural fallen man has lost that polarity which always points toward God. He will point in any direction except toward God. The carnal mind is enmity against God. The direction of his nature is totally twisted or depraved, so that he twists truth, holiness, and righteousness into a thousand other things which miss the mark. Sometimes the fallen man is obviously headed in the opposite direction, but the most dangerous kind of twisting is when it closely resembles the real thing. To be almost true, almost holy, almost righteous is the very worst of all perversions. The well-developed carnal mind is fully-formed in its enmity against God – whether grossly or subtly. We're not talking about the failures of the saints to live up to God's standards. That is a failure of strength, not of direction. They truly seek God – their compass points true north – but their carnal fallen nature points another way and perverts their path (Romans 7:14-25). Our job is to overcome the inner Canaanites of our own carnal fallen nature.

As we are transformed on the inside, we begin to transform things on the outside. First, our own behavior is transformed. Then our immediate environment is brought into order. Then our family. Then our social neighborhood. Then our community. Then the institutions of the community – commerce, church, and civil government. The potential for a true change of our culture lies with those people who renew and transform the family, because the family is God's instrument of choice for transforming a culture. Only through the transformation of the family can a society be restructured to agree with Christian order and the rule of God's law.

The Steps of Transformation

What are the steps of transformation? The Scriptures describe the transformation of men from darkness to light, and we may take this as a model for the transformation of other things from the service of darkness to the service of light.

1. Remove an item from its dark surroundings and expose it to the light of God's truth.
2. Separate the precious from the vile and breathe new life into it – the Spirit of Christ.
3. Set it at liberty by putting it into lawful service within the correct order of things under God.

These three steps are actually principles for redeeming anything for Christ.

The Opinion of Scripture on Classical Greek Education

What do the Scriptures tell us about the classical world's education? Let's gather up a few comments of Paul which may shed light on the subject. Consider Paul's words before the learned tribunal of Athens.

After describing how men in general – and Athenians in particular – had ignored and degraded God and dishonored themselves, Paul summarily dismisses it all with these words:

> And the times of this ignorance God winked at; but now commandeth all men every where to repent: — Acts 17:30

In the minds of many, Athens is the mother of all the best that the world has to offer in education – both ancient and modern. Yet Paul dismisses this all as "this ignorance" and says that God "winked at" it. Literally, God "looked beyond" it, much like a man looks beyond another man whose presence is an offense to him, completely ignores him, and acts as if the offending man doesn't deserve to exist. The Creator of all things has every right to be offended at the behavior of the Athenians and other pagans. Paul presses his point by declaring that God now commands these men to repent of "this ignorance." The very height of all human culture was Athens, but God declared that they have been headed for a long time the wrong way down a one way street, and He demands that they completely and absolutely redirect their thinking. So, in a word, all of ancient culture and education, including the very height of ancient learning, is "this ignorance."

The Apostle Paul made a few other comments upon this subject to the saints who lived in the great centers of learning in the ancient world. Paul's first comment on Greek education was to the Corinthians, who lived at another center of learning.

> For after that in the wisdom of God the world by wisdom knew not God, it pleased God by the foolishness of preaching to save them that believe. — First Corinthians 1:21

Paul contrasts the world's wisdom with Christian faith. It was by their carnal wisdom that the world knew not God. Their education was the agent which caused their great ignorance, because they were educated without reference to God.

> The wicked, through the pride of his countenance, will not seek *after God*: God *is* not in all his thoughts. — Psalms 10:4

No true education can take place without reference to God. Education is for a purpose. If the purpose does not have God in view, then it is godless education, and it will eventually produce godless results. The objective of education is not service to self, the community, business, church, or state, but service to God. Education which does not serve God is an empty education, and that emptiness will be filled by other gods to serve. To develop capacities for service, but to omit the One Who is to be served, is to manufacture a monster.

Modern government education does what ancient education did – teach without reference to God. Hence it creates ignorance.

The Apostle Paul had more to say to the Romans about this profound ignorance.

> For the wrath of God is revealed from heaven against all ungodliness and unrighteousness of men, who hold [/suppress] the truth in unrighteousness; Because that which may be known of God is manifest in them; for God hath shewed *it* unto them. For the invisible things of him from the creation of the world are clearly seen, being understood by the things that are made, *even* his eternal power and Godhead; so that they are without excuse: Because that, when they knew God, they glorified *him* not as God, neither were thankful; but became vain in their imaginations, and their foolish heart was darkened. Professing themselves to be wise, they became fools, And changed the glory of the uncorruptible God into an image made like to corruptible man, and to birds, and fourfooted beasts, and creeping things. . . . Who changed the truth of God into a lie, and worshipped and served the creature more than the Creator, who is blessed for ever. Amen. . . . And even as they did not like to retain God in *their* knowledge, God gave them over to a reprobate mind . . . — Romans 1:18-23,25,28

As you can see, God is not happy about this inexcusable ignorance which proudly professes itself to be wisdom, while it changes the truth of God into a lie and worships the thing created over the One Who created it, thereby inverting all of created order. As they did not approve of having God in their knowledge, so God delivered them over to a reprobate mind – literally, a mind which does not pass the test and is therefore worthless, like the dross or slag removed when purifying metal. God says their kind of wisdom is worthless.

We'll look at one more of Paul's opinions of classical education. This time his opinion was delivered to the saints at Ephesus – the last of the three great centers of learning in ancient Greece.

> This I say therefore, and testify in the Lord, that ye henceforth walk not as other Gentiles walk, in the vanity of their mind, Having the understanding darkened, being alienated from the life of God through the ignorance that is in them, because of the blindness [\hardness] of their heart: — Ephesians 4:17,18

Their minds were full of vanity, not wisdom; their understanding was darkened, not enlightened; and they were full of ignorance, not knowledge – which made them total strangers to the spiritual life which comes from God. And all of this was because of the hardness of their hearts. Paul is careful to contrast this with Christian education.

> But ye have not so learned Christ; If so be that ye have heard him, and have been taught by him, as the truth is in Jesus: That ye put off concerning the former conversation the old man, which is corrupt according to the deceitful lusts; And be renewed in the spirit of your mind; And that ye put on the new man, which after God is created in righteousness and true holiness. — Ephesians 4:20-24

The Gentile mind, which lacked wisdom, understanding, and knowledge, is contrasted with the renewed spiritual mind, which is taught in Christian truth, and thereby restored in *wisdom* to do righteousness, restored in *understanding* to discern truth, and restored in *knowledge* to observe holiness.

> For this cause we also, since the day we heard *it*, do not cease to pray for you, and to desire that ye might be filled with the knowledge of his will in all wisdom and spiritual understanding; — Colossians 1:9

Modern education, which prohibits any reference to God in the classroom, rivals ancient education for the skepticism which it breeds in the minds of children. Nothing can be truly known and understood correctly without reference to God.

> The fear of the LORD *is* the beginning of knowledge: *but* fools despise wisdom and instruction. — Proverbs 1:7

> The fear of the LORD *is* the beginning of wisdom: and the knowledge of the holy *is* understanding. — Proverbs 9:10

Much of modern science is taught from the perspective of the philosophy of naturalism, which begins with the presupposition that all things must be explained only in terms of natural observable phenomena. This philosophy should be called anti-supernaturalism, because it is precisely formulated to exclude the supernatural and the God of the Bible before it ever begins. It is studied ignorance. It is pure skepticism.

Distinctives of the Biblical Model of Education

If we are supposed to transform education for Christ, then we need to renew our minds with the distinctives of a Biblical model for education.

1. ALL TRUE EDUCATION MUST BEGIN WITH THE REVELATION OF GOD.

The Scripture is sufficient to educate us in all necessary areas of life.

> O how love I thy law! it *is* my meditation all the day. Thou through thy commandments hast made me wiser than mine enemies: for they *are* ever with me. I have more understanding than all my teachers: for thy testimonies *are* my meditation. I understand more than the ancients, because I keep thy precepts. I have refrained my feet from every evil way, that I might keep thy word. I have not departed from thy judgments: for thou hast taught me. How sweet are thy words unto my taste! *yea, sweeter* than honey to my mouth! Through thy precepts I get understanding: therefore I hate every false way. — Psalms 119:97-104

> And that from a child thou hast known the holy scriptures, which are able to make thee wise unto salvation through faith which is in Christ Jesus. All scripture *is* given by inspiration of God, and *is* profitable for doctrine, for reproof, for correction, for instruction in righteousness: That the man of God may be perfect, throughly furnished unto all good works. — Second Timothy 3:15-17

This is our first presupposition. God's word gives us the correct way to view the world, and directs us how to live in the real world. It tells us the proper order of things, defines the role relationships, gives us the true presuppositions to establish our knowledge, imparts the holy values to guide our understanding, and establishes the righteous goals to guide us in a walk of wisdom. Therefore, knowledge of the Scriptures is of first importance. An education which does not always give Scripture a place, and always makes that place the first place, does not measure up to the standard.

John Wycliffe wrote,

> "There is no subtlety, in grammar, neither in logic, nor in any other science that can be named, but that it is found in a more excellent degree in the Scriptures."

Everything can be taught from a beginning place in the Word of God. This establishes the authority for all of education. The Scriptures must be the foundation of all studies, the guide through all studies, and the final test for all studies. Of Him and through Him and to Him are all things. The Word of God contains, in seed form, everything necessary to completely educate a man: all true principles, all worthy values, all proper goals. All other learning must be brought into conformity with the Word of God. Many persons balk at the notion that everything must bow before the Word of God. This displays how the views of the world have overwhelmed their minds, and how small a part the Scriptures have been allowed to play in their own lives. The Word of God does indeed speak to every issue. We just need to listen. Experiential learning is not absolute. The study of natural phenomena must be a tool, never a master. The humanistic method is to draw answers out of man and nature, without reference to God. Man is the measure of all things – so they say. The Biblical method is to draw the answers out of God through His Word – God is the measure of all things. We must believe God in His Word, and be skeptical of man's word.

2. THE FAMILY AT HOME IS GIVEN SOLE JURISDICTION OVER THE EDUCATION OF CHILDREN.

> Therefore shall ye lay up these my words in your heart and in your soul . . . . And ye shall teach them [to] your children, speaking of them when thou sittest in thine house, and when thou walkest by the way, when thou liest down, and when thou risest up. — Deuteronomy 11:18,19 (Compare 4:9,10; 6:4-9; Genesis 18:19)

> And, ye fathers, provoke not your children to wrath: but bring them up in the nurture and admonition of the Lord. — Ephesians 6:4

The Scripture is most explicit about the exclusive jurisdiction of the family in education. Education is the father's jurisdiction, carried out by the father and the mother and whomever they choose to employ for attaining specific goals. The priests, and later the synagogues, were primarily to teach men, who would teach their families. More will be said about this in Chapters Two and Three.

3. EDUCATION IS TO FULLY PREPARE CHILDREN FOR ADULT LIFE.

> Train up a child in the way he should go: and when he is old, he will not depart from it. — Proverbs 22:6

> For I know him, that he will command his children and his household after him, and they shall keep the way of the LORD, to do justice and judgment . . . . — Genesis 18:19

> That the aged men be sober, grave, temperate, sound in faith, in charity, in patience. The aged women likewise, that *they be* . . . teachers of good things; That they may teach the young women to be sober, to love their husbands, to love their children, *To be* discreet, chaste, keepers at home, good, obedient to their own husbands, that the word of God be not blasphemed. Young men

> likewise exhort to be sober minded. — Titus 2:2-6

> I will therefore that the younger women marry, bear children, guide the house, give none occasion to the adversary to speak reproachfully. — First Timothy 5:14

> According as his divine power hath given unto us all things that *pertain* unto life and godliness . . . . — Second Peter 1:3

There is more to life than what is styled "academic education." Indeed, all education should prepare students for mature adult life. Education is to involve all of the affairs of adult life – where you sit, where you walk, where you lie, where you rise. We are not interested in reviving the Greek or Roman civilizations on an academic model. True education will establish a culture on the foundation of God's word, according to God's order and structure, directed by God's law and policies.

4. THE ULTIMATE GOAL OF EDUCATION IS HOLINESS – SEPARATION TO GOD FOR HIS SERVICE.

> And ye shall be holy unto me: for I the LORD *am* holy, and have severed you from *other* people, that ye should be mine. — Leviticus 20:26

> For God hath not called us unto uncleanness, but unto holiness. — First Thessalonians 4:7

> But as he which hath called you is holy, so be ye holy in all manner of conversation; Because it is written, Be ye holy; for I am holy. — First Peter 1:15,16

All education is essentially religious, and the sooner we realize this, the better. By the things which we learn, and by the way which we learn them, we will be separated to one thing or another. Any education which is truly Biblical will teach how to distinguish good from evil, truth from falsehood, right from wrong, holy from profane.

> And that ye may put difference between holy and unholy, and between unclean and clean; — Leviticus 10:10

> And they shall teach my people *the difference* between the holy and profane, and cause them to discern between the unclean and the clean. — Ezekiel 44:23

> But strong meat belongeth to them that are of full age, *even* those who by reason of use have their senses exercised to discern both good and evil. — Hebrews 5:14

Scripture requires us to maintain a separation from the world and its ways.

> Blessed *is* the man that walketh not in the counsel of the ungodly, nor standeth in the way of sinners, nor sitteth in the seat of the scornful. — Psalm 1:1

> Enter not into the path of the wicked, and go not in the way of evil *men*. Avoid it, pass not by it, turn from it, and pass away. — Proverbs 4:14,15

> Be ye not unequally yoked together with unbelievers: for what fellowship hath righteousness with unrighteousness? and what communion hath light with darkness? And what concord hath Christ with Belial? or what part hath he that believeth with an infidel? And what agreement hath the temple of God with idols? for ye are the temple of the living God; as God hath said, I will dwell in them, and walk in *them*; and I will be their God, and they shall be my people. Wherefore come out from among them, and be ye separate, saith the Lord, and touch not the unclean *thing*; and I will receive you, And will be a Father unto you, and ye shall be my sons and daughters, saith the Lord Almighty. Having therefore these promises, dearly beloved, let us cleanse ourselves from all filthiness of the flesh and spirit, perfecting holiness in the fear of God. — Second Corinthians 6:14-7:1

We must always labor to maintain the line of demarcation. We must not entertain the notion that there is any crossover from darkness to light, unless there has first been a thorough transformation,

> To open their eyes, *and* to turn *them* from darkness to light, and *from* the power of Satan unto God . . . . — Acts 26:18

All of the imagined light which is in the world is actually darkness.

> . . . If therefore the light that is in thee be darkness, how great *is* that darkness! — Matthew 6:23

> Take heed therefore that the light which is in thee be not darkness. — Luke 11:35

> Professing themselves to be wise, they became fools . . . . — Romans 1:22

We cannot walk by the imagined light which the world claims to have. Despite their claims, without a transformation, there can be no light in them.

> To the law and to the testimony: if they speak not according to this word, *it is* because *there is* no light in them. — Isaiah 8:20

So all things must first be exposed to the light.

> The entrance of thy words giveth light; it giveth understanding unto the simple. — Psalms 119:130

When we were turned "from darkness to light, and from the power of Satan unto God," we left a sinful world of imagination and we entered into the real world. Before we can use things in our real world, we must first bring them into our world – we must square them with reality, redeem them and cleanse them, and make them serviceable to our Lord. We must never be so foolish as to think that those things have any light to give us while they remain in the world of darkness. We may gather from darkened pagan culture many things which will serve us as useful tools, but they will serve us only after they have been transformed.

> . . . if thou take forth the precious from the vile, thou shalt be as my mouth . . . . — Jeremiah 15:19

Before we can speak for God, we must separate what is precious – what has redeemable value – from what is vile – what is corruption beyond redemption.

Why Follow a Classical *Model and Method?*

1. *Academics*. Certainly, some parents choose a classical style of schooling because they are attracted by the academic achievement. They want their children to achieve high academic goals in classical languages, in logic, and in communications skills. They want them to study a very high level of material. Perhaps some of this is driven by a sort of academic snobbery, but much of it is driven by a sincere desire to see their children challenged and excel for the glory of God.

2. *Results*. The classical Trivium – Grammar, Logic, and Rhetoric – is a very effective means to prepare to serve God in the world. By mastering these basic tools of learning, the classical method creates self-teaching students who are able to move forward and master any area of learning on their own. Whatever our goals may be, the classical approach lays the broadest and most solid foundation for achieving them.

3. *Methodology*. The best reason for choosing the classical style of schooling is simply because this is actually the Biblical model written into reality. So what if the pagans stole it? We simply take it back and clean it up and put it to our own use. The classical style has been successful for millennia because it conforms to the created nature of things. It works well because it matches reality. If we ever learned anything, then we learned it by the Trivium method – whether we knew it or not. But it's always better to know what we're doing, and in this Book we

explain and apply the Trivium model and Trivium method for classical education.

DON'T TRY THIS AT HOME

If you try to do homeschool like a classroom school – using their course of study, their scope and sequence, their curricula, their class format, their teaching methods – then you will probably buckle under the burden and give up. And you will be right – that kind of schooling does not fit in a homeschool. Rare is the pair of parents who have the time and the talents to bear such burdens. It will truly test your commitment to Homeschooling. The great advantage of tutoring your own children at home is that much of what goes on in classroom schooling is rendered completely unnecessary.

We want to show you that you can tutor at home in a classical style. Our purpose in this book is to convey to the reader some of what we have learned in our many years of Homeschooling. We have made many mistakes, so in this book we have combined what we did do and what we would do if we could do it over. We have attempted to consistently apply Christian truth – Biblical philosophy – to the family in general, and to education in particular.

We homeschoolers are raising a generation of custom built children – no factory models here. We want to keep it that way. The academic goal of Homeschooling is not to teach a multitude of things to an adequate level, but to tutor in the most important things to an excellent level. There is room for different approaches within the broad classical model, and we are not afraid to incorporate them where they fit and are useful.

FIGURE 1A, SCHOOL IN THE HOME

FIGURE 1B, HOMESCHOOL

THE ARRANGEMENT OF THIS BOOK

We have assembled this book in the way which we thought would be most useful. Chapters One through Ten form an argument for a classical style of education on Biblical principles. Chapters Eleven through Sixteen apply those principles in a practical and workable way. Appendix One contains numerous articles on education which enlarge on specific issues addressed in various Chapters. Appendix Two lists curricula and resources, and is indexed back to the Chapters of the book.

Chapter Two

Who Should Control Education: Parents, or the State?

. . . Render therefore unto Caesar the things which be Caesar's,
and unto God the things which be God's.
— Luke 20:25

INTRODUCTION

EVERY DAY, CHRISTIAN parents send their children off to be educated in schools controlled by the state. Most of these parents turn a deaf ear to other options for education. We could explore the many reasons which they might give for preferring socialized education for their children – cost, time, social pressures, cultural norms, school programs, credentials, etc. We've heard them all. We could explore these reasons, but we won't bother. Instead, in this Chapter, we make a Biblical argument that socialized education should never even be considered as an option for the education of our children.

The First and Great Commandment

When one of the scribes asked Jesus what was the first commandment of all, Jesus replied,

> . . . First of all the commandments *is this*: Hear O Israel, ***the* Lord our God, *the* Lord is One**. And thou shalt love *the* Lord thy God with thy **whole** heart, and with thy **whole** soul, and with thy **whole** mind, and with thy **whole** strength. . . . — Mark 12:29,30 (v.l.t.)

Jesus called this "The first and great commandment" (Matthew 22:38). It is first in position and importance, and it is great because, in principle, it encompasses all other commandments. Jesus was quoting the first portion of a much larger passage of Scripture. When an Israelite heard the words, "Hear O Israel," he immediately recognized this as a reference to the entire *Shemah* (pronounced sheh-MAH) – that one passage out of God's Law which every Israelite memorized before he was five years old, and which he repeated numerous times throughout each day.

> Hear, O Israel: The LORD our God *is* one LORD: And thou shalt love the LORD thy God with all thine heart, and with all thy soul, and with all thy might. And these words, which I command thee this day, shall be in thine heart: And thou shalt teach them diligently unto thy children, and shalt talk of them when thou sittest in thine house, and when thou walkest by the way, and when thou liest down, and when thou risest up. And thou shalt bind them for a sign upon thine hand, and they shall be as frontlets between thine eyes. And thou shalt write them upon the posts of thy house, and on thy gates. — Deuteronomy 6:4-9

So, the first and great commandment requires 1) that we confess that the Lord is One, and 2) that we love the Lord with all of our being – our whole heart, soul, and strength. But it does not end there. It also requires 3) that we keep the Lord's commandments in our hearts and 4) that we diligently teach them to our children. In other words, our whole life is to be filled with:

1) Confessing the Lord.
2) Loving Him.
3) Memorizing His word.
4) Teaching His word to our children.

In the words of the *Pulpit Commentary*:

> *Truth and godliness* [are] *to be perpetuated by means of home training.* In this paragraph, the aged lawgiver [Moses] . . . is showing what provision God had made in the structure of society for the maintenance and perpetuation of truth and godli-

> ness. . . . Here is a special arrangement divinely appointed, to conserve and perpetuate both.
>
> 1. The home is here supposed to be a centre in which the conserving forces of truth and godliness are to be themselves conserved. What a profound principle Moses here indicates, viz. That a nation will be good or bad according to its home life! . . . – our land will be as our homes are!
>
> 2. In the home, our God looks to the parent to give it its character, tone, and influence. . . .
>
> 3. [These truths] are to be in the parents' heart, that they may be poured out anew from thence as rivers of living water. . . .
>
> 4. By a variety of ways, the parent is to see his child's spirit early saturated with the truths of God. . . . Divine truth is to be ever before him, night and day, indoors and out. Those who gave him birth and who love him best, are to mould his young life for God. . . .
>
> — Rev. C. Clemance, Pulpit Commentary, in loc., n.d. (19th Century).

The Whole Commandment

But some will say, "Jesus quoted only a part of that commandment. The rest of that is Old Testament stuff." We strongly disagree. In the ancient land of Israel, the vocalization of the first word or two – "Hear O Israel" – would begin the congregational recitation of this entire passage – not just on the Sabbath day, but several times on each and every day. The Hebrews would bind this entire passage (Deuteronomy 6:4-9) upon themselves as one of their four "phylacteries." (See Exodus 13:9,16; Matthew 23:5) To a Hebrew, it was absolutely impossible to disconnect verses 4 and 5 from their context. It all stood as one continuous and indivisible unit. Jesus meant to draw the whole passage into the memory of His hearers when He quoted the first few words. Without entering into an extended theological discussion, suffice it to say that, whether or not this passage is "Old Testament," the principles which it teaches have universal application.

AN EXPOSITION OF DEUTERONOMY 6:4-9

The following is a brief exposition of the first and great commandment, focusing upon its importance for Homeschooling.

The Unity Commandment

|6:4| HEAR, O ISRAEL: THE LORD OUR GOD IS ONE LORD [OR: THE LORD, OUR GOD, THE LORD IS ONE].

The Hebrews call this the *Shemah,* which is the first Hebrew word of this confession, translated "hear." The Hebrews also called this "the witness of God." The text does not say that Jehovah is the only God. That is assumed. The word "one" ('ehad) means a compound unity made up of more than one, in contrast to another word (yahid) which means a single one. The text says, "Jehovah, our Elohim, Jehovah is united." It implicitly declares that the Lord our God is not a single person, but is an eternal self-existent indivisible unity of being. (Compare the same use of the word for *one* in Genesis 2:24; Exodus 26:6,11; Ezekiel 37:16-19.) Some ancient Hebrew expositors concluded from this passage alone that the Godhead was a trinity of persons. Jesus said, *"I-myself and the Father are one in essence."* (John 10:30, Literal) The third person of the Tri-unity is the Holy Spirit (Matthew 28:19). The Father, the Word or Son, and the Spirit are One in essence, Jehovah (First John 5:7).

|6:5| AND THOU SHALT LOVE THE LORD THY GOD WITH ALL THINE HEART, AND WITH ALL THY SOUL, AND WITH ALL THY MIGHT.

The Lord our God is the foremost object toward Whom we are to direct all of the energy of our being. As we worship a unity in trinity, so we are also to be a unity within ourselves. We are to love and worship 1) with our whole heart; 2) with our whole soul; 3) with our whole might. Just what do these three things mean?

1) *With our whole heart* does not mean with an emotional gush. The world has attached such notions as this to the heart, but the Hebrews did not understand it so. To the Hebrew, the *heart* generally referred to all of the faculties of the inner life of a man: the intellect, the emotion, and the will. It especially referred to the *mind* which supplies the energy to the whole mental life, much like the physical heart which supplies the energy to the whole physical life. Our intellect, emotion, and volition are to be wholly united in undivided devotion to the Lord.
2) *With our whole soul* refers to our self-consciousness and personality – who we are recognized to be – that part of our essence which distinguishes us from other individual persons.

3) *With our whole might* must refer to all of our resources of energy. We must put all which we have into loving the Lord.

> Our desire must be towards him, our delight in him, our dependence upon him, and to him we must be entirely devoted. — Matthew Henry, Commentary, 1706, in loc.

The Apostle Paul may be referring to this commandment when he declares:

> Now the end of the commandment is charity [/love] out of a pure heart, and *of* a good conscience, and *of* faith unfeigned: — First Timothy 1:5

In other words, the goal of *the great* commandment is love proceeding from a heart which is wholly pure, a soul or conscience which is entirely good, and a faith which is of full strength.

Wherever this passage is quoted in the gospels, "the mind" is added to the list, without any explanation or objection. The mind is the premier faculty which controls or leads all other parts of man, and is therefore assumed to be behind all of these, and is therefore supplied by our Lord according to the figure of speech known as pleonasm – where, in order to clarify and emphasize a thought, it is repeated or expressed more fully in different words.

> . . . Thou shalt love the Lord thy God with all thy heart, and with all thy soul, and with all thy **mind**. — Matthew 22:37

> . . . thou shalt love the Lord thy God with all thy heart, and with all thy soul, and with all thy **mind**, and with all thy strength . . . . to love him with all the heart, and with all the **understanding**, and with all the soul, and with all the strength . . . . — Mark 12:30,33

> . . . Thou shalt love the Lord thy God with all thy heart, and with all thy soul, and with all thy strength, and with all thy **mind** . . . — Luke 10:27

The Apostle Paul said it all in a different sort of way:

> I beseech you therefore, brethren, by the mercies of God, that ye present your bodies a living sacrifice, holy, acceptable unto God, *which is* your reasonable service. And be not conformed to this world: but **be ye transformed by the renewing of your mind, that ye may prove what *is* that good, and acceptable, and perfect, will of God**. — Romans 12:1,2

|6:6| AND THESE WORDS, WHICH I COMMAND THEE THIS DAY, SHALL BE IN THINE HEART.

The words of the *Shemah* – that God is a Unity; and the words of the commandment – to love God with our whole being; these words are to be "in our heart," meaning "in our mind" by the Hebrew idiom (Mark 12:33). They are to be solemnly inscribed upon our memories and foremost in our consciences, so that our thoughts and our meditations and our conversations are filled with the knowledge of God.

The Education Commandment

|6:7a| And thou shalt teach them diligently unto thy children.

The word translated *teach diligently* literally means *to sharpen by repeatedly rubbing.* The picture is one of repeatedly rubbing against a sharpening stone, and resharpening whenever the edge is becoming dull, so that the edge remains sharp at all times. We are to teach our children the *Shemah* and the command to love God. But the command to love God encompasses all of God's commands. Jesus said that the second commandment, to love our neighbor, was implicit in the first commandment, to love God, and "On these two commandments hang all the Law and the Prophets" (Matthew 22:40). He also said that if we love Him, then we would keep His commandments (John 14:15). We are commanded to bring up our children in the nurture and admonition of the Lord (Ephesians 6:4). We are commanded to make our children sharp, ready and expert in applying the Word of God to all areas of life. This is not optional. *Our children are to be well-honed in God's commandments – sharp and accurate in applying them.*

This requires that we parents be sharp as well, ready and expert in the commandments of God. The pupil is not above his master. The parent and child both benefit from this commandment. Sharpening our children will keep us sharp as well. *Our children are indispensable to our own spiritual growth.*

Many Christians have cut off these blessings because they have delegated to others their parental duty to educate their own children. According to the Bible, the home is to be the center of all education. Education is the God-ordained function of the family. No one else is given the responsibility to teach children: not the government, nor the church, but the parents. *It takes a family, not a village, to raise a child.*

Of course there are appropriate ways for others to help parents in the process. We do not deny this. We only wish to emphasize that the work of educating children is what the family is all about. When parents are left in observer status, the family is damaged – greatly. Both the parents and the children are cheated out of a huge portion of God's ordained process for spiritual growth. As we continue down this road of separating children from their parents, we are tearing apart the very sinews and ligaments of our culture. Families are falling apart because we are tearing them apart. We need to teach our children – *for our sake.* Our children need to be taught by us – *for their sake*. The way to destroy the family is to divide the children from the parents. And the way to divide the children from the parents is to remove from the family its authority in education.

The Presbyterian theologian, Robert L. Dabney, wrote 125 years ago:

> It is the teaching of the Bible and of sound political ethics that the education of children belongs to the sphere of the family and is the duty of the parents. . . . Now, by what apology does the State . . . justify itself in stepping in to revolutionize that order? — *Discussions* by Robert L. Dabney, Vol. IV. Secular, 1876. p. 194.

For whatever excuse they may give, and no matter how others may have contributed to the problem, nevertheless the bottom line is that the parents have shrunk from their God-ordained responsibility to educate their own children. The schools have become orphanages full of children who have been educationally abandoned by their own parents. Children are no longer in the hearts of their parents.

The failure of the family corresponds directly to the rise of state-controlled education. This is because God intended for parents to be the primary educators, and because He never intended for the government to be an educator at all. Under God, education has never been within the government's jurisdiction.

> The theory that the children of the Commonwealth are the charge of the Commonwealth is a pagan one, derived from the heathen Sparta and Plato's heathen republic, and connected by regular, logical sequence with . . . the dissolution of the conjugal tie. — *Discussions* by Robert L. Dabney, Vol. IV. Secular, 1876. p. 194.

In other words, state controlled education eventually works to destroy the bond of marriage by dividing the children from their parents and dissolving the order and authority which God ordained for the family. In the new order, because the nurturing state takes the place of the natural nurturing family, marriage and legitimacy become unimportant. We are now reaping, in our culture, the fruits of several generations of unfaithfulness to God's revealed order in education. The best way to help the family is not to step over jurisdictional boundaries which God has ordained and do the family's job for it, but to get out of the family's way and to let it return to its God-ordained function of educating those children with whom God has blessed it.

The Method of Education

|6:7B| AND SHALT TALK OF THEM.

This is what is to characterize our diligent teaching of our children: *thou shalt talk about them*. Repetition is an important part of inscribing the words upon the memory, but this commandment is not limited to rotely reciting the words of God's commands. We should also verbally meditate upon their meaning, their implications, and their applications to all of the varied situations, circumstances, and happenings of life. We speak freely and fluently what is in our heart. If God's word is our great interest, then it will be reflected in our daily speech.

> A good man out of the good treasure of his heart bringeth forth that which is good; and an evil man out of the evil treasure of his heart bringeth forth that which is evil: **for of the abundance of the heart his mouth speaketh**. — Luke 6:45

> The lips of the righteous feed many: but fools die for want of wisdom [/ heart]. — Proverbs 10:21

A specimen of this instruction is offered a few verses later:

> *And* when thy son asketh thee in time to come . . . . Then thou shalt say unto thy son . . . . — Deuteronomy 6:20,21

Our instruction should be characterized by free and fluent godly conversations which invite open inquiry by our children.

|6:7C,D| WHEN THOU SITTEST IN THINE HOUSE, AND WHEN THOU WALKEST BY THE WAY.

Hebrews would sit together at mealtimes, at times of leisure, rest, and visitation, at times of instruction, and at times of light labor. This implies that every family should do such things together, or else they would rule out opportunities to obey this commandment. The Hebrew means of transportation was primarily walking. Travel time is often leisure time, which allows much time for the discussion of the things of God. We are not to alter our religious manner of life when we are outside of the home. "Sitting" and "walking" are token expressions which encompass all of the activities of the waking hours. Families should be doing things together all of the day. Parents should be using these moments as opportunities to relate all of their activities to the one activity of loving

God through keeping His commandments. How many homes throw these opportunities away by inordinately pursuing amusements – sports, television, videos, shopping? How many parents release each child to pursue his own things alone and apart from the family? Yes, there is a balance to be found, but the balance must always be in favor of the family. Please notice that this text does not say, "when thou sittest in thine temple of worship and in thine synagogue or school." Such things were not necessarily excluded, but they were by no means the focus – as if that was where we primarily did these things.

|6:7E,F| AND WHEN THOU LIEST DOWN, AND WHEN THOU RISEST UP.

The Hebrew day began at sunset. (Compare Genesis 1:2 *"And the evening and the morning were the first day."*) The Lord was to be remembered in the evening – when one day ended and another day began; and in the morning – which was the middle of the twenty-four-hour day. The Hebrew family set apart a time every evening and every morning for prayer and instruction in the things of the Lord. The beginning, the middle, and the end of the day belonged to the Lord. These last four phrases – *when thou sittest, when thou walkest, when thou liest down, when thou risest up* – teach us that we are to take every opportunity throughout the entire day to teach the commandments of the Lord. We are not to be overtaken by amusements, but we are to muse upon God's word. The family life of the parent and child is to be thoroughly filled with the knowledge of the Lord. The home is to be the center of education. *It takes a parent to teach a child.* (Stick that on your bumper!)

|6:8| AND THOU SHALT BIND THEM FOR A SIGN UPON THINE HAND, AND THEY SHALL BE AS FRONTLETS BETWEEN THINE EYES.

The hand was a symbol of active service, and the eyes and the forehead were symbols of guidance and conscience. This commandment is to be like a string around our finger which constantly reminds us that our acts and our thoughts are to be devoted to God. It is a universal custom in all cultures that when we cannot trust our minds to remind us, then we place something where we will meet it, in our usual course of the day, which will serve to continually remind us. "Tie a string around your finger so you won't forget." Some Hebrews took these words so literally that they wore parchment scrolls on their hands and bands on their foreheads with the words of Deuteronomy 6:4-9 and 11:13-21 written upon them.

|6:9| AND THOU SHALT WRITE THEM UPON THE POSTS OF THY HOUSE, AND ON THY GATES.

Where other religions would adorn their property with idolatrous symbols, the Hebrews were instead to inscribe the word of the Lord. The Hebrews were to be a Bible-literate people. The Word of God was to be posted wherever anyone would enter or leave their property. The Scriptures were not so easily obtained in times past because writings were copied by hand, not printed on a press. So the Hebrews wrote their lessons where everyone in the home would pass every day. Hebrews attached a parchment scroll of Deuteronomy 6:4-9 on the posts and gates of their houses. Unfortunately it became the custom to roll the scroll up before it was attached, and every day they touched it or kissed it as if it were a protective charm – but they did not read it! How is this any better than persons today who carry their Bibles with them everywhere, but never read them or expound them to their children? Or missionaries who teach other families how to keep God's commandments, but put their own families into boarding schools? Symbolism over substance is the modern formula for hypocrisy.

To summarize: We must avail ourselves of every possible means in order to become familiar with the Word of God, in order that it will be available to us when necessary, useful, and profitable – which is all of the time. We should never be ashamed of the Lord and His Word, but we should display His Word openly and boldly.

> My son, keep my words, and lay up my commandments with thee. Keep my commandments, and live; and my law as the apple of thine eye. Bind them upon thy fingers, **write them upon the table of thine heart**. — Proverbs 7:1-3

If anyone should slight us for using the Bible throughout our school curriculum, then we should correct them with the first and the great commandment. How grievously this contrasts with state-controlled schools, where God is not to be mentioned – at least not with reverence – all the day long. The school day thus becomes a daily lesson in *practical atheism*, which has a subtle and insidious, yet nevertheless cumulative and disastrous effect upon us all. Our culture has thereby lost the knowledge of God, and because of this, we suffer in every area of life.

THE IMPLICATIONS OF THIS COMMANDMENT FOR THE FAMILY

The first and great commandment requires that parents teach their children the truth of God's word. Both parents and children benefit from this commandment enormously. Our own knowledge and understanding of the truth increases as we communicate truth to our children. Our children's appreciation and trust of us parents increases as they receive instruction from us. Some may object that this task is best left to "professionals." God didn't think so when He gave this commandment. God created a massive professional staff of priests and Levites, some of whom were assigned the task of teaching the parents. Yet God did not entrust the task of teaching *children* to these professional teachers, but to the professional *parents*. Through day-to-day living, families can communicate things across generations in a way which no hired teacher is capable, let alone authorized. (The socialist educators recognize this principle, and are now reforming elementary schools into, in their words, "the new family.") When the work of instruction is taken from the family, both the parents and the children are cheated, and the family as a whole suffers.

> Then why resign into a stranger's hand A task as much within your own command, That God and Nature, and your interest too, Seem with one voice to delegate to you? — from *Tiriconium; or, A Review of Schools* by William Cowper, 1785.

This commandment is also given to insure the purity and perpetuity of the faith. A religion of truth which is faithfully handed down from generation to generation by a multiplicity of devoted families will be more pure and less open to widespread corruption than a religion handed down by a small staff of self-interested "professionals." Is it mere coincidence that the fall of true family devotion is inversely proportional to the rise of professional religious education? The best way to help the family is to get out of its way and to let it do the job for which God has designed it. Education is the God-ordained function of the family, and who are we to render useless the commandment of God in order to keep our tradition? (Matthew 15:6; Mark 7:9) It takes godly parents and grandparents to teach and train a godly child.

> I thank God . . . . . . when I call to remembrance the unfeigned faith that is in thee, which dwelt first in thy grandmother Lois, and thy mother Eunice . . . . . . knowing from whom thou hast learned them; and that from a child thou

hast known the holy Scriptures which are able to make thee wise unto salvation through faith which is in Christ Jesus. — Second Timothy 1:3,5; 3:14,15

THE BROADER IMPLICATIONS OF THIS COMMANDMENT

Our culture is being manipulated to worship the state. We see the state as a god, with the right to control everything which it chooses. The state is being endowed with powers for controlling the destiny of its human resources – the power of predestination. Our culture teaches us to think of the state as having a natural right to control the education of children for the sake of society, because, after all, the democratic state is the embodiment of society. Our culture teaches us that the state has a *compelling interest* in its own survival and success. Hence the state must own the children, for the children are the future. Though this doctrine is rarely stated in such explicit terms, it is nevertheless the implicit declaration of virtually all state programs. The state seeks to be omniscient – to know everything about us. The state seeks to be omnipresent – to be everywhere in our lives. The state seeks to be omnipotent – to control everything in society. *The state is the incarnation of the god of humanism*. Man, through the state, has become the measure of all things. The promise of the tempter in the Garden of Eden is at last fulfilled in the socialist state. Man is as a god, determining for himself what is good and evil – measuring everything by his own invented standards, apart from God's revealed standards.

There is only one way to defeat the socialist state. It is not with political machinery and votes. It is not with petitions and protests. It is with godly, parent-controlled education of their own children. Socialism breaks down the natural bond between parents and children – that is a necessary part of the socialist program. Unless those bonds are broken, the state cannot gain power to control the future. Parent-controlled education thwarts that purpose. Hence the socialist state has worked hard to turn the parental bond into a liability and to make it desirable for parents to sever that bond wherever and whenever it is possible.

From a practical point of view, Homeschooling is strongly out of favor with the socialist state, because it strengthens that parent-child bond which controls the future. The family is socialism's public enemy number one, and practicing Biblical Christianity is a hate crime against the state.

The state did not give birth to our children, neither did it give our children to us, neither can we trust it to raise them for us, neither should we let the state take them from us.

> Lo, children are an heritage of the Lord: and the fruit of the womb is His reward. — Psalm 127:3

Children are placed under the authority, and protection, and tutelage, not of the government, nor of the church, but of the parents. Parents are accountable to God for how their children are raised. Barring unusual and unavoidable circumstances, we – the parents – will answer to God for who raises our child, and for how they are raised. God is not going to place the primary blame for any failures upon the government, or upon the church, but upon us, the parents.

> Children, obey your parents in the Lord: for this is right. . . . And, ye fathers . . . bring them up in the nurture and admonition of the Lord. — Ephesians 6:1,4

In 1973, when we were just married, we both agreed at that time that we would never send our children off to schools controlled by the state. Our commitment was not a reaction to the condition of socialized education. At that time, the state-controlled schools were not nearly so overtly-dangerous as they are today. Our conscious commitment to parent-controlled and parent-directed education began when we both took a marriage vow to raise our children in the fear of the Lord. Our commitment at that time was philosophical. We alone, as parents, have the authority under God, and the responsibility before God, to raise our children in the knowledge and fear of God.

Since that time, we have developed many other reasons for Homeschooling, but all reasons remain subordinate to this one. We know some people do not like it when we speak against state-controlled education. But our opposition to public education is not to the academic quality of the education – as bad as that can sometimes get, nor is it to the godlessness of the curriculum – though that also is a serious consideration, nor is it to the dangers of the classroom – though that has become a very serious consideration as well. All of these things are only the inescapable moral consequences of one fundamental error: acting contrary to God's order by removing from parents their control in education, and giving it to someone else, such as the state or the church.

> *This duty rests with the parent.* Such is the Protestant doctrine – the Bible doctrine. Neither State nor Church are to usurp it; but both are to enlighten,

encourage and assist the parent in his inalienable task. — *Discussions* by Robert L. Dabney, Vol. IV. Secular, 1876. p. 223.

Though there are many other practical reasons for withdrawing from the state-controlled system of education, all of these other reasons are subservient to this one.

I am sure as I am of Christ's reign, that a comprehensive and centralized system of national education, separated from religion, as is now commonly proposed, will prove the most appalling enginery for the propagation of anti-Christian and atheistic unbelief, and of antisocial nihilistic ethics, individual, social, and political, which this sin rent world has ever seen. — A. A. Hodge, Princeton Theologian, circa 1869

Thou wouldst not, deaf to Nature's tenderest plea,
Turn him adrift upon a rolling sea,
Nor say, – "Go thither;" – conscious that there lay
A brood of asps, or quicksands, in his way;
Then only governed by the self-same rule
Of natural pity, send him not to school.
— from *Tiriconium; or, A Review of Schools* by William Cowper, 1785.

Objection: Parents should put their children in the state-controlled school as "salt" to the system.

Response: This refers to Matthew 5:13, which says, "Ye are the salt of the earth." But that verse goes on to say, "but if the salt have lost his savour, wherewith shall it be salted? It is thenceforth good for nothing, but to be cast out, and to be trodden under foot of men." What follows is a little lesson in historical chemistry.

If we tried to wash the taste out of ordinary table salt, the salt would all dissolve and wash away, and there would be nothing left. That is because today's table salt consists of pure crystals of the chemical compound which we call sodium chloride. But the "salt" of Biblical Palestine was not pure sodium chloride. It contained sodium chloride; but it also contained many other compounds and impurities. One could actually wash the sodium chloride out of ancient salt, which would remove the salty taste, but there would still be a substantial "residue." It would still look like "salt," but it would lack the salty taste or "savor." This washed out "salt," lost all of its beneficial properties: to preserve food, to fertilize the ground, to cleanse wounds, to enhance flavor, and, above all, simply to sustain life. With the sodium chloride removed, this "salt" was worth no more than sand – in fact, it actually was sand. Men literally paved paths with this sand – hence Jesus said it was "good for nothing, but to be cast out, and to be trodden under foot of men."

Now the real question is: "Will our children act as salt in the state-controlled school, to sustain, preserve, fertilize, cleanse and flavor it; or will the state-controlled school wash the taste and usefulness out of our children and make them worthless salt?" Just who is washing — or teaching — whom in the state-controlled school? Socialist educators may not always be effective in teaching academic skills, but they are highly skilled and very effective in transmitting – in ever so subtle ways – the humanist worldview. The father of modern socialist education is John Dewey. Dewey was a dedicated humanist and author of the first humanist manifesto. The humanists have openly declared their intent. They intend to salt our children with the philosophy of humanism. Charles F. Potter, a leading humanist, wrote in the *Humanist* magazine (1930):

> Education is thus a most powerful ally of Humanism, and every American public school is a school of Humanism. What can the theistic Sunday schools, meeting for an hour a week and teaching only a fraction of the children, do to stem the tide of a five-day program of humanistic teaching?

Another leading humanist, John Dunphy, wrote in the Humanist Magazine (Jan/Feb 1983):

> I am convinced that the battle for humankind's future must be waged and won in the public school classroom by teachers who correctly perceive their role as the proselytizers of a new faith: a religion of humanity. . . .The teacher must embody the same selfless dedication as the most rabid fundamentalist preachers, for they will be ministers of another sort, utilizing a classroom instead of a pulpit. . . . The classroom must and will become an arena of conflict between the old and the new – the rotting corpse of Christianity, together with all its adjacent evils and misery, and the new faith of humanism.

Our children do not come with salt. Our God given task as parents is to fill our children with salt. We call this process education.

> Train up a child in the way he should go, [that is, fill him with salt] and when he is old he will not depart from it. — Proverbs 22:6

> And ye, fathers, provoke not your children to wrath, but bring them up in the nurture and admonition of the Lord. — Ephesians 6:4

Literally, this says "nourish them in the correction and counsel of the Lord." In other words, do not provoke them to wrath, but provoke them to righteousness. When we nourish our children, we act as salt upon our children – preserving their integrity, fertilizing their mind, cleansing their walk, and giving them a distinctively Christian taste of life.

Are our children prepared to do battle with the Philistine Giant of Humanist Education? David first proved himself with a sling before lions and bears before he took on the Giant Goliath. Have our children proven themselves with the weapons of Christian warfare? (Romans 13:12; Second Corinthians 10:4,5; Ephesians 6:10-18) Only after our children have matured and are proven in the correction and counsel of the Lord – only then may we send them out to do battle with the Humanist Philistines. But if we send our children out to be discipled by the humanist system, then we may expect any salt which we may impart to them to be steadily washed away by a constant stream of polluting humanism. The salt will soon lose its taste and be good for nothing. No wonder Christians are being cast off and trodden under foot of men. If we had any salt, then our enemies would try to kill us. Instead, they just walk all over us.

A century of Christians sending their children off to state-controlled schools has washed away the saltiness of Christianity, so that now we have a generation of Christians who do not even know what a Christian culture is. Now we are struggling to raise up Christian parents to be "the salt of the earth" by salting their children in the fear of the Lord.

SUMMARY AND CONCLUSION

So why should Christian parents control their children's education? Briefly, parents should control their children's education because this is their responsibility before God. It is not the responsibility of the state, nor of the church, nor of the economy, nor of society at large. Though there are many practical reasons for withdrawing from the state-controlled system of education, these other reasons are subordinate to the issue of responsibility and control.

Chapter Three

Should Christians Prefer a Classroom School?

And, ye fathers, provoke not your children to wrath:
but bring them up in the nurture and admonition of the Lord.
— Ephesians 6:4

One that ruleth well his own house,
having his children in subjection with all gravity.
— First Timothy 3:4

INTRODUCTION

AT AN INCREASING rate, Christian parents are choosing to take back some of the control over their own children's education. Many parents consider their primary or preferred option to be to send their children to a private school. In this Chapter, we will explore the problems with this option.

The Biblical Order

As we have already explained in Chapter Two, the Biblical order is for parents to control and direct the process of their child's education. Some may argue that classroom schools can be parent-controlled and parent-directed. Perhaps – but not in the same sense, way, or degree as the homeschool.

In Homeschooling, the parent is directly involved in the process. In private tutoring, the parent relinquishes some of the control and direction, but only to a trusted tutor; on a limited basis; with direct accountability to the parent who can easily stick his nose directly into the process where he determines it is necessary. How does this compare with a classroom school? Parents may carefully and conscientiously choose a classroom school; the school's board may include some parents; the parents may even have some input regarding who are hired as teachers and what curriculum is used. And, of course, the parents may exercise the final veto power with their feet by pulling their child out of the school and enrolling him elsewhere. Nevertheless, the control which parents exercise in such a classroom school is several steps removed from direct control of the education of their own children. Multiple levels of intermediaries in all directions, insulating barriers of many sorts, and conflicting interests of various magnitudes, come between the parent and his child. Such things are a functional requirement in any efficiently run classroom school. They unavoidably come with the territory. They are "necessary evils" of the graded classroom process, and they cannot be avoided.

Adults often choose to attend private classes in order to be trained in specialized academic information. This can be a very efficient use of specialized teachers. Adults can handle this process. But it would be an error of enormous magnitude to suppose that the academic training of children through their high school years should be handled in the same manner as adult education. A very different process is going on during those years. To use a computer analogy: Adults should have all of their operating system and basic software in working order. But children are still receiving their elementary programming. Formatting errors will abound if we simply input raw data – mere academics, before the programming is completed. Much more is involved than mere academics. And only occasionally do the academics touch on such specialized training as would require a specialized teacher.

> And O ye fathers, **do not aggravate** [/exasperate] your children, rather, nurture them to full maturity in *the* correction and counsel of *the* Lord. — Ephesians 6:4 (v.l.t.)

> O ye fathers, do not *over*stimulate [/provoke *too far*] your children, in order that they should not be broken in spirit [/disheartened]. — Colossians 3:21 (v.l.t.)

The Greek words for *aggravate* [παροργίζετε] and *stimulate* [ἐρεθίζετε] convey the idea of pushing the child too far, beyond his capacity, to the point of justifiable anger and broken desperation. (An exaggerated example of this in English literature would be young Paul Dombey, a Charles Dickens character who was taught to death – literally.) Fathers are to nurture their children to full maturity, not drive them there. The process is different with each and every child, requiring plenty of micromanagement. Young children cannot be treated like little adults. We cannot just run them down an academic conveyor belt and expect them to emerge at the end like well-manufactured machines. The factory is a model for efficient manipulation of many inanimate objects to manufacture multiple look-alike products. The fragile nature of our children's character is such that it demands they be custom built, not mass-produced look-alike factory models.

In addition to these Biblical considerations, some of the reasons not to put children into state-controlled schools apply, in different degrees, to all classroom schools – whether controlled by the state or by private interests.

Why not Classical School?

The question occurs to some parents: "Why not just send our child to a graded classical classroom school?" We are not opposed, in principle or theory, to the existence of private tutors for any profitable subject. In many circumstances, the private tutor, under the direction of the father, is to be preferred. And in emergency situations, other possibilities may be allowed to fulfill critical and absolute necessities. But a private tutor placed over one or over a very small number of students is not the same as a classroom – especially a classroom composed of mixed families and mixed genders, and most especially a large classroom of age-segregated peers. We do not believe that the classroom should be preferred above the parent or the special tutor.

We recognize that we are now entering into the controversial zone. Let it be said at the outset that we are not in the business of judging other Christians for their decisions. They are answerable to the Lord, and they should understand best their own circumstances and the direction in which the Lord is leading them. In the process of sanctification, there may be many halfway measures which, in an ideal sense, do not appear to fit, but in a practical sense, they are nevertheless necessary. We may belong in New York. We may have started a journey from Los Angeles to where we belong. Now, if you should find us in Chicago, do not be too quick to judge. Chicago may only be a stopping place on the way to where we belong. Just point us in the right direction and help us to make some progress on our journey.

TEN PROBLEMS WITH CLASSROOM SCHOOLS

We list below a few of the problems which persist in large gender-mixed, age-segregated, day-long classroom schools. (As long as we are stirring up controversy – many homeschoolers have awakened to the fact that the following problems also apply to gender-mixed and age-segregated Sunday schools, youth groups, and similar situations. But that's the subject of another book.)

1. Classroom schools create bonds which can easily cross and oppose the proper bonds of authority and affection.

For example:

The teacher-to-student bond may weaken the parent-to-child bond.

The school-to-student bond may weaken the family-to-child bond.

The student-to-student bond may weaken the sibling-to-sibling bond.

The parent-to-school bond may weaken the father-to-mother bond.

There is enormous potential for the alienation of appropriate lines of affections, and the engendering of inappropriate lines of affections. Under the Lord, parental authority is the whole foundation for instruction. Respect for parental authority is undermined, diluted, and broken down, when, in the minds of the children, other authorities are exalted above their parents. Do the children understand who has authority over them? Trust is undermined whenever authority is confused.

In 1985, we were involved in an attempt to found a private school. Despite working very hard at setting up this school, organizing schedules, and deciding upon a curriculum, one problem persisted: no students. Efforts at arousing sufficient interest in such a school failed. Our own children would undoubtedly have attended the school. Instead, we moved away and continued to pursue Homeschooling. At that time, we were quite disappointed. We did not then understand, as we do now, the real value of Homeschooling.

Most children who attend a classroom school – private or government, Christian or secular, classical or modern – are pulled toward their peers. They bond with their peers, and they are drawn away from their parents. The authority of the parents is undermined – subtly and perhaps quite unintentionally, but nevertheless most unavoidably. In *The Socialization Trap*, Rick Boyer remarks, "Peer socialization breaks down family relationships. . . . [it] separates kids both from their siblings and their parents through time commitments, interests and emotional bonding." Oh, sure, the child stills loves mommy and daddy to some degree. But the heart, the affections, the attentions, the very life of the child becomes bound up with his peers. Parents lose the hearts of their children.

If you had asked us in 1980 why we homeschooled our children, we would have responded that we wanted our children to receive a good education. We wanted them to learn Latin and Greek. Today, we would tell you that we homeschool because we don't want our children to be socially bonded to their peer group. We want to keep the hearts of our children where they ought to be, with their parents and family, until it is time for them to marry and to leave home. We parents need the sanctification which comes from teaching our children, and our children need the same from us. So, even if we couldn't teach them Latin and Greek, we would still homeschool them.

2. Classroom schools can create an atmosphere of ungodly rivalry instead of godly challenge.

When peers are put together in a graded context, the natural result is comparison – not against an absolute standard, but against each other, which breeds a fleshly competition and rivalry.

We quote here a passage which appears to illustrate this point. During the Civil War, Augusta Jane Evans wrote the book, *Marcaria; or, Altars of Sacrifice*. Evans was educated at home by her mother. She had studied Latin and Greek and was well read in the classics. The main character of her book is Irene, a sweet southern belle of fifteen years, who was sent off to a prestigious boarding school in New York.

> As tall tyrannous weeds and rank unshorn grass close over and crush our slender, pure, odorous flowerets on a hill-side, so the defects of Irene's character swiftly strengthened and developed in the new atmosphere in which she found herself. All the fostering stimulus of a hot-bed seemed applied to them, and her nobler impulses were in imminent danger of being entirely subdued. . . . and the associations which surrounded Irene were well calculated to destroy the native purity and unselfishness of her nature. The school was on an extensive scale, thoroughly fashionable, and thither pupils were sent from every section of the United States. As regarded educational advan-

> tages, the institution was unexceptionable; the professors were considered unsurpassed in their several departments, and every provision was made for thorough tuition. But what a Babel reigned outside of the recitation-room. One hundred and forty girls to spend their recesses in envy, ridicule, malice, and detraction. The homely squad banded in implacable hatred against those whom nature had cast in moulds of beauty; the indolent and obtuse ever on the alert to decry the successful efforts of their superiors; the simply-clad children of parents in straightened circumstances feeding their discontent by gazing with undisguised envy at the richly-appareled darlings of fortune; and the favored ones sneering at these unfortunates, pluming themselves on wealth, beauty, intellect, as the case might be; growing more arrogant and insufferable day by day. A wretched climate this for a fresh, untainted soul; and it is surprising how really fond parents, anxious to promote the improvement of their daughters in every respect, hasten to place them where poisonous vapors wreathe and curl about them. The principals of such institutions are doubtless often conscientious, and strive to discharge their duty faithfully; but the evils of human nature are obstinate, difficult to subdue under even the most favorable auspices; and where such a mass of untrained souls are turned into an enclosure, to amuse themselves at one another's expense, mischief is sure to follow. — Augusta Jane Evans, *Marcaria; or, Altars of Sacrifice*

Objection: I made it through school and turned out okay.

Response: At least you think you did. When we compare ourselves with ourselves, we don't look so bad, do we? By the world's standards, we may look okay, and our families may appear just fine. Compared to a century ago, we may look a little pale. But we need to measure ourselves by the absolute standard of God's word, and by that standard we are afraid that most of us look more like Lot acclimated to Sodom. Those who are unaware are unaware that they are unaware.

3. Classroom schools create a cross-cultural exchange outside of the parents' control, establishing values which may conflict with those of the parents.

The artificial environment of a classroom school becomes a pool of cultural values from various students, various teachers, various administrators. In the adult setting of the church, this may be an appropriate and welcome challenge. But in the childhood setting of the school, this can undermine the authority of the father and the family.

Objection: Children need to learn to deal with the real world.

Response: Adults need to learn to live righteously in the real world. Children do not have the maturity to properly respond to sophisticated cultural pressures. It is the job of the parents to instruct them and to test them in controlled situations, not simply sprinkle them with a few choice words of advice, then immerse them in an adverse world. If we taught swimming this way, most students would drown.

4. Classroom schools can be academically inferior in many cases simply because of the inefficiency of teaching the identical material to multiples of children at different learning levels.

Classroom teaching has the inevitable long-term effect of dumbing down the curriculum, reducing the method to minimums, and lowering the quality of results. So, specialized programs must be introduced. Of course, that can happen in Homeschooling as well, but not as the result of an inherent weakness in the institution of the family itself, but rather as the result of personal indolence, or of mimicry of the classroom, in place of personal tutoring.

Objection: Classroom classical schools are able to provide more talented professional teaching than any parent can provide.

Response:

1) Rare is the school which is filled with talented teachers. Talented or not, if they graduated from a teacher training program, they were probably filled with the latest methods in educational psychology. It is our observation that former school teachers usually have the greatest difficulty adjusting to Homeschooling – by their own admission. What they've been taught doesn't match reality.
2) Such teachers would be more effective as private tutors.
3) The effectiveness of talented teachers in a classroom situation applies better to adult education than to childhood education. A Ph.D. in physics does little to enhance elementary physics – indeed, it may unintentionally work as a hindrance for many students.
4) There is no great difference between a parent instructing his child in elementary physics using materials prepared by a talented professional, and that same instruction being given directly by that professional. Now, if you want to teach advanced quantum mechanics, that would be another matter.
5) Parents who served their twelve-year sentence in state institutions – elementary, junior and senior high schools – may remediate their resulting lack of education by teaching their own children these classical subjects. Sending children to classroom schools does nothing to remediate this problem. Ho-

meschooling is also for parents!

6) When a decision is made on the sole grounds of academic value, then academic pursuit becomes the highest authority, and respect for parents and their authority is undermined.
7) Even if this objection were generally true, it would still be no justification. Certainly, if all things were equal, then providing more talented professional teaching would be a valid criterion – yet only after many other questions had been settled. This certainly is not the first and foremost criterion upon which to decide the question.

5. The age segregation of classroom schools encourages peer groupings as the proper way of partitioning society.

It creates an artificial and impractical one-size-fits-all standard within age segments, while it divides families and generations. We do not recommend any such group socialization for children. It develops the wrong type of appetite – an appetite for being surrounded by one's peers, and shunning the presence of adults, while creating a culture void of age-integrated relationships. It is frequently a formula for foolishness.

> His intercourse with peers, and sons of peers – There dawns the splendor of his future years. — from *Tiriconium; or, A Review of Schools* by William Cowper, 1785.

The age-segregated classroom finds its origins in evolutionary and socialist philosophy, and it ends in an artificial youth culture which is glamorized for its breaking with cultural tradition. (Read *Critique of Modern Youth Ministry* by Christopher Schlect.)

Objection: Children at school mix with other children of different ages in the playground, on the bus, and at other activities – much more than do homeschooled children.

Response: That's exactly where the problem comes – first the sorting and labeling, followed by the mixing. The sorting creates a sociological age-peer adhesive, and the mixing proves (and often improves) the quality of the adhesive which segregates them. The larger the classes, the more exaggerated the problem becomes. We need more family bonding and less peer bonding.

6. The gender mixing of classroom schools can create situations which are inappropriate.

Boys and girls from different families should only mix together in controlled environments fully under the authority of their parents. Period.

(For that matter, boys and boys, or girls and girls, should likewise be so controlled, though for somewhat different reasons.) Our girls have no business developing independent relationships with other boys, and our boys have no business developing independent relationships with other girls, apart from our knowledge, advise, and consent. (The same with girls and girls, or boys and boys, though again for different reasons.) What we call "co-education" is a breeding ground for cultural disintegration through the breaking down of parental authority. It essentially has created the context which sustains the culturally idolatrous and emotionally fornicative "dating" mentality which prevails in our society. (Read *The Pattern of Courtship* by Natali Miller.)

7. *Time at school away from home, other after-school programs away from home, and schoolwork brought home from school – these all draw order and commitment to the school and away from the family.*

Timing is a large part of life, and someone else's timing is an enormous imposition. The entire family life is made to conform to the daily, weekly, monthly, yearly time schedule of an outside institution. The school becomes the center of life, replacing the home. Children grow up with allegiances forged more strongly with the educational institution than with their own blood relatives.

Objection: Homeschooling disrupts the home, so we should choose to go the classroom school route.

Response: This is like saying, "housing cows disrupts the cow barn." Perhaps it does – if you don't want to use the cow barn for what it was designed. Our concepts of "home" and "family" have been so fundamentally altered by the artificial culture created by socialized education that we have forgotten the true purposes of the family. The real problem is that the modern cultural concept of "home" and "family" are disruptive to the legitimate Biblical family function of Homeschooling, not vice versa. We are not saying anything about private classroom schools and hired tutors when we say this. Each father can sort out what that place is with respect to his family's calling and conditions and circumstances. But every family is a Homeschooling family – whether they realize it or not, whether they like it or not, and whether they do little or much of it. So let the cows into the cow barn and stop thinking of what transpires thereafter as a "disruption." "Oh mess and bother!" Sorry, but that's the real world. The next thing we'll hear is that having children is disruptive of marriage. Oh, wait, this culture is already teaching that.

8. There is an inherent contrast between:
1) the tutorial-discipleship model, and
2) the teacher-classroom model.

The first is an organic covenant model. The second is an artificial manufactory model. The first begins with persons in their ordinary and natural environment and follows a pattern of organic growth, adjustment, and development. The second begins with persons severed from all ordinary relations, and it follows a pattern of imposed conformity, efficiency, and productivity. Let's face it, other things being equal, the very best classroom school is the one most like home, and the very worst homeschool is the one most like a classroom. What do we call the reaction of little tykes to being coldly ripped from their natural relations and institutionalized at a young and tender age? Psychologists call it *separation anxiety* or *juvenile separation syndrome*. Educators call it kindergarten. Adults can easily adapt to teachers and classrooms. But to expect this from children is just plain unnatural and cruel. It should be considered a necessity only in emergencies.

Objection: Private school is just a supplement to parental administered education.

Response: Let's see if we have the redefinitions correct: Day-long teachers are just *supplementary* parents. Day-long classmates are just *supplementary* siblings. Day-long school is just *supplementary* family. Other things being equal (though they aren't), we think you're right – except for one thing: We may eat a meal and take dietary supplements to enhance the nutrition value. If the nutrition value of the meal goes down, then the quantity of supplements goes up. At what point do the supplements become the meal, and the meal becomes the supplement? We'll let you be the judge of that.

9. When learning is artificially separated from real life,
many things are left unlearned, creating a vacuum void
of things which need to be learned by daily example.

Both parents and children need to learn these things, but neither parents nor children can learn these things as they ought when they are separated from each other all day, and when, while they are together, their activities largely center around preparing the child for his separated activities at school. (By the way, doesn't this breed a child-centered culture instead of a family-centered culture? Sure, we try to counterbalance this. Why should we have to?) Pity the student who grows up thinking life should be as it was experienced in the classroom. Life is cooking and cleaning, caring for infants and toddlers, feeding the animals and planting the garden, grocery shopping and running errands, visiting the sick and the elderly, and lessons are learned in these things which are altogether missed in school.

There is a net loss of culture across each generation. The loss, at first, is relatively small. Children come to school with some discipline and respect for authority, some notions of perspective and proportion to life, some courtesy and etiquette, some politeness and consideration, some morality and sense of shame, etc. But the losses grow exponentially as well as accumulate over time, until the culture finally reaches a degenerate level at which all values precipitate, all sense of direction is lost, and competing cultures take over. We are about at that point in America today. Maybe we are past that point. Yes, we think we are past that point.

The reason for Israel's captivity in Babylon was ultimately ascribed by God to the failure of fathers to pass on instruction to their children.

> And Moses made an end of speaking all these words to all Israel: And he said unto them, Set your hearts unto all the words which I testify among you this day, **which ye shall command your children to observe to do, all the words of this law**. For it *is* not a vain thing for you; because it *is* your life: **and through this thing** [*that is, through commanding your children to observe to do the Law*] ye shall prolong *your* days in the land, whither ye go over Jordan to possess it. — Deuteronomy 32:45-47

Passing on the instruction of the Law to their children would prolong their days in the land. This was part of the first and the great commandment to love the Lord God with all their heart, and to diligently teach their children His commandments. This is the very thing which they failed to do, which led inevitably to their captivity.

After their captivity in Babylon, because so much instruction had been lost, the fathers had no idea what to pass on to their children. The generation after the Babylonian captivity had never heard the words of the Law. Thus we find in the book of Nehemiah that dramatic scene of the renewal of the feast of tabernacles which required that the book of the Law again be read to the people.

> And all the people gathered themselves together as one man into the street that was before the water gate . . . And Ezra the priest brought the law before the congregation . . . . And he read therein . . . And Ezra the scribe stood upon a pulpit of wood . . . . And Ezra opened the book in the sight of all the people; (for he was above all the people;) and when he opened it, all the people stood

> up: And Ezra blessed the LORD, the great God. And all the people answered, Amen, Amen, with lifting up their hands: and they bowed their heads, and worshipped the LORD with their faces to the ground. . . . **So they read in the book in the law of God distinctly, and gave the sense, and caused them to understand the reading.** And Nehemiah [the governor] . . . . and Ezra the priest and scribe, and the Levites that taught the people, **said unto all the people, This day is holy unto the LORD your God; mourn not, nor weep. For all the people wept, when they heard the words of the law**. — Nehemiah 8:1-6,8,9

The synagogue was instituted after the exile, not to replace the instruction of the family by the father, but to help the fathers to learn the Law so that the fathers could then instruct their own families in the Law. The synagogue was primarily for the fathers.

We will not recover our heritage so long as we are contented to follow the example of the Greek academy in education. We are not instead advocating a narrow Amish sort of culture which retreats from any formal education beyond the eighth grade, and which shrinks from knowledge about anything beyond the Bible or practical things. The liberty of the New Covenant frees us from the childish micro-regulated life, yet it requires us to take the very same principles once applied in a childish way in Israel, and to apply them now in a mature and responsible way to new and different circumstances. The modes may change, but the principles remain the same. Our culture has lost the fundamental principle of parental instruction of children. The business world, the religious world, the political world, the educational world – they all avoid it, work against it, and in many ways they rule it out – it will not fit into their order of things. Family *is* culture, and parental instruction of children is the God-ordained means of passing culture across generations. We interrupt that order only at our own peril. Naturally, there is stress between the world's ways and God's ways. Giving in to the world is not the solution. Giving in to God is.

Objection: Children need to grow up sometime, don't they? You're not operating in the real world. You're trying to shelter your children.

Response: That's exactly our point. The so-called "real world" isn't *real* according to God's standards. Children need to grow up in God's real world, not in man's fantasy world. God's real world requires parents to shelter their children and protect them from the elements while they are growing. Adam and Eve were the only persons born as adults.

10. Resources are imprudently consumed.

From the point of view of the parent, education in a classroom school is obtained at a premium rate. Unlike private classroom schools, Homeschooling does not cost from one thousand to three thousand dollars per student (or even more). You certainly could spend that much if you desired, but you would eventually accumulate a treasure of resources which would be the envy of any private school.

From the point of view of the student, time at a classroom school is consumed at a discount rate. After time for transportation, administration, interruption, and rearrangement is factored out, actual teaching and learning time in the most efficient of classroom schools could not be more than one half – more like one third – of the time elapsed between when the child left for school and when he returned home. In many public schools, this is actually far below a quarter of the total time elapsed. Six hours needed at a classroom school translates into perhaps two or three hours needed at homeschool. At homeschool, better quality time is available, and much less time is needed for pursuing studies, which leaves lots of time for other worthwhile activities, such as visiting the nursing home, or preparing a thoughtful treat for dad when he gets home. Though, in some respects, the classroom system may be considered a more efficient use of the teacher's time (teaching several students one subject at one time), it is not a more efficient use of the student's time – especially on the juvenile level.

The family which homeschools has greater freedom of time and movement for special family activities such as academic research, specialized tutoring, ministry to others, extended travel, or even family emergencies. Such opportunities are greatly decreased when the family is tied to the schedule of the classroom school.

The Problems with Classroom Schools – A Conclusion

We have arbitrarily cut off our list of problems with the classroom schools at ten. In making this short list, our purpose has been to awaken parents to some real issues concerning which the culture may have made them dull. We've left out such issues as health and safety, conformity and uniformity, lines of communication, conflicts in academics, behavior, and discipline, and the list goes on.

In summary, the long term effect of classroom schools is to take the child from his parents and to give him to himself, to his peers, to his teachers, to his school, and to a family-neutral culture. This necessarily leads to an improper and disorderly cultural transformation. The proper orderly transformation of culture comes from teaching adults at church and elsewhere, who in turn teach their children at home. The ordinary classroom of today is fundamentally an usurpation of proper lines of authority. We fully understand that this is not the expressed or implied intent of those who found, fund, and function in private schools. But good intentions are not the question. The question is whether its end is good and its means are lawful and proper. In an emergency, perhaps. Yet we would argue that the nature of the present cultural emergency drives us away from any institutional separation of children from their parents. We should never have adopted such institutions as a regular practice. (Why we did so is a large discussion in itself. Every violation of jurisdiction, if it passes unrecognized and is not stopped in the bud, will always grow and assume its own authority until it finally displaces the original jurisdiction.) We should never have forced minors to learn by an adult mode of education. We should help parents to do their duty, not facilitate their neglect of duty

THE HOMESCHOOL ADVANTAGE

> The home education has so much more potential than that of the school, that the little *modicum* of training which a "common-school" system can give to the average masses is utterly trivial and impotent . . . — *Discussions* by Robert L. Dabney, Vol. IV. Secular, 1876. p. 197.

Many and varied are those who have sung the praises of Homeschooling. The advantages have been treated by many authors. We have elsewhere written about *Seven Undeniable Truths of Homeschooling*:

1. Homeschooling is not alternative education. We were here first and we've been here the longest.
2. Every parent homeschools – but some parents homeschool more than others.
3. Parents are accountable directly to God for the education of their children.
4. Homeschooling produces by far the best academics.
5. Homeschooling produces by far the best socialization.
6. Homeschooling produces by far the best values.
7. Homeschooling is by far the best for parents as well as for their children.

We believe God's blessing today rests upon much of the modern Homeschooling movement because it conforms most closely to God's order for families, which is His chosen way to restore godly foundations to culture and society.

SOME QUESTIONS

Can Parents Handle Classical Education?

Question: Can parents really handle the classical subjects? Wouldn't the best option be a good classical Christian school?

Answer: The attitude of some homeschool parents is, "We can't do the classical approach. We have to leave that to the experts." They unknowingly throw out one of the many strong arguments for Homeschooling: private tutoring is much more effective than classroom teaching. Is there something about classical education which nullifies this argument? Not at all. Is classical Homeschooling not practical? Indeed, it is practical.

In the past, private tutoring in classical subjects was common. Some parents question whether they can act as a competent tutor when they have little or no experience in teaching such subjects as Greek, Latin, Logic, or classical literature. But today there are many friendly, digestible, self-teaching materials available in these subjects. Any parent with little or no familiarity with classical education can indeed act as a competent tutor with an ordinary amount of effort – a hurdle which he has already jumped when he entered the ranks of Homeschooling. No special degrees are required, except a Ph.D. (Doctor of Parenthood).

Furthermore, if we parents value a classical education for our children, why should we not value it for ourselves as well? Just because we *did not* learn these things in our youth does not mean that we *should not* learn them now, nor that we *cannot* learn them as we teach them to our own children. We never learn anything so well as when we ourselves have to teach it. What a blessing it is to have children to teach these things. We twentieth century graduates of government education were cheated out of much. We need to teach these things to our children – for our own sake!

How Long to Homeschool?

Question: How long do you plan to Homeschool?

Answer: God gave parents jurisdiction over the education of their children. If we fear we are failing in the task of educating them ourselves, then we must seek the Lord's help, and He may direct us to employ the help of others. Unfortunately, we do not have many relatives who are able or willing to help. Nevertheless, we cannot expect the Lord's help to come outside of His order and contrary to the way of His commandments. We grant that these times are emergency times which may justify some emergency measures. But we maintain that the nature of the emergency is such as militates *toward* rather than *against* Homeschooling. We hope to help our own children to homeschool their children. And we hope to continue to help other homeschoolers as well. We don't think we can ever stop Homeschooling. Why should we?

Our Child Doesn't Want to Homeschool

Question: Our child wants to go to school. Why should we still homeschool him? We are afraid we will *lose* him if we don't allow him to have his way.

Answer: This is a question of authority, and it is entirely separate from the question as to which mode of schooling is best.

Children don't know what's best for them – that's why God placed them into the care of parents. Teenagers sometimes think they know everything. That is all of the evidence which we need in order to prove that they don't. He who knows a little is sometimes worse off than he who knows nothing.

Here are the kind of decisions which a thirteen-year-old can make: Do you want to read *Swiss Family Robinson* or *Ben Hur*? Do you want to do a research paper on Benjamin Franklin or Patrick Henry? Do you want to memorize Romans or Hebrews first? But life-altering, major family-changing decisions – such as sending a child off to a school – are to be made by the parents, without even considering the momentary "felt needs" of the child. How we wish our own parents had made some good decisions for us when we were in high school, instead of leaving it up to us under the *wise* advice of our school counselor. (We did not know what was best for us, and our high school counselors knew less than we did.) God bless those wise parents who make their children do things which children do not want to do. ("Am I ever glad they *made* me take Latin.")

Parents do not need to support another program outside of the home – whether it should be a Sunday School, a Youth Group, or a private day school. What we really need are ministries to parents to help them raise and school their children at home. In other words, we need ministries which actually help parents to perform their God-given duties. What a concept! Furthermore, we need examples for fathers to follow in managing their own households and teaching their own families. We can skip some of the homeschool mother's meetings and homeschool student enrichment days for a while in order to concentrate on restoring fatherhood to the cultural vocabulary.

It is still true that

> He that walketh with wise men shall be wise: but a companion of fools shall be destroyed. — Proverbs 13:20

It is still true that

> . . . evil communications corrupt good manners [/bad companionships corrupt good morals].— First Corinthians 15:33

It is still true that

> . . . a little leaven leaveneth a whole lump. — First Corinthians 5:6; Galatians 5:9

Sure, the Lord can protect our child if he is cast into a lion's den, or into a fiery furnace. The Lord may some day throw him precisely into such circumstances, for his obedience to His word, in order to test, purify, and strengthen his faith. But if we ourselves throw our child into such circumstances, we have no reason to expect the Lord to deliver him. The Lord might, but not because He has promised to – because He has never promised any such thing. If He does deliver him, it will only be because He has chosen to show him mercy – but to our humiliation.

> Thou shalt not tempt the Lord Thy God. — Matthew 4:7

You must do what is right, and leave the result to God. If you must let your child have his own way, then you have already lost your child's heart, haven't you?

> . . . a child left *to himself* bringeth his mother to shame. — Proverbs 29:15

What About Emergencies?

Question: We have an emergency in our family (an extended illness, care for a grandparent, a pregnancy, etc.) which will demand much of my time. I fear that I will not have enough time to adequately prepare to teach my children. Though I do not want to put any of my children in a classroom school, I also do not want them to have less than they need in an education. My first reaction is to enroll them in a school. How should I decide?

Answer: Decisions are best made on the basis of established principles, values, and goals. Many of these are worked out over time, though often this is not done quite so deliberately, and seldom are they actually written down. In a situation such as you describe, it is best to think through carefully and write down what principles, values, and goals apply to the situation.

Let's suppose that high among your goals is, "My children will get a high school diploma." You might satisfy this goal in a government, a private, or a homeschool. Financial and time constraints might then cause you to favor sending your children to a government school. Time constraints alone might cause you to favor sending them to a private school. You might homeschool if there were no other constraints.

Let's suppose that high among your values is, "My children will have the best curriculum, no matter what the cost." You might satisfy this value in a private school, or in a homeschool. Time constraints might then cause you to favor enrolling your children in a good private classical school.

Let's suppose that one of your principles is, "My children should be bonded to their family, not to their peers." Since God gave you responsibility over the education of your children, therefore you will homeschool your children, regardless of financial and time constraints. If this is one of your principles, then your decision to homeschool would be firm, and, regardless of the circumstances, you would work out the details as to curriculum.

Principles take priority over values, and values take priority over goals. We need to shift from being goals driven (outcome-based), and toward being principles driven (standards-based). We may have a goal which seems very worthy, but no end justifies pursuing any means necessary for obtaining it. Standards justify means, and means justify ends, and when a golden chain of standards, means, and ends (principles, values, and goals) is forged, only higher purposes in the Lord's plan can cause them to fail.

So, when confronted with an emergency situation, such as an ill and elderly grandparent, or a nine-month-long pregnancy, then after you have determined your principles, values, and goals, if you determine that you should homeschool, then you would simply prepare as you can, teach what you are able, and leave the results to the Lord. Perhaps the Lord wants your children to learn some special skills in helping to care for the ill and elderly, or in helping mom to homeschool from the living room couch. These are valuable lessons too – valuable enough to interrupt a regular schedule for.

What About an Only Child?

Question: As parents of an only child, we would be interested in good solid answers to the socialization arguments which we endure the most from family and friends: "he needs to learn to play with other children; to be patient with others who do not catch on as quickly; to tolerate others who are from very different backgrounds than he; to interact with children who have social or physical disabilities; to raise his hand and wait to be called upon; to patiently listen to others answer; to understand that it is not always his turn."

Answer: It sounds like some social-psychologist with too much time on his hands, and sensing a need to justify his existence, or his research budget, has been out there in the culture promoting silly ideas which make his philosophy look important. What does it take to learn how to properly relate to and interact with other people? It takes other people. So if you've got some other people around, you probably have everything you need to accomplish what you want. One child plus two parents makes three people. Do you need any more? There will be plenty of opportunities to relate to and interact with other people. Indeed, there will be too many opportunities. You will need to limit those opportunities, though you may desire to plan a few. What your only child is really missing is brothers and sisters. So do you have a brother or sister who believes like you, who homeschools, who lives close by, and who has an orderly family, so that you can spend a day together every now and then and your only child can sort of adopt his cousins as semi-brothers and sisters? If you don't have a blood brother and sister whom you can do this with, then how about a brother and sister in the Lord? Remember, in the sovereign providence of the Lord, He has chosen to make your child an only child. He has a unique purpose in this. The Lord wants you to learn something different with this child. As far as learning to play with other children, to be patient with others, to tolerate others who are different, to interact with those who have disabilities, to wait patiently for an opportunity to speak, to patiently listen to others answer – what's the big deal? Just think of all of the people in the world who have to learn to get along with an only-child! With a first-born! With a last-born! With a middle child! Not to mention the misfit families which dominate our culture today – multiple divorces and multiple marriages, etc. Being an only child is not nearly as unique nowadays as being one child of twelve. So how does the one-of-twelve child adjust? Well, as a matter of fact, each of us is rather unique in some way or another, so how does anyone ever survive? This is the kind of worrywart thinking promoted by social-psychologists. None to worry. God is in control. Just follow His lead and you'll keep on the right path. He knows what your child needs more than you do. Remember, your child was His before your child was yours! You only have him as a temporary stewardship.

SUMMARY AND CONCLUSION

So why do Christian parents choose to homeschool their children?

Obviously, parents choose, for a plethora of reasons, to tutor their children at home, rather than send them to a private school. There may be no satisfactory private school within the financial or transportation limits of the family. Actually, homeschool is about as private a school as we can get. It could, in fact, be considered an exclusive boarding school where each pupil has his own specialized program and dedicated personal tutor. Students thrive in such an environment. Many parents are attracted to Homeschooling for social reasons, and some for academic reasons. But more and more parents are choosing to homeschool simply because they wish to follow Biblical principles, values, and goals for education, and the Homeschool model fits this best.

According to the Biblical model for education, parents are to be directly in control and directly involved in the education of their children. Under God, neither the state nor the church has any jurisdiction in the matter.

Private tutoring and specialized classes may be usefully adapted to direct parental control and involvement. However, the classroom school – whether controlled by the state or by private interests – takes another step beyond this by creating an artificial microculture of age segregation, gender integration, reorientation of personal commitments and time commitments, cultural and academic value alterations, social peer pressures, and ungodly rivalry. The classroom usurps the proper lines of parental authority.

Socialists have promoted the classroom school as the incarnation of their model for cultural transformation – weakening the family bonds, separating children from their parents, and culturally transforming the children into human resources for the state. Christians should stop mimicking the socialist culture. We should begin to transform culture through a Biblical model. We must stop conforming our thoughts to this world's standards and prejudices. Instead, we must allow our minds to be transformed in order to prove what is that good, and acceptable, and perfect will of God (Romans 12:1,2).

This culture in which we live is in ruins because of its unbiblical ideals. These ideals simply will not stand on their own. So why do many Christians still feel some cultural obligation to keep propping up these ruins? We do not need to repair, reform, or reconstruct our culture.

> . . . Know ye not that a little leaven leaveneth the whole lump? Purge out therefore the old leaven, that ye may be a new lump, as ye are unleavened. — First Corinthians 5:6,7

We need to remove the corrupting influence of the culture, and rebuild the family from the foundation up – not on the model of our crumbled culture, but on the biblical model of God's order. We need to reconstitute biblical culture from the foundation up – a new lump, unleavened.

The "classical" model of education – the Trivium – happens to be the Biblical model written into the very nature of things. Though the pagans stole it and used it to help prop up their classical culture, there is nothing essentially pagan about the model itself. Removed from its pagan context, and reunited with reality – genuine Christianity – it will serve well Christian parents who desire to enculturate their own families in order to develop a distinctly Biblical and Christian culture. (To learn how the Emperor Julian attempted to stamp out Christianity by forbidding Christians to teach the Trivium, see Appendix One, Article Twelve, Outcome-Based Education versus Trivium-Based Education.)

SOME FINAL WORDS

In the providence of God, private classroom schools have served as an intermediate launching pad for many of the materials which later lifted Homeschooling off of the ground, up, and into orbit. But now that Homeschooling is increasing, we believe it is time for classroom schools to decrease.

> And he spake also a parable unto them; No man putteth a piece of a new garment upon an old; if otherwise, then both the new maketh a rent, and **the piece that was *taken* out of the new agreeth not with the old**. And no man putteth new wine into old bottles; else **the new wine will burst the bottles, and be spilled**, and the bottles shall perish. But new wine must be put into new bottles; and both are preserved. No man also having drunk old *wine* straightway desireth new: for he saith, The old is better. — Luke 5:36-39

Those who have grown up in a world which knew nothing better than the classroom school, tend to think that classrooms must be better. When homeschoolers experience "burnout," it is often because they have tried to sew the new patch of home-tutoring upon the old and familiar garment of the classroom school. They have tried to "bring school home." Many parents hold to a ridiculous conception of what is required for tutoring their children, so they overburden themselves with all kinds of activities and studies which are either redundant or unnecessary. Home-tutoring and classroom schools are, in many ways, two very different worlds.

It is time to put the new wine into new wineskins. We must not bring the classroom home. That is only a hindrance which we must get beyond. When our children finally do face classroom situations, they will adjust quickly and easily. It is the classroom school children who commonly have difficulty adjusting to a disciplined Homeschool setting. With exceptions which prove the rule, classroom schools create a dependency which is sometimes very difficult to overcome. It can require three years or more for a classroom student to adjust to Homeschooling.

Perhaps you think that we have overstated the case. We'll allow you to be the judge. We are satisfied that every parent should prefer Homeschooling. We are most sympathetic to the practical difficulty of pursuing such an ideal within a culture which excludes normal family life from its agenda.

The home should always be considered the normal and ordinary center and setting for childhood education, and those who honor God's order will receive the blessing. The future of godly education is not served by centralizing the process, but by diversifying it. We do not expect the classroom day-schools to largely disappear on our recommendation. We do suggest that they be thoroughly restructured into a resource for Christian parents. Faculties could be greatly reduced and converted into *think tanks* to produce materials for Homeschooling parents, to provide a few specialized part-time classes for parents, and to provide specialized tutorial services where special help is needed. That would be a very efficient use of talents within a Biblical framework for education.

Chapter Four

What is the Trivium?

For the LORD giveth wisdom:
out of his mouth *cometh* knowledge and understanding.
— Proverbs 2:6

INTRODUCTION

AFTER SHIFTING ASIDE a mountain of modern educational philosophy, removing the corruptions and incrustations which have accrued through time, and sifting all of the ancient rubble through the critical screen of the Scriptures, we have reduced our findings down to some valuable nuggets and gems of educational wisdom. Refined and molded under the fire of God's providence, cut and polished under the light of God's Word, they are transformed into fine coin and rare jewel – precious principles for education. In this Chapter, we begin to share with you some of these treasured tools for teaching known as the Trivium. We will explain the classical model and method for education, and we will show how modern education does not measure up to classical standards.

THE CLASSICAL TRIVIUM

Trivium is a Latin word which means "where three roads meet." Both ancient and mediaeval schools structured their curriculum around three roads of learning which they taught by means of three formal subjects:

1. The first subject which they taught was called *Grammar*. By means of Grammar, a student was taught the mastery of the elements of a language (usually Greek or Latin). Teaching Grammar gave the student skill in comprehension. He learned to accurately receive knowledge.
2. The second subject which they taught was called *Logic* (or *Dialectic*). By means of logic, a student was taught the mastery of statements, definitions, arguments, and fallacies. Teaching logic gave the student skill in reasoning. He learned to critically analyze and to understand.
3. The third subject which they taught was called *Rhetoric*. By means of Rhetoric, the student was taught the mastery of creative and persuasive speech. Teaching Rhetoric gave the student skill in communication. He learned to wisely and effectively express and practice what he had learned.

These three subjects: Grammar, Logic, and Rhetoric, constituted the *formal* Trivium in the *classical* sense.

THE APPLIED TRIVIUM

At Oxford University in 1947, Dorothy Sayers delivered an essay entitled *The Lost Tools of Learning.* (Her essay is reprinted in Appendix One, Article One.) Only a generation later, her essay has sparked a revival in the classical method of learning. Though we do not venerate Miss Sayers, and we must never fail to sift everything through the critical screen of the Scriptures, nevertheless we acknowledge that she has made some valuable observations.

In her essay, Miss Sayers lamented the inability of modern educators to educate. She made the following observations:

1. Students are taught more subjects, but they know less about everything.
2. They cannot divide fact from opinion, or plausibility from proof.
3. They are incapable of directly addressing a point, or staying on point without introducing irrelevant material.

4. They do not define terms, and they cannot understand different senses in which a term can be used.
5. They speak the language with inaccurate syntax.
6. They cannot learn a new subject on their own.
7. They do not make the connection between different subjects.

In other words, the miracle of modern education has rendered our culture intellectually impotent. We have lost the tools for thinking and for learning on our own.

Miss Sayers proposed a remedy for the problem. She suggested that we return to what had worked in the past. Specifically, she applied the three subjects of the formal mediaeval Trivium – Grammar, Logic, and Rhetoric – as both an educational model or philosophy and as a teaching method or technique. We call this the *Applied Trivium.*

The Trivium Model of Child Educational Development

First, Miss Sayers applied the Trivium to the progressive steps of a child's educational development. She observed that every child passes through three stages of development:

1. A Grammar Stage, when the child absorbs factual information like a sponge.
2. A Logic Stage, when the child is more inquisitive and analytical.
3. A Rhetoric Stage, when the child is more creative and expressive.

We call this the *Trivium Model of Child Educational Development*. Here is how Miss Sayers described the different stages:

> *Grammar Stage:* "The Poll-Parrot stage is the one in which learning by heart is easy and, on the whole, pleasurable; whereas reasoning is difficult and, on the whole, little relished. At this age one readily memorizes the shapes and appearances of things; one likes to recite. . . . one rejoices in the chanting of rhymes and the rumble and thunder of unintelligible polysyllables; one enjoys the mere accumulation of things."

> *Logic Stage:* "The Pert Age, which follows upon this (and, naturally, overlaps it to some extent) is only too familiar to all who have to do with children: it is characterized by contradicting, answering-back, liking to "catch people out" (especially one's elders) and propounding of conundrums (especially the kind with a nasty verbal catch in them)."

Rhetoric Stage: "The Poetic Age is popularly known as the "difficult" age. It is self-centered; it yearns to express itself; it rather specializes in being misunderstood; it is restless and tries to achieve independence; and, with good luck and good guidance, it should show the beginnings of creativeness, a reaching-out towards a synthesis of what it already knows, and a deliberate eagerness to know and do some one thing in preference to all others."

The Trivium Method for Teaching Subjects

Miss Sayers also applied the Trivium to the steps of the development of each individual subject. Each subject goes through three stages of development:

1. Every subject has its own Grammar, or a knowledge of the basic facts, and fundamental rules – in other words, all of the individual parts.
2. Every subject has its own logic, or an understanding of the relationships between these facts and rules – in other words, how all of the parts fit together.
3. Every subject has its own Rhetoric, or wisdom in verbally expressing and practically applying what we know and understand – in other words, how to put this all to good use.

We call this the *Trivium Method for Teaching Subjects*. The student must learn each subject by progressing through these three steps:

First, the Grammar of the subject – the facts – the *who, what, where and when*.

Second, the Logic of the subject – the theory – the *why*.

Third, the Rhetoric of the subject – the practice – the *how*.

Here are a few examples. Let us begin with the subject of Mathematics:

1. The *Grammar* of mathematics would include learning the Arabic number system, memorizing the math facts of addition, subtraction, multiplication, and division, learning measurement systems – inches and feet, quarts and gallons, cents and dollars.
2. The *Logic* of mathematics would progress from such things as story problems to the proofs of algebra or theorems of geometry.
3. The *Rhetoric* of mathematics would apply mathematics to surveying, accounting, engineering, or astronomy.

Now let us consider the subject of English language:

1. The *Grammar* Stage of English would be phonics, vocabulary, and spelling.

2. The *Logic* Stage of English would be what we call *formal grammar* such as the parts of speech, the construction of sentences, and proper syntax.
3. The *Rhetoric* Stage of English would include paragraph construction, essay development, composition, and public speaking.

Finally, let us look at the subject of history:

1. The story part of history, which includes names, places, and dates, would be the *Grammar* of history.
2. Study and research to determine the reasons for such things as wars, migrations, or inventions would be the *Logic* of history.
3. Applying historical research and conclusions to views in politics, economics, religion, or science would be the *Rhetoric* of history.

THE SCRIPTURAL TRIVIUM

The *formal* Trivium in the *classical* sense (the three subjects of Grammar, Logic, Rhetoric) is an ancient method of education which has been highly successful for millennia. The mediaevals did not invent the Trivium. They obtained it from the Romans, who acquired it from the Greeks. But they were not the first to use it. The Hebrews recognized these principles in their teaching. So what is the actual source of the Trivium?

We believe the classical Trivium is rooted in our created nature. Many ideas in ancient times are actually remnants of ancient truths which came from God. For example, over three hundred cultures in the world have accounts of a worldwide flood, and though these stories themselves are pagan in origin, who can doubt that many of them were passed down from the original accounts given by Noah and his family? Nevertheless, we do not believe in the flood because of these accounts. We believe in the flood because of Scripture. So it is with the Trivium.

The learning process naturally falls into this three step progression:

1. The first step is to accumulate the facts. We call this *Knowledge*.
2. The second step is to comprehend the relationships between these facts. We call this *Understanding*.
3. The third step is to put to practical use and expression what we know and understand. We call this *Wisdom*.

Knowledge of the facts corresponds closely to the *Grammar Stage* of the Trivium. *Understanding* of their relationships corresponds closely to the

Logic Stage of the Trivium. *Wisdom* in applying what we know and understand corresponds closely to the *Rhetoric Stage* of the Trivium.

We will find this refrain of *Knowledge*, *Understanding*, and *Wisdom* interwoven throughout the Scriptures, though especially in the book of Proverbs. For example:

> For the Lord giveth **wisdom**: out of His mouth cometh **knowledge** and **understanding**. — Proverbs 2:6

> The LORD by **wisdom** hath founded the earth; by **understanding** hath he established the heavens. By his **knowledge** the depths are broken up, and the clouds drop down the dew. — Proverbs 3:19,20

God's Wisdom is creative, founding the earth (Genesis 1:1), His Understanding is powerful, dividing the firmament of waters into the oceans below and the heavens above (Genesis 1:6-8), and His Knowledge is detailed, moving fountains everywhere from out of the earth and dropping rain everywhere from out of the heavens.

> Through **wisdom** is an house builded; and by **understanding** it is established: and by **knowledge** shall the chambers be filled with all precious and pleasant riches. — Proverbs 24:3,4

The practical *Wisdom* of the builder brings about the house's construction. The *Understanding* of the principles of building establishes the house's integrity. The *Knowledge* of the particulars fills the house with beautiful materials.

Our Creator worked the fundamental structure of the Trivium into the very fiber of our natural being. We come to *know* things in the natural world through our natural *senses*. We come to *understand* these things with our *minds*. We put our understandings into *wise practice* through our *muscles*.

We will only give here a brief introduction to the Trivium in Scripture. (For more development of the Trivium in Scripture, see Appendix One, Article Two)

Analogy of the Trivium to a Building: Foundation, Structure, and Use

Though Knowledge, Understanding, and Wisdom can be studied as separate concepts, these three concepts are not isolated from each other. Rather, all three grow together and build upon one another (which is why we rarely find them in Scripture in a simple one-two-three order.) Let us look at their relationship.

1. Knowledge (or Grammar, or the facts) is the foundation. Without first acquiring Knowledge, we cannot go on to build an Understanding.

Apply thine heart unto **instruction**, and thine ears to **the words of knowledge**. — Proverbs 23:12

2. After we have laid the foundation of Knowledge, we can begin to build an Understanding (that is, logic, or the theory). But as we build an Understanding, we also create a need and desire for more Knowledge.

The heart of him that hath **understanding** seeketh **knowledge**. — Proverbs 15:14

3. After we have the foundation of Knowledge, and the structure of Understanding, we can move on to the practical use of what has been built – the Wisdom (that is, Rhetoric, or the practice). But this creates a need and desire for still more Knowledge and still more Understanding.

I, **wisdom**, dwell with **prudence** [/understanding], and [I] find out **knowledge** of witty inventions [/*of* learned thoughts]. — Proverbs 8:12

The heart of the **prudent** [/one with understanding] getteth **knowledge**; and the ear of the **wise** seeketh **knowledge**. — Proverbs 18:15

ANALOGY OF THE TRIVIUM TO A BUILDING

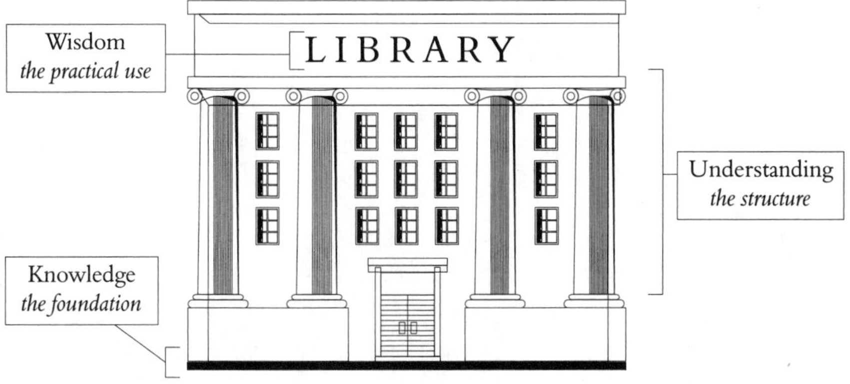

FIGURE 4A

Analogy of the Trivium to Computers: Input, Processing, and Output

A comparison to computers may help to explain the idea: *Knowledge* would be the *input*. *Understanding* would be the *processing*. *Wisdom* would be the *output*.

1. *Knowledge requires input*. The Knowledge or input level engages our input devices – reading, hearing and experiencing with our senses – in order to *key in* the data or information.
2. *Understanding requires processing*. The Understanding or processing level utilizes the central processor of our mind to dissect, compare, discuss, and debate the data in order to discover relationships.
3. *Wisdom requires output*. The Wisdom or output level turns to the practical use and expression of the material through our output devices – *printing out* through performing, producing, and creating with our voice, our hands, our feet, etc. We are applying all of the data which we have read in, and all of the relationships which we have processed, in creative, meaningful, and practical ways.

ANALOGY OF THE TRIVIUM TO A COMPUTER

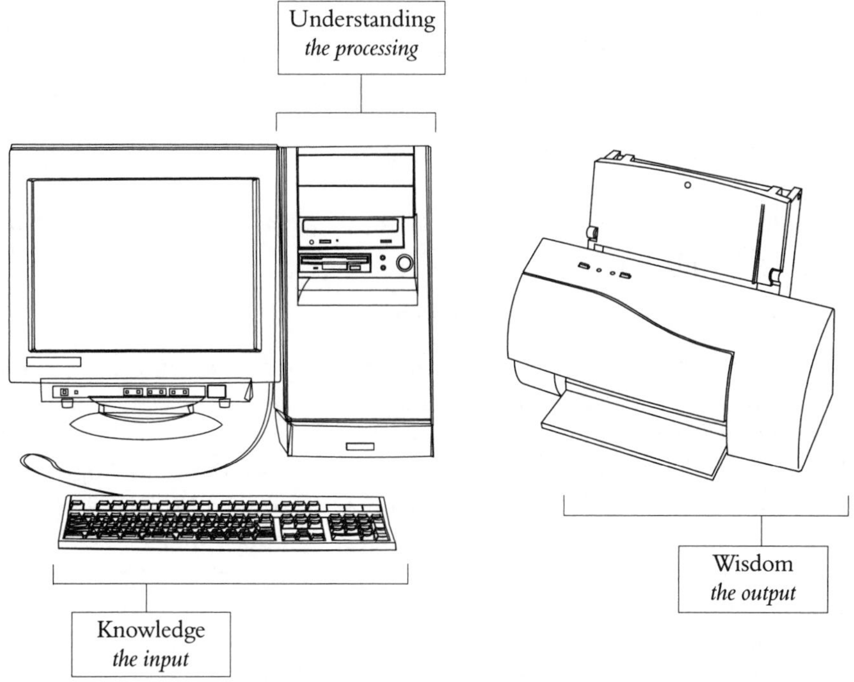

FIGURE 4B

The Development of Knowledge, Understanding, and Wisdom

A large portion of a child's early years are spent soaking up Knowledge. This is the Knowledge Level (or Grammar Stage).

Once the child has accumulated a fair amount of Knowledge, and his mind has developed, he becomes able and eager to reason on things. So by age twelve or thirteen, the child is entering the Understanding Level (or Logic Stage). He continues to accumulate Knowledge, of course, but more of his choices as to what Knowledge to pursue are determined by his growing Understanding.

By the later teens, the student has filled enough of his Understanding that he becomes able and eager to express himself in creative and effective ways. This is the Wisdom Level (or Rhetoric Stage). In order to feed his desire to express himself, he needs still more Knowledge and still more Understanding.

What we are talking about here is not some brand new and different educational philosophy. All education, from the far-removed past up until this century, has been built upon these three roads of learning. We call it the six-thousand-year-old curriculum. This is simply the natural progression of learning. It is the way in which God made us, and nobody can improve upon it no matter how hard they might try. Anybody who ever learned anything necessarily learned it by this Trivium progression, whether they knew it or not. But it is usually better to know what you are doing, and that is why we have written this book.

(For an historical look at the Trivium, see Appendix One, Articles Three through Seven.)

Trivium Terminology

Dorothy Sayers led the way in attempting to coin a terminology for the levels (or stages) of learning. She suggested *Poll-Parrot*, *Pert*, and *Poetic*. Her terminology has never caught on. Because Dorothy Sayers applied, by analogy, the three formal classical subjects – Grammar, Logic, and Rhetoric – to the three levels of development, those who have followed her application have – probably by default – simply appropriated these same terms for the three levels of development. Back in 1989, we suggested that the terms *Knowledge*, *Understanding*, and *Wisdom* would serve better to describe the three levels of development. Well, that never caught on either. So as to avoid confusion with others who have written on these subjects, we will try to work with both terminologies – though we still prefer Knowledge, Understanding, and Wisdom.

MODERN EDUCATION IS DYSFUNCTIONAL

Harvard, 1643

In 1643, the first college entrance requirements in this country were established by Harvard College as follows:

> "When any scholar is able to understand Tully, or such like classical author extempore, and make and speak true Latin in verse and prose, . . . and decline perfectly the Paradigms of Nouns and Verbs in the Greek tongue; let him then and not before be capable of admission into the college."

Few Harvard graduates today could have entered the Harvard freshman class back then. Students often entered Harvard around age 16, and graduated around age 18 or 19. These were their College Graduation Requirements:

First Year: Logic, Physics, Disputes, Greek, Hebrew, Rhetoric.

Second Year: Ethics, Politics, Disputes, Greek, Hebrew, Rhetoric.

Third Year: Arithmetic, Geometry, Astronomy, Nature of Plants, History, Greek, Composition, Hebrew, Rhetoric.

They required no Latin. They were to have mastered Latin before college. Many of the college textbooks were written in Latin.

Three Observations on Modern Education

Once we become familiar with the classical Trivium, it becomes apparent to anyone with eyes to see that the problems with modern education are systemic.

1. Trivia, not Trivium.

Our first observation is that modern education majors on the minors. It pursues Trivia, not Trivium. True education should not be like filling an empty bucket. It should be like lighting a fire. Alas, modern education tries to fill a bucket. It creates a twelve volume "scope and sequence" encyclopedia of everything it wants every child to learn – one volume for each year of school. Then it expects every child to be on the same page of that encyclopedia at the same time. If a child's bucket isn't filled to the prescribed level, then he must have some kind of learning dysfunction.

Our disagreement is not so much with the scope and sequence approach, as with the factory method of education by which the scope and sequence is applied. Educational bureaucrats have reduced education to the synchronized memorization of an entire encyclopedia of knowledge as it comes down an educational conveyor belt. Every child on the assembly line is expected to be in perfect synchronization with the conveyor belt. But we know that no two children develop at exactly the same rate in exactly the same areas. Some will be ahead of the pace, and others will be behind – and both will miss what is on the conveyor belt. As a result, there will always be children who miss some pages, others who miss some chapters, and still others who miss entire books. Educators often try to eliminate this problem by slowing down the conveyor belt – eliminating some of the contents of the encyclopedia. As a result, the children ahead of the pace become bored, and the children behind the pace miss even more. (Thomas Edison was considered by such educators to be ineducable.) The problem is not so much the encyclopedia as it is the conveyor belt.

Modern education teaches a multitude of subjects, but it does not teach children to master the skills of 1) comprehending, 2) reasoning and 3) communicating (that is, the Trivium) by which one can master any subject on his own. By contrast, classical education focused first upon learning these three skills of the Trivium, while practicing with these Trivium skills upon various "subjects." The modern student is spoon-fed many subjects – but never taught how to learn. The ancient student was first taught how to learn, then he applied that skill of learning to many things.

The student who masters the Trivium can teach himself anything. But many products of modern schools need to be spoon-fed everything. The Trivium is lifelong self-learning. Modern education is lifelong task-learning, or we might say, lifelong serf-learning.

2. Interrupting the Learning Process.

Our second observation is that modern education interrupts the natural progression of learning.

Children are naturally curious. They are natural learners. Children teach themselves to speak a highly complex language in their first few years – English! In fact, there is strong evidence that the ear of a child is trained to discern the sounds of his native language while he is still in his mother's womb. (But we do not want educational bureaucrats to learn about this, or we are likely to have prenatal speech therapists before too long!)

It takes a lot of modern education to stifle a young child's natural ability to learn. If a child learns anything, then he learns it by the natural Trivium progression of learning, no matter what else we may try to impose upon the learning process. But if we interrupt the natural Trivium progression of learning, then we will create a learning dysfunction. That is what modern education does: it creates learning dysfunctions by omitting parts of the learning process.

To begin with, formal education is begun too early. Young children need more training than teaching. When we take a young child out of the natural environment of his own home under his own parents, and we place him in a formal institution, then we train him to look to his peers and to his teachers and to the power of the state as the authorities in his life, while we undermine the authority of his parents. Early socialization is very important to modern socialist educators. It is anti-family social training. For over a half of a century, social psychologists and educators have been telling us that they must "weaken the family" –

those are their words – in order to accomplish their socialist goals for our children.

The reasoning (Understanding or Logic) skills of young children are not highly developed, and their creative (Wisdom or Rhetoric) skills are still at an elementary level. Sure, young children are capable of some reasoning and they can be quite creative, but they are still largely down at the basic *Knowledge Level* until about age twelve or thirteen. They need more training than they need teaching. This is the time to lay a proper foundation for future education. But in modern education, the time is squandered. When we should be filling our child's mind with useful facts and training his spirit in self-discipline, instead, the educators are overstimulating the child's senses with all kinds of things which he either does not need to know, or he is simply too young to handle. (Some of the sex-education material to which the young children are exposed in the socialized schools constitutes child abuse of the worst sort. It destroys the child's innocence and it violates the child's purity. Such questions do not normally arise in a young child's mind.)

When a child reaches the early teens he is at the *Understanding Level* – he is entering the Logic or reasoning stage. He needs to develop the critical apparatus for thinking. But in modern education, this Logic Stage of learning is overridden by what we like to call "programmed thinking," where certain understandings are imposed on the child's thinking without factual knowledge, and without training the mind to correctly reason them out.

We are referring, in part, to the way children are brainwashed into accepting politically correct ideology – socialism, environmentalism, feminism, multiculturalism, etc. The teaching of evolution is another good example. Evolution is mythology disguised as science. The success of the theory of evolution is proof that intelligent persons can be led to believe anything! These children are not taught to logically evaluate the presuppositions which lie behind the politically correct ideology or evolutionary teaching. Instead, these things are treated as if they were infallible revelations directly handed down to us from the gods of Political Correctness. This is mind-neglect, and it constitutes intellectual child-abuse.

Many students become frustrated, bored, and burned out because they are not allowed to think. Not only are they not trained to think, they are actually trained not to think. If you ask a product of modern education to evaluate something for you – perhaps a movie – he can tell you his sensory perceptions, but don't expect him to go much further than the sensory level. ("Hey, man, like, this movie was just like, ya' know, totally awesome.") Ask him for some analysis of the plot (if there is any) or whether the movie was trying to make some point or to teach some lesson (they all do that). His thinking will come to a screeching halt. ("Huh! What'cha mean man? It's just, like, a movie, man.") He does not possess the critical apparatus to intellectually evaluate what his senses are receiving. He cannot discern between good and evil; only between pleasant and unpleasant sensory perceptions. No wonder that products of modern education are so easily swayed by propaganda in the media. Their mental development never properly matures. Many of them never go beyond the childish level.

The *Star Wars* movies are a good example of this. While the audiences are soaking up entertainment, their little minds full of mush are being impregnated with the seeds of New Age pantheistic dualism – the equal divinities of Light and Darkness. The dark side of The Force speaks through the character Darth Vader and asks, "What is your bidding, my master?" The light side of The Force speaks through Obewan Kenobe and says, "If you strike me down now, I shall become more powerful than you could possibly imagine." Evolution and reincarnation are also interweaved throughout the movie.

When children are taught so-called "thinking skills" they are actually being taught "unthinking skills;" that is, they are being programmed to think a certain way. Though the programming may involve some superficial reasoning, nevertheless, it is not logic based. Instead, it is emotionally based. You may have heard of "phony phonics." We call this "lazy logic."

You must understand, that unless we reason from the propositions of Scripture, all of our reasoning is eventually going to break down into logical contradictions. We will say more about this later in the book, but for now, we want to give you a few examples.

Children may be programmed with lazy logic to "say no to drugs" for many reasons – physical and psychological health, etc. But because their motivation for not taking drugs is not based upon clear reasoning from moral absolutes, they are actually being prepared to "say yes to drugs" under the right mixture of circumstances. By training a child to "say no to drugs" for wrong and inadequate reasons we are actually laying a weak and faulty foundation. When the wind and rain of strong emotional pressures come against this house built upon sand, the foundation will crumble because it is not built upon solid logic.

Here is another example. If your boy studies Bicycle Mechanics, then would you be surprised to find him out in the garage one day with his bicycle torn apart? Of course not! If your girl takes a course in Cooking, then would you be amazed to find her in the kitchen one day trying out a new recipe on her own? Of course not! You would expect it. You would be disappointed if she did not! Yet children who have been taught no moral absolutes, nor have they been taught how to correctly reason from moral absolutes, are put into Drug Ed 101, Sex Ed 101, and Death Ed 101. Then, surprise! These children are coming home drugged and diseased, pregnant and perverted, morbid and suicidal. What is truly surprising is that any of these children ever come home normal!

When students enter the later teens they reach the *Wisdom Level*. They should be learning to creatively and effectively express things and to put them into practice. However, modern educators have encouraged self-expression from children since preschool, yet without training them in self-discipline. After a dozen or more years of mental abuse imposed upon them by educational bureaucrats, many older teens simply express their frustrations with this whole abusive system in undisciplined and destructive ways.

In other words, the state's schools run every child through their mental meat processing plant, and unless something interrupts the process, the children will all come out the same size baloney.

By contrast, classical education conforms to the very nature of mental development. Education in any subject naturally develops through these three levels:

1) Mastery of the facts.
2) Mastery of their relationships.
3) Mastery of their uses and applications.

We must overcome all of the dysfunctional impositions of these disastrous modern learning theories – imposed upon our children as the experiments of social psychologists, without any honest critical analysis – and we must return to the natural progression of learning which has worked for multiple millennia.

3. Regressive Education.

Our third observation is that modern education is not *progressive*. It is *regressive*. It does not move *forward*. It moves *backward*.

If we train a child in those disciplines which equip him for self-education, then we will open all doors for him. The first and the greatest masters in any discipline of learning were all self-taught. There was no one else ahead of them to teach them! In order to progress beyond the limits of their teachers, students must be given the tools for self-teaching which will enable them to go forward and to become creative on their own. Trivium-based education is the only truly "progressive" education because it alone gives students the basic tools for self teaching which can guarantee progress.

Trivium Based Education versus Outcome Based Education

All of these distinctives of modern education – that it majors on the minors; that it interrupts the natural progression of learning; that it is regressive, not progressive – all of these distinctives, at their best, can only inhibit the normal learning process. But at their worst, they create serious learning dysfunctions.

One effective way to explain something is to contrast it with its opposite. The opposite of the Trivium is a modern development called *Outcome Based Education*, in which students are taught to perform or produce in a certain way, regardless of their understanding of the fundamentals. We will explain with an example.

Let us pretend that we are going to teach you to play Beethoven's *Moonlight Sonata* on the piano by the Outcome Based Education method. We will call this the "whole music" method. We will sit you down at the piano, and we will begin with the *Moonlight Sonata*. We will tell you where to put your fingers, and we will take you by rote through the piece. We might break the piece up into smaller and simpler portions at first. We might introduce some "look-play" flash cards. Eventually you will learn to play the Moonlight Sonata. And you will receive your certificate of mastery sooner than if we had taught you by the Trivium method.

What if you want to learn another song? This is where the differences in these two methods will become noticeable. Under Outcome Based Education, you will have to come to us, and we will have to teach you. "We are the toastmasters; you are the task-performer." You will be dependent upon your instructors for everything which you learn.

Of course, there will be a few students who will learn by ear, and who will catch on to the technique after a few songs – just as there are a few students who figure out some of the English phonetic code and spelling and grammar rules on their own. But most students are not going to figure this all out on their own.

That is the Outcome Based Education method. We obtain good looking results, and we obtain them faster! But these results are shallow, and they do not last long. But what is most important of all, Outcome Based Education creates intellectual cripples who are dependent upon the educational system for everything they learn. Why is that? Because they never master the basics! They only master the outcomes! Creativity is tremendously stifled, because the student is never given the tools with which to create anything on his own.

Now, let us say that we are going to teach you Beethoven's *Moonlight Sonata* by the Trivium method. First we will teach you how to read music. That is the Knowledge Level (or Grammar Stage). Then we will teach you the proper fingering. That is the Understanding Level (or Logic Stage). Then we will teach you the proper technique and expression. That is the Wisdom Level (or Rhetoric Stage). Once you have mastered these three levels, then we can begin to work on the Moonlight Sonata.

Using the Trivium method will take much longer to master the piece than will the Outcome Based Education method. But let us look at the long term benefits. What if you want to learn another song? You have all of the basic tools, so you can teach yourself! You no longer need your instructor. In fact, you can write your own music, because you have mastered those arts of the piano which *liberate* you from your teacher so you can learn on your own.

That is why Grammar, Logic, and Rhetoric are called "*Liberal* Arts." These are the arts which *liberate*! *Liberal Arts* is what this book is all about. How many have graduated from so-called "Liberal Arts Colleges" without ever learning these "Liberal Arts?" Too many!

A true liberal arts education is the mastery of those skills which liberate us from our teachers so that we can learn on our own. The liberal arts were designed to liberate us from taskmasters. Outcome Based Education is designed to chain us to our tasks. What will you have: lifelong self-learning or lifelong task-learning? Dignity or drudgery? Freedom or Serfdom? "Hi. I'm an educator from the socialist state, and I'm here to help you."

If we have been taught to read and write by the "look-say" or "whole language" method, then we have been taught the "outcome" – we memorized the "look" of the words, instead of mastering the basics – the phonetic code and spelling rules. What kind of a vocabulary can we develop with that handicap?

We have had Outcome Based Education in the language department for decades. Now that people cannot read and write, the social engineers can implement Outcome Based Education in all the other departments with little resistance. In fact, with so much functional illiteracy, O.B.E. has become a practical necessity.

If we first mastered the alphabet and phonetic code, then the spelling and grammar rules, and finally style and composition, then we would truly master the "whole language." But if we begin where we ought to end – with the "whole language" – do not be surprised if we end up not knowing our beginning from our end.

Even the three R's are an elementary version of the Trivium: reading is the Grammar, arithmetic is the Logic, and writing is the Rhetoric.

THE WHOLE TRIVIUM IN A CAPSULE

Everything about the Trivium which you've read in this Chapter, *and more*, is encapsulated in the remainder of this section. If you don't understand it yet, then you have one more chance. And if you have understood it well, then there is still more here to learn.

The *formal* Trivium in the *classical* sense is Grammar, Logic, and Rhetoric. This is reflected in the Biblical terms of Knowledge, Understanding, and Wisdom.

Each child goes through three levels of development, and each subject has three levels of development, and these three levels (or stages) correspond to the formal Trivium and the Biblical Trivium.

We will describe the three levels from the point of view of the individual child's development, but keep in mind that this also applies to the development of each individual subject which is taught, and that the development of each subject is not necessarily age-bound.

The Picture

Here is the picture: Man has three mental capacities:

One for gathering up information – *Knowledge*.

A second for arranging the information in a logical order – *Understanding*.

A third for putting this information and this ordering into practical use – *Wisdom*.

The Early Knowledge Level (or Grammar Stage)

These three capacities are mutually dependent upon each other, but there is nevertheless a logical and developmental order among them. All three capacities are developing in the child from before birth. The child is always learning facts, relating the facts to each other, and using these facts and relations in practical ways.

The Knowledge Level (or Grammar Stage)

During the child's early years, while all three capacities are growing, the capacity for Knowledge experiences the greatest growth. At about age nine or ten, the developmental parts have reached such a state of maturity that *the light bulb goes on* and the capacity for Knowledge makes a growth spurt – a quantum leap – into an intensive period when capacity and ability for formal academic study of Knowledge-related materials is most profitable.

When the child is at this level, we teach him the skill of comprehension – to accurately receive information – to gather the facts. Knowledge is imparted through telling, and demonstrating. It comes through the senses. We develop a vocabulary of facts and rules. At this level, we do not need to separate subjects. We can combine 1) language with literature and fine arts 2) mathematics with natural sciences 3) history with geography and social studies. Our goal is to develop competence in the tools of inquiry: reading, listening, writing, observing, measuring.

The Understanding Level
(or Logic Stage)

The intensive Knowledge period lasts about three years, and when it is over, Knowledge, of course, continues to grow and develop, but the capacity for Understanding – which has been developing all along – emerges as the frontrunner in this race. With a large foundation of Knowledge laid, and the developmental parts of Understanding reaching a level of maturity, another light bulb goes on, and the capacity for Understanding makes a growth spurt – a quantum leap – into an intensive period when a capacity and ability for formal academic study of Understanding-related materials is most profitable.

When the child is at this level, we teach him the skill of reasoning – to critically question, analyze, evaluate, and discern causes, motives, means, purposes, goals, and effects – to investigate the theory. Understanding is imparted through coaching, correcting, drilling. We develop a vocabulary of relationships, order, and abstractions. Our teaching will become more sequential and systematic, separating the different branches of learning. Our goal is to develop competence in the tools of investigation: analyzing, comparing, contrasting.

The Wisdom Level
(or Rhetoric Stage)

The intensive Understanding period lasts about three years, and when it is over, Understanding, of course, continues to grow and develop, but the capacity for Wisdom – which has been developing all along – emerges as the frontrunner in this race. When a large foundation of Knowledge and Understanding have been laid, and the developmental parts of Wisdom reach a level of maturity, then a third light bulb goes on, and the capacity for Wisdom makes a growth spurt – a quantum leap – into an intensive period when a capacity and ability for formal academic study of Wisdom-related materials is most profitable.

When the child is at this level, we teach him the skills of prudent judgment and effective expression – through communication and practical application. Wisdom is imparted through encouraging individual initiative and innovation, asking questions, and leading discussions. We develop a vocabulary of philosophical ideas and values. We begin to recombine the knowledge and skills from separate disciplines. We seek the application of principles, values and goals.

The intensive Wisdom period lasts two or three years, and when it is over, Wisdom, of course, continues to grow and develop, but all three capacities – Knowledge, Understanding, and Wisdom – which have been developing all along, emerge as a fully developed team of tools.

The Final Finishing Level (or Stage)

During the next couple of years, the moral capacity of conscience – which has been developing all along, is brought to full measure, so that the capacity for accountability should be fully developed by the completion of the full Biblical age of twenty years. Of course, all of the capacities will continue to grow, but the basic tools, which will be used throughout life, should all be developed by this time.

Summary

In summary, the capacities for Knowledge, Understanding, and Wisdom are not neat little compartments with sealed doors between them. Rather, they all develop at the same time from the very beginning, yet they each pass through successive periods of intensive development, until they finally catch up with each other and work harmoniously together.

To summarize it all in one sentence: we first instruct the child in Knowledge or Grammar; then we guide the child in Understanding or Logic; and finally we challenge the child in Wisdom or Rhetoric.

QUESTION

How Can a Victim of Public School Remediate?

Question: How can a victim of public school prepare himself and his children for this type of Homeschooling?

Answer: The hurdle in front of you is yourself. You will need to overcome your bad habits and deficiencies. Thank the Lord that He gave you children for an excuse to learn all the things you should have learned anyway. We can only give a few suggestions to begin with:

1. *Kick the entertainment habit*. Turn off the television. You cannot develop your mind under a television addiction. An occasional educational video may be profitable, but set rules and standards to discipline yourself, and stick to the rules and standards.
2. *Start reading*. If you don't like to read, then start learning to like it. Besides reading to yourself, start reading aloud to your children – not just the *ten-minutes-before-bedtime-let's-read-Green-Eggs-and-Ham* type of reading, but the *this-week-let's-read-the-unabridged-version-of-Treasure-Island* type of reading – to the six-year-old!
3. *Ask the Lord to give you an inquiring mind*. Investigate, with the children, the world around you. Search through all of the libraries in your area and find out what are the special features of each. Attend concerts of the visiting artists who come to town. Find out what you can about the men black topping the road outside you house. Ask questions and learn from the experts.
4. *Build vocabulary*. Don't talk baby-talk to your children. Throw out the grade-level mentality. Continually test your children's level of understanding. Read books to them which are a step above what you think is their level. Encourage them to listen to adult conversation.
5. *Have discussions with your children*. Argue with your children – not in the sense of fight, but in the sense of debate. Making them think things through will be a great exercise in making yourself think things through.
6. *Make sure your children obey you*. First time obedience promotes good internal discipline in the children, brings order to the home, and makes learning easier. Children must have this internal discipline developed within them before they are academically prepared. You will find your own weaknesses and develop your own self-discipline as you do the work of developing this internal discipline in your children. Discipline is a disaster if yourself you do not master.
7. *Establish family worship*. This is not just a nice thing to add on at your convenience. It should be the cornerstones of the

> day – morning and evening, establishing the order of the whole day – and the whole life. Don't expect the Lord's presence in your family if you do not regularly invite His presence into your midst.

The practical part of this book – Chapters Eleven through Sixteen – are full of more detailed suggestions. Remember, Homeschooling is for parents. From teaching your children, you will learn, learn as much or more, and learn it better than you ever learned in school.

Chapters Five through Seven give arguments for teaching, respectively, Languages, Logic, and Rhetoric – the three formal subjects which constitute the Classical Trivium. Following each argument is a brief introduction to teaching the subject. Chapter Eight discusses Literature, Chapter Nine discusses History, and Chapter Ten discusses different approaches to Homeschooling.

Chapter Five

Teaching Languages

. . . Canst thou speak Greek?
— Acts 21:37

AN ARGUMENT FOR TEACHING CLASSICAL LANGUAGES

EACH AND EVERY SUBJECT has its own *grammar* – its basic elements and fundamental rules. There is a grammar of mathematics, of geography, of history, etc. But the most basic of all the grammars is our own native language grammar, because this gives us the building blocks with which we build our understanding of every other subject. Failure to master native language skills will cripple a student's ability to learn any other subject.

If we wanted to overthrow the educational system of an entire country, where would we begin? We would begin with the language department. If we introduced an *outcome-based* reading program, we could stymie young students' ability to learn. For example, if, instead of teaching children the English phonetic code, we taught them to recognize words as glyphs – "picture words," then we could greatly reduce their vocabulary. Vocabulary is the primary index of intelligence. Once we reduced their vocabulary and intelligence, and, over a couple of generations, weeded out the remnants of cultural intelligence which stubbornly survived, eventually we could reduce a culture to the point where we could introduce outcome-based education into all the other subjects, and eventually reduce all learning to a functional (or dysfunctional) minimum. The result would be cultural suicide. We wonder if this has ever been tried?

All knowledge and culture is transmitted through language. Nothing can transmit language abilities more effectively than the family. As the state has encroached upon the family's task of education, the fundamental language skills have rapidly declined. That's because the family is no longer transmitting them. High schools, and even colleges, are graduating many students who cannot read and write. As this progresses, our culture can only disintegrate. It will eventually be taken over by a competing culture. Hopefully, it will be the Christian Homeschool culture.

Why Study Other Languages?

I trust everyone reading this Chapter is convinced of the fundamental need for good English language skills. But what about the study of other languages?

Europeans all live in close proximity to people who speak another language. They need to know those languages just to do business. We, in America, have been largely insulated from this. We have some French speaking people north of us in Quebec, and some Spanish speaking people south of us in Mexico, but this is of limited – though growing – significance to most of us in the United States.

English is the native language of 350 million persons in the world, but it is the second language of another 700 million persons, so over a billion persons in the world speak English. We Americans have been spared the necessity of learning a second language. So why learn another language?

If we were interested in studying the cultures of the past, we might be driven to learn ancient languages, such as classical Greek or Latin; or European languages, such as French or German.

On the other hand, if our interests focused more on the contemporary and the practical, we might want to learn a modern foreign language in order to apply ourselves in business, pleasure, correspondence, research, missionary work, or simply as a link to our own ethnic heritage.

The state's socialized schools stress languages as part of *global multicultural education*, in order "to create better appreciation of life in other cultural and linguistic environments." (Quoted from *Minimum Standards for Ohio Elementary Schools*, 1970.) You no doubt recognize that this statement was written in a foreign language. It is called "Obscuranto," and it is spoken only by professional bureaucrats. Loosely translated, it means they are preparing students for a one-world mentality, which is the trend in all socialized education.

Christians Should Have Some Overriding Considerations

The world has a number of criteria for determining language choices. But Christians are commanded not to be pressed into the world's mold.

> And be not conformed to this world: but be ye transformed by the renewing of your mind . . . . — Romans 12:2

As Christian parents, we are called by God to develop a distinctly Biblical and Christian culture – a transformed culture – for our family, for our church, and for our community. Culture is embedded in language. When culture changes, language changes, and when language changes, culture changes. The two are inextricably bound together.

The influence of language can be subtle, but powerful. In order to successfully change a culture, we must change the language – we must change the words people use, and the meanings which they assign to those words. This will alter how people think, and what they think about, and – most important of all – what they do *not* think about.

That is precisely what is being done to us in our culture. We are now being taught to speak politically correct, nonsexist, multicultural English. We will soon have a socialistic, neutered, and totally disoriented culture.

God inscribed and embedded all culture which is distinctly Biblical and Christian in the language of Scripture. Therefore, the study of Scripture in the original languages is an essential and indispensable part of developing a genuinely and distinctly Christian culture. Because God's Word must remain basic to all of Christian education, a Christian language program must stress the Biblical languages.

Now, we are not suggesting that we completely throw away all of our English Bibles and study aids, and study only in the original languages. We are suggesting, however, that Christians have become intellectually atrophied. In Old Testament times, of course, every Hebrew spoke

Hebrew. And in New Testament times, the whole Mediterranean world spoke Greek. The early Christians knew and studied the Greek Scriptures in their own native tongue. But as the knowledge of the Biblical languages diminished among the common people, a darkness crept over professed Christianity. The people became more and more dependent upon religious professionals, and those professionals became less and less accountable to the people. The two greatest periods of the spread of the Gospel were in the first century and in the sixteenth century. By the time of the apostles (A.D. 30-70), the whole world knew and spoke the Greek language due to Alexander the Great's conquest of the Mediterranean world (about 330 B.C.). Due to the fall of the capital of the Greek Empire, Constantinople (in 1453 A. D.), Greek scholars fled with their manuscripts to western Europe, so that by the sixteenth century there was a revival of Greek studies in Western Europe. This prepared the way for the unearthing of a marvelous old book which had not been seen for a thousand years. That book was the Greek New Testament. The republication of the Greek New Testament by Erasmus in 1516 was immediately followed by the greatest period of the spread of the gospel since the days of the apostles.

We are persuaded that a genuine renewal of the Gospel in our own day awaits a renewal of the study of the Greek Scriptures. In the not too distant past, Christians in general, and ministers in particular, were competent students of the Scriptures in Greek and Hebrew. But most evangelical ministers today do not commonly study the Greek and Hebrew Scriptures with any proficiency. Many seminaries do not even require the study of the Biblical languages for graduation. Some evangelical seminaries do not even offer courses of instruction in the Biblical languages. If a minister does happen to learn these languages – even a little, he does not often continue his studies in the languages. Instead, he relies upon the same English study-aids as does everyone else. Indeed, a common joke on seminary campuses is, "Who will be the first to forget these languages?" – which illustrates how seriously many students regard their study of the Biblical languages.

The plethora of English translations in our day would never have seen the light of day if more Christians were familiar with the Greek Scriptures. The truth of the Scriptures was once hidden in the language of scholars, and the truth was largely lost to the people. Today, we fear that the truth is lost in a multitude of "well, it might mean this" translations (including the most popular translations).

Only a century ago, a majority of high school graduates in the United States had studied Greek. In fact, only a century ago, no seminary in the

United States even offered a course in Greek. Students were expected to have mastered Greek before they entered seminary. In the last century, Christians have largely lost the tools with which to personally examine the actual Word of God. We have gradually become dependent once again upon an elite priesthood of scholars and specialists, most of whom – quite frankly – are infidels. The subtle influence of their skeptic philosophy upon Biblical studies has been cumulatively ruinous to the foundations of Biblical faith.

In April of 1997, we were in an old bookstore in Fresno, California, and we asked the proprietor to direct us to the language section. He said, "That has become the most popular section of my bookstore. People involved in witchcraft and the occult want to read their literature in the original languages." What a revealing comment! People involved in the occult understand the power of studying their literature in the original languages, but we Christians – we go galloping after the latest translation, as if it were somehow a better translation. The fact is, most of the new versions inject a large amount of unmarked interpretation into the text. If we are reading a translation of a novel, we can appreciate the need for some freedom in interpretation. But if we are reading a translation of a legal document, we want to be able to identify what the text literally says, and what is merely an interpretation of the text. The Scriptures are legal documents, the most legal of all documents: the inspired and infallible record of the covenants of God, to which we are all accountable. The Scriptures require some interpretation, but nobody should identify their interpretation with the actual word of God.

If we are to educate our children in the words of the Lord, in order to prepare them to live from an aggressively Christian perspective, then we should see the Biblical languages as both foundational and practical for the remainder of their lives. It is foundational, because nothing is more foundational to Christian education than the study of the Scriptures.

> All Scripture *is* given by inspiration of God, and *is* profitable for doctrine, for reproof, for correction, for instruction in righteousness: that the man of God may be perfect, throughly furnished unto all good works. — Second Timothy 3:16,17

And it is practical, because nothing will prepare the student for practical service to the Lord better than the careful study of the words of the Lord in their original languages.

> The cloak that I left at Troas with Carpus, when thou comest, bring *with thee*, and the books, *but* especially the parchments. — Second Timothy 4:13 (The Hebrew Scriptures were written on parchments.)

Those who pursue the study of the Greek New Testament will become the vessels of God for the recovery of His truth.

Further Argument for the Study of Greek

1. Cultural literacy. We think Greek is a foreign language written in a foreign alphabet. Yet we speak and write Greek every day without realizing it. Our alphabet comes from Greek. Our Vocabulary is filled with Greek. Much can be said of the broad understanding of language and culture which can be gained through studying Greek. But honestly, such thoughts do not move most persons to study Greek.

2. Mental discipline. Studying Greek demands mental effort. It trains the mind to observe details, to recognize patterns, and to draw conclusions. As we study the etymology of a word, or meditate upon the significance of a preposition, or parse a verb, we develop the powers of the mind.

Mental discipline is important to serving the Lord. We are to gird up the loins of our minds (First Peter 1:13) by diligently searching the Scriptures. A diligent search requires the tools with which to search. The better the tool, the better the searching, and one of the best tools is a knowledge of the language of Scripture – Greek.

Though these reasons offer more motivation to study Greek, yet, for most of us, this is still not enough.

3. Serving the Lord. There is no more important reason for studying Greek than its usefulness in understanding the Word of God. God has chosen to record the words and acts of our Lord and His Apostles in the Greek language. The ability to read the Greek New Testament increases our capacity to be taught from God's Word with an accuracy and authority which can never be obtained through a translation.

Here are just two little examples.

In Galatians 1:6,7, we read in the King James, "I marvel that you are so soon removed from him that called you into the grace of Christ unto ANOTHER gospel: which is not ANOTHER. . . ." The word *another* is used twice in English, yet two very different words are in the Greek text. The first *another* (ἕτερος: heteros) means *of another kind or quality*. The second *another* (ἄλλος: allos) means *of the same kind but numerically distinct*. In other words, Paul is saying emphatically that there is only one gospel. This other "*hetero*dox" (heteros) gospel is in no way an *all*y (allos) of the one true gospel – in fact, it counts as no gospel at all! The King James does not make this clear. The Greek makes it unavoidably clear.

In Galatians 6:2,5, we read the apparent contradiction, "Bear ye one another's BURDENS. . . . For every man shall bear his own BURDEN." The first *burden* (*βάρη*: barE) refers to those things which weigh us down or oppress us, especially grievous sorrows and miseries. The second *burden* (*φορτίον*: phortion) refers to a load – often a soldier's kit, or sometimes it refers to a task which a soldier is expected to perform. Hence we are all to share the many difficulties of life, but we each must pursue ourselves that particular task which the Lord has placed upon our shoulders.

Jim Elliott, the martyr of Ecuador, wrote in his diary that although John 19 was quite familiar to him in English, when he read it in the Greek, it seemed as if he was reading it for the first time, so much more vivid was it than any English translation. When you learn the details of Greek vocabulary and grammar, God will speak to you through the New Testament with greater accuracy and authority, and you will speak to others with greater certainty and precision.

"This is all well and good," you may say, "but I'm afraid I need a little more incentive to get moving." Okay, consider this.

4. Preparation for revival. Great revival begins with a closer, more careful examination of the word of God. The great Hebrew revival under King Josiah occurred when Hilkiah the priest uncovered the Book of the Law.

> And Hilkiah the high priest said unto Shaphan the scribe, I have found the book of the law in the house of the LORD. And Hilkiah gave the book to Shaphan, and he read it. . . And Shaphan the scribe shewed the king, saying, Hilkiah the priest hath delivered me a book. And Shaphan read it before the king. And it came to pass, when the king had heard the words of the book of the law, that he rent his clothes. — Second Kings 22:8,10,11 (Compare Second Chronicles 34:14-19)

The restoration of Israel under Ezra and Nehemiah likewise involved the rediscovery of the Book of the Law.

> And Ezra the priest brought the law before the congregation both of men and women, and all that could hear with understanding, upon the first day of the seventh month. . . . and the ears of all the people *were attentive* unto the book of the law. . . And Ezra blessed the LORD, the great God. And all the people answered, Amen, Amen, with lifting up their hands: and they bowed their heads, and worshipped the LORD with *their* faces to the ground. . . . and the

> Levites, caused the people to understand the law . . . . So they read in the book in the law of God distinctly, and gave the sense, and caused *them* to understand the reading. And Nehemiah . . . and Ezra . . . and the Levites that taught the people, said unto all the people, This day *is* holy unto the LORD your God; mourn not, nor weep. For all the people wept, when they heard the words of the law. — Nehemiah 8:2,3,6-9

We mentioned earlier how the Greek New Testament was rediscovered and became the basic text for the Reformers of the sixteenth century. Other, more local revivals can also be traced to the study of the Greek New Testament – and declines can be traced to its neglect.

Though a knowledge of the Greek language was once considered an indispensable part of a good education, in the past century these standards have so deteriorated that Greek is no longer considered a part of any education – even a theological education. Our culture has been so "dumbed down" that we have lost the basic tools of Biblical scholarship. We have again allowed the Greek Scriptures to be covered over with the speculations of men.

By taking up the task of learning together the language of God's Word, Homeschooling parents along with their children are laying the foundation for a great revival.

Further Argument for the Study of Hebrew

1. The cultural key. We argued earlier that language is the vehicle of culture. The Hebrew nation was formed and transformed through more than a millennium of direct revelation from God. Its basic cultural institutions were revealed by God.

> Behold, I have taught you statutes and judgments, even as the LORD my God commanded me, that ye should do so in the land whither ye go to possess it. Keep therefore and do *them*; for this *is* your wisdom and your understanding in the sight of the nations, which shall hear all these statutes, and say, Surely this great nation *is* a wise and understanding people. For what nation *is there so* great, who *hath* God *so* nigh unto them, as the LORD our God *is* in all *things that* we call upon him *for*? And what nation *is there so* great, that hath statutes and judgments *so* righteous as all this law, which I set before you this day? . . . For ask now of the days that are past, which were before thee, since the day that God created man upon the earth, and *ask* from the one side of heaven unto the other, whether there hath been *any such thing* as this great thing *is*, or hath been heard like it? Did *ever* people hear the voice of God speaking out of the midst of the fire, as thou hast heard, and live? Or hath God assayed to go *and* take him a nation from the midst of *another* nation, by temptations, by signs, and by

> wonders, and by war, and by a mighty hand, and by a stretched out arm, and by great terrors, according to all that the LORD your God did for you in Egypt before your eyes? — Deuteronomy 4:5-8,32-34.

> He sheweth his word unto Jacob, his statutes and his judgments unto Israel. He hath not dealt so with any nation: and *as for his* judgments, they have not known them. Praise ye the LORD. — Psalms 147:19-20

> What advantage then hath the Jew? or what profit *is there* of circumcision? Much every way: chiefly, because that unto them were committed the oracles of God. — Romans 3:1-2

With the coming of the New Covenant, the force of the Old Testament Scriptures as a covenant is altered, but its authority as revelation remains the same. Its revealed truths are foundational to our understanding of all things. For example, we simply cannot understand the nature of the world without the account of origins in Genesis.

> For whatsoever things were written aforetime were written for our learning, that we through patience and comfort of the scriptures might have hope. — Romans 15:4.

> Now all these things happened unto them for ensamples: and they are written for our admonition, upon whom the ends of the world are come. — First Corinthians 10:11

> All scripture *is* given by inspiration of God, and *is* profitable for doctrine, for reproof, for correction, for instruction in righteousness: That the man of God may be perfect, throughly furnished unto all good works. — Second Timothy 3:16,17.

The revealed principles of just law and godly order are examples to us as to how we should form law and establish order for our own culture. If we are to accurately apply them to our times – as we must – then we must study them in the form by which God revealed them: in Hebrew.

2. The original language. It is believed by some that Hebrew is a surviving representative of the original language – *lashon haqodesh*, the holy language.

> And the whole earth was of one language, and of one speech. — Genesis 11:1

Noah's father would have known Adam, and Noah and his sons would have known Eber, for whom the Hebrew language is named. Eber means "the region beyond" and Hebrew means "one from the other side." Hence it is supposed that Hebrew is the language which survived from the other side of the flood and the tower of Babel. The etymology of the names Adam, Eve, Cain, Noah, etc. is Hebrew. God gave the direct revelation of the Old Testament in the Hebrew language. That we all will be speaking Hebrew in heaven is debatable, but it seems quite likely that Hebrew is akin to the language spoken by Adam – the language revealed by God to Adam. This would make Hebrew the most natural of languages – separated from the confusion of Babel. It would also make it the purest language for expressing thought. The forms of a language reflect the way of thinking in the culture to which it is attached. Hence, Hebrew may have a way of re-ordering and purifying our way of thinking. This may not be the strongest reason to study Hebrew, but it is a most interesting one.

3. Christian heritage. The New Testament is written in Koine Greek, the common language of the day; nevertheless, the vocabulary – and even the grammar – is stamped with a distinctly Christian character. Words are used and sentences are constructed in ways which are often adapted to Hebrew meaning. (The Greek version of the Old Testament had already established some of this "Jewish Greek." Joseph Yahuda wrote a book, *Hebrew is Greek*, which shows the root relationship between the Hebrew and the Greek languages.) The Holy Spirit worked providentially to form the Greek language of the first century to receive the revelation of God, but when He did so, He infused it with many Hebrew expressions – personal names, place names, Hebrew words (abba, alleluia, amen, hosanna, messiah, rabbi, sabbath, etc.) and Hebrew ideas expressed in Greek words (abomination, almighty, angel, baptism, Christ, covenant, devil, glory, head, idol, sin, truth, etc.) So even the Greek New Testament is in many ways a Hebrew book.

Early Christians acknowledged the value of Hebrew. But within a century or so after Jerome's translation of the Bible into Latin (the Vulgate, A.D. 404), until some time after Johannes Reuchlin's first Hebrew grammar (*De rudimentis hebraicis*, A.D. 1505), the Latin Vulgate was the standard Christian text of the Bible, and the original Hebrew and Greek texts were ignored. In other words, the Hebrew and Greek Scriptures were largely lost to Christians for a millennium.

> Without this language, there can be no understanding of Scripture, for the New Testament, although written in Greek, is full of Hebraisms. It is rightly said that the Hebrews drink from the fountains, the Greeks from the streams, and the Latins from the pools. — Martin Luther (A.D. 1483-1546)

4. Direct Access. Translations can be treacherous. They are secondary sources, and are therefore subjective in many places. There are things of nuance and connotation, such as color and emphasis, which are in the original, but which do not pass through translation. These same things also appear in a translation, though they are not from the original. So direct access to the original text should be a high priority with Christians in order to be able to discern what is the original, what is left out in translation, and what is added in translation.

Many consider the study of Hebrew to be too difficult, or irrelevant to their goals. Of course, your priority level for learning Hebrew will be determined by your needs, resources, values, and goals. As far as learning the language itself is concerned, the main obstacle is the first obstacle – mastering the unusual system of symbols for the language. And modern Hebrew is not the same as Biblical Hebrew. The modern form of the language has been greatly simplified, and the cultural context, of course, has greatly changed.

Further Argument for the Study of Latin

Beyond Greek and Hebrew, Latin becomes important. Scripture enjoins us to make the best use of our time:

> Redeeming the time, because the days are evil. — Ephesians 5:16

> Walk in wisdom toward them that are without, redeeming the time. — Colossians 4:5

The days are evil and they will consume our time. We can easily waste our time pursuing an outsider's agenda. We need to apply wisdom in order to buy back some of that time for the Lord's use.

We believe the study of Latin can be a good use of our time. Consider some of the following advantages for studying Latin. Most of these reasons also apply, in a different measure, to studying Greek as a classical language (not just as a Biblical language).

1. *Latin is basic to English.* Over half of English vocabulary (some estimate 60 to 70 percent) comes from Latin. For example, most of our prefixes (such as mono-chrome, mono-logue, mono-tone) come from Latin and Greek. The study of Latin develops English Vocabulary and Grammar and even improves pronunciation.

Students who have taken Latin tend to score higher on standardized tests than other groups of students. Here are the average scores for students who took the SAT exam. (Notice, the scores for 1996 and after are the dumbed-down scores.)

SAT Scores for Students who Study Languages

	All Students	Spanish	German	French	Hebrew	Latin
1991	422	497	548	544	545	571
1992	423	497	540	544	545	574
1993	424	499	541	548	560	576
1994	423	502	540	549	552	579
1995	428	501	545	553	551	579
1996*	504	576	625	625	622	648
1997	505	581	624	623	629	647
1998	505	583	617	627	634	654
1999	505	590	623	632	636	662
2000	505	589	621	636	623	665

*SAT scores were re-centered in 1996.

Statistics supplied by Bolchazy-Carducci publishers from College-Bound Seniors – A Profile of SAT Program Test Takers.

Figure 5A

Latin students scored 144 to 160 points above the average of all students, and 18 to 29 points above the next highest class of scores. Latin students are 33% above average. We are not here arguing a *post hoc ergo propter hoc* (which is Latin for "it happened after this, therefore it happened because of this"). We are not saying the fact that they studied Latin necessarily caused their scores to be higher. We readily grant that it may often work the other way around: better students with higher scores may choose to study Latin over other languages. We suspect that it works both ways – the better students choose Latin and the Latin students become better students – so that each way strengthens the other.

2. *Latin is a springboard for mastering other inflected languages, such as Greek or German.* It broadens our understanding of the structure of other languages. If we wanted to learn any of the Romance languages (Spanish, French, Italian, Portuguese, Romanian, etc.), we would find that 80 per

cent of the vocabulary of each of these languages is Latin! It is like having a ticket to Europe or to South America with an 80 per cent reduction in price.

3. *The study of Latin sharpens the mental processes.* It demands mental effort. Therefore it develops mental strength and attention. The task of searching for words and structures in our own language to compare with that of another language, develops and trains skills of accurate observation and logical analysis.

> "Now there has been found nowhere a better training for the thinking apparatus of the young than the study of Latin and Greek." — Dr. Victor C. Vaughan, former president, American Medical Association

4. *Everything in a culture is embedded in its language.* When we study the Latin language, we also study the Latin history and culture, some of which, of course, survives in our own culture. Such things as government, religion, art, literature, economic customs, ideas, and values have some of their roots in Latin culture and history.

> I will say at once, quite firmly, that the best grounding for education is the Latin grammar. I say this, not because Latin is traditional and mediaeval, but simply because even a rudimentary knowledge of Latin cuts down the labour and pains of learning almost any other subject by at least fifty per cent. It is the key to the vocabulary and structure of all the Romance languages and to the structure of all the Teutonic languages, as well as to the technical vocabulary of all the sciences and to the literature of the entire Mediterranean civilisation, together with all its historical documents. — Dorothy Sayers

5. *Technical language is Latin.* Medical, scientific, and legal terms are all Latin and Greek. Because a great deal of these studies is terminology, then, if we know the terminology of these three disciplines, we will have a lifelong advantage over others.

> "In my opinion, Latin and Greek (especially) are the most valuable subjects in the college curriculum. . . . Personally, I would unhesitatingly accept as a medical student one who is long on the Classics, especially Greek, and short on science." — Fred C. Zappfe, Secretary, Association of American Medical Colleges

6. *Latin is also valuable for further studies in all disciplines.* Because Latin is embedded in Western culture, especially in professional terminology, the study of Latin is also important in the study of history, theology, literature, art, architecture, ad infinitum. (*Ad infinitum* is a Latin expression!)

7. *Latin is useful in English.* Many of us learned some Spanish, German, or French in high school or college. How much of it do we use? Most of us use it very little, if at all. The general rule applies well to languages, "If we do not use it, then we will lose it." So, for many of us, much of this effort went to waste. We could have used the time much more wisely studying Latin, because everyone who learns Latin vocabulary and grammar will use it often, even if he continues his studies only in English.

For millennia, the classical languages were considered an essential part of education. Why? Because of all of their benefits to learning. Many of those benefits survive until today in different strengths.

Here are some interesting quotes on the study of classical languages.

> "I have become convinced that of all that human language has produced truly and simply beautiful, I knew nothing before I learned Greek. . . . Without a knowledge of Greek there is no education." — Leo Tolstoy, Russian novelist, author of *War and Peace*. (He learned Greek at the age of 42.)

> "I began to realize as I read the Greek classics that I could not really draw valid inferences from translations. So I began to study Greek. I am having a wonderful time! I did not intend to get drawn in this far, but the further I get, the more enchanting it is." — I.F. Stone, Journalist, Writer, Distinguished Scholar in Residence, American University. (He taught himself Greek at the age of 70, beginning a new career.)

> "I would make everyone learn English; then I would let the clever ones learn Latin as an honor – and Greek as a treat." — Sir Winston Churchill, Writer, Prime Minister of England.

Our conclusion is: generally speaking, ones time is best spent learning Latin, Greek and Hebrew. Latin, because it is most useful for further studies in English as well as in other languages. Greek, for the same reasons, and because it is most useful in understanding Scripture. Hebrew, because it is most useful in understanding Scripture and Biblical culture.

Knowing these three languages will give the student a large and useful tool kit for all of his studies. We will now attempt to present some practical information on teaching languages.

PRINCIPLES FOR LEARNING LANGUAGES

Which Languages to Study?

We believe that Greek, Latin, and Hebrew should receive first consideration of all the classical languages. These three languages hold the most practical usefulness for ordinary Christians.

Nevertheless, on a realistic level, one student or one family may not be able to pursue the classical languages as aggressively as others might. You are the best judge of your own resources, circumstances, and the Lord's special direction for your family. You may have special reasons for pursuing other languages in addition to or instead of any or all of the three classical languages which we have recommended. Perhaps you are assured that you will spend a few years in Germany. You would then have a special reason for giving the study of German a higher priority. You may be adopting a Russian child. You would then give a higher priority to gaining some familiarity and skill with Russian.

We know that God calls each of us to specific venues, and we have no authority to impress a "one-size-fits-all" curriculum upon everybody. Each family must determine its own goals. Some classical "snobs" might look down upon a decision to drop one or more of these classical languages. That is their problem, and not necessarily yours. In this section, we want to give you some criteria for determining your priorities in pursuing the classical languages.

If Only One Language, Then Greek

If you choose to pursue only one language, then we recommend *Koine Greek* (also called *Hellenistic Greek*), which is the language of the New Testament. We recommend Koine Greek because of its value in Biblical study. Not only is the New Testament written in Koine Greek, but there is also a Koine Greek version of the Old Testament. The early church fathers also wrote in Koine Greek, as did the Jewish historian Josephus. Koine Greek is not exactly the same as classical Greek, but the bridge between the two is short, should anyone need to cross it.

If Two Languages, Then Latin and Greek

If you choose to pursue two languages, then we recommend first Latin, then Greek. Latin uses the same alphabet as English, but with a slightly different pronunciation. The Latin vocabulary alone will prove very valuable in other studies – studies in English proper, as well as specialized studies in science, medicine, law, and other disciplines. Because most of the structure and some of the vocabulary of Latin is similar to Greek, Latin study will also prepare you to study Greek. Hence, Latin will act as a bridge to make the trip to Greek a little easier.

If Three Languages, Then How About: Latin, Greek, and Hebrew?

We admit that this is an ambitious program, especially for Americans who have been educated (or dys-educated!) during the last fifty years. If Latin is a step away from English, and Greek is two steps away from English, then Hebrew is at least three steps away from English. Hebrew has a very different alphabet, a very different vocabulary, and a very different grammar than either English, Latin, or Greek. But it is the language of the Old Testament, and as such, it will prove valuable in understanding the Bible.

Language and culture are inextricably intertwined. During the Renaissance, when the culture of the classical world was being revived, then, of necessity, the classical languages were also being revived. The first generation restored classical Latin from its degenerated form. The second generation rediscovered classical and Koine (Biblical) Greek. The third generation recovered classical (Biblical) Hebrew. Perhaps the Homeschooling renaissance in learning, if it is not quashed by the imposition of socialism, will follow a similar pattern.

The amount of time which we commit to learning the languages will, over a lifetime, reap a more than compensatory reward. Consider only this one compensation: access to the original documents. Without some knowledge of the original languages, we must be satisfied with the English translation and explanation of a passage. We will not have the tools with which to investigate and compare the translation or the explanation of that passage with its original. In other words, we will always be dependent upon others to interpret the passage for us, with no realistic ability to check their work and hold them accountable. This is important with regard to all kinds of literature, but it is especially important with regard to the Scriptures. In our opinion, the downgrade in the knowledge of the original languages since 1900 has led to the flood of over a hundred entirely new English translations of the New Testament, and over forty entirely new English translations of the Bible. We are treated to a smorgasbord buffet of translations from which we can pick and choose to fill our plate and please our appetite, as if Koine Greek were so pregnantly expressive that it becomes thoroughly uncertain and ambiguous. What does that do to the authority of Scripture?

Levels of Proficiency

The goal for language learning is to acquire a familiarity and skill with a language at one of the following three levels:

1. *Lexical Skill*. When we acquire this level, we have developed a working knowledge in the basic elements of the language, such that we can read words, pronounce words, and find words in a lexicon.
2. *Grammatical Skill*. When we acquire this level, we have developed a working understanding in the connecting structure of the language, such that we can use both the lexicon and the grammar to read literature in the language.
3. *Fluency Skill*. When we acquire this level, we have developed a working wisdom in the flow of meaning of the language, such that we have confidence to read and translate in the language with little dependence upon a lexicon or grammar.

We must determine which level of proficiency we wish to acquire. For example, if our goal is Biblical study, we would need Fluency Skill in Greek and at least Grammatical Skill in Hebrew. If our goal is study in ancient literature and philosophy, we would need Fluency Skill in both Latin and Greek.

What we do not use, we will lose. These three levels of skill act as thresholds. Once we have begun the task of acquiring a certain level of skill, we should stick to it until we have reached that level, or else we are likely to fall back to the last level which we have acquired. For example, if we have reached Lexical Skill in Hebrew, and we aspire to Grammatical Skill, what will happen if we only do half of the work for acquiring Grammatical Skill, then quit? Because we have not completed that level, we will not enjoy working at that level, and we will frequently be frustrated by our lack of proficiency. As a result, most likely we will not use much or any of whatever portion we did complete. Instead, we will rely upon the Lexical Skill which we have mastered and which we therefore enjoy using. The effort which we expended on the uncompleted level may then be lost for lack of use. So, once we have made a measurable beginning on a new level, we should stick to it until we have completed it. Even if we must slow down and take smaller steps, we should not abandon our efforts.

Where Should We Begin?

What do Latin, Greek, and Hebrew have in common? They are all dead languages! Yes, Latin has many modern descendants, Greek has a modern descendant, and Hebrew has been "re-invented" for modern use. But there are no cultures on the earth who speak the classical form of these languages. The classical form must be learned from scratch – which presents a major problem to language learning.

The *spoken* part of a language is best learned at as early an age as possible – when the ears and the tongue can best be trained to the special sounds of the language. We learn our native language with the ear (hearing) and the tongue (speaking) before we move on to the eye (reading) and the hand (writing). When a child is confident of his grasp of the spoken language, he can move more easily into the written language. So the written part of a language is best learned when the child is developmentally prepared – anywhere between ages five and nine (with no necessary relationship between intelligence and how early a child learns to read). Becoming familiar with the written language prepares the student for formal grammar. Around age ten (ages nine through eleven), the abstract abilities of the child's brain should be developed well enough to handle formal grammar on an elementary level.

We learned to read and write English after we were already familiar with spoken English. We studied English grammar and composition after we were already familiar with written English. The more familiar we are with a language, the easier will our studies come. So, ideally, training in any language should begin with the ear and the tongue, and training in these things comes easiest at an early age. How do we do that with a dead language which nobody speaks? "Therein lies the rub," as Shakespeare would say it. Perhaps in the second or third generation of homeschoolers, we will have multilingual families – proficient enough to speak and write in Greek, Latin, or Hebrew. Then children will grow up with some familiarity and skill with speaking and writing these languages before they tackle the formal grammar of these languages. But until we arrive at such a time, we will need to adjust to the circumstances with some replacement measures.

A GENERAL COURSE OF STUDY

We will now explain some practical ways to apply the principles which we have just discussed. Our examples will refer to learning the three classical languages:

Classical Latin
Classical and Koine (Biblical) Greek
Classical (Biblical) Hebrew.

Level One: Focus on Lexical Skill – Learning the Sights and Sounds of the Language.

Unfortunately, most of us do not have the luxury of learning to speak fluently the ancient languages before we learn to read and write them. Hopefully, the next generation of homeschoolers will be better prepared for the journey than we pathfinders. In the mean time, during the present cultural emergency, we need to create some synthetic substitutes.

Before studying the grammar of these languages, we must first become thoroughly grounded in their alphabet and phonetic system. We must first learn to read and pronounce the letters of the alphabet, then learn to read and pronounce letter combinations, then syllables, then words. When a child is capable of doing this in English, he is capable of doing this in other languages as well.

We are not talking about reading with full comprehension. When we learned to read in English, we also comprehended much of what we read because we already had been speaking English for a few years, therefore we possessed a large English vocabulary on the auditory level. But such is not the case with the ancient languages. When we begin to read in these ancient languages, there will be very little which seems familiar to us. With Latin and Greek, parts of the vocabulary will seem familiar. But we will not be familiar with the structure of the words and the sentences. So we will have very little comprehension as we begin with the written language.

Apart from actually speaking the language fluently in your home – which is beyond the capabilities of most of this first generation of homeschoolers – about the only way to provide some comprehension on this first level is to memorize passages both in English and in the language which you are studying. Of course, you must master the pronunciation of the alphabet before you can even do this.

AN INTRODUCTION TO ANCIENT ALPHABETS

The ancients would begin the literary language learning process by memorizing their whole alphabet – first forwards, then backwards – learning the sounds of each letter. In other words, they believed in phonics. Of course, the ancient alphabets were more strictly phonetic – one symbol for one sound – than the English alphabet. (But don't be too disparaging of English. English is by far the largest language the world has ever known, incorporating so many words from other languages that it carries an enormous lexical burden – all on one simple alphabet originally designed only for the little language known as Latin.) Let's take a glance at the three ancient alphabets.

LATIN ALPHABET & CORRESPONDING ENGLISH LETTERS

Latin Alphabet	A B C D E F G H I J K L M N O P Q R S T U V — X Y Z a b c d e f g h i j k l m n o p q r s t u v – x y z
English Letters	A B C D E F G H I J K L M N O P Q R S T U V W X Y Z a b c d e f g h i j k l m n o p q r s t u v w x y z

FIGURE 5B

As you can see, the Latin letters directly correspond, one-to-one, with the English letters, except no Latin letter corresponds to our English W. (Actually, Double-U is related to U and V.) (Also, K, X, Y, and Z were rarely used, and J and V are modern inventions to take the place of the consonantal use of I and U.) Most of the consonants are pronounced the same in both languages, except Latin has only one sound for each consonant (C and G each have only one sound). The vowel pronunciations are the main difference. Each Latin vowel has only one basic sound, but two lengths: short and long. (Compare English, where, for example, the letter *a* has three basic sounds: *bat, bait, ball.*) In modern Latin grammar texts, macrons (a horizontal line) are placed above the long vowels ā ē ī ō ū. (We explain the vowels in more detail in Appendix One, Article Eight, A Comparison of Ancient Alphabets.) So with Latin, we do not need to learn a new alphabet; we only need to learn a few different pronunciations.

Our comments are based upon the *restored classical* system of pronunciation for Latin. This is a reasonable attempt to restore the way the ancients pronounced the language. Unless you have some special reason for adopting the *ecclesiastical* (Italian) system of pronunciation, as is used in the Roman Catholic church, or some other more modern system of pronunciation, we recommend the restored classical for two simple reasons: 1) in the long run, it will be less confusing; 2) most of the new literature is based upon it.

Greek Alphabet & Corresponding English Letters

Greek Alphabet	Α	Β		Γ	Δ	Ε		Ζ	Η	Θ	Ι		Κ	Λ			
	α	β		γ	δ	ϵ		ζ	η	θ	ι		κ	λ			
English Letters	A	B	C	G	D	E	F	Z	H		I	J	K	L			
	a	b	c	g	d	e	f	z	h		i	j	k	l			

Greek Alphabet	Μ	Ν	Ξ	Ο	Π		Ρ	Σ	Τ	Υ	Φ	Χ	Ψ	Ω			
	μ	ν	ξ	ο	π		ρ	σ	τ	υ	ϕ	χ	ψ	ω			
English Letters	M	N	X	O	P	Q	R	S	T	U					V	W	Y
	m	n	x	o	p	q	r	s	t	u					v	w	y

Figure 5C

The letters are listed in Greek alphabetical order, which, as you can see, does not necessarily agree with English alphabetical order. For example, the Greek letters Γ Ζ Ξ correspond to the English letters G Z X, but are out of English order. Many Greek letters look like English letters: Α Β Ε Ζ Η Ι Κ Μ Ν Ο Ρ Τ Υ Χ. But they don't necessarily correspond to the English letter which they look like. What looks like a P is actually an R. What looks like a Υ is actually a U. And the letters which look like English letters do not necessarily sound the same as the English letters. For example, Greek H is a vowel with the long A sound. Greek X has a hard rough KH sound. There are seven Greek vowels, Α Ε Η Ι Ο Υ Ω, which sound like Latin vowels. No English letters directly correspond to the Greek letters Θ Φ Χ Ψ Ω, and no Greek letters directly correspond to the English letters C F J Q V W Y.

So the Greek alphabet is quite a bit different from English. The pronunciation system also is different. What is worse, if we picked ten Greek grammars from our shelf, we might find ten different systems of pronunciation. Though Ancient Greek was pronounced different ways at different times in different places, there is a way to sort through these pronunciations and arrive at a consistent system. We recommend a system which is consistent within itself, and which accommodates well with ancient Latin. (We explain the pronunciation system in more detail in Appendix One, Article Eight, A Comparison of Ancient Alphabets.)

HEBREW ALPHABET & CORRESPONDING ENGLISH LETTERS

Hebrew Alphabet	נ	מ	ל	כּ		י	ט	ח	ז	ו	ה	ד	ג		בּ	א
English Letters	N	M	L	K	J	I		H	Z	F	E	D	G	C	B	A

Hebrew Alphabet						ת	שׂ	שׁ	ר	ק	צ	פּ	ע	ס		
English Letters	Y	X	W	V	U	T		S	R	Q		P	O			

FIGURE 5D

If you think Greek is quite different from English, then what do you think of Hebrew? Hebrew has only capital letters, and is written from right to left. Several of the Hebrew letters look so similar to each other that our English-trained eyes can hardly distinguish them from each other:

SIMILAR HEBREW LETTERS

בּ and כּ and פּ

ג and נ

ה and ח and ת

ו and י

ל and ק

ע and צ

שׁ and שׂ

FIGURE 5E

Without exercising a great deal of imagination, none of the Hebrew letters have a shape which bears any recognizable relationship to our English letters. Beyond that, no English letters directly correspond to the Hebrew letters: שׁ צ ס ט, and no Hebrew letters directly correspond to the English letters: C J U V W X Y.

The Hebrew consonants are more closely related to Greek. (Both Hebrew and Greek developed from the Phoenician language.) Many of their names are similar:

GREEK & HEBREW LETTER NAMES

Greek	**Hebrew**	**Greek**	**Hebrew**
Alpha	Aleph	Lambda	Lamedh
Beta	Beth	Mu	Mem
Gamma	Gimel	Nu	Nun
Delta	Daleth	Xi	Samekh
Epsilon	He	Omicron	Ayin
Zeta	Zayin	Pi	Pe
Eta	Heth	Rho	Resh
Theta	Teth	Sigma	Sin
Iota	Yodh	Tau	Tau
Kappa	Kaph		

FIGURE 5F

Originally, there were no Hebrew vowels. Instead, vowels were interpolated, which is a fancy way of saying that they were inserted by the reader's best guess, based upon the context. Later, Hebrew scribes invented vowel points, which they placed below the consonants in order to fill in the pronunciation.

HEBREW POINTED & UNPOINTED TEXT

Pointed	Unpointed
אַבְרָהָם	אברהם
‘aB-RaaHaaM	‘BRHM

FIGURE 5G

As with Latin and Greek, so with Hebrew, there is more than one system of pronunciation. Some grammars adopt the pronunciation system of Modern Hebrew, which was invented by simplifying Ancient Hebrew. Unless you have some special reason for adopting the modern system of pronunciation used in Israel today, we recommend a classical pronunciation for two reasons: 1) in the long run, it will be less confusing; 2) most of the literature is based upon it. (We explain the pronunciation system in more detail in Appendix One, Article Eight, A Comparison of Ancient Alphabets.)

When we study Greek or Hebrew, the first thing we must learn is the alphabet. We must spend time thoroughly learning all the symbols of the alphabets and the sounds which these symbols represent. Only after we have mastered the alphabets, will we then be prepared to begin the study of Greek or Hebrew grammar. With Latin, this preparation in the alphabet is not quite so difficult. We are already familiar with the symbols. We only need to master a few changes in the sounds.

BEYOND THE ALPHABET

After we have developed a fundamental skill in the alphabet and phonics, then we can move on to the mastery of that skill. This can only be done through reading. Remember, the *natural* way to learn a language is to speak it from an early age. We don't have that advantage, so we must find some way to at least approximate that skill.

1. Syllabary. After mastering the alphabet, the next step for the ancients was a syllabary. This is an arrangement of consonants and vowels into syllables in order to practice pronunciation. We have something similar in our old English spellers. For example, here are some excerpts from Noah Webster's Speller:

ba	be	bi	bo	bu	by
ab	eb	ib	ob	ub	
bla	ble	bli	blo	blu	bly

spla sple spli splo splu sply

She fed the old hen.
She put her hat on the bed.
Ann can hem my cap.

2. Interlinear, etc. The next step after a syllabary is to read from an *interlinear*, an *intercolumnar*, or an *interleaved* text. An interlinear text places the English translation line-by-line below the ancient language text.

LATIN–ENGLISH INTERLINEAR

In principio erat Verbum,
In the beginning was the Word,

et Verbum erat apud Deum,
and the Word was with God,

et Deus erat Verbum.
${}_{1}$And ${}_{5}$God ${}_{4}$was ${}_{2}$the ${}_{3}$Word.

FIGURE 5H

GREEK-ENGLISH INTERLINEAR

’Eν ἀρχῇ ἣν ὁ λόγος,
In the beginning was the word,

καὶ ὁ λόγος ἣν πρὸς τὸν Θεὸν,
and the word was with God,

καὶ Θεὸς ἣν ὁ λόγος.
${}_{1}$And ${}_{5}$God ${}_{4}$was ${}_{2}$the ${}_{3}$Word.

FIGURE 5I

HEBREW-ENGLISH INTERLINEAR

בְּרֵאשִׁית הָיָה הַדָּבָר
$_{5}$*the* $_{6}$*word,* $_{4}$*was* $_{1}$*In* $_{2}$*the* $_{3}$*beginning*
וְהַדָּבָר הָיָה אֵת הָאֱלֹהִים
$_{6}$*God,* $_{5}$*with* $_{4}$*was* $_{1}$*and* $_{2}$*the* $_{3}$*word*
וֵאלֹהִים הָיָה הַדָּבָר
$_{2}$*the* $_{3}$*Word.* $_{4}$*was* $_{1}$*And* $_{5}$*God*

FIGURE 5J

We can cover the page with a piece of paper, slide the paper down to expose a line of Latin, Greek, or Hebrew text, read the text out loud, then slide the covering down to expose a line of English text, and read the English translation out loud. After we have practiced this for a while, we will not know the language well enough to understand or translate on our own, but we will certainly become familiar with the sound and the form, and with some of the vocabulary of the language. (For interlinear versions, see our Resource List in Appendix Two .)

An intercolumnar or interleaved text places the English translation beside the ancient language text, either in an adjoining column, or on the facing leaf or page. Here is one way to use an interleaved: familiarize yourself with the content of a selected portion by reading it in English, then read the same portion in the classical language.

LATIN-ENGLISH INTERCOLUMNAR OR INTERLEAF

In the beginning was the Word, *and the Word was with God,* *And the Word was God.*	In principio erat Verbum, et Verbum erat apud Deum, et Deus erat Verbum.

FIGURE 5K

GREEK-ENGLISH INTERCOLUMNAR OR INTERLEAF

In the beginning was the Word, *and the Word was with God,* *And the Word was God.*	Ἐν ἀρχῇ ἦν ὁ λόγος, καὶ ὁ λόγος ἦν πρὸς τὸν Θεὸν, καὶ Θεὸς ἦν ὁ λόγος.

FIGURE 5L

HEBREW-ENGLISH INTERCOLUMNAR OR INTERLEAF

In the beginning was the Word,	בְּרֵאשִׁית הָיָה הַדָּבָר
and the Word was with God,	וְהַדָּבָר הָיָה אֵת הָאֱלֹהִים
And the Word was God.	וֵאלֹהִים הָיָה הַדָּבָר

FIGURE 5M

Reading from an interlinear or interleaved text will help the student to develop a "feel" for the language itself. Though there are a multitude of new vocabulary words and inflections with which to become familiar, nevertheless, reading aloud the English followed by reading aloud the classical language will help. (For intercolumnar and interleaved versions, see our Resource List in Appendix Two.)

Some college and seminary professors frown upon the interlinear approach. But if we ask them how many of their students ever become sufficiently familiar with the language to read it fluently every day, then the professors respond with silence. In all fairness, the professors fear that adult students will use the interlinear text as a crutch which hinders them from developing a real skill in the vocabulary, grammar, and syntax of the language. Compare this to giving a child a calculator, who then becomes dependent upon the calculator, thus he never develops the real skill of working with numbers. Well, how about giving the child the calculator so that he can punch in numbers and learn his sums: 4 + 4 = 8; 4 + 5 = 9; etc. Once he learns his sums, you do not let him use the calculator for anything except practicing his sums. In the same way, when your young student becomes familiar enough with the language that he can sound it out easily and read along fluently, then he is ready to move on to formal grammar, and he can reserve the interlinear for use only to keep up his fluency in reading the language.

3. Chrestomathy. Another tool which was common in times past, but is little seen today, is the Chrestomathy. Chrestomathy is from *χρηστός* (useful) and *μάθεια* (learning). A Chrestomathy is a collection of select and exemplary literary passages used in studying a language. It is like a high class Graded Reader where you pronounce, hand copy, memorize, and translate very good examples of the language.

4. Memorization and Copywork. Memorization and copywork may prove valuable in helping your family to develop a familiarity and skill with these dead languages. If you memorize and recite multilingual passages, or if you read and copy a multilingual interlinear, then your mind will begin to fill with examples of the language. You may, for example, copy and memorize important Biblical passages in English, Greek, Latin, and Hebrew. As the members of your family memorize short pieces of a dead language, they may have fractional exchanges in that language. Actually, we have fractional exchanges in foreign languages every day. Et cetera. Eureka. Shalom. Faux pas. Gesundheit.

5. Vocabulary Studies. Finally, vocabulary studies teach you the Latin and Greek which you already know – that is, they identify Latin and Greek vocabulary words which also appear in an English form. Because a considerable amount of English vocabulary is rooted in Latin and Greek, studying English word derivations from Latin and Greek is a suitable preparation for formal study in these languages. Even those who, for whatever reason, cannot pursue a formal course in these languages, will nevertheless benefit from such studies. Below is an example. If you knew the Latin word or Greek word in the left column, would you then recognize its relationship to the English words in the right column?

VOCABULARY STUDIES

Classical Word		English Derivative
aqua	= water	*aquatic* (having to do with water) *aquarium* (enclosure for aquatic animals) *aqueduct* (a channel for drawing water over long distances) *aqueous* (pertaining to water)
manus	= hand	*manicure* (literally: care for the hand) *manual* (pertaining to the hand) *manufacture* (literally: to make by hand, hence to produce in a mechanical manner) *manuscript* (something written by hand)
ὕδωρ hydor (hydro-)	= water	*hydrant* (water outlet) *hydraulics* (the movement of fluid, especially water, under pressure in a tube) *hydroelectric* (generating electricity with water) *hydrogen* (an element which generates water when oxidized) *hydrophobia* (fear of water, a characteristic of the disease called rabies)
χείρ cheir (chiro-)	= hand	*chirality* (right or left handedness) *chirography* (handwriting = penmanship) *chiropteran* (a class of animals with hands for wings, such as bats)

FIGURE 5N

Such studies may prove valuable in preparing for the study of formal Latin and Greek grammar. You must appraise whether your time is better spent on vocabulary studies or on something else. (For vocabulary studies, see our Resource List in Appendix Two.)

Level Two: Focus on Grammatical Skill – Learning the Grammar and Syntax of the Language

At some point, perhaps while you are still acquiring some familiarity and skill with the spoken and written forms of the ancient language, you will move on to a formal study of its Vocabulary, Grammar, and Syntax.

We are satisfied that the formal study of grammar is best begun sometime around age ten (ages nine through eleven). Here is a good test as to whether your child's brain has developed to the point where he can handle formal grammar: Can he discern *easily* the different parts of speech? For example, can he tell how the word *look* is used differently in these two sentences:

I *looked* at John.

I gave John a *look*.

The first use of *look* is as a Verb, describing a manner of action, change of condition, state of existence, or attitude of mind. The second use of *look* is as a Noun, naming a person, place, thing, quality, or idea. When your child understands this distinction *easily*, then he is ready to learn the formal grammar of a language.

We want to avoid cramming our child's mental file drawers full of grammar before he is developmentally prepared to receive it. If we teach him grammar too early, he will take the information and store it in his brain in a different way than he would store it he were to learn it later – learn it after the connections of his brain were more fully developed. The process can be compared to putting information into a simple linear filing system as distinguished from putting the information into a complex multidimensional array. The world which the young child understands is largely a world of concrete ideas. He is physically prepared to handle first verbal, then written, communication; but mostly with a concrete vocabulary. Sure, he will develop some more abstract understandings, but until around age ten, he is greatly limited as to his comprehension. His ability to handle a large number of complex abstract ideas is greatly limited, unless he reduces those ideas to a linear version. You ask, "What's so bad about storing the information differently?" Well, it makes the information less accessible after the brain is fully developed. In fact, there is evidence that it may actually do physical harm to the brain. (See our article History and Research on the Teaching of Math, found in Appendix One, Article Eleven.) Actual physical learning disabilities may develop. But even if we suppose that all of this talk about the physical development of the brain is a bunch of poppycock, there is nevertheless no particular advantage to teaching formal grammar early.

Notice, we are not saying that there is no advantage to teaching *language* early. There are many advantages to that. We refer only to teaching *formal grammar* early. Instead of consuming your time with formal grammar instruction, your time would better and more efficiently be spent on other things. When the child is ready, he will learn formal grammar easily enough, and he will avoid the pains and possible injury to the brain caused by forcing him beyond the normal physical limits of his early capacities. A few children may be ready earlier, and if so, that will be quite obvious to you. But do not force the issue upon a child who, from a developmental point of view, is physically unprepared.

If you study some basics of English grammar before you move on to Latin, Greek, or Hebrew grammar, then familiarity and skill with the concepts of English grammar will give you the basis upon which to compare the other languages.

Formal Latin grammar could begin around age nine, ten, or eleven – it's your call, based upon the child's development and your own priorities. Formal Greek grammar could begin around age thirteen or anytime thereafter – again, it's your call. Hebrew? Well, unless you have unusual priorities, you will probably want to wait until after you've mastered some of the Greek.

A COMPARISON OF GRAMMARS

In a simple active English sentence, we identify the subject, verb, and direct object by observing its order in the sentence. The subject comes first, then the verb, then the direct object. Hence, these three sentences say different things.

Flowers love blossoms.
Love blossoms flowers.
Blossoms flowers love.

But in the classical languages, the word-order does not necessarily identify the subject, verb, and direct object. Instead, the form – the actual spelling – of the word is changed in order to show its function in the sentence, or its relationship to other words. In Latin, for example, one determines the function of a noun by its ending, regardless of its position in the sentence. Below is a simplified example:

LATIN NOUN PARADIGM

Case	Function	Singular	Plural
Nominative	*Subject*	canis	canēs
Accusative	*Direct Object*	canem	canēs
Ablative	*Object of a Preposition*	cane	canibus
Dative	*Indirect Object*	canī	canibus
Genitive	*Possessive*	canis	canum

FIGURE 5O

This change in the form of the word is called *inflection*. The ancient languages are all highly inflected languages. Modern English has some inflection, but English is not a highly inflected language. For example, the singular English noun is usually changed to the plural by adding an *s* or *es*, or by changing the spelling (book, books; fish, fishes; fly, flies; wife, wives; goose, geese; child, children; exceptions: sheep, sheep; deer, deer). The possessive of the noun is created by adding an apostrophe and *s*, or, if the noun already ends in *s*, then by adding only an apostrophe (book's, books'; fish's, fishes'; fly's, flies'; wife's, wives'; goose's, geese's; child's, children's; sheep's, deer's). The English personal pronoun is about the only thing which remains fairly highly inflected.

I, me, my, mine; we, us, our, ours.

[Thee, Thou, Thy, Thine]; [Ye], you, your, yours.

He, him, his; she, her, hers, it, it, its; they, them, their, theirs.

In the ancient languages, nouns, verbs, pronouns, adjectives, and other words have an inflection for nearly every function – including functions we don't even think about in English. Because word-order plays less of a grammatical role in ancient languages, word-order in ancient languages is free to play the role of expressing emphasis – a role which is more difficult to play in written English.

So, not only do the symbols and sounds of ancient languages differ from English, but the structure of the words and sentences also differ. The grammatical structure of Latin is very different from English, the structure of Greek is very similar to Latin, and the structure of Hebrew is very different from either English, Latin, or Greek.

As you can see by now, studying an inflected language forces the student to think in different categories than those to which he is accustomed.

THREE BASIC APPROACHES TO FORMAL GRAMMAR STUDY

There is more than one way to study the formal grammar of a language. You will need to choose which approach to grammar study fits your circumstances best. There are three basic approaches to consider.

1. The Traditional or Deductive Approach

The first basic approach to language learning is the Traditional or Deductive Approach. With this approach, the basic facts and fundamental rules of the language are taught in a logical and systematic fashion. We learn Vocabulary, Noun and Verb paradigms, rules of grammar and syntax, and so forth. The student memorizes the facts and rules, and is tested with exercises. He learns the fundamental details of the language before he attempts to read larger pieces. It is like learning piano: one first learns to read the music and finger the notes and chords, then he practices technique and expression on small pieces. He does not attempt large pieces until he has first mastered the fundamentals. In the same way, the language student cannot read extensively in the language until he has first mastered the fundamentals of the language.

We know that the Deductive approach works, because it has worked for at least two millennia. The earliest grammar textbook we know anything about was entitled τέχνη γραμματικη΄ (techne grammatike = grammar arts). It was written by Dionysius Thrax around 100 B.C., and it was used as a textbook until the eighteenth century A.D. (They must have had good copyright laws back then.)

The Deductive approach is effective to the degree that it is clear, comprehensive and digestible. Unfortunately, this approach has become less digestible to products of modern culture who are not trained to think deductively and systematically; who lack self-discipline; and who find it difficult to sustain an interest in something without an entertaining stimulus and an immediate reward. Studies will become tedious, painful, and boring to the student if there are no pretty colored pictures and a smorgasbord of activities to stimulate the student's interest.

We are not speaking against the Deductive approach when we say all of these things. We are only speaking against the degeneracy of our culture. The overall culture has dragged everyone down to such an extent that what was once accomplished with moderate effort is now accomplished only with great effort.

Latin is a dead language, as dead as it can be.
First it killed the Romans, and now it's killing me.

With the Deductive approach, most students will need an experienced teacher who knows the language, who can explain each lesson, who can tell the student what to do, and who can competently check the work.

TRADITIONAL OR DEDUCTIVE GRAMMAR, LATIN NOUN PARADIGM

	Number			
Case	*Singular*		*Plural*	
Nominative	mundus	=*world*	mundī	=*worlds*
Accusative	mundum	=*world*	mundōs	=*world*
Ablative	mundō	=*by/with world*	mundīs	=*by/with worlds*
Dative	mundō	=*to/for world*	mundīs	=*to/for worlds*
Genitive	mundī	=*of world*	mundōrum	=*of worlds*

FIGURE 5P

There are numerous Deductive curricula for teaching Latin, Greek, and Hebrew. In a typical Deductive grammar textbook, the first two chapters might cover the first declension, nominative case, genitive case, ablative case, the first conjugation, direct object, ablative of accompaniment, and apposition. In other words, much grammar is covered in a short period of time. A good understanding of English grammar ordinarily helps much in using a Deductive grammar. Some Deductive grammars offer much help, and some offer little, but all require a considerable degree of self-motivation on the part of the student for a successful completion of the course. Without an experienced teacher to help, the success rate drops off abruptly. So purely Deductive grammars are used in classroom schools with experienced teachers.

Question: Isn't the Deductive Approach the classical approach; therefore, shouldn't we use this approach?

Answer: The Deductive Approach is the classical approach to writing about formal grammar. Dionysius Thrax wrote a deductive grammar. We very much favor a deductive approach to describing grammar, because grammar is by its very nature deductive and systematic. But how formal grammar is written is not quite the same thing as how it is taught. To begin with, the people of ancient times were already familiar with these languages before they learned the formal grammar. The Greeks knew Greek before they studied Greek Grammar. The Latins knew

Latin before they studied Latin Grammar. (The English know English before they study English Grammar.) The fundamentals of expression were already known to the students. Grammar described in detail, in a systematic way, what the students were already practicing. So the method of instruction would follow a deductive course. This must necessarily be distinguished from modern students who study a language quite unfamiliar to them. The method may still follow a deductive course, but it will need to employ various techniques – unnecessary to the ancients – which will create in the student a familiarity with the language. So, just to say that something is deductive is not to say that it is necessarily effective. It may be, but that will depend upon how it is used.

2. The Natural or Inductive Approach

The second basic approach to language learning is the Natural or Inductive Approach. Someone had the idea of learning new languages the way we all learned our native language – by trial and error. The natural approach to teaching languages is to give a sentence or a paragraph in the language; then to supplement this reading with helps in pronunciation, vocabulary, grammar, and syntax. It is somewhat like throwing someone in the middle of the swimming pool to teach him how to swim, then shouting instructions to him from the pool side. Interest is held because the information is immediately useful.

We know the Inductive approach has always worked with children in learning their native language. However, with older children, and with adults, it has had different degrees of success. It has been very successful in teaching modern foreign languages – Spanish, French, German – on a conversational level. It has been less successful in establishing a deep and firm grasp of all the complexities of a foreign language. It has been the least successful in teaching classical languages.

Why would this be? It is because the goals of a conversational language course are different from the goals of a classical language course. The goal of a conversational language course is to produce rapid results: rapid understanding – not complete understanding; and rapid expression – not full expression. We learn how to have functional conversations within a culture which speaks that language. For example, we may learn how to order our dinner in French or Italian. (Hopefully, we will learn how to pay the bill as well.)

With classical languages, however, we are entirely on the receiving end. We are not going to speak or write letters to persons who have been dead for millennia. Classical authors did not write for a conversation level understanding. They wrote for full comprehension. So the primary goal of a classical language course is not rapid reading, but full comprehension. Instead of focusing on how we might say something in the classical language, we focus on what precisely is meant by the classical author. The Inductive approach does not often succeed with full comprehension as its goal.

With the Inductive approach – just as with the Deductive approach – most students will need an experienced teacher who knows the language, who can explain each lesson, who can tell the student what to do, and who can competently check the work.

NATURAL OR INDUCTIVE GRAMMAR, LATIN PARAGRAPH

> et pastores erant in regione eadem vigilantes et custodientes vigilias noctis supra gregem suum. et ecce angelus Domini stetit iuxta illos et claritas Dei circumfulsit illos et timuerunt timore magno. et dixit illis angelus, nolite timere: ecce enim evangelizo vobis gaudium magnum quod erit omni populo: quia natus est vobis hodie salvator, qui est Christus Dominus in civitate David. et hoc vobis signum invenietis infantem pannis involutum et positum in praesepio. et subito facta est cum angelo multitudo militiae caelestis laudantium Deum et dicentium. gloria in altissimis Deo et in terra pax in hominibus bonae voluntatis.

FIGURE 5Q

There are very few Inductive curricula for teaching Latin, Greek, or Hebrew. In a typical Inductive grammar textbook, the first chapter might begin with a short Latin paragraph, like the one above (Luke 2:8–14). The student is expected to translate the passage, using the supplied list of vocabulary words, along with a few grammatical hints. The paragraph is the swimming pool, and the vocabulary and hints are the instructions from the pool side. Again, without an experienced teacher to help, it requires a considerable degree of self-motivation on the part of the student for a successful completion of the course. Purely Inductive grammars are most often used in classroom schools with experienced teachers.

Question: If we want to have a natural understanding of the language, shouldn't we follow the inductive approach?

Answer: This may sound good in theory, but in fact, no inductive program actually teaches a dead language within a living culture. To be sure, they do the best they can to artificially "induce" such a culture, but everything is contrived. We aren't suddenly dropped into Athens 400 B.C., or Rome 100 B.C., and expected to learn our way around – safely, without a guide! Inductive programs, under the direction of a good guide, can create some familiarity with the language. Nevertheless, it is less likely that they will develop great precision in understanding the language. Grammar is, by its very nature, deductive and systematic, so we recommend to those who follow the inductive approach, that they also keep a systematic deductive notebook of everything which they learn. The work involved in maintaining the notebook will require disciplined categorical thought, which does as much or more for the student as learning the language itself.

3. The Programmed-Interactive Approach

The third basic approach to language learning is called the Programmed-Interactive Approach.

Both the Inductive and Deductive approaches have their advantages and their disadvantages. One advantage of the Deductive approach is that it follows the natural progression of learning – first describing the simple elements, then showing how those elements are put together, then showing how these constructions are used. One advantage of the Inductive approach is that it produces faster results – the student is using the language almost immediately. But a major reason why both of these approaches fail – particularly with classical languages – is because, as the brain develops, it establishes neuron-synapse routes, and these routes are changed only by very painful means. (No fair using electric shock treatment!) Do not bother buying any book entitled, "Classical Hebrew, Greek, or Latin *Made Easy*." We might compare this to the title, "Learn Brain-Surgery By Mail in Three Easy Lessons." Unless we have a natural aptitude for language learning, it is never going to be easy for us.

However, the Programmed Interactive Approach has been proven to be the least painful and the most effective. "Programmed" means that the text is arranged to take the student step-by-step through the normal learning process, introducing information, then explaining how the pieces of information fit together, then showing him how to use the information. (That is the Trivium method, in case you missed it.) "Interactive" means that the text is written in a way which simulates a teacher who continually interacts with the student, asking him questions, then confirming or correcting his answers as he studies. This immediately strengthens skills in analysis (taking things apart) and synthesis (putting things together). The process is repeated in small steps, and the student learns at his own speed. Eventually, the facts and skills are mastered. The Result: "Classical Hebrew, Greek, or Latin Made Easi–*er*."

A Programmed Interactive approach will incorporate both the Deductive and the Inductive approaches, but in a more effective way. With the Programmed Interactive approach, we do not need to know the language in order to teach it, and we do not need to have a teacher in order to learn it – because the text *is* the teacher. The text explains each lesson, it tells the student what to do, and it competently checks the work.

PROGRAMMED-INTERACTIVE GRAMMAR, GREEK GRAMMAR

What is a Noun?

The name of anything which has a name.

Say out loud and write all of the Nominative and Accusative forms of the Greek Article, both Numbers, all three Genders.

Nominative Singular: *ὁ, ἡ, τό*; Nominative Plural: *οἱ, αἱ, τά*
Accusative Singular: *τόν, τήν τό*; Accusative Plural: *τούς, τάς τά*

Translate the sentence: *Πέτρος βλέπει τὴν ἔρημος*.

Peter sees the desert.

FIGURE 5R

There are only a few Programmed Interactive curricula for teaching Latin or Greek. In a typical Programmed-Interactive grammar textbook, the material to be learned is divided into small particles (called frames); is presented in sequence; requires continuous, active student responses; and each response is immediately checked before the student is allowed to proceed. Students progress at their own individual rate. To learn another language requires a degree of self-motivation from most of us, but the Programmed-Interactive program supplies, in the program itself, an experienced teacher to help with the successful completion of the course.

Question: Isn't programmed learning the same as behavioral psychology? Should we be using animal behavior techniques on our children?

Answer: The behavioral psychologists employ stimulus-response training. First, they observe how stimulus-response techniques work in training animals. Their evolutionary presuppositions drive them to treat men like animals. So they employ these same stimulus-response techniques on men. Because there is enough similarity of natural design between men and animals, these same techniques often work – in varying degrees – on men. But there is a moral issue involved here. The behavioral psychologists are, in practical philosophy, if not in actual profession, atheists. They treat men as if they were merely animals, with no mind or spirit. In fact, the way in which they use their techniques may cause men to be driven more by their animal nature than by their mind and spirit.

Well, when little Bobby's hand has been caught playing with the knobs on the gas stove, or making uninvited fishing expeditions into the cookie jar, if we apply a negative stimulus to his hinder parts, we might also be accused of using behavioral psychology. We may also be accused of applying a little positive stimulus when we praise him for doing his lessons well. There may also be a legitimate use of behavioral training in limited medical situations for treating some physical disabilities. But there is a huge chasm between these uses and the philosophy of the behavioral psychologists. We might say that these psychologists have taken a technique which is only natural, which is perfectly legitimate within proper parameters, and which has been used effectively for millennia, and they have refined and improved it, but they have also perverted it to serve their own nefarious philosophical ends.

How does programmed-interactive learning resemble this stimulus-response training? Well, a program – a course of study – is laid out step-by-step to accomplish a particular end. The steps involve interaction – inquiry and response – to test the success of learning at each step, to correct errors, and to re-enforce the correct learning. Isn't this really how we all learn anything? Of course it is – especially a language. And this is precisely the methodology of a private tutor. We simply do not learn best when we passively read, or try to memorize, then perform a series of exercises. Rather, we learn best when we actively respond with the teacher, being held accountable during the teaching by requiring ongoing responses, and immediately confirming or correcting those responses. The better we can perfect such a technique, the better we can learn.

This is similar to the Socratic method, where two or more persons pursue a discussion, through question and answer, in order to achieve a better understanding of some subject. It stimulates the reasoning by constantly challenging the reasoning in a variety of ways and situations. If the programmed-interactive learning were to bypass the reasoning and attempt to achieve merely an *animal* response, then it would be nefarious indeed. Though programs will differ in the degree to which they engage the reasoning powers, we are not aware of any program which bypasses the reasoning and works for an animal response – like an animal trainer, instead of a personal tutor. Indeed, we judge some of the programs which we have examined to be quite engaging and challenging. In developing some programmed-interactive curricula, the machinery of behavioral psychology has been picked over for useful parts. Not the nefarious philosophy, but some useful technique, has been used. This may be compared to classical Christian education, which does not use the pagan philosophy of the ancients, but only the useful parts of the Trivium technique. Of course, we must always keep our eyes open for how a particular thing is being used in any given situation, and we must make adjustments where necessary.

> All things are lawful for me, but not all things do benefit. All things are lawful for me, but I-myself will not be brought under the control of anything. All things are lawful for me, but not all things do benefit. All things are lawful for me, but not all things do edify. — First Corinthians 6:12; 10:23 (v.l.t.)

SOME TIPS AND HELPS

If you are familiar with one of the classical languages, and you can explain the grammar well to your child, then you may find any of these approaches useful in teaching that language. But if you are not familiar with a language, then most likely the interactive self-teaching grammar will work best for you. We have found that *Artes Latinae* by Waldo Sweet is the best self-teaching Latin grammar available to Homeschooling families.

Once you have chosen a grammar text, the text itself should provide you with the form and substance to begin your formal study. But here are a few ideas which may prove helpful.

1. Alphabetics and Phonetics.

For some unrevealed reason, most language materials are extremely weak in the most fundamental characteristic of a written language – the letter-symbols and their sounds. In a random survey of twenty out of over forty elementary Greek grammars in our library, we found the following number of pages devoted to teaching the alphabetic and phonetic system (in ascending order) 1, 1, 2, 2, 3, 3, 3, 3, 3, 3, 4, 4, 4, 4, 5, 6, 6, 8, 9, 10. (Of course, size of print, size of page, and white space on the page, are not here considered.) In our opinion, the grammars with 8, 9, and 10 pages were approaching adequacy. Now, just because a grammar spends little time and space on mastering one of the basics – the alphabet, does not mean it is otherwise a poor grammar. But if you choose such a grammar, then you must supplement this weakness with other material.

2. Readings in the Language.

Elementary deductive grammars usually stick to studying the mechanics of the language, while ignoring the activity of reading the language. Some of the translation exercises may be based upon sentences from actual literature, but there is no regular practice provided for actual reading. You may enter into the process of studying grammar thinking that you will learn everything you need to know, but when you come out at the other end of the process, you may be wondering what to do with what little you retain. If you had been reading all the time, you would have applied your lessons to what you read, and have gained a familiarity which is impossible to gain otherwise. So, if you choose a grammar which neglects reading, then you must supplement this weakness with other material.

3. Language Notebook

No matter which approach you choose to study grammar, we recommend that you create and maintain an orderly and systematic language notebook. The student should have a notebook for each language he studies. This is his lifelong Greek or Latin or Hebrew notebook. A medium sized three-ring binder with subject dividers and notebook paper should work well. The notebook is divided into separate sections. Here is a suggested list of sections:

a. *Sounds and Symbols of the Language* (including such things as the names of the letters of the alphabet and how to pronounce them, as well as special accent rules and punctuation, etc.).
b. *Technical Terms and Definitions* (including such words as Declension, Conjugation, Ellipsis, Pronoun, Antecedent, Tense, etc.).
c. *Substantive Syntax* (which includes how to use Nouns and words which are like Nouns: Noun Declension Paradigms, Rules

of Agreement, etc.).

d. *Verbal Syntax* (which includes how to use Verbs and words which are like Verbs: Verb Conjugation Paradigms, Explanation of Tenses, etc.).

e. *Vocabulary* (including Noun, Adjective and Verb paradigms, etc.).

f. *Translation and Memorization Exercises* (Phrases or Expressions, etc.).

g. *Tests.*

Because everything – test papers, translation exercises, vocabulary words, etc. – will be in one place, language study will be simplified

Whatever is entered into the notebook must be done in a neat, orderly, systematic manner. As the student learns the grammar, he will need to add, change, and rearrange divisions in his notebook, and he may rewrite pages into better order. The exercise of rewriting the notebook has the added advantage of forcing him to rethink his Latin, Greek, or Hebrew in an orderly manner, which impresses the mind with the order of the grammar. This will teach the student to be neat, systematic, and orderly. We give an example of a Latin notebook in Chapter Twelve, under Section 6.

4. Vocabulary Cards

For each word which we entered into our language notebook, we copy the same information onto a 3 x 5 note card. We put the Latin, Greek, or Hebrew on one side, and the English translation on the other. We recite both sides out loud as we move through our deck each day. At first, our deck may be small, so we can recite the whole deck daily. As the deck grows, we may take several days to recite the whole deck. We may also have someone else read one side of each card to us, then we respond with what we recall of the other side, with our partner cuing or correcting us. Then we may exchange places with our partner. Exercises like this help us to build our vocabulary, and they make learning other parts of the language easier.

5. Reading and Memorizing

Continue regular reading and memorizing in the language. The more familiar you are with the language, the easier the grammar will come to you.

6. Student Pace

Younger students may take as much as two years to progress through a normal sized grammar text. Older students may complete it in a year. Diligent and gifted students may master it in a semester or less. The goal is to master the material, not to finish the material in as short a time as possible.

7. Reference Grammar

You may sometimes have difficulty understanding a concept. It may be helpful to you to compare another grammar text which explains the concept another way. No matter which of the three different approaches to grammar study is used by the grammar which you choose, comparing with another grammar will often be helpful. So obtain a second text – a deductive text – for reference purposes and for comparing treatments and explanations of various topics. (For information on grammars, lexicons, and other helps, see our Resource List.)

8. Practice, Repetition, and Hard Work is Classical.

The old adage says, "You can't get out of it what you don't put into it." Other things being equal, the measure of the benefit which you acquire from your studies will be proportional to the measure of effort which you expend toward them. Language materials may be classified on a continuous scale from *easier* to *more difficult*, from *spoon fed* to *exasperating*. But in the final analysis, it is what you make of it. You can breeze your way through an easy curriculum on the cheap, but you will end up with cheap results. Or you can add value to the program by adding repetitions and practices, and you will end up with valuable results. You can also cut corners on your way through a difficult curriculum, but you will end up with less than a whole piece of pie in the end. Or you can add some sugar to sweeten, and some oil to smooth friction between some of the parts, and you will have a sweet and smooth piece of pie to dine upon.

Level Three: Focus on Fluency Skill
– Learning to Translate and Interpret the Language

At some point, perhaps while you are still acquiring some of the skills in vocabulary, grammar, and syntax, you will move on to a practical use of your knowledge in translating and interpreting in the classical languages. It makes no sense to master a language, then, through years of disuse, to lose what you have gained. Those who learn to read fluently in the language are more likely to keep up their proficiency in the language. So once you have acquired some proficiency in grammar, it is a good choice to strive to acquire an adequate level of fluency in reading with comprehension. By *fluency in reading* we mean you are able to spend more time simply reading, less time consulting a lexicon or grammar. By *comprehension* we mean reading with confidence, so that you understand what you read. The ultimate goal in a classical language program is to learn to understand and accurately translate most any passage without continually looking up vocabulary and grammar.

If you pursue this goal with diligence, then it could be accomplished, in at least one language, by the age of eighteen. Some ambitious students may reach the fluency level in less time – perhaps in as little as five years. Depending upon what goals you set, a few students may reach fluency level in more than one language in this amount of time. That may be too ambitious a program for many families. As proficiency in these languages is recovered within the Homeschool culture, the task will become easier with each generation. Of course, those who begin the program as adults may take much longer.

You will encounter more specifics on language study in the practical section of this book.

Chapter Six

Teaching Logic

. . . no lie is of the truth.
— First John 2:21

AN ARGUMENT FOR TEACHING LOGIC

THE SECOND PART OF THE TRIVIUM is Logic. Every subject has its own *logic* – the proper order and relationship between all of the parts. Logic is the way things fit together – or at least the way they ought to fit together. We want to describe the subject which we call *Logic*, because all of our understanding of every other subject is built upon the framework of this thing we call Logic.

What is Logic?

Logic is the simplest and most elementary of all exact sciences. It is the science of correct reasoning. Every science is occupied with detecting and describing the necessary and unalterable laws which rule a particular field of knowledge. Considered as a science, Logic detects and describes the necessary and unalterable laws of correct reasoning.

The apparatus which reasons – or performs logic – is the mind. Logic is, in a limited sense, a science of the mind. To the extent an individual is incapable of logical analysis and conclusion, he is to the same extent *mindless* – that is, he does not use the powers of his mind.

Some persons want to make a strong division between the powers of the mind and spiritual things. But the powers of the mind are powers of the spirit.

> And be renewed in the spirit of your mind. — Ephesians 4:23

> For God hath not given us the spirit of fear; but . . . of a sound mind. — Second Timothy 1:7

What affects the mind, affects the spirit; and what affects the spirit, affects the mind. So logic is a spiritual power, and without that spiritual power called *logic*, we are incapable of discerning truth from error. We will return to the power of logic a little later.

Words, Sentences, and Meaning

Man's mind is not blank at birth. Well before we are born, while we are still in our mother's womb, God gives us minds which have the power to evaluate all of our sensory experiences according to a systematic logic which has already been structured and programmed into our minds by God. This natural logic is thus an inborn faculty for reasoned judgment and inference. But like any other native faculty, its capacity may be developed through use, its power strengthened through training, and its precision fine tuned through testing.

As infants, when we began to learn the language, we assigned meanings to words according to our logical analysis of how we observed those words being used in sentences. So, let us talk about words and sentences for a moment.

Standing all by themselves, words have meaning. For example, here is a word:

> Horse.

It has more meaning within a sentence. Here is that word used in sentences:

> I would love to ride a palomino horse.

> I enjoy watching a Clydesdale horse work.

However, when words are illogically combined in a sentence, they become meaningless. For example, consider this sentence:

Draw a square circle.

The sentence is grammatically correct. Standing by themselves, the two words "square" and "circle" make sense. But when these two words are combined as they are in this sentence, they make no sense. The sentence is nonsense. By definition, something circular cannot also be square. We call this an oxymoron, or a contradiction in terms.

Sometimes we are confronted by a contradiction in terms, but we do not recognize it. For example, someone might ask, "Can God make a stone too heavy for Himself to lift?" The idea is absurd. We might as well ask God to make a god greater than Himself, such that He must bow before that god which He had made. It is not possible in the very nature of things.

Yet, we are surrounded by attempts to impose such absurdities upon us. Feminism, homosexuality, multiculturalism – such ideas are logical absurdities, contradictions in terms which we are expected to absorb into our thinking. (Feminism? – Making women to be men would be Masculinism. Homosexual ? Sex means they're different, not the same. Multiculturalism? Many cultures may be in contact with each other, and affect each other, but they cannot inhabit the same population – something must give.) – Such ideas cloud our minds in order to corrupt our thinking, and to lead us into a whole world of absurdities. Our culture is being filled with these absurdities of language.

For example, consider the man who thought he could fly. So he jumped off of the top of the Sears Tower. Sure enough, he was flying. As he passed each story on his way down, he cried to those who were looking through the windows, "So far, so good. So far, so good." Everything seemed to be going just fine. He was even gaining speed as he flew. He had proven that he could fly. But as he approached the pavement below, he suddenly realized that he had overlooked the question of whether he could land.

What was the man's problem? He knew the meaning of "fly" and he knew the meaning of "man" but he made a connection between them which was contrary to the nature of things. But that was not nearly so bad as when he tried to put this connection into practice. The law of gravity seemed to play on his side – for a while. But once he encountered the pavement below, the law of mass inertia was enforced. He suddenly had a concrete understanding of the matter.

Feminism, homosexuality, multiculturalism, ad nauseam, may seem to fly – "So far, so good." And some things may seem to play on their side, but eventually they will be arrested by the laws of nature, and of nature's God, the Creator, to Whom they must inevitably give an account. They are absurdities which contradict the logic of reality.

So words may have meaning, but truth is not in the meaning of words. Truth is in the meaning of sentences. A logician would say it this way: "Truth is not in terms. Truth is in propositions." A word or a term by itself is neither true nor false. For example, the word *broccoli* has meaning, but by itself it is neither true nor false. However, a sentence or a proposition about *broccoli*, such as "broccoli is edible," is either true or false. (We each have our own opinion about that proposition, don't we?) Truth is not in *words*, or *terms*, but in *sentences* or *propositions* which say something about those terms.

Why is it Important to Study Logic?

Let us consider the most basic law of logic, called the Law of Contradiction. (Some prefer to call it the Law of *Non*-Contradiction.) Aristotle expressed it in this manner:

> "The same attribute cannot at the same time both belong and not belong to the same subject and in the same respect."

Philosophers always speak in such plain language, don't they? Perhaps we can make it more plain with a simple illustration.

A candle may be both lit and not lit, but not at the same time, nor in the same respect. It may be lit in the night time, but not lit in the daytime. Or it may be lit on one end, but not lit on the other end. Or it may be lit on both ends, but not lit in the middle. But wherever it may be lit or not lit, it cannot be both *lit* and *not lit* on the *same* end at the *same* time, because that would be a what? *A Contradiction!*

A dove cannot have all white feathers and all black feathers at the same time. A person cannot be both completely dead and totally alive at the same time – or at least, not in the same respect.

Without this Law of Non-Contradiction, words or terms would no longer have specific meaning. If an attribute may at the same time both belong and not belong to the same word and in the same respect, then that word may be twisted to mean anything. (We may trust politicians to supply us with ample examples of this phenomena. For example, a budget surplus is really a reduction of the rate of deficit spending.)

If we disregard this basic rule of logic – that a word cannot have contradictory meanings at the same time – then the distinctions between black and white; right and wrong; good and evil; is and is not, will slowly grow fuzzy, and may eventually dissolve completely.

> Woe unto them that call evil good, and good evil; that put darkness for light, and light for darkness; that put bitter for sweet, and sweet for bitter! — Isaiah 5:20

> He that justifieth the wicked, and he that condemneth the just, even they both *are* abomination to the LORD. — Proverbs 17:15

> . . . If therefore the light that is in thee be darkness, how great *is* that darkness!— Matthew 6:23

Where there is no logic, there can be no absolute standards, but only relative personal values. If truth becomes relative in our thinking, then it follows that morality must also become relative in our thinking. Our values must then be clarified from the perspective of our own personal choice, instead of from the perspective of God's Word – His logos, His logic, which is the logic of reality, the only logic that really counts. Ethics must then be determined by the situation, and not by the revealed absolute standard of God's law.

Polylogism

In our culture, we have now arrived at the philosophy of polylogism – many logics. We are told that there is no such thing as absolute truth. All truth is relative. There is no single logic; there are many different logics, and *all* of them are *equally* valid. This, of course, means that *no* logic is *actually* valid. Apparent contradictions among the different logics must be resolved – so they say – by some force other than reason, because reason itself is the cause of the contradictions. We shall all be like gods, deciding for ourselves – individually or collectively – what is good and what is evil. Where did that teaching come from? (Genesis 3) Instead, we should refine out reasoning tools so that we can discern the apparent contradictions from the real ones.

This polylogism is the kind of absurd nonsense which is being taught in government schools today. Though this was once largely confined to the University, now elementary schools are being filled with this nonsense. Polylogism forms the foundation of modern thinking. With polylogism, absolute truth is absolutely ruled out. The only way to establish any truth is to decree it. Truth is whatever we decide it to be. Evolution is a fact, if we decide it is a fact. Never mind that this does irreparable damage to the word "fact." What we *want* to be true is our standard for what *is* true. If it fits with our preferences, then we say, "Let it be so," and it is so. And the evening and the morning were not day at all, for the light which was in them was all darkness.

Logic and Morality

The rejection of genuine logic leads inevitably to the abandonment of genuine morality, to be replaced – not with *im*-morality, we have always had plenty of that, but – with *a*-morality. A-morality is the idea that there is no right or wrong, there are only personal choices. Why? Because there is no logical standard by which we may judge anything. Like the serpent in the garden, a-morality says that we shall determine for ourselves what is good and evil. This is exactly where we have arrived in this culture — moral relativism. We have no right or wrong, only personal choices. "Nothing is innately good or bad, it is all in the way we think." There is no outward absolute standard. We define right and wrong only for ourselves. Our moral codes have all been personalized and privatized. The moral code for society considered as a whole is entirely arbitrary and negotiable. Anything goes, unless someone creates a force to stop it.

> ". . .every imagination of the thoughts of his heart *was* only evil continually."
> — Genesis 6:5

The only public sin is to violate the code of the politically correct. Politics has become the tool of choice to force upon everyone the personal choices of some – whether a few or many.

When we remove the true standards, something else must move in to fill the vacuum. But when it does, it necessarily creates other vacuums and imbalances. Eventually everything must collapse upon itself because it is all supported by nothing. The only order which will be left standing in the end is the one order which was standing from the beginning – the true order established by God's standards.

Logic and A-morality

The ultimate "morality" in our culture is now *the right-to-choose*. This is not limited merely to the so-called right-to-choose an abortion. No, we now have the right-to-choose our own sexual preference, or our own family lifestyle, or our own standards of private morality, ad nauseam.

Logical pro-life arguments are an attack upon that ultimate "morality" – the "right to choose," because we, as Christians, seek to define the term *life* according to the logical Law of Non-Contradiction. A baby in the womb cannot be both alive and not-alive at the same time and in the same respect. When we logically propose that a woman's "right-to-choose" ends where another life begins, we are attacking the morality of our age – the morality of a-morality. We cannot win the argument until we force our opponent to acknowledge *first*, that there are moral absolutes, and *second*, that we can reason logically from those moral absolutes.

Our culture has abandoned logic. If what is true for us is not, for others, their personal choice for truth, then what is moral for us may not be, for others, their personal choice for morality. If we do not first maintain a standard of *logic*, then we can never maintain a standard of *morality*.

Do you now understand what the politically-correct and double-speak language is all about? If the logic of our words and our sentences can be corrupted, then our language and our culture can be corrupted.

> "All the day they pervert my words:" — Psalm 56:5a

That is a matter of logic – the twisting of words.

> "All their thoughts are against me for evil." — Psalm 56:5b

That is a matter of morality – the intention of their heart.

When people tell us not to impose our "Christian" *morality* on them, they are really telling us not to impose our Christian *logic* on them. They prefer to remain *mindless*. They do not want to use their mind. They choose, instead, to follow the mindless multitude. But God commands us in His word to follow a different standard:

> "Thou shalt not follow a multitude to do evil. . . ." — Exodus 23:2

So much for peer pressure and social democracy.

The Spiritual Power of Logic

As we said earlier, logic is a spiritual power, and by the spiritual power of logic we discern truth from error.

In Second Peter 3:16, we are warned of "those who are untaught and unstable" and who "wrest," or "twist," the Scriptures "to their own destruction." This *twisting* refers to the torturing of a witness in order to extract a false confession from him. The twisting of the meaning of words involves errors in logic.

In Second Timothy 3:7, we read of those who are "always learning," yet they are "never able to come to the knowledge of the truth." They cannot discern truth from error. They are incapable of logical analysis. We do not mean to diminish the spiritual element in the discernment of the truth. We only mean to assert that logic must never be divorced from that spiritual element.

Second Timothy 4:4 describes those who "turn away their ears from the truth," and, having nowhere else to turn, it says that they "turn unto fables." The theory of evolution would be an example of a fable which men turn to because they refuse to be held accountable to a Creator.

What is Our Responsibility?

As Christians, we have an important responsibility to maintain the standard of logic. What is our responsibility?

> For *while* we are *yet* walking around in *the* flesh, we never wage war according to *the* flesh. For the weapons of our warfare *are* not fleshly. Rather, *they are* powerfully enabled by God for *the* pulling down of strong defensive *barriers*: *for* pulling down reasonings [/logical arguments] and every high *defensive barrier which* raises itself up against the knowledge of God; and *for* capturing every thought [/all intellect] to the obedience of Christ. — Second Corinthians — 10:3-5 (v.l.t.)

The weapons of Christian warfare are not those taken up by military forces. Our weapons are those which defeat false reasonings, and which expose false gods, and which capture the thoughts and intellect for service to Christ.

Why are Christians not winning the culture war? It is because we are not using the weapons which God specifically designed for our warfare. We have retreated. We should be aggressively engaging the culture – overturning false words and arguments with logic, and pulling down false ideas and philosophies with truth. Instead, we pass out weak little tracts filled with emotional arguments for a cheap gospel requiring psychological works instead of the spiritual grace of faith. We should not throw away our minds when we become Christians. Indeed, this is precisely when we should really begin to use them!

We are repeatedly commanded in the Scriptures to reason and dispute from the Scriptures with persuasive and convincing logical arguments. We are commanded to prove our doctrines. Romans 12:1 literally says that our service to God is to be logical or rational (λογικὴν, logikEn). We are to be ready always to give an answer to every man who asks us the reason – literally: the logical defense – for the hope which is in us (First Peter 3:15). We have no better example of this than Jesus Himself, Who repeatedly engaged in logical arguments from the Scriptures. The Gospel of Matthew alone (chapters 12, 19, 21, 22, and 23) contains a miniature textbook in logical argument.

What is Logic Useful For?

Logic is useful to understand the sciences. Every science – whether it be chemistry, physics, geography, history, or theology – is (or at least it should be) the application of the science of Logic to observations made in that particular field of knowledge. Hence the study of the exact science of Logic is foundational to the study of every other subject. The ancients called logic the *organon*, the instrument presupposed by every other science. The formal study of Logic should therefore be considered a foundational and indispensable part of every educational curriculum. And in the past it was.

Logic is useful to discern the truth. In the past, Logic was the first course required of all college freshman. Why? Because logic is the means for getting at the truth of propositions, the soundness of arguments, and the possibility or plausibility of assertions. How could we arrive at sound conclusions about what God commands if we had no ability to reason soundly from the Bible? Indeed, our degree of obedience and service to God is a direct function of our ability to reason from His Word. How could we detect illogical arguments which may lead us away from the truth? How could we judge other men's reasoning about things in this world? Without skill in logic, we are

> . . . children, tossed to and fro, and carried about with every wind of doctrine, by the sleight of men, *and* cunning craftiness, whereby they lie in wait to deceive; — Ephesians 4:14

Of course, if we reject the notion that there is any truth to get at, then our interest in getting at the truth plunges rather rapidly. If we reject the notion of revelation from God, then we necessarily reject the concept of absolute truth. So logic is ultimately unnecessary.

Logic is useful in the proper development of the brain. Our brain can be compared to a muscle in this respect: no pain, no gain. A certain radio commentator likes to describe school-age children's brains as "skulls full of mush." We presume he is pointing to their lack of intellectual development due to their improper diet (input of Knowledge), lack of exercise (processing of Understanding), and extracurricular activity (output of Wisdom). Of course, the mind must have something good to chew on, and it must have a reason to be chewing. But right now, we're only talking about the chewing itself – the logic.

Whenever we interrupt the natural Trivium progression of learning – leaving out one of the steps – we create a learning dysfunction. This is the age of learning dysfunctions. This is the age of interruptions. For example, when we omit teaching the basic principles of phonics, then we interrupt the natural development of written phonetic language learning, and we thereby create the learning dysfunction which we call *dyslexia* – the inability to read. Well, if we omit teaching the basic principles of logic, then we will create the dysfunction which we might call *dyslogia* – the inability to think! Put dyslexia and dyslogia together, and what do you have? Disaster.

The Rejection of Logic Leads to the Rejection of God

Logic is thoroughly dispensed with in modern curricula – except as a tool for manipulation. Nebulous social skills are considered more important than precise thinking skills. Feeling is valued more than discernment. And where some kind of thinking is taught, it is a programmed thinking, not a genuine critical thinking. The child is trained to think with the herd, like an animal, then socialized to run with the animals in the herd. Beware of stampedes – known today as "group consensus." "Thou shalt not follow a (mindless) multitude to do evil." (Exodus 23:2)

The child is programmed not to question certain concepts – precisely because they are *not provable*. They have been handed down from the politically correct *gods* by infallible revelation, and none may dare to deeply explore their reasoning.

It is through some form of logical study that we become skilled to discern between truth and error, and therefore between good and evil, and right and wrong (Hebrews 5:14). We cannot obey the truth before we know the truth (Psalm 143:8; John 8:32). We cannot know the truth apart from logic (First John 2:21 – the Law of Non-Contradiction). To reject logic is to reject truth, and to reject truth is to reject God. And that is what modern education is all about – the rejection of the standard of logic, the rejection of absolute truth, and the rejection of the sovereign God. At the heart of everything is the rejection of God, and without the knowledge and fear of God, there is no education.

> . . . Behold, the fear of the Lord, that *is* wisdom; and to depart from evil *is* understanding. — Job 28:28

> The fear of the LORD *is* the beginning of wisdom: a good understanding have all they that do *his commandments*. . . . — Psalm 111:10

> The fear of the LORD *is* the beginning of knowledge: *but* fools despise wisdom and instruction. — Proverbs 1:7

> The fear of the LORD *is* the beginning of wisdom: and the knowledge of the holy *is* understanding. — Proverbs 9:10

(For more arguments from a Christian point of view for studying logic, see the Article, The Christian Use of Logic, found in Appendix One, Article Ten.)

PRINCIPLES FOR LEARNING LOGIC

Defining and Describing Logic

The study of Logic is divided into two parts: *Formal Logic* and *Informal Logic*. We are not talking about a formal *tuxedo* type of logic and an informal *blue jeans* type of logic. The words *Formal* and *Informal* are here used as technical terms.

Formal Logic is the study of the systematic form or structure of argument, such as syllogisms. This includes the abstract rules of logical reasoning which logicians have reduced to a system of mathematic-like formulas. Formal Logic is the foundation for all reasoning, and is therefore also the foundation for what is called *In*-formal Logic.

Informal Logic includes everything which is not classified within in the narrow limits of what we call *Formal* Logic. So *In*-formal, in this instance, simply means *Not*-Formal. *In*formal does not mean it has no form or system, but only that it deals more with the substance of an argument than with its systematic formulation. We might say it is less theoretical and more practical. The subject called Informal Logic includes such things as Logical Fallacies and Propaganda. We encounter bad verbal arguments everyday (especially if we are listening to politicians), and Informal Logic is concerned with developing methods to detect such arguments and to deal with them.

In this section, we will provide a small taste of logic, along with a few practical ideas about teaching the subject of Logic.

Formal Logic

Formal Logic divides into two fundamentally different types of reasoning: *Deductive* and *Inductive*.

1. *Deductive Reasoning* is the kind of logic which proves things for certain. It describes the laws of necessary inference. With Deductive Reasoning, we begin with a few statements which are presumed (for the sake of the argument) to be true, and from these statements we construct an argument which we know (because of the form) must reach a true conclusion. An argument which does not have the correct form is necessarily not valid, and its conclusion cannot be trusted.

Deductive Reasoning includes such things as the study of Categorical Logic and Propositional Logic.

Categorical Logic, developed by Aristotle and others, involves statements which have terms which are quantified: "all" "some" or "none." This includes syllogisms such as:

All men are mortal.	[All M is P.]
Socrates is a man.	[All S is M.]
Therefore, Socrates is mortal.	[∴ All S is P.]

Syllogisms may also be represented by Euler circles, which are diagrams representing the various quantities and their relationships.

Propositional Logic, developed by Gottfried Leibniz and others, translates ordinary reasoning into symbols. It involves statements which are not quantified, but which relate two possibilities: "and" "or" "if – then" or "only if." This includes symbolic formulae such as:

$p \supset q$	[If p is true, then q is true.]
p	[p is true.]
$\therefore q$	[Therefore, q is true.]

It may not look like there is much here to study, but once we dig into the subject, we will find that it can be quite involved. Computer programming is an application of this kind of symbolic logic.

2. *Inductive Reasoning* is the kind of logic which describes the laws of possibility and probability, but which proves nothing for certain. With Inductive Reasoning, we begin with many observable facts, and from these we speculate as to possible causes and their effects. No Inductive argument is considered necessarily true unless it accounts for all possible facts – which is usually not possible. For example:

Ten thousand dogs were examined.

All ten thousand dogs had fleas.

Therefore it is possible that all dogs have fleas.

All which is certainly known is that some dogs have fleas. Perhaps only the ten thousand dogs examined had fleas – and no more. Perhaps the thousand and first dog will not have fleas. The only way to prove that absolutely all dogs have fleas is to examine absolutely all dogs – a most unlikely endeavor. Nevertheless, the generalization that perhaps all dogs, or at least most dogs, have fleas may prove very useful for persons who are allergic to flea bites.

The Experimental Scientific Method and Statistical Probability are a couple of practical applications for Inductive Reasoning.

Informal Logic

Informal Logic involves everyday reasoning, and may be classified into perhaps seven categories:

1. CLASSIFICATION

Classification is the analyzing of relationships between things in order to organize them into classes according to their similarities or differences.

2. DEFINITION

Definition is the explanation of the essential properties of a thing. The elements of a definition are: a. The *Genus*: Which identifies the general class to which the thing defined belongs. b. The *Species* (or Differentia): Which describes the specific characteristics which distinguish the thing from others in the same general class.

Example of a bad definition:

> A bicycle is something children ride to school.

This definition gives the General Class (the Genus), but not the Distinguishing Characteristics (the Species). It could be a school bus, a train, a horse, etc.

Example of a bad definition:

> A bicycle has two wheels and handlebars and is powered by peddling with one's feet.

This definition gives no General Class from which to distinguish these characteristics. It could be a game, an exerciser, or a power generator.

Example of a better definition:

> A bicycle is something children ride to school, which has two wheels and handlebars and is powered by pedaling with one's feet.

(Of course, homeschooled children do not usually ride bikes to school.)

3. ARGUMENT

Argument can be divided into:

a. *Recognizing* – identifying what is the argument; distinguishing its parts.
b. *Diagramming* – laying out the reasoning in a visual way.
c. *Evaluation* – analyzing the truth, validity, and soundness of what is being said.
d. *Argumentation* – constructing effective logical arguments in an efficient manner.

4. PROBLEM SOLVING

Problem Solving is the method for solving complex puzzles.

5. INFORMAL LOGICAL FALLACIES

Informal Logical Fallacies are common errors which we make in reasoning. (Informal Fallacies may be distinguished from *Formal Fallacies,* which are violations of the rules of Syllogisms.) Though Informal Fallacies involve faulty reasoning, they are nevertheless often quite persuasive. Here is a Fallacy Sampler of selected Logical Fallacies which you, no doubt, will recognize:

(1) Argument to the Man (Abusive Argumentum ad Hominem).

This is an argument which appeals to a man's personality, character, or features, instead of addressing the real issues.

a. Favorable: We should elect Jack president because he seems so compassionate. (Never mind where his proposed policies will lead.)

b. Unfavorable: I'm taking you in, young man, because you look like someone who could have committed this crime. (You're under arrest because you look guilty.)

(2) (Inductive) Fallacy of Hasty Generalization.

This is an argument based upon an inadequate sampling of instances. This is also called "Jumping to Conclusions."

a. I bought a Goodstone tire once and it went bad. I'll never buy another Goodstone tire.

b. I knew a homeschool student who used poor grammar. Homeschooling is bad.

c. I knew a homeschool student who memorized Shakespeare. Homeschooling is great.

(3) Fallacy of the False Dilemma.

This is an argument which limits the question to only two possibilities, when in fact there are other possibilities. (This is also called "Either-Or Reasoning.")

a. If you don't like the government's school, then you'll have to send your children to a private school somewhere far away. (Ever hear of Homeschooling?)

b. "Tell us therefore, What thinkest thou? Is it lawful to give tribute unto Caesar, or not?" (Matthew 22:17) (There's another option: "Render therefore unto Caesar the things which are Caesar's; and unto God the things that are God's." Matthew 22:21.)

(4) Fallacy of the False Cause (Post Hoc Ergo Propter Hoc – literally: after this, therefore because of this).

This is an argument which confuses time with cause. It is supposed that one event *caused* another to happen because the second event happened *after* the first event.

a. The rooster crows every morning. Then the sun rises. Now do you understand why roosters are so important?

b. I've eaten carrots and onions, carrots and garlic, and carrots and chives. Everyone tells me that I have bad breath. I'm never eating carrots again!

(5) Fallacy of Equivocation.

This is an argument which builds on dual meanings of words.

a. Of all creatures on earth, only men are rational. Therefore women are not rational. (The expression "men" is generic, ordinarily including males and females, unless the context separates the genders. But an inordinate gender-consciousness may take "men" as gender-specific where it is completely unwarranted.)

b. Give me your gun and I'll take care of you. (Does he mean "I'll protect you," or does he mean "Bang! There, you're taken care of.")

(6) Fallacy of Pettifoggery.

This is an argument which avoids the obvious sense of a word, phrase, or detail. A pettifog is a lawyer. Some call this fallacy "Lawyer-talk" or "Splitting Hairs."

a. God helps those who help themselves. So I'll help myself to this pie.

b. I did not lie when I said that I was alone when I took the pie. It all depends on what you mean by "was" and "alone."

(7) Fallacy of Begging the Question (Petitio Principii).

This is an argument which presupposes the very thing which it ostensibly proves. This is also called "Circular Reasoning."

a. The president is innocent because he is not guilty.

b. Question: How do you date fossils? Answer: Fossils are dated by the rocks in which they are found. Question: Then how do you date the rocks? Answer: Rocks are dated by the fossils which they contain.

(8) Fallacy of Composition or Division.

This is an argument based upon the false assumption that the characteristics of each individual part must also be the characteristics of the whole, or vice versa.

a. Sodium is a poison. Chlorine is a poison. Therefore sodium chloride (table salt) is twice as powerful a poison.

b. Sodium chloride is ordinary and harmless table salt. Therefore sodium is harmless and chlorine is harmless.

(9) Fallacy of the Hidden Question.

This is an argument which asks someone to give only one answer to what amounts to two questions, one question expressed and the other question not expressed. (This is also called "Loaded Question" or "Complex Question.")

a. Where did you hide all of the cookies you stole? (If we answer, "Nowhere," then it sounds like we ate them all. The separate question is, "Did you steal the cookies?")

b. What do you believe the Bible teaches about flying saucers? (The hidden question is, "Do you believe the Bible teaches about fly saucers?")

(10) Fallacy of Diversion.

This is an argument which leads us away from the subject of the original argument. This is often called the "Red Herring," which is a smelly fish which leads the bloodhound onto the wrong trail.

a. I can't accept your solution because I never agree with anything which you say.

b. Why should I read the Bible? I don't want to become a preacher.

(11) Argument to Pity (Argumentum ad Misericordiam).

This is an argument which appeals to the power of the arguer to arouse sympathy in order to manipulate another.

a. If you don't marry me, then I'll be heartbroken and suicidal.

b. Aborting unwanted fetuses is better than letting them be born into a life of unwanted misery. (This is also a Fallacy of False Dilemma and Hidden Question.)

(12) "Proof" By Failure to Find Contrary Evidence.

This is when something is thought to be true because a counter example cannot be found. This is a form of Argument from Ignorance. If the argument is to be proven, then it must be proven on other grounds.

a. Of course women can have abortions, because you can't find one place in the Bible which explicitly says that they can't.

b. Of course women can't have abortions, because you can't find one place in the Bible which explicitly says that they can.

The study of fallacies is just one part of the study of informal logic, but those who have a good handle on them will have a practical advantage, both in Homeschooling and in life after Homeschooling.

6. PROPAGANDA TECHNIQUES

Propaganda Techniques such as, "Gloria Cinemastarr only uses this perfume, so you should also."

7. METHODS OF MANIPULATION

Methods of Manipulation, such as Diapraxis, or the Delphi technique, are what we see on television and hear from politicians every day.

Learning to identify errors in logic – such things as Informal Logical Fallacies, Propaganda Techniques, and Methods of Manipulation – often proves useful in evaluating the words of politicians, theologians, plumbers, and neighbors.

Informal Logic will prove quite useful in Rhetoric. Though the distinction between Informal Logic and Rhetoric may sometimes seem blurred, it is still best to teach the branches of Informal Logic separately.

BRANCHES OF LOGIC

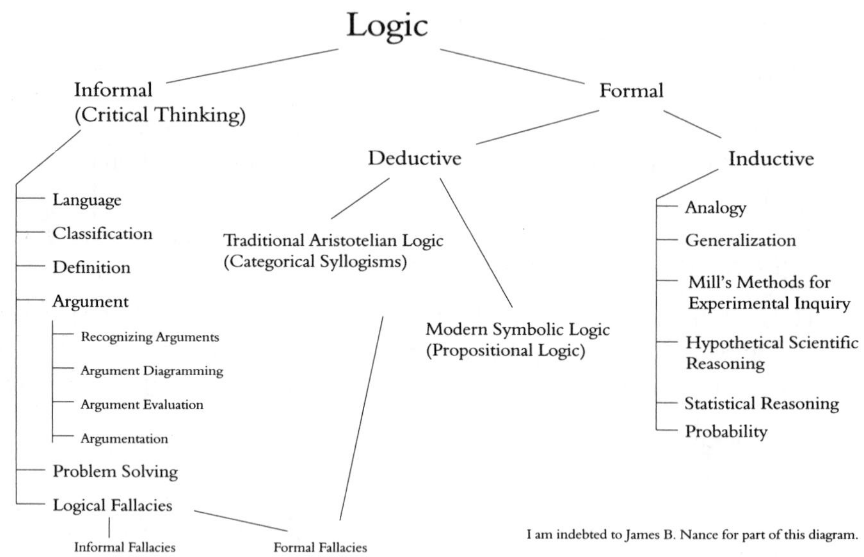

FIGURE 6A

OVERALL OBSERVATIONS FOR LEARNING LOGIC

Logic Materials

The perfect logic book has not been written, but many useful ones have, and what is best for one student may be less than best for another student. The most useful logic curriculum which we could put together for homeschoolers would follow this description:

1) It touches on all branches of logic.
2) It is self-teaching, containing all of the necessary information to master the subject.
3) It is distinctively Christian – both in philosophy and examples.
4) It regularly shifts to the practical use of things.

Since no available curriculum does all of these things, we must mix and match as best we can with what we have.

Pride, Sarcasm, Cynicism and Logic

We do not study logic in order to put others down, and to make them feel small. We learn logic so that we can glorify God in good works. Showing others how to reason a matter through, or pointing out an error in someone's reasoning – these skills go beyond the mere mechanics of logical reasoning. A moral curriculum must accompany a logic curriculum. People who put their logic on display as a proud ornament are being fleshly, and they are not "adorning the doctrine of God our Savior in all things." (Titus 2:10) They are like a golden ring in a pig's snout.

Sarcasm literally means "to tear the flesh," and that's exactly what proudly applied logic tends to do. When we employ scornful sarcasm in our rebuttal to what we suppose are errors, we often stir up the wrong reaction in others. We actually tear at their fleshly nature, and we thereby invite their fleshly response. We provoke others to sin. There is a sanctified use of boastful sarcasm (e.g. First Corinthians 4:8-14; Second Corinthians 11:1-12:11), but it is rare and it must be handled carefully. Certainly, developing a spirit of sarcasm is itself a fleshly pursuit. When done in the right spirit, the study of Logic should engender a humble, not a proud, spirit.

> Before destruction the heart of man is haughty, and before honour *is* humility. . . . He that answereth a matter before he heareth *it*, it *is* folly and shame unto him. . . . *He that is* first in his own cause *seemeth* just; but his neighbour cometh and searcheth him. . . . Go not forth hastily to strive, lest *thou know not* what to do in the end thereof, when thy neighbour hath put thee to shame. — Proverbs 18:12,13,17; 25:8

We heartily recommend a study of the wisdom of Proverbs, with appropriate memorization of selected verses, to accompany any study of Logic.

As we develop skill in logic, we will view the world with more critical eyes. We will no longer be satisfied by the same shallow reasoning. Theological or political arguments which once seemed convincing to us will no longer satisfy us, but often will be revealed as very shallow reasoning indeed. If we are tempted to become cynical, then we must reflect on the humbling fact that, in our natural self, we are no less prone to error than others. We must ask God to use us to raise the level of reasoning in the culture.

Logic Notebook

All students should begin a *Lifelong Logic Notebook* in their first year of formal study of Logic. This notebook may include such things as:

a) Rules and formulas which they learn.
b) Technical terms with their definitions.
c) Answers to quizzes, problems, exercises and tests.
d) Outlines or summary for each chapter of each book which they study.

This notebook will help students to organize and restate the information as they learn it. Later in life, the notebook will serve them as a handy reference tool.

Study Logic Together

Though students can study the materials by themselves, we believe there is great value in setting a regular time for the parent to meet with the student for answering quizzes and discussing problems. Video and audio lessons are best done with parent and child together. Three things to consider are:

1) Children will become discouraged when they encounter problems which they cannot solve on their own.
2) Parents need to learn the logic as much as their children.
3) Parents do not want their children far out ahead of them on this subject.

So parents may want as much direct involvement in the lessons as is reasonable. (Is that a pun?)

Before Age Thirteen — Focus on Elemental Logic Skills

Man is a logical being, separated from all other earthly beings by his capacity for deductive logic. Though man uses his capacity for logic from before his birth, this capacity for logic develops slowly and in steps. Children enjoy elementary logic skills such as collecting things, sorting things, connecting things, and putting things into order. About age ten, the brain begins to develop more complex connections to perform logical operations, and this capacity continues to develop until about age thirteen, when the child is in the full Understanding Level (or Logic Stage). So, between ages ten and thirteen, Elemental-Logic materials can be used to exercise and develop and sharpen the child's innate thinking tools. A child practices and develops handwriting skills before he practices and develops written composition skills. We might call handwriting and copywork *elemental-composition skills*. In the same way, he develops some logic skills before he develops formal logical reasoning skills. We call these *Elemental-Logic skills*.

In years past, these Elemental-Logic skills were satisfactorily developed in the natural environment of the home. Common games and everyday activities develop our child's powers for thinking. Checkers, chess, dominoes, card games, scrabble, and strategy games strengthen the mind. Listening to thought-provoking adult conversation does as much as anything to help the mind mature. (So the next time you have someone over, keep your children around, instead of sending them out to play.) Reading and listening to good literature – not literary junk food – gives children a larger and deeper perspective on the world around them. Memorization and narration also exercise and build the mind. (See *Ten Things to Do Before Age Ten*, in Chapter Eleven.)

Unfortunately, our supposedly *education enriched* culture is actually dumbed down and getting dumber by the day. The things which used to develop the mind – books and games – have been replaced by television and the computer. During early developmental stages, a two-dimensional opaque image on the surface of a cathode ray tube does not help develop the brain properly. Rather than develop logic skills, it can work in quite the opposite way – especially at early ages. We are not against computers. We wrote this book on a computer. But we believe exposure to computers and television screens at early ages can be counterproductive. (See Chapter Eleven.)

Some things must take precedence over others, and there is only so much time in the day, so we must understand that as long as our child is involved in such activities as sorting, connecting, and ordering – on both physical and verbal levels – he should develop adequately. In other words, in most cases special Logic-skill-building activities are good, but optional. In Chapter Twelve, we will discuss specific Elemental Logic curricula and how to use them.

Age Thirteen and Beyond

By age thirteen (sometimes earlier), children undergo a *growth-spurt* in their capacity for logic. This is the full Understanding Level (or Logic Stage). Earlier, they amazed us with the things they remembered (and we forgot). Now they amaze us with the things they conclude (and we overlook). This is time for more formal training in logic. So grasp the opportune moment for teaching teenagers to think. But beware – they may learn to out-think you. So be sure to inculcate in them a polite and gentle manner, and a humble and respectful attitude, especially toward elders and authorities.

A GENERAL COURSE OF STUDY

A Three-Step Curriculum

The Logic curriculum could be spread out over several years – much like the math curriculum. We will here give a brief description of a course of study for Logic. You will want to modify it to fit your schedule, priorities, and individual needs. We have broken the course of study up into three steps. The age divisions are arbitrary. Because the majority of materials for Logic are written for college age and beyond, the strategy here is to find the most usable materials, and to make the materials more usable. In Chapters Thirteen and Fourteen, we will discuss specific Logic curricula and how to use them.

Step One: Beginning About Age Thirteen — Focus on Informal Logic

As the student begins his formal study of the discipline of Logic, the focus should be on understanding and evaluating how, with the vocabulary and grammar of the English language, we express logic. We suggest a study of the logical uses of words and expressions, of definitions and assumptions, of facts and opinions, of possibilities and probabilities. This should be accompanied with a survey of the characteristics and methods of Argumentation, Informal Fallacies, Propaganda Techniques, and Advertising Schemes.

All of the topics we have so far listed are classified under Informal Logic. Though we do not recommend a full course in Formal Logic during this step, you may include an elementary introduction to selected topics in Formal Logic. You may introduce, in a simplified form, Deduction, including *"And, Or, If – Then, Only – If" Reasoning* (Propositional Logic) and *Syllogistic Reasoning* (Categorical Logic). This will whet the appetite of the student and prepare him for a more comprehensive study of Deductive Reasoning later. You may also use the Scientific Technique to introduce the student to a simplified form of Inductive Logic.

Though all of this may be squeezed into two years, it is more comfortably stretched into three years. (See Chapter Thirteen for more specific recommendations, and a discussion of how to use certain materials.)

Step Two: About Age Fifteen or Later
— Focus on the Practice of Logic

Once the student has become familiar with the branches of Logic, he may focus on specific branches. We suggest a full length Christian treatment of the values and uses of logic, a full length treatment of Logical Fallacies, and a full length treatment of Argumentation. This may be the time for specific analysis of how logic is applied to other disciplines. Though Christian Theology and Philosophy will have been discussed in Family Devotions and in the gathered Assembly, the student may be ready for a more systematic survey of some of the branches of these disciplines (e.g. Epistemology, Hermeneutics, Theology, Apologetics). Curricula which apply logic to history or to music or to debate would be useful. This may take two years or possibly less. (See Chapter Fourteen for more specific recommendations, and a discussion of how to use certain materials.)

Step Three: About Age Sixteen or Later
— Focus on the Finer Details of Logic

After the student is well grounded in the basics of the logical disciplines, and the application of logic to other disciplines, he may polish up his understanding of the discipline of logic with a full length study Formal Logic (Deductive and Inductive Reasoning), and a full review of Informal Logic. We recommend a full length study of Categorical Syllogisms, a full length study of Propositional Logic, and a full survey of the branches of Inductive Reasoning. You may use an upper level Logic text (or texts) which reviews the whole field of Logic, and which covers specific subjects in greater detail. More extensive studies in Christian Theology and Philosophy may accompany this. This may actually take two or three years. (See Chapter Fourteen for more specific recommendations, and a discussion of how to use certain materials.)

SOME QUESTIONS

Question: Is a formal study of logic within the reach of ordinary people?

Answer: We use language every day, but the study of grammar sharpens and expands our speech and writing skills. We use numbers every day, but the study of mathematics sharpens and expands our use of numbers. Plain ordinary reasoning is basic to both language and grammar; to both numbers and mathematics. We use reasoning every day, but the study of logic sharpens and expands our use of reasoning, and therefore our use of speech and writing skills, and our use of numbers. In this culture, one thing which will transform us from ordinary people into extraordinary people is the study of logic. So the answer to the question is, "Yes, logic is within the reach of ordinary people." But once they reach it, they will no longer be ordinary. If we do not accept the challenge, then we will not receive the reward.

Question: Don't we naturally develop the ability to think logically?

Answer: We naturally develop language skills and skills in working with numbers, and some people appear to have more natural talent in these skills, such that, if they were left to themselves, then they would probably develop further than others. But formal study tends to make the skills of men more equal, by stretching men with less natural talent further than their talents would otherwise take them. If we should cease to study language or numbers, but leave this only to natural development, then we would cease to be a civilization, and we would become like simple savages living in the woods. (But this would not last long. The clever savages would build a civilization around themselves and their superior talents, and would probably enslave everyone else who did not study logic. Maybe that has already happened.) What is true for language and number skills is also true for logic skills. The improvement of natural talents is a part of culture. We are required by the Lord Jesus to improve ourselves in the graces of the spirit, and in the talents of the flesh, and we do Him disservice if we neglect the improvement of what He has given us (Matthew 25:14-30).

Question: Don't we learn to reason well by simply reading great books written by great men?

Answer: Great men advise us to study logic, and their great books can best be evaluated, and their errors exposed – for great men do make many errors – only through careful analysis of their logic. Logic develops the tools with which to analyze the works of all men, great or not.

Question: Wasn't logic invented by an ancient pagan philosopher named Aristotle? Should we be following pagans?

Answer: The light bulb was invented by a pagan named Edison. We don't accept his philosophy, but we do accept his light bulb as a useful application of the real laws of God's universe – laws which Edison did not invent. Likewise, we do not accept Aristotle's philosophy, but we do accept his descriptive science of reasoning as a useful formulation of the real laws of God's universe – laws which Aristotle did not invent. We redeem what is useful in Aristotle for the service of Christ. In God's universe, God uses pagans to unknowingly serve God's people.

Question: Who should study logic with the children: fathers or mothers?

Answer: Either parent can teach logic, and both parents should learn it in some measure, even if they do not teach it. Nevertheless, Father is usually the best equipped with natural talents for teaching logic, and in teaching logic, his natural talents will be enhanced for the benefit of the whole family. Eventually, logic will become a part of the family's culture – everyone in the home will be reasoning more accurately, and will be continually applying reasoning skills – skills which they will pick up informally before they ever study logic formally. As family logic rubs off on the younger children, they will be much easier to teach – not just logic, but all subjects. But while you're getting started, it is probably best to put the matter in the hands of the one who has the most talent from God, by natural gift. If Father hasn't formally studied logic before, then this will make him a better man, husband, and father; a better citizen, saint, and elder; a better worker, boss, and tradesman; and the list goes on.

Chapter Seven

Teaching Rhetoric

. . . an eloquent man, *and* mighty in the scriptures, . . .
For he mightily convinced the Jews, *and that* publickly,
shewing by the scriptures that Jesus was Christ.
— Acts 18:24,28

AN ARGUMENT FOR TEACHING RHETORIC

EVERY SUBJECT HAS ITS OWN "Rhetoric" – the creative expression of sound conclusions. There is also a formal subject which we call *Rhetoric,* which includes such things as persuasive composition and public speaking.

A few years ago, there was a radio commercial for a product called *Verbal Advantage*. It went something like this:

> People judge you by the words you use. To make a powerful impression you need a powerful vocabulary. You need Verbal Advantage.

Well, that is a useful application of Rhetoric:
The effective choice of words.
To have a command of the language.
To be skilled in phrasing.

To be clear and precise in our expression.

To be both accurate and interesting at the same time.

And at times:

To be eloquent, and impressive and persuasive in our speech.

(I mean, like, really, man. Like, ya' know.)

How important is the skill of effective communication? Without effective communication, our cultural principles, values, and goals would not be transmitted from one generation to the next, and our culture would collapse. Perhaps that's one reason why our families are disintegrating and our culture is collapsing.

But isn't this the age of communication? Yes, but what is being communicated? This is the age of *mass* communication and of *inter-personal* communication, but it is not the age of *meaningful* communication of those things which are important to maintaining a living culture.

Effective communication is also the tool with which one can transform a society and a culture. In the first century, the preaching of the gospel, accompanied by God's grace, turned the world right side up. In the present century, the preaching of the modern media, under the devil's spell, is again turning the world upside down. Why do you suppose that effective communicators of traditional, or conservative, or Christian values are shouted down in our society? Why are they denied an audience? We're told they are "dangerous right-wing extremists," part of a "massive right-wing conspiracy." And we're told not to listen to them. Why? Because the men in the media understand the power of effective communication. If we listen to those whom they tell us are "extremists," that may interrupt the mass media's regularly scheduled programming of our minds. If we were to begin to think for ourselves, why, that would be dangerous for those who want to do the thinking for us.

If all we have is Grammar and Logic, we will have frustrated purposes, because Grammar is no goal, and Logic is no goal. It is like a computer – we can feed in data, and we can process data, but if we have no output, then we have nothing.

In her essay on the *Lost Tools of Learning*, Dorothy Sayers wrote, "It is difficult to map out any general syllabus for the study of Rhetoric." We heartily concur. But we will attempt to present some practical information on teaching the subject of Rhetoric.

PRINCIPLES FOR LEARNING RHETORIC

Defining and Describing Rhetoric

What is this thing called *Rhetoric*? The term is frequently used as a rough synonym for sophistry, propaganda, pettifoggery, or demagoguery, describing political speech or writing which argues impressively or persuasively, but insincerely. That is rarely the proper use of Rhetoric. (But see Second Samuel 15:31,34; 17:5-14.) The Greek words ῥητορικὸς τέχνη (rhEtorikos technE) literally mean *the art of oratory*, or *skill in public speaking* – in order to advance an idea or a cause in the minds of an audience. In ancient times, effective communication was primarily by means of speech, not writing. When the invention of the printing press made possible a larger audience for the written word, writing was raised to a primary means of effective communication. The invention of radio, movies, television, and recordings of audio and video, have increased the audience for public speaking. Nevertheless, writing remains the unseen basis for most public speaking. Indeed, writing may be considered the transcribing of what would otherwise be spoken. So, while the classical definition of Rhetoric was limited to *skill in public speaking*, our modern definition is more inclusive: *Rhetoric is the art of effective communication, the competent and forceful composition and delivery of oral, visual, or written expression*. This would include the study of all elements of literature and public speaking, such as content, structure, style, and delivery. Rhetoric teaches how to compose essays, reviews, and prose, how to prepare and to perform speeches, and how to construct arguments and to participate in debates.

The formal subject which we call *Grammar* involves analyzing words and sentences (noun, verb, direct object, etc.) in order to read, write, and spell in a technically proper way. The formal subject which we call *Logic* involves putting words together into statements which make logical sense in order to construct sentences in good logical form. The formal subject which we call *Rhetoric* involves making those sentences take on a clear, attractive, and forceful form in order to write, speak, and argue incisively, eloquently, and effectively.

Rhetoric is somewhat of an art. There are principles which rule over the endeavor of drawing sketches or painting pictures, but there is much variety in how those principles may be applied. The same is true of Rhetoric. Some persons have special talents and gifts for drawing and painting, and for speaking and writing, but almost anyone can learn enough of the basic principles to make an identifiable effort, or to construct an understandable message. Not everyone is called upon to show some skill in drawing pictures, but everyone is called upon to show some skill in expressing himself, and the more effectively you express yourself – well, that's Rhetoric.

The Five Parts of Classical Rhetoric

Historically, the classical study of Rhetoric is divided into five parts:

1. *Inventio* – How to determine topics and arguments for speech or composition.
2. *Dispositio* – How to arrange topics and arguments.
3. *Elocutio* – How to deliver a speech or to write a composition in the most appropriate, attractive, and powerful style.
4. *Memoria* – How to memorize speeches.
5. *Pronuntiatio* – How to manage the voice and gestures while delivering a speech.

By the repetitive "how to" in the five points listed above, anyone can see that Rhetoric is a very *output-based* subject. As long as we have not neglected the input (Grammar), and the processing (Logic), then we should have assembled all of the necessary parts in order to generate the output (Rhetoric). And output, there should be plenty of. One does not learn to express himself by reading and outlining books. As faith, without works, is dead, so mere head-knowledge, without actual practice, amounts to little or nothing. You should expect the trees which you planted and nursed in years past to finally bear their fruit in these Rhetoric years.

The parts of Rhetoric called *Inventio*, *Dispositio*, and at least part of *Elocutio*, are covered in standard curricula for writing or composition. Any of the many "How to Write" books can serve as a supplement to help hone certain details of composition.

But Rhetoric goes beyond mere writing. Any Rhetoric curriculum must include activities in public speaking. Here, *Elocutio*, *Memoria*, and *Pronuntiatio* step forward with important roles. The family and friends may be the only audience available, though a more objective audience would be a better test of how a student's skills are developing.

SOME OVERALL OBSERVATIONS FOR LEARNING RHETORIC

The following are some general observations on teaching and learning Rhetoric. More specific recommendations and applications are made in Chapters Eleven through Fourteen.

1. Early Bloomers.

Don't expect a child at the Grammar Level to exhibit Rhetoric Level ability. There may be some early bloomers here who show some advanced ability, but early bloomers often slow down later, and the last thing which we want to develop is a precocious prodigy who is pugnaciously pedantic. Special abilities require special humilities, lest the gift destroy the gifted. Just because a boy can speak like a man does not mean he is a man. Maturity still requires the experience of years. Do not focus on the development of one special gift as if that gift justifies all other imbalances.

> Pride *goeth* before destruction, and an haughty spirit before a fall. — Proverbs 16:18

> And lest I should be exalted above measure through the abundance of the revelations, there was given to me a thorn in the flesh, the messenger of Satan to buffet me, lest I should be exalted above measure. — Second Corinthians 12:7

> Not a novice, lest being lifted up with pride he fall into the condemnation of the devil. — First Timothy 3:6

> For who maketh thee to differ *from another*? and what hast thou that thou didst not receive? now if thou didst receive it, why dost thou glory, as if thou hadst not received it? — First Corinthians 4:7

2. Late Bloomers.

Parents must develop Rhetoric skills in a child without exasperating him. A child at age ten or twelve may show no appreciable ability to write, but that does not mean that he will not be a good writer by the time he is fifteen or seventeen. Late bloomers happen – often. Require enough to press him, but not to break him. The younger years require patience and trust, yet firmness and steady pressure. Reluctant writers need more nudging and encouragement than driving and demanding – but the parent is the best judge of the balance.

3. Preparing Future Rhetoric Students

Here are a few principles for preparing students in their early years for Rhetoric in their later years:

a. The child needs to be well grounded in the elements of the language before he can use them in an effective manner. Poor reading, spelling, and grammar skills will be a drag on him and will discourage him from writing. So the foundation must be well laid in an intensive phonics system, in spelling, and in English grammar.

b. A love for learning and a sense for creativity, developed in the Knowledge (Grammar) and Understanding (Logic) Levels, will bear its greatest fruit in the Wisdom (Rhetoric) Level. The child's mind absorbs good written and oral language skills by being regularly exposed to them. What a child reads and what is read aloud to him, and what he sees and hears, will determine what he writes and how he speaks. What goes into his mind, by and large, is what comes out of his pencil, by and by. Don't talk baby talk. Read a step beyond the child's level of full comprehension. Watch videos and hear recordings which set good examples. Developing the student's own special interests often fosters these qualities – though the parent must balance their child's interests with essential skills. Reading good literature aloud to young children, and limiting their exposure to pictures – especially pictures moving on a two-dimensional screen – will encourage the "verbal advantage," while warding off brain-rot.

c. Copywork, dictation, simple outlining, summarizing, and written narration – all of these things prepare a child for learning to write creatively. How? By constantly filling his mind with good examples. In written narration, the student reads a paragraph or passage, then attempts to rewrite it in his own words. In written summaries, the student reads a passage, then attempts to write down, briefly and concisely, the author's main points. All of these activities also train small motor skills. As the child grows older, let him know that you expect more of him – more complex and detailed outlining, more extensive summaries with titles and subtitles, etc. (We will discuss these things further in Chapter Eleven.)

d. Oral narration, oral recitation from memory, and oral interpretation, will help to develop and sharpen the mind and the voice. In oral interpretation, the student learns to pronounce words clearly and audibly, to use proper inflection and emphasis, and to be comfortable reciting in front of an audience – even if it's only the family. This is an elementary step toward public speaking. (We will discuss these things further in Chapter Twelve.)

e. Letter writing and journal writing is a first step in composition. Some parents will have no problem teaching elementary composition skills, while others will be more comfortable with a structured curriculum. Eventually the child should submit articles and editorials to newsletters and newspapers; enter writing contests; begin a newsletter.

f. Introduce and acquaint the student with live speeches, rhetoric competitions, speech tournaments, Toastmasters, homeschool speech and debate tournaments, etc. Teach him the standards by which to distinguish good speech from poor speech. In written form, through reading and copying them, expose the student to classic speeches (Demosthenes' *The First Philipic*, Isocrates' *The Panegyricus*, Pericles' *The Funeral Speech*, etc.) and modern speeches (Patrick Henry's *War is Inevitable*, George Washington's *Farewell Address*, William Jennings Bryan's *Cross of Gold*. See Chapter Nine for more names of ancient speeches.) Some modern speeches are available in audio recordings and video tapes. When he has established some self-confidence, then begin or join a speech and debate club, enter speech competitions, then debates.

g. Do not introduce keyboard typing until after the child has mastered the skill of handwriting. The word processor will eventually become an invaluable tool, but if it is introduced too early, important and necessary skills are shortchanged, and their absence can slow, if not cripple.

h. While you are helping your child to accumulate the tools he will need for good rhetoric skills, do not neglect logic. Continuously encourage the application of the logic which he is learning to all of his other studies and to situations in life as they occur. If he is constantly analyzing, looking at the different angles, and thinking things through, then he will find his thoughts flow more easily, which should make it easier for him to express his thoughts.

4. Learn Rhetoric by Doing It.

The Rhetoric Level is full of output. Learning is full of doing. In many ways, Rhetoric is more caught than taught. A project oriented approach to Rhetoric may be the most effective. The student cannot merely read a book and take a test. He must find avenues for productive output. He may be encouraged to enter speech and writing competitions, history fairs, debates, and the like.

5. Hard Work Will Pay in the End.

With some persons, putting words together in an elegant and effective manner takes little effort – its seems as natural as breathing. With the remainder of us, it is a skill learned after repeated trial and practice. Students who have some natural advantage still must study and practice in order to develop their skill to an optimum level. Students who lack the natural advantage will need to study and practice harder. But in the end, the students who have done all of the work have the real advantage, regardless of the natural talent. Many of the finest writers and speakers will tell you that, when they began to write or speak, their work was a miserable mess of meaningless mumble. It often takes years to develop real skill, character, and style of expression, and those who appear prodigies in rhetoric, if they rely only upon their natural talent, will eventually be passed by those who, slowly and steadily, improve themselves as they plod along through the race. Slow but steady wins the race.

6. Bible Principles for Rhetoric.

Everyone speaks, writes, and argues; therefore everyone uses Rhetoric skills – good or bad. How well you speak and write and argue is an outward measure of your ability to think. You may suppose that some persons think better than they express themselves, and that others express themselves better than they think, but in the final analysis, with all other things being equal, the two balance each other. In other words, apply yourself to effective expression, and you will improve your intelligence.

> "The wise in heart shall be called prudent: and the sweetness of the lips increaseth learning." — Proverbs 16:21

Apply yourself to intelligence, and you will improve your expression.

> "The heart of the wise teacheth his mouth, and addeth learning to his lips." — Proverbs 16:23

Apply yourself to both, and you will excel.

> "Bow down thine ear, and hear the words of the wise, and apply thine heart unto my knowledge. For *it is* a pleasant thing if thou keep them within thee; they shall withal be fitted in thy lips." — Proverbs 22:17,18

Apply yourself to neither, and both will worsen.

"The words of a wise man's mouth *are* gracious; but the lips of a fool will swallow up himself." — Ecclesiastes 10:12

Some may excel in writing over speaking.

For *his* letters, say they, *are* weighty and powerful; but *his* bodily presence is weak, and *his* speech contemptible. — Second Corinthians 10:10

And we are certainly to put no trust merely in technical speaking or writing ability, but in the Lord.

And I, brethren, when I came to you, came not with excellency of speech or of wisdom, declaring unto you the testimony of God. For I determined not to know any thing among you, save Jesus Christ, and him crucified. And I was with you in weakness, and in fear, and in much trembling. And my speech and my preaching *was* not with enticing words of man's wisdom, but in demonstration of the Spirit and of power: — First Corinthians 2:1-4

7. Called to Communicate.

Christians have a special calling to be good communicators.

Let your speech *be* alway[s] with grace, seasoned with salt, that ye may know how ye ought to answer every man. — Colossians 4:6

But sanctify the Lord God in your hearts: and *be* ready always to *give* an answer to every man that asketh you a reason of the hope that is in you with meekness and fear: — First Peter 3:15

In all things shewing thyself a pattern of good works: in doctrine *shewing* uncorruptness, gravity, sincerity, Sound speech, that cannot be condemned; that he that is of the contrary part may be ashamed, having no evil thing to say of you. — Titus 2:7,8

Why shouldn't Christians be interested in learning Rhetoric? We have both outward command and inward compulsion to communicate Biblical truth to every area of life. We must not depend solely upon our skill, but we must make good use of everything which our Lord gives us in order to promote His interests.

8. Establish High Standards for Grammar and Logic

The formal science of Rhetoric is founded upon the formal sciences of Grammar and Logic.

a. Grammar discovers the facts and the rules for the correct use of the language.

b. Logic discovers the facts and the rules for the correct use of reasoning.
c. Rhetoric discovers the facts and the rules for the correct use of expression.

By *correct use*, we mean *application which conforms to an accepted standard.* We should establish high standards, then conform our curriculum to those standards. And the first standard of a Rhetoric curriculum must be high standards in Grammar and Logic, because without high standards in the use of language and reasoning, the student will lack the necessary tools to meet high standards in Rhetoric.

9. Standards for Rhetoric.

The available Rhetoric curricula vary greatly, especially as to how much they cover. Some curricula cover only writing, and do not cover speaking. Others handle composition, but do not review important grammatical points. So you may need to supplement your curricula.

We suggest the following standards:

a. *Accuracy in Details*. On written work, or work done on a word processor, spelling, grammar, and punctuation mistakes must be rewritten until perfect. Discipline in one area promotes discipline in other areas, and sloppiness promotes sloppiness.
b. *Good Form*. Establish a form – a manner of presentation – which is expected for every assignment, and enforce the form. Creativity must always be bound by limits, and one of your limits is your form. If the student believes he must alter the form for a particular purpose, he must have your permission.
c. *Punctuality*. Establish reasonable deadlines, and allow extensions only for extraordinary reasons. Life is full of deadlines, and Rhetoric should not be an exception. Penalties for overtime should be established ahead of time.
d. *Improvement*. You cannot insist that every student meet the same high level of standards, but you can always insist upon improvement in each student no matter what their level. With each assignment, specifically state what you expect the student to improve upon, and do not be satisfied with less. A war is won through a series of battles.
e. *No Lazy Logic*. Never allow fuzzy thinking, politically correct terminology, or unbiblical reasoning to pass. Always insist that the student think through the implications of his asser-

tions. The more he is forced to rewrite, the more he will think it through thoroughly to avoid another rewrite. Don't let up on this. We win the war with the world when we write with wise words. (That may be a tongue-twister, but it is also a truth-tester.)

f. *Criticism*. Whenever feasible, employ, as independent judges, at least both parents, possibly older siblings, and others outside the immediate family. Even parents who are skilled in the arts and accuracies of Rhetoric can be bettered by more objective judges.

g. *Reward*. Good writing is a reward in itself – creating satisfaction and self-confidence in the student. (Notice, we did not say *self-esteem*.) For a student who has accomplished a degree of excellence, praise by others is an encouragement for the student, and for the teacher, and for anyone else who had a part in it. So you should find an outlet for fine work so that others can contribute to the encouragement of excellence.

10. Boys and Girls

Ability in public speaking should be considered a worthy goal for every student, boy or girl. Scripture is most clear and explicit that there are venues where no man, whether male or female, has jurisdiction to speak.

> How that he was caught up into paradise, and heard unspeakable words, which it is not lawful for a man to utter. — Second Corinthians 12:4

And there are venues where a woman does not have jurisdiction to speak.

> Let your women keep silence in the churches: for it is not permitted unto them to speak; but *they are commanded* to be under obedience, as also saith the law. And if they will learn any thing, let them ask their husbands at home: for it is a shame for women to speak in the church. — First Corinthians 14:34,35

> Let the woman learn in silence with all subjection. But I suffer not a woman to teach, nor to usurp authority over the man, but to be in silence. — 1 Timothy 2:11,12

Nevertheless, there are other venues where women are free, or even required to speak.

> And it shall come to pass in the last days, saith God, I will pour out of my Spirit upon all flesh: and your sons and your daughters shall prophesy, and your young men shall see visions, and your old men shall dream dreams: —

> Acts 2:17
>
> And he began to speak boldly in the synagogue: whom when Aquila and Priscilla had heard, they took him unto *them*, and expounded unto him the way of God more perfectly. — Acts 18:26
>
> And the same man had four daughters, virgins, which did prophesy. — Acts 21:9
>
> But every woman that prayeth or prophesieth with *her* head uncovered dishonoureth her head: for that is even all one as if she were shaven. — First Corinthians 11:5

There are even some venues where it is especially a woman's place to speak.

> The aged women likewise, that *they be* in behaviour as becometh holiness, not false accusers, not given to much wine, teachers of good things; That they may teach the young women to be sober, to love their husbands, to love their children, *To be* discreet, chaste, keepers at home, good, obedient to their own husbands, that the word of God be not blasphemed. — Titus 2:3-5

Indeed, the role of a mother as the primary tutor of her children virtually requires the best development of her communication skills.

> I will therefore that the younger women marry, bear children, guide the house, give none occasion to the adversary to speak reproachfully. — First Timothy 5:14

We write this to counter the notion that daughters do not need to study Rhetoric. Though by no measure are we the champions of any kind of Christian feminism, we are nevertheless champions of Christ and His orderly Kingdom, and His Kingdom is well served by well-prepared mothers, wives, and witnesses for Christ.

That being said, it is necessary to note that, especially in speech, it may be inappropriate for genders to mix, except in the case of siblings. We are not the judges in these matters, and every situation has its own special circumstances, but God honors those who honor Him in everything, and one way to honor Him is to honor His order. Fathers should be the best judges of what would be appropriate.

A GENERAL COURSE OF STUDY

We will here discuss the course of study in a general way. It is the job of a Rhetoric text or curriculum to lay out and explain the parts of the subject. We will discuss specific curricula in Chapters Eleven through Fourteen.

Before Age Ten
— Focus on Vocabulary

Of course, reading and writing are of fundamental importance, and they will come in time. Spelling and grammar are also fundamental, and they will need continual development. But vocabulary is the one thing which should be stressed in the early years. Vocabulary will drive reading and writing, spelling and grammar. We're not talking about an abstract list of words to memorize. Children develop a large and rich working vocabulary from what they hear, in context, then repeat, in their own conversation. Yes, you can reinforce this with some drill and examples, but the force of drills is not the same as regular use. Where are they going to pick up this vocabulary? Primarily from your reading to them, but also from hearing adult conversation, hearing adult teaching in church, hearing audio tapes, reciting prose and poetry. If you can teach the child to speak, read, and write a foreign language (we're not talking about formal grammar here), that will also do much to build his English vocabulary. We will give more specific recommendations and discuss these matters further in Chapter Eleven.

Ages Ten Through Twelve
— Focus on Spelling and Grammar

If you have built a good vocabulary before age ten, then vocabulary should take care of itself from this point on. (If you have any doubts, then take appropriate measures.) Now, the focus should turn instead to refining the technical tools of expression: spelling and grammar. If you begin a foreign language grammar (such as Latin), then vocabulary, spelling, and grammar will advance rapidly. The student should advance from reciting prose and poetry to the oral interpretation of prose and poetry. Typing skills should be established here. As soon as the student becomes accustomed to using the word processor, then he can incorporate this as one of his writing tools. Be careful not to let him use the spell checker to avoid good spelling skills. He may use it to assist him, but he should not be encouraged to rely entirely upon it. We will give more specific recommendations and discuss these matters further in Chapter Twelve.

Ages Thirteen Through Fifteen — Focus on Composition, Argumentation, and Speech

Spelling and grammar should be well in control, and the student's own notebooks should be full. Nevertheless, have a good English handbook on hand, and make sure your child knows how to use it. Your child has already been doing all kinds of little writing projects – maybe some bigger ones, if you thought he was capable of them, or else he was motivated to do them on his own. But now is the time to begin requiring regular writing projects of gradually increasing complexity and great variety. Formal speech should also begin at this level. We will give more specific recommendations and discuss these matters further in Chapter Thirteen.

Ages Sixteen Through Eighteen — Focus on Research and Debate

Composition, argumentation, and speech skills should be well developed by this age. The student has already been doing all kinds of research, but now is the time to begin requiring large projects and much more output. If you decide to pursue debate, that alone will be one large project. (See Appendix One, Article Fifteen, Beginning A Homeschool Speech and Debate Club.)

If the student has studied grammar thoroughly, there should be no need for formal grammar at this point, unless some weakness persists. However, there is profit in reading through books which focus on correcting particular common errors or inadequacies in expression, and upon building style of expression. You may consult our Resource List for information on such books as *The Elements of Style* by Strunk and White, or *The King's English* by Fowler.

The student should begin reading through a rhetoric textbook, and write a summary outline of each chapter. You must assign projects which correspond to the material which he is studying.

During the Understanding Level (or Logic Stage), the student studied separate subjects with a focus on the logic of those subjects. For example, he studied history, focusing on the reasons for events and the connections between events. He might write a report on the Civil War, focusing on the timeline and the geography. During the Wisdom Level (or Rhetoric Stage), the student focuses on communicating and practically applying what he is learning. For example, he may write a research paper on history, recombining what he has learned into a new thesis, and communicating that thesis with its practical implications. He might rework the earlier material into a research paper on the political and economic circumstances which created the tensions leading to the War Between the States.

Each year in Rhetoric, the student will combine all of his learning – in science, logic, history, or literature – into several small projects and a few larger projects, developing and demonstrating his skill of expression. The student could produce two or more lengthy research papers in different fields of study, or he may substitute debate, or possibly a major contest, for a research paper. We will give more specific recommendations and discuss these matters further in Chapter Fourteen.

A WORD ABOUT POLITICAL CORRECTNESS

The current culture war is being fought on the level of language itself. One of the ways this is being done is through an assault upon race, gender, and economic status – in the name of defending race, gender, and economic status. Few people realize the subtle but immense power of this assault. He who defines the terms wins the argument. The enemies of truth are busy redefining the terms, building a brick wall, and Christians are asleep at the wheel while they are headed straight for a collision with that brick wall. If we allow the redefinition of our language, we lose. We must use our Rhetoric to hold and tenaciously defend the Christian definition of words and expressions.

One example of the culture war is the assault on gendered language. The monstrous invention of such terms as *chairperson* and *gingerbreadperson* is an assault upon women in the name of defending them. Adam, in his sinless state, declared "she shall be called *wo-man* (Hebrew: *ish-shah*) because she was taken out of *man* (Hebrew: *ish*)." (Genesis 2:23) The Hebrew term for woman (*ish-shah*) corresponds to the Hebrew term for man (*ish*) just as the English term *wo-man* corresponds to the English term *man*. God sees *wo-man* as being within *man* and created out of *man*, but never as being separate from *man*. Neither is *man* separate from *wo-man*, but he comes into being through the *wo-man* (First Corinthians 11:11,12). The Hebrew terms for man (*ish, adam, enosh, enash*) refer generically to anyone of the species, whether male or female (*ish* Genesis 9:5; *adam* 1:26,27; 2:5; *enosh* 17:23; *enash* Ezra 6:11), unless the context distinguishes the male (*zakar, zakur*) from the female (*ishshah, neqebah, nashim*) (Genesis 2:23,24; 3:6; etc.). Likewise, the Greek term for man (*anthrOpos*) refers generically to anyone of the species (Acts 17:30) unless the context distinguishes the male (*anEr, arrEn*) from the female (*gunE, thElus*) (Matthew 19:5; First Corinthians 7:1; etc.).

Whenever anyone contradicts the truth, he (including she) will eventually contradict himself (including herself). The Feminists at one moment want to completely separate the genders, and at the next moment they want to remove all distinction of gender. And why do they want to remove the inclusion of the female *woman* from the generic use of the word *man*, but they say nothing of removing the inclusion of the male *bull* from the generic use of the word *cow*?

The Feminist reconstruction of English grammar is a rebellion against God's grammar. Though God most clearly moved the prophets and apostles to reinvent their language in order to make new distinctions in meaning, He never moved them to reinvent the language to distinguish the genders in the way which it is being done today. Unless there is, within a context, a clear differentiation between male and female, the word "man" and the pronouns "he, him, his" are inclusive of male and female, and every female should take solace in that protective covering. The invention of so-called Gender-Specific language, such as *chairwoman* or *gingerbreadwoman*, is an assault upon women, and should be resisted at every encounter. Undue attention to gender (or race, or economic status) is a corruption which creates disharmony, envy, strife, and division, and such is immitigably reprobated in the Word of God.

> But if ye have bitter envying and strife in your hearts, glory not, and lie not against the truth. This wisdom descendeth not from above, but *is* earthly, sensual, devilish. For where envying and strife *is*, there *is* confusion and every evil work. — James 3:14 -16

> If any man teach otherwise, and consent not to wholesome words, *even* the words of our Lord Jesus Christ, and to the doctrine which is according to godliness; He is proud, knowing nothing, but doting about questions and strifes of words, whereof cometh envy, strife, railings, evil surmisings, Perverse disputings of men of corrupt minds, and destitute of the truth, supposing that gain is godliness: from such withdraw thyself. — First Timothy 6:3-5

So we argue that Christians should have nothing to do with such monstrous concoctions as: *she or he, he/she, s/he, congressperson, humankind, parenting* (in place of *mothering* or *fathering*).

While we are on the subject, when stereotypes are properly used, they are perfectly acceptable. Jesus called the Scribes and Pharisees, "Hypocrites" (Matthew 23:13 etc.), and Paul affirmed the sentiment that, "Cretans are always liars" (Titus 1:12). While the so-called multiculturalist (that is an oxymoron) decries the stereotypical humor, he displays not the slightest compunction about stereotyping Christians. He thereby reveals his real agenda, which is not multiculturalism. Cultural-confusionism (that's what multiculturalism really is) is simply the means which is employed to reach an end. The means is to gather different peoples into opposing special interests groups, then pit these groups against each other – senior citizens against boomers, minorities against whites, workers against employers. The end is to divide society in order to disintegrate culture and prepare the way for the new culture. So when you are assaulted in an English Handbook or Rhetoric text about "stereotypical language" and "sexism" and the like, please recognize that these transformations of language are not without power. The opposition themselves claim they are countering the tremendous power of what they call "prejudicial" language. Their new language alters the structure of society – that is its openly-stated purpose, and it will accomplish that purpose if it is allowed to stand. If we are to take every thought captive (Second Corinthians 10:5), then we ought to take captive every word which represents many thoughts.

We must not allow ourselves to be intimidated by the subtle linguistic manipulations of the culture war. We are actually being tortured by their twisting of words – to own destruction. The "war of words" is the war of ideas. We must recognize the false notions and evil motives which are behind the choice of words, and we must take every thought captive to the obedience of Christ. While they advocate the corruption of speech, we must recommend the refinement of speech. In the end, the culture war will be won with words.

Chapter Eight

Principles for the Study of Literature

. . . of making many books *there is* no end . . .
—Ecclesiastes 12:12

INTRODUCTION

SHOULD WE STUDY the ancient classical authors? Some say, "Never!" Others say, "Always!" Can they both be right? And if so, then how should we undertake the assignment? Before we can answer these questions, we must determine our Principles, our Values, and our Goals.

Cultural Principles

What is *culture*? Culture consists of those products of work and thought, from a given community of men, which are transmitted across generations. This includes customs, habits, traditions, language, literature, arts, skills, technologies, beliefs, philosophies, governments, laws, institutions, and anything else which characterizes the activities of men.

The primary *vehicle* for transmitting culture is *language*. When a culture has achieved a level of complexity which requires a *literature* to fully transmit itself, then it may be classified as a *civilization*. A "savage" is literally *one who lives in the woods*. Those who live out in the back woods, away from other families, must have some culture simply to survive, but they do not need a literature to transmit their culture. Because they do not depend upon the culture and inventions of others for living, their ways are often more simple. They may be refined in their own way, but they are not civilized in a cultural way.

The primary *institution* for transmitting culture is the *family*. The family transmits the elementary and fundamental principles of government, religion, and economics for a culture. Whatever educates functions as the family.

When the usages of language and the nature of the family are changed, the foundation of a culture is shifted. Its customs, arts, philosophies, laws, etc. will fundamentally shift with this change in its foundation. Hence, from the point of view of transmitting culture, it is the family and the language which we must pay the closest attention to.

Some people argue: "Since we know more than those of the past, why should we waste our time studying things from our past?" This is a one-dimensional view of history. Such a view of progress would burn the historical bridges behind it – they are no longer needed.

This argument lacks breadth and depth. The knowledge of the present is built upon the knowledge of the past. If we remove the past entirely, then we remove the foundations upon which we have built. If we do not, in some sense, first *know* the writers of the past – their ideas, then we cannot know *more* than writers of the past – we cannot build upon their ideas. When we cease to know them, then we cease to know more than them. We cannot stand above their shoulders if we do not stand upon their shoulders. To stand upon their shoulders is to benefit from culture – to benefit from the transfer of knowledge accumulated from one generation to the next. This is a civilized culture – a culture built upon a literature.

Man without civilized culture is man without a past to build upon. He starts from scratch. He has only the present. He has stranded himself in the cultural woods. He is without civilization. Because he has erased the past upon which he might have built, he is a savage, who must re-invent everything.

Man without culture is man without the materials to build a future. There is no progress without culture. It is the culture which carries us along. Like the Egyptian culture of the time of the Exodus, which "knew not Joseph," so decades of socialized education have washed over our culture and eroded the foundations of many cultural absolutes that we now have a culture which *knows not reality*. We have a political system which *knows not the Constitution*. We have an economic system which *knows not real money*. We have a Christianity – even a Bible-believing Christianity – which *knows not the Scriptures*. And we have families which *know not the fundamentals of education*. Our culture is held together by bureaucracy and technology – its only parts which remain civilized. We live only to serve ourselves. We care neither for our progenitors nor for our posterity. We live only for the present, and we are therefore the cultural prey of every ravenous bird.

Biblical Christianity produces the *only* civilized culture which is transmitted through an infallible written record handed down and lived out by families. It is the only culture which builds upon a true past and toward a true future. It is the only culture which serves God with all of its heart and soul and strength. All other cultures fail because they are built upon shifting sand.

Cultural Values

Generally speaking, the more experience we have, the more refined our knowledge and understanding becomes. But refinement is not necessarily a good thing. One can progress in righteousness, or he can progress in wickedness – and sometimes it is hard, outwardly, to tell the difference. The man who gets better and better at blaspheming, or burglarizing, or swindling can be easily identified as progressing in wickedness. But the man who gets better and better at lying, or cheating, or hypocrisy – the more he progresses in his wickedness, the harder he is to detect. The same is true of cultures. The culture which degenerates into open idolatry and debauchery is identifiably declining. The culture which refines its monetary deceit and intellectual fraud is likewise declining, but the decline is identifiable only to those who have absolute cultural standards by which to measure.

From where do such absolute cultural standards come? Humanism declares that man is the measure of all things. But Scripture declares that the Lord, man's Maker, reveals the standards for measuring man and his culture. There is no truly passive, objective, or neutral ground:

> He that is not with me is against me; and he that gathereth not with me scattereth abroad. — Matthew 12:30

nor is there any shared middle ground:

> No servant can serve two masters . . . . — Luke 16:13

The notion that there is common ground between believers and unbelievers is a lie. In the Lord's providence, the unbelievers share many good things with believers.

> . . . for he maketh his sun to rise on the evil and on the good, and sendeth rain on the just and on the unjust. — Matthew 5:45 (Compare Luke 6:35; Psalm 145:9)

> Who in times past suffered all nations to walk in their own ways. Nevertheless he left not himself without witness, in that he did good, and gave us rain from heaven, and fruitful seasons, filling our hearts with food and gladness. — Acts 14:16,17

But the unbeliever takes the gifts which the Lord provides to him, and he uses them from the framework of his false philosophy – his erroneous worldview, which leaves the true and living God out of the picture. His facts are not the same as the believer's facts. The facts may appear the same on the surface, but they have an entirely different meaning, because they are interpreted from an entirely different framework. No matter what superficial similarities may appear to exist between them, at the base and core, the unbeliever's philosophy drives him in any direction except towards the one true and living God. He does not love God with all his heart, soul, and strength. His fleshly mind is enmity (it is not *at* enmity, it *is* enmity) against God and cannot truly be subject to the Law of God (Romans 8:7). As he continues to interpret his experience by wrong – unbelieving, skeptical, humanistic – presuppositions, he actually becomes more and more ignorant – that is, he builds up more and more false interpretations of the reality over which he blindly stumbles. He progresses in building a false culture. But those who evaluate their experiences by true presuppositions – presuppositions drawn from the Bible – revise their understanding more and more to conformity to the truth revealed to them. They progress in building a true culture.

Then, have we no lawful use for the works of unbelievers? We certainly do. But that which is common and unclean must first be tested and purged with fire and purified with water of separation (Numbers 31:23; Psalm 66:12) before it can be set apart for lawful use. It must first be washed and reshaped for the Master's use before it can be used "in house," that is, among Christians, or before it can be used "outside the house," that is, in apologetic evangelism, calling out the Lord's people from among the world.

Cultural Goals

We cannot communicate with the dead, but they can communicate with us.

. . .he, being dead, yet speaketh. — Hebrews 11:4

When we study the language and the writings of those now dead, we overhear their conversations, and we learn to understand their thoughts. Civilized culture is the body of knowledge and understanding and wisdom which is accumulated and passed along as presuppositions from generation to generation. This body of collected knowledge constitutes the fabric of culture. The practices of the members of a society are determined by its culture. To the degree which we pass on the knowledge and presuppositions of Scripture, to that degree our society will be permeated and held together with Biblical ideas. To the degree which Christians fail to pass these on, to that degree our society will lose its salty savor and become fit for nothing but to be cast out and trodden under the feet of men.

When Israel failed to pass on the culture revealed to them through Moses, the Lord sent them into captivity. As the knowledge of the Scriptures has waned in America, the values of other cultures – particularly, humanist culture – have moved into the vacuum, have trampled over Christian culture, and have taken up temporary residence over its grave.

What about the remnants of Christian tradition? We should not be committed to mere tradition. Tradition can never be allowed to stand on its own authority. A culture held together merely by tradition – even if that tradition reflects Scripture – is doomed to collapse. Culture must continually be informed by the authority of Scripture, or it will eventually die and will either turn into a hard fossil or will decay and disintegrate. Many institutions in America, such as the church denominations, were once informed and corrected by Scripture, but as they drifted from the authority of Scripture, either they have turned their well-bred traditions into fossils, or they have decayed from inward corruption.

Tradition is the vehicle which brought us through time to where we are. But our philosophy must not be, "It seemed to work in the past, so let's return to it." We do not need to throw away tradition, but we do need to continually test it by the Scriptures. We may gain much from reviewing the traditions of our cultural past, but only if we are able to discern the tried and true principles which are represented in our culture. When such principles are properly, consistently, and forcefully applied, then, over time, they can create a force which cannot be resisted.

What about our tradition of literature? Our literature is our history – but only if we read it. If we cease to read it, then we no longer belong to it. The present generation has been cut off from our history by being cut off from its literature. They cannot read it because they cannot read, because it is removed from the bookshelves, and because the general knowledge of its existence is removed from our culture. Worse, the history which they are taught is the product of the imagination of social engineers. We may laugh at the non-historical myths of the ancients, but our orphaned culture has invented and taught itself its own non-historical myths. Rome had its pantheon of gods and licensed religions, but we have our own pantheon of evolution and licensed teachers. The only way to nourish historical reality is to feed on the record of the past – but that past must be handled correctly.

We must let the dead speak to us. They have valuable lessons for us, if we will only listen. But we must try their words before the tribunal of the Word of God. We must respect our ancestors, but we must not worship them. We can hear tradition, but we must not canonize it. If we redeem their words, cleanse them, and put them to lawful use, we can build a civilization which honors our Lord. But we dare not use their words apart from their trial and cleansing by the Word.

How Should We Deal with Other Cultures?

If Biblical Christianity is the only true culture, then how should we deal with other cultures which we will encounter in literature? In Scripture, there are several examples of Christian encounters with Greek culture, and perhaps the most exemplary is that of the Apostle Paul at the city of Athens, recorded in Acts 17:16-34. Let us examine that record carefully, then see what lessons we can learn from the record. (The translation of this passage is our own very literal translation — v.l.t.)

PAUL AT ATHENS

> |17:16| NOW, WHILE PAUL *WAS* EXPECTING THEM [SILAS AND TIMOTHY] AT ATHENS, HIS SPIRIT WAS SHARPLY MOVED WITHIN HIM *UPON* SEEING *THAT* THE CITY WAS FULL OF IDOLS. |17:17| THEREFORE, FIRST OF ALL, HE WAS DEBATING: – *BOTH* IN THE SYNAGOGUE, WITH THE JEWS AND THOSE *GENTILES WHO* WERE DEVOUT, AND IN THE MARKETPLACE EACH AND EVERY DAY, WITH THOSE *WHO* WERE HAPPENING BY. — (V.L.T.)

Athens was both the intellectual and the religious center of the ancient world. Petronius, a contemporary of Paul, remarked in jest, “Our country is so full of deities, that you may more frequently meet with a god than a man” (*Satyr*, 17). Pausanius said, “There was no place where so many idols were to be seen” (*In Attica*, 17.24). (Compare Cicero, *De Responsis Aruspicum*; Xenophon, *De Athen. Polit.*) Athens was the height of human culture. Indeed, the whole civilized world spoke the language of Athens – Greek. If man, by wisdom, could find out God, most certainly he would have done it in Athens.

Paul was left alone in Athens. Upon seeing the magnificent grace and beautiful form of the artwork displayed throughout the city – the statues, the altars, the shrines, the temples – was Paul moved to develop a deep and full appreciation for the very highest of Greek culture? Not at all. Instead, his spirit was sharply moved within him – he was greatly provoked – against what these things represented: the idolatrous blasphemy, the bottomless ignorance, the intellectual deformity, the moral depravity. Idolatry is devotion to anything above devotion to the one true and living God. And idolatry inevitably leads to distortion and degradation. The worship of beauty deified art while corrupting human nature. The proper place of art is to serve the true God and to purify human nature.

Paul's first reaction to this idolatry was to enter into reasoned discourse (*διαλέγομαι*: exercising skill in the art of dialogue which draws answers from an opponent in order to prove a conclusion). He debated with Jews in the synagogue on the Sabbath day and with Gentiles in the marketplace on the other six days. Hence he confronted the grosser idolatry of the Gentiles, who worshiped graven images and the more refined idolatry of the Jews, who were cured of graven images, and instead worshiped their nationality – their Jewishness – their tradition.

|17:18| FURTHERMORE, SOME PHILOSOPHERS FROM AMONG THE EPICUREANS AND FROM AMONG THE STOICS CONFRONTED HIM. AND SOME SAID, "WHAT MAY THIS SEED-COLLECTOR WISH TO SAY?" BUT THESE *OTHERS SAID*, "HE SEEMS TO BE A PROCLAIMER OF FOREIGN DEMONS." (BECAUSE HE PROCLAIMED TO THEM THE GOSPEL OF JESUS AND THE RESURRECTION).

Paul had one more kind of idolatry to confront. This was the idolatry of philosophy, which is the worship of man – both individually and collectively. *Epicureans* (followers of Epicurus, 341-270 B.C.) acknowledged that gods existed in name only, but denied that they exercised any power in the world. They denied the resurrection and immortality of the soul, and they asserted that the chief good in life was to gratify the appetites of sense. *Stoics* (followers of Zeno, 334-262 B.C.) held that all human affairs were determined by fate, believed in a creator god, did not deny that the gods existed, but did not believe men received any good from the gods. A good man was as good as any god. Virtue was its own reward. They also denied the resurrection, but held to the immortality of the soul. Most likely, *Academics* (followers of Socrates and Plato) and *Peripatetics* (followers of Aristotle) were also present, but the Epicureans and Stoics were most numerous, and their philosophies were most opposed to the Gospel. They were the Sadducees and Pharisees of the Greek world.

When these Epicureans and Stoics confronted (*συμβάλλω*: made war with, Luke 14:31) Paul in the Athenian marketplace, they contemptuously called him a *spermologos* (*σπερμολόγος*: seed-collector). Spermologos was the name of a small crow-like bird or rook which is known for its incessant cawing and which lived by picking up seeds on the road. The name was applied to persons who, without order or method, collected the sayings of others, then repeated them to others in the same way which they collected them – without order or method. Apparently Paul's arguments lacked so much of the Greek art of rhetoric that they sounded like a disorderly concoction to these philosophers. That, in itself, was not a crime. Indeed, the Athenians rather liked new stories. However, the law of Rome strictly forbade proclaiming foreign deities without proper license by decree of the senate – religio licita. (Compare Acts 16:21; Tertullian, *Apology*, 5: ". . . no one should be consecrated a god by an emperor till he had been approved by the senate." Eusebius, *Ecclesiatical History*, Book 2. Section 2: ". . . no one could be regarded by the Romans as a god unless by vote and decree of the senate." Cicero, *De Legibus*, Book 2, Chapter 8: "No person shall have any separate gods, nor new ones; unless they be publicly allowed.")

Theos (*θεός*: god) referred to a god by nature. *Daimonion* (*δαιμόνιον*: demon) referred to a deified man. "Romulus, father Bacchus, with Castor and Pollux, for their eminent services, have been received into the temples of the gods." (Horace, *Second Epistle*, 1.5) Because Paul proclaimed to them the gospel of Jesus – a man resurrected and raised to the throne of God, the philosophers accused Paul of introducing foreign demons. To a Greek, this sounded like the deification of a hero – a new and foreign demon. Oddly enough, later in Ephesus, Paul was opposed for his a-theism (Acts 19:26), while here he was opposed for his neo-theism.

Paul must have listened carefully to the arguments of the Epicureans and Stoics, because the argument which he was about to give before the Athenian Tribunal contradicted their philosophies. Indeed, he used their own idols and their own poets to prove his points.

> |17:19| MOREOVER, HAVING TAKEN HOLD OF HIM, THEY LED *HIM* TO THE TRIBUNAL [AREOPAGUS], SAYING, "WE ARE COMPETENT TO KNOW WHAT THIS NEW DOCTRINE WHICH IS SPOKEN BY THEE *IS*. |17:20| FOR THOU DOST CARRY CERTAIN FOREIGN THINGS TO OUR EARS. THEREFORE, WE WISH TO KNOW WHAT *FORM* THESE THINGS MAY

CHOOSE TO TAKE."

Paul was taken and led to the Areopagus, the supreme Tribunal in Athens. The Areopagus officially met at night so that they could not be distracted by the sight of the accused. Pleaders were strictly forbidden any speech which would move the members of the Tribunal to pity or passion, but were restricted simply to stating the facts and their relations. Parties were placed under oath to tell the truth, invoking horrible imprecations upon themselves and families should they perjure themselves, calling upon the Furies to witness. Judges expressed their decisions by throwing pebbles on tables, one for acquittal, another for condemnation. The justice was so strict and impartial that both plaintiff and defendant never dared to question it. Apparently, Paul was allowed this "hearing" to determine if any formal charges should be made against him.

|17:21| NOW ALL ATHENIANS AND THE FOREIGNERS SOJOURNING *THERE* WERE TAKING THEIR GOOD TIME FOR NOTHING OTHER THAN TO TELL SOMETHING AND TO HEAR A NEWER THING.

The Athenians showed a remarkable degree of worldliness in that they wanted to know every new thing which came along. Those who are well grounded in the truth have no such preoccupation, for the simple reason that they know there is really nothing new, only new versions of the old (Ecclesiastes 1:9; 3:15; 7:10), and they have better ways to spend their time.

> See then that ye walk circumspectly, not as fools, but as wise, Redeeming the time, because the days are evil. — Ephesians 5:15,16

The evil days will consume you if you don't redeem them. You can be consumed by every new thing, or, in the same sort of way, by every old thing which is new to you.

|17:22| AND PAUL, HAVING STOOD IN *THE* MIDDLE OF THE TRIBUNAL [\AREOPAGUS], SAID, "MEN, ATHENIANS, I OBSERVE HOW, IN EVERY RESPECT, YE *ARE* MOST REVERENT TO DEMONS; |17:23| FOR PASSING THROUGH AND CONSIDERING YOUR OBJECTS OF VENERATION, I FOUND EVEN *AN* ALTAR ON WHICH HAD BEEN WRITTEN, 'TO THE UNKNOWABLE GOD.' THEREFORE, WHOM YE UNKNOWINGLY VENERATE, THIS ONE I-MYSELF ANNOUNCE TO YOU.

Paul appears to pay them a compliment of some sort for their religiosity.

Oecumenius indicates that the full inscription on this altar may have read,

> *θεοῖς Ἀσίας καὶ Εὐρώπης καὶ Λιβύης, θεῷ ἀγνώστῳ καὶ ξένῳ.*
>
> To the gods of Asia, and Europe, and Africa: To the unknown and foreign God."

Apollonius of Tyanna, a contemporary of Paul, took note of the altars bearing the inscription,

> *ἀγνώστοις θεοῖς,*
>
> unknowable gods.

Lucian uses this oath:

> *νὴ τὸν ἀγνώστον τὸν ἐν Ἀθῆναις,*
>
> I swear by the unknown (god) at Athens.

and he declares:
ὑμεῖς δὲ τὸν ἐν Ἀθῆναις ἀγνώστον ἐφευρόντες καὶ προσκυνή σαντες, χεῖρας εἰς οὐρανὸν ἐκτείναντες,

> We have discovered the unknown god at Athens, and worshiped him with our hands stretched up to heaven.

(*Philopatris*, 13.769; 29.180.) (Such altars are also mentioned by Philostratus, *Apollon*. 6.3; Pausanias, *Attica* 1.4; Minutius Felix; Tertullian.) It is said that Epimenides suggested to the Athenians the erection of statues to "unknown gods."

The Jews considered God's name to be ineffable, a name which was not known and must not be pronounced. The Gentiles called the Jewish God *πάγκρυφος*, all hidden one.

It was a capital offense to introduce a new god. Paul's argument is a fine legal point: This was no new God. This was a God Whom they already acknowledged among their altars – at least in a formal way. But he was a God as yet unknowable to the Athenians. They would soon receive knowledge, through Paul, for which they would be held accountable.

> |17:24| THE GOD WHO MADE THE WORLD AND ALL THE THINGS IN IT – THIS ONE BEING *INTRINSICALLY* LORD OF HEAVEN AND OF EARTH – HE DOES NOT DWELL IN HANDMADE SHRINES, |17:25| NOR IS HE TENDED BY MEN'S HANDS *AS THOUGH* NEEDING SOMETHING. HE-HIMSELF GIVES TO ALL LIFE AND BREATH IN EVERY RESPECT.

In proclaiming a God Who made all things, Paul contradicted the Epicureans, who believed the world evolved through a chance combination of atoms. In claiming there was but one eternal God Who is Lord of all things, Paul contradicted their polytheism. In claiming that the Creator does not dwell in such sacred shrines as surrounded them in Athens, Paul contradicted their idolatry. In claiming that the true God was sovereignly independent and needed nothing from men, Paul contradicted their false forms of worship. Finally, in claiming that God gave life and breath to all, Paul contradicted their false philosophies of human independence from God.

|17:26| WHAT IS MORE, HE MADE, FROM ONE BLOOD-*LINE*, EVERY NATION AMONG MEN, TO DWELL UPON ALL THE SURFACE OF THE EARTH, HAVING MARKED OUT PREARRANGED SEASONS AND THE BOUNDARIES OF THEIR DWELLING,

In claiming that every nation comes from one blood-line, Paul contradicted the Athenian notion that they were a separate and self-made race of men. Not only did God make every nation, He also predetermined where and when they would be (Genesis 9:25-11:9). Hence the repelling of Persian conquest by the Greeks, and the Greek conquest of the world, and the Roman conquest of the Greeks were all predetermined by Paul's God.

> When the most High divided to the nations their inheritance, when he separated the sons of Adam, he set the bounds of the people according to the number of the children of Israel. — Deuteronomy 32:8

In other words, Paul's God is in control of everything from the smallest – each man's life and breath – to the largest – world empires. This is the one sovereign and almighty Creator God Who owns all things and therefore to Whom all things are due. God, not man, is the measure of all things. Paul is arguing against Stoic fate and Epicurean chance, and toward total human accountability.

|17:27| FOR TO SEEK THE LORD, IF, CONSEQUENTLY, INDEED, THEY MIGHT GROPE *IN THE DARK* FOR HIM AND THEY MIGHT FIND *HIM*, ALTHOUGH, IN REALITY, *HE* IS INTRINSICALLY NOT FAR FROM EACH ONE OF US.

Paul says that, although God is always there, these wise Athenians, who call Him the "unknowable God," have been forever stumbling about in the dark, groping for what they are unable to find.

> The way of the wicked *is* as darkness: they know not at what they stumble. — Proverbs 4:19

They've been looking in all the wrong places. They knew God, but they didn't know Him *as* God.

> Because that, when they knew God, they glorified *him* not as God, neither were thankful; but became vain in their imaginations, and their foolish heart was darkened. Professing themselves to be wise, they became fools, And changed the glory of the uncorruptible God into an image made like to corruptible man, and to birds, and fourfooted beasts, and creeping things. — Romans 1:21-23

Furthermore, without revelation from God, they never will be able to find Him.

> But if a man walk in the night, he stumbleth, because there is no light in him. —John 11:10

Finally, Paul's God marks out the time and place that anyone does truly seek and find Him.

> Having made known unto us the mystery of his will, according to his good pleasure which he hath purposed in himself: That in the dispensation of the fulness of times he might gather together in one all things in Christ, both which are in heaven, and which are on earth; *even* in him: In whom also we have obtained an inheritance, being predestinated according to the purpose of him who worketh all things after the counsel of his own will: – Ephesians 1:9-11

The assertion that God is a Person separate from His creation, though intimately in touch with it, contradicted the pantheism of the Stoics.

Though God is not far from each man, and the things which He has created make up all of what man is and what man possesses, and He did not leave himself without a witness to them (Acts 14:15-17), nevertheless the heathen can never find Him. What they lack is revelation – both inward and outward (Second Corinthians 4:6; Ephesians 5:8; First Peter 2:9).

> |17:28| FOR IN HIM WE LIVE AND WE MOVE AND WE EXIST, AS ALSO SOME OF THE POETS – ACCORDING TO YOU – HAVE SAID, 'FOR WE ARE ALSO FROM AMONG HIS OFFSPRING.'

The Stoics were pantheists, believing God was everything in everything. Paul contradicted this by saying that God created everything separate from Himself, and that everything was in Him. Their existence depended upon Him, and should He cease to pronounce their existence, they would cease to exist. And he used their own religious poets to make his point.

Some assert that the expression, "For in Him we live and we move and we exist," is a poetic quotation from Epimenides (whom we will discuss later). There is no surviving manuscript of a Greek poet saying this, and the statement does not follow a Greek poetic form, and the connection to Epimenides is very conjectural. Perhaps in his discussions in the Athens marketplace, or in remarks previously made by others at the Areopagus, Paul heard a similar expression. Perhaps it was from a Greek poet. Perhaps he reformulated it here to serve his purposes. Perhaps.

Paul did not overwhelm the Greeks with his knowledge of their philosophy, but he did know enough to address them with what they needed to hear in the way which they needed to hear it. Paul appears to have quoted his interrogators when he said, "as also some of the poets – according to you – have said."

> *τοῦ γὰρ καὶ γένος ἐσμέν*
>
> for we are also from among his offspring

That phrase matches, word-for-word, the first half of the fifth line of a half-hexameter "Hymn to Zeus (Jupiter)" found in *Τὰ Φαινόμενα* (5), an astronomical poem written about 270 B.C. by Aratus, a native of Solis, a city of Cilicia, not far from Tarsus, where Paul was born. A similar expression (*ἐκ σοῦ γα`ρ γένος ἐσμέν*) is attributed to a "Hymn to Jove (Jupiter)" (5), written by Cleanthes of Assos (300-220 B.C.) who taught at Athens, and who was the successor of Zeno, founder of the Stoics. A similar expression is also found in Aratus the astronomer, and in the poet Homer, and in other places. We, in fact, are emphatically *not* Jupiter's offspring, as Aratus and others asserted. Paul conceded no authority to the quotation itself, but reframed it in order to serve his own purpose. This is precisely what Christians must do with everything which they use from the world – we must reframe it into the Christian worldview in order to serve our purposes. Paul's purpose was to point to the sentiment – which existed even among the heathen – that we are all related to deity by creation. In this incident, it served Paul's purpose to quote out of context!

There is one other place where Paul directly said he quoted a Greek author. In Titus 1:12, Paul apparently quoted a poem entitled, "Per^ crhsmîn," "*Concerning Oracles*," written about 500 B.C. by the pagan prophet and fortune-teller Epimenides, a Cretan by birth, of the city of Cnossus. It is a hexameter line, quoted by Callimachus in a "Hymn to

Zeus," (5.8) and quoted by others elsewhere.

> *εἶπέν τις ἐξ αὐτῶν ἴδιος αὐτῶν προφή'της,*
>
> *Κρῆτες ἀεὶ ψεῦσται, κακὰ θηρία, γαστέρες ἀργαί.* — Titus 1:12
>
> A certain one of themselves, a prophet of their own, said,
>
> Cretans are always liars, evil wild-beasts, lazy gluttons.

This was everywhere the Cretan reputation, such that to "krht…zein," "Cretanize," meant to tell a lie. This saying became a very common syllogistic puzzle called "The Liars."

> Epimenides said, "All Cretans are always liars."
>
> Epimenides is a Cretan.
>
> Therefore Epimenides says he is always a liar.
>
> If we **do** believe what Epimenides says about Cretans being liars, then we **must not** believe what Epimenides says about Cretans being liars.
>
> But if we **do not** believe what Epimenides says about Cretans being liars, then we **must** believe what Epimenides says about Cretans being liars.

Paul solved the puzzle in the only way possible, by declaring not that Epimenides was truthful, but only that "this testimony is true," shifting the focus to the saying, regardless of the messenger. This is what Christians must always do with all information emitted by non-Christian worldviews. They are all, in character, liars, and what they say is a lie because of its connection to their false worldview, but we can convert it to truth by putting it in its proper place in our own worldview, which is reality. In other words, the framework is what gives every word or fact or message its absolute truth value. The fact that dogs wag their tails is a lie in any other framework of interpretation than the Christian framework. The Christian framework says that they were created to do so for the glory of God (among other things). The naturalist framework says that they evolved so by chance and are chemically determined to do so for no ultimate reason. The agnostic framework says that we know neither how it happens nor why it happens – it just happens. So when an unbeliever says a dog wags its tail, we interpret that from our framework and formally agree to its truth. But when it is placed within the unbeliever's framework, it actually becomes a lie. There is no evolved dog wagging its tail by chemical determination. There is no dog wagging its tail for completely inexplicable reasons. There is only a dog created by God to wag its tail. Everything which is not understood in its proper relation to God is a lie. Teaching anything – no matter how innocuous it may seem – while leaving out its relation to God, is a lie. Writing a book on classical education, while leaving out its relation to God, is a lie.

From a Christian worldview, when Epimenides, a Cretan, said Cretans are always liars, he pointed to the inherent contradiction within any non-Christian worldview. Nevertheless, when reinterpreted from a Christian worldview, both Epimenides and Cretans are characteristically liars, and indeed, all men in their fallen condition are always liars walking about in darkness (Psalm 58:3; 62:9; 116:11; Romans 3:4; First John 1:6).

Worldliness is simply a failure to make this distinction by creating a so-called neutral zone of shared providences and "uninterpreted" facts. But the facts are indeed interpreted – as being neutral! The lie is that there is no difference between a fact in the Christian worldview and any other worldview – as if it is all relative. No. Whatever form of knowledge which the unbeliever has regarding God, he suppresses it (Romans 1:18,19). There is an absolute perspective, and God communicates His absolute perspective to us by His Word, and we spend our lives interpreting the world according to the perspective of His Word, not the perspective of anyone else's word.

"Cretans are always liars" (Titus 1:12) is the only passage where Paul identifies his words as a quote from a pagan prophet/poet. "For we are also his offspring" (Acts 17:28) is more likely Paul quoting his interrogators, though this is arguable. There is a third passage (First Corinthians 15:33) wherein many believe Paul was quoting a Greek poet.

Φθείρουσιν ἤθη χρηστὰ ὁμιλίαι κακαί — First Corinthians 15:33

bad company corrupts good manners

This appears to be a quote from Menander, the comic poet, who himself probably lifted his expression from Euripides.

There are a few other passages which are sometimes asserted to be quotes or allusions by Paul:

To Greek authors (First Corinthians 9:16 – Socrates; 12 – Menenius Agrippa; First Timothy 6:10 – Bion, or Democritus, or Diogenes the Cynic, etc.).

To the Jewish Greek Apocrypha (First Corinthians 6:2; Ephesians 6:11,13; Romans 9:21 – Wisdom of Solomon 3:8; 5:17; 15:7).

To Jewish Pseudepigrapha (Galatians 5:6; 6:15; First Corinthians 7:19 – Revelation of Moses).

Some even claim that Jesus was a scholar of Greek tragedies ("kick against the goads" Acts 9:5; 26:14 – Aeschylus' *Agamemnon*, 1624). Well, it must be conceded that the resurrected Jesus, in His divine omnipotence, knows all things, including Aeschylus' writings. But Jesus was conceding no authority to Aeschylus. This, and all of the other alleged quotations or allusions, were simply well-known and customary expressions – they were passed about like coins of the realm, and we have no idea whether or not the author to whom the quote is first assigned is actually the first to use the expression. How many of such heathen expressions were originally Hebrew, or Noahic, or Adamic? For that matter, it is not impossible that the expression was independently coined more than once. All we know is that somebody somewhere seemed to say something similar.

Does the apostle Paul quote these pagans to display his great learning? Not at all. Indeed, since he expected his listeners and his readers to readily recognize them, these quotes must have been quite common among the expressions men would toss about. These expressions were often quoted in literature before and during Paul's earthly lifespan.

If we said the words "government of the people, by the people, for the people," would that mean that we had thoroughly studied the literature of what is called the Civil War era, or even Lincoln's life and works, or would it simply mean that this selection from the Gettysburg address is a common expression? (For that matter, did Lincoln craft this expression himself, or did he overhear it from some unknown source, or did he borrow it from John Wycliffe, who had used this identical expression five hundred years earlier?)

Paul was not trying to impress his audience with his own pagan learning, nor with the authority of the pagan authors whom he cited. He simply borrowed a common expression from a pagan context, and he put it to his own use. Indeed, the Greek vocabulary of the New Testament could be said to be appropriated from the pagans for Christian use. (Some have also argued that Paul borrowed his vocabulary from Greek philosophers.) We also appropriate the English vocabulary for our own Christian use – even as we are doing at this very moment. If Paul was an erudite scholar of Greek literature, then what truly needs to be explained is why he only quotes a very few common Greek expressions which everyone was likely to recognize or understand.

Somewhere along the line, Paul picked up on elementary "classic rhetoric," as witnessed by his fondness for classic Greek rhetorical figures of speech such as alliteration, antithesis, asyndeton, chiasmus, climax, euphemism, hyperbaton, litotes, oxymoron, paradox, paronomasia, zeugma, etc.

Paul also adopted matters of heathen life for the illustration of Christian truth.

Greek Theater – First Corinthians 4:9; 7:31; Hebrews 10:33

Greek Athletics – First Corinthians 9:24-27; Philippians 3:12-14; First Thessalonians 2:19; First Timothy 6:12; Second Timothy 2:5; 4:8

Roman Law – Galatians 3:15-18; 4:1-5; Ephesians 1:5; Romans 7:2

Roman Military Triumph – Second Corinthians 2:14-16

But none of this is evidence that Paul was formally schooled in Greek or Roman literature, history, or philosophy. Paul simply used to his advantage whatever he had learned from living in the Greek and Roman culture.

|17:29| THEREFORE, EXISTING *INTRINSICALLY AS* OFFSPRING OF THIS GOD, WE ARE NOT OBLIGATED TO SUPPOSE HIS DIVINE NATURE TO BE LIKE GOLD OR SILVER OR STONE, AN ENGRAVING OF MAN'S ARTFUL CRAFT AND CLEVER REASONING.

The logic runs thus: If we are the offspring of God, then God is much greater than us. Since we are much greater than the clever engravings of men, then how could we suppose that God, our Father-Creator, is somehow like an engraving? How can the progenitor be infinitely inferior to the offspring? (Compare Isaiah 44:9-20.)

|17:30| THEREFORE, INDEED, LOOKING BEYOND THESE TIME *PERIODS* OF THIS IGNORANCE *OF HIM*, THIS *UNKNOWN* GOD AT THE PRESENT *PERIOD* IS COMMANDING ALL MEN EVERYWHERE TO REPENT, |17:31| ON THIS ACCOUNT: HE APPOINTED A DAY IN WHICH 'HE INTENDS TO JUDGE THE INHABITABLE WORLD IN RIGHTEOUSNESS,' BY A MAN WHOM HE MARKED OUT; HAVING FURNISHED CREDIBLE EVIDENCE TO ALL, HAVING RAISED HIM FROM AMONG *THOSE* DEAD."

The Creator of all things has every right to be offended by His offspring ignoring and degrading Him, and thereby dishonoring themselves. Paul summarily dismisses it all as "this ignorance" and says that God "looked beyond" this long period when they ignored Him, much like a man looks beyond another man who is an offense to him, ignoring him, acting as if the offending man doesn't at all deserve to be in his presence, or even exist.

> . . . the living God, which made heaven, and earth, and the sea, and all things that are therein: Who in times past suffered all nations to walk in their own ways. Nevertheless he left not himself without witness, in that he did good, and gave us rain from heaven, and fruitful seasons, filling our hearts with food and gladness. — Acts 14:15-17

Paul declares that God now commands these men to repent of their ignorance. He has opened up an aperture of opportunity – a light shining in a dark place – for them to be released from their ignorance. He now commands all men everywhere to repent, (*μετανοέω*: metanoeO), literally, change their mind, alter their intellect, redirect their thinking. Their minds have been heading in every conceivable direction – except toward God. All of the so-called "grand" accomplishments of Greek culture – the very height of all human culture to the Athenian mind (and still so in the minds of many today) – have been for the glory of anything except the true God Who made all things.

But there is a Judgment Day coming. The whole culture will be judged. In case they had any doubts, the Judge Himself rose from the dead, proving that He had power over life and death (Matthew 26:24; John 5:27; Acts 2:22; 10:40-42).

> |17:32| AND HAVING HEARD *OF* A RESURRECTION FROM AMONG *THOSE* DEAD, SOME INDEED RIDICULED, YET SOME SAID, "WE WILL OURSELVES HEAR THEE AGAIN CONCERNING THIS *MATTER*." |17:33| AND *DISMISSING HIM* IN THIS WAY, PAUL WENT OUT FROM THEIR MIDST. |17:34| HOWEVER, SOME MEN, *THROUGH* FASTENING THEMSELVES TO HIM, BELIEVED; AMONG WHOM *WERE* BOTH DIONYSIUS, THE TRIBUNAL-MEMBER [\AREOPAGITE], AND A WOMAN, DAMARIS BY NAME, AND OTHERS WITH THEM.

Paul carefully observed the Areopagan rule against exciting passion in his discourse. He merely asserted the doctrine and connected the logic (Contrast his discourses in Acts 24:10-25; 26:1-29). However, it is his pure doctrine and clear logic which nevertheless moved his audience in the end to break off the discourse. Epicureans would be among those who ridiculed any future state after death. Stoics might be less skeptical, believing in a future state after death, but quite probably their words, "we will hear thee again," were about like Felix, who said the same words, but never did (Acts 24:25). This disagreement apparently ended the proceeding. Paul therefore was politely dismissed. They could not convict him of a crime without condemning themselves also. Paul elsewhere used a similar method to split the Pharisees and Sadducees (Acts 23:6).

An Areopagite was a member of this Tribunal for life, and no man became a member who was not first an Archon – a chief governor of Athens. Hence a renowned government official of the highest reputation for intelligence and conduct – Dionysius – was converted, and others with him – perhaps his family and friends. Also a woman named Damaris was converted, and others with her.

Athens was so full of philosophy and idolatry that it attracted every kind of foul mind to the city. Though God has power to convert anyone He chooses, it is nevertheless true that He does not call many wise men of this world (First Corinthians 1:26). At Athens, both the Jewish synagogue and the Gentile Tribunal were too disinterested to persecute Paul. Paul's preaching didn't even raise the city against him. Their minds were so corrupted that Paul's preaching stirred up only a momentary interest. Hence Paul's evangelism had little effect – much like Jesus, who was amazed at His listeners' unbelief (Mark 6:6). But the abiding effect of Paul's preaching cannot truly be measured unless we can trace what became of Dionysius and Damaris. A few seeds sown may grow great harvests in time.

Lessons to Learn from Paul at Athens

Though this passage contains many valuable lessons, we wish only to point out these four:

1. To serve his purposes, Paul redeemed what he chose from the darkness of Athenian culture. However, he needed to give new meaning to what he did redeem, because its old meaning was determined outside of the reality of the Christian worldview. This is absolutely true of all things in the world. All things – stones, love, light bulbs, government – have a different meaning in the world of unbelief than they do in the world of belief.
2. Paul's knowledge of Greek lore was of the most elementary sort – the kind which was casually picked up from contact with the culture. His knowledge of Christ was of the most advanced sort – which enabled him to know how to pick and choose among the scraps of Greek to serve his purposes. He did not need to know the deep darkness of Greek philosophy – the depths of Satan, in order to preach the heights of Christ. A little grammar, a little logic, and a little rhetoric go a long way.
3. Some places attract the kinds of people who love darkness, and these are often the most "religious" and "philosophical"

places. Jerusalem had its Sadducees and Pharisees. Athens had its Stoics and Epicureans. Washington has its Conservatives and Liberals. Paul's arguments do not impress the worldly. They love their lies – their worldviews – too much to come to the light.

4. Things of the world will consume our time. The Athenians spent their time collecting new information. In other words, though they accused Paul of being a seed-collector, they were the seed-collectors and scavengers who searched to find something new to feed upon. (Those who accuse the innocent are usually guilty of the crime which they project upon others.) We must not become caught up in the world's endless search for something new. We must be content with pursuing our calling from the Lord and limit our searching to those things which come within our calling, and depend upon God to bring what else we may need into our path. We must not pursue miscellaneous and worthless knowledge for the sake of knowledge.

WHAT ARE THE CLASSICS?

In a narrow sense, the term "classics" may refer to the noted works and authors of ancient Greek and Roman literature. Strictly speaking, these are the "humanist classics." But we use the term "classics" in a broader sense to mean *what is of good form and lasting value* – regardless of the time period. There are Greek classics and Roman Classics, Mediaeval Classics and Renaissance Classics, Reformation Classics and Modern Classics. Because the two criteria – *good form* and *lasting value* – are subjective, there will always be disagreements about what books meet these criteria. Someone may question the form of a piece of literature, and another will question its value. You will need to sort these things out for yourself, but we will give you a few pointers before this Chapter is done.

You can find numerous lists of classics, great books, recommended reading, desired reading for college, required reading for cultural literacy, and so forth. We would collapse in financial and emotional bankruptcy if we read all of the books on these lists. Some suggest that we should at least be familiar with the substance – the plots and characters, the themes and contents – of all the books on these lists. It is not possible for the ordinary person to do that and also have a life.

Who expects us to know everything? Who binds us to these lists? Do we want to follow men's lists, or do we need to devise our own lists? They say, "When in Rome, do as the Romans." The question is, do we want to go to Rome, or do we want to go to Zion? In the end, we must bring all *classics* into obedience to serve Christ, or they are useless. If we cannot use them to promote the Biblical standard within the Biblical worldview, then we cannot use them.

HOW TO CLASSIFY LITERATURE

Four Categories of Literature

We can divide literature into four distinct categories: faith, fact, fiction, and fantasy.

1. *Faith* – the record of God in Scripture. This is fact, but it is a perfect record of fact. It is in a category all by itself, and must always be treated so. Yes, there are problems of text, translation, and interpretation, but these are problems created by men, not problems inherent in Scripture itself. We must look to the Scriptures themselves, not to the theories of men, for how we should deal with those problems.

The Scriptures are divided into the Old Testament and the New Testament. The Hebrews divided the Old Testament into twenty-three books:

1. Five books of the *Law* (Torah): Genesis through Deuteronomy.
2. Seven books of the *Prophets* (Nevi'im), including the three early prophets: Joshua, Judges, Samuel & Kings (four considered as one book); the three later prophets: Isaiah, Jeremiah, Ezekiel; and the twelve minor prophets: Hosea through Malachi (twelve considered as one book).
3. Eleven books of *Writings* (Kethuvim): Psalms, Proverbs, Job, Song of Songs, Ruth, Lamentations, Ecclesiastes, Esther, Daniel, Ezra & Nehemiah (two considered as one book), Chronicles (two considered as one book).

The more common Greek division of the Old Testament rearranges the same material into thirty-nine books:

1. Five *Books of Moses* (Pentateuch): Genesis through Deuteronomy.

2. Twelve *Historical Books*: Joshua through Esther.
3. Five *Poetic Books*: Job through Song of Songs.
4. Seventeen *Prophetic Books*, including the five major prophets, Isaiah through Daniel; the twelve minor prophets, Hosea through Malachi.

The New Testament is divided into:

1. Five *Historical Books*: including the four Gospels, Matthew through John; the Acts of the Apostles.
2. Twenty-one *Doctrinal and Practical Epistles*: including the fourteen Epistles of Paul, Romans through Hebrews; the seven General Epistles, James through Jude.
3. One *Prophetic Book*: Revelation.

2. *Fact* – the record of men about their understanding of reality. All records of fact are necessarily selective, and the author's perspective selects and arranges the facts. Because of the darkness of sin, what is presented by men as factual is never quite the actual – it is always colored and shaded in some way by our false perceptions. This is what we must always be looking for. There are honest mistakes – which the faithful are making all of the time, and there are dishonest mistakes – which are deliberately worked into the record in order to deceive. Both must be detected and corrected.

The types of fact-literature include: letters, essays, speeches, periodicals, books, encyclopedias.

The subjects of fact-literature include:

– *Philosophy* – Metaphysics, Logic, Ethics, Psychology, etc.
– *Religion* – Churches and Sects, Theology, Other Religions, etc.
– *Social Science* – Politics, Economics, Law, Education, etc.
– *Language* – Linguistics, ancient and modern Languages, etc.
– *Pure Science* – Mathematics, Earth Science, Physics, Astronomy, Chemistry, Biology, Zoology, Anthropology, Paleontology, etc.
– *Technology* – Engineering, Construction, Manufacturing, Agriculture, Home Economics, Business, Medical Science, etc.

– *Arts* – Music, Drawing and Painting, Sculpture and Printing, Decoration, Photography, Architecture and Landscaping, etc.
– *Literature* – Ancient literature, Foreign language literature, English and American literature, etc.
– *History* – Ancient history, World history, American history, Biography, Geography, etc.

3. *Fiction* – the invention of men, but based upon reality. If fiction were necessarily evil, then Jesus' parables would prove He was a sinner. We are continually inventing what we will say, and fiction writing is an extension of this. It is subject to the same faults as fact, but it has the additional dimension that much of it cannot be checked against other records of the fact.

The varieties of fiction-literature include: stories, parables, poetry, drama, essays, humor, satire, etc.

4. *Fantasy* – the invention of men, but not based upon reality. Just as Scripture is fact, but a special class of fact, so fantasy is fiction, but a special class of fiction. Fantasy is fiction which has crossed the borderline into a world which operates differently than reality. We must discern the character of that world. If it is based upon real principles and parallels real things, then it may serve a real purpose. Animal fables which play on some characteristic of an animal, but which also give human personality to the animal, may be compared to Solomon's proverbs, which compare men to some distinctive characteristic of an animal. ("Go to the ant.") But we must be very careful with any fantasy which distorts and perverts relationships, or which invents supernatural forces, or which changes the moral consequences of human action. We could invent such a fantasy to show how contradictory and self-destructive such a world would be, in order to contrast this with the marvel of God's order. But the purpose of many such fantasies is to invent a world apart from God. This is the first phase of false religion and mythology (like evolution). It is the invention of a new faith, in competition with the true faith – the faith of Scripture, which was our first category of literature. Because the true faith and the new mythical faith cannot stand together, the new mythical faith must necessarily treat matters of reality as if they were myth – whether it ever actually says so or not. Many children have

become so involved in this mythological fantasy life that they have lost touch with the true moral consequences of their actions.

Obviously, the lines between these four categories of literature are not absolute or distinct. For example, a poem could be fact, fiction, or fantasy – or all three. It is certainly true that many things in philosophy and science might better be classified as fiction, or even fantasy. We say this with some humor, but also with much seriousness.

CHOOSING WHAT TO READ

To Burn or Not To Burn?

When the Israelites entered the Promised Land, they were commanded to wipe out all of the Canaanite literature.

> . . . When ye are passed over Jordan into the land of Canaan; Then ye shall drive out all the inhabitants of the land from before you, and destroy all their pictures, and destroy all their molten images, and quite pluck down all their high places: — Numbers 33:51,52 (Compare Exodus 23:24,32,33; 34:12-17; Deuteronomy 7:2-5,25,26; 12:2,3,30,31; 20:16-18; Joshua 23:7; Judges 2:2.)

In the New Testament, the repentant Ephesians burned their books of sorcery.

> Many of them also which used curious arts brought their books together, and burned them before all *men*: and they counted the price of them, and found *it* fifty thousand *pieces* of silver. — Acts 19:19

It does not say that they burned all of the books there were, but only that there were some books which, regardless of their worldly worth, were better burnt. Likewise, there may be some things which the world considers of "literary value," but which, because of their ability to cause little ones to stumble, we are better off leaving alone until a mature age, or, in some cases, leaving alone altogether.

> And if thy right eye offend thee, pluck it out, and cast *it* from thee: for it is profitable for thee that one of thy members should perish, and not *that* thy whole body should be cast into hell. And if thy right hand offend thee, cut it off, and cast *it* from thee: for it is profitable for thee that one of thy members should perish, and not *that* thy whole body should be cast into hell. — Matthew 5:29, 30

We must be willing to give up everything of this world before we can redeem any of it back for the Lord's use.

> So likewise, whosoever he be of you that forsaketh not all that he hath, he cannot be my disciple. — Luke 14:33

The world's values cannot be our values.

Ten Principles for Choosing What to Read

Here are some of the principles which we have developed for our family in order to discern which literature to "redeem" and which to "burn."

1. DO WHAT IS PLEASING TO THE LORD.

> That ye might walk worthy of the Lord unto all pleasing, being fruitful in every good work, and increasing in the knowledge of God. — Colossians 1:10

> But without faith *it is* impossible to please *him* . . . . — Hebrews 11:6

If you go places you ought not go, and see things you ought not see, and hear things you ought not hear, you'll end up doing things you ought not do. We can hear someone say, "Well, the Bible is full of descriptions of wicked deeds of men." True, but the Bible also tells us what to think about all of that wickedness. And though the Bible is not particularly graphic in description of depravity, there are sections of the Bible which we simply do not read to young children. The Hebrews would not allow a young child to read the Song of Solomon – not that the Song of Solomon is wicked, but that some of the material is not appropriate for a little child. We must not cause little ones to stumble.

> But whoso shall offend one of these little ones which believe in me, it were better for him that a millstone were hanged about his neck, and *that* he were drowned in the depth of the sea. Woe unto the world because of offences [/stumblings]! for it must needs be that offences [/stumblings] come; but woe to that man by whom the offence [/stumbling] cometh! — Matthew 18:6,7

2. DO NOT FOLLOW THE WORLD.

> And be not conformed to this world: but be ye transformed by the renewing of your mind, that ye may prove what *is* that good, and acceptable, and perfect, will of God. — Romans 12:2

We do not need to adopt the world's values and standards in order to fit in and to prove to the world that we are not inferior. We are not looking for their friendship or approval. Do not allow the world to define you. If you are a Christian, then you must allow the Lord to define you and all that you do, as you seek to please Him. Do not decline to define all things from a Christian perspective.

Worldliness is bred by a lack of mature separation from the world. We are not saying "be Amish" – indeed, the Amish have their own peculiar form of worldliness, in their own peculiar little world. The Old Testament had childish rules – touch not, taste not, handle not – fitting their primitive culture made from the elementary principles of the world (Colossians 2:20,21; Galatians 4:3). The New Testament requires maturity – not childish rules, but fuller understanding. Under the Gospel, all things are lawful when used lawfully, but the liberty of the gospel is a law of maturity (James 1:25) to do things to the glory of God, not to indulge the flesh.

3. DO NOT ALLOW THE WORLD TO FOLLOW YOU.

> Pure religion and undefiled before God and the Father is this, To visit the fatherless and widows in their affliction, *and* to keep himself unspotted from the world. — James 1:27

> Keep thy heart with all diligence; for out of it *are* the issues of life. — Proverbs 4:23

The world wants to be your friend – but only on their terms. There is no neutrality. If a piece of literature cannot be used to build Christian culture in our children, then, no matter how neutral it may seem, it will be used to build something culturally anti-Christian in our children. The world will defile us, spot us, with ungodliness and worldly lusts. The comedy plays of Aristophanes, for example, are full of perverse topics which defile the imagination and the conscience. Even the pagan Plutarch criticized Aristophanes' plays as disgusting and degrading (*Morals*, X, 1.467 and 4.471-473). Where do we go to get our purity back?

4. THERE IS ONLY SO MUCH TIME IN THE DAY.

> Walk in wisdom toward them that are without, redeeming the time. — Colossians 4:5

There are many things which we can do, but how is our time best spent? Wasting time is anti-Christian.

5. OLDER DOES NOT NECESSARILY MEAN BETTER.

> Beware lest any man spoil you through philosophy and vain deceit, after the tradition of men, after the rudiments of the world, and not after Christ. — Colossians 2:8

The better things are often older things, but just because something is "old" does not mean it is good.

Have you ever read any of the works by John Bunyan? Have you read *Robinson Crusoe*? These are wonderful pieces of literature which you will want your children to read over and over.

The Greek historians such as Xenophon or Thucydides may prove useful in studying history – though we must understand that they are writing from their unbelieving perspective, and they are mere men reporting the lies and distortions of themselves and others.

The Canterbury Tales is full of gross and profane babble unfit for little eyes or ears, and anything one might miss by not reading it will be made up by what he will get from reading something else. There may be sections which would prove of some value, but we have better use for our time than to pull on the chore boots and wade through the muck for a few kernels of corn.

Do you have a copy of Ovid's *Metamorphoses* in your house? We suggest that you put it on a very high shelf.

We made the children read *Beowulf* in its unabridged form, then write a paper on it. Hans' paper was entitled *Beer-wulf: A Story of How God Used a Monster to Rid the Land of the Beer Halls.* Enough said.

6. IS THIS PROFITABLE?

All things are lawful for us as Christians – but only so long as we use them lawfully.

> All things are lawful for me, but not all things do benefit . . . . — First Corinthians 6:12 (v.l.t.)

All things are lawful for us as Christians, but only if we use them lawfully – according to their proper use.

But we know that the law *is* good, if a man use it lawfully; — First Timothy 1:8

> Meats for the belly, and the belly for meats: but God shall destroy both it and them. Now the body *is* not for fornication, but for the Lord; and the Lord for the body. — First Corinthians 6:13

We cannot abuse things in a way which contradicts God's law.

Paul narrows the field of uses down to those things which do benefit. The word translated *benefit* literally means *to bring things together* so as to make a helpful contribution. What we use must bring things together for us in a helpful and profitable way. Pythagoras and Euclid may have developed useful geometry, but their philosophy is foolishness. A study of their philosophy would be useful only as a study in the carnal speculative mind – a study which has much more limited use than geometry. All things must be made to serve the Lord Jesus, or they serve no good purpose. Lest you think we are advocating some extremely narrow and strict philosophy of use, well, we aren't – Jesus is. We are not judges of other men's uses. They must answer for their own uses. There may be things which they can use but we cannot, and vice versa, simply because of the differences in our constitutions, abilities, and experiences.

7. DOES THIS PROMOTE GOOD HABITS?

> . . . All things are lawful for me, but I-myself will not be brought under the control of anything. — First Corinthians 6:12 (v.l.t.)

What we study should not be of a nature which can take control of us – as an addiction, an obsession, or a dominating habit which makes such demands upon us that godly ways are no longer in control. We must not be made servant to ungodliness. One application to classical literature is that we must not put classical and Biblical together on an equal basis. This constitutes an unequal yoke, and the classical will always emerge as dominant. We must make all things serve the Biblical. We must never make the servant the master.

8. WILL READING THIS FURTHER MY EDUCATION?

> . . . All things are lawful for me, but not all things do edify. — First Corinthians 10:23 (v.l.t.)

Edify means to build up, to promote proper growth. Some things do not promote healthy growth. Some things promote perverted growth. It may serve some edifying purposes to be aware, at a mature age, that some perversions exist, but it is never edifying to dwell upon and explore the depths of depravity. Never.

> Enter not into the path of the wicked, and go not in the way of evil *men*. Avoid it, pass not by it, turn from it, and pass away. — Proverbs 4:14,15

> And have no fellowship with the unfruitful works of darkness, but rather reprove *them*. For it is a shame even to speak of those things which are done of them in secret. — Ephesians 5:11,12

There are some works which, if they are to be read – particularly by children, then they should be expurgated. Expurgated means the graphic obscenities are purged out – either in the text itself, or when the parent reads the text out loud. Though the Greek and Roman historians and biographers (such as Herodotus, Livy, Plutarch, and Diogenes Laertius) must be read if you want any idea of ancient history, nevertheless, now and then, you will find passages which will make you blush.

9. DOES THIS MATERIAL HAVE LASTING VALUE.

> And they that use this world, as not abusing *it*: for the fashion of this world passeth away. — First Corinthians 7:31

Only those things which are of the Lord are of lasting value. Everything else will pass away. If something cannot be redeemed for His use, then it is useless. If it cannot serve Biblical goals, then it will necessarily work to undermine Biblical foundations by pursuing other worldly goals. Some of the speeches of Pericles, Isocrates, and Demosthenes are significant examples for historical, political, and rhetorical content, but only so long as they are redeemed for the Master's use.

10. WHEN IN DOUBT, LEAVE IT OUT.

> . . . for whatsoever *is* not of faith is sin. — Romans 14:23

Like the stuff that's been in the refrigerator for a long time, and it doesn't look – or smell – quite right, "When in doubt, throw it out." Life is too short, and things are too many, to be fretting over a few little things which, if we discover they are really so important, can always be picked up in more mature years. We never reach the point where we say, "There's nothing to do." There are too many things to do, and we almost relish the opportunity to eliminate something.

Whether or not you agree with our understanding of these principles, you should agree to the value of establishing some principles. Parents are subject to peer pressure as well – even classical Homeschooling peer pressure. If someone shares their long list of classics which their children are reading, then do not begin to doubt or fret, but look back at your list of principles and stick to them.

We once followed lists. We were using a curriculum which required the reading of Greek mythology. Our children observed that it was full of immorality and they did not think they should be reading it. We had never read it, but we trusted the curriculum, and suspected that they wanted to escape the assignment – until we read it! We repented. It did not agree with our principles on how to evaluate literature.

Require your child to read those classical works which agree with your family's principles, and forget the rest. There are a large number of classical works which are good reading, and there is only so much time in the day.

Where to Draw the Line

We all recognize that it is necessary to draw the line somewhere, but sometimes it can be difficult to see where that line should be drawn. There is no rulebook which gives us exhaustive directions. Different situations call for different judgments, and those judgments must be made in a mature way, by applying sound principles. Here are some of the borders:

1. Between the *sacred* and the *profane*. We must not treat the Bible as if it is just another book. All works of men are profane. The Bible is sacred, and though men have, through faulty copying, introduced incidental errors into the text, the Bible is not fundamentally harmed by man's mistakes. It has been preserved through the ages as the only infallible guide to all truth. So we don't treat the Bible, God's Word, to the same kind of criticism as we do man's word.
2. Between the *godly* and the *ungodly*. Though John Bunyan and Aesop are both men, *Pilgrim's Progress* and *Aesop's Fables* are in different leagues. They aren't even playing the same game. One is from a man who knew the light and walked in the light, the other is from a blind man who stumbled in the darkness. The first may be improved upon, but the second must be redeemed and transformed under the light.
3. Between the *decent* and the *indecent* – the coarse, crude, lewd, obscene, pornographic, outrageous, unconscionable, unprincipled, corrupt, unscrupulous – well, you get the idea. The writings of Sophocles, one of the great Greek tragic dramatists, reflect his sexually perverse and immoral life. Sigmund Freud appropriated the plot of one of his plays, *Oedipus Rex*, for his perverse theories of sexuality.

4. Between *what is appropriate for children*, and *what adults may be able to tolerate*. Young children ought not to be exposed to indecencies. This even applies to some portions of the Bible. Though the adult may be able to wash away the incidental indecency, no adult is able to withstand a steady bath of the indecent.
5. Between the *worthwhile* and the *worthless*. The world is full of "decent" but worthless things. The devil doesn't need to keep us busy with pursuing evil. So long as he can keep us from pursuing the worthwhile, his purpose is accomplished. Work your way through *Pilgrim's Progress* before you dream along through some brainless novel or detective story.
6. Between the *good* and the *best*. Life is short, and there is only so much time in the day. How may we best redeem the time? These are hard decisions to make, and we learn this only by experience, and we never learn this perfectly.
7. Between the *best* and the *best*. You will eventually discern that God is calling you in a certain direction in life. When confronted with many of the best choices, you will eventually learn to choose many things according to what literature best fits your calling.

These rules should apply to ancient as well as modern literature. If we wouldn't allow our children to read *Tom Jones* or *Heather Has Two Mommies*, then why should we allow them to read *The Iliad* by Homer or *The Frogs* by Aristophanes?

There is some literature which is worthy to be burnt. Whatever causes you or your children to stumble should be "burnt" to you. We are not suggesting that we burn *all* classical literature of every sort. It's too late to do that anyway. But we do think *some* of it could be burned with no great loss. (There are plenty of modern writings of the same type to which we would gladly put a match.) But if we burned it *all*, then we would need to reinvent some of it – in a redeemed form.

Appropriate Ages

Question: What things are appropriate at what age levels?

Answer: The Scriptures repeatedly draw the line between the worship of the true God and all other religion. Little children are not held accountable for this kind of knowledge because they cannot fully understand it. Parents are held accountable for what they teach their children. Causing one of these little ones to stumble is a major offense.

> Then said he unto the disciples, It is impossible but that offences will come: but woe *unto him*, through whom they come! It were better for him that a millstone were hanged about his neck, and he cast into the sea, than that he should offend one of these little ones. – Luke 17:1,2

Because of the continual warnings to Israel to leave no knowledge of false gods in the land, we must understand that this is no small matter in God's eyes. We must understand the principle and apply it carefully.

There is no "one size fits all" way of looking at this. Different families are at different levels of cultural maturity, and they will handle different things differently. Because of their cultural environment, some families are more frequently assaulted with offensive views, so they may be forced to teach more extensively on the offenses. There should, however, be some common lines of demarcation.

1. Different age-levels can handle different materials.
2. Different children can handle different materials.
3. Nothing should engender an improper or ungodly appetite.
4. The explicit description of acts of degenerate depravity must be omitted.

With young children, we should proceed on a need-to-know basis. This is true even with Scripture. When we read about the false god Baal, children do not need to know the details of the degenerate depravity to which men went in worshiping this false god. One way to handle references to Greek and Roman mythology used in curricula or vocabulary studies is simply to explain what the words mean and what they describe, then give God's perspective on it. This way, you are not glorifying idols and false gods by making the study of them overly interesting and entertaining. Consider carefully the following observations regarding exposure to pagan teachings:

1. *The young child may become confused.* A child may say he can tell the difference between Biblical miracles, angels, and gods and their heathen counterparts, but the counterparts were invented by the demons precisely to confuse adults – not to mention children. It does not matter whether our children "believe" the myths; what matters is that the myths leave an impression upon our children. (Many pagans did not believe the myths, but nevertheless insisted upon their value. Even the unbelievers who regard the Bible as myths use the Bible to leave "moral" impressions.) It does not matter that you distinguish between "fictitious" pagan myths and "real" Bible history. The children will be confronted with the similarities. Satan "inspired" them to be similar. A counterfeit dollar bill won't go very far if it looks like a cartoon charac-

ter. The contrasts which an adult sees may not be so obvious to young minds, regardless of their ability to repeat your insistence that there is a difference. A young child will have difficulty telling the difference between play money and real money, between counterfeit money and real money, between photocopied money and real money.

2. *The child may become insensitive to immorality*. It is argued that many children have become insensitive to violence and murder because of their exposure to it on television. Exposure to the immorality of heathen literature may likewise create a callous indifference to it.

> Were they ashamed when they had committed abomination? nay, they were not at all ashamed, neither could they blush . . . . — Jeremiah 6:15; 8:12

Everyone must find the correct balance between knowledge of the truth and knowledge of the corruptions in the world, but the youngest should have more of the truth, and never should knowledge of corruptions take a dominant position. Thorough familiarity with the truth will help children to spot an error when they encounter it. But a steady diet of error without Biblical criticism is dangerous.

> Can a man take fire in his bosom, and his clothes not be burned? Can one go upon hot coals, and his feet not be burned? — Proverbs 6:27,28

Then how can a child at an impressionable age read literature about immoralities and be left untouched? It is one thing to stumble off a cliff, then pray the Lord to save you. It is another thing to jump, then expect Him to help.

3. *The child may fail to distinguish the holy from the common*. Regrettably, we adults seem to have little sense of this ourselves, so we fail to teach this to our children. When the people of God meet to worship, do we treat the meeting (not the building, but the meeting) as the inner sanctuary of the temple of the living God? (First Corinthians 3:16,17; 6:19; Second Corinthians 6:16; Ephesians 2:21,22; Hebrews 3:6; First Peter 2:5) Or do we treat it more like another public meeting? We need to regain this distinction ourselves, and teach it to our children. They will never learn to tell the difference between the clean and the unclean, the common and the holy, if we are not careful, not just to point it out to them, but to live it out to them. We must never treat the Scriptures and what they teach in the same way as we treat other literature.

> Her priests have violated my law, and have profaned mine holy things: they have put no difference between the holy and profane, neither have they shewed *difference* between the unclean and the clean, and have hid their eyes from my

sabbaths, and I am profaned among them. — Ezekiel 22:26

Reading Critically

Literature appreciation – what does that mean? Well, it does not necessarily mean liking the literature. It means interpreting and evaluating the literature – determining what it is really worth. Of course, unbelieving literature is actually worthless except as it is used to serve God.

While you are reading the literature, be sure to:

1. *Collect your knowledge* – the facts of the literature. You may use some oral narration or question-and-answer to check this – whether privately with yourself when reading by yourself, or mutually when reading together.
2. *Build your understanding* – the reasoning of the literature. What are the connections which are being made? Why are they being made?
3. *Develop your wisdom* – the purpose, direction, goal, or effect of the literature. What is this all leading toward, and how does the author work to accomplish this?

Each family will develop its own distinctive criteria for evaluating literature, but to help you to begin, here are some criteria which we think should be included:

1. What are the author's intentions in writing, and how are those intentions displayed?
   a. What is his worldview, and how does it show in his writing?

   – From his point of view, how is reality constructed, what is correct behavior, what is the source of truth?
   – What principles does he believe in, what things does he value, what goals does he pursue?
   b. Is he frank and open in expressing his intentions, or are they subtle, or even hidden?
2. How does the Lord use this literature to serve Himself – regardless of the author's intentions?
   a. To form good or poor communication skills in the righteous or in the wicked.
   b. To corrupt men's minds and ripen them for judgment, or to edify their minds and equip them to serve Him.

c. To inform and warn the righteous or the wicked of the fruit of their ways.

3. How can we redeem this literature to intentionally use it to serve the Lord?
    a. By injecting criticism as a lesson in detecting and understanding godlessness.
    – The primary godless philosophy which pervades almost all literature, ancient or modern, is the absence of speaking of things – objects, thoughts, emotions, actions – with reference to God.
    – Godless philosophies which particularly infuse modern works include a focus on the worldly, an emphasis upon self-esteem, gushy, maudlin emotions, feminism, entertainment orientation.
    b. By pointing out the good or poor examples of literary communication – figures of speech, choices of words, manner of phrasing, structure of the work.
    c. By evaluating the information contained in it and its value for serving the Lord.

Every reader must be careful not to imbibe of the poisonous spirit of ungodly literature – or of ungodly ways and notions which appear in professedly Christian literature. The way to strengthen your carefulness is to develop a spirit which continuously evaluates and criticizes everything you read (or hear, or watch). Set a watchdog at the door, and when he barks, go and find out what he is barking at.

QUESTIONS

In the remainder of this Chapter, we will address a number of questions under the following four topics:

1. Don't godly men in the Bible pursue the world's wisdom?
2. Don't we need to be culturally literate?
3. How should we approach classical literature?
4. How can we maintain a proper separation?

1. Don't Godly Men in the Bible Pursue the World's Wisdom?

EXAMPLES OR EXCEPTIONS?

Question: Didn't Moses and other great men learn the ways of the heathen?

Answer: Exceptions do not make rules.

> And Moses was learned in all the wisdom of the Egyptians, and was mighty in words and in deeds. — Acts 7:22

Moses spent forty years *programming* in Egypt, then forty years *deprogramming* on the back side of the desert in the company of Jethro the priest of God at Midian, then forty more years *reprogramming* Israel in the desert. In the government school system, we ourselves were trained in the culture of atheistic naturalism. The Lord saved us out of those lies, but we still haven't fully recovered from their influence. We have not been reprogramming quite so long as Moses. We would never advocate that Christian parents raise their children the way we were raised. We teach our children about atheism and naturalism and their implications, but we do not drown our children in them.

Daniel, Hananiah, Mishael, and Azariah were

> Children in whom *was* no blemish, but well favoured, and skilful in all wisdom, and cunning in knowledge, and understanding science, and such as *had* ability in them to stand in the king's palace, and whom they might teach the learning and the tongue of the Chaldeans. . . . And in all matters of wisdom *and* understanding, that the king enquired of them, he found them ten times better than all the magicians *and* astrologers that *were* in all his realm. — Daniel 1:4,20

About fifteen years before Daniel and his companions were taken into captivity, during the days of Josiah the King of Judah, Hilkiah the priest found the book of the law in the house of the Lord. In the providence of God, Daniel and his companions were given about fifteen years to study God's law and gain their extraordinary knowledge, understanding, and wisdom. They could not have been younger than their late teens or early twenties when they were taken into captivity. These young men purposed not to defile themselves from the King's table, which shows that they were very principled in their behavior and careful to draw the line of separation between the sacred and the profane. Who, among all young men, were better prepared than these young men? For they had learned the ways of Lord before they had ever learned the ways of the heathen! In this sense, they were much better prepared than was Moses. Would to God that we raised such remarkable young men in these days.

PAUL'S EXAMPLE

Question: Surely you are wrong. Wasn't Paul a great scholar of the Greeks, and doesn't he declare himself to be an example for us to follow?

Answer: Let us grant, for just a moment, the premise that Paul was indeed an erudite of Greek literature and philosophy. What would this prove? Would it prove that we can or should become the same? Well, Paul was raised to be a Pharisee of Pharisees, and he often used his extensive knowledge of Pharisaism. Does this prove that we should become Pharisees? All that this proves is that, when it was necessary, Paul used to his advantage what he happened to possess, regardless of how he came to possess it. He exposed the errors of the Pharisees for the purpose of displaying the truth. We do not find him advocating that Christian children be raised in the ways of the Pharisees, but rather, in the way of Christ.

> Be ye followers of me, even as I also *am* of Christ. — First Corinthians 11:1

But, in fact, we grant no such notion that Paul was an erudite of the Greeks. As we argued in the exposition of Acts 17, Paul displays a paucity of Greek learning.

> The notion that he [Paul] was a finished classical scholar is, indeed, as we have shown already, a mere delusion; and the absence from his Epistles of every historical reference proves that, like the vast mass of his countrymen, he was indifferent to the history of the heathen, though profoundly versed in the history of Israel. — F. W. Farrar, *The Life and Work of St. Paul*, page 296.

Paul's quotations and allusions are as ordinary as our ability to quote the proverb, "A penny saved is a penny earned." Is this any proof that we are well read in all of the literature of the American founding fathers? (Even this assumes that Benjamin Franklin originated this expression – which itself is doubtful.) When a writer makes a "literary allusion" – if that is indeed what it is – he expects his audience to recognize and understand it – unless he is endeavoring to be obscure and expecting to be understood only by the initiates of some esoteric mystery. If a writer suspects his audience may not understand, then he attaches a little explanation – that is, unless his purpose is to display his mastery of obscure learning. We ascribe no such purposes to Paul. When Paul writes things "hard to be understood" (Second Peter 3:16), the difficulty does not lie in his literary allusions, but in the nature of the subject. So much for the arguments of those who have awarded Paul an honorary Ph.D. in classical literature and philosophy. There is no evidence for any New Testament writer being well read in Greek writers. If they were, then they were not at all burdened to display it. Their burden was different.

> For I determined not to know any thing among you, save Jesus Christ, and him crucified. — First Corinthians 2:2

> Let no man deceive himself. If any man among you seemeth to be wise in this world, let him become a fool, that he may be wise. For the wisdom of this world is foolishness with God. For it is written, He taketh the wise in their own craftiness. And again, The Lord knoweth the thoughts of the wise, that they are vain. — First Corinthians 3:18-20

2. Don't We Need to be Culturally Literate?

CULTURAL RESPONSE

Question: Don't we need to know our culture in order to work within it and to respond to it?

Answer: Are we going to conquer the culture for Christ, or are we going to let the culture conquer us? Though we may benefit from studying what *has* shaped us, we will benefit more from studying what *should* shape us. Our calling is to advance the cause of Christ. Our calling is not to advance western culture. Western culture is a mixed bag. It may contain many Christian influences – but those influences are impure, and fading fast away. Western culture is not something to be worshiped, but something to be redeemed. We want real religion, not tradition. The real source of all that is good is neither the Greeks nor the Romans, neither the Mediaevals nor the Renaissance, neither the Reformation nor the Enlightenment, but the Bible. Why drink from the polluted stream when you can drink from the pure source? The ancients, mediaevals, and moderns may have many things of relative value, depending upon how they are used, but they have nothing of absolute value which we cannot do without. If all of western culture and civilization were somehow wiped from the face of the earth and from the folds of men's minds, then what would we need of western culture to restore in order to establish a Christian culture? That's the kind of question we should ask ourselves before we defend traditions of western culture.

> It is one of the curiosities of our civilization that we are content to go for our liberal education to literatures which, morally, are at an opposite pole from ourselves: literatures in which the most exalted tone is often an apotheosis [deification] of the sensuous, which degrade divinity, not only to the human level, but to the lowest level of humanity. Our hardest social problem being temperance, we study in Greek the glorification of intoxication. While in mature life we are occupied in tracing law to the remotest corner of the

> universe [in hope of justice], we go at school for literary impulse to the poetry that dramatizes the burden of hopeless fate. Our highest politics aim at conserving the arts of peace; our first poetic lessons are in an Iliad that cannot be appreciated without a bloodthirsty joy in killing. We seek to form a character in which delicacy and reserve shall be supreme, and at the same time are training our taste in literatures which, if published as English books, would be seized by the police. — Richard G. Moulton, *The Literary Study of the Bible*, page xii.

We suppose someone might accuse us of endeavoring to reinvent the wheel. Not at all. We are not saying that we should throw it all away. But we do not need to use every wheel we find in order to get the wagon rolling. Some wheels need some cleaning up, some wheels aren't worth fixing, and some wheels just don't belong. Do not misunderstand. God, in His providence, has left these things in this fallen world for us to pick through and use. But from what Scripture do we receive the impression that we should be constantly preoccupied with picking over this dust heap for seeds of thought, when the pure and nourishing grains of truth are all collected in one field for us to harvest? There is no experience of man, no philosophy of man, no emotion of man, and no truth that man needs, which is not inscribed in some form in Holy Writ. So we do not say, "throw it all out." We say, "dismiss those works which are not redeemable, and redeem those works which are." None of the literature has intrinsic worth. Its worth comes only from its usefulness to Christ. So let us gather up what valuable classics – first class works – men have made, and put them to practical use as we move along in our work of building a Christian culture. Anything which we cannot use, let us not cling to it as a precious relic, but let us drop it as a weight which hinders us in our task. The devil delights in keeping us occupied at seemingly good but actually quite useless tasks.

LITERATURE AND HISTORY

Question: Don't we need to understand all kinds of literature in order to understand history?

Answer: We advocate the careful and critical study of history, but we must acknowledge that, outside of Scripture, history is the word of man. It cannot be entirely trusted. Every attempt to understand the past involves interpretation and speculation. We aren't suggesting that we will one day discover that Alexander the Great really didn't conquer the Mediterranean world, that it was really his otherwise unknown twin brother, Fredrick the Fraud. But remember who writes history, and you'll see what we mean. Some call Herodotus the father of history. Others call him the father of lies. Mark Twain said that history is a lie agreed upon. (There we go, quoting another pagan – but for our own purpose.) Our point is, there is much disagreement about history. These things all will perish. They have no lasting significance.

This having been said, it remains true that to more fully understand someone, we must understand where they are coming from. If we study the Greeks, then we need to know about their beliefs, about their laws, about their families, about their language, about their history – even if the record of these things is not absolutely reliable. Try to reconcile the following two quotes.

> Those who cannot remember the past are doomed to repeat it. — George Santayana, *A Life of Reason, Book One: Reason & Common Sense*, 1916.

> Who controls the past controls the future; who controls the present controls the past. — George Orwell, *1984*

George Santayana seems to say that those who don't learn the necessary lessons from past mistakes are more likely to repeat those mistakes. George Orwell seems to say that those who control the present are able to manipulate the record of the past to make it support their philosophy, which will control how people view the world, which will control how they will act in the future. Presuming the general accuracy of George Santayana's statement, we would want George Orwell's history to be in the control of people who have a Biblical worldview which informs them how to understand and to record history. So we would want Christians who operated consistently on the basis of a correct worldview to dominate the study of history. Otherwise we would have a more unreliable history upon which to build our understanding and learn our lessons, so as to avoid repeating the mistakes of history. History recorded by Marxists is very unreliable. Nevertheless, we must acknowledge that Scripture is the only thoroughly accurate record of history, and ultimately the only history which counts when all else fails.

CULTURAL ACQUAINTANCE

Question: Don't we need to be thoroughly familiar with the ancient authors, poetry, drama, and myths in order to recognize and understand them when they are referred to and discussed in literature and in every day life?

Answer: Studying tomes of ancient material so that we won't miss an infrequent reference to something? That's not a very good use of our time. Should we know all of the rock music groups of the fifties and sixties with their hit songs in order to recognize and understand them when they pop up? That would have been a poor use of our resources. How about yours?

This is no argument against any Christian ever studying any such things, and we make no such argument or assertion. We only point out that, for most people, it is not necessary, it is not a good use of resources, it has potential for evil, and there are much better ways to spend your time.

More than knowing all of the philosophers, one must know the true philosophy and how to go about recognizing and refuting any philosophy which contradicts it. We'll let you in on a secret: there are really only a few lies – with a multitude of variations; and there are really only a few refutations – with a multitude of variations. So you don't need to learn everything there is. Life is short. Learn what's useful, and put it to good use. You'll never run out of good uses. If you need to know some more about one particular form of a lie – well, you know the Trivium: gather your facts, analyze their relationships, and put your arguments in good form. It works.

MYTHOLOGIES: ANCIENT AND MODERN

Question: Isn't there educational value in the ancient pagan myths?

Answer: Let's examine modern mythology, then apply the principle backwards to ancient mythology. Evolution is indeed modern mythology disguised as science. We may visit a museum or a park, and be confronted with geological myths which presume millions and billions of years. The authors of these myths deny the Word of our Lord concerning the perfection of the original creation, the entrance of the curse of death through the fall of Adam, and the destruction of the earth's surface in the flood of Noah's time. Because they ignore revealed truth, and they speculate with a bias toward excusing themselves from accountability to God, they produce absurd theories, and ignore, hide, manipulate, or destroy the enormous amount of contrary evidence, while inventing – even faking – their own evidence. In modern culture, because we are constantly confronted with this myth of evolution, it is necessary to teach evolution to our children in contrast to the revealed truth of God's creation. Nevertheless, we do not teach to our young children the most degenerate notions of and excuses for evolution. They will learn or discover these notions and excuses soon enough without being confronted with them in childhood.

The modern myths, such as evolution, explain some of our modern culture, and the ancient myths explain some of ancient culture. We cannot avoid the ancient myths without avoiding the history with which they connect. So part of the process of teaching history is teaching the myths. But even as we are selective in teaching history, so we must be selective in teaching its most degenerate, depraved, or corrupting elements – especially the myths. We do not want to stir up the muddy bottom of the pool by dwelling upon a knowledge of the pagan myths. We must keep them in their museum cage, and display them when they serve the purpose of explaining something, such as an object lesson for contrast with the Biblical worldview.

We should focus on teaching a cohesive body of inseparable knowledge to be logically understood and wisely applied. Some mythological god may be an integral part of explaining that body of knowledge – and that's where it belongs. Remember, though Scripture notes that the plagues of the Exodus were against Egypt's gods, nevertheless, Scripture gives no details about these gods.

So let's not get bogged down with identifying the pagan gods after whom the months and weekdays are named. This trivia may seem interesting, and it may prove valuable to somebody, somewhere, sometime. But so might a million other things. We cannot know everything. Let's make sure we know the most important things. We have yet to hear of someone whispering with his dying breath, "I wish I had mastered more of my mythology."

3. How Should We Approach Classical Literature?

RAIDERS OF THE LOST ARTS

Question: Shouldn't we "plunder the Egyptians" and other pagans of their treasures?

Answer: We certainly agree with this principle:

> This is the portion of a wicked man with God . . . . Though he heap up silver as the dust, And prepare raiment as the clay; He may prepare it, but the just shall put it on, And the innocent shall divide the silver. — Job 27:13,16-17

> . . . the wealth of the sinner is laid up for the righteous. — Proverbs 13:22

God, in His providence, causes the wicked to labor and store, then he delivers their labors over to the righteous. This happens with individuals as well as with nations. The nation Israel came into the Promised Land and took over the Canaanite civilization.

> . . . to give thee great and goodly cities, which thou buildedst not, And houses full of all good *things*, which thou filledst not, and wells digged, which thou diggedst not, vineyards and olive trees, which thou plantedst not . . . . — Deuteronomy 6:10,11

It is important to note, however, that when they took possession of the land, they were commanded to clean up.

> . . . ye shall drive out all the inhabitants of the land from before you, and destroy all their pictures, and destroy all their molten images, and quite pluck down all their high places: — Numbers 33:52

The Israelites were to make a thorough break with the civilization of the Egyptians out of which they came, and to keep clean from the civilization of the Canaanites which they were invading. They were to make no mention of the names of their gods; they were to remove their altars, images, and places of worship; they were to take no silver and gold from them; and they were to enter into no covenants, leagues, or marriages with them, lest these things became an entangling snare.

In other words, the Israelites were to keep certain useful items of physical culture – built cities, filled houses, dug wells, planted vineyards and orchards; but they were to make a clean separation from their intellectual culture – matters of worship, idols made of precious metals, family relations.

Augustine of Hippo said:

> If those who are called philosophers, and especially the Platonists, have said anything which is true and in harmony with our faith, then we are not only not to shrink from it, but we are to claim it for our own use from those who have no lawful possession of it . . . . — Augustine, *De Doctrina Christiana* 40.

Though we agree with Augustine that all truth is our lawful possession as Christians, we must be careful about what we claim as our property. Unbelievers never say anything which rings true to us unless they borrowed it from our reality in the first place. Whatever we might find in pagan philosophers which seems true to us, was first stolen from reality, then adapted by the philosopher to his irrational worldview, where it was turned into falsehood. Such stolen goods will never become truth again until they are first removed from the philosopher's godless worldview and put back where they belong – back inside reality, which is the Christian worldview.

We must not love pagan literature for its own beauty, because its own beauty appears only in its own light, which is darkness. Only what is redeemed and displayed in Christian light is truly beautiful.

We are not saying that we must avoid all Greek and Roman literature. We are only saying that if we are going to plunder Egypt, then we must do just that. We shouldn't be picking over Egypt for every last crumb, but we should be riding off with the precious metals and jewels. Not everyone will draw the line at the same place, but here are some principles to help us to recognize where to draw the line.

1. NEW COVENANT USE.

Much of Old Covenant law was the application of moral principle to a childish nation. The "touch not, taste not, handle not" rules of the Old Covenant may be compared to our telling our little children "touch not the stove, taste not the wine, handle not the glassware." These rules keep them safe when they cannot understand the principles for using these things lawfully. Under the law of the Old Covenant, pagan literature was under a total ban. This ban was not itself an absolute moral *law*, but it was the "childish" application of the absolute moral *principle* that we must separate from those cultures which are built upon pagan presuppositions. The New Covenant is the era of maturity, where the believing remnant is removed from the bondage of children into the freedom of mature sons of God. If we bound ourselves by the wineskins of childish Old Covenant applications, then those childish constraints would burst when they were filled with the wine of mature New Covenant liberty. So what would be the mature New Covenant adult manner of applying this same principle?

> Casting down imaginations [/reasonings], and every high thing that exalteth itself against the knowledge of God, and bringing into captivity every thought to the obedience of Christ; — Second Corinthians 10:5

Because every thought of pagan origin is placed in the setting of the wrong worldview, it is an enemy which must be taken captive and made to obey Christ. In other words, every thought must either be polished and made to shine in the light of Christ's glory, or else it must be tossed into the rubbish heap filled with examples of the vanity of the ungodliness, and unrighteousness of men who suppress the truth in unrighteousness.

2. PRACTICAL USE.

Some of the works of pagans, when they are redeemed and sanctified, have a lawful and most practical use in Christ's service. We are to make them slaves to serve Christ. For example, the unbelievers, such as

Aristotle, who have labored to develop the science of reasoning, are our servants, giving us this technical tool for discerning the truth. We must always be careful, however, that we do not allow the unbelievers to deceive us into lies or traps, or to fool us into giving these tools an unlawful use.

3. APOLOGETIC USE.

Logic is also a worthy weapon in our arsenal, and we are glad to have our enemies help us to develop our weaponry against them. We may use logic lawfully when we press the claim that their world of unbelief is out of line with reality. When we point out the contradictions which abound within their very own words, the Lord may use this as a very effective means of either leading them to conversion, or at least stopping their mouths so that others can hear us.

4. EDUCATIONAL USE.

Some truths are better understood when they are contrasted with an opposing error. The countering of an error, point by point, with truth, will display the beautiful logic of the truth, and will glorify God. A good example of this is the contrast of the ancient myth of evolution along with all of its implications, both ancient and modern, with the Scripture account of creation.

We must be the true "raiders of the lost arts," redeeming what is redeemable, while not having bought what is best forgotten. Remember the fall of King Saul.

> . . . and Saul said unto him [Samuel], Blessed *be* thou of the LORD: I have performed the commandment of the LORD. And Samuel said, What *meaneth* then this bleating of the sheep in mine ears, and the lowing of the oxen which I hear? . . . the LORD . . . said, Go and utterly destroy the sinners the Amalekites, and fight against them until they be consumed. Wherefore then didst thou not obey the voice of the LORD, but didst fly upon the spoil, and didst evil in the sight of the LORD? And Saul said unto Samuel, Yea, I . . . have utterly destroyed the Amalekites. But the people took of the spoil, sheep and oxen, the chief of the things which should have been utterly destroyed, to sacrifice unto the LORD thy God in Gilgal. — First Samuel 15:13-14,18-21

Saul's error was in not obeying the commandment of the Lord to destroy all. We may not be commanded to destroy all, but in keeping back what some may consider the best, indulging some fleshly or worldly notions of good, we may fall into the same error as Saul by not destroying what we should.

Remember, some things out of pagan culture may be useful – perhaps very useful, but nothing of pagan culture is absolutely necessary. Nothing. So, if there are any reservations as to the usefulness of something, then "when in doubt, throw it out."

> . . . without faith *it is* impossible to please *him* . . . . — Hebrews 11:6

> . . . for whatsoever *is* not of faith is sin. — Romans 14:23

Tertullian (A.D. c.160/170- c.215/220) was considered a brilliant defender of the Christian faith, a Christian rhetorician of the highest order. He wrote,

> What, indeed, has Athens to do with Jerusalem? What concord is there between the Academy [the philosophy of Plato] and the Church? . . . Away with all attempts to produce a mottled Christianity of Stoic, Platonic, and dialectic composition! — Tertullian, *De Praescriptione* 7.

> What likeness is there between the philosopher and the Christian, the disciple of Greece and the disciple of heaven, the trader in reputation and the trader in salvation, the doer of words and the worker of deeds, the builder up and the destroyer of things, the friend and the enemy of error, the corrupter and the restorer and exponent of truth, its thief and its guardian? — Tertullian, *Apology* 46.

Tertullian was by no means alone in this opinion. It was the common opinion in his day. Nevertheless, Tertullian and Justin Martyr, Tatian and Aristides, Athenagoras and Lactantius, and many other apologists, were not afraid to quote or allude to the philosophers and poets. Indeed, the Christian apologists were as well educated in rhetoric and the law as any men in the Roman Empire. But they were careful how they used these things.

In the final analysis, we ourselves prefer to allow someone other than our own children to trod through the hog lot of classical literature, to muddle about in the dung of perverted reason and practice, and to bring back the few kernels of corn or the pearls of wisdom which may be found there. Notice, we are not saying that no one has any business in the hog lot. A few have a special calling to work in these things. What there is of worth has been salvaged, collected, and, for the most part, improved upon, and we all appreciate what pearls they have found. We may show our children those pearls in the brilliant light of the gospel. But we do not need to send our children down to the hog lot of human depravity in order to work like scavengers to find these things for themselves. Our time is better spent on the collected and improved product.

Aristotle is worse than worthless unless his work is evaluated by Scripture and transformed for lawful use. But even Popeye the Sailor can be of some worth when evaluated in the light of Scripture. So instead of a *Great Books* curriculum, we recommend, first of all, a *Great Book* curriculum – the Bible. No other book holds a candle to it. The Bible is not just one of many great pieces of literature. It is the only great piece of literature. It is the Word of God. If all other literature was lost, then we could rebuild the greatest civilization upon the foundation of the Word of God alone.

4. How Do We Maintain a Proper Separation?

How Do We Stay Pure?

Question: How can we walk about in pagan culture and not have some rub off on us?

Answer: In painting a room, no matter how carefully we handle the brush and the paint, somehow the stuff finds a way of getting on us. So when we are done, what do we do? We don't immerse ourselves in the paint. We scrub down in the shower and wash all of the contaminants away. It is impossible that the world – ancient, mediaeval, or modern world – will not drop spots of paint on us. Nevertheless we must keep ourselves "unspotted from the world" (James 1:27). So we need to scrub down regularly.

> Wherewithal shall a young man cleanse his way? by taking heed *thereto* according to thy word. — Psalms 119:9

> Now ye are clean through the word which I have spoken unto you. — John 15:3

> Sanctify them through thy truth: thy word is truth. — John 17:17

> That he might sanctify and cleanse it with the washing of water by the word, — Ephesians 5:26

> Seeing ye have purified your souls in obeying the truth through the Spirit unto unfeigned love of the brethren, *see that ye* love one another with a pure heart fervently: — First Peter 1:22

Purification only comes by a separation process – whether by sifting, sorting, burning, melting, skimming, distilling, washing, rinsing. It is the Word of God which performs that separation process on us.

> For the word of God *is* quick, and powerful, and sharper than any two-edged sword, piercing even to the dividing asunder of soul and spirit, and of the joints and marrow, and *is* a discerner of the thoughts and intents of the heart.
> — Hebrews 4:12

The world has a mindset – a habit of mind, whether it's the ancient world, the mediaeval world, the modern world, or any of the sub-worlds within these worlds. We are to be the light of the world and the salt of the earth. We are to affect the world, not be infected by the world. The only way which we can affect the world is to preach and teach, live and work the Word of God, and the only way we can protect ourselves from being infected by the world is to continually wash ourselves with that same Word. So a constant immersion into the corrupting world – its literature, its philosophy, its habits – must be avoided, while a frequent affusion by the cleansing Word – its principles, its rules, its doctrines – must be invited.

Chapter Nine

An Application of Principles for the Study of Historical Literature

The thing that hath been, it *is that* which shall be; and that which is done *is* that which shall be done: and *there is* no new *thing* under the sun. — Ecclesiastes 1:9

THIS CHAPTER IS AN APPLICATION of the principles discussed in Chapter Eight. In this Chapter we will discuss some specific principles which apply to the study of history, then we will give a synopsis of world history from 753 B.C. through 323 B.C., listing events with their literary and historical resources, and giving our opinion as to which portions of these sources may be valuable to read.

THREE UNDERLYING PRINCIPLES FOR THE STUDY OF HISTORY

1. Knowledge Level: "History repeats itself."

To state this in Biblical terms: God so rules over circumstances that similar actions regularly have similar consequences.

> The thing that hath been, it *is that* which shall be; and that which is done *is* that which shall be done: and *there is* no new *thing* under the sun. — Ecclesiastes 1:9

2. Understanding Level: "The past is key to the future."

If you know what has happened leading up to the moment, then you will know where things are likely leading. To state this in Biblical terms: Given the circumstances, we cannot escape the consequences. As we stand in the stream of events, what we see coming down the stream will eventually pass by us.

> That which hath been is now; and that which is to be hath already been; and God requireth that which is past. — Ecclesiastes 3:15

3. Wisdom Level: "He who does not study history is doomed to repeat it."

If we do not study history and learn its lessons, then we are less likely to interrupt the pattern discerned by those who do study history. If we know how similar things have concluded, and we know what has happened leading up to the present moment, then we may know how to intervene to change events and to interrupt the pattern.

> . . . the children of Issachar, *which were men* that had understanding of the times, to know what Israel ought to do . . . . — First Chronicles 12:32

But if we do not know these things, then we are less likely to recognize the significancy of the moment and to act in order to alter the pattern. Therefore, we will repeat the pattern.

> . . . O *ye* hypocrites, ye can discern the face of the sky; but can ye not *discern* the signs of the times? — Matthew 16:3

To state this in Biblical terms: If God should grant repentance, then we can change the given circumstances and the resulting consequences.

> *At what* instant I shall speak concerning a nation, and concerning a kingdom, to pluck up, and to pull down, and to destroy *it*; If that nation, against whom I have pronounced, turn from their evil, I will repent of the evil that I thought to do unto them. And *at what* instant I shall speak concerning a nation, and concerning a kingdom, to build and to plant *it*; If it do evil in my sight, that it obey not my voice, then I will repent of the good, wherewith I said I would benefit them. — Jeremiah 18:7

> And Jonah began to enter into the city a day's journey, and he cried, and said, Yet forty days, and Nineveh shall be overthrown. . . . Who can tell *if* God will

turn and repent, and turn away from his fierce anger, that we perish not? And God saw their works, that they turned from their evil way; and God repented of the evil, that he had said that he would do unto them; and he did *it* not. — Jonah 3:4,9,10

AN INTRODUCTION TO THE STUDY OF HISTORY

History is the teller of stories. It is a narration of events in the order in which they occurred, and an attempt to explain their causes and their effects. Apart from the record of history revealed in Scripture, history is an inexact science. The activities of the past can only be reconstructed from the remains of the past – historical sources, in whatever state of preservation. So history must depend upon the development of other sciences in order to improve its accuracy.

Historical fact and *historical record* must be sharply distinguished. The historical fact is what indeed actually happened. The historical record of the fact is what someone believes happened from his own narrow perspective. (The historical record of a magician's show may be very different from the historical fact.) First, an objective historical event takes place. Then the event is subjectively recorded in one or more ways, from one or more perspectives. Ignorance, prejudice, passion, and the tricks of the mind and memory become a part of the record – along with any physical defects in the way the record is preserved. Even if the record is relatively objective, it is nevertheless always incomplete – the event cannot be perfectly recreated from the record. The historian collects the physical remains of an event, and the recorded descriptions of the event, and he attempts to interpret these sources. This adds still another level of subjectivity to history. Because of this interpretive element, absolute certainty about historical fact is impossible, apart from direct revelation from God.

The one great history book is the Bible. It is an anchor in the midst of man's conflicting records of history. The Bible teaches historical facts – such as the origin of all things, the division of races, and the causes of God's judgements upon men and nations – which form principles which can be applied to historical events in order to discern the truth of a matter.

One approach to the study of history is to study how the philosophies of men have worked their way out into their actions. What men believe eventually works out into what they do. If we can discern the philosophy which prevails in any given age, then we can observe what the fruits of that philosophy are within that age. The next step is to study God's philosophy and actions which explain man's philosophy and actions. Only the Bible can explain universal history, because only the Bible is the word of the universal God.

AN OUTLINE FOR EVALUATING HISTORICAL DOCUMENTS

The Value of Primary Sources

Perhaps the most important part in determining the trustworthiness of an historical account is knowing how far the writer or historian was removed from the event. In other words, is he a primary or a secondary source? As Ken Ham would put it, "Were you there?" Primary sources are the meat and potatoes of an historian's diet. They are where he obtains the essential information.

What is a Primary Source?

A *primary* source is a direct link between us and someone or something which was actually present when the event which we are studying occurred. Eyewitness accounts, original documents, surviving objects, photographs, audio or video recordings are all examples of primary sources.

What is Important About a Primary Source?

Primary sources are valuable because they are closest to the action – as close to the action as anyone can be. A primary source has not been "handled" by others, each contributing his own interpretations and biases to the record. Therefore, a primary source is ordinarily a more accurate record of the original event as the eyewitnesses originally experienced it. An account of the burning of Rome would be more credible as to detail if the author was actually there when it happened.

What is a Secondary Source?

In the courtroom, a *secondary* source is called "hearsay evidence." It is information given by someone who was not at the original scene, but who heard about it from someone else, who in turn may have heard about it from someone else, eventually tracing its way back to the original event. The more times a story has been handled, ordinarily the less reliable it becomes, because interpretations and biases are usually attached with each handling. History textbooks, encyclopedias and historical novels are all examples of secondary sources.

If we wrote a history of WWII, that history would be a secondary source because we were not alive during WWII, and our record is "second hand."

If we have only one early record of an event, and it is a secondary source, then we call this a *principle* source. This is less reliable than a primary source, but it is all we have. Homer could not be considered a primary source for the Trojan war because he was not there, but we have no record from someone who was there, so Homer is our most useful source. Regarding ancient history, much of the literature we have is not primary in the strictest sense, but because it is all we have, most historians refer to the ancient literature as primary.

Biases, Interpretations and Other Distortions

Even if we begin with a primary source, this is no guarantee that the record is characteristically accurate. A secondary source which has passed through one or more intermediaries may actually be more accurate than a primary source. How can this be? Our secondary source may have received its information from a primary source which was less biased than our primary source.

Criteria for Critical Evaluation of Sources

Here are some questions to consider when evaluating sources:

1. *Does the witness have any peculiar biases or agendas*? The witness himself does not need to be aware of his bias for it to affect his record. A witness who grew up in Alabama may express an unconscious bias in his account of the battle of Gettysburg. This fact needs to be carefully weighed, but it must also not be stereotyped. ("He says the south was right only because he is from the deep south.") The fact that one is from the losing side does not mean he cannot give accurate information, nor does it mean the winning side is more accurate.
2. *Does the witness have a reason to lie or distort the evidence*? Someone present on Lexington Green in 1775 may have a reason to lie about who fired the first shot, depending upon what side he was on. Someone with no discernible reason to distort or lie about an event is a more desirable witness.
3. *Was the witness knowledgeable enough concerning a subject to be capable of describing it accurately for our purposes*? An ordinary landsman may not know enough about ships to correctly

describe a naval battle.

4. *Was the witness telling us what he saw* – "Russians don't smile very much" – *or what he inferred* – "Russians are a depressed race."
5. *Was the witness in a good position to accurately chronicle the event?* He may not have been close enough, or the conditions may have been too difficult for him to have fully grasped the events. ("He said it was a good play, but he was too far away in the balcony to see it well." "He may not have been close enough to have known why the president made the decision.") For the same reasons, even tape recorders, video cameras and other solid evidence may give us improper or incomplete evidence. An artifact which has been found may be uncharacteristic of others found in the same area.

More Than One Point of View

Was there more than one witness to an event? If so, do the witnesses agree? If they do not agree, then the matter must be investigated more deeply. Two persons may view the same event from different angles, and their description from their perspective may be accurate, yet they may not seem to agree. If we watched a magician perform from the perspective of the audience, we would see one thing. If we were backstage, or one of the magician's assistants, then we would see it all another way. The audience may have seen quite accurately, but incompletely, which, in their minds, produced an illusion contrary to fact. When we have apparently conflicting accounts, it would be necessary to disqualify at least a portion of the testimony – unless a way is found to reconcile them. In the case of the magician, the conflicting accounts could be reconciled by taking into account the different perspectives.

Historical Fallacies

When analyzing historical events, we are more likely to commit certain errors in reasoning:

1. *Post hoc ergo propter hoc.* (After this, therefore, because of this.) This argues that if one thing happened after another, then the first thing must have caused the second. "The Boston tea party caused the War for Independence because it happened right before the war."
2. *False scenario.* Arguing that if something in history had not happened, then all the events following it would never have happened either. "If General MacArthur had never been born,

then we would all be speaking Japanese now."

3. *Faulty analogy*. Arguing that two things which are similar in some ways, are similar in virtually all ways. "Both the American revolution and the French revolution involved an unhappy populace getting rid of a king, therefore both revolutions must have pursued the same ideals."
4. *Hasty generalization*. Over generalizing without enough of a sample. "Cretans are all liars, evil beasts and lazy. I've met several that were that way."
5. *Proof by failure to find contrary evidence*. Assuming something has been proven true just because it has not been proven false yet. "Cretans are all liars, evil beasts and lazy. I have yet to meet one that wasn't."
6. *Proof by obviousness*. Something must be true because "everybody knows" it. "Everybody knows that Cretans are all liars, evil beasts and lazy."
7. *Proof by mass*. Proving an argument's validity by the sheer number of arguments or evidence in favor of it – even though all the arguments or evidence may be based on false assumptions. "We have checked literally hundreds of documents, and they all say the Romans had bad plumbing."
8. *Appeal to authority*. Arguing based on views of people in authority. "This historian says that the cause for the fall of Rome was because of their lack of proper plumbing. He must be right. After all, he's famous."
9. *Either or reasoning*. Presenting an issue as if there were only a few possible explanations, when there could be more. "The fall of Rome was either caused by their lack of plumbing, or aliens from outer space infiltrating them. Rome had a very good plumbing system so it must have been the aliens."
10. *Ad hominem attack*. Discrediting a man's argument by discrediting the man, not his argument. "Don't trust what that man says. He's a Cretan. Everybody knows they are all liars, evil beasts and lazy."

This is obviously only a partial list, but we all understand the principle that historians are subject to the same infirmities of fallacy as are we all.

A SAMPLE MODEL FOR COMBINING HISTORY AND LITERATURE:

Ancient Greece and Contemporary Civilizations

When we study history, we must consider primary sources first. People who actually witness an historical event are considered primary sources for the time period of the event, and the literature which was written during a particular time period is considered primary sources for that time period. Here is an example. In about 472 B.C. a man named Aeschylus wrote an historical play called *The Persians*, which presents in dramatic form the invasion of Xerxes (King of Persia) and his overthrow by the Greeks at Salamis. This play is considered a primary source of the highest quality for two reasons: first, this play was written only a few years after the battle of Salamis (literature written during a time period is considered a primary source for that time period); and secondly, Aeschylus was actually present at the battle of Salamis (eye witnesses to an historical event are considered primary sources). Here is another example. Herodotus wrote a book called *The History*, which is an historical account of the wars which Persia waged against Greece from the time of Cyrus to about 479 B.C. Herodotus is also considered a primary source, but not of as high a quality as our previous example. Herodotus was born in about 484 B.C., so he was not even alive for most of the time about which he wrote. He was not an eye witness to the events he described. Yet, historians prefer to consider Herodotus a primary source because he wrote his history shortly after the events he described and we have almost no other records of the events for that time period. So he is sort of a primary source by default. Technically, he would be a principle source, but not a primary source. Much of ancient historical literature falls into this category.

In order to show you how to study history using primary sources and also to show you how to combine the study of history with the study of literature, we have constructed a study of the time period from the founding of Rome (753 B.C.) through the death of Alexander the Great (323 B. C.) – 430 years. We have covered the civilizations of Israel, Egypt, Assyria, Babylonia, Persia, Greece, and Rome.

In the charts on the following pages, we have placed a timeline on the left hand page, noting the major events and personalities. On the right hand page, we have listed the literature which was written during that time period – or in some cases, literature which was written shortly after that time period but still close enough to be considered by historians to be primary sources. This is a skeleton of a timeline, with only the major events and personalities listed.

We list the Biblical literature first. It should be treated as the highest quality primary source because it is the inspired record of God. Next to the Biblical literature we list the secular literature. Some of the secular literature which we list can be read by Knowledge Level students, but most of it should be left until the Understanding and Wisdom Levels.

Warning: Reading classical literature, especially Greek and Roman literature, can be dangerous. Though we have purged out of our lists the worst examples of obscenity and perversion, it is nevertheless a fact that an occasional instance of this is found in almost any of the literature of this period. Though we give our own opinion as to which pieces of literature may be profitable reading, we do not endorse every word in this literature as profitable, and you the parent must proceed with all due caution and reserve.

In the Resource List at the back of the book we direct you to where you can find copies of all of the primary sources.

B.C.	*Judah*	*Israel*	*Egypt*	*Assyria /Babylon /Persia*	*Greece*	*Rome*
753	Jotham (crowned 758)	Pekah (crowned 759)		Ashur-nirari (crowned 754) Assyria is world power		Rome founded/Romulus first king
752 751 750 749 748 747 746						
745				Tiglath-pileser III crowned		
744 743						
742	Ahaz crowned					
741						
740		Pekah slain/no king till 729				
739 738 737 736 735 734 733 732 731 730						
729		Hoshea crowned				
728						
727				Shalmaneser crowned		
726	Hezekiah crowned					
725 724 723 722						

B.C.	*Biblical Literature*	*Secular Literature*
753	Jotham: 2 Kings 15; 2 Chr onicles 27; Isaiah 1-6; Hos; Mic 1-2 Pekah: 2 Kings 15, 16; 2 Chr onicles 28; Hos; Mic	Ancient Geography by Strabo (Greek geographer b.66BC d.24AD) Bk 5.3 (Founding and grandeur of Rome) "Romulus" in Parallel Lives by Plutarch (Greek biographer b.50AD d.125AD) Antiquities of the Jews by Josephus (Jewish priest/historian b.37AD d.95AD) Bk 9, Ch11 (Jotham, Pekah) Ancient Geography by Strabo Bk 17.1.4 (The Nile) The History by Herodotus (Greek historian)Bk 2.1-2.98 (Egyptian history) History of the Peloponnesian War by Thucydides (Greek historian) Bk 1.2-1.11 (Primitive Greece) Natural History by Pliny the Elder(Roman historian b.23AD d.79AD) Bk 3.6, 3.38-3.42 (Early Rome) Republic by Cicero (Roman historian and orator b.106BC d.43BC) Bk 2.5-2.17 (Romulus) The Early History of Rome by Livy (Roman historian b.59BC d.17AD) Bk 1 The Roman Antiquities by Dionysius of Halicarnassus (Greek historian and rhetorician b.55BC d.7BC) Bk 1.1-2.56 (Early Rome through Romulus)
742	Ahaz: 2 Kin 16; 2 Chr 28; Is 1, 7-10, 17; Hos; Mic	Antiquities of the Jews by Josephus Bk 9, Ch 12 (Ahaz, Pekah)
729	Hoshea: 2 Kin 17, 18; 2 Chr 30, 31; Is 28; Hos 5-14; Mic	Antiquities of the Jews by Josephus Bk 9, Ch 13 (Hoshea, Hezekiah)
726	Hezekiah: 2 Kin 18-20; 2 Chr 29-32; Is 11-16, 18-27, 29-66; Mic 3-7	

B.C.	*Judah*	*Israel*	*Egypt*	*Assyria /Babylon /Persia*	*Greece*	*Rome*
721		Israel carried away captive to Assyria by Sargon		Sargon crowned		
720 719 718 717 716						
715						Numa (2nd king of Rome) rules
714 713 712 711 710 709 708 707 706 705						
704				Sennacherib crowned		
703 702 701 700 699						
698	Manasseh crowned					
697 696 695 694 693 692 691 690						
689				Sennacherib destroys Babylon		
688 687 686 685 684						

B.C.	*Biblical Literature*	*Secular Literature*
721		Antiquities of the Jews by Josephus Bk 9, Ch 14
715		"Numa" in Parallel Lives by Plutarch The Roman Antiquities by Dionysius of Halicarnassus Bk 2.57-2.76
713		Antiquities of the Jews by Josephus Bk 10, Ch 1-2
698	Manasseh: 2 Kin 19, 21; 2 Chr 33; Is 22, 37; Mic	Antiquities of the Jews by Josephus Bk 10, Ch 3

B.C.	*Judah*	*Israel*	*Egypt*	*Assyria /Babylon /Persia*	*Greece*	*Rome*
683					Creon first archon of Athens	
682						
681				Esarhaddon crowned		
680 679 678 677 676 675 674 673 672 671						
670						Tullus Hostilius (3rd king of Rome) crowned
669						
668				Asurbanipal crowned		
667 666 665 664 663 662 661 660 659 658 657 656 655 654 653 652 651 650 649 648 647 646 645 644						

B.C.	*Biblical Literature*	*Secular Literature*
670		The Roman Antiquities by Dionysius of Halicarnassus Bk 3.1-3.35

B.C.	*Judah*	*Israel*	*Egypt*	*Assyria /Babylon /Persia*	*Greece*	*Rome*
643	Amon crowned					
642						
641	Josiah crowned				Thales (Greek philosopher)born	
640 639						
638						Ancus Marcius (4th king of Rome) crowned
637 636 635 634 633 632 631 630 629 628 627 626 625						
624					Draco (Greek archon) draws up code of laws	
623 622 621						
620					Aesop wrote and compiled fables	
619 618 617 616 615						
614						Lucius Tarquinius (5th king of Rome) crowned
613						

B.C.	*Biblical Literature*	*Secular Literature*
643	Amon: 2Kin 21; 2 Chr 33	Antiquities of the Jews by Josephus Bk 10, Ch 4
641	Josiah: 2 Kin 22-23; 2 Chr 34-35; Jer 1-12; Nah 1-3; Hab; Zeph 1-3	"Thales" in Lives of the Philosophers by Diogenes Laertius
638		The Roman Antiquities by Dionysius of Halicarnassus Bk 3.36-3.45
624		Constitution of Athens by Aristotle Ch 2-4
620		Aesop's Fables
614		The Roman Antiquities by Dionysius of Halicarnassus Bk 3.46-3.73

B.C.	*Judah*	*Israel*	*Egypt*	*Assyria /Babylon /Persia*	*Greece*	*Rome*
612				Nabopolass-ar rules/Babyl-on now world power		
611						
610	Jehoahaz crowned/taken captive to Egypt/died		Necho begins rule/inva-des Judah			
609	Jehoiakim crowned					
608 607 606						
605	Jehoiakim submits to Nebuchadnezzar/Dan-iel and others taken to Babylon			Nebuchadn-ezzar crowned		
604 603						
602	Jehoiakim rebels against Nebuchadnezzar					
601						
600					Sappho (female lyric poet) born	
599						
598	Jehoiakim killed by Nebuchadnezzar/Jeho-iachin crowned/Neb takes Jerusalem and deports Jehoiachin and others to Babylon					
597	Zedediah crowned/subject to Neb					
596 595						

B.C.	*Bibilical Literature*	*Secular Literature*
610	Jehoahaz: 2 Kin 23; 2 Chr 36; Jeremiah 22	Antiquities of the Jews by Josephus Bk 10, Ch 5
609	Jehoiakim: 2 Kin 23-24; 2 Chr 36; Jeremiah 13-20, 22, 25-27, 35-36, 45-49, 52; Daniel 1-2; Habakkuk 1-3	
605		Antiquities of the Jews by Josephus Bk 10, Ch 6 Ancient Geography by Strabo Bk 16.1.5 (Babylon)
598	Jehoiachin: 2 Kin 24-25; 2 Chr 36; Jeremiah 22; Ezekiel	Antiquities of the Jews by Josephus Bk 10, Ch 7
597	Zedekiah: 2 Kin 24-25; 2 Chr 36; Jeremiah 21-24, 27-30, 31-34, 37-39,51-52; Ezekiel 1-24, 26-31; Daniel; Obadiah; Lamentations 1-5	

B.C.	*Judah*	*Israel*	*Egypt*	*Assyria /Babylon /Persia*	*Greece*	*Rome*
594					Solon's (Greek statesman) reforms in Athens creates Democracy	
593 592 591 590						
589	Zedekiah makes treaty with Egypt					
588	Neb. lays siege to Jerusalem					
587						
586	Neb. burns temple/destroys Jerusalem/takes Zedekiah and others captive/Zed. dies in Babylon			Nebucha-dnezzar destroys Jerusalem temple		
585 584 583						
582					Pythagoras (Greek philosopher) born	
581 580 579 578 577						
576						Servius Tullis (6th king) crowned
575 574 573 572 571 570 569						

B.C.	*Bibilical Literature*	*Secular Literature*
594		"Solon" in Parallel Lives by Plutarch Select Fragments of poetry by Solon The History by Herodotus Bk 1.29-1.33 (Solon) The Constitution of Athens by Aristotle Chaps 5-12 (Solon)
586	Captivity under Nebuchadnezzar: 2 Kin 25; Jeremiah 39-44, 46, 52; Ezekiel 25, 28-30, 32-48; Daniel 3-4	Antiquities of the Jews by Josephus Bk 10, Ch 8-10
582		"Pythagoras" in Lives of the Philosophers by Diogenes Laertius Ancient Geography by Strabo Bk 10.3-10.10
576		The Roman Antiquities by Dionysius of Halicarnassus Bk 4.1-4.40

B.C.	*Judah*	*Israel*	*Egypt*	*Assyria /Babylon /Persia*	*Greece*	*Rome*
568 567 566 565 564 563						
562	Jehoiachin favored in Babylon			Evil-Merodach crowned		
561						
560				Neriglissar crowned	Pisistratus rules Greece	
559 558 557						
556				Nabonidua/Belshazzar rules		
555 554 553 552 551 550 549 548 547 546 545 544 543 542 541 540						
539				Cyrus defeats Babylon/Persia now world power		
538 537						
536	Judah returns from captivity/rebuilding of temple begun by Zerubbal and Joshua					
535 534 533						

B.C.	*Bibilical Literature*	*Secular Literature*
562	Captivity under Evil-Merodach: 2 Kin 25; Jeremiah 52	Antiquities of the Jews by Josephus Bk 10, Ch 11
560		The Constitution of Athens by Aristotle Chaps 14-17 "Pisistratus" (at the end of "Solon") in Parallel Lives by Plutarch
556	Captivity under Belshazzar: Isaiah 13; Jeremiah 25, 50-51; Daniel 5, 7-8	
539	Captivity under Cyrus: 2 Chron 36; Ezra 1-6; Nehemiah 7, 12; Isaiah 44; Daniel 1, 6, 9-12	The Education of Cyrus the Great by Xenophon The History by Herodotus Bk 1.45-1.216
536		Antiquities of the Jews by Josephus Bk 11, Ch 1

B.C.	*Judah*	*Israel*	*Egypt*	*Assyria /Babylon /Persia*	*Greece*	*Rome*
532						Tarquinus II (7th king) crowned
531						
530				Cambyses crowned		
529 528						
527			Persia conque-rs Egypt			
526						
525					Aeschylus born Greek tragedian	
524 523						
522				Darius crowned	Pinder (lyric poet) born	
521 520 519 518 517						
516	temple completed					
515 514 513 512 511 510						
509						Tarquin kings expelled /Republic begins
508						first treaty between Rome and Carthage
507 506 505 504 503 502 501						

B.C.	*Bibilical Literature*	*Secular Literature*
532		The Roman Antiquities by Dionysius of Halicarnassus Bk 4.41-4.53
530	Captivity under Cambyses: Ezra 4	The History by Herodotus Bk 2.99-2.182 Antiquities of the Jews by Josephus Bk 11, Ch 2
527		The History by Herodotus Bk 3.1-3.88
525		Aeschylus wrote 6 tragedies based on the myths (not recommended) and one historical tragedy about the battle of Salamis (a valuable primary source since Aeschylus was present at this battle).
522	Captivity under Darius I: Ezra 5-6; Haggai 1-2; Zechariah 1-8	Pinder was connected with the worship of Apollo and wrote victory odes. Not recommended. The History by Herodotus Bk 3.89-6.93 Antiquities of the Jews by Josephus Bk 11, Ch 3
516	Restoration under Darius I: Ezra 6; Zechariah 9-14	The Behistan inscription of King Darius (engraved in rock in ancient Persia) Antiquities of the Jews by Josephus Bk 11, Ch 4
509		The Early History of Rome by Livy Bk 2 The Roman Antiquities by Dionysius of Halicarnassus Bk 4.54-4.85 and Bks 5-11
508		The Histories by Polybius (Greek historian b.200BC d.123BC) Bk 3.22

B.C.	*Judah*	*Israel*	*Egypt*	*Assyria /Babylon /Persia*	*Greece*	*Rome*
500					Cleisthenes' (Greek statesman) influence in politics	
499 498						
497					Sophocles (Greek tragedian) born	
496 495 494 493 492 491						
490					Battle of Marathon/Themistocles rules	
489 488 487						
486				Xerxes crowned		
485					Herodotus (Greek historian) born	
484 483 482						
481					Euripides (Greek tragedian) born	
480					Battle of Thermopolae/Antiphon (Greek orator) born	
479					Battle of Salamis/end of Persian wars	
478 477 476 475 474 473 472 471						
470					Socrates (Greek philosopher) born	
469					Pericles rules Athens	
468 467 466 465						

B.C.	*Biblical Literature*	*Secular Literature*
500		The Constitution of Athens by Aristotle Chaps 20-22
495		Sophocles wrote 7 tragedies based on myths. Not recommended.
490		The History by Herodotus Bk 6.94-6.140 "Themistocles" in Parallel Lives by Plutarch
486	Restoration under Xerxes: Esther	The History by Herodotus Bks 7-9 Antiquities of the Jews by Josephus Bk 11, Ch 5
481		Euripides wrote 17 tragedies based on myths. Not recommended.
480		First and Second Tetralogies and select speeches by Antiphon
479		Historical Library by Diodorus Siculus (Sicilian historian b.90BC d.21BC) Book 11 "The Persians" by Aeschylus (historical play)
478		The History of the Peloponnesian War by Thucydides Bk 1.12-1.146 (history of time between Persian Wars and Peloponnesian War)
469		"Pericles" in Parallel Lives by Plutarch The Constitution of Athens by Aristotle Chaps 24, 26-27

B.C.	*Judah*	*Israel*	*Egypt*	*Assyria /Babylon /Persia*	*Greece*	*Rome*
464				Artaxerxes I crowned		
463 462 461						
460					Hippocrates(Greek physician) born	
459						
458	Return of Ezra to Judea from captivity					
457 456						
455					Thucydides (Greek historian) born	
454 453 452						
451						Dece-mvirate
450 449 448 447						
446					Aristophanes (Greek comedian) born	
445	Return of Nehemiah to Judea					
444 443 442 441 440 439 438 437						
436					Isocrates (Greek speech writer) born	
435 434 433 432						

B.C.	*Biblical Literature*	*Secular Literature*
464	Restoration under Artaxerxes I: Ezra 7-10; Nehemiah 1-9, 11, 13	Antiquities of the Jews by Josephus Bk 11, Ch 6
460		Selected works by Hippocrates: The Oath; On the Sacred Disease; On Airs, Waters and Places; On Ancient Medicine; etc.
451		The Early History of Rome by Livy Bk 3
450		Historical Library by Diodorus Siculus Book 12
446		Aristophanes wrote 11 comedy plays. Not recommended.
432		"First Speech" by Pericles found in History of the Peloponnesian War by Thucydides Bk 1.140-1.144

B.C.	*Judah*	*Israel*	*Egypt*	*Assyria /Babylon /Persia*	*Greece*	*Rome*
431					Peloponnesian War starts	
430					plague in Athens/Xenophon (Greek historian) born	
429						
428					Plato (Greek philosopher) born/Alcibiades rules Athens	
427 426 425 424						
423				Darius II crowned		
422 421 420 419 418 417 416 415 414 413 412 411 410 409 408 407 406 405						
404				Artaxerxes II crowned	Peloponnesian War ends/Athens falls/Sparta rules	
403 402 401 400 399						
398					Agesilaus rules Sparta	
397						
396						capture of Veii

B.C.	*Biblical Literature*	*Secular Literature*
431		"Funeral Speech" by Pericles in History of Peloponnesian War by Thucydides Bk 2.34-2.36; History of Peloponnesian War by Thucydides Bk 2
430		"Third Speech" by Pericles in History of Peloponnesian War by Thucydides Bk 2.59-2.64
429		Early History of Rome by Livy Book 4
428		History of Peloponnesian War by Thucydides Bk 3; "Alcibiades" in Parallel Lives by Plutarch
427		"Lysander" in Parallel Lives by Plutarch
425		History of Peloponnesian War by Thucydides Bk 4
423	Restoration under Darius II: Mal 1-4	
422		History of Peloponnesian War by Thucydides Bk 5
415		Historical Library by Diodorus Siculus Bk 13; History of Peloponnesian War by Thucydides Bk 6-7
413		History of Peloponnesian War by Thucydides Bk 8
411		Hellenica by Xenophon Bk 1.1.1-2.3.10
410		The Constitution of Athens by Aristotle Chaps 34-41
404		Hellenica by Xenophon Bk 2.3.11-5.1.36; Historical Library by Diodorus Siculus Bk 14
401		The Anabasis by Xenophon
400		Crito by Plato (we suggest that only mature Christians read Plato)
399		Phaedo by Plato (we suggest that only mature Christians read Plato); The Constitution of Athens by Aristotle Chaps 42-69; Apology of Socrates by Plato (we suggest that only mature Christians read Plato)
398		"Agesilaus" in Parallel Lives by Plutarch
396		The Republic by Plato (we suggest that only mature Christians read Plato); The Early History of Rome by Livy Bk 5

B.C.	*Judah*	*Israel*	*Egypt*	*Assyria /Babylon /Persia*	*Greece*	*Rome*
395 394 393 392 391						
390						Gauls sack Rome
389 388 387 386 385						
384					Aristotle (Greek philosopher) and Demosthenes (Greek orator) born	
383 382 381 380 379 378 377 376 375 374 373 372 371 370 369 368 367						
366						first plebeian consul at Rome
365 364 363 362 361 360						
359				Artaxerxes III crowned		

B.C.	*Biblical Literature*	*Secular Literature*
395		The Laws by Plato (we suggest that only mature Christians read Plato)
389		The Early History of Rome by Livy Bk 6
386		Hellenica by Xenophon Bk 5.2.1-end Historical Library by Diodorus Siculus Bk 15
384		"Demosthenes" in Parallel Lives by Plutarch
380		"The Panegyricus" by Isocrates
366		The Early History of Rome by Livy Bk 7 (Frontier Wars)
360		Historical Library by Diodorus Siculus Bk 16

B.C.	*Judah*	*Israel*	*Egypt*	*Assyria /Babylon /Persia*	*Greece*	*Rome*
358 357 356 355 354 353 352 351 350 349 348 347 346 345 344						
343					Aristotle tutor to Alexander the Great	
342					Epicurus (Greek philosopher) born/Menander (Greek comedian and poet) born	
341 340 339						
338					Philip of Macedon defeats the Greeks	
337						
336					Philip is killed/Alexander the Great crowned/Zeno (Greek philosopher) born	
335				Darius III crowned		
334					Alexander the Great defeats Persians	
333 332 331 330 329 328						
327					Alexander the Great invades India	
326 325 324						
323					Alexander the Great dies	

B.C.	*Biblical Literature*	*Secular Literature*
354		"On the Areopagiticus" by Isocrates
351		"First Philippic" by Demosthenes
346		"To Philip" by Isocrates
342		"Epicurus" in Lives of the Philosophers by Diogenes Laertius "Letter to Herodotus" and "Letter to Menoeceus" by Epicurus (we suggest that only mature Christians read Epicurus)
341		"Third Philippic" by Demosthenes The Early History of Rome by Livy Bk 8 (the first Samnite War and settlement of Latium)
336		"Zeno" in Lives of the Philosophers by Diogenes Laertius Antiquities of the Jews by Josephus Bk 11 Ch 8 Ancient Geography by Strabo Bk 17.1.6-17.1.8 (description of Alexandria)
335		Ancient Geography by Strabo Bk 1.4.9 (character of Alexander) Historical Library by Diodorus Siculus Bk 17
334		"Alexander" in Parallel Lives by Plutarch Anabasis of Alexander by Arrian Bks 1-7 The Early History of Rome by Livy Bk 9
330		"On the Crown" by Demosthenes
329		selected works by Aristotle (we suggest that only mature Christians read Aristotle's philosophical works; his other works are for upper Wisdom Level students or older)
323		Historical Library by Diodorus Siculus Bk 18 The Histories by Polybius Bk 6.2-6.18. 6.43-6.57

Chapter Ten

Different Methods and Approaches to Homeschooling in the Light of the Trivium

For who maketh thee to differ from another?
and what hast thou that thou didst not receive?
— First Corinthians 4:7

INTRODUCTION

MOST HOMESCHOOLERS ARE FAMILIAR with the different methods and approaches to Homeschooling, and they may employ several of them. We wish to examine these approaches in order to see what light the Applied Trivium sheds upon them. Before doing so, let us review the Trivium Model of Child Development. (See Chapter Four for a fuller development of this model.)

Children are continually developing in Knowledge, Understanding, and Wisdom. Though these three capacities are developing in the child from before birth, and they are mutually dependent upon each other, nevertheless, children pass through several developmental stages, or levels of learning, where one capacity experiences greater growth:

1. Before age ten, children are at the *Early Knowledge (or Grammar) Level.* They are largely learning the language, building their vocabulary, and filling up their basic understanding of the world. These children need more training than they need teaching. They should be trained in self-discipline and filled with useful information. This lays a proper foundation for more formal studies later.

2. At about age ten, the light bulb goes on, and these youngsters enter the *Later Knowledge (or Grammar) Level.* They develop the capacity for more abstract thinking. They can handle abstract mathematical concepts. They can discern the difference between a noun and a verb. From ages ten through twelve their knowledge begins to grow on the abstract level, but their reasoning and their creative communication skills are not very highly developed yet.

3. Youths, from ages thirteen through fifteen, are at the *Understanding (or Logic) Level.* They begin to develop their reasoning skills. They can handle algebra and geometry. They should be developing the critical apparatus for thinking. They should be more inquisitive and analytical. Their minds should be trained to correctly reason things out – to logically evaluate presuppositions and conclusions.

4. Older youths, from ages sixteen through eighteen, are at the *Wisdom (or Rhetoric) Level.* They begin to develop their skills in communication and application. They want to creatively and effectively express what things they have learned and to put these things into practice.

5. Young adults, ages nineteen and twenty, are at the *Final Finishing Level.* The capacities for Knowledge, Understanding, and Wisdom should be fully developed, and, during this level, these capacities are brought into unison under the moral capacity for conscience, as they develop the full Biblical accountability described by Moses – those age twenty and up who were held accountable for the decision not to enter Canaan, and consequently died in the wilderness (Numbers 14:29, etc.).

These ages are only approximate, and your child may be on either side of the line. A fuller summary of this model is given at the end of Chapter Four.

At the end of this Chapter is a chart of the *Trivium Matrix*, which lays out this Trivium Model for Child Development in a way which corresponds to the different methods and approaches to Homeschooling which we will discuss in this Chapter.

1. THE SCOPE AND SEQUENCE METHOD

Most of us who were taught in a graded classroom are familiar with the *Scope and Sequence Method*. The first assumption of this method is that there is an encyclopedia of information which every child must learn. The second assumption is that we can divide this encyclopedia down into efficient little increments according to twelve grade levels and 180 daily installments. The third assumption is that every child should be able to regularly digest these installments with other children whose age falls within nine months of their own. So, like an automobile assembly plant, as each child goes down the educational conveyor belt, he has various parts attached along the way, and he comes out of the academic assembly plant a completed product at twelfth grade. This is the factory model of education. It neglects a number of things, such as *training* in proper behavior and moral character. As long as families were supplying the behavioral and moral training, the factory model was still productive. But as more and more products of this system became parents themselves, the family began to break down. Therefore the family supplied less and less of the proper behavior and moral character to keep this factory model operating. Hence the assembly line has begun to turn out products which do not run properly. The factory itself will *never* be able to supply the necessary behavioral and moral *training* – it can never replace the family.

There is nothing wrong with the notion that there are certain things each child should learn (the scope), and that there are different levels of learning (the sequence). (Notice, we are not saying that we necessarily agree with anyone's notion of what that scope and sequence for each child should be.) The problem is not with the scope and sequence, but with how it is applied. We cannot squeeze every child into the same mold. All other things being equal (and they never are), the program of scope and sequence must be adapted to the child, not the child to the program. In other words, we must abandon the efficient factory model – which may work well for automobiles, and we must adopt an organic family model – which works well for real, living and growing children.

Traditional Textbook publishers (A Beka, Bob Jones, Rod and Staff, etc.) use the Scope and Sequence Method, producing textbooks for each subject for each year of grade-level. These textbook materials were originally written for use in a formal graded classroom. Some of the correspondence schools (Christian Liberty, Seaton, Calvert, etc.) assemble textbooks from various sources. In order to work with the grade-level textbooks (and especially with the grade-level packages from the correspondence schools, with their teacher's manuals and tests, etc.), the homeschooler will need to adapt his method of teaching, making it conform to the time and frequency limits expected by the textbook curriculum.

A different form of the Scope and Sequence Method is the *Worktext.* (Alpha Omega, Christian Light, School of Tomorrow, etc.) The student's lessons and tests are not located in separate teaching materials, but they are incorporated into the student's text. (The teacher still has the answer key.) The text is broken into small units which must be mastered. Because the student can do the work largely on his own, the worktext reduces the need for teacher supervision. A specialized form of the worktext is the *Programmed-Interactive text* (*Artes Latinae* by Waldo Sweet, *Homeschool Greek*), which takes the student step-by-step through the normal learning process (knowledge of facts, understanding of how the information fits together, wisdom in how to use the information), while continually confirming or correcting the student's response. The Programmed-Interactive method is primarily used with languages.

The Applied Trivium gives us a general "scope and sequence" of Knowledge, Understanding, and Wisdom. For each subject, the facts (Knowledge) must first be mastered, then the theory (Understanding), and finally the practice (Wisdom). Also, each child passes through an early Knowledge Level of development and training (before age ten), a later Knowledge Level (ten through twelve), an Understanding Level (thirteen through fifteen), a Wisdom Level (sixteen through seventeen or eighteen), and a final level where the conscience is fully developed (nineteen through twenty-one). Anyone teaching from a Trivium Approach will, of course, be using some textbooks and workbooks. However, the teacher will edit and rearrange materials to fit them into the developmental levels of the Trivium. Scope and Sequence materials are particularly useful for the separate and more intense study of individual subjects. For example, Scope and Sequence texts often work well for chemistry and physics, or geometry and algebra. A Scope and Sequence history text may serve as the framework for the study of history.

2. THE HABITUAL "CHARLOTTE MASON" METHOD

The *Habitual Method* of teaching was developed in the nineteenth century by Charlotte Mason. This method seeks to instill habits of self-discipline in children through daily routine, concentration, truthfulness, self-control, cooperation, and unselfishness. Children should be exposed to the best sources of knowledge, and be required to orally narrate the material back, in order to develop attention, concentration, and understanding.

Narration is an essential part of the Habitual Method of Charlotte Mason, but it also fits very well into the Applied Trivium. Narration builds and strengthens the mind, which is what both methods strive for. The Habitual Method encourages children to have a love for learning which leads them to self-education. Again, this idea is at the center of the Applied Trivium. There is an emphasis on "whole books" and "living books" in the Habitual Method. No argument here with the Applied Trivium. Charlotte Mason encouraged nature walks and the making of nature notebooks. This fits very well with the Grammar Level of the Applied Trivium. We want our children to learn to observe and record their observations.

Karen Andreola noted in her article "Learning From the Inside Out" in *Practical Homeschooling* (Nov/Dec, 1997) that ". . . Charlotte's method is in disagreement with Dorothy Sayers' strong emphasis on memory work in the early grades." "A true intellectual life is not achieved by exercising children's minds as if they were nothing but memory machines." We also would diverge from Dorothy Sayers here. Though there may be some value, at a young age, to memorize groups of facts (dates, geographical facts, Latin chants, etc.), there is much more value in memorizing passages of literature – both prose and poetry – and in more than one language. An early and high degree of mastery of the language is more valuable than an early mastery of the presidents. Besides that, facts are better learned and are less of a drudgery when they are placed within a setting instead of isolated as abstractions.

For the most part, the Habitual Method of Charlotte Mason and the Applied Trivium fit together quite well. They complement and reinforce each other. When combined, they enrich the homeschool experience.

3. THE ENVIRONMENTAL "UNSCHOOLING" METHOD

The *Unschooling Method* (John Holt) seeks to provide an unstructured and unguided environment of books and resources. Parents 1) provide a model of interest in learning, 2) involve their children in their own adult experiences, 3) surround them with a rich environment of resources, 4) make themselves available to answer questions and suggest things to help the children to explore their own interests. Here, in the words of the proponents of unschooling, are definitions of the term unschooling:

> . . .Where unschoolers differ from other homeschoolers is the extent to which we let children be responsible for their own education. . .Unschoolers believe that the natural curiosity of a healthy child, given access to a rich environment, will lead the child to learn what he or she needs to know . . . Child-driven learning is fundamentally active. Children are doing things because they have taken responsibility for carrying out the actions needed to fulfill their desires. Unschooling is centered around the idea of learning, with the student as the center of action and the source of activity, rather than on the idea of teaching (with the teacher as the center of action and the source of activity) . . . . The child learns that if he wants something to happen, he has to make it happen . . . . Unschooling families do not set up miniature classrooms, with time set aside for studying, a parent playing the role of teacher, formal lesson plans and imposed curricula. Beyond that limit, we differ in how much order we try to lend to the learning process. "Radical" unschoolers impose little or no structure, though books and such are available to act as guides. Others allow children to learn what they wish, but provide strong organizational assistance to help the children reach their goals. (Assistance can take the form of lessons, or workbooks, or even assigned projects.) Some families use curricula for some subjects (often math) but are freer with others. Most try to squeeze learning out of the activities of everyday life. — *Unschooling Undefined* by Eric Anderson, http://www.olin.wustl.edu/Staff/bradford/unschool.html

> . . . A better way to state the unschooling position is that children should not be forced to learn something against their will. . . . Unschoolers trust children to choose to learn and they recognize that the deepest and most satisfying learning comes about when someone is at least fascinated with, if not passionate about, a subject. . . . Unschooling does mean that parents have consciously decided to leave many, most, or all decisions about what and how to learn up to the learner. . . . Unschoolers believe that there is so much that is worth learning and so many ways to learn anything that there is no good reason to force anyone to learn certain materials at certain times or in certain ways. Across this spectrum, unschoolers are distinguished by their high degree of confidence that children will benefit from being allowed tremendous amounts of freedom to choose their own educational paths. — *Defining Unschooling* by Pam Sorooshian, http://www.comenius.org/chn/netnews/unschool.htm

> I believe that we learn best when we, not others, are deciding what we are going to try to learn, and when, and how, and for what reasons or purposes; when we, not others, are in the end choosing the people, materials, and experiences from which and with which we will be learning; when we, not others, are judging how easily or quickly or how well we are learning, and when we have learned enough; and above all when we feel the wholeness and openness of the world around us, and our own freedom and power and competence in it. What then do we do about it? How can we create or help create these conditions for learning? — John Holt, from *What Do I Do Monday*

> John Holt's ending in the book "How Children Learn" is a good definition of unschooling. "Birds fly, fish swim, man thinks and learns. Therefore, we do not need to motivate children into learning by wheedling, bribing or bullying. We do not need to keep picking away at their minds to make sure they are learning. What we need to do, and all we need to do, is bring as much of the world as we can into the school and classroom; give children as much help and guidance as they ask for; listen respectfully when they feel like talking; and then get out of the way. We can trust them to do the rest." — http://www.unschooling.com/

> Then what is unschooling? I can't speak for every person who uses the term, but I can talk about my own experiences. Our son has never had an academic lesson, has never been told to read or to learn mathematics, science, or history. Nobody has told him about phonics. He has never taken a test or has been asked to study or memorize anything. When people ask, "What do you do?" My answer is that we follow our interests - and our interests inevitably lead to science, literature, history, mathematics, music - all the things that have interested people before anybody thought of them as "subjects." — *What is Unschooling?* by Earl Stevens

The primary tenet of the advocates of unschooling is that the child be left to determine his own direction. The whole tenor of the Scriptures disagrees with such a notion.

> The rod and reproof give wisdom: but a child left to himself bringeth his mother to shame. — Proverbs 29:15

The first half of this verse tells us that a child must be disciplined with the rod and reproved for his misbehavior. Misbehavior may be manifested in a multitude of ways, including intellectual misbehavior.

> Train up [/catechize] a child in the way he should go: and when he is old, he will not depart from it. — Proverbs 22:6

We are to intellectually train up our children. They are not to be left to determine their own direction.

> . . . A wise son maketh a glad father: but a foolish son is the heaviness of his mother. He that begetteth a fool doeth it to his sorrow: and the father of a fool hath no joy. A foolish son is a grief to his father, and bitterness to her that bare him. — Proverbs 10:1; 17:21,25

We are not to raise fools, and fools are those who are left to themselves, not trained in the ways of the Lord. We would not limit this wisdom and foolishness to outward behavior and misbehavior. It includes inward and intellectual behavior.

> . . . out of the abundance of the heart the mouth speaketh — Matthew 12:34

We should focus on the second half of Proverbs 29:15 – "a child left to himself bringeth his mother to shame." Children are not to be left "unschooled." They are to be trained and taught. We have often said that "a young child needs more training than he needs teaching." Notice, we did not say "a child needs only training and no teaching." Training and teaching go hand in hand, but with younger children, the training predominates, and this need for training gradually gives way to more teaching as the child matures. If we have done our training at an early age, then an older child will be prepared for plenty of teaching and will need very little training. But in neither the training nor the teaching do we advocate leaving the child entirely to his own interests. Children are not little adults.

On the basis of Scripture, we thoroughly reject the notion of unschooling – in principle and practice – especially before age ten. The Scripture doctrines of original sin and total depravity should forever end the discussion. We affirm disciplined age-appropriate schooling for all ages. A child must be trained in self-control and self-discipline, and he must acquire the tools and equipment which he needs before he can embark upon a guided exploration of the world around him. He also needs some academic training in order to be able to use these resources to the best advantage.

Once we have instilled such disciplines in our child, then providing an open environment rich with resources may be the best thing we could do for him. As a child matures, especially at the Wisdom Level, he should gradually be allowed more freedom in what he pursues. But even students approaching adulthood – age twenty – need some structure in their environment. So we propose, in strong contrast to unschooling, a *Resource-Rich Environment for Disciplined Students*. The more disciplined the student, the freer his access to resources.

4. THE UNIT STUDY APPROACH

Studying a particular topic or theme – examining it from the perspectives of science, fine arts, mathematics, language, history, and literature – this is called a *unit study*.

When all subjects are blended together around a common theme, this is called the *Thematic-Directed* unit study. Unit studies have been created around personal character (Konos, Advanced Training Institute), scientific interests (Alta Vista), and history (Weaver).

Or the parent could construct his own *Interest-Directed* unit study, employing all subjects to pursue a particular interest. For a child who is less motivated in his studies, perhaps constructing a unit study around a subject in which he has a strong interest will serve to spark his interest in other subjects. If a child has a particular interest in guns, then studies can be designed in the *history* of guns, the *physics* and *chemistry* of guns, the *mathematics* of guns, the *language* and *literature* of guns, the *laws* regarding guns, etc.

The Unit Study Approach works well in the early and later Knowledge Level, when the child is soaking up factual information. The mind tends to retain information more accurately and comprehensively when it is not just a collection of isolated facts, but is part of an interrelated whole. The young brain packs this information together in little connected units, which is conducive to making profitable associations later. Even if we do not use a unit study approach, it would be most profitable to make early learning into miniature unit studies – little file drawers of associated facts.

During the Understanding Level, it is important to separate subjects in order to teach the disciplines of the subject – language, logic, mathematics, the separate sciences, etc., and these subjects are time-intensive. This may greatly limit the amount of time free to follow a unit study. Composition, literature, history, and geography may be pursued as a unit study, but the other subjects may only touch on the unit study while they are mostly pursuing their separate course.

This approach may work well in the later Wisdom Level, when the student harnesses his Knowledge and Understanding to pursue a particular application or project. For example, if the student is involved in debate, his studies may be especially modeled to follow the debate topic.

5. THE FORMAL CLASSICAL APPROACH

The *Formal Classical Approach* encompasses the three formal subjects of the classical Trivium: Grammar (Latin and Greek, etc.), Logic (informal fallacies and formal propositional logic, etc.), and Rhetoric (composition, oratory, and debate, etc.). These subjects give students the three formal tools with which to teach themselves. Chapters Five, Six, and Seven of this book are concerned with the subjects of the Formal Classical Approach. Though the three formal subjects of the Trivium comprise the essence of this approach, technically speaking, this approach may also include the mathematical Quadrivium, along with a curriculum of Great Books. (In the Seven Liberal Arts, the Quadrivium is the complement of the Trivium. The Quadrivium is described in Appendix One, Article Four.)

The Formal Classical Trivium must be distinguished from the Applied Trivium, which is an educational model and a teaching method, not a subject curriculum. Are you confused? Unfortunately, the terminology aggravates the confusion. The Applied Trivium takes the idea or philosophy behind the three formal subjects of the classical Trivium, and it adapts this philosophy to matters of child development and subject development. The three stages or levels of learning which children pass through – Grammar, Logic, and Rhetoric, or as we call them Knowledge, Understanding, and Wisdom – this is the educational model of the Applied Trivium. The three steps or levels for teaching a subject – Grammar, Logic, and Rhetoric – or, the facts, the theory, and the practice – this is the teaching method of the Applied Trivium.

This book is mostly about the Applied Trivium, but it incorporates within this Applied Trivium the three formal subjects of the classical Trivium. We might say that the Formal Classical Trivium is now swallowed up somewhere inside of its child, the Applied Trivium. The advantages of the Formal Classical Trivium are argued in Chapters Five, Six, and Seven.

6. THE PRINCIPLE APPROACH

The *Principle Approach* began with Rosalie Slater in 1965, when she published her big red book: *Teaching and Learning America's Christian History: The Principle Approach*. In this book, she distilled seven principles of American Christian history and government which are derived from the Bible.

1. *The Principle of Individuality*. God maintains the unique identity and role of each individual thing which He creates. The westward movement of Christianity expanded both inward and outward individual liberty wherever it went.
2. *The Principle of Self-Government*. Godly rule is from the inside out. True liberty is to be self-governed, not outwardly restrained. All true liberty begins with individual self-government, expanding to the family, then to the community, then to the institutions of a nation – church, business, civil government.
3. *The Principle of Christian Character*. One's internal character will affect his external environment. The Christian character of self-government, personal accountability and productivity produces fruits which will bring his outward environment under God's order and rule.
4. "*Conscience Is the Most Sacred of All Property*" — James Madison. Each individual governs himself by consenting to do right by his own conscience, which is a property which God has given us as a stewardship.
5. *The Principle of a Biblical Form of Government*. Scripture teaches a representative form of government, bound by laws, with the separation and balance of powers.
6. *The Principle of Local Self-Government*. "Liberty is an individual responsibility . . ." — Samuel Adams. Governmental action begins with the individual, and works its way outwardly. Self-government is a seed to be planted.
7. *The Principle of Political Union*. Inward agreement in principle produces outward agreement in practice. All spheres of government will work in union when they are agreed in spirit – in their beliefs, in their principles, and in their goals.

The goals of the Principle Approach are to educate children in a Biblical worldview, to develop their ability to think Biblically and to apply God's word to all areas of their lives, to create in them proper self-disciplines, including the responsibility of self-education.

With the method of the Principle Approach, a student researches a subject such as history, or government, or literature, focusing upon God's government in the world. The student discovers:

a. The *Providence* of God in history.
b. The *Principles* of self-government that protect liberty.
c. The *Persons* who preserve, guide, regulate or direct in those areas of life covered by this subject.

This method utilizes a notebook approach organized around *the four R's*:

1. *Researching* – to identify God's principles and purposes with regard to a particular subject.
2. *Reasoning* – from these truths to determine the significance and importance of the subject in God's government.
3. *Relating* – applying these principles to each student's character.
4. *Recording* – writing individual applications of biblical principles to life.

The Principle Approach can be understood as an application of the natural Trivium, though narrowed to the focus of God's government in the world. The method emphasizes collecting the facts from primary sources, analyzing these sources to discern the principles, then applying these principles to our lives.

1. Researching is recognizing the elemental facts – the Knowledge – of God's Providence.
2. Reasoning is looking for the theory – the Understanding – of self-government.
3. Relating and Recording is the practical application – the Wisdom – of the responsible use and extension of God's government to all of life.

The seven-principles approach is based upon a study of American history, but both it and the four-step practical method can be expanded to include all other disciplines, and be adapted to the different levels of a child's development.

7. FORMAL VERSUS NON-FORMAL EARLY ACADEMICS

There are some who believe we should introduce every child to formal, structured, classroom-like instruction from as early an age as possible – by four years of age, or even earlier. They believe time is wasted if we wait. The early years are academically very important. Others believe we should delay such formal academic instruction until eight to ten years of age.

Research, and You Will Find

Research indicates that if we begin such formal instruction too early, then it causes developmental problems. Stress is placed on the child's systems – such as vision, hearing, nerves, and coordination – which are not yet fully developed. In the early years, the brain is not yet formed to handle complex abstract thought. It is better adapted to receive lineal instruction. If it is strained to go beyond its development, it will lack proper comprehension, and it will store the information in less accessible places than if it is taught these same things when the brain has properly developed and is prepared to receive it. (For more discussion of this, see Appendix One, Article Eleven, History and Research on the Teaching of Math.)

A Moral Foundation for Academics

If we lay a good foundation of self-discipline and moral character in the early years, the academic instruction of later years will be more productive. Instead of focusing solely upon academic concerns in the early years, we should also be training our child in proper behavior and developing his moral outlook by teaching him household management chores, involving him in doing service for others, and pursuing special projects with him which are designed to instill traits of diligence, perseverance, attention to detail, and the like. (For more discussion of this, see Chapter Eleven.) The more we read to children, the larger their minds will be – larger vocabulary, larger store of categories of thought, and a greater love of learning. We are talking about the polar opposite of "unschooling."

> Train up [/catechize] a child in the way he should go: and when he is old, he will not depart from it. — Proverbs 22:6

Against Indulgences

Because some, such as we, do not advocate early formal structured academics, others have speculated that we must recommend an indulgent, non-demanding, even negligent approach to schooling before age ten. Would anyone say that doing such things as reading and narrating Charles Dickens, memorizing Greek and Hebrew alphabets, memorizing and reciting passages of Biblical and classical literature, learning to speak, read, and write foreign languages – that doing such things before age ten fits into the category of indulgent or non-demanding? Definitely not! Yet these are all things done by those who take a later formal-academics approach. We agree wholeheartedly that early instruction is important. We disagree only with the notion that it is necessary to follow the modern methodology of early formal academics. Instead, we advocate the classical method of instruction which prevailed until the twentieth century, which emphasized informal instruction until an age when formal instruction is developmentally comprehendible. Why attempt to stuff things into a child's mind at a time or in a manner which renders the material less digestible?

The last century of education has been an ever-expanding experiment in earlier and earlier formal academics, accompanied by ever-multiplying "learning disabilities" and such things as were never heard of before. The evidence suggests a direct connection between early formal academics and learning disabilities, and this warrants considerable caution regarding this modern methodology. Again, we recommend something closer to the classical methodology of delayed formal academics as a general rule, but there are many and varied exceptions, and the parent is most qualified to discern what is best for his own child.

Imagine these two extremes: On the one hand, we have a strict, constrained, starched, rigid, formal, military academy classroom setting. On the other hand we have the casual, loose, offhand, perfunctory, come-as-you-are-and-do-as-you-please-and-go-as-you-may hippy-dippy setting. Now we tell you that you must choose between these two settings. What have we done? We have suggested that there are only two possibilities. This is known as the Either-Or Fallacy. It is like saying, "If you are not a fascist, then you must be an anarchist." Well, there are numerous possibilities other than just fascist or anarchist. The early formal-academics people are not necessarily like the military academy, and the later formal-academics people are not necessarily like the hippy-dippy setting. We believe forcing young children into too rigid a structure is counter-productive, but too little structure is also counter-productive. We are not talking about rigid opposites, but different points on a scale, and the best point is different for different families and different children at different ages and in different circumstances.

Brain Strain

We emphasize that the physical properties of the brain should be fully developed before engaging in those activities which place stress on those properties. When this rule is followed, learning progresses very rapidly and more satisfactorily. If there were some simple but accurate diagnostic tests to assess whether the mind is physically ready, we might recommend them. As it is, the best test we know of on the market is the parental assessment – the homeschool hunch – a carefully designed method whereby mom and dad, after working with the child, come to agree, "Yep, he's ready for this," or "Nope, we're going a bit fast, we'll hold back a little here." Please notice that the parent is being trained through this process as much as the child. We suspect this was the original design.

Some parents are a bit compulsive. They want to drive their children like Hebrew slaves without supplying straw for their bricks. (That may be the child's view of it, anyway.) These parents may be driven by their desire to show off their children's progress, or they may expect their children to perform at adult levels of ability. Or they may simply be trying to find ways to keep the curious little rascals plenty busy and out of trouble. But children are rather resilient creatures, and as long as we are in tune with what's happening, and we don't try to force things too strongly before their time, then a little too much here or there won't burn the little tykes brains out, and they'll progress along at a nice pace.

There is, however, the opposite difficulty of doing too little or being too lax. This can be due to laziness or an indulgent spirit on the part of parents. Or it may be weariness with the work of raising lots of rambunctious little rug rats. Guess what? Children have resiliency in this direction as well. As long as we don't soften things too far, then a little laxity here or there won't turn the little lads' and lassies' brains into cornmeal mush.

They'll survive the minor flood or the minor drought.

Now, can you name the parents who are not guilty of both of these tendencies? What keeps us in balance? Our love for God and for our children. What gets us out of balance? Our lust for the world and our flesh. You see, this is a spiritual problem at its core. We cannot teach our children discipline if we do not have it ourselves. One of the reasons God has given us children is to goad us into self-discipline. Everything rests on us doing our jobs as parents.

The Downside-Up Solution

Our culture is turned upside down. We are taught to believe that everything rests on the government, or on the economy, or on the church. We become dependent upon those things which are, in fact, dependent upon us. Those who will not rule themselves will be ruled by others, and treated like children. Once we break the pattern of being conformed to the external structure which this world imposes upon us, then the internal structure and self-discipline, which have been built into us through the operation of the Spirit of Christ, will begin to work out of us to transform the things around us. When we restore the Biblical jurisdiction and order to the family, we will find parents behaving much more responsibly – like mature adults should. Then order should grow outward from the family into all of society. We will then be able to restore Christian order and the rule of law.

We lament the cultural slide which has made it necessary for parents to rely upon external structures to keep order in their own families – whether it is rigid programmed curriculums, or classroom schools, or other. The solution to this situation is not to give them more outside structure. The solution is to build structure within them, which will make the outside structure less necessary. The solution is to promote the self-discipline of the parents. In other words, the solution is to get the parents to grow up. Then the structure inside the parents will generate the outside structure which the children need while they develop their own internal structure under the nurture and admonition of the Lord administered by their parents. This will make children more greatly honor and admire their parents, which means they will love them more. Proper order will be re-established. God's order. And God will be glorified.

Filling Buckets Versus Lighting Fires

Chris Davis of Elijah Company quotes W.B. Yeats, "Education is not the filling of a bucket, but the lighting of a fire." (Or maybe it was Plutarch who said it.) The light bulb for formal academic learning does not go on until about age ten. Before this time, we can waste much time teaching simple things, often to the exasperation of both pupil and parent. Instead of teaching a five-year-old to count by fives – and take five days to do it, we can wait until the child is age nine or ten and teach him in ten seconds – if he has not already figured it out on his own.

Pushing formal-academics at an early age may destroy more promise than it creates. Those children who have been pushed in very early years often experience a jet-lag of academic burnout in later years. Of course we should never discourage a child from learning, but neither should we over press academics to the point of strain or exasperation. We should stretch and challenge our child in order to strengthen him. When your child is ready to learn something, then teach him. When he has a question, then answer it. Encourage questions – and teach him the proper manners for asking questions.

Every child is different, and there are precocious little prodigies who take to academics and go farther and faster than others. But these children still need more *training* than *teaching* in their early years. A bright young child who is undisciplined, ill-mannered, and amoral can be a genuine grief, especially if he is also academically learned. Formal academic *teaching* is not the same thing as child *training*.

Preparation for Academic Progress

God invented the family to *train up* and enculturate the child with godly principles, values, and goals. There is no legitimate substitute for the family. What we most want to do with children during their early years is to *train* them to function in the Scripture-controlled Christian culture of our own home, raising them to eventually take their own self-governing place in godly culture. The early child *training* and development of the physical and mental faculties are preparation for more formal-academics. At about age ten, after the child has learned to read, and his vocabulary and categories of thought have been well-developed through informal academics, the formal subjects of the Trivium can easily and readily be taught, and academic progress is a joy to the child.

So our focus before age ten is building language skills – speaking, reading and writing – especially vocabulary. This is the primary index of intelligence throughout life. Do things in a concrete way. At age ten, when the brain physically changes, and begins to make the complex connections, we begin the more complex and abstract learning. With this emphasis in the early years, we lay a proper foundation for a full academic load later.

The Ideal and the Real

In our opinion, the ideal would be to learn to speak and write several languages and to become familiar with a wide scope of literature before age ten, which would lay a wide and solid foundation for formal math and grammar beginning around age ten. Everything seems to point to this as the best course to take. But we have never said "don't ever teach math before age ten." The whole idea is as ridiculous as it sounds. You cannot avoid exposing your child to arithmetic concepts. They will discover it on their own at a very early age. Teach them what they are ready to learn. But teach them in a concrete way, not in an abstract way. That's what informal math is. It is not leaving the child to discover what he wants. Also, we have never said, "don't ever teach formal math before age ten." We have always said that was a judgment call to be made by the parent, and if we should have a precocious little tyke who wants to learn math and works well with workbooks, then we would probably be mistaken if we were to hold him back. But if we force him beyond his developmental capabilities, then we are more prone to cause developmental abnormalities. In other words

> And O ye fathers, do not aggravate [/exasperate] your children, rather, nurture them to full maturity in *the* correction and counsel of *the* Lord. — Ephesians

6:4 (v.l.t.)

O ye fathers, do not *over*stimulate [/provoke *too far*] your children, in order that they should not be broken in spirit [/disheartened]. — Colossians 3:21 (v.l.t.)

Don't Bring the Classroom Home

The Apostle Paul gives these warnings in Ephesians and Colossians precisely because it is necessary and ought to be heeded. Just because something can be characterized as "disciplined" does not mean that it is the most profitable in the end. We discourage the *formal abstract workbook* type of rigor as an "aggravation" to the proper development of the child. We encourage other avenues and other time schedules which reach precisely the same goals with as much or more discipline, but with less time commitment and with more satisfactory results. In other words, don't bring the classroom school home, but tutor your child instead. This frees up time for other good and important things, such as reading aloud. Nevertheless, as we have always said, the parents are the best judges of what is best for their own family, and what may be too much for one family may not be enough for another. The socialist one-size-fits-all academics are incompatible with Homeschooling!

(For more on this subject, see Chapter Twelve, under *Arithmetic*.)

Summary

1. We thoroughly reject unschooling in principle and practice. "Lax learning lacks learning."
2. We affirm disciplined age-appropriate schooling for all ages. No, we *insist* upon it. But disciplined does not necessarily mean *formal narrow abstract workbook academics*.
3. Before age ten, we encourage – as a general rule – building language skills, general knowledge, and concrete perspectives, while training the character in godly attitudes and personal discipline. This builds a broad and sound foundation for later formal academics.
4. Before age ten, we discourage – as a general rule, but not as an absolute rule – a load of formal narrow abstract workbook academics. This is ordinarily not the best use of one's time, and it has potential for causing trouble in the long run.
5. We insist that the parents are the best judges of their own family's needs. There is no "one-size-fits-all" plan. God planned for parents to be in charge.

EACH METHOD AND APPROACH HAS ITS PLACE

TRIVIUM MATRIX

Incorporating Different Approaches Within the Applied Trivium

<table>
<tr><th>Early Knowledge
Before Age 10</th><th>Knowledge
Ages 10–12</th><th>Understanding
Ages 13–15</th><th>Wisdom
Ages 16–18</th><th>Maturing Concience
Ages 19–20</th></tr>
<tr><td></td><td colspan="3">**1. Scope and Sequence Methods**
Traditional Textbook & Programmed-Interactive</td><td></td></tr>
<tr><td colspan="3">**2. Habitual Method**
Charlotte Mason</td><td colspan="2">**3. Resource-Rich Environment**
For Disciplined Students
Contrary to Unschooling</td></tr>
<tr><td colspan="5">**4. Unit Study Approach**
Thematic Directed . . . . *Interest Directed*</td></tr>
<tr><td></td><td colspan="3">**5. Formal Classical Approach**
Grammar, Logic, & Rhetoric</td><td></td></tr>
<tr><td></td><td colspan="3">**6. Principle Approach**
Researching, Reasoning, Relating, Recording</td><td></td></tr>
</table>

FIGURE 10A

In the chart above, we have placed each method or approach in the age column where we thought it fit best within the Applied Trivium. This is not to say that it cannot be used at other times, when properly adapted. There is nothing hard and fixed about this chart. Obviously, most of the methods or approaches will extend, in some form and measure, into adult years.

Our point is this: Teaching the Formal Trivium – Grammar, Logic and Rhetoric – could be considered a separate approach – the Formal Classical Approach (Number 5 on the chart). But we must not confuse the *Formal* Trivium with the *Applied* Trivium. The Applied Trivium should be the larger framework or matrix upon which we build our whole system of education, simply because this is the way which we learn – even if we never actually teach the Formal Trivium.

As you can see, all of these methods and approaches are not mutually exclusive. The Trivium should be the matrix upon which we build our own curriculum, while we match each approach with each child's style of learning and the resources and constraints of our life as a family.

Question: How rigid are these age divisions for each level of the Trivium?

Answer: They are not rigid, but they do follow a regular progression through the three levels. Different persons have broken them up in different ways and have given them different names. We shift the age breaks a year later than Dorothy Sayers. (See Appendix One, Article One, The Lost Tools of Learning.) Others shift the ages one or more years earlier than Dorothy Sayers. The differences are largely due to differences in definitions and differences in how each person assesses the average progress of a child's development. When we evaluate the differences, we find we're only trying to measure how wide the middle is. By stretching or squeezing the length of each level (or stage), everyone ends up at about the same place, completing the Wisdom Level (or Poetic Period, or Rhetoric Stage) by age seventeen or eighteen.

We can compare these differences to the differences between *Strong's Concordance* and *Young's Concordance* – same material, different arrangement. We simply approach the same problems from different perspectives.

Our own divisions are based primarily upon:

1) Some hints in Scripture.
2) Scientific research – particularly in brain development.
3) Personal observation – with our own children.
4) Anecdotal evidence – the observations of many others.
5) Just plain common sense – our notions of order and proportion.

With us, the primary divisions are:

1) Age ten, when the brain undergoes a remarkable physical change.
2) At some time during his thirteenth year (he was already twelve), Jesus was found independently questioning his elders, and this appears to mark a point of growth in His wisdom (Luke 2:41-52).
3) Age twenty, which is the Biblical age of *full* accountability (Numbers 14:22-35; 32:11; Deuteronomy 2:14-16; First Corinthians 10:5; Hebrews 3:8-4:5; Jude 5, etc.; Exodus 30:14; Leviticus 27:3,5 etc.), and is also the approximate age of maturity in brain development.

Our divisions – ten, thirteen, sixteen, eighteen, twenty – are to be understood as *upper thresholds*, not *lower limits*. In other words, the child should be in the:

Later Knowledge Level no later than age ten;

Understanding Level no later than age thirteen;
Wisdom Level no later than age sixteen;
Maturing Level no later than age eighteen or nineteen;
Adult Level of Full Accountability no later than age twenty or twenty-one.

Again, this is not rigid. There may be a very few children who go beyond these ages, but the great majority will meet or beat these ages.

Part Two

The Practical Trivium

Chapter Eleven

The Early Knowledge Level: Ten Things to Do Before Age Ten

Train up a child in the way he should go: and when he is old, he will not depart from it. — Proverbs 22:6

INTRODUCTORY REMARKS

THE GOAL OF TEACHING by the Trivium is to give students the tools with which to learn on their own – to liberate them from the drudgery of task-performance and to make them independent scholars. In previous chapters we have:

1. Explained how the Trivium can serve as both a method for learning any subject, and as a model of how the learning of a child develops (Chapter Four).
2. Argued the importance of the three formal subjects of the Trivium, and supplied some introduction to those three subjects (Chapters Five, Six, and Seven).
3. Discussed the importance of literature and history, laid out some principles for studying them, and given an example for the study of the literature of an ancient historical period.

(Chapters Eight and Nine).

4. Offered a survey of different approaches to Homeschooling, showing where they all fit into the Trivium model of development (Chapter Ten).

There is more than one legitimate way to approach teaching by the Trivium. In this chapter, we explain how we, as a Homeschooling family, have put the principles of the Trivium into practice. Other classical educators may apply the Trivium differently, emphasizing different methods and principles. Most of the things we recommend come from our own experiences. This does not mean that we followed every one of our recommendations all the years we have taught our children. It has taken us almost three decades to fully develop our philosophy of education – and we're not done yet. We made the most mistakes with our first children – they were our guinea pigs. Some of the things we recommend are what we would do if we could begin again. In this chapter you will read the culmination of our long journey.

Education does not occur on a factory assembly line. We disagree with the "one formula fits all" approach, which seeks to press every child into the same mold. Each and every child is one-of-a-kind, growing up in the unique family where God has placed him. You, the parents, must determine for yourselves, under the direction and guidance of the Lord, what is the best approach for your own family and for each of your own children. We suggest that you should not limit yourselves to our recommendations. We certainly do not know everything, and we may know very little about what may fit your particular circumstances.

Some classical educators have had little or no experience with Homeschooling. Classical private schools apply the principles of a classical education to a classroom environment. This influences their methods significantly, as well it should. We would not expect them to necessarily regard our Homeschooling experience as applying to a classroom. These are two greatly different experiences. When compared to classroom schools, Homeschooling operates under a very different set of circumstances and by a very different philosophy of education. Teachers and principals in a classroom school would use teaching methods which differ significantly from the one-on-one methods which a mother would use in teaching her own children. Discipline would significantly vary between the two different situations. Classical classroom educators tend to focus more on competitive academic achievement in the classical subjects (Latin, logic, Greek, rhetoric, etc.). Because less can be achieved in a classroom situation in a given amount of time than can be achieved by one-on-one tutoring in the home, classroom educators are driven to pursue academics at earlier ages. Homeschooling tends to release parents from these restrictions, so they can focus more upon the classical method of the Trivium. This freedom allows them to pay more attention to the principles of child development. In other words, in a Homeschooling situation, teaching by the Trivium becomes more than just an academic discipline. It becomes a way of life.

There is a wide variety of ways to implement the Trivium model and method of teaching in the homeschool. In this *Course of Study*, we have laid out *general principles and plans*, not detailed and micro-managed instructions. Who knows better how to bring order to your own homeschool and family life than yourself? If we tried to take in every possibility, this Chapter would resemble a phone book. If we laid out any one possibility in every little detail – which day of the week to teach each Latin verb – it would be a workable plan for practically nobody. Those who produce individual curricula often lay out these details. But whether you are following a pre-planned curriculum, a recommended reading list, or your own collection of materials, you still must adapt it to your own circumstances, which you should learn to do rather easily. We have mapped out the road ahead of you. We have left it to you to lay out your traveling schedule and to explore some of the side roads. You must figure out on your own when and how to eat your breakfast in the style of a truly classical education – as if that actually mattered. Though teaching by the Trivium may seem a bit daunting at first, it is not necessarily more difficult than other approaches to education, and in some ways is actually easier than most. So do not feel overwhelmed. Average parents with average children – like us and ours – can certainly succeed and thrive while teaching by the Trivium. We have found it rewarding and enjoyable.

Because our ideas are built one on top of the other, we suggest that you read this and the following Chapters from beginning to end, rather than skipping to the parts which focus on the particular needs or ages of your children.

A SUGGESTED COURSE OF STUDY

Before age ten, the child is at the Early Knowledge Level, where he is mostly dependent upon his concrete sensory experiences for learning. To put it in computer lingo, he is still *booting up*. Around age ten, the child enters a more intense phase of the Knowledge Level, where his brain becomes physically able to make more complex connections, which, among other things, makes the child more able to handle abstract concepts, and which helps the child with self-management and self-control.

Force feeding academic studies before age ten is not an efficient use of your time, it is not going to accomplish all of the good which you desire, and it may actually work some harm. Of course the exact age differs from child to child, but about age ten the child becomes developmentally mature enough to pursue studies which are more academic. *Before* age ten, the focus should be on building a good foundation for the later academics. We suggest that formal academics should be the focus *after* age ten. If we exercise those parts of our child's mind which are developing, we will strengthen and enlarge his capacities. In the early years, we want to sow such seeds as:

Honoring God and parents.
Developing the capacity for language.
Developing the appetite for learning.
Enriching the memory.
Encouraging creativity.
Instilling a good work and service ethic.

These are the kind of things which will lay a good foundation for the formal academics later. First things come first. Academics must be built upon a good moral foundation.

At age ten, with a well prepared mind, you can choose the curriculum which best suits both your child and your circumstances. If you lay a firm foundation, then you can build upon it a mighty edifice. But if you begin hastily on the building while skimping on the foundation, then the building may sag and lean, and parts may fall, as the foundation sinks or crumbles beneath it.

The following is a general list of ten things we believe are important to teach your children before age ten. After this, we will outline a suggested daily schedule. Questions which are inserted into the text are actual questions which we have received.

1. Reading and Writing

PHONICS

Sometime before your child reaches the age of ten, you should teach him to read, using a good intensive phonics method.

The first question is: "At what age should I begin?" A few children will learn to read at age four, while a few may be fully ten years old before they can confidently read a basic reader. Most children, however, will learn to read sometime between the ages of five and eight. The age at which a child learns to read is no indicator of how intelligent he is or how well he will do later in academics. Our own children learned to read between ages five and nine. We suggest that you begin phonics instruction at age five. If, after a reasonable amount of time, you find that your child is not retaining any of the instruction, even though he is putting forth an effort, then you may want to put the curriculum aside, and wait a few months before attempting it again, and continue this routine until it sticks.

The second question is: "What materials should I use?" There are many good intensive phonics reading programs. Some families will use one, find it does not work, then use another, find it does not work, then use another, and at last it works. So, to the parents' mind, this last program is the best program, while in reality, the child was finally old enough and had developed to the point where he was ready to read. A child simply cannot blend letter-sounds together into words until he has physically developed to a certain point.

Here is how I (Laurie) began to teach our oldest child, Nathaniel, to read. This is by no means a recommendation, but only the story of a small part of our journey through the school of hard knocks. When Nathaniel was just an infant, I read the book *How to Teach Your Baby to Read*, by Glenn Doman. This book teaches a pure form of the "look-say" or "whole language" method for learning how to read. Back in the 1950's, I was taught to read with the Dick and Jane "look-say" sight readers, so I recognized Doman's method as the way I had been taught to read. Since I did not know any better, I latched onto this method of teaching reading. Following the book's instructions, when Nathaniel turned two, I began to teach him to read. As the book directed, I made up large flash cards, with vocabulary words printed on them: mommy, daddy, house, school, etc., and I drilled Nathaniel several times each day. Yes, he learned to "read" those words on the flash cards, but I found that if I skipped a day's instruction, then he forgot all the words, so I had to begin all over again. My sister suggested that I teach him the alphabet first. I simply parroted the instructions of Mr. Doman by replying, "Oh, no, teaching the alphabet would just confuse him."

I think I lasted about three months with this method. It was an exercise in futility, not unlike pouring water into a bucket full of holes. As long as I spent large and precious amounts of time each day drilling him with the flash cards, he continued to "read" them back to me. But if I failed to fill his bucket by drilling him with the cards, then his level of reading ability would drop as his vocabulary would drain out of the holes.

At about this time, I heard a radio talk show program on the subject of teaching reading by a method they called "intensive phonics." The guest that day was Benita Rubicam, president of the Reading Reform Foundation. What she said made sense, and she immediately converted me. I read everything which that organization had to offer, and I began my search for the best intensive phonics program to use with my children. That all happened back in 1978. I finally decided to use *The Writing Road to Reading*, by Romalda Spalding. At that time, it was considered to be the best intensive phonics curriculum. Back then, the many helps and teacher's manuals available today did not exist. When I first looked the curriculum over, I was overwhelmed. I thought, "How am I ever going to learn *all of these rules*?" It was not nearly as hard as it first seemed. Mom had to learn the phonics system herself – which she did, as she taught her first couple of children to read. After that, it was easy. Remember, mom was never taught the phonics system herself! Once mom had correctly learned the phonics system, she could teach reading with just about any curriculum – or even with no curriculum, using whatever was at hand.

Homeschooling families have many good intensive phonics programs from which to choose. You should locate an intensive phonics curriculum which best fits the needs of your family. Here are some criteria for choosing a phonics curriculum:

1. *Expense*. The teaching of reading does not need to be costly. Because many of us parents were not taught phonics, we need a full curriculum to teach ourselves first! Once we have learned the system, then we can easily teach our children by using a small chalkboard and a few easy readers.
2. *Method*. Despite what some persons want us to believe, English is a phonetic language. The problem with English is that it has the largest vocabulary, manifold larger than any other language which has ever existed. As a consequence, English has incorporated spellings from many different languages. Therefore, the way a particular word spells its sound may also display some of its history. This is the great cultural treasure of the English language – a treasure which is rapidly being lost as our vocabularies swiftly shrink under "look-say" or sight reading – a method of teaching reading which was invented for the deaf! You cannot build a large vocabulary upon the foundation of sight reading. Intensive phonics teaches the sounds of each letter or letter combination, and builds up a full system of pronunciation. (Yes, there

are some quaint little exceptions, and they are taught also.) Intensive phonics is the only method which fits English. Do not be fooled by the phony phonics programs which are based upon "look-say" sight reading, but which sprinkle in some incidental phonics as "auditory-clues." Most of the reading curricula used in the state-socialist schools are phony phonics.

3. *Usability*. If you are unfamiliar with the English phonetic system, then make sure that the curriculum which you choose has plenty of teacher's helps. Back in the seventies and eighties, when we used *The Writing Road to Reading*, the parent was expected to take a course at a college in order to learn how to use it. Today, numerous helps have been added. We recommend using a phonics curriculum which is easy to understand and use, such as *TATRAS* or *Alphaphonics*.

Here are a few suggestions to reinforce whatever phonics curriculum you choose: When your child studies a particular sound, bring it before his mind in different ways. For example: Write the letter "B" on the blackboard, or write it on paper and hang it in the living room. Talk with him about words which begin with "B." When the children and I would play on the swing set, I would sing to them the alphabet song, and they would sing along. When we played with clay, I would make the clay into shapes of letters and encourage them to make them also. We were often making cards to send to the relatives, and I would encourage the little ones to write their letters on the cards. I would give them a pile of macaroni or rice or beans, and we would glue these items onto paper in the form of letters. We would line their toys up on the floor in the shape of letters. Our family worship time doubled as phonics instruction time. The little ones who were just learning to read would be required to find in their Bible a letter which they could recognize – such as the initial letter of their name. Later they would sound out words. As the children become proficient in reading, they should be reading aloud some each day, perhaps out of one of the old-time readers. Our youngest child went from sounding out letters to reading fluently the King James Bible in about one year.

ARTIFICIALLY INDUCED DYSLEXIA

Question: Several of my children do not seem to think deeply, despite the fact that they have been homeschooled. We reached a crossroads recently with my thirteen-year-old son, and we finally put him into a classroom school full time. I found that I could not do this job by myself. I needed my husband's help to do it. But my husband has "dyslexia," and so does his whole family. He does not think in words, but in pictures, which makes our communication difficult at times. My husband has been so adversely affected by the teaching methods of the secular school system that he is not a reader – not by his choice. My husband is willing to read several hours a week in order to set an example. Since my husband is already well past the normal age to learn reading, where should he begin?

Answer: This appears to be a classic case of artificially induced dyslexia. I would suggest that you pick out an intensive phonics program and teach him to read phonetically instead of pictographically. Your biggest problem will be to break his habit of looking at words pictographically. Encourage him to practice sounding out words aloud (or mouthing the words silently). Find easy books for him to read which will interest him.

Concerning the problem of not thinking: people who do not read, and who spend their free time watching television and movies, playing video and computer games, or who otherwise spend their time seeking entertainment, will not be able to think critically. Documentation for this is given in Jane Healy's two books, *Endangered Minds: Why Children Don't Think and What We Can Do About It* and *Failure to Connect: How Computers Affect Our Children's Minds for Better and Worse*.

ENGLISH LANGUAGE NOTEBOOK

We recommend that each student maintain an English language notebook (which we will discuss in more detail later). The notebook can begin with his study of phonics. Because pages can be taken out easily and replaced, three-ring binders often work better than spiral notebooks. Fill it with notebook paper, blank paper (white and colored) and subject dividers. Each child should have his own notebook. If phonics is new to mom, she may need one also. The student will add to his notebook each week.

At about the same time you are teaching your child to read, you should also teach him to write his letters. Most phonics curricula include instructions for how to teach writing. You begin with printing each letter of the alphabet. He may fill a page or two of his notebook with each letter of the alphabet. Decorate the pages with your child's own drawings, or with cutouts from magazines: apples on the "A" page, buttons on the "B" page, etc. Have your child add pages of his practice letter writing to his notebook. You will add consonant digraphs, diphthongs and other letter combinations later. This notebook will *supplement* a phonics curriculum, but will *not take the place* of it.

COPYWORK

When your child becomes reasonably proficient at printing his letters, and he is on the road to learning how to read, you can begin him on copywork. The practice of Copywork dates back to ancient times, and is, along with oral narration, the first step in teaching a child how to write.

> Christ also suffered for us, leaving behind for us a copyhead [ὑπογραμμόν: hupogrammon], in order that ye should trace over his tracks. — First Peter 2:21 (v.l.t.)

Copywork is a good way to practice handwriting skills, reinforce phonics instruction, introduce grammar and proper sentence structure, and lay a foundation for creative writing. In copywork, the child copies on his own paper, word for word, from a sentence or paragraph which someone else has written. Whose sentences and paragraphs should your child copy? Use the finest literature. Begin with the Bible. For more advice on selections, consider,

> Finally, brethren, whatsoever things are true, whatsoever things *are* honest, whatsoever things *are* just, whatsoever things *are* pure, whatsoever things *are* lovely, whatsoever things *are* of good report; if *there be* any virtue, and if *there be* any praise, think on these things. Those things, which ye have both learned, and received, and heard, and seen in me, do: and the God of peace shall be with you. — Philippians 4:8,9

Your child should spend some time each day doing copywork. Ruth Beechick (*A Strong Start in Language*) and Cindy Rushton (*Language Arts... The Easy Way*) outline how to incorporate copywork into your curriculum. Copywork could be kept in his English language notebook, or it may deserve its own separate notebook. Your child may copy from the Bible one day, copy poetry or literature the next day, copy famous speeches or sayings of important men another day. He may maintain all of his copywork in one notebook, or he may maintain different notebooks for different kinds of literature.

How much time should he spend in copywork? As always, it depends upon your child. Some little girls, who are born with pencils in their hands, will write the day away, and you must set some upper limits. Some little boys, who find it a struggle to even hold a pencil, let alone use it – even at the age of nine! – will require some minimal "you're not free until this is done" time. Writing just one verse of Scripture may reach the upper limit of their ability. You want to teach these little ones diligence and perseverance and challenge them, but without discouraging them. How do you determine what to require of your child? Here is a principle: once you have found a level at which he can work, then steadily challenge him to do a little more, a little better, a little further, yet never pushing beyond his level of abilities. If you require far too much, then you will certainly discourage him. If you require far too little, then you will spoil him. There is a band in the middle, and it is your job to find it. Some children reach a plateau for a while, until a couple things click, then they are off again. Attempt that in a class of thirty students, then you will understand why one-on-one tutoring is so superior. Normally a five-year-old may spend perhaps fifteen minutes a day in copywork, while a nine-year-old may spend thirty minutes each day.

HOW MUCH WRITING IS ENOUGH

Question: We have been using X Curriculum as the foundation for our history and reading. Their language arts program, especially creative writing, seems overwhelming. There are weekly assignments, poems, dialogues, outlines, imaginative writing, etc. It is a bit daunting for my eight-year-old and seven-year-old. Instead of dictation, we have been doing copywork two to four times per week, using a variety of sources: poetry, Psalms, Proverbs, and passages from the books we are reading. My children will occasionally, without any initiation, add dialogue to pictures they have drawn, tell silly stories, put on plays with puppets, etc. So I know they are not completely devoid of creative abilities. Since my husband is in the habit of maintaining a journal, we plan to give them nice journals at the end of the year and make journal writing a family affair. Are we on the "right track" with copywork, journal writing, oral narration, and their occasional creative writing impulses? My instinct is to encourage their other creative pursuits, and not to require any creative writing at this point – except what they initiate themselves. My husband is concerned that if we do not require the creative writing assignments at this time, then they will miss out on something.

Answer: Copywork, oral narration (which we will talk about later), and their occasional spontaneous creative writing – this seems like plenty for children at the Early Knowledge Level (below age ten). There's only so much time in the day. We encouraged our children to combine art with copywork. They made little booklets of their copywork, of the Greek or Hebrew alphabets, of little stories which they wrote and illustrated with pictures, of science projects or history projects. Children can cover their booklets with scraps of fabric or paper out of wallpaper sample books.

2. Oral Narration

In Britain, at the close of the nineteenth century, Charlotte Mason developed the concept of narration as a method of teaching. In her book, *For the Children's Sake*, Susan Schaeffer Macaulay has reintroduced narration to Homeschooling families. Karen Andreola followed this with *A Charlotte Mason Companion*. In oral narration, the parent reads to the child, or the child reads to himself, then the child "tells back" to the parent, in his own words, what was just read. It is best to begin narration at an early age, when the child is four or five years old, to practice it on a daily basis, and to continue the practice through the later teens. 

Narration is an exercise which builds mental stamina. According to Karen Andreola, ". . . narration takes the place of questionnaires and multiple choice tests, it enables the child to bring all the faculties of mind into play. The child learns to call on the vocabulary and descriptive power of good writers as he tells his own version of the story."

Narration is very difficult to do. Could you, without notes, narrate the sermon which you heard last Sunday? Most of us – including the pastor who preached the sermon – would have trouble remembering even the text of the sermon. Our adult minds have not been trained to listen to something, remember it, and then retell it. We were never trained in the skill of narration.

It is best to begin small. Read to your child one short paragraph from a simple story, then ask him to retell the story in his own words. In the beginning, you may need to prompt your child with questions about the passage. As the child becomes more practiced in the skill of narration, he will be able to narrate longer and more detailed passages.

Narration can serve three functions.

1. To periodically test how well a child is comprehending the material which he reads or hears. The more a child must say in his narration, the more thoroughly he has understood the material. If he does not remember much about the material, then he probably did not listen well or read carefully.
2. To develop and sharpen the mental capacities. As jogging down the physical road exercises the body, so jogging down the memory channels exercises the mind. Using the information through telling it back strengthens the child's grasp of it.

3. Copywork, when combined with oral narration, constitutes the first step in teaching a child how to write. The process of creative writing involves two skills: the actual physical work of taking pencil in hand and putting the words on paper, which your child learns by copywork; and the work of creating in the mind the ideas to write about, which is developed in your child through oral narration. If you develop these two skills in your child before age ten, then, when your child has matured, he will have these two "tools" at hand to work with creatively when writing.

Do not let your child be a passive observer. If you read to him, ask him questions about what he has heard. Tell him to narrate the material back in his own words. Make him address any moral value issues which may come up. Develop his mind, not simply in the direction of absorbing, but in the direction of responding. The mind which can respond must also absorb, in some measure, but the mind which simply absorbs – as in front of a television or computer screen – is too passive in the learning process, learns to take without giving, and it is questionable how much it really does absorb anyway. Computers do not offer learning experiences which require real human responsiveness. Programmed learning has its uses, and it can be very effective at later ages, but at this age, your child needs interaction with an adult (and not with groups of children his own age).

HOW TO DEVELOP NARRATION

Question: All my children are reading well and we are managing to read aloud together. My eleven-year-old is doing well with narration, but my nine-year-old twin boys struggle with it immensely. I think they are listening, but they can't put thoughts into words. What is the best way to develop this skill?

Answer: If your boys are struggling with oral narration, then I suggest that you take smaller bites for them to narrate. One sentence, then two sentences, then three.

Sometimes the problem is less a difficulty in narrating, and more a difficulty in obeying. The child doesn't want to put forth the effort for you. Oral narration requires that we make our brain work. It takes an effort to force the mind to listen attentively, knowing that you will later be asked to narrate back what you heard. Don't we all hate to put forth great effort? Doesn't it require strong motivation to overcome our reluctance to endure the pain? You, as an adult, see the value in narration, but the child may see only the pain, and if he's not used to obeying you, it may be difficult to motivate him to put forth the effort. This would be an example of how obedience is a foundation for all of education. But if your child is an obedient child, the problem can perhaps be overcome by reducing the pain by making the narration short, and helping him at first by prompting him with some questions. If he remembers the questions, they will help him to narrate on his own.

There are, of course, some people who find oral narration to be easy and fun and can go on and on narrating. They still need training to improve their narrating. They may need to learn how to cut their narration down to what is important. Regardless of how easy or difficult it comes, all children should be required to narrate. It should be done cheerfully and willingly just like all chores – brushing your teeth and making your bed – and anything else Daddy and Mommy want them to do.

If oral narration is a real chore, then you may let the children know ahead of time when you will be requiring narration – always being "on call" for narration, wondering when mother will call for narrations, might take the fun out of hearing you read.

3. Memorization

Memorization should be begun when your child is young – even as young as two or three – and continued throughout life. (It is good for us old folks, also). Time should be spent everyday reciting memory work. Encourage your child to memorize such things as the Greek and Hebrew Alphabets, passages from the Bible, poetry, catechisms, excerpts from literature. Your child could memorize passages of the Bible in Greek or Latin, and the same passages in English, in order to give them a feel for those languages. Memorizing passages of literature will prepare your child for the study of formal grammar at age ten. This gives him a feel for the way sentences are put together, and it helps him to build his vocabulary. Memorizing also prepares your child to be a good writer. What goes into a child's head as a little one, will come out later as he writes.

Perhaps your child can recite his memory work in front of the family  or a larger group. This may prepare your child for competitions in oral interpretation and speech and debate when he is older. Together, memorization and narration train, sharpen, and strengthen the mind, which prepares your child for more rigorous studies later on. That is precisely what we want to do in the early years of a child's life. By contrast, television, videos, and even much of the educational software, actually works in the opposite direction.

There is some discussion over *what* to have the child memorize. Some say the time should be spent memorizing facts: dates, Latin verb endings, miscellaneous scientific and geographic data, etc. Maybe so, but there is only so much time in the day, so we, as the parents, need to determine what is the best use of that time. If it is important to you that the child have all the states and capitals memorized by age ten, then by all means do it. Both parents could sit down and write out a list of those things they think are important for their children to memorize, and adjust this list as different priorities emerge. Bare facts, divorced from their contexts, can become a drudgery. Facts are best planted as seeds in the fertile context of their story. Christopher Columbus, discoverer of America on October 12, in the year 1492 – those facts are much better memorized when linked to the story of Columbus. The Greek paradigm for "I believe" – *πιστεύω, πιστεύεις, πιστεύει, πιστεύομεν, πιστεύετε, πιστεύουσι* – is much better memorized when linked to the actual usage of the words:

πιστεύω, I believe.

And immediately the father of the little child, crying out with tears, said, "**Πιστεύω**, *κύριε*, **I believe**, Lord. *Βοη'θει μου τῇ ἀπιστίᾳ.* Relieve my unbelief." — Mark 9:24

πιστεύεις, Thou believest.

And Philip said, "*Εἰ* ***πιστεύεις*** *ἐξ ὅλης τῆς καρδίας, ἔξεστιν.* If **thou believest** from the whole heart, it is lawful." And answering he [the Ethiopian] said, "**Πιστεύω** *τὸν υἱὸν τοῦ θεοῦ εἶναι τὸν Ἰησοῦν Χριστόν.* **I believe** Jesus Christ to be the son of God." — Acts 8:37

Et cetera.

Because of the way that the brain is structured before age ten, we believe that memorizing passages of literature in Latin or Greek, and their translation in English, would be much more profitable than memorizing deductive paradigms in the language (which is formal Latin and Greek grammar). Indeed, the ideal is to be a multilingual family where the children learn to speak and read all of these languages in their early years long before they ever study the grammar – just as they learn English before they ever study the grammar! The time for formal grammar – paradigms and such – is at age ten or after. If they've trained their mind to memorize, and they have become familiar with the language, then they should be able to memorize the paradigms at age ten with relative ease. More on that subject later.

Spend some time – maybe five to ten minutes per child, once or twice each day – listening to each child recite his memory work. Daily exercise for the memory, like daily exercise for the body, helps to maintain its strength. Certainly, the child will not need to review every day everything that he has ever committed to memory. After he has mastered something, bring on something new, and review the old masters once a week or so. After a fair amount of old masters are accumulated, then review the oldest once a month or so. Over the years, many things may fade, though their impression will always be there, yet some things will never be forgotten.

4. Hearing and Listening

By reading aloud to your child, he learns the sound of words, he increases his vocabulary, he enlarges his conceptions of the world, and he develops his imagination. We suggest that you read to your child at least two hours a day (not necessarily consecutive). Read from a wide variety of good literature, biographies, and historical fiction. Include books on science, geography, art, music, and history. Some parents combine narration with read aloud times.

THREE DO NOTS:

1. Do not be afraid to read to young children books with long chapters. A five-year-old is capable of attending to and understanding much of such books as *Treasure Island* or *Journey to the Center of the Earth*.
2. Do not waste your time reading "fast-food" type books (e.g. *Babysitter Club* books or Nancy Drew mysteries).
3. Do not require your children to sit beside you on the couch perfectly still while you read. As long as they stayed in the room and were not distracting or interrupting, we allowed our children to play quietly with their toys, or to work on cross-stitching, or to draw, or some similar quiet project, while we read aloud. Many children listen much better when they are doing something with their hands – indeed, it seems some little boys cannot sit still long enough to listen unless they are holding something.

We do not often read aloud in one uninterrupted two-hour-long stretch. We read some in the morning, some in the afternoon, and some at night. There are notable exceptions. I remember one day when we read *The Long Winter* by Laura Ingalls Wilder in one long stretch, skipping everything else which would interrupt our reading the day away.

Reading aloud is my (Laurie's) favorite part of Homeschooling. How many others have had this experience: I am sitting on the couch (a chair would never do) reading a good book, such as *Men of Iron* by Howard Pyle. One child sits on my right, and one child sits on my left, and one child sits on the back of the couch behind my neck, and one child sits on my lap. The fifth child must make do. Everyone *must* to be situated, just so, in order to see all of the pictures – which *must* be examined minutely before the page is turned. This is one of the ways God taught me patience. Let them look at the pictures and ask their questions. We will eventually find out if Miles wins the joust. My oldest daughter, Johannah, painted this cozy scene for us, collaging photos from long ago, putting us all into one memorable picture. I was wearing braids and sitting on that old brown couch which long ago met the rubbish pile after much good use. If I could have just an hour of that time again, right now, I would gladly read *Corduroy* fifteen times in a row and not complain.

When I read a book which includes dialogue written in a dialect, I attempt to imitate the foreign accent. This tends to spill over into other conversations – even when answering the phone. The children are embarrassed when we drive into the McDonald's drive through, and I order the hamburgers in a Scottish brogue.

TIMELINE

You can develop your child's idea of the continuity of history by marking those things you study or read about on a timeline. Stretch some paper out on your living room wall, draw a line down the middle, mark it off in fifty or hundred year increments, then leave it there for the next twenty years. You could have one family timeline, or each child could make his own timeline. Every time you read something historical, mark it on your timeline. When you read about the life of Bach, mark his birth and death on the timeline. When you read about the invention of the printing press, mark that point on the timeline. The children could illustrate the timeline. Some families put their timelines into three ring binders. That makes them more portable, and more revisable. A timeline displays a continuous view of history, especially when it is placed where the children can always look at it. If memorizing dates is important to you, this may make it easier. More importantly, it gives your child a better notion of the time relationship between events. Daddy and Mommy were not even married when men first landed on the moon! Daddy lived before there were superhighways or rockets. Great grandpa lived before there were jet airplanes. *The Wall Chart of*

World History, by Edward Hull, is a valuable resource to have in order to consult. This looks like an oversized hard cover book, but it folds out into a chart over fifteen feet long, and it includes Biblical and world historical events. The chart presents a visual overview of history. It will help you to put into context the historical fiction and biographies which you read aloud. It will also help you to compose your own timeline.

HISTORY NOTEBOOK

We suggest that each child should maintain his own history notebook. He could begin this notebook when he is in the Early Knowledge Level, though many will wait until he is older before introducing this. A three-ring binder filled with subject dividers and paper (white and colored) will allow for adding and removing pages. We will discuss the history notebook in more detail under the Later Knowledge Level (Chapter Twelve).

ABRIDGED VERSUS UNABRIDGED BOOKS

Question: Why is it important to read classic literature in unabridged versions? Isn't the version abridged in order to prevent readers from becoming "bogged down" and "giving up?"

Answer: Here are the four phases of a book: 1) the original unabridged version, 2) the abridged version, 3) the comic book version, and 4) the movie version. Why shouldn't we skip the first three phases and only require that our children watch the movie version? I hope the answer is obvious. If our children only watched movies instead of reading, they would not develop literary-mindedness. They would not develop vocabulary, grammatical construction, paragraph construction, development of thought, etc. They would not develop their mental imagery – they would only be seeing pictures, interrupted by dialogue.

What if we only required our children to read the comic book version of a book? They would still gather in some of the story, but the vocabulary, sentence construction, etc. would be at the pabulum level. This sort of thing may be acceptable for children first learning to read, but older children must be challenged in their thinking.

We could stop at the abridged versions. That is where most of America stops anyway. Read this:

> Mrs. Swift was waiting for them in front of the house, as the car shrieked to an abrupt halt.

This was taken from *Tom Swift and His Flying Lab* – a typical fast-food type book. It takes no thought to read that sentence. You know all the words and their meanings. Your mind absorbs the sentence easily. In fact, reading aloud this type of sentence is tiring. It doesn't take long before fatigue sets in and the book is put down. It dulls the mind. Now, read this:

> By the time the boat came back to Hall's, his arms were so numb that he could hardly tell whether his oar was in or out of his hand; his legs were stiff and aching, and every muscle in his body felt as if it had been pulled out an inch or two.

This was taken from *Tom Brown at Oxford*. This type of sentence holds the attention. It engages the mind. The sentence structure challenges, yet does not overwhelm. Abridged versions commonly dumb down the language to an elementary level. There are exceptions, of course – but that is exactly what they are – exceptions.

How do you develop an appetite for a good, lean steak if all you eat is soybean imitation meat? One develops the fast-food appetite by reading the fast-food edited versions. They write those abridged versions because most people today cannot read the good literature. They never learned to read properly, and their vocabulary is frozen at the fifth grade level. But we should not allow the unbelieving culture to drag us down with their adulterated versions.

NON-CHRISTIAN BOOKS

Question: What good purpose is served by reading books which are written by non-Christians? We know homeschoolers who do not read anything which is not by a Christian author, and even then, they reject many books if they appear to have too much "conflict or evil." This would include, but not be limited to books such as *The Hobbit* and *Silas Marner* or authors such as George MacDonald and Charles Dickens.

Answer: I first heard this question many years ago in Houston, Texas. A woman was looking over our booklet, *Hand That Rocks the Cradle* (our list of books of fiction which we have read and recommend) and she wondered why we recommended a book all about war: *Johnny Tremain*.

Some of the books which we read and enjoyed fifteen years ago, we would not necessarily approve of today. Several years ago, we read the *Jeremy* books by Hugh Walepole, and I remember loving them. I recently reread one of them, and I could not believe I ever liked it. Jeremy, the main character, is quite disrespectful of his parents, and what is worse, his disrespectfulness is approved of by the author. In other words, if the boy showed disrespect and was punished for it and this conflict was resolved in the book, then that would be right. But in this story, the boy showed disrespect, and the author allowed that to be a part of Jeremy's character without showing that it was wrong. Fifteen years ago, I did not see that problem. Today, I see the problem very clearly. We took the books off of our list.

Each book should be read critically, pointing out its good points as well as its problems and faults, and analyzing the author's philosophy. Use each book as an example to show the children what to look for. Though you should never read anything uncritically, yet you also do not want to spend all of your time criticizing. You must determine for your own family what is the proper balance for each book. This is a judgement call, and we cannot fault families who choose not to read some literature. The label "Christian" is by no means a guarantee that the material is not offensive, let alone that it is of good quality. Many Christian authors write pabulum.

We read theological authors with whom we disagree. We read very critically, and they often end up being much more profitable than authors with whom we agree – precisely because they make us think.

The works of Robert Louis Stevenson are some of the most excellent English literature ever written, and there may be much value in reading them, but he does not appear to be a Christian.

Do not make a steady diet of one author. Read critically. Do not live for entertainment.

I CANNOT KEEP UP WITH MY CHILD'S READING

Question: My son, age nine, devours books. He does manage to put up with my reading aloud, and even seems to enjoy it, but I can tell that he would rather just zoom through the books himself. I have told him that we will continue to do both. The problem is, he reads so fast (and can narrate back accurately) that I can hardly keep him in books! I used to be able to read books before I gave them to him, but I can no longer keep up with him. I am uncomfortable with just handing him books which I have not read. What if he comes across something which I would not want him to read, or which I think would not be appropriate for his age?

Answer: You are right in feeling uncomfortable with just handing a nine-year-old a book to read without knowing what is in the book. It is better not to read at all than to read garbage. I never allowed my children to read books with which I was unfamiliar. When they did want to read something with which I was not familiar, then I would read it aloud, commenting on any bad ideas presented in the story, and skipping over any inappropriate parts. Sometimes I would just stop reading – the book was not worth the bother. The book which taught me this lesson was *Tarzan*, by Edgar Rice Borroughs. Nathaniel was young when he wanted to read this book, and because it is an old book, I thought it must be acceptable. After Nathaniel finished reading the book, he told me that the main character in it committed adultery. He did not think he should read any more books by Borroughs. I was rather upset that Nathaniel had not stopped reading the book immediately when he came upon that incident, but I was nevertheless glad that he told me about it. It taught me that I need to be more careful concerning what the children read, and that just because a book is old does not mean it is good. If you cannot keep up with the boy's reading, then you may choose to have him reread approved books.

As your son listens to father or mother read aloud to all the children, he will strengthen his auditory learning skills, and he will help him to develop his imagination. He will also be sharing time with the family, instead of being off by himself, indulging his own ways.

QUIET WHILE READING ALOUD

Question: I have four children. I read to my ten and seven-year-old together, and I read separately to my four-year-old. The four-year-old is wonderful, but he is also strong-willed, and he is inclined to test the waters whenever and wherever he can. Having a seven month old baby on top of this has made schooling very challenging. Since the four-year-old is no longer napping, it is even more challenging. Though I have attempted to include him in the room while I read, it seems very difficult for him to avoid making interruptive noises while I read. I have tried puzzles, and this worked the best, but he does not have the attention span of the older two. It is hard to continue reading while he constantly switches activities. I can read for about an hour when he is with us, but it is a very challenging hour. It is difficult for the older two to narrate against the background noise of his activities.

Answer: Imagine this scenario: mother calls up the stairs, "I will be reading in five minutes." Instantly, five little munchkins come tumbling down the steps, ever anxious for the next installment of *Island of the Blue Dolphins*. Intent on working with the new markers which Uncle David gave him, nine-year-old Nathaniel quietly sits down at the art table which mother has positioned next to the art shelf in the living room. Seven-year-old Johannah picks up her cross-stitch project she is hoping to finish for this year's county fair. Five-year-old Hans plays quietly in the corner with his Legos. Three-year-old Ava happily sits near mother on the couch sucking her thumb and holding mother's hair. And little Helena crawls around, examining the furniture, and falls asleep on the floor an hour into the reading. All the children work and play quietly, never causing mother a moment's worry or distraction. She never has a need to tell anyone to be quiet or to stop fighting. All is peace and calmness. Mother reads for two hours, stopping occasionally to call for narrations, and then stops to prepare dinner. Is this reality? I think not.

Here is reality. Mother is reading *Two Little Confederates*, by Thomas Nelson Page. Twice, she stops to tell the girls to please stop talking. Then the boys came in from working on the barn roof to check on what had come in the mail. Then grandma calls to tell mother the latest news. By the time mother puts down the phone, her audience has disappeared. If you wait for the perfect time to read aloud, you'll still be waiting. When the children are small, you will have interruptions. The smaller the children and the larger the number of children, the more the interruptions. But what is motherhood all about but a training of these children. When you're through with the brood, and your nest is empty, then you'll miss those times, and you won't care about the interruptions. My hope now is that my sons and daughters will let me help with their broods.

My daughter Helena just asked me if I told you to keep a fly swatter next to your chair as you read. I guess I must have done that when they were young, but I really don't remember. Children do remember the strangest things.

Here are some suggestions which may help. You may require a three or four-year-old to stay in one area – on a blanket or small rug, kept busy for half of an hour with Legos or some such toy. After this, switch his places and his toys and require him to play quietly for another fifteen minutes. By that time, mother will need a break from reading, so everyone can move on to the next thing on their schedule. Perhaps you could hold back some special toys just for read-aloud times. If the child becomes noisy in his play, then stop reading, and gently remind him to "modulate your voice," as Laura Ingalls Wilder's mother used to say. At times, you will need to use the switch. The process for obtaining the end is as important as the end itself. We would like to obtain the end point of no interruptions when we read, but we must employ appropriate means, even if we never quite obtain that end. Children remember *how* we mothers did things, and sometimes *why* we did things, regardless of how often the perfect result was actually obtained. Were we gentle and kind in our training? Were we consistent in how we disciplined? Was it important to show respect by keeping quiet and not interrupting her, so that everyone could listen? When it's time for them to raise their children, they'll follow our example. Let's bless them with better examples for them to follow.

BOOKS RECORDED ON TAPE

Question: What do you think of children listening to books recorded on tape as a partial substitute for mom reading aloud one to two hours per day. My eight-year-old boy has latched onto several very good books, at least two grades above his reading level, which he has gobbled up because he can listen to the tape and follow along in the book.

Answer: Our family occasionally listens to books on tape, especially while traveling long distances in the van. Many libraries have a large selection of books recorded on tape. Your suggestion of having the child follow along in the book as he listens to the tape may be very good. This combines the auditory with the visual. But do not allow this to become a total substitute for his own reading, and for father and mother reading aloud. You still need to do this, for your sake, and for your family's sake.

5. Family Worship

Contrary to the old saying, "the family which prays together, stays together," studies have shown that the family which only prays together – that is, worships together only at church – does not usually stay together. The family which stays together is the family which prays and studies the Bible together regularly as a family at home. The father should lead the family in prayer and Bible studies, morning and evening, if possible. This will strengthen the father's role as the accountable head and moral guide of the family. The mother teaches her children the proper role of submission to their parents by her example of submission to their father. Mothers are not to be the spiritual leaders of the family. With regular family worship, the mind is developed along spiritual and moral lines in a way which cannot be accomplished by Bible workbooks, private devotions, or regular church attendance.

Here is a method of Bible study which we believe is Biblical and profitable. Have someone read a passage of Scripture, then have everyone in the family, perhaps in turn, ask the father a question about the passage. Before age ten, you may expect a child to ask mostly Knowledge Level questions of fact and details. By age thirteen he will ask more Understanding Level questions of theory and implications. By age sixteen he will ask more Wisdom Level questions of practice and application. If you accomplish all of the academics, but leave out family worship, then you will raise well educated practical agnostics. Family training in God's word should be your top priority – far above academics. (See Appendix One, Article Fifteen, Family Bible Study by the Trivium.)

Do not let your child ignore God. God is the ultimate reason for why he is alive. When God speaks, He must always have the child's attention. So do not indulge in frivolous Bible story books which degrade God's word to entertaining comics, or reduces Bible history to nice little tales on the level of myths and fables. The standard must not be entertainment value, but faithfulness to God's word.

6. Arts and Crafts

Young children learn more through their senses. They need more hands on manipulatives before age ten. Provide children with the place, the tools, and the time for their art work.

Make sure you have a space in your home where the children can easily pull out these art materials and work on projects. In the main room of your house, or wherever it is you read to the children and spend the most time, maintain a low shelf stocked with good quality colored pencils, crayons or markers, paints, brushes, paper, scissors, glue, clay, wallpaper sample books, fabric sample books, matting board scraps, stitching, sewing, knitting, and crocheting supplies. Next to this shelf, you may have a small table with chairs where the children can easily work on their projects while you read to them. Younger children can do crafts, while the older ones are being helped with math or science. Art and craft projects can be sent to relatives, made into gifts, given to residents at the nursing home, entered into contests, taken to the county fair, or simply displayed in the home. In our home, we have framed many of the children's works, and the walls are covered with the results.

Give them plenty of time to experiment with arts and crafts and thereby develop their elementary creativity. Some children could spend one or two hours a day on arts and crafts, while other children won't be able to give it more than a few minutes attention. If you sit down and work beside them, they'll spend more time.

One of the most useful things I ever purchased for my girls was a bag of fabric scraps from a lady who did sewing and alterations. The bag cost me only five dollars, but was filled with all kinds of scraps of silks, satins, velvets, and wools. The girls were quite young at the time, and they had very elementary skills at sewing, but those first few efforts at turning the scraps into doll clothes fed their desire to learn more. They quickly passed me in ability, and eventually taught themselves tailoring and pattern making, such that now they make vintage clothing reproductions. All this came out of a bag of scraps. I made sure that they had all of the time and the materials which they needed for their projects, and I provided the place for them to work. The sewing machine, the art shelf, and the tables were always handy and accessible for all of the children. Their projects could be left setting out until finished. Nothing may be more discouraging to a budding young artist than to be required to put away a half finished project. When they're done with the project, they can clean up, and the house can return to order.

Do not allow your child to do arts and crafts on the computer. The mouse does not teach manipulation nearly so well as a lump of clay or a square block. Computers may be wonderful tools in their place. This is not their place.

Our children primarily learned to draw by copying. They copied famous drawings and paintings, pictures out of *The Art-Literature Readers*, or the *McGuffey Readers*, books from Dover Publications, or just anything we had around the house. When our children were young and just learning to draw I bought for them the Dover book, *Animals: 1,419 Copyright-Free Illustrations of Mammals, Birds, Fish, Insects, etc., A Pictorial Archive from Nineteenth-Century Sources Selected by Jim Harter*. This book is full of black and white pen and ink drawings (with short descriptions) which the children copied into their own little art booklets. They also entered these drawings at the fair.

7. *Field Trips*

Take field trips frequently. Take time to attend concerts and plays, museums and exhibits. Visit workplaces. Give your child experiences from which to build his understanding of the world – experiences he will draw upon and perhaps revisit when he is older.

Do not let your child explore the world only from a cathode ray tube. Children need real experiences to relate to. Seeing a jet take off on television is not the same as seeing a jet take off in front of you. Hearing an orchestra on television or radio is not the same as hearing an orchestra in person. Watching a computer simulation of a scientific experiment, or watching a video of it, is not the same as doing it in front of your very own eyes. Yes, you can learn some things by the tube. But it is not the same — there are also some things which you are not learning.

When your child is four or five, begin attending your local Science and Engineering Fair. Observe all of the different kinds of projects and experiments. Encourage the child to think of what kind of experiment he could enter when he is thirteen (at the Understanding Level).

Early on, form the habit of visiting the library on a weekly basis. At a young age, the child will become familiar with where to find the different assortments of books, and how to ask the librarian for help. Later, you will teach the child to use the computer catalog and the reference section of the library. Around age thirteen (which is the beginning of the Understanding Level), take your child to a good college library and familiarize him with doing research, using the Library of Congress system. At age fifteen, take him to a large university library. By the time a child is in his later teens, he should know how to perform research in any library.

When I was no more than eight years old, Grandma Haigh took me to one of the tiny branches of the Des Moines Public Library. To this day, I can recall the wonder and amazement which filled me when I saw all of those books. After that visit, I yearned to have a library card of my own. It was another three years before my wish was fulfilled. In 1963, when I was eleven, my family moved to San Diego, and there we were given a free card to the public library. For the next year, every Monday night, after doing the grocery shopping, we would visit the library. I began at the "A's" in the juvenile fiction section, checking out six books every week. I do not remember how far I went down the alphabet, but that "year of the library" provoked in me a life time love for reading.

PROTECTING A CHILD IN THE LIBRARY

Question: Our library children's room is largely filled with light reading and pop-culture rubbish. My seven-year-old son loves to read, and he will read anything, so I must be careful when I take him to the library. Though I direct him to the good books, he often ends up with some rubbish. What is the point in my taking him to the library if I then refuse to take home the books which he picks out? He loves to go to the library, and I do not want to quench his desire.

Answer: Libraries have become dangerous places for children. The covers alone on some books on display are very wicked. It is no longer safe to allow a child to wander about in a library – particularly because of the magazine section, the Internet access, the videos, and now, even the books on display in the window. It may come to the point where you must pick out the books for the children and bring them home. It may even come to the point where you do not want to be seen in the library yourself. But then how will your children learn to do library research? Since you are in a situation where you have only one library to which to go, then you must work with the situation. The Caldecott books are usually safe. Do they have these books in a separate section of the library? Is there a little table somewhere in the library where you could all park your things, and the children could sit and look at the books which you bring to them? If you are unsure of which books would be good for your children to read, then find and work through a recommended reading list from someone whom you trust. You will teach your son how to pick out the good books by picking out the books for him at first, explaining to him what kind of books you do not want him to read. Explain to him that if he is not sure whether you would approve of a particular book, then he must bring it to you and ask. Explain to him that you are teaching him to be a discerning reader. I am afraid Christians must eventually abandon the libraries some day. We need to build our own libraries. If possible, build up your own personal library. I am buying books for my grandchildren.

8. Work and Service

Develop in your child a love for work and service. From the time a child is able to walk and talk, he should be given regular chores to perform. We do not mean simply feeding the dog and making his bed. A five-year-old is quite capable of putting the dishes away and folding the laundry. A ten-year-old can prepare simple meals from start to finish. Children of all ages can clean and straighten the house. The mother should not be picking up things from off of the floor. Your goal should be that, by the time the children are in their teens, they are able to take over the work of the household, from cooking to cleaning to caring for their younger brothers and sisters. This not only teaches them to appreciate work while removing some of the burden from the parents, but it is good training for when they have their own households.

Do not do for your child what he can do for himself. We need to reject all of this popular *self-esteem* stuff. The world's problems can be summarized in one simple expression: too much self-esteem. Too many people think they are too good for what they receive in life. They think they deserve better. And among the things which foster such notions is parents fawning over their little children. For the first year of his life, you pretty much need to do everything for him. But after that, the situation should begin to change rapidly. He can learn to do many things for himself in the next couple of years. He can clean up his own messes.

An important corollary to this is: Do not do for yourself what your child can do for you. Your child needs to esteem himself lower than others, beginning with his parents. He can gather the clothes for laundry, and he can fold the laundry. Then he can do the laundry. He can set the table and wash the dishes. Then he can help fix the meals. He can vacuum the floor and dust the furniture. Then he can wash the windows. If you do all of this for him, then he will develop a notion of self-*esteem*: "I am so important that everyone ought to do things for me." But if he learns to do it for himself, then he will develop a notion of self-*confidence*: "I can do it myself." And if he learns to do it for you, then he will develop a notion of self-*usefulness*: "I can be helpful, and I am needed around here."

We suggest that you write out a schedule of chores for each child. Some families rotate chores on a weekly basis, while other families prefer to give each child permanent chores, changing them only after several months, or when needed. However you choose to do it, the schedule should be well organized, listing who does what and when. You should post the family schedule in a prominent location. Make sure the results for not obeying are clearly understood. When our children were young, I did not write out a chore schedule. I would give out orders randomly and inconsistently. Because the children did not know what was expected of them, I ended up doing the majority of the work. Later, when we put together an organized schedule, dividing up the work among all five children, our life moved much more smoothly. At first, all five children took turns cooking the main meal. After suffering with the boys' cooking for a few months, we rearranged the schedule so that only the girls cooked. It will take a while for you to fine tune your chore schedule. Be flexible: make changes as children grow older and more mature.

Along with work, children should be taught to serve. We visited the residents of a nursing home on a regular basis. When we visited, we simply walked in and began talking to one of the elderly people. Most of the residents were not able to communicate, so we continue until we found someone with whom we were able to communicate. Some cannot communicate, but enjoy having someone holding their hand. We would eventually find two or three people with whom we wanted to be friends. If you should attempt nursing home visitation, I suggest during your first visits, that the mother and father do the talking, and the children just walk beside and listen.

Other volunteer opportunities abound. Our girls crochet from thread tiny baby booties for different pro-life organizations. When a mother has a positive pregnancy test, she is given a pair of these booties as her first baby present. Many of these mothers have every intention of getting an abortion, and it is our hope that the sight of these tiny booties will bring them to their natural senses. Another area of need is in the neonatal Intensive Care Unit of your local hospital. They need hospital gowns for the tiny babies born there and clothes for the babies going home. There is also a need for bereavement gowns for babies which die.

9. Discipline

We have found, in our own experience, that if the area of discipline is neglected, then we may as well forget about academics. Children will never learn self-discipline if parents do not train them in it. The child who does not develop self-discipline will fail in many things – including the academics for which you hope to prepare him.

Ask yourself these questions: Am I satisfied with the obedience of my children? Do I enjoy being around my children? Do my children honor and respect me? If your answer is "no" to any of these questions, then you should re-evaluate your priorities. If you do not have first time obedience from children of all ages, then your homeschool journey will be beset with all number of difficulties. Regarding first time obedience, we highly recommend a book originally published in 1833, *The Mother At Home*, by John S.C. Abbott. This book is a most valuable resources for training young women, from a Biblical perspective, on the art of mothering. Another resource is, *Letters on the Education of Children*, by John Witherspoon, published by the MacArthur Institute.

Do not allow your child to ignore you. You are the immediate reason for why he is alive. When you tell him something, make sure he hears you. When you read to him, do not let his attention wander too far. Of course, be sensitive. There are going to be times when he has something he needs to think about, and you may need to leave him do so. But do not let him shut you out. You must always have his attention when you speak. You must always have something for him to hear. No, we do not live up to that standard. But that should be the standard by which we measure.

Do not let your child rule you. Let him rule himself. A man must rule himself before he can rule others. (Think of all of the public offices which have become inverted and perverted because of men who could not first rule themselves.) Nobody learns to rule himself by obeying his own desires. He can only learn to rule himself by obeying another's desires. There must be something larger than himself to serve. (That is why the concept of God is inescapable. If you do not follow the true God, then you must invent a substitute god to serve a similar function.) If you can teach your child to know himself and rule himself, then he will be able to rule that part of the world which you give to him, and eventually that part of the world of which God places him in stewardship

During one of our trips, we visited a family which lived a very simple life in a very modest home, and homeschooled their five small children. The parents were quite soft spoken and gentle in manner, always speaking to the children in a calm, quiet way. From the very beginning of our visit, it became obvious that the children attended to the voices of their parents. The parents had first time obedience from even the youngest, and this obedience was obtained with a quiet voice and manner. In all my life, I have never witnessed anything like it. On one occasion, the one-year-old began to climb up on the kerosene heater. I saw the father give an almost imperceptible shake of the head and heard him say in a whisper, "Isaac, huh, uh." Immediately the child shifted into reverse and backed away from the heater. The child attended to and obeyed the very whisper of his father. It moves me to tears to recall that scene and the affection which the children and parents had for each other. Oh, that I had trained my children so well when they were young. God wants first time obedience from us, and we should form the same habit in our children. When we resort to speaking in a loud voice when we want something of our children, or when we form the habit of repeating our requests, we train our children to ignore us when we speak. If we could only begin at the very beginning to train our children to attend to our voice – to listen for it no matter what they are doing, and to immediately obey, how well we will prepare them to listen to their heavenly Father as well.

If we were to accomplish this, then our children would view their parents as servants view their masters, and as subjects view their king. They would have great respect and honor for their parents, wanting only to please them. Of course, the king would be a benevolent and kind master who cared most for his subjects, always treating them with tenderness and love. Yes, we are kings and queens, our homes are our castles, and the little ones are the servants training one day to be masters of their own homes. Does a queen need to resort to yelling to have something accomplished? Not likely in a well ordered kingdom. How much better our world would be if we rendered first time obedience to our Lord.

SOCIALIZATION AND YOUNG GIRLS

Question: My oldest (age eleven) does not want to go to the library during the day, because "school kids" are not there. I am worried about her. We moved here two years ago, and we have not found any homeschool friends in the area.

Answer: I assume, from your letter, that your daughter likes to be around other children. She feels lonely. Perhaps she even would like to go to school. Young children like yours actually need *very little socialization*. In fact I would avoid it, except for occasional, controlled situations when you have another family over to visit and your children play with their children. The notion that every child needs another child of his same age to play with all of the time is an idea invented in the twentieth century. Whether children like it or not, it is nevertheless generally a bad idea. Involve your daughter in crocheting, knitting, sewing, and other craft work. Perhaps she can make things to give away, or even sell. My girls sew costumes. Teach your daughter to cook. An eleven-year-old girl is perfectly capable of cooking an entire meal, from start to finish. Obtain a large hope chest for your daughter and have her begin making things to fill it. A profitable use of time for young ones is raising food in the garden and storing it up for the winter. Is she good at drawing or painting? She could produce little booklets on a variety of subjects (birds, dogs, flowers, etc.) to sell or give away. Incorporate this into her school work. She needs to get busy doing things for others and to worry less about her own little desires and comforts.

Around age ten or eleven, many girls go through a phase where they are hard to get along with. When this happened with my first daughter, I did not understand what was happening, and I allowed her rebellion, incommunicativeness, coldness, moodiness, etc. to go without proper correction. I found myself attempting to please her and to make her comfortable. I thought I was not a very good mom. I could not figure out what I was doing wrong. Because she always seemed so unhappy and out of sorts, I would go to great lengths to make her happy. Finally, after several years of heartache, the Lord showed me what was happening, and we resolved the problem.

You cannot allow a child to show disrespect to his father or mother. Ask yourself this question: Am I satisfied with his behavior? If the answer is no, then you must take action. There are many ways a child can show disrespect: rolling of the eyes; exasperated sighing; delayed obedience; questioning; stalking out of a room; slamming doors; non-communicating attitude. You must force them to talk with you and to tell you what they perceive is wrong or what is bothering them. Often, they don't really know themselves until you force them to think about it, when they realize how stupid their ideas are. I insisted that my daughter sit on the couch with me until she told me what was bothering her. Sometimes we sat there for several hours. Many times it all boiled down to the fact that she just felt irritable and did not even have a reason for it. She learned to recognize and repent of her irritability and moodiness and disrespect. Of course, all of this led me to recognize that I, as her mother, must be a good example for her. I also must learn to recognize and repent of my own irritability.

DOES NOT WANT TO WORK

Question: I find myself "putting up" for far too long with the rolling of the eyes, the unhappiness, the stomping. Now, what do I do with a young lady, sixteen, who wants to read all day and do nothing else – no cleaning, no chores, no cooking, no gardening? Did you come across this with your children, and if so, how did you deal with it?

Answer: Do you mean that she will not obey you when asked to clean or cook? Or is it that she only does the minimum that you require and spends the rest of her time reading? I picture a sixteen-year-old daughter as being able to take over the running of the household. If the mother must be gone for a few days, the daughter should be able to take care of the house: the cleaning, cooking, laundry, answering the phone, and perhaps caring for one or two little ones. Perhaps she will not keep the house as thoroughly clean as mother does, and perhaps the meals will not be as elaborate, but at age sixteen, she can run a relatively orderly household. All this should be done cheerfully and willingly.

Some mothers will expect these things of their daughters, but not give the child any freedom in making some of the decisions as to how these things are done. For example, the daughter is expected to prepare the meals, but is not allowed to decide what she will serve. I suggest that a sixteen-year-old could be planning the meals (with some of mother's help), shopping for the food, and preparing the meals. That is how we do it in our house. I allow the girls to decide when they will do the laundry. As long as it is finished before bedtime, they can do it whenever they want. I do not tell them when to clean their rooms, but they know they are to keep them neat. I am referring to older children here. Little ones need to be trained, so you would have more rules and time schedules, but older children have already been trained and need less "do this now, and this way" type rules.

I think children find more satisfaction in their chores if they know they are "in charge" of something, and they know they have full responsibility. My older daughters love it when I give them the food money for the week and let them take charge. I do have a problem with them not wanting to use up all the zucchini I harvest from the garden, but we are working on that.

Now, perhaps your problem is that the sixteen-year-old just will not obey. If you write out and explain to her exactly what is expected from her – which goes, beyond chores, to attitudes and behaviors – and what will happen if she does not do them, then she has no excuse. You know what you must do. The Bible tells you that you must respond to the disobedience. The time for spanking is long past by the time a child reaches sixteen. I do not think that is appropriate. There are other ways to discipline her. Take away her reading time. Fine her money. Take away privileges. Require more work from her, such as picking up trash on the roadway. Apply academics to the problem and have her write an essay concerning her disobedience. This will require her to think it through.

How much of the problem is you? Who is boss in your family? Often we parents do not consistently enforce obedience. Sometimes we make them obey, and at other times we are too tired, or it is too inconvenient to make them obey. Perhaps we are at the store, or we have company, or we have been working all day, or we are just plain weary. We make excuses for the child, or for ourselves. Homeschooling is more than Latin and Logic. It is a way of life. And that way of life includes having disciplined children, and encouraging loving relationships within the family. We want peace in our homes. Peace comes with one price – God's order.

PEACE IN THE HOME

Question: You said the goal is to have peace in the home. How do you accomplish that? I grew up in a non-Christian home where everyone was always fighting, and I do not want our family to turn out that way. Our children are much better behaved than my siblings and I were, but they still spend too much time fighting and crabbing at each other.

Answer: In our travels we have stayed with quite a few families. Here are some of our observations:

In families where peace reigns, we notice that the children have respect for father and mother. You can see it in their faces. The children want to please their parents. They know father is in charge, and they look to him for answers. Father knows what is best. They know that their mother controls the household to serve their father, and they understand that father rules the family to serve the Lord. When children are made to understand the order and purpose of things, and they live out their role in that order and purpose – that is peace. Of course, wise parents rule and control their family and household with kindness and gentleness and tender loving care. They are fallen creatures themselves, and are not always wise. But the more the family matches the ideal, the more peace reigns.

In families where peace does not reign, we notice that the children lack respect for the father and mother. The household revolves around the children and their likes or dislikes, their moods, their desires. They know that their parents are intent on pleasing them, and they use this as a manipulative tool. When the child is displeased, uncomfortable, or inconvenienced, the parents consistently go out of their way to please the child. They think their little child is so smart, or cute, or witty. In other words, the order and purpose and roles of this family are inverted, and anything which might resemble peace for a moment is just a temporary lapse in the ongoing war over who is in charge.

Children may know how to speak and understand words, but this does not mean that communication is happening at the level which it should. We cannot assume that they will come to us and tell us what is bothering them. If we detect something wrong with an attitude or an action, then we need to discuss it with our child. Do not wait until the action or attitude gets unbearable. There was a time when our older daughter began to treat her younger sister very coldly. She was excluding her from things, not confiding in her any more, and siding up with the youngest daughter. It began slowly, and we did not really notice it until it had been happening for perhaps four or five months. The younger daughter had to come to me and point it out. Only when she pointed it out did I see it. Something can begin so small, yet if you do not catch it, it can grow very big, and you still must have it pointed out to you. By the time I began to address the issue, the younger daughter was angry with her sister for treating her that way. It took several weeks to straighten out the matter. The older daughter did not even realize what she was doing. She repented, her sister forgave her, and we had to go through several weeks of pointing out to the older daughter when she was exhibiting the undesirable behavior (acting coldly to her sister). She had developed the habit of treating her sister that way, and I had to help her break the habit. Praise God, He put the desire in her to change. But, what if the older one did not repent, but preferred to treat her sister coldly – for whatever reason? Then I must enforce proper behavior.

IRRITATED OBEDIENCE

Question: Regarding the eye-rolling and 'humphs,' with a little puff of air which blows her hair up: Am I at fault for asking my daughter to do various chores, keeping her "on call" for things which need to be done at her own convenience, though not on the chart? Do I verbally correct her on the spot? Even that little "humph" can grow into something more as a child gets older, so I think it does need some punishment, but what and how? Should I have a planned "punishment" for every little "humph?"

Answer: I think you have already answered your own question. The little "humph" clearly communicates disrespect. What would have happened to a lady-in-waiting at Queen Victoria's court if she had responded with a "humph" to one of the Queen's requests? You are the Queen in your house and Daddy is the King. All the little ones are servants in training.

It is good to have a schedule of chores and activities and responsibilities posted so that everyone knows what is expected of them, but there will always be extra things to do which cannot be put on a chart. The children should be happy (if not inwardly, at least outwardly) to perform these tasks for Mommy. A "humph" from a young child needs a visit from the switch. You will need to determine for yourself at what age the switch is put away and other forms of discipline are imposed.

WAIT UNTIL DADDY GETS HOME

Question: What about discipline for the eight-year-old boy? If he does not do his chores, or if he does something he has been told not to do, then is waiting until his father gets home for the discipline a good idea, or is that waiting too long?

Answer: The father rules the family. The mother administrates the household according to father's rules. Punishment delayed loses its proper force, and introduces other forces. So explain the law, administer the punishment, and go on with the day. Otherwise, the day may be ruined as everyone is just waiting "until father gets home." There may be some things which need to be adjudicated by father, but mother should be able to handle most matters. Mother can give her court report when father gets home, and he can make any further adjustments at that time.

UNMOTIVATED SON

Question: My thirteen-year-old son is slower in math, so I let him set the pace. He is also "allergic" to pencils and I am wondering how much is enough writing for him this year. I do not want to encourage laziness, but I also do not want to exasperate him!

Answer: One of the most challenging things which I have dealt with in our Homeschooling is a boy (ages ten to fifteen) who seemed allergic to academic pursuit. One of our five children was like this. He has plenty of inertia. If he is at rest, then he tends to stay at rest, but once you start him moving, he keeps on moving. It is the "get him moving" part which is the difficulty. Somewhere along the way, someone failed to install a starter motor, so we had to crank him to "get him moving." Like you said, we certainly did not want to encourage his laziness, nor exasperate him, yet we needed to "get him moving" and challenge him. If it is any encouragement to you, our son is now a good writer. When he turned fifteen, he discovered that he could write creatively, and he even discovered he enjoyed writing – somewhat, though we are still laboring to make that newly installed starter motor work more consistently.

Here are some of the right things I think we did with him:

1. Up until about age fourteen or so, we did much of his math orally, and sometimes I would do the writing for him. He dictated to me the problem and the steps to the answer, and I held the pencil and did the writing. This in no way interfered with his understanding of math, but on the contrary, I think it helped him to learn to enjoy math. Later, he was able to go through the Saxon algebra books, Jacobs Geometry, and Saxon Advanced Math book with no help at all.
2. I think television, video games, and computer games and most computer software are especially dangerous to boys like this. I am very thankful that we kept our son away from these influences.
3. I am thankful the Lord moved us into the country when the children were young. Peer influence seems to be stronger on unmotivated boys.

10. Play and Exploration

Give the child plenty of time to explore and play. Do not buy "toystore" toys – they are expensive and are usually forgotten after the newness wears off. Invest in real things. Garage sales and auctions are an unending source for things like sewing machines, small tools for working in the garden, hammers, nails, and things for building, some wooden blocks, and dress-up clothes. Buy tools for exploring (a good microscope, telescope, binoculars, dissecting equipment, basic chemistry equipment, etc.), not toys for adoring. Teach your children how to use them responsibly (safe, neat, and orderly – clean up when you are done), and make them readily available for when they want to use them.

When your children are young (at the early Knowledge Level), spend your money on the tools of exploration, and motivate them to learn how to use the tools and enjoy using the tools. If I had to do it all over again, I would have bought our microscope and dissecting kit when my children were young (age six or seven), and would have taught them to use this equipment even at that young age. I would also have bought for them a good telescope, binoculars, basic chemistry equipment (beakers, test tubes, burners, etc.). Of course, they would be taught how to keep everything safe and neat and orderly.

It is not only important that you do some things, it is important that you not do some things. It always seems like there are more do not's than there are do's. Do not set your child in front of a television screen. Television is bad. We mean the screen itself. It is unhealthy for the body, and especially for the eyes. Visual strain is the number-one problem of frequent computer users. Studies estimate that anywhere from fifty to ninety percent of regular computer users experience visual deterioration.

The material on the screen is also bad. The entertainment method of learning creates an entertainment addiction – the child wants to be entertained all of the time – he wants his visual and auditory senses stimulated (overstimulated). Every child needs to learn through touch and taste and smell, and through interaction with real human beings who smile and answer back. He needs to learn while in submission to the authority of real parents, not the authority of glamorized, always-happy, limitlessly-resourceful, never-tired substitutes who have absolutely no accountability. Need we say more?

Do not let your child waste away. You must discover the happy medium between giving your child enough time of his own and giving your child too much time of his own. If he has too little time, he will not develop his own thoughts. If he has too much time, he will pursue mischief, or at least no profitable ends. Give him something to think on when he has nothing to do. Memorization fills the mind with things to teethe his mind on and ponder.

Do not let your child play in a cyber world. He can play in a miniature world. He can play in a pretend world. But it must be made up of objects which exist in the real three-dimensional world, not electrons hitting an opaque, two dimensional phosphorescent screen. Why? Because – though he may learn something from the screen image, there are nevertheless many things which he is not learning precisely because it is only a screen image. Besides the missing sensory experiences (touching, tasting, smelling, hearing, seeing – three dimensionally), there are logical things missing (such as consequences for actions in the real world).

When the computer substitutes for the functions and processes which the brain normally supplies, the brain is left to atrophy. It does not develop its brain muscles, as it were. No pain no gain. If you don't use it, you lose it.

Excessive use of computers, especially at early ages, will restructure the way the brain processes information, often for the worse. It also causes the underdevelopment of the emotional and social dimensions of the child. Young children are developing many parts of their understanding, and "holes" can occur in their development if they are deprived of certain experiences during critical periods of time. These may not be discovered until much later. For example, a child may test perfect for hearing. Yet he had a period of head colds earlier in his life, at the same time that his discernment of speech sounds was developing. Because he was not hearing properly at that time, his discernment of speech is underdeveloped. He hears speech perfectly, but he does not properly discern in his mind what his ears are perfectly hearing. Because you know he can hear well, you think he does not pay careful attention, so you punish him. You do not realize that he cannot pay careful attention, and that you need to train him in a missing skill.

Televisions and computers can be useful tools under the proper circumstances and controls. But they are like fire – a useful servant, but a terrible master. There are many legitimate reasons to doubt their value for children below the age of ten, especially in preparation for classical academic education.

A MOM FOR ALL SEASONS

Question: I'm looking for suggestions on how a mom can best divide, share or even multiply her time among several little ones. My four sons are between two and eight years, with another on the way. Two sons need my time and attention for learning to read and write. I find that I spend less time in puzzles and play dough with the younger two than I did when the older ones were little. I should add that my eldest has some special needs which require one-on-one exercises twice a day. Even when I am reading, or when we are all doing a project together, it seems we serve the interests of the younger sons, or else older sons, but never both. I tell myself that when the older boys are reading, they will have more productive independent time.

Answer: Probably most conscientious young mothers worry about this at one time or another. A mother does not always need to be actively participating with the child in his play in order to satisfy his need for mother's attention. Mother's presence is usually enough. When the children are small, they really don't care to be playing in their bedrooms. They would rather be in the living room or kitchen where mother is. Our children just need to be near us. They need to hear our voice and feel our presence. My friend, who has twelve children, suggested that what is really happening is not that mother's love is being divided more and more as she has more children, but rather, as more siblings are added to the family, love is multiplied, because there are more people to love each child. The family is composed of father, mother, and children. It's not just mother's love that goes around, but father's love and the siblings love for each other. A child in a family of twelve children has thirteen people loving him – mother, father, and eleven brothers and sisters.

TEN THINGS TO DO BEFORE AGE TEN

1 Reading & Writing	*Intensive Phonics* program, beginning at age five or when the child is ready. Old-time readers – when proficient. *Copywork* – at age five: fifteen minutes per day; by age nine: thirty minutes per day. *English Language Notebook*, containing phonics, copywork (or separate copywork notebook).
2 Oral Narration	Begin at age four or five, practice on a daily basis.
3 Memorization	Begin as young as age two or three, recite five to ten minutes daily from Alphabets, selections from the Bible, catechisms, poetry, or literature. Review old memory masters once a week.
4 Hearing & Listening	*Read aloud* at least two hours per day (not all at once) from a variety of fiction and non-fiction. *Timeline* – mark which things you read. *History Notebook* – record things you read.
5 Family Worship	Family Bible Study morning and evening, using Knowledge level questions.
6 Arts & Crafts	Provide the place, the tools, the time, develop elementary creativity.
7 Field Trips & the Library	Investigate the world. Attend concerts, plays, science and engineering fairs, visit museums, exhibits, workplaces. Begin to learn elementary library research.
8 Work & Service	Schedule children's chores, visit nursing homes, develop attitude of service to others.
9 Discipline	Establish first time obedience.
10 Play & Exploration	Develop the imagination.

FIGURE 11A

For books and curriculum materials mentioned in this chapter, and other resources, see our Resource List at the very end of this book.

A SUGGESTED DAILY SCHEDULE FOR FAMILIES WITH CHILDREN ALL UNDER THE AGE OF TEN

Schedules are made as a standard to serve you, not as a master to break you. Do not be a slave to the schedule, but also do not be a slave to the emergency mindset which always interrupts the schedule. The following is only a suggested guideline. It gives you some of the categories from which to work out your own schedule. Sometimes there are days which are so disruptive that you must simply list priorities, rotate through the list, and perform triage wherever necessary.

Principles to consider: The children should be doing much of the housework, which will free the parents to give attention to personal or administrative tasks. "Early to bed, early to rise" is generally a good policy, though a father's work schedule or other considerations may not allow for this.

5:00-6:30	Parents rise, children rise, showers, dressing, early morning chores.
7:00	Breakfast. Morning Family worship.
8:00	Daily Chores (predetermined schedule).
8:30-9:30	General School Meeting: 1. Recite memory work: All children could recite their memory work (including Greek and/or Hebrew alphabet). 2. Practice reading: Each child who is able will read aloud a portion of something while all others listen (Bible, history, Constitution, poetry, etc.). 3. Practice narration: All children practice narration (if there are several children, then break it up – half in the morning, half in the afternoon).
9:30-10:15	Mother reads aloud to all children (narration could be included). Children can work on arts and crafts while Mother reads.
10:15-11:30	1. Phonics instruction for children learning to read and entries made in English language notebook. (This could be moved to the afternoon when infants are sleeping.) 2. Copywork, history notebook, and timeline.

11:30	Prepare lunch. Straighten house.
12:00	Lunch. Midday chores.
1:00	Naps.
2:00-2:45	Mother reads aloud and finishes narration (children can work on arts and crafts).
2:45-4:30	Same as 10:15 period; play outside; go for walks; once a week volunteer work (nursing home, etc.), field trips; library.
4:30-5:00	Prepare supper. Straighten house.
5:00	Supper. Evening chores.
6:30	Evening Family worship.
7:00-7:45	Father reads aloud to family.
7:45-8:30	Family activities.
8:30-9:00	Prepare for bed.
9:00	Lights out.

Chapter Twelve

The Later Knowledge Level: Ten Things to Do With Children Ages Ten Through Twelve

Apply thine heart unto instruction, and thine ears to the words of knowledge. — Proverbs 23:12

And by knowledge shall the chambers be filled with all precious and pleasant riches. — Proverbs 24:4

INTRODUCTORY REMARKS

WHAT ARE OUR goals for a child at the Later Knowledge Level? During the entire Knowledge Level (birth through age twelve) the child is gathering Knowledge. In this later part (ages ten through twelve), academic discipline becomes more structured and formal, and the study of formal language grammar and the study of mathematics is begun.

Consider this basic maxim of Homeschooling: "There is only so much time in the day." Keep this maxim in mind as you consider which of the many subjects your child will study throughout his school age years. What is the wisest use of your time?

In our last Chapter, we discussed the ten things to do with children in the Early Knowledge Level, before age ten. "Formal" academics – a stack of textbooks and workbooks – are not necessarily the most important use of our time with children before age ten. But by age ten, most children are entering the Later Knowledge Level. This is approximately the age when children are ready for more *formal* academics. Around age ten, the light bulb goes on. The brain becomes physically able to make more complex connections, which, among other things, makes your child more able to handle abstract concepts, and helps your child with self-management and self-control. During the Later Knowledge Level, from ages ten through twelve, the parent will be the most intensely involved in his child's education

The following is a list of ten things which we believe are most important for children in this Later Knowledge Level.

A SUGGESTED COURSE OF STUDY

1. Family Worship

Regular family worship is not just an add on. It is central. By age ten, your child is able to grow rapidly in the knowledge of the Scriptures, through his father's instruction. The child will obtain an overall view of the Bible, and will continue memorizing Scripture. Your study of history may be designed to coincide with your study of the Old Testament. For more discussion, see Appendix One, Article Fifteen, Family Bible Study by the Trivium, or our booklet, *On Family Worship*.

2. Literature and Reading Aloud

Daily require your child to read something in the area of classical fiction, poetry, or short stories. Of course, many children are already doing plenty of reading on their own by this age. Old readers, such as McGuffey's, are good sources for this type of literature. We bought the *McGuffey Readers* in 1978, and we used them until they wore out. I love these Readers, and I would recommend them to anyone. We have used them as beginning readers, as material for instruction in oral interpretation, for copywork, for literature study, as examples for art copywork, and for fun reading. It is not necessary to buy graded reading textbooks. Use the library instead. We suggest that you stay away from light reading (Jeanette Oake, Hardy Boys, The Boxcar Children, American Girl, etc.). Develop in your children an appetite for "nutritious" literary "food," not literary "fast-food."

Though your children are now reading on their own, continue to read aloud to them two hours per day. It might be one of your favorite parts of Homeschooling. Our Resource List (at the back of this book) contains a few booklists and book sources. We suggest reading such books as *Lorna Doone* by Richard Blackmore, *Thirty-Nine Steps* by John Buchan, *The Door in the Wall* by Marquerite De Angeli, *Robinson Crusoe* by Daniel Defoe, or any of the G.A. Henty series. Continue requiring oral narration.

There is more than one way to study literature.

1. *The Unplanned Method.* There will be seasons in a family's life when you must abandon any notions of an all-encompassing order to your reading. You may have limited access to libraries, or there may be prolonged stresses or disruptions such as relocation, health, or pregnancy. This may be the time to just pick from the list of good books.
2. *The Historical-Order Method.* Combine history with literature while you survey the historical periods in chronological order. You can use one of the prepared unit studies, or you can design your own study. You must do a little planning to combine literature with history, but the benefits include an overall sense of order, the reinforcement of factual material, and the time you will save from combining subjects. (We will discuss this more later.)
3. *The Follow-A-Theme Method.* Read material of different types from different historical periods, but on a particular subject of importance or interest (inventions, character qualities, horses). Again, you can use one of the prepared unit studies, or you can design your own study.

MEMORIZATION AND INTERPRETIVE READING

Continue memorizing and reciting aloud passages of literature or poetry. Recitation of poetry or literature before an audience is called "oral interpretation" or "interpretive reading." Here's how it works: The student will choose a poem or a piece of prose which he likes. (An example might be the poem *Casey at the Bat*, by Ernest Lawrence Thayer.)

He will practice reading it aloud, paying attention to such things as:

- Articulation. (Example: sen-si-ble, not sen-sub-ble; or, bags of gold, not bag sof gold.)
- Inflection. (Example: "The language of emphasis generally requires the falling inflection.")
- Proper breathing.
- Quality of voice.
- Loudness.

When he has perfected the piece, he will perform it before an audience. The student can tape record himself reading his piece so that he may make necessary corrections. Then he can ask others to evaluate his readings. The student does not need to memorize the material, but he must know the piece well enough that he can make regular eye contact with his audience. The student may perform the piece in front of his family, his homeschool speech and debate club, a church function, or a more formal setting, such as a speech competition.

Students should attempt to interpret a variety of literature:

- humorous poetry (*Jabberwocky*, by Lewis Carrol)
- dramatic poetry (*O Captain, My Captain*, by Walt Whitman)
- poetry with a regional dialect (*To a Mountain Daisy, On Turning It Down With a Plow*, by Robert Burns, or *Foreign Views of the Statue*, by Fred Emerson Brooks)
- classic speeches (*Speech on the Trial of a Murderer*, by Daniel Webster)
- short essays (*Description of a Storm*, by Benjamin Disraeli, or *A Second Trial*, by Sarah Winter Kellogg)
- excerpts from plays or books (*The Quarrel of Brutus and Cassius*, by William Shakespeare, or *Father Hires a Cook* from *Life with Father*, by Clarence Day.)
- duet readings (*An Encounter With an Interviewer*, by Mark Twain).

You will find a variety of forms of literature at the library if you research Dewey Decimal numbers 808.8 to 900. Selections for oral interpretation, including choral readings, begin at Library of Congress PN4199.

Interpretive reading is a simple method to ease students into speech and debate. It accustoms them to standing before an audience and practicing eye contact. Formal speech and debate competitions include categories for interpretive reading. After interpretive reading, your student may write his own poem or prose and read it. Next, your student may write and perform his own speech.

In Appendix One, Articles Fifteen and Sixteen, we give suggestions for forming a homeschool speech and debate club, pointers for public speaking, and a bibliography for interpretive reading.

3. History

History is a large subject with many variables. It is man's record about man's activities in time. No man can master all of recorded history, but everyone should master some of it. The questions are: when to begin, which part to study, and how to study it. Through your reading, your child will have already become familiar with many events and periods of history. Many families focus specifically on reading history during their family reading times.

By age ten, your child should be reading from history and narrating it back to you. Biographies, autobiographies, and historical fiction are ideally suited for this purpose. You can search the library for many of these books. Be careful to critically evaluate what books you select for him. You may study history in chronological order, or you may study history according to interest, or you may do both, depending upon what your goals in history are.

THE CHRONOLOGICAL STUDY OF HISTORY

A chronological study of history would begin in the most ancient times, and work, period by period, up to modern times. For many, this is the ideal way to study history. Some study all of history in two years, others stretch it out over three or four years or more. If you haven't studied history in any chronological order, then you may choose to begin when your oldest has turned ten. A mother, with only one or two children, can probably organize a chronological study of history with no great difficulties. However, as you add more children, especially little ones, your study of history may lose some of its chronological character, and it may take some interest-directed side streets – at least until the little children add some years. The timeline can serve to correct some of possible discontinuity of your approach by displaying the continuity of history. Maps can do for spatial continuity what timelines can do for chronological continuity, so post maps on the walls and locate the events about which your children read in both time (chronology) and space (geography).

A history textbook, such as *Streams of Civilization*, may serve as your framework and guide while you work through a chronological study of history. This will only be the skeleton upon which you attach other history sources. You should supplement the history textbook with reading primary sources, biographies, autobiographies, journals, historical fiction. (We will discuss primary sources later.) You may maintain a history notebook and pursue history contests or other such projects.

PRINCIPLES FOR CHOOSING AND USING A HISTORY TEXTBOOK

1. The bias of the author and publisher will be expressed in the book in some way. As long as you are aware of it, you can compensate for it.
2. No history text can be exhaustive. So every text will omit some things which others will include. Do not rely entirely upon one text. Compare other texts to determine what you may need to supplement.
3. History texts must be brief in order to cover many things. The larger the period of history covered, the more brief the treatment. On historical events or periods which you consider important, find a resource with a fuller treatment than the textbook.
4. Very few textbooks attempt to apply Biblical principles to explain or evaluate historical events. Do not allow this ignoring-God-bias to creep into your way of treating history. Always evaluate history from God's perspective.
5. Man's record of history is imperfect, and often contradictory. After evaluating sources, do not be afraid to conclude that there is not enough evidence to be confident about what happened, how it happened, or why it happened.

THE INTEREST-DIRECTED STUDY OF HISTORY

You may not be able to stick to a strict schedule of chronological study without some significant deviations from the stream. Many who begin down the main stream of history find it profitable to explore one or more of the tributaries along the way. So the schedule is interrupted for a short spell in order to study Austrian history, or the history of warfare, or the history of dog breeding and training.

One of our goals for the study of history is to give our children the tools for learning a new subject on their own. The subject of history is perfect ground for learning these tools. We want them to be able to study history, even when they are grown and have children of their own. We hope to give them a survey of all of history at least once. We hope to give them the tools to fill in the spaces which are between the lines of history. Only if they learn to love the study of history will they pursue the study of history on their own. This is where following a strict chronological study of history might interfere. We'll give you an example.

Suppose you plan to spend the first year of your chronological plan studying the ancient Greeks and Romans. Now, suppose your children are wired for a different plan. Your lads spend all of their spare time making swords, armor, and castles, or your lassies are busy sewing Civil War costumes. Ancient history can be a bit boring to young children who are interested in mediaeval times or civil war times. You may be able to redirect your children's interests to ancient history, but should that fail (or you clearly see it failing before you have tried it), then you may choose instead to strike while the iron is hot, and interrupt your own studies to meet their interests. As a general rule, one learns best when he pursues his interests. You can't do that with a classroom of thirty children, but we homeschoolers have the flexibility to do this. Will you force the child to study ancient history for a year when his heart is really with the knights in shining armor? I think a good teacher will combine discipline and structure and schedule with sensitivity to the needs and desires of the student. We will return to ancient history later. There are limits to this, of course. No, we're not going to study World War II for twelve years straight, like Hans would like, but we will keep in mind his love for this subject as we plan our study of history.

HISTORY NOTEBOOK

By the time your child enters the Later Knowledge Level, he should have his own history notebook. This notebook could contain:

1. Drawings (freehand or tracings) which illustrate the historical events of which he has learned in historical novels or nonfiction books.
2. Copywork or dictation of an historical nature.
3. Photographs taken on field trips, which appropriately belong with what you have studied in history. Your child should accompany his photographs with short descriptions of their historical significance.
4. A child in the Later Knowledge Level can do history projects and enter history competitions (See Appendix One, Article Thirteen, for a list of history competitions.) After he finishes a project, his written work and drawings can be put into his notebook.
5. As you teach basic outlining, some of his exercises may concern history, and he can put these into his history notebook. (Outlining exercises which do not concern history may belong in his English language notebook.)
6. Drawings or pictures of costumes.

The history notebook will serve not only as a memorial of your child's studies, but it will help him to develop his creativity and sense of order. His notebook will be the repository for all of his ideas concerning the study of history. Each family must decide what its own standards will be for what goes into the notebook, and how it is maintained, taking into consideration each child's developed abilities, so as not to indulge nor to exasperate him. Some mothers may be tempted to impose a standard of perfection too high for their child's capabilities, while other mothers may be satisfied with too low a standard. So be careful what you do. Most children will not need their notebook to be a showcase of history, where everything is perfectly written and organized better than a doctoral thesis. That would be one extreme. The other extreme would be the sloppy, disorganized, and seldom used grab bag which vaguely resembles a notebook. We want to find the happy medium which best fits our goals. Above all, we want to promote in our children a love for learning history, and we want the notebook to serve that goal.

Even if you are not currently studying history chronologically, you will want to maintain the history notebook in some kind of chronological order, using subject dividers where necessary.

HISTORY FAIRS AND CONTESTS

Reading and studying history is a favorite part of our Homeschooling. For many years, our family organized a city wide History Fair for homeschoolers. Each of our children, from about age ten and up, was required to produce a history project. In preparing a history project, the child will perfect his library research skills. A history project can involve any number of things. Ours generally looked something like science fair projects, with the three-sided display boards covered with pictures, timelines, text, genealogies, and such. The child would dress in an appropriate costume and display various artifacts or items relating to the project. After presenting the project at the History Fair, we often took it to the library for additional display. One year, the girls did a project on the history of hats. I have part of the project taped to the wall here in the office, and I look at it all of the time. It is a poster with pictures and descriptions of all of the different hats of the nineteenth century.

LEARNING TO USE THE LIBRARY

Question: You have mentioned teaching your children to use the library. I am ready to take my son through the steps required to do a research report. Would you please give some practical tips here?

Answer: Your local public library is your first step in learning library research. You might want to establish the habit of visiting it on a weekly basis and become familiar with where the different kinds of books are: fiction, nonfiction, biographies, magazines, newspapers, reference books, special collections, recorded books. Learn how to ask the librarian questions, how to do a search on the computer or to use the card catalog (card catalogs are becoming obsolete), and how to use the different reference books. The easiest way to begin is to think of some subject that the child is especially interested in, such as airplanes, guns, horses, dolls, etc., and research that subject. Your goal at first is not necessarily to write something about the subject which you are researching. At first, you are learning to investigate for the love of learning itself. Perhaps the child wants to build a birdhouse, and you need to find the building plans. Library research will help your child to develop an inquiring mind and to love learning.

After you are comfortable using your local public library, then visit your local college library. You might wait until your child is twelve or thirteen before you do this. Local public libraries are organized by the Dewey Decimal system, but college and university libraries are organized by the Library of Congress system. These are two different systems for organizing books, but neither are difficult to learn. The first time you go to a college library, you may be disappointed if you intended to do a great amount of research. Unless your research involves only one small corner of the library, it is likely that it will take you several visits before you become thoroughly acquainted with the system that you can immediately find whatever you are looking for.

Next, you can visit a big university library, perhaps when your child is fifteen or sixteen. We first had our children follow us around as we did our own research on various subjects. Next, they would branch out and pursue some of their own interests. Hans has always been interested in maps and geography so you would find him in the map room. The girls could be found with the old magazines where they could look up vintage crochet and knitting patterns. Nathan spent most his time in the several science libraries. At least once a year, each child would do a history or science project or contest. At first, we would direct their research. Eventually, they could do it all on their own.

In thinking back to the years when I took all five of the children with me to the library, there is one thing which stays in my mind – how irritated I became with the little ones while the older ones and I tried to look things up. It grieves me now to think on it. I tried everything back then to occupy them. Some years I took a laundry basket with me to set the baby in (I don't think strollers were allowed in libraries at that time), and, oh, what a challenge to keep them quiet, especially at the university, with all the students staring at us. "I need patience, Lord – right now!" "This is a good way to learn it," He responded. It only took me twenty-four years to get my attitude adjusted. Library research takes patience and time.

4. Composition

By age ten, your child should be writing something everyday. During the Later Knowledge Level (ages ten through twelve) you should keep it simple: copywork, dictation, letters to relatives or pen pals, journal entries, and simple outlining skills. All of this is in addition to the writing which they will do every day in math, spelling, Latin, and English grammar. You may be able to combine their composition with parts of these other subjects.

COPYWORK AND DICTATION

By age ten, the student should be proficient at copywork. Some students at this age will be ready take the next step up, from copywork to dictation. Others will need another year. You will need to determine when the child needs to make that move. Dictation requires something more from the child than does simple copywork. In copywork, the child uses pencil and paper to reproduce what he sees. In dictation, the child reproduces what he hears, not what he sees. He translates the spoken sounds to spelled words, which involves more steps and more practiced memory.

JOURNALS AND LETTERS

The next step in the process of learning how to write is journals and letters to relatives and pen pals. Here, the child combines the skill of copywork with that of oral narration. He only applies pencil to paper, but he now creates in his mind what he puts on his paper. Some children have no problem with this. Others need more time to develop this skill. The student's first letters to Grandma and Grandpa can be an extension of copywork. First, Mother may do most of the composing of the letter, and may write out the text for the child to copy. From here, you move by steps to the point where the child composes and writes his own letters. We required our children to bring a rough draft of their letters to us. We would make corrections, then they would rewrite the letters before sending them.

Writing in a journal daily is like writing a letter to yourself. Some parents correct journal entries, while others allow the child to keep his journal entries private. Here is an excerpt taken from *Life, Administration and Times of John Quincy Adams, Sixth President of the United States.*

> John Quincy Adams was homeschooled by his mother in American classical education, learning to read from the Bible and studying poetry and literature, French, and history up to the age of ten. Here follows a letter written by John Quincy at the age of eleven. . .
>
> Honored Mamma, My papa enjoins it upon me to keep a journal, or a diary of the events that happen to me, and of objects that I see, and of characters that I converse with from day to day; and altho' I am convinced of the utility, importance, and necessity of this exercise, yet I have not the patience and perseverance enough to do it so constantly as I ought. My papa, who takes a great deal of pains to put me in the right way, has also advised me to keep copies of all my letters, and has given me a convenient blank book for this end; and altho' I shall have the mortification a few years hence to read a great deal of my childish nonsense, yet I shall have the pleasure and advantage of remarking the several steps by which I shall have advanced in taste, judgment, and knowledge. A journal book and a letter book of a lad of eleven years old can not be expected to contain much of science, literature, arts, wisdom or wit, yet it may serve to perpetuate many observations that I may make, and may hereafter help me to recollect both persons and things that would otherwise escape my memory.
>
> —*Life, Administration and Times of John Quincy Adams, Sixth President of the United States*, by John Robert Irelan, 1887, page 17, as reported in the Principle Approach Education newsletter (800-352-FACE):

SIMPLE OUTLINING SKILLS

Most families will need help in teaching outlining skills. This may be included in your writing curriculum (which is our next topic), or you may wish to buy a book on how to do outlining. You would begin to teach outlining skills around age twelve.

USING A COMPOSITION CURRICULUM

Some families will be able to teach writing using the steps outlined in this Chapter. Other families will prefer more structure, and will want to use a writing curriculum. There are numerous writing curricula available to Homeschooling families. Principles for choosing a writing curriculum include:

1. Expense. Curricula may range from twenty dollars to well over a hundred dollars.
2. How much structure do you need? Curricula range from very detailed – tells you every step, to sketchy – just gives you suggestions.
3. Philosophy. Some are secular and may contain politically correct assignments or pop culture assignments.

A Bible-based Christ-centered curriculum for all grades which fits these criteria is *Understanding Writing*, by Susan Bradrick.

HATES TO HOLD THE PENCIL

Girls usually have no problem writing. Some girls will take up writing poetry and short stories from a very young age. Boys often need more help and encouragement to put even the first word down on paper. It seems that some boys are allergic to pencils. I remember one morning when I was attempting to persuade Hans, who was about ten years old at the time, to write something on a piece of paper. He was sitting at the dining room table, and I was standing behind him, attempting to force a pencil into his hand. There was a struggle, but I finally molded it into his hand, at which time he cried out, "I can't breathe, I can't breathe." It always baffled me that this boy of mine hated writing. I personally never had that problem, and our three girls always seemed to view writing as a natural and easy exercise.

If you have a reluctant writer, write his thoughts down for him as he narrates them to you. (Or he may narrate his thoughts into a tape recorder.) You have now created an inertia in the direction of writing. There will still be friction, but that will be overcome as you gain speed. The trick is to start out short and simple, and to know how large to increase each increment. The child may be a reluctant writer due to immaturity or from just plain laziness and disobedience, or probably both, but either way, you'll overcome it by boiling the frog slowly – if you know what we mean.

Our children loved to shop at office supply stores. We would buy little pads of special colored paper and fancy writing utensils for them to use in copywork. We hired them to produce all of our greeting cards. Their cards had artwork on the cover, and a poem or Bible verse inside. Have them copy the Greek alphabet on a card – that's a surefire way to impress unapproving relatives. An exceptionally good personal greeting card could be copied on a color copier and sold. (Money is a motivator.) Bible verses can be copied onto narrow strips of nice paper, decorated, laminated, and used as book markers, sold, or given away. Several pages of copywork can be assembled into a little book.

MATH AND PENCILS

Question: I have a ten-year-old boy who has done very little formal academics. He is very creative by nature, devours books (although he did not "learn" to read until nine years old), draws continually, has an inventor's mind (like his beloved daddy), can recite anything he has read from a book, is fascinated by history, but despises using the pencil! He is very obedient, and will do whatever I ask, but is growing to despise math because of the continuous demand for writing. We have done much mental math over the years, and I write plenty of word problems out on the board, and he will do them. But we began with Saxon 54 this year. When he sees me pull out the book, his face does these strange contortions! He will complete the pages and arrive at the correct answers, but he loathes it! Any suggestions? Is it time for him to just buckle down and do it?

Answer: It's nice to know our boy is not alone – there are other boys who hate holding a pencil. Perhaps someone at a university should do a study to discover why. On second thought, that would only mean more taxes and more government programs – and we'd probably never find out the real reason. Forget I ever mentioned it.

Little boys are wired to jump, roll, and chatter. Perhaps they are uncomfortable holding the pencil "just so," or maybe they are discouraged because their letters do not look "just like" in the books, or possibly just sitting completely still through all of this is beyond their control capabilities.

Your son sounds like a delightful laddie who is willing to please his mommy and daddy in most anything. Help him out with his weaknesses. A ten-year-old should be doing some writing every day, no matter how little, but you may allow him to do as much of the math orally as is reasonable. In another year or so, he will be ready to write out his math exercises without a hitch. In fact, he'd probably be embarrassed if you offered to do it for him. In other words, don't make too much of a fuss. He'll grow out of it.

DICTATION

Question: I have tried dictation with my eleven-year-old daughter and she absolutely hates it. Not knowing where the punctuation marks go frustrates her. We have compromised by giving her hints.

Answer: Dictation is less exact than copywork. You can't always be sure that what you are writing is correct. Some children are perfectionists who want to do things just right. Do not put too much pressure on the child to have everything perfect. We often have unrealistic expectations – especially for our first child. We sometimes wonder how they ever survived. Instead of striving for first time perfection, strive for continuous improvement. I wanted Nathaniel to have perfect handwriting, read at a high school level, write with creative wit, carry on advanced conversations with the neighbors, and draw like Michelangelo – by the age of five. I think that's why the Lord gave us five children in eight years. It mellowed me out fast. Notice, I am not saying we should have low standards, but that we should establish realistic standards, and realistically raise those standards with time. In our travels, I have seen many perfectionistic Mothers putting unrealistic burdens on their children. Perfectionism can break the spirit of a child.

When I would dictate to my children, I sat next to them on the couch, watching everything they wrote. If there was supposed to be a comma in the sentence and they didn't know it, then I would tell them where it went, and we would write down that particular rule in their English language notebook. If they take dictation in pencil, then their mistakes can be easily erased. Spelling can also be taught during dictation. Dictation should be a teaching session, not only a testing session to see what they know. Later, when the child is older and more skilled at dictation, you'll be free to back off a few steps from the immediate process.

5. Spelling and English Grammar

By age ten, your child can comprehend the abstract grammatical concepts of noun, verb, participle, and gerund. English grammar, or any language grammar, can be readily learned.

Some begin the formal study of English grammar in the first grade (age six). We would recommend beginning at age ten (grade level five). The abstract concepts of formal mathematics and formal grammar are best left until the child is developmentally most ready to handle them. (You may compare Appendix One, Article Eleven, History and Research on the Teaching of Math.) Before age ten, memorization, oral narration, reading aloud, and copywork will build a solid foundation for the study of formal grammar later.

There is a difference between learning a language and learning grammar. Children begin to learn their native language from their earliest age, and they can develop skill in speaking several languages while they are still in their youngest years. Indeed, this is the optimal time for developing spoken proficiency in a language. Formal grammar, however, is the study of the structure of a language, and such study should be delayed until the brain is developed to handle it.

One part of the brain handles the language, and another part of the brain handles the grammatical analysis of the language. The part which handles the language is well developed by age four or so. The child learns inductively that the subject comes before the verb and the direct object comes after the verb, even though he has no way of conceiving what a subject, a verb, and a direct object are. He learns vocabulary and style without any way of conceiving what a noun, a verb, a preposition, or what iambic pentameter is. He just enjoys language. The part of the brain which handles the formal grammar is developed by age ten or so. If you force formal grammar too early, then you will put the information in odd places of the brain, and it is more difficult for the brain to assimilate and to make use of the information. Three years (ages ten through twelve) for studying English grammar and spelling are usually sufficient. Your child will be studying Latin or Greek grammar by age thirteen, which renders the study of English grammar largely superfluous.

TWO METHODS FOR STUDYING GRAMMAR AND SPELLING

During the three years in which the student studies English grammar and spelling, you could use one of two methods:

1. Work through a prepared English grammar and spelling curriculum appropriate for the age of the child. This would be the preferred course to take if you are new to Homeschooling, or you are not proficient in English grammar yourself. *Spelling Power*, by Beverly L. Adams-Gordon and *Easy Grammar*, by Wanda C. Phillips are two programs which are inexpensive and thorough.
2. Use an old speller such as *Webster's Elementary Spelling Book* or *McGuffey's Speller* to teach both English grammar and spelling.

Either way, the student should maintain his English language notebook.

USING OLD SPELLERS

A century and more ago, students may have possessed only one textbook, *Webster's Elementary Spellingbook*. Using this little book, students learned reading, spelling, grammar, handwriting, and vocabulary. In the preface of this book we read,

> This little book is so constructed as to condense into the smallest compass a complete system of elements for teaching the language; and however small

> such a book may appear, it may be considered as the most important class book, not of a religious character, which the youth of our country are destined to use.

Judging from the large number of great writers produced in the nineteenth century, this book must have been adequate to teach these subjects well. With a little improvisation, Webster's Speller can be just as useful to us.

If you go into an old book store, you will find several old spelling books, but Noah Webster's speller was one of the first written for Americans, and it was certainly the most popular. What made Webster's so popular was his sentences. They are beautiful masterpieces. Here is a sampling:

> "God will impart grace to the humble penitent."
>
> "Examine the Scriptures daily and carefully, and set an example of good works."
>
> "To revere a father is to regard him with fear mingled with respect and affection."
>
> "Before you rise in the morning or retire at night, give thanks to God for his mercies, and implore the continuance of his protection."
>
> "Strong drink leads to the debasement both of the mind and the body."

Webster had a way with language which you will never find in any textbook written in this century. These sentences are good examples of writing which you will love your children to imitate by copywork, dictation, diagramming, and narration. McGuffey's Speller is also fine to use, but his sentences are not quite so beautiful as Webster's.

Here are some advantages to studying the English language using this method. (When I speak of "the English language," I include handwriting, grammar, vocabulary, and spelling.):

1. Inexpensive – you need only Webster's Speller (or any of the old spellers, such as McGuffey's) and an English handbook which contains grammar rules and spelling rules (such as the Bob Jones *English Handbook*). These books can be purchased once, and used over and over again with each of your children.
2. It helps to develop creativity in the child.
3. Mom learns grammar as she teaches the children.

Here are some disadvantages of using this method:

1. It may take more of Mom's time.

2. It may be more difficult with the first child, if Mom has forgotten much of the grammar which she learned in school and must relearn it as she teaches her first child.

A good candidate to use an old speller to teach English grammar and spelling would be the person who likes old books, is not afraid to improvise and invent, has a basic understanding of spelling and English grammar, has twenty to thirty minutes (depending on the ages of your children) each day to devote to these subjects, and is interested in saving money. If you are just beginning Homeschooling, have forgotten all which you learned about grammar and spelling from school, and are feeling a bit overwhelmed, then, for your first year or two, a prepared curriculum may serve you adequately. Webster's does not *teach* spelling or grammar. It just provides the lists of words, sentences, and paragraphs for you to use when *you* teach the child spelling and grammar. There are some spelling rules along with some rules for punctuation and capitalization included in the book.

Nobody knows exactly how parents and school teachers used these old spellers in their daily teaching of reading and spelling. We can only guess and improvise. I used Webster's speller to teach not only spelling, but also grammar, vocabulary, and handwriting. Apparently, it was also used to teach reading, though I never used it that way. The English handbook will help refresh your mind about the grammar rules, and will show you how to diagram sentences. Our own *Handy English Encoder/Decoder* lists all of the spelling and phonics rules we were able to find in the world – for English. This may help you to find the rule which applies to the spelling words which you happen to be studying.

ENGLISH LANGUAGE NOTEBOOK

Here are a few ideas on how to develop an English language notebook. A three-ring binder filled with notebook paper and subject dividers works well. If you began this notebook in the Early Knowledge Level, then you already have a section on the rules of phonics. You may also have included the student's copywork in this notebook. Our notebook had separate sections for:

1. *Word Dictation*. Containing spelling words, dividing each word into syllables.
2. *Sentence Dictation*. Containing sentences, diagramming each sentence.
3. *Spelling Rules*. Containing the rules which applied to what we were studying, using the *Handy English Encoder/Decoder*.

4. *Paragraph Dictation*. Containing the paragraphs in Webster, no diagramming.
5. *Grammar rules*. Containing the rules which applied to what we were studying, using the Bob Jones *English Handbook*.
6. *Punctuation and Capitalization Rules*.
7. *Vocabulary Studies*.

Each child produced his own little handbook of all of the things which he needed to know about English.

USING WEBSTER'S SPELLER

Webster's *Elementary Spellingbook* begins with two sections entitled "Analysis of Sounds in the English Language" and "Key to the Pronunciation." Webster's analysis of the sounds of the consonants is fairly easy to understand, and is similar to such phonics programs as *Alpha-Phonics* or *The Writing Road to Reading*. Though his descriptions of the sounds of the vowels may not have been confusing to people in the nineteenth century, they are confusing to those of us who are used to twentieth century phonics programs. Webster differentiates seven sounds for the letter "A," five sounds for "E," four sounds for "I," eight sounds for "O," and four sounds for "U." Twentieth century phonics programs simplify this to only two or three sounds for each vowel. Many modern programs differentiate:

Three sounds for "A:" fat, fate, father.
Two sounds for "E:" wet, we.
Two sounds for "I:" fin, find.
Three sounds for "O:" tot, tote, too.
Three sounds for "U:" putt, repute, put.

On pages 15-16, Webster shows the student how to form the letters of the alphabet: Roman, Italic, Old English, and Script. A section of the child's notebook can be labeled "The Formation of Letters".

I begin on page 20 (Lesson 12), dictating to the child the first ten words. The words are in word families (cab, dab, nab, etc.). We are not teaching reading (decoding), but spelling (encoding). As I dictate these words, I explain to the child why the words are spelled that way. The child can add spelling rules to his notebook. You will find help with spelling rules in the back of Webster, your English handbook, or the *Encoder/Decoder*. I continue dictating ten words a day until I have used all of Webster's one syllable, short vowel words.

As the child writes these ten words from dictation, I show him the proper way to form the letters in cursive. Some children need more instruction in this area, while other children, from their previous phonics instruction, are completely familiar with handwriting. Make clear to the child that whatever he does not neatly enter in his notebook you may make him rewrite.

After the ten words are dictated, then I dictate a sentence to the child. (I guess that makes me a dictator.) At the beginning, I simply make up the sentences, since Webster does not have simple sentences with only a subject and a verb. I use these dictated sentences to teach English grammar. This is where the English handbook proves useful. The first sentence which I dictate is something simple, such as, "Mary ran."

At this point, I begin to teach what a noun is, what a verb is, and what the subject and predicate are. I also introduce some capitalization and punctuation rules here (pages 168-169 Webster). The Grammar section of their notebook can dedicate a page for each part of speech: Noun, Verb, etc. At the beginning, the only thing the child has on his Noun page is the definition: A noun names a person, place, thing, quality, or idea. (Or perhaps, A noun is the name of anything which is given a name.) The child adds more information regarding nouns as I teach them. The same is true with other parts of speech, such as his Verb page.

Next, I show the child how to diagram the sentence, Mary ran:

DIAGRAMMING A SENTENCE

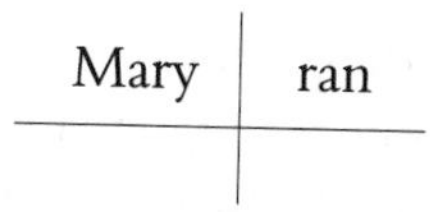

FIGURE 12A

I dictate three sentences per day, and the child diagrams all three sentences. After a few days of simple subject-verb sentences of my own, I introduce Webster's more difficult sentences. I do not move on to the next concept until the child has mastered the current concept.

I introduce the long vowel words (Lesson 17-20 and Lesson 33) when the child is ready. The same with two syllable words. At an appropriate time, I introduce Webster's spelling rules on pages 159-164, and dictate words from these pages (or supplement with my own words).

On pages 139-146, Webster includes paragraphs for dictation. On pages 146-155, he lists words spelled alike and words pronounced alike (along with their definitions and plenty of sentences). On page 165, he lists Roman numerals. On pages 166-167, he lists words and phrases from foreign languages. On pages 167-168 he lists abbreviations.

Noah Webster's *Elementary Spellingbook* works as a basic text, supplemented with an English handbook and other sources. As your child learns spelling, grammar, handwriting, and vocabulary, he will compile his own notebook. This eliminates the need to buy a multitude of graded workbooks for each of these subjects, and for each grade level. You will be there to watch and guide your child in his growth in knowledge and understanding, and you will probably relearn a few things you forgot along the way.

WHY SENTENCE DIAGRAMMING?

Sentence diagramming is just one method for teaching grammar. There are other ways. In Laura Ingalls Wilder's time, they "parsed" sentences. *Easy Grammar* has the student label and underline, in different ways, the words in sentences. I like diagramming, because it is so organized and precise, as it lays out the logic of the sentence grammar. Two sources for diagramming are *Diagramming: The Key to Understanding Grammar*, by Ellen Hajek, and *The Complete Book of Diagrams*, by Mary Daly.

6. Latin and Greek

Chapter Five was concerned with learning languages, and if you haven't read that Chapter, then we suggest that now is the time to do so. The discussion below will, in an abbreviated fashion, touch on some of the contents of that Chapter, adding a few practical things here or there.

You can introduce your children to alphabets at a very early age, but if you haven't done it by the Later Knowledge Level, then we suggest that the time is slipping away for you to do this. The Greek alphabet can be learned right along with the English alphabet. When the child is skilled in writing the Greek alphabet, then copywork exercises can include passages from the Greek New Testament. Latin grammar can begin by age ten or eleven (using *Artes Latinae* by Waldo Sweet), and Greek grammar can begin by age thirteen or fourteen. We recommend that you study both Latin and Greek, but circumstances for your family may suggest strong reasons to follow other language choices.

LATIN AND GREEK FOR YOUNG CHILDREN

Studies which assess the value of learning foreign languages at an early age show that persons who learned a foreign language before the age of ten used the same part of the brain to think in that language as they did to think in English. Persons who learned a second language after the age of ten used a totally separate part of the brain to process that language. It seems far better and easier to learn a foreign language before the age of ten. Well, these tests only confirm what we already know intuitively: that the best way to learn *any* foreign language is to learn it from childhood as a spoken language. This trains the ear and the tongue. The reading and writing of the language will then come easier, because the student is already familiar with the sounds. And the grammar, which is learned later, and goes in a separate part of the brain, will still come much easier, because the student already has a working knowledge of the language. This applies to any language, not just classical languages. So it would be best to learn Latin or Greek as a *spoken* language right along with English. Unfortunately, most families are not conversant in Latin and Greek. We must wait a generation or two into Homeschooling before we can expect much early language learning to occur.

The next level up from learning Latin or Greek as a *spoken* language would be to learn Latin as a *written* language right along with English. The English alphabet is the Latin alphabet, with some modification. So when we teach a child to read and write English, we are also preparing him, in a small way, to read and write Latin. It would be profitable to be reading and writing Latin from as early an age as possible – right along with reading and writing English. Of course, we must learn the Latin phonics, but that is not difficult for the young. (It is more difficult for us older folk.) I am not talking about learning formal Latin grammar, any more than I am talking about learning formal English grammar. At an early age, the child should become familiar with good literature in English. The same would be true of Latin. Because the parents are probably unfamiliar with Latin, it would be best to begin with classical expressions in Latin, or Bible passages in Latin. At an early age, I think this would be more profitable than simply memorizing Latin paradigms unconnected to the language. The child does not really understand the formal grammar, and he cannot use the paradigms. But he can use the expressions and the Bible passages with some understanding, and when it is time for paradigms, he will already have developed a meaningful familiarity with the language which will make the paradigms more understandable and digestible. (Our Resource List gives information on some catechisms available in Latin and English.)

Though the Latin and the English alphabet are derived from the Greek Alphabet, there is nevertheless quite a difference in the orthographic system, and an even greater difference in the phonetic system. If you wish, you could begin teaching the Greek alphabet – the names of the letters and their sounds – as soon as you begin the English alphabet. However, the whole phonetic system – the classification of sounds and the combination of letters – you will probably want to delay until about age ten. After that, reading Biblical passages in a Greek-English Interlinear Bible would serve as good practice in preparation for Greek grammar.

SUGGESTIONS FOR STUDYING GREEK

Here are some suggestions for studying the Greek alphabet: For an eight-year-old, take one or more letters per week, depending on the child. Once you complete the alphabet, begin again. Your goal is to become thoroughly familiar with the Greek alphabet. Write the letters, practice saying the sounds (you may use the tape and / or flash cards), make posters of the alphabet, make greeting cards and decorate the edges with Greek letters (this will impress the grandparents), make your own flash cards, compare the sounds of the Greek letters with the corresponding English letter sounds (Alpha and "A," Beta and "B," etc. – some letters in Greek have no corresponding English letter), make up a simple song of the alphabet (some sing it to Onward Christian Soldiers, and we have heard others as well), make your own tape of the sounds, make up the game of "Concentration" or some other such game with the Greek alphabet (some games are in our book). Do one of these activities each day. Make a Greek language notebook to hold the student's copywork exercises. This notebook will actually be a rewriting, in the student's own words, of our book *A Greek Alphabetarion*.

After the student knows the alphabet (sounds and symbols), then practice reading Greek (there are a few exercises in our book). Since he has not studied Greek grammar yet, he will only be reading Greek at this point, not translating from Greek to English. Of course, by the time he is proficient at reading Greek, he will have begun to recognize some of the Greek vocabulary, especially if he is practicing reading his *Greek-English Interlinear Bible*. (In an interlinear text, each line of Greek text has the English translation on the line immediately underneath.) A good exercise would be to memorize passages from the Greek New Testament which he has already memorized in English.

Once the student has become proficient at pronouncing Greek – that is, at recognizing the letters and sounds so as to be able to fluently pronounce each word, then he should begin his study of Greek grammar. If the student does not master the alphabet before beginning grammar, then he will find grammar to be most difficult.

We recommend that you delay the study of formal Greek grammar (or Latin grammar or any language grammar) until at least age ten. Our own Greek program (*Homeschool Greek*) is written for age thirteen and above.

BEGINNING THE FORMAL STUDY OF GREEK AND LATIN

Formal Latin grammar could begin as soon as the child can easily recognize the grammatical distinction between Noun, Verb, Participle, and Gerund. This happens somewhere between ages nine and eleven. We recommend that the student maintain a Latin notebook of all of the grammar he learns. This forces him to rehearse the material and categorize it.

Because the structure of Latin is so similar to Greek, a couple of years of Latin grammar may serve as preparation for Greek grammar. We recommend waiting until about age thirteen before beginning formal Greek grammar. If you began Latin at age thirteen or later, then you could teach Latin and Greek concurrently. The student will not be confused. However, the parent might be confused, and the burden of two languages may be too much for one parent. So the father can teach Greek, and the mother can teach Latin.

A ten-year-old could spend fifteen minutes per day on Latin, while a twelve-year-old might increase to thirty minutes per day. While studying Latin, your child should continue to regularly review the Greek alphabet and pronunciation system – practicing his pronunciation with some interlinear reading.

All foreign languages need to be studied on a regular basis – at least four times a week, but every day is better. Don't take the summer off unless you must. If you stop for any length of time, then it is normal to feel lost and need some extensive review. Such is the nature of language study: if you don't use it, you tend to lose it. Steady study – evenly paced advancement – is what we want. Language study develops the mind, much like math. We won't all produce Ph.D. Latin scholars, but we will produce students who learn to think in other categories, and who are better prepared to study even in English.

CREATING & MAINTAINING A GREEK OR LATIN LANGUAGE NOTEBOOK

No matter what language you study, or what curriculum you use, you should make your own language notebook. Buy a medium sized three-ring notebook and fill it with notebook paper and subject dividers. Each student will have his own notebook. If Mom or Dad is learning along with the children, then they will need a notebook also. This will be the child's lifelong Latin (or Greek or French) language notebook. If the student is studying two languages, then he should have two notebooks. To simplify things, we will confine our examples to a Latin notebook. The same principles will apply to other languages.

The notebook will be divided into sections. Here are some suggestions on how to label the subject dividers. (This list is modified from the example given in Chapter Five.)

1. Alphabet and Pronunciation.
2. Technical Terms and Definitions.
3. Nouns. (Subdivide this section into the five Latin Declensions.)
4. Adjectives. (Subdivide this section into the two Latin Declensions.)
5. Verbs. (Subdivide this section into the five Latin Conjugations.)
6. Pronouns.
7. Miscellaneous Words. (Subdivide this section as you learn more grammar.)
8. Memorization Exercises.
9. Translation Exercises.
10. Test Results.

You may develop better divisions for your notebook as you advance, but these suggestions should help you to begin. As you learn more, you may want to rewrite parts or sections and rearrange the material in a better order. The process of rewriting the notebook has the added advantage of forcing you to rethink your Latin in an orderly manner. If you are like us, then you will learn the most about Latin as you write and organize your notebook.

For an example, let us pretend that we are just beginning our study of Latin. As we learn our first few vocabulary words – probably Nouns – we will need to enter them into our notebook. Because we may need to do some erasing later, we will use pencil. We enter the first Noun we learn on the first line of the Noun section of our notebook. Nouns are divided into five main groups, called Declensions, and each Noun may have a dozen different inflections (forms) to show Case and Number, but our grammar text may not give us all of this information at first. Because we need to leave room for adding information later, we put only one Noun per notebook page. Later, we may have room to fit a second Noun halfway down the page. We write the Noun, with its meaning. As we learn the inflections for each Case and Number of each Noun, we will record them on this page in our notebook. After we have learned the different Declensions, we can sort the Noun pages according to Declension. Here is an example of a Noun paradigm.

EXAMPLE LATIN NOUN PARADIGM

	Number	
Case	*Singular*	*Plural*
Nominative	aqua	aquae
Accusative	aquam	aquās
Ablative	aquā	aquīs
Dative	aquae	aquīs
Genitive	aquae	aquārum

FIGURE 12B

Verbs are entered into the Verb section of the notebook. There are five main groups of Verbs, called Conjugations, and each Verb has a multitude of inflections reflecting different Tenses, Voices, Moods, Persons, and Numbers. In other words, if we fully conjugate each Verb, then we will take much more space for each Verb than we did for each Noun. We may eventually take several pages for each Verb. We may rewrite these pages more than once. After a while, we may abbreviate our entries somewhat, but in the beginning, we want to write out all Verb Conjugations (also, all Noun Declensions) in full. Here is an example of a Verb Conjugation.

EXAMPLE LATIN VERB CONJUGATION

	Number	
Person	*Sigular*	*Plural*
I love	amō	amāmus
you love	amās	amātis
he/she/it loves	amat	amant

FIGURE 12C

Adjectives are similar to Nouns in that they are divided into Declensions. But they are different in that they have the added dimension of three Genders. We may fit two Adjectives for each page. Later, we will sort the pages according to Declension. Here is an example of an Adjective paradigm: (These are First/Second Declension Adjectives)

EXAMPLE LATIN ADJECTIVE PARADIGM

	Masculine		**Feminine**		**Neuter**	
	Singular	*Plural*	*Singular*	*Plural*	*Singular*	*Plural*
Nominative	cautus	cautī	cauta	cautae	cautum	cauta
Accusative	cautum	cautōs	cautam	cautās	cautum	cauta
Ablative	cautō	cautīs	cautā	cautīs	cautō	cautīs
Dative	cautō	cautīs	cautae	cautīs	cautō	cautīs
Genitive	cautī	cautōrum	cautae	cautārum	cautī	cautōrum

FIGURE 12D

Communicate to the student at the beginning of his language study that whatever is entered into the notebook should be done in a neat, orderly, systematic, manner. Language study will be simplified because everything will be in one place – test papers, translation exercises, vocabulary words, etc. Also, maintaining a notebook teaches the student to be neat, systematic, and orderly.

7. *Early Logic*

By age ten, children are in the Later Knowledge Level, and they are capable of only elementary logic activities. A formal course in logic would be beyond their developmental capacity. There are a number of "early logic" activities which may be helpful.

Building Thinking Skills (Critical Thinking Books and Software) is an excellent series of workbooks to develop these early logic skills and to prepare children for a more formal course in logic by age thirteen. The usual assignment of these books is:

ten-year-old: *Building Thinking Skills, Book 2.*
eleven-year-old: *Building Thinking Skills, Book 3 Figural.*
twelve-year-old: *Building Thinking Skills, Book 3 Verbal.*

Your child may be a step ahead or behind this assignment. If you begin with *Book 2*, but your child is struggling with it, then you may need to put it aside and try it again in a few months. Then again, if your child is breezing through it like a hot knife through soft butter, then you may want to jump to the end of the workbook, or move on to the next workbook. These workbooks are optional and are not absolutely necessary for preparation to the study of formal and informal logic, but they can be enjoyable and will help build up the logic powers of the mind to make the transition to the formal study of logic more gentle and easy. There is a Book 1 for a nine-year-old, but we regard this as too early and quite unnecessary. If you have time or resources for only one book in the series, then we recommend *Building Thinking Skills, Book 3 Verbal* for the twelve-year-old. ●

8. Arithmetic

BEGINNING ARITHMETIC (MATH) AT AGE TEN

A ten-year-old is perfectly capable of jumping right into a sixth grade math textbook, such as *Saxon 65*, with no previous experience with math workbooks or textbooks. Skipping Kindergarten through fifth grade in math will in no way hinder your child's success in math. You do not need to wear out your child's interest and your own patience attempting to make him understand what his brain is not yet wired to handle. Waiting until age ten, when your child is developmentally prepared to handle mathematical concepts readily, makes instruction in arithmetic very easy. What was painfully spread over five previous years, may here be compressed painlessly into as little time as a month.

We are *not* saying that you should keep your child away from numbers before age ten. Not at all. By age four, most children have discovered money, and you will not be able to hide numbers from them after that. Children encounter numbers all of the time. If you encourage learning, then they will be asking plenty of questions, and you will have plenty of opportunities for *informal* instruction in numbers and measurements. But we would not encourage *formal workbook* instruction before age ten unless the child shows a genuine interest and genuine competency to handle the work.

Before age ten, the child is largely acquiring the verbal skills of language, and your time is better spent developing his vocabulary – which is the primary index of intelligence. Remember the maxim: *There is only so much time in the day*. Your time may be much better spent reading aloud to your children than struggling with math concepts which your child simply is not developmentally prepared to handle.

OUR RESEARCH ON EARLY INFORMAL MATH

We have often been asked about our suggestion that math before age ten is best taught "informally." This seems most uncustomary to many. We very much want to learn if there is any contrary research or historical evidence. Everything which we encounter on the question continues to confirm this common sense view on the matter. We continually receive positive and enthusiastic feedback from families which have followed these suggestions – though many at first were somewhat apprehensive. Now, if a family is generally lax or unschooling in its approach, they cannot blame their math troubles on our recommendations. We recommend no lax learning. Lax learning lacks learning.

WHAT WE RECOMMEND FOR MATH (AND GRAMMAR TOO)

What we and others recommend regarding math is basically what was practiced with outstanding success until the twentieth century, when formal math before age ten was largely introduced into the world. Cultural math failure coincides with the innovation of early formal "workbook" math. We argue that it's the method. We believe in math before age ten. But we believe the evidence is against *workbook* math before age ten. The developmental evidence appears very supportive of that view. The same is true with grammar – not language, but formal grammar. It is best to learn to speak and to read and to write a language before age ten. But grammar – identifying gerunds and participles – is best left until approximately age ten.

THE FILE DRAWER ANALOGY

Math and grammar can be "learned" – sometimes "learned" well – before age ten, but it's not the kind of learning which we want. We may compare this to putting information in the wrong file cabinet – we have trouble later finding the information and using it. By age ten, the information is literally stored in a different part of the brain than before approximately age ten. Learning math in an abstract workbook fashion before age ten literally causes the brain to be structured differently. If the child depends upon his early math learning drawer, and does not develop a new file draw for later math learning, then he runs into a brick wall when he encounters algebra. (We like to mix our metaphors.) Now, if he learns abstract workbook math before age ten, then he will either develop a second math memory after age ten (and, hopefully, not have a cross-indexing problem), or else he will begin to fail in upper math. But if he learns math in a concrete – not abstract – way before age ten, and he begins to learn abstract workbook math by age ten, then the brain will develop properly, the right connections will be made, and – assuming normal abilities and developments elsewhere – he will advance in math at a regular pace without unusual difficulties. The same is true with grammar.

THE COMPUTER ANALOGY

Or, to put it in computer terms, some word processors can handle some simple calculations. We can type in the data, and it will work with numbers on a simple level. But if we want to do complex calculations, then we must load a much more complex program on the hard drive. Until about age ten, children only have word processors. About age ten, the more complex spread sheet program begins to be loaded up on the hard drive. If we enter all of our math information in the word processor, then it is likely that when the child switches to the spread sheet program, the data will not be compatible. Formatting errors will abound. We'll need to re-enter the data. Why not do something more profitable until the spread sheet program is up and running?

TIME BETTER SPENT

We are satisfied that the time spent studying math – which the young child is not yet developmentally equipped for – could better be spent developing verbal skills – which the child is a sponge for at these early ages. Deal with numbers in a concrete and verbal way until age ten. Use actual objects when you can, and when you can't, then use words and names for actual objects. Our culture is so full of numbers and measurements, that we let them pass without notice. Teach the names for numerical values with dominoes. Teach counting with cards or Rummikub. Teach addition with checkers or chess. Teach base ten and place value with money or Cuisenaire rods, or other manipulative math programs. Teach measuring systems with tape measures, measuring cups, weight scales, odometers. Teach fractions with pies and cakes and cooking. Teach area by garden plotting and room arranging. One mom who had struggled with waiting in math wrote us that her son wrote down on a Sunday school form that math was his favorite subject. Since they didn't do math, she was surprised and puzzled. When she asked her son why he wrote down math, he said, "What do you mean, Mom? We talk about numbers all the time." When she sat down with her son and looked through a math program, she discovered that he already knew it all. This may be a little more intuitive and less structured than we have in mind, but it demonstrates well how these things are taught as part of life.

Much more could be said on this subject. Suffice it to say that formal instruction in math before age ten is historically a very recent phenomena. So are all of the problems which have developed in math instruction. This has encouraged the invention of the more "informal" manipulative curricula – exactly what we advocate. (See Appendix One, Article Eleven, History and Research on the Teaching of Math.)

EIGHTEENTH CENTURY ATTITUDE TOWARDS MATH

Here is an excerpt taken from *Drums*, an historical novel by James Boyd (published in 1925). This excerpt will show you the general feeling towards mathematics among classicists of the colonial period. The time period here is about five years before the War for Independence. The place, North Carolina. Thirteen-year-old Johnny has been sent from his backwoods home to the nearest city in order to be tutored by Dr. Clapton, a pastor of the Church of England. He had been homeschooled up to that point. In this passage, Dr. Clapton is determining where Johnny stands academically:

> "Now," he said, "fetch down your school books and we shall see." What Dr. Clapton saw by the end of the morning was this: that Johnny wrote a fair hand and spelled within reason, that he read the easier passages in Caesar's Commentaries passably but with no pretensions to elegance; and that his efforts to write Latin were uniformly deplorable. In the realm of science he could add, subtract, divide and multiply infallibly if given ample time, but of fractions the less said the better. "You must learn to cipher, Johnny. It is unfortunate that gentlemen's sons should employ their time in the commercial branches, and I should never subscribe to a young man's going a step beyond fractions and decimals, unless, of course, he were to enter his Majesty's navy, and even there I consider that the mathematics should be left as far as possible to the lower ranks. But with clerks and stewards what they are nowadays, a gentleman must know fractions if he would protect his affairs."
>
> "Yes, seh. Dadder said I must learn fractions."
>
> "I have no doubt. A knowledge of ciphering is commonly demanded by the parents of this Province." His eye wandered. "I have concluded," he murmured, "that ciphering is one of the unavoidable disadvantages of a new country. Yes. . . . as to Latin exercises; that is more serious. When I was a Colleger at Eton the meanest scholar your age could do his fifty lines a day with never a false quantity."

This is not quoted to encourage less study of mathematics, but only to demonstrate the provincialism of those who advocate very early formal instruction in arithmetic and mathematics.

MATH BEFORE AGE TEN

Before age ten, our children studied math informally. We taught them to count and write their numbers. By the time they were ten, they had learned how to add and subtract, and had memorized many of the math facts without any formal instruction.

Your average Homeschooling family lifestyle comes complete with a full array of informal arithmetic exercises. Here are just a few examples of how children learn math informally:

1. Setting the table (How many people to serve?) and cooking (How many times should I increase the recipe?) and chores (How many scoops to fill the dog's dish?).
2. Helping Dad around the house. This often involves measurement systems and fractions: inches and feet, ounces and pounds.
3. Helping Mom around the house. Teach fractions and measurement systems with cooking: teaspoons and tablespoons, pints and quarts. Teach area by garden plotting.
4. Playing games such as Rummikub, chess, checkers, card games, dominoes, jacks, pick-up-sticks, and hopscotch. In all of these games, children must count and keep score.
5. Playing store and restaurant. (Base ten, place value, money systems.)
6. Building calculators and cash registers out of cardboard or matting board scraps.
7. Collecting coins.
8. Playing with Cuisenaire rods. (Sizes and fractions.)
9. Observations while driving in a car. (Mileage signs, advertisements.)
10. Baseball statistics.

MATH BY AGE TEN

By age ten, I made for the child two arithmetic grids – one for addition and subtraction, and one for multiplication and division. Each grid consisted of a square piece of paper, with the digits 1 through 9 running in a column along the left side of the page (with 1 at the top and 9 at the bottom), and again in a row along the top of the page (with 1 at the left and 9 at the right).

The Addition and Subtraction Grid: Where the "1" column and the "1" row come together, you write the digit "2" (1 + 1 = 2). Where the "1" column and the "2" row come together, and where the "2" column and the "1" row come together, you write the digit "3" (1 + 2 = 3 and 2 + 1 = 3). You continue writing in the sums until the grid is filled. (Compare the chart for mileage between cities which is found on many road maps.)

ADDITION & SUBTRACTION GRID

	1	2	3	4	5	6	7	8	9
1	2	3	4	5	6	7	8	9	10
2	3	4	5	6	7	8	9	10	11
3	4	5	6	7	8	9	10	11	12
4	5	6	7	8	9	10	11	12	13
5	6	7	8	9	10	11	12	13	14
6	7	8	9	10	11	12	13	14	15
7	8	9	10	11	12	13	14	15	16
8	9	10	11	12	13	14	15	16	17
9	10	11	12	13	14	15	16	17	18

FIGURE 12E

The Multiplication and Division Grid: This is similar, except you are filling in the products instead of the sums (1 x 1 = 1, 2 x 2 = 4, etc.). These grids function as an answer key for the math facts.

Multiplication & Division Grid

	1	2	3	4	5	6	7	8	9
1	1	2	3	4	5	6	7	8	9
2	2	4	6	8	10	12	14	16	18
3	3	6	9	12	15	18	21	24	27
4	4	8	12	16	20	24	28	32	36
5	5	10	15	20	25	30	35	40	45
6	6	12	18	24	30	36	42	48	54
7	7	14	21	28	35	42	49	56	63
8	8	16	24	32	40	48	56	64	72
9	9	18	27	36	45	54	63	72	81

Figure 12F

By age ten, we began the children in formal math with a sixth grade math textbook. We allowed the children to use the two grids when doing their math lessons. We took away the Addition and Subtraction Grid by age eleven, and the Multiplication and Division Grid by age twelve. By then, they weren't using it anyway. (It's much easier to remember it than to keep looking it up.)

Now, if a child lives in a home where neither parent is home much, where the child is watching television or videos most of the day, and he is not given time to explore and investigate the world around him, and where the love of learning is never encouraged, then that child will probably not be able to begin a sixth grade math book by age ten. Most Homeschooling families interested in pursuing the classical approach will not have homes like this.

Math at Ages Eleven and Twelve

If the child does not have the addition and subtraction facts memorized by age eleven, then we drill him until he does. The same with the multiplication and division facts by age twelve. No problems.

One of our boys began formal math at age eleven. I remember he liked for me to sit with him while he did math. It was not that he did not understand the concepts; he just wanted someone there by him.

Sometimes we would do the problems orally. Sometimes I would write out what he dictated to me. He was one of those who was allergic to pencils. But by the time he was in Algebra I, he was doing the math lessons by himself. After that, I seldom needed to help him with math. The girls almost never needed my help, even from the beginning.

TEXTBOOK MATH

There are plenty of perfectly good math programs available to Homeschooling families. I do not know that one is more classical than another. We used *Saxon Math* textbooks with our children, but there is nothing magical about Saxon. Different children will learn differently, and you will need to use the program which best suits your child. Before buying any math program, test a few pages to see if you can work with it. This is how we progressed with math in our family:

Age ten – Saxon 65 (sixth grade)
Age eleven – Saxon 76 (seventh grade)
Age twelve – Saxon Algebra ½ (eighth grade) – this is Pre-Algebra.

This "one size fits all" mentality about textbooks is for the birds. We are raising a generation of custom built children – no factory models here. If you have a child who is struggling with math, then just slow down the pace and take longer to finish. You may even take one step back and begin with a lower level textbook, or you may delay beginning for a few months. If he is a whiz at math, then step up the pace until he meets his point of challenge. We want our children to enjoy learning, to understand the mathematical concepts being taught, and to be challenged, but not exasperated, in their work. If your goal is only "to finish the book in the specified amount of time," then you may fail in the real goals of education. Do not let adult peer pressure rule you. Just because someone says to you that their child finished a certain book by a certain age does not mean that your child must finish that same book by the same age. An hour of math a day is plenty. You may require less, but do not require more. If your child really wants to do more, then you may allow it, but do not require it. Even of good things, there is still such a thing as too much.

JOHN QUINCY ADAMS AND MATH

Here is a correspondence between John Quincy Adams and his father John Adams, written when John Quincy was twelve years old and attending school in France.

John Quincy Adams to John Adams: My Work for a day. Make Latin, Explain: Cicero, Erasmus, Appendix. Peirce Phaedrus, Learn greek Racines, greek Grammar. Geography, Geometry, Fractions, Writing, Drawing. As a young boy can not apply himself to all those Things and keep a remembrance of them all I should desire that you would let me know what of those I must begin upon at first. I am your Dutiful Son, John Quincy Adams.

John Adams to John Quincy Adams: My dear Son, I have received your Letter giving an Account of your Studies for a day. You should have dated your Letter.

Making Latin, construing Cicero, Erasmus, the Appendix de Diis et Heroibus ethnicis, and Phaedrus, are all Exercises proper for the Acquisition of the Latin Tongue; you are constantly employed in learning the Meaning of Latin Words, and the Grammar, the Rhetorick and Criticism of the Roman Authors. These Studies have therefore such a Relation to each other, that I think you would do well to pursue them all, under the Direction of your Master.

The Greek Grammar and the Racines I would not have you omit, upon any Consideration, and I hope your Master will soon put you into the Greek Testament, because the most perfect Models of fine Writing in history, Oratory and Poetry are to be found in the Greek language.

Writing and Drawing are but Amusements and may serve as Relaxations from your studies.

As to Geography, Geometry and Fractions I hope your Master will not insist upon your spending much Time upon them at present; because altho they are Useful sciences, and altho all Branches of the Mathematicks, will I hope, sometime or other engage your Attention, as the most profitable and the most satisfactory of all human Knowledge, yet my Wish at present is that your principal Attention should be directed to the Latin and Greek Tongues, leaving the other studies to be hereafter attained, in your own Country.

I hope soon to hear that you are in Virgil and Tully's orations, or Ovid or Horace or all of them.

I am, my dear Child, your affectionate Father, John Adams

P. S. The next Time you write me, I hope you will take more care to write well. Cant you keep a steadier Hand?

— *Our Sacred Honor*, edited by William J. Bennett. New York: Simon and Schuster, 1997, pp. 230-232.)

MATH UNDERDEVELOPED?

Question: I just received your set of booklets a couple of days ago. In the article on math, I've been reading all of the quotes concerning how math was not a subject in the grammar school. I might not know history well enough where math is concerned, but math as a science was still being developed, wasn't it? So it wasn't even at the point of being 'teachable,' was it? Also, if children can understand an abstract symbol system like alphabets and reading, then why can't they understand an abstract symbol system of numerals and arithmetic?

Answer: We receive many questions about math. When we do our seminars, at one point we ask, "How many of you did not like math in school?" Every time, no matter which state we are in, about half of the people raise their hands. Why is it so many people dislike math?

If you read the article on the history of teaching math, then you noticed that until the twentieth century, math was not taught in a formal way to children before age ten. Before the twentieth century, children under age ten learned math (actually arithmetic) informally. They began their formal math studies – in schools or at home – around age ten. A man named Pestalozzi changed all that at the turn of the century by introducing some new ideas about education.

It is true that some highly developed concepts of mathematics have been developed in the last few centuries – such as the calculus. But none of that is the subject matter of elementary arithmetic.

When you teach a child that the symbol "a" is a letter which stands for the sound in bay, you are correct to call than an abstract concept. There is one step of abstraction from the sound to the symbol. When you teach a child that the symbol "2" is a digit which stands for the concept of "two," you must also go one step further and teach him that the concept of "two" stands for two things – any two things. It seems to me that math is somewhat more abstract than the teaching of reading. There are two steps of abstraction from the digit to the things.

The symbols of the alphabet are phonetic, linked to the auditory-speech mechanism which the child has been experiencing and practicing with since his goo-goo-gah-gah days. The concept of number, and the concept of performing arithmetic operations on numbers, and the symbols used for representing these arithmetic operations – well, we're straying further and further into abstractions.

The more complex combinations of abstractions are physically more difficult for the brain of a young child to handle. The child's brain will store the information where it can best use it *at the time* – which is in a linear file. Unfortunately, at an early age, because of the lack of physical development of the brain to handle such abstractions, that information is stored in a place which, when the brain becomes more highly developed, is less accessible. At a later age, the brain will develop multidimensional arrays, and this information is more accessible when so stored. (Please notice that we are using abstract mathematical concepts for our analogies!)

Some people mistakenly believe that we were the ones who originated the idea of delaying the study of formal math until age ten. Not at all. This idea has been around for a very long time. In the 1970's, others, such as Raymond Moore, reintroduced this idea back into American education. Some people read what people such as ourselves have written about delaying the formal instruction of math until age ten and conclude that we are opposed to teaching any math to any child before the age of ten. Not so. When the child asks questions, answer them. If he asks for a math workbook, then buy one for him. But this is different from systematically working through a math curriculum with a child every year from age five through age nine, doing every page, teaching every concept according to a preset, age designated, scope and sequence schedule developed by Megabucks Textbook Corporation of the World.

MATH AND TESTING

Question: If we don't teach formal textbook math before age ten, then isn't it likely that our children will miss some math concepts? Which means they won't do well on testing!

Answer: At any and all costs, we would avoid the so-called academic testing of young children. There is a place for private diagnostic tests where it is obvious there is some problem, but most of the testing which is being done to children is either of little value or validity, used as a manipulative tool, or downright a violation of the child's innocence and purity.

Only a few states require testing of young children. With many, it is an option – though they often do not tell the parents that they have other options. (By the way, how does a school system teach honesty to children when, in fact, it is continuously practicing base dishonesty such as this?) If you must test, then you might need to be satisfied with lower test scores in math during the younger years. However, everywhere we have traveled and discussed this topic, parents have told us that their children did do very well in math with no formal workbook instruction.

Once again, we do not believe in delayed math. We believe in delayed *workbook* math. Much big difference. Distinguo!

HARD WORK VERSUS EXASPERATION

Question: My husband and I are convicted that our boys must learn that, although there is great joy in learning, it is not always fun. We want them to know that worthwhile things are worth working hard for. We don't want school to always be 'fun' at the expense of their learning the value of hard work. However, I recognize what you are saying about the developmental aspects of this math issue. Math is the only subject we are struggling with. So I sense that you are on the right track. If only this were one of those issues where the Bible says, "Thou shalt not teach arithmetic before age ten."

Answer: Remember when your oldest was learning to walk? At six months you might have held onto his hands and stood him up on the floor to test the strength of his legs. Maybe you even helped him "walk" a few steps. You put him through the motions, but he wasn't really walking. But you didn't become all worried because he couldn't take off walking all by himself. You knew he wasn't developmentally ready to walk yet. You simply waited until he was ready. I've heard that some children walk as early as nine months, but most will walk at about a year, while a few will be fully sixteen months before they take their first step. The age that a child learns to walk really has no bearing on his future intelligence. A child who walks at sixteen months may often be more intelligent than a child who walks at nine months. It's simply a matter of physical development.

It's the same with learning to read. A few will learn to read by age four and a few by age ten, while most will learn sometime between the ages of six and eight. The child who learns to read by age nine may often be "smarter" than the child who learns to read by age four. The age when a child develops skill in reading is no necessary index of intelligence.

Some of us have higher expectations of our children than their physical development allows. Like driving too heavy of a load over too light of a bridge – the bridge sags and shakes from the overburden, and may not fully recover from the experience. Sometimes we unnecessarily hurry the process. We may even force the child to read before he is able. Rather than gently introducing the letters and their sounds little by little as the child is ready, we are intent on our goal of the child "learning to read by the first grade."

Learning math is also a matter of development. Some children seem to understand the mathematical concepts at what seems an early age, others understand at what seems a late age, but for most children, the light bulb goes on at about age ten. If we press children to perform before they are developmentally able, then we will discourage them and cause them to fail, which in turn sets them up for further discouragement. No amount of hard work on the part of a four month old child will result in the ability to walk. No amount of hard work on the part of a wee five-year-old who is not developmentally able to blend (putting the sounds of letters together to read a word) will result in reading. Similarly, sitting at the kitchen table with the same first grade math workbook page before him for forty-five minutes will not help a developmentally unready six-year-old learn to subtract. Perhaps you can encourage him to memorize the procedures of subtraction and "walk" him through the page, but the light bulb is still not on. Why not wait until age ten, when all of those procedures of addition, subtraction, multiplication, and division are clear to the child and he understands it in a flash.

Yes, we want our children to learn the value of hard work. But there is a difference between hard work and exasperation.

> Fathers, do not provoke your children, lest they become discouraged. — Colossians 3:21

Exasperation is placing a greater burden upon someone than they are developmentally able to bear. This is the closest we will come to "Thou shalt not teach arithmetic before age ten." We have the example of our Heavenly Father to follow.

> . . . God *is* faithful, Who will not leave you alone, *so as* to be tested beyond what *level* ye are capable *of bearing*; rather, along with the testing, He will also make an overload escape [★], in order for you to be able to bear up under *the load*. [*ἔκβασις: a place to step out, an out of bounds, an end or limit, an escape.] — First Corinthians 10:13 (v.l.t.)

SITDOWN MATH

Question: My oldest, a girl, is having a hard time working independently. More specifically, she has a difficult time reading directions or explanations, and understanding what is required of her. She will read through her Saxon math lesson, and tell me she doesn't understand it. If I sit down and read it to her and walk her through the examples, then she gets it perfectly, and can do the problem set without any difficulty.

This happens with other subjects also, such as Wordsmith, so I know it is not just a problem with math. Any suggestions? Is there something I could do to determine what the problem is? How do I go about teaching her, at this stage in her development, to think for herself? Please help! I feel a case of the "homeschool guilts" coming on!

Answer: Probably the government school professionals would call it a disability or some such learning problem and give it a complicated sounding label, but it's well within the range of normal behavior. Both my boys were like that until they were thirteen or fourteen. They wanted me sitting with them when they did math and grammar and Latin. I think my being near helped them to focus their attention. I remember that when Nathaniel did his math alone, he would later come to me with a "?" next to half of the problems, meaning he couldn't figure out how to do them, but if I sat next to him, then he had no problem at all figuring out even the most difficult problem. There is nothing wrong with sitting near the child and helping. It gives him confidence and motivates him to work diligently. And that's exactly what we are seeking to do with our children, teaching them to work diligently and to be confident in all their work. With some children, it takes longer to learn this, so we must be patient.

9. Science

The Knowledge Level is the observation level of science. Provide your child with the time, the tools, and the opportunities for experimental observation and exploration. For the Later Knowledge Level, studies in science could remain interest directed, supplemented with experiments, collections, nature studies, copywork, art, and reading.

Here is a suggested list of activities for teaching science to a Later Knowledge Level student. Do not think you will need to do all of these activities. Use this list simply to generate ideas:

1. Require the child to read something every day touching on science or nature. The library may have useful materials here, or you can purchase some of the nature readers reprinted by Christian Liberty Academy, or the creation science materials from the Institute for Creation Research. Subscribe to elementary science or nature magazines. Read to the children books from the library about various science subjects, including biographies of scientists. Practice narration.
2. View creation science videos regularly.
3. Purchase a booklet of blank pages and encourage your child to make little drawings of bugs, plants, or animals as a na-

ture study notebook. He could label each drawing with its Latin name. A good example of a nature study notebook is *The Country Diary of An Edwardian Lady*, by Edith Holden.

4. Do simple experiments at home. There are plenty of books for this at the library. Visit your local Science and Engineering Fair every spring, and observe all of the different science projects. This will help develop ideas for science projects he can present when he is thirteen.
5. Give children plenty of time to explore, observe, and collect. Help the child develop an interest and love for the outdoors. Interact with nature. Take walks. Visit parks. Go camping. Children should be spending at least an hour a day outdoors. See the Elijah Company catalog for suggestions on nature walks.
6. Begin bug, rock, and plant collections. Allow your children to collect to their heart's content. Forget about having a Better Homes and Gardens home. We once stayed with a family which specialized in collecting things. Their boys had large collections of snakes, lizards, spiders and rocks – all very neatly organized and mounted in boxes and labeled. It was a wonder to behold. Discuss with your children what they would like to study and collect first. Rocks are a good thing with which to begin. Begin at the library, checking out books on rocks and anything you can connect to rocks. Talk to people who make rock collecting a hobby, and find out how they organize their specimens, and where they obtain them. Use Newsgroups and mailing lists on the Internet to do your research.
7. Take field trips to college/university laboratories, veterinary clinics, radio stations, museums.
8. Get your novice license in ham radio and set up a station.
9. Build and launch model rockets.
10. Train dogs for obedience and show goats or rabbits at the state and county fairs.

We believe science in the Later Knowledge Level should be interest directed, whetting the appetite, developing creativity, and encouraging a love for learning. It is at the Understanding Level where science will become more structured.

10. Art and Music

If you want your children to be familiar with classical art and music, check such things out from the library, buy some prints or recordings, take them to the art museum or the orchestra. At this age, you will need to critically evaluate and select things for them.

You may choose to pursue a formal art curriculum, or to begin formal instruction in a musical instrument.

I think the best way to develop art creativity in your child is to continue to provide your children with the tools, the space, and the time for art projects. Ease of availability of art materials and encouragement from the parent are what the Knowledge Level child needs in order to pursue art. A table and chair in the corner of the living room, along with a nearby shelf lined with good quality art and craft supplies, will draw most any child. I bought my children matting board scraps to use in their art projects. These pieces of hard colored cardboard can be used to build castles, cash registers, computers, doll houses, boxes, and any number of objects. Matting board scraps can be purchased from most art stores.

A Few More Thoughts

CLASSICAL COWBOYS

Question: Thank you for the reminder that we do not need to compete, not even with other homeschoolers. Periodically, we have a day (like today!) where I am not organized, and the boys capitalize on my lack of input. Right now, all three (nine, seven, five) are in the backyard, dressed as cowboys, putting on packs, making camp, and plowing ground for a small garden. On these days, my spirit tells me that this is an excellent use of time, although my mind nags at me to call them inside to work. We seek to find a balance. Today, my nine-year-old began school work, and both boys spent about an hour to an hour and a half covering math, copywork, spelling, reading, grammar, and Spanish. We will read aloud in a little while, and my nine-year-old will read on his own, but meanwhile they can ride their horses (well, they are actually bikes) around the backyard. A nine-year-old in jeans, chaps, bandana, cowboy hat, boots, and pack, on a horse-bike is more pleasing to me than a beautifully written report. In my way of thinking, we will have time for those reports later on.

Answer: It seems like only yesterday that Hans (now twenty-one) was dressed in his cowboy outfit and sitting on his horse (the living room couch armrest). I have a picture of it. He would sit there by the hour riding his horse. I wish I could go back fifteen years and watch him again. Savor the moment. Enjoy their youth. It doesn't last long.

WHAT DO I DO WITH THIS BOY

Question: I have a boy who manifests the following behaviors:

1. Hates to hold a pencil and has terrible handwriting.
2. Is not motivated.
3. Does the minimum required – seems lazy.
4. Wanders around with seemingly nothing to do.
5. Must be continually reminded.
6. Does not read much.
7. Does not like academics.
8. No project appeals to him.
9. Has a narrow field of interests.
10. Has a short attention span.
11. Often seems "hyper."
12. Always must be doing something with his hands or his feet.
13. Does not want to do any of the things which I suggest.
14. If enrolled in a classroom school, then he might be labeled.

What do I do with this boy? I feel very frustrated.

Answer: Here are a few suggestions:

1. Do not allow television, movies, computer games, music which contains any kind of a syncopated beat, sugar and caffeine. Allow him only supervised contact with peers.
2. Make him repeat back to you what you have told him to do.
3. Work with him until you are satisfied with his obedience. This is of the utmost importance.
4. Make a list of the things he needs to accomplish each day, and have him check them off as he does them, and hold him accountable daily.
5. Wait until age eight or nine before teaching him to read if necessary. Do not begin formal workbook academics until age eleven. Read to him at least two hours each day. If he hates to write, then allow him to dictate to you his letters and journal entries, or use a tape recorder.
6. Exploit the child's one or two chief interests. Use it as an avenue to other things. (e.g. Link guns to the Second Amendment to the Constitution to principles of sound government, to history of warfare.) Start him in his own business involving his interests. For example, if the child's interest is fenc-

ing (with a sword), then you might suggest that he give fencing lessons to other children, develop a web page on fencing, write a newsletter on fencing, do a display at the library on fencing, write an introductory booklet on fencing, produce fencing equipment, do a fencing seminar for the farm-boys club. He can become the Homeschooling expert on fencing.

7. Give him plenty of physical work to do – regular household chores and special jobs. But do not dump it all on him at once – he probably is the kind of person who is easily overwhelmed and frustrated. Break everything down into parts and mete them out one or two at a time. Use a chart to hold him accountable.
8. If possible, move to the country so you can raise animals and there will be more outside work to perform. Raise rabbits, goats, or chickens, display these projects at the fair, obedience train your dog and show at fairs, raise earthworms to sell or for your garden, raise berries to sell or barter, raise some specialty animal such as a certain breed of horse, and become the local expert on that breed, have him practice carpentry skills by rebuilding a small shed or outbuilding.
9. Involve the child in some kind of community service. Visit the nursing home every week for one hour, cook meals for the elderly, do repair work for the elderly, pick up the trash around your neighborhood, make small wooden toys and give them to children in the hospital, make greeting cards and give them away, write letters to relatives or others.
10. If possible, Dad can take him to work once or twice a week.
11. Do unit studies instead of the traditional textbook approach to academics.
12. Become involved in history re-enactments (Civil War, Buckskinners, Mediaeval, World War II), make costumes and equipment, attend events.
13. Teach him to hunt and fish.
14. Buy the family good mountain bikes so they can all explore with him.
15. Hold the child to a regular schedule (flexible, but regular).
16. This suggestion we list last, but it is really our first: the child should be part of your daily family Bible studies led by the Father.

God gave you this child to teach you something. You need to recognize early on that your child is probably one of these “late bloomers.”

Their timing just doesn't follow the norm, and he needs your special attention. You do not want to wake up to this fact when the child is seventeen or eighteen and has already developed numerous unprofitable habits and wasteful ways of thinking. Motivating a seventeen-year-old is much more difficult than motivating a ten-year-old. Molding a seventeen-year-old is much more difficult than molding a ten-year-old.

With any child, you must build a solid foundation before you begin academics. With a late bloomer, the foundation takes longer to build and more patience must be used, because the bricks tend to be less than square. But, trust me, by the mercy of God, if you persist, then the structure which is built on this foundation will be worth all the blood, sweat, and prayers.

I think the secret to this is in the diagnosis. The earlier you can spot the problem and work on a remedy, the better. We have one child who was like this, and we did not really catch on to it until rather late. And then it certainly does not help that my husband and I approach the problem differently. I tend to take a more hard-line condemnation approach about it: *I can't believe it! The compost bucket has been sitting on the kitchen sink since yesterday, and you haven't emptied it yet!* While my husband would simply remind him to do it. We need to find out where their weaknesses lie and then train to those weaknesses. They do not always think ahead, so we need to somehow devise a way to help them develop the skill of thinking ahead. They put off doing what you ask them to do and then in a short while they forget that you even asked them, so we need to develop their understanding of the fact that putting things off has bad consequences, so they should do what you ask immediately, without questions. They are overwhelmed by multistep directions, so we at first avoid giving them multistep directions, and we gradually build them up in handling multistep tasks. All this takes patience, perseverance, and energy. Plenty of energy. And if a mother has more than one child like this, then it can be wearying. This is one way in which the Lord teaches us patience and perseverance. It is in the process of being forced to exhibit patience and perseverance that we learn to be truly patient and to truly persevere. The alternative is to use duct tape.

HOW MUCH TIME TO SPEND ON ACADEMICS

How do we count up the time a child spends on academics? Do we count the time spent thinking about a subject for an essay? Do we count the time researching a topic at the library? Do we count the time the twelve-year-old boy spends rolling on the floor and complaining that he cannot think of anything to write about? Some children can zoom through their math lesson, while others take the full hour. So, any time-frames which we suggest are only that: suggestions. I'm not going to consider the two hours of reading aloud, family worship time, personal devotion time of the student, or any extra reading done by the student (beyond what is required in literature, science, or history) as academics. That is just "living." It seems to me that two to three hours of "pure" academics for a ten to twelve-year-old is plenty. It is certainly much more time than is actually spent on academics in most classroom schools.

TEN THINGS TO DO FROM AGES TEN THROUGH TWELVE

1	**Family Worship**	Family Bible Study morning and evening; Knowledge Level questions; memorization.
2	**Literature & Reading Aloud**	Continue to read aloud two hours per day; memorization and oral narration; student reads good literature; oral interpretation.
3	**History**	History Notebook; outlining; maps; timeline; could begin studying chronologically; use primary sources; biographies; history contests and projects.
4	**Composition**	Copywork; dictation; letters; journals; simple outlining.
5	**Spelling & English Grammar**	English Language Notebook; could use a prepared grammar and spelling course, or use Webster Elementary Spelling Book
6	**Latin & Greek**	Begin Latin grammar at age ten or eleven; continue Greek and/or Hebrew Alphabet system; practice reading Greek from an interlinear.
7	**Early Logic**	Building Thinking Skills: Book 2 – age ten ; Book 3 Figural – age eleven; Book 3 Verbal – age twelve.
8	**Arithmetic**	Math Text: Sixth Grade – age ten; Seventh Grade – age eleven; Pre-algebra – age twelve.
9	**Science**	Interest directed; read books and watch videos on science and creation; simple experiments and projects; collections; visit science fairs; provide tools.
10	**Art & Music**	Provide materials, space, and time. Could pursue formal music lessons

FIGURE 12G

For books and curriculum materials mentioned in this Chapter, and other resources, see our Resource List at the very end of this book.

A SUGGESTED DAILY SCHEDULE

For Families with One or Two Children
In the Later Knowledge Level (Ten through Twelve)
And Some in the Early Knowledge Level (under Ten)

Schedules are made as a standard to serve you, not as a master to break you. Do not be a slave to the schedule, but also do not be a slave to the emergency mindset which always interrupts the schedule. The following is only a suggested guideline. It gives you some of the categories from which to work out your own schedule. Sometimes there are days which are so disruptive that you must simply list priorities, rotate through the list, and perform triage wherever necessary.

Principles to consider: The children should be doing much of the housework, which will free the parents to give attention to personal or administrative tasks. "Early to bed, early to rise" is generally a good policy, though a father's work schedule or other considerations may not allow for this.

5:00-6:30	Parents rise, children rise, showers, dressing, early morning chores.
7:00	Breakfast. Morning Family worship.
8:00	Daily chores (predetermined schedule).
8:30-9:30	General School Meeting: 1. Recite memory work: All children recite memory work. 2. Practice reading: Each children who is able will read aloud a portion of something while all others listen (Bible, history, Constitution, poetry, etc.). 3. Practice narration: All children practice narration (if there are several children, then break it up – half in the morning, half in the afternoon).
9:30-10:15	Mother reads aloud to all children (narration could be included). Children can work on arts and crafts while Mother reads.

10:15-11:30	1. Phonics instruction for children learning to read (or in the afternoon, when infants are sleeping). 2. Mother helps children ages ten and up (as necessary) with academics. (★★ See below.) 3. Independent academic work for ages ten and up. (★★See below.) 4. Copywork, history notebook, and timeline.
11:30	Prepare lunch. Straighten house.
12:00	Lunch. Midday chores.
1:00	Naps. Independent academic work for ages ten and up.
2:00-2:45	Mother reads aloud and finishes narration (children can work on arts and crafts).
2:45-4:30	Same as for 10:15 period; play outside; go for walks; once a week volunteer work (nursing home, etc.); field trips; library.
4:30-5:00	Prepare supper. Straighten house.
5:00	Supper. Evening chores.
6:30	Evening Family worship.
7:00-7:45	Father reads aloud to family.
8:00-8:30	Family activities.
8:30-9:00	Prepare for bed.
9:00	Lights out.

Children from ages ten through twelve need the most personal attention. You should plan on working one-on-one with them from one to two hours per day per child. By the time the child is thirteen, he should be doing much of his studies independently. Fathers could assume the task of teaching their children Greek and logic.

★★Some children can, from the beginning, do the following subjects independently, with only occasional help. Other children, for the first year or two, will need Mother to sit beside them while they do their work.

Fifteen minutes of Spelling & English Grammar per day.

Fifteen minutes of Latin per day.

Sixty minutes of Arithmetic per day.

After Mother has helped the child with the following subjects for the first week or two, the child can do them independently.

Fifteen minutes of early logic per day.

Fifteen minutes of writing per day.

Forty-five minutes of independent reading per day (fiction, history, and science).

Chapter Thirteen

The Understanding Level: Ten Things to Do With Children Ages Thirteen Through Fifteen

I have more understanding than all my teachers:
for thy testimonies *are* my meditation. – Psalms 119:99

And all that heard him were astonished at his understanding
and answers. — Luke 2:47

INTRODUCTORY REMARKS

When children reach the Understanding Level, Homeschooling becomes more interesting! Early teens are developing into thinking, reasoning, questioning creatures. They are no longer content to know *what* happened; they want to know *why*.

Alas, at the Understanding Level, many parents become distressed, because the curriculum is becoming more difficult, and the children are asking more complex questions. We are no longer allowed to teach mere capitalization rules and addition facts. We must now begin to exercise our minds with our children. Because these children are developing the ability to think abstractly, we parents are being challenged to move out of our post-secondary-school-days comfort zone. As a result, many parents retire from Homeschooling, and send their children off to a classroom school.

But this is not at all the time to give up. We encourage parents to persevere to the end. Remember, Homeschooling is for parents. The children are coming along for the ride. How many of us went through school without learning anything in general, or without remembering anything in particular? We were neither interested nor motivated. We were simply serving our twelve year sentence. We now have another opportunity to learn these things as we teach them to our children. We have the opportunity to learn such things as:

The math we never understood.

The science from a Christian instead of from a naturalistic perspective.

The history they never taught us.

The classical language they never offered us.

The logic they never allowed us to use.

Homeschooling saves two generations: first the parents, then the children.

Children in the Understanding Level should be more independent in their studies, and, in certain subjects, they should need less academic one-on-one attention from their parents. At this level, the amount of time the parents spend teaching hinges upon what kind of curricula they use. In some subjects, self-teaching materials are available, which may reduce the amount of input needed by the parent.

A SUGGESTED COURSE OF STUDY

1. Family Worship

In the Understanding Level, the child should be developing theologically. He does not just know what the Bible says – the story line; he is developing an idea of what it means – the more subtle connections and their implications. God is three Persons in one Essence. Christ is one Person in two Natures. Only in Christ can God be both just and gracious to the sinner. The child begins to ask questions, and the father needs to learn the answers. The father will be challenged to become the resident theologian.

Family worship is more than just a nice thing to add on at your convenience. We suggest that at least forty-five minutes be spent each day with the family together in worship. The child's personal devotions may take a minimum of fifteen minutes per day. We are not talking about self-teaching Bible materials which parents let children do on their own. You will want to continue with memorization of Scriptures.

Beyond their personal studies in the Scriptures, children at this level can be reading devotional literature such as: *Thoughts for Young Men* by J.C. Ryle; *Letters to Young Men* and *Letters on Practical Subjects to a Daughter* by W.B. Sprague; *Stepping Heavenward* and *Aunt Jane's Hero* by Elizabeth Prentiss; *Female Piety: a Young Woman's Friend and Guide* by John Angell James; *Pilgrim's Progress* by John Bunyan; biographies of Christians such as Patrick Henry, Robert E. Lee, Mrs. Robert E. Lee, and Mary Bunyan.

2. Reading Aloud

Continue to read aloud to all of your children for a couple of hours per day. Read from a wide variety of literature, and continue with the oral narration. Reading aloud may be your favorite part of Homeschooling. The books you read aloud will frequently coordinate with the time period in history which you are studying, or the books may spark the children into some exciting study in science or art.

3. History and Literature

We are combining the study of history and literature in the Understanding Level because they perfectly compliment and enhance each other.

1. CHRONOLOGICAL VERSUS INTEREST-DIRECTED

Some families begin at the Knowledge Level to survey history chronologically, and they repeat their survey every so-many years. Others introduce the chronological survey at the Understanding Level. Still others are content at this Level to move back and forth on their timeline while pursuing interest-oriented or project-directed studies, and wait until the Wisdom Level to do a comprehensive chronological survey.

To review: At the Knowledge Level we lay the foundation by encouraging a love for learning in our child and developing their enquiring mind. Here, you want to give him the basic tools for a lifetime of studying history. What are these tools? A sharp, creative, enquiring mind; well honed research skills; a love for writing. The study of history and literature will develop those tools in your child. While the children are young, and Mother is yet inexperienced in the art of Homeschooling, a rigid chronological survey of history and literature might be a great burden than some can bear. It is important at the foundation that the child's creativity and sense of wonder about things historical and literary be developed and expanded. Reality dictates that when our children are young, even the most organized Mother won't always be able to stay within the borders of a strict chronological survey of history.

Similar circumstances may also prevail in the Understanding Level – especially in families where there is a wide range in ages and there are children in both Knowledge and Understanding Levels. It may be best for all children to study the same time period at the same time, and this may require more shifting than a strict chronological survey will allow. In a classroom school, a room of same-age children studying history chronologically delivers results – to the satisfaction of parents and school boards. The child has studied all the way through history. But in a homeschool environment, with children at various ages and levels, it may be better to survey certain periods of time, or certain geographical regions, then use the timeline and the map to orient the child regarding time and place in history. For example, when you study the Peloponnesian War, you locate it on your timeline in relation to other events in history, and locating it on your world globe and your map of the Mediterranean area, showing its relation to other areas. Make sure that your child understands the overall sequence of events and has not missed any major events. We will discuss a chronological survey of history and literature in the next Chapter.

2. SUGGESTIONS FOR COMBINING HISTORY AND LITERATURE

Below are eight key elements to the study of history and literature – whether studied chronologically or not.

(1) A history textbook, such as *Streams of Civilization*, can be used as a framework for your history studies. It can be your guide to give you ideas on what to study, and it will hold you on track if you are studying history chronologically. If the textbook *Streams of Civilization* is not available to you, then we suggest visiting your local old book store and find a pre-1960s World History text to use as your guide. It would be best to use one written from a perspective which was not outwardly hostile to Christianity.

(2) Consult primary sources as often as possible. This includes literature written during the time period being studied (fiction, essays, plays, orations, etc.). For example, when you study early American history, read Bradford's *History of Plymouth*. When you study the history of the American Constitution, read the *Constitution* and the *Federalist Papers* and *Anti-Federalist Papers*. When you study Greek history, read

Xenophon's *Anabasis*. Your child could write outlines or narrations or summaries of these pieces of literature. Some will wonder how to coordinate the historical time periods with the primary sources and literature. Today we have numerous resources which can help us. Unit study curricula such as *Konos* and *Beautiful Feet* can prove very useful in coordinating your studies in history and literature. The *Critical Thinking in United States History* series teaches students how to apply logic to history by analyzing and evaluating primary sources.

(3) A timeline serves the student well to locate events in the overall scheme of time in relation to other events. You should have begun a timeline back in the early Knowledge Level. Other resources which are useful for timeline study are: *The Timetables of History*, by Bernard Grun; *Chronological and Background Charts of the Old Testament*, by John H. Walton; *The Wall Chart of World History*, by Edward Hull; and *The Reese Chronological Bible*, by Edward Reese.

(4) Consult maps, historical atlases, and globes.

(5) Each child should maintain an organized history notebook filled with his notes, outlines, drawings, essays and narrations. He may have begun this notebook earlier in the Knowledge Level.

(6) Read aloud biographies, autobiographies, and journals of persons who lived during the historical period which you are studying. Have your children write outlines or narrations or summaries of some of the books which you read or assign them to read. More reading and writing can be done by students in the Understanding Level than in the Knowledge Level.

(7) Read historical fiction and other nonfiction books from the library for the era which you are studying.

(8) Turn your study of history and literature into a project. This may spark the child's interest and love for studying history and literature. History projects require library research. We have done projects on The Lost Dauphine, Leonardo Da Vinci, Napoleon, the life of J.R.R. Tolkien, the history of fighter planes, Illinois women in WW II, Queen Victoria, the Great Exhibition, and the Illinois Central Railroad. Our girls did projects on queens and princesses and anything which concerned costumes. The boys enjoyed studying wars and

great men of history. In younger years we would all work on the same projects. When the children were older, each worked on separate projects. You can display your project at your local public library, a homeschool project fair, or enter it in history competitions such as National History Day.

3. EXAMPLE OF A HISTORY AND LITERATURE LESSON

Here is an example of how to apply these eight key elements to the time period from 431 through 404 BC:

(1) Read the section from a history textbook which corresponds with your time period. If you are using *Streams of Civilization*, then you would read pages 124-131.

(2) Read aloud to your children, or have your children read to themselves, primary sources and literature from the time period. It is not necessary to read every one of these listed below, but only a selection. You may wish to combine some composition assignments with this part of the study. Readings:

   a. *Israel* – the book of Malachi 1-4 (all ages).

   b. *Greece* – Peloponnesian War – *The History of the Peloponnesian War*, by Thucydides, Books 2-8 (which includes the *Funeral Speech* and the *Third Speech*, by Pericles) (ages thirteen and up); "Alcibiades" and "Lysander" in *Parallel Lives*, by Plutarch (ages thirteen and up); *Historical Library*, by Diodorus Siculus, Books 12-13 (ages thirteen and up); *Hellenica*, by Xenophon, Book 1.1.1-2.3.10 (ages ten and up); *The Constitution of Athens*, by Aristotle, Chapters 34-41 (ages thirteen and up).

   c. *Rome* – *The Early History of Rome*, by Livy, Book 4 (ages thirteen and up); *Historical Library*, by Diodorus Siculus, Books 12-13 (ages thirteen and up).

(3) Write in the major events and births and deaths of notable people on your timeline. Use the *Wall Chart of World History* and your textbook to help you with this. For 431-404 BC, you will add Pericles, Darius II, the Peloponnesian War, Alcibiades, Lysander, among others.

(4) Locate the events on a map. If possible, use an historical map showing the kingdoms as they existed at that time.

(5) Organize all of the work which they produce in a notebook. All composition assignments which deal with history and literature will be included in this notebook. If you have a child who is artistic, then his notebook will hold drawings.

(6 and 7) Read aloud to your children, or have your children read, biographies and historical fiction of the time period. The historical fiction you choose may drift a little from the exact time period, but it should be close. We list some resources for biographies and historical fiction in Appendix Two, Resource List, under Literature: Booklists.

(8) Produce projects about some aspect of that time period for display at the library or other events. Here is where Homeschooling shines. Let the creative juices flow and incorporate the child's natural interests in with your time period. Costumes, models of ships, weapons, architecture, and oratory can all be used to communicate what you are learning about this time period. You can't produce a project for every section of the timeline. Depending on talents and other interests being pursued, some children may only have time for one history project per year, while others may produce several.

4. Composition

Children in the Knowledge Level followed these steps in learning to write: (1) Oral Narration, (2) Copywork, (3) Dictation, (4) Letter writing, (5) Journals, and (6) Simple outlining skills.

Now, in the Understanding Level, the child is capable of more difficult composition, including: (1) Written Narration, (2) advanced Outlining and Written Summaries, (3) Essays and Creative Writing.

1. WRITTEN NARRATION.

Written narrations are similar to oral narrations, except the pencil is now in their hand and the paper is on their desk and their mind must work. Here is an excerpt from *How I Taught Myself to Write*, from *The Autobiography of Benjamin Franklin.* This will give you an idea of how other people used written narration.

> From a child I was fond of reading, and all the little money that came into my hands was ever laid out in books. Pleased with the Pilgrim's Progress, my first collection was of John Bunyan's works in separate little volumes. I afterward sold them to enable me to buy R. Burton's Historical Collections; they

were small chapmen's books [paper bound books sold by peddlers], and cheap, forty or fifty in all. . . . Plutarch's Lives. . . I read abundantly, and I still think that time spent to great advantage.

This bookish inclination at length determined my father to make me a printer. . . . I . . . signed the indentures when I was yet but twelve years old. . . . I now had access to better books. An acquaintance with the apprentices of booksellers enabled me sometimes to borrow a small one, which I was careful to return soon and clean. Often I sat up in my room reading the greatest part of the night, when the book was borrowed in the evening and to be returned early in the morning, lest it should be missed or wanted.

And after some time an ingenious tradesman, Mr. Matthew Adams, who had a pretty collection of books and who frequented our printing-house, took notice of me, invited me to his library, and very kindly lent me such books as I chose to read. . . . [A]s prose writing has been of great use to me in the course of my life and was a principal means of my advancement, I shall tell you how in such a situation I acquired what little ability I have in that way.

There was another bookish lad in the town, John Collins by name, with whom I was intimately acquainted. We sometimes disputed, and very fond we were of argument and very desirous of confuting one another. . . . A question was once, somehow or other, started between Collins and me. . . . As we parted without settling the point and were not to see one another again for some time, I sat down to put my arguments in writing, which I copied fair and sent to him. He answered, and I replied. Three or four letters of a side had passed when my father happened to find my papers and read them. Without entering into the discussion he took occasion to talk to me about the manner of my writing; observed that, though I had the advantage of my antagonist in correct spelling and pointing (which I owed to the printing-house), I fell far short in elegance of expression, in method, and in perspicuity, of which he convinced me by several instances. I saw the justice of his remarks and thence grew more attentive to the manner in writing and determined to endeavor at improvement.

About this time I met with an odd volume of the Spectator. It was the third. I had never before seen any of them. I bought it, read it over and over, and was much delighted with it. I thought the writing excellent and wished, if possible, to imitate it. With this view I took some of the papers and, making short hints of the sentiment in each sentence, laid them by a few days, and then without looking at the book tried to complete the papers again by expressing each hinted sentiment at length and as fully as it had been expressed before in any suitable words that should come to hand. Then I compared my Spectator

> with the original, discovered some of my faults, and corrected them. But I found I wanted a stock of words or a readiness in recollecting and using them. . . . Therefore I took some of the tales and turned them into verse and after a time, when I had pretty well forgotten the prose, turned them back again. I also sometimes jumbled my collections of hints into confusion and after some weeks endeavored to reduce them into the best order before I began to form the full sentences and complete the paper. This was to teach me method in the arrangement of thoughts. By comparing my work afterwards with the original I discovered many faults and amended them; but I sometimes had the pleasure of fancying that in certain particulars of small import I had been lucky enough to improve the method or the language, and this encouraged me to think I might possibly in time come to be a tolerable English writer, of which I was extremely ambitious.
>
> . . . While I was intent on improving my language, I met with an English grammar (I think it was Greenwood's) at the end of which there were two little sketches of the arts of rhetoric and logic, the latter finishing with a specimen of a dispute in the Socratic method. . . .

A couple of times a week, throughout the Understanding and Wisdom Levels, students should do some written narration. Here are some suggestions for those beginning with written narration:

Have the child read a short paragraph from a piece of classical literature. Begin with something very simple and very short (two sentences at most). Ask the child to read and reread this passage. Then lay the book aside and ask the child to rewrite this passage in his own words. At first, the child might write the passage nearly word for word from the original. This is fine. Later, when the passages become more lengthy and complex, the child will rewrite more in his own words. Slowly increase what you expect from your child. Be flexible here. This is a process which will take time to perfect. You may allow your child to write his narration quickly at first, then to rewrite it more neatly before he hands it to you. Once your child becomes somewhat proficient in written narration, then he can begin to practice it on the books which you require him to read for history or literature.

Before beginning written narrations, some students in the Understanding Level may need to continue with copywork, dictation, journaling, and letter writing (as in the Knowledge Level) for another year or so. One of our sons was a reluctant writer. He hated to hold a pencil. He could never think of anything to write about. His handwriting was poor. This continued until he was about fifteen, at which time something happened. We do not know what it was. Maybe he was struck by lightening, or maybe he just woke up out of a coma. He began writing some very creative pieces. His letters were entertaining. We would say he is now an excellent writer – when he wants to be. We tell you this to encourage you not to give up on your children if at age thirteen or fourteen they still hate writing.

Question: I hope this year to begin written narration with our thirteen-year-old, but I am unsure about the ultimate goal of the exercise. Is it merely to copy the piece from memory? Is it to emulate the vocabulary used in the piece? Am I simply looking for the fact that the child comprehends the piece? How does one critique paragraph rewrites?

Answer: When you begin written narration, it is best to pick out a short and simple paragraph from a book or story with which the child is familiar and which he enjoys. Have him read it several times, then put it aside. Instruct him to write the paragraph in his own words. It may be almost word for word at first, but impress upon him the need to develop a variety of ways of expressing himself. The more he practices, the more capable he will become. A thirteen-year-old might write narrations from books such as *Strawberry Girl*, the *Narnia* series, or the *Little House* series. His paragraphs could begin with two sentences, then progress to several sentences by the end of the year. A fifteen-year-old might write narrations from *Little Women*, *The 21 Balloons*, or *The Story of Rolf and the Viking Bow*. He should be expected to narrate paragraphs several sentences in length. An eighteen-year-old might write narrations from *Lorna Doone*, *Kidnapped*, or *The Hobbit*. He should be expected to narrate longer paragraphs. Do not use these as hard and fast rules. Each child is different, and each has his own unique capabilities. If a child has genuine difficulties, then you may prompt him with little hints as he writes. If the child shows himself capable, then expect more of him. Perhaps, to give encouragement, you will want to write your own narration along with him. The goal of the exercise is exercise – of the mind, that is. We want to exercise the mind, stretch the mind, strengthen the mind, sharpen the mind. If the body is not exercised, then it becomes flabby. If the mind is not exercised, then it becomes dull. Also, this exercise will improve his writing skills – which is what motivated Benjamin Franklin.

2. WRITTEN SUMMARIES

Written summary is a step up from written narration. It is a much more difficult skill to learn, and it is usually perfected only after years of practice. Most adults have a hard time writing summaries. Good newspaper writers have perfected this skill.

How is a written summary different from a written narration? In a written summary, you are concerned with content. Your goal is to condense the content of the material. You might have the child practice written summaries of passages from the history and literature which you are studying. In a written narration, you are more concerned with style. Your goal is to imitate the style and vocabulary of the author whom you are narrating. It is an exercise to help you learn how to write with polish, so you choose writers with polish.

3. ESSAYS, CREATIVE WRITING, AND BEYOND

Besides copywork, dictation, journaling and letter writing, written narrations, and summaries, the student in the Understanding Level should be learning more advanced outlining skills, practicing creative writing, and learning to write essays. Some parents will feel more confident in teaching composition if they have a prepared composition curriculum to guide them through the process – at least with their first few children. A curriculum which may serve this purpose well is *Understanding Writing*, by Susan Braderick. Whatever you need to do, do it.

The student who is more advanced in their writing abilities may choose to enter one of the numerous creative writing contests.

With some students, just motivating them to pick up the pencil is a major accomplishment. It is your job as the parent to provide the motivation and to stimulate the desire. Keep in mind that the hardest step in inducing the reluctant student to write is to get him to begin. Once he is over the hump and has begun to move, it is easier to keep him moving. You need to examine your own and your spouse's attitude toward writing. Do you like to write? Do your children ever see you writing anything besides what is absolutely necessary? Your answer to these questions may give you insight into why your child does not like to write.

Be sure your child is reading good literature and avoiding excessive "pictures" (television, videos, and computer games). What goes into a child's head when he is young will come out later in his writing. If nothing literary is going in, then don't expect something literary to come out.

Where does creative writing come in? Actually, journaling and letter writing are the first steps in creative writing. Many children vault ahead in their creative writing abilities at some time during the Understanding Level, while others advance at a slow and steady pace – sometimes too slow for our expectations. You cannot force creative writing, but you can encourage it incrementally. Make the assignments small at first, and perhaps entertaining. Write a parody of some favorite song or poem.

Describe a funny event which happened to the family.

Children in the Understanding Level should be writing something everyday. One notebook page of writing per day is plenty to require for most children this age. Some children will not be able to stop at one page. Ideally, the child's composition assignment will coordinate with his history and literature assignments.

5. Speech and Debate

In the Knowledge Level, the student practiced oral interpretation on a regular basis. Now, in the Understanding Level, he will continue with oral interpretation, and he will add Speech and possibly Debate.

Age thirteen: Oral Interpretation; Speech.
Age fourteen: Oral Interpretation; Speech.
Age fifteen: Oral Interpretation; Speech; (Debate optional).

ORAL INTERPRETATION AND SPEECH

You may require your child to write and present one speech and one oral interpretation per month. It would be ideal to have your child perform these in front of a group – your homeschool support group or your church, but if that is not possible, then in front of the family is fine. A thirteen-year-old's speech might be something simple, such as a report on heartworm in dogs, or a description of last summer's vacation. You would expect much more from a fifteen-year-old.

THE BENEFITS OF DEBATE

Some children in the Understanding Level will be ready to begin Debate, while some will need to wait until the Wisdom Level. If you are like most of us, then you were never involved in Debate in high school or college, have never even attended a debate, and don't have the slightest idea how to begin.

A debate is a contest where two or more speakers present their opposing arguments with the hope of convincing an audience.

> He [the student debater] learns to use a library, and to find the exact information he needs in the shortest possible time. He learns to be thorough and accurate. He learns to analyze; to distinguish between the vital and the unimportant. He learns the need of proving his statements; of supporting every statement with valid evidence and sound reasoning – and he learns to demand the same sort of proof for the statements of others. He learns to present ideas in a clear and effective manner, and in a way which wins others to his way of thinking. He learns to think under pressure, to "use his head" in a time of

> need, to make decisions quickly and accurately. In a word, the essential point in any debating situation is that of convincing the listener that your side of the proposition is desirable. — Harrison Boyd Summers, *How to Debate*

Debate is the ultimate mind exerciser. In his *Autobiography*, referring to a discussion group, which was similar to a debate squad meeting, John Stuart Mill said, "I have always dated from these conversations my own inauguration as an original and independent thinker." If your child can participate in Debate even one year, sometime between the ages of fifteen and eighteen, then we doubt that either he or you will regret it. One word of caution: Debate takes much of your time. Plan on spending a minimum of seven hours per week on Debate.

SPEECH AND DEBATE RESOURCES

Excellent speech and debate resources are now available to Homeschooling families. The National Christian Forensics and Communications Association is an outgrowth of the Home School National Debate Tournament that was begun in 1997 by Home School Legal Defense Association. The NCFCA organizes speech and debate competitions, and it networks with interested Homeschooling families from across the nation. They hold a yearly national tournament, and are involved in developing materials in various forms of media to help families pursue forensics, including coaching and judging videos.

There are articles on speech and debate in Appendix One, Articles Fifteen and Sixteen, and Appendix Two is a Resource List which includes resources for speech and debate in the appropriate place.

6. Languages

Children in the Understanding Level should continue studying Latin grammar, and may now add Greek grammar. Continue with the language notebooks. Since English grammar is best learned by studying a foreign language, the study of English grammar can be discontinued if the child is studying Latin or Greek grammar. There will be some students who will complete Latin grammar by the end of the Understanding Level.

Age thirteen: Begin Greek grammar; continue Latin grammar.
Age thirteen: Continue Greek and Latin grammar.
Age fifteen: Continue Greek and Latin grammar.

7. Logic

Age thirteen is an ideal time to begin the study of Formal and Informal Logic. The perfect Logic textbook for homeschoolers has not yet been written. At this time, the most user-friendly texts are *Critical Thinking Books 1 and 2.* These books include some political correctness, but you will recognize it immediately so as to point it out and teach around it. It takes two to three years to complete the series. Here are our general recommendations for studying the subject of logic:

Age thirteen: *Critical Thinking Book 1.*

Age fourteen: *Critical Thinking Book 2.*

Age fifteen: *Critical Thinking Book 2.*

Critical Thinking Book 1 introduces many of the most basic concepts in Informal Logic and some topics in Formal Logic. *Book 2* further develops the concepts of *Book 1.*

You should spend twenty to thirty minutes per day on logic. Review lessons at the end of each chapter may take a little longer. The review lessons could be used as chapter tests. *Critical Thinking* is a discussion course, so one parent, or an older child, will need to take the child through the course. Each lesson can be read individually, then you will sit together, discuss the lesson, and do the problems. Each student should maintain a logic notebook from his first year of logic.

When you do come to a difficult lesson, then try the following:

(1) Review that lesson, and possibly the lesson before – you may have missed something.

(2) Go on to the next lesson – it may explain further.

(3) In your own words, explain to someone else what you don't understand. The process of putting the problem into your own words often makes the matter clearer to you.

(4) Find help elsewhere – another textbook, or someone more experienced.

Logic confronts us in all communications – television, radio, magazines, newspapers, books. Point out logical fallacies and propaganda techniques when you encounter them. Distill arguments to their premises and conclusions and determine their validity.

8. Mathematics

Since algebra and geometry are an application of logic to arithmetic, they will be best understood by students in the Understanding Level, which begins for most students at about age thirteen. The study of math will be the same in the classical approach as in most any approach.

As you study the concept of the Trivium, you will understand *why* you do not attempt to teach algebra or geometry to a ten-year-old .

Age thirteen: Algebra I.
Age fourteen: Algebra II.
Age fifteen: Geometry.

Thirteen and fourteen-year-olds will study Algebra I and II. A fifteen-year-old will study Geometry. We suggest spending no more than sixty minutes per day on mathematics, unless, of course, you have a child who asks for more time. Math is one area where self-teaching materials are valuable. We used Saxon's *Algebra I* and *II*, and *Geometry* by Harold Jacobs, but there are numerous other good mathematics textbooks available to Homeschooling families.

9. Science

When students were in the Knowledge Level, they made observations, investigated things they discovered in the world around them, and generally learned to love science. In the Understanding and Wisdom Levels, students can continue to observe and investigate, but they will also begin a systematic study of the different scientific fields (earth science, biology, chemistry, and physics) and they will learn to conduct experiments in each of these fields. At age fifteen you might consider having your child work through a prepared course in earth science. We recommend the *Exploring Creation* series by Jay Wile, produced by Apologia Educational Ministries.

Age thirteen: Science Fair Project or Science Contest; interest directed.
Age fourteen: Science Fair Project or Science Contest; interest directed.
Age fifteen: Science Fair Project and Earth Science course. (Earth Science could be begun at age fourteen and stretched out over two years.)

SCIENCE FAIRS AND CONTESTS

We recommend that the student enter a Science Fair or Science Project contest each year. (See our list of national contests in Appendix One, Article Thirteen.) This type of project usually takes several months to complete, and it will incorporate grammar and logic, library research (collecting data), verbal communication skills (interviewing people and talking to the Science Fair judge), writing (each project will be written up), deciding on an hypothesis, analyzing the data and coming to a conclusion. A thirteen-year-old could begin with a simple project involving some special interest which he has (rock collecting, cooking, growing flowers). A fifteen-year-old's project would be more complex.

During the first year your child does a Science Project, this will probably be such new and uncharted territory to him that you will need to walk him through it. That will be the year in which you, the parent, will become an expert in how to do a Science Project. (Remember, Homeschooling is for parents.) By age fifteen, your child will be much more independent, and you will need to intrude yourself into his project in order to find out what is going on. So enjoy it while you can. Actually, we love helping with projects. It is one of our favorite parts of Homeschooling. We enjoy doing research at the big university libraries.

Nathaniel, our oldest, was always ready to study science. When he was thirteen, we read in the newspaper about a Science Fair to be held in two weeks at the local mall. It was open to all students in the area, even homeschooled students. We made an attempt at some projects to enter in the fair. Since Nathaniel was interested in model rockets, he devised an experiment to measure how high a rocket would fly with different weights in its payload. He built a tool which used angles and geometry to measure how high the rocket flew. His project was very simple, and his write-up and display were very simple. He won first place over all the other government school eighth graders – there must have been about twenty other children. Johannah's project was something about making bread using different ingredients. She won third place. Their projects were so simple that we were quite surprised they did so well. I think it was the simplicity, yet the thoroughness, which impressed the judges. So every year, for the next five years, Nathaniel and others entered a Science Fair. When Nathaniel was fourteen, he grew plants under hyperbaric (high air pressure) conditions, and at fifteen he made wine under hyperbaric conditions. At sixteen he grew bean plants under Extra-Low Frequency electromagnetic waves, and at age seventeen he entered the NASA Space Science Mars project. It was so much fun! We loved going to the different libraries in order to research each project. It was challenging to conceive and devise each project. Some Science Fairs will allow students to display projects which are more like demonstrations (how a volcano works) or collections (the different kinds of insects found in my yard) in place of a real science experiment with hypothesis, procedure, data, and conclusion. Demonstrations and collections are good beginning projects for a student in the Knowledge Level (ages eight through twelve), while students in the Understanding or Wisdom Levels should be doing real science experiments.

CREATION SCIENCE

You do not want to neglect the wealth of creation science resources which are available – science videos, books, and tapes. Our Resource List has many of these resources.

10. Art and Music

Families vary in their priorities here. If neither parent has any special abilities in music or art, then you could pursue formal music or art lessons under a professional tutor, or you could attempt one of the "learn at home" courses. If your child shows no particular talent or interest here, then you should nevertheless develop his appreciation for matters of music and art. This will be difficult if the child has no particular interest, and even more difficult if Mom and Dad are not particularly talented or interested either. Expose the family to good music and good art. When our children were young, we bought some inexpensive instruments – an autoharp, a dulcimer, some recorders, and a guitar. We have spent many hours playing instruments together. You will find materials for art and music appreciation in our Resource List.

FATHER'S ROLE

We have covered the academics for the Understanding Level, but there is more to say. The classical homeschool is not just Latin and logic. It is a way of life. We have made our share of mistakes in our Homeschooling. Here is one of them:

Fathers should be more than figuratively the head of your school. Children in the Understanding Level need their father. Of course, children of all ages need their father's attention, but the early teens even more so. We have not always been aware of this in our own family. Oh, to go back and do things right! But perhaps others can learn from our mistakes. If junior is supposed to be writing out his spelling words, but Daddy wants him to help him with the lawn mower, then by all means let the lawn mower win. Daddy only has so much time with the children, so make the best use of it.

We suggest Fathers assume the task of teaching the children Greek. It will not only help the children, but it will also help him – in his study of God's Word, and in numerous other ways. Logic is also best taught by the Father. Here is an excerpt from an essay our oldest son Nathaniel recently wrote: "When I was about thirteen, my parents announced that we were going to study logic. What thoughts flitted through my anti-intellectual mind I cannot rightly say, but I imagine they were not good. Back then, my father had not yet taken on much of the responsibility for our schooling, and so the burden fell upon my mother's shoulders. If you do not know what it is to learn logic with a woman, then how can I describe it to you. . ." We quote this, not to imply that mothers cannot teach logic, but only to suggest that perhaps fathers are more often better equipped for the task.

TEN THINGS TO DO FROM AGES THIRTEEN THROUGH FIFTEEN

1 Family Worship	Family Bible Study morning and evening; Understanding Level Questions; Memorization.
2 Reading Aloud	Continue to read aloud approximately two hours per day; Oral Narration.
3 History & Literature	Combine these two subjects; read classics; Written Narration; Memorization; Outlining; History Notebook; study history chronologically if possible; use primary sources.
4 Composition	Written Narration, Outlining, Summaries, Essays, Creative Writing. Could use prepared curriculum.
5 Speech & Debate	Oral Interpretation; Speech; Debate.
6 Languages	Finishing Latin Grammar and Notebook; Beginning Greek Grammar and Notebook.
7 Logic	Critical Thinking Books 1 and 2.
8 Mathematics	Age thirteen: Algebra I; Age fourteen: Algebra II; Age fifteen: Geometry.
9 Science	Ages thirteen and fourteen: Science Fairs, projects, and contests; Ages fourteen and or fifteen: Earth Science.
10 Art & Music	Could pursue formal Music lessons; interest directed.

FIGURE 13A

For books and curriculum materials mentioned in this Chapter, and other resources, see our Resource List at the very end of this book.

A SUGGESTED DAILY SCHEDULE FOR FAMILIES WITH AT LEAST ONE CHILD IN THE UNDERSTANDING LEVEL

The following is only a suggested outline to give you a framework for forming your own schedule.

Principles to consider: The children should be doing much of the housework, which will free the parents to give attention to personal or administrative tasks. "Early to bed, early to rise" is generally a good policy, though a father's work schedule or other considerations may not allow for this.

5:00-6:30	Parents rise, children rise, showers, dressing, early morning chores, personal devotions.
7:00	Breakfast. Morning Family worship.
8:00	Daily chores (predetermined schedule).
8:30-9:30	General School Meeting: 1. Recite memory work: All children recite memory work. 2. Practice reading: Each child who is able will read aloud a portion of something while all others listen. 3. Practice narration: All children practice narration (if there are several children, then break it up – half in the morning, half in the afternoon).
9:30-10:15	Mother reads aloud to all children (narration could be included). Children can work on arts and crafts while Mother reads.
10:15-11:30	1. Phonics instruction for younger children (or in the afternoon, when infants are sleeping). 2. Mother helps children ages ten and up (as necessary) with academics. 3. Independent academic work for ages ten and up. 4. Copywork, and history notebook, and timeline.
11:30	Prepare lunch. Straighten house.
12:00	Lunch. Midday chores.
1:00	Naps. Independent academic work for ages ten and up.
2:00-2:45	Mother reads aloud and finishes narration (children can work on arts and crafts).

2:45-4:30	Independent academic work for ages ten and up. Same as for 10:15 period; play outside; go for walks; once a week volunteer work (nursing home, etc.); field trips; library.
4:30-5:00	Prepare supper. Straighten house.
5:00	Supper. Evening chores.
6:30	Evening Family worship.
7:00-7:45	Father reads aloud to family.
8:00-8:30	Family activities.
8:30-9:00	Prepare for bed.
9:00	Lights out.

By the time the child is thirteen, he should be doing much of his studies independently. After age twelve, Logic will always be done one-on-one or in a group with other siblings of close ages. Fathers could take over teaching (and learning) Greek and Logic.

Chapter Fourteen

The Wisdom Level: Ten Things to Do With Children Ages Sixteen Through Eighteen

Wisdom *is* the principal thing;
therefore get wisdom . . . . — Proverbs 4:7

So teach *us* to number our days, that we may apply
our hearts unto wisdom. — Psalms 90:12

INTRODUCTORY REMARKS

THE TRIVIUM MODEL for child development may be explained in computer terms. Children are:

Booting up at the Early Knowledge Level (birth through about age nine).

Keying in the information at the Later Knowledge Level (about age ten through twelve).

Processing at the Understanding Level (about age thirteen through fifteen).

Printing out at the Wisdom Level (about age sixteen through eighteen).

From about age sixteen onward, children are quickly advancing toward adulthood. We call this the Wisdom Level.

There are academic subjects which are commonly studied at this level, but in this Chapter we will also include some considerations in preparing students for mature adulthood – considerations which are not necessarily academic. Remember, we are not seeking to reconstruct classical education the way the ancient Greeks and Romans did it. We are not interested in reviving the Greek and Roman civilizations. We do not emphasize the classical *subjects* and *literature*, which were products of their pagan culture. We emphasize the classical *model* and *method*, which are not limited to any specific culture. We are seeking to apply, in practical ways, and to all areas of life, those pressed and proven principles which were expressed – however imperfectly – in ancient classical education.

The goal of a classical liberal arts education was to give the student the basic skills or tools with which to educate himself. But academic education is not sufficient. In order to fill this out and balance it, we need to add three goals pursued in a classical Hebrew education: 1) teaching our children the Word of God, 2) preparing them for marriage, and 3) training them for a practical trade (men) or for managing their household (women).

The Wisdom Level is the most creative level. The Wisdom Level takes the facts (Knowledge) and theories (Understanding) and begins to apply them. Teaching will advance from the coaching and correcting level to the coaxing and directing level. You will be asking questions, leading discussions, and encouraging individual initiative and innovation.

What we offer in this Chapter is merely a working model which each family will expand and adapt to fit its particular needs, interests, strengths, and weaknesses.

A SUGGESTED COURSE OF STUDY

1. Family Worship

Family worship should take about forty-five minutes to an hour total per day. In addition to family worship, father may take his older students through a systematic survey of the whole course of theology. He may use a commentary based on either a Confession of Faith or a Catechism, or he may use a theology textbook, supplementing that with other books on specific subjects. In the evenings, Father may wish to read aloud from devotional material or Christian biographies.

Personal devotions should take your student no less than fifteen to thirty minutes per day. He may wish to outline books of the Bible during this time, or study a particular topic, finding passages related to specific topics by using a topical Bible or *The Treasury of Scripture Knowledge*. Or he may do word studies in Greek or Hebrew. The student may also read devotional material such as *Through Baca's Vale*, by J.C. Philpot; *Profiting from the Word*, by A.W. Pink; or biographies of Christians such as *The Mercies of a Covenant God* by John Warburton.

The student may wish to expand his interests in theology. Students should probably be steered away from the speculative areas of theology, and kept to foundational topics such as the doctrines of God, of Christ, of Man, of Sin, and of Salvation, and practical topics such as Hermeneutics and Apologetics. This will provide a broad and firm foundation upon which to build later in life. If the student is interested in the history of the Christian religion, then he will be encountering controversy. Children at this age are often prone to follow one point of view to the exclusion of others before they are truly capable of discerning the issues. We therefore recommend reading a wide range of opposing viewpoints, which will sharpen the students powers of conscience and discernment, while serving as a means for balance and depth.

2. Reading Aloud

Continue reading aloud to the family about two hours per day. Without reading aloud, Homeschooling could become rather dreary. There is one drawback to reading a good book – the fear that you may never find another book as good as this one!

By the time your children are in the Wisdom Level, you will find yourself rereading many of the good books which you read when they were younger. That's okay. They are just as good the second time around. The *Little House* books by Laura Ingalls Wilder and *The Wreck of the Grosvenor* by W. Clark Russell can be safely read more than twice.

We always leave the funny books, such as *Life With Father* by Clarence Day and *Penrod* by Booth Tarkington, for Daddy to read in the evenings. When he reads a funny part and begins to laugh, we all begin to laugh, whether it is funny or not, and that makes him laugh even harder, and by then Nathaniel is on the floor holding his stomach and rolling around, and pretty soon Daddy must remove his glasses to wipe his eyes. There is something about a good solid belly laugh which cleans out the soul from the weariness of the day.

3. History and Literature

As far as history and literature are concerned, except for the increase in the level of challenge, there is not much difference between the Understanding and Wisdom Levels. We explained in our last Chapter how to combine the chronological survey of history with a survey of literature. In the Wisdom Level, there is much advantage to the chronological approach. By this time, the student has become familiar with many periods and places of history, oriented them chronologically on his timeline and geographically on his maps, has studied many of the details of these periods, and has logically evaluated many of the sources of the record.

Up to this point, your family may have been studying history in an interest-directed manner. Now is a good time to string this all together into one comprehensive survey which reviews everything, and which fills in pieces which previously may have been passed over. You can begin with ancient history and proceed through to modern times, filling in the gaps by spending more time on those periods you skipped in earlier years, and less time on those periods you already covered in detail.

EXAMPLE OF A HISTORY AND LITERATURE LESSON

In Chapter Thirteen, we gave an example of how to apply eight key elements in the study of history and literature. Here is another example, this time for the time period 721 through 586 BC:

(1) Read the section from a history textbook which corresponds with your time period. If you are using *Streams of Civilization*, you would read Chapter 5.

(2) Read aloud to your children and have your children read to themselves, primary sources and literature from the time period. It is not necessary to read every one of these listed below, but only a selection. You may wish to combine some rhetoric assignments with this part of the study. Readings:

a. *Israel* – Use a *Chronological Bible* to help you find the exact Bible readings: 2 Kings 18-25; 2 Chronicles 29-36; Micah; Isaiah; Jeremiah; Ezekiel; Zephaniah; Nahum; Habakkuk; Daniel; Obadiah; Lamentations; *Antiquities of the Jews*, by Josephus, Book 9 Chapter 14, Book 10 Chapters

1-10 (all these sources are for all ages).

b. *Assyria/Babylon* – *Ancient Geography*, by Strabo, Book 16.1.5 (ages thirteen and up).

c. *Greece* – "Thales" in *Lives of the Philosophers*, by Diogenes Laertius (ages thirteen and up); *Aesop's Fables* (all ages); "Solon" in *Parallel Lives*, by Plutarch (ages thirteen and up); "Select Fragments" of poetry by Solon (ages thirteen and up); *The History of the Persian Wars*, by Herodotus Book 1.29-33 (ages thirteen and up); *The Athenian Constitution*, by Aristotle Chapters 2-12 (ages thirteen and up).

d. *Rome* – "Numa" in *Parallel Lives*, by Plutarch (ages thirteen and up); *The Roman Antiquities*, by Dionysius of Halicarnassus, Book 2.57-3.73 (ages thirteen and up);

(3) Write in the major events and births and deaths of notable people on your timeline. Use the *Wall Chart of World History*, *Chronological and Background Charts of the Old Testament*, *The Timetables of History*, and your textbook to help you with this. For our example, you will need to add the kings of Israel and Judah for this period, Sargon, Sennacherib, Numa, Esarhaddon, Creon, Asurbanipal, Tullus Hostilius, Thales, Ancus Marcius, Necho, Nabopolassar, Nebuchadnezzar, Draco, Aesop, Lucius Tarquinius, Solon, Israel carried away captive by Assyria, democracy in Athens, Judah carried away captive, among others.

(4) Locate the events and places on a map. If possible use an historical map, which shows the kingdoms as they existed at that time. For example, locate the extent of the Babylonian and Assyrian empires.

(5) Maintain a well-organized notebook. All rhetoric assignments which deal with history and literature will be included in this notebook. If you have a student who is artistic, then his notebook will have drawings.

(6) and (7) Read aloud to your children, and have your children read, biographies, autobiographies, journals, other nonfiction books from the library, and historical fiction of the time period. We list some resources for biographies and historical fiction in our Resource List, under Literature: Booklists.

(8) Produce projects about some aspect of that time period for display at the library or other events. The seeds sown in the

Knowledge and Understanding Levels should now have grown and be bearing their fruit in the Wisdom Level. Students should be able to pursue some wonderful projects which combine history, literature, and rhetoric. Enjoy the fruit of all of your labors. You can't produce a project for every section of the timeline. Depending on talents and other interests being pursued, some children may only have time for one history project per year, while others may produce several.

4. Rhetoric (Includes Composition, Speech, and Debate)

Students in the Wisdom Level will be (1) reading everyday out of one of the books listed below, (2) writing something every day, (3) performing speeches and interpretive readings each month, and (4) perhaps spending one year studying debate.

(1) *Reading.* What the student learns from these books will be put to use in all of his studies and throughout his life. Recommended rhetoric books to read:

How to Read a Book, by Mortimer Adler, along with the *Study Guide for How to Read a Book*, by Maryalice B. Newborn.

The Elements of Style, by Strunk and White. This little paperback was first published around 1919. In a brief space, this "little book" (as it was called at Cornell) gives the principle requirements of plain English style. Table of Contents: Elementary Rules of Usage; Elementary Principles of Composition; A Few Matters of Form; Words and Expressions Commonly Misused; An Approach to Style.

Classical Rhetoric for the Modern Student, by Edward Corbett. This is the standard rhetoric text for high school age students. It is an excellent book, now in its fourth edition. 230 pages are devoted to *Inventio*, 80 pages to *Dispositio*, and 146 pages to *Elocutio*. *Memoria* and *Pronuntiatio* are not covered. The last chapter is called *The Progymnasmata*, which was the sequence of prose compositions in which Greek students were exercised. For those who want to study classical rhetoric more thoroughly, the book ends with a selective bibliography which lists primary texts (books written by Greeks and Romans on the subject of rhetoric), books on the history and theories of rhetoric, collections of articles on rhetoric, and books on style.

On Writing Well, by William Zinsser.

The Classic Guide to Better Writing, by Rudolf Flesch.

(2) *Writing*. In the late 70s, before we actually began Homeschooling, we received a publication called *Home Education Newsletter*, published by the Bergman family. This publication recommended that older students should be writing at least one notebook page per day. I have always remembered her advice as a rule of thumb when deciding whether my child was doing enough writing. Types of writing:

Type 1: Outlining, Summaries, Written Narration.

Type 2: Book reviews (as opposed to book reports), Research Papers, Argumentative Essays and other types of essays.

Type 3: Newspaper articles, short stories and novels.

Writing assignments may coordinate with history, literature, science, or logic studies.

HOW TO WRITE A RESEARCH PAPER

Our favorite book on how to write research papers is *The Research Paper: Process, Form, and Content*, sixth edition, by Audrey J. Roth. This 300 page paperback takes the student step by step through the process of writing a research paper, from choosing the topic, narrowing the topic, searching for information, recording information, organizing ideas, writing the paper, documenting the paper, preparing the works cited, to final presentation. At the beginning of the book is a timetable and checklist for preparing the research paper and a research paper process log. This book breaks down a seemingly overwhelming project into bite-sized pieces.

For those students interested in learning how to write fiction, consider *Learn to Write the Novel Way*, by Carole Thaxton. This easy to use curriculum takes the student through the steps to write his own novel: coming up with an idea; putting the words on paper; editing, including a review of grammar; and publishing the final product. I would have loved to use this with my own kids when they were younger.

(3) *Speech and Interpretive Reading*. The student could prepare and perform one speech and one oral interpretation per month. This may be coordinated with your history and literature studies. Ideally, the student can perform these for some event, such as a farm club meeting, a contest, Young Author's Night, Speech Club, or Toastmasters Junior. Or perhaps your family can create their own event with relatives or neighbors.

(4) *Debate*. At least a year of debate would serve well to sharpen the student's research and communication skills. Debate research would involve seven or more hours per week.

5. Government, Economics, and Law

Government, Economics, and Law are important subjects in our day and age. They were just as important in past ages. A classical education would not be complete without these. At the time of America's founding, every man knew enough about basic law and government to be his own lawyer. Today, most people have never even read the Constitution, let alone have the knowledge to make out a deed for property for themselves. If we cannot move our country back to those days, we can at least teach ourselves to be more legally and politically independent and self-sufficient in order to take our own stand for Biblical principles in Government, Economics, and Law.

Age sixteen: American Government
Age seventeen: Economics
Age eighteen: Law

GOVERNMENT AT AGE SIXTEEN

Basic American Government, by Clarence B. Carson, is a textbook written from a constitutionalist perspective which teaches how our American Government works and how it came to be the way it is now.

> *Basic American Government* gives an account of the general government as established by the Constitution, of the state governments which preceded or came after it and their constitutions. More, it details the ancient and modern foundations, scriptural and secular, on which these constitutions and governments rested. The Founders of the United States built on a great foundation, and the story of that is told in these pages. The story is told, too, how the Constitution of 1787 became venerated and accepted as a Higher Law in the nineteenth century. The account ends with a sobering description of the massive departures from the Constitution in the twentieth century, on the way to constructing a Leviathan, which government is now out of control. —from the back cover of *Basic American Government*

Plymouth Rock Foundation and Bluestocking Press carry numerous materials for teaching American Government.

ECONOMICS AT AGE SEVENTEEN

Resources here include *Basic Economics* by Clarence B. Carson, the *Uncle Eric* series by Richard J. Maybury, and materials from the Foundation for Economic Education such as *Economics in One Lesson* by Henry Hazlitt. Bluestocking Press also carries numerous materials for teaching Economics.

LAW AT AGE EIGHTEEN

> When attorneys are employed, they must be paid; and their charges are not always regulated either by their abilities, or their services to a client, but by their own desire to make as much as they can. This evil can only be remedied by making their clients well informed on common subjects, and able to see what course they are taking in matters of more intricacy. Thomas Wooler, *Every Man His Own Attorney*, 1845.

Most Law books published in early America were for laymen, not lawyers. Besides the one quoted above, another popular title was *The Farmer's Assistant; or, Every Man His Own Lawyer*, by John McDougal, 1815. Self-help Law is an American tradition. There even was a time in the not-so-distant past when public high schools offered classes in Law.

Because modern laws are much more vast and complex than those of the past, we cannot be as legally self-sufficient as our forefathers. However, we do recommend that students understand the foundational principles of our legal system, and know a smattering of layman's law. If students understand the principles of Constitutional Law, basic legal terminology (which is largely Latin), know how to perform simple legal research, and have experience watching a courtroom trial, they will know the beginning steps for resolving any legal controversies they may have in their life. If one of your children wants to go a little further, let him read some of the self-help Law books, such as those on making a personal will, small claim's court, or buying and selling land. This will save him from being "lawyered" later in life.

You could begin your studies in Constitutional Law with the audio tape series offered by the Plymouth Rock Foundation, *An Overview of Constitutional Law* and the *American Civics and Constitutional Law Course*, by Paul W. Jehle. Other sources you may consult include, *The Making of America*, by Cleon Skousen; *Lex Rex, or the Law and the Prince*, by Samuel Rutherford; the *Federalist Papers*, the *Anti-Federalist Papers*; *The Federal Government: Its True Nature and Character; Being a Review of Judge Story's Commentaries on the Constitution of the United States*, by Abel Upshur; *A Familiar Exposition of the Constitution of the United States*, by Joseph Story; *God, Man, and Law, the Biblical Principles*, by Herb Titus. You can find books on layman's law at your local library. The materials from Nolo Press include *Nolo's Encyclopedia of Everyday Law* and *Legal Research*.

6. Languages

Just because your child is long past the Knowledge Level does not mean he must set aside the study of language. The skills of language grammar will apply to everything he does. Unless the student plans on regular encounters with a modern foreign language, such as in missionary work, the study of ancient Latin and Greek will prove much more useful than the study of, for example, modern French, Spanish or German. Latin will prepare the student for professional terminology, for understanding much of English vocabulary and grammar, and it will serve well as a platform upon which to learn any Romance language. Greek, of course, will prepare the student to study the Bible. If there is time for only one language, then we suggest Biblical Greek would prove the most profitable for most families. If two languages, then Latin first, and add Greek later.

If you have not begun one of these languages by this time, then do not delay, begin Greek today. We wrote our *Greek Alphabetarion* (Greek Alphabet Primer) and our *Homeschool Greek* with homeschoolers in mind.

If the student lacks motivation for studying Greek or Latin, he may need to see its usefulness. In Chapter Five, we gave several arguments for studying these languages.

7. Logic

Just because your child has passed from the Understanding to the Wisdom Level does not mean Logic must be set aside. The principles of logic apply to absolutely everything. The more he studies logic, the clearer it will become to him, and the more adept he will become at applying it to all of his studies. In fact, it is at ages sixteen through eighteen where the greatest understanding of logic is gained. The subject of Logic is similar to Mathematics in this way: each year, more advanced concepts are built upon those going before. By age eighteen, a student should have a good understanding of both branches of deductive reasoning, and have some familiarity with inductive and scientific reasoning. Informal Logic – fallacies, propaganda and the like – serve as a strong foundation for defending the Christian faith and worldview in all arenas of life. A capacity for good reasoning should grow and increase throughout all of life.

LOGIC AT AGE SIXTEEN

We recommend going through *With Good Reason*, by S. Morris Engel, *A Rulebook for Arguments*, by Anthony Weston, and *Introductory Logic*, audio series by R.C. Sproul. These books and tapes give a good foundation in Formal Logic. *With Good Reason* teaches Logical Fallacies, and *A Rulebook for Arguments* introduces Argumentation. It has excellent suggestions for writing an Argumentative Essay. R.C. Sproul gives an introduction to the Christian philosophy of logic.

LOGIC AT AGE SEVENTEEN

We recommend going through the *Introductory Logic* video series, by Douglas Wilson and James Nance. Mr. Nance teaches traditional Aristotelian Logic in the form of syllogisms. This is traditional deductive reasoning.

LOGIC AT AGE EIGHTEEN AND BEYOND

We recommend reading through *The Art of Reasoning*, by David Kelley. This is a standard textbook for upper high school or college, and it teaches all major subjects in Logic, including Inductive Reasoning and Symbolic Logic. *The Art of Reasoning* focuses more on practical skills than do other texts.

ABOUT USING LOGIC MATERIALS

Logic is definitely doable if you use the right materials. You need to use materials specifically designed for or easily adapted to self-study, and used successfully by other Homeschooling families. *Learning Logic at Home*, by Nathaniel Bluedorn, gives clear and practical suggestions on how to use all of the Logic materials which we have listed. Don't forget to maintain your Logic notebook.

HOW TO USE INTRODUCTORY LOGIC, BY WILSON AND NANCE

The *Introductory Logic* video course by Wilson and Nance is made up of: 1) a textbook with exercises, 2) an answer key booklet for the exercises, 3) a test booklet with answers in the back, 4) three video cassettes. The material in the text is divided into thirty sections, with exercises for each section. There are six tests which are to be used periodically throughout the text, and there is a comprehensive final test. The videos are divided into twenty lessons; each lesson covers one or more sections of the text.

Here are Mr. Nance's suggestions for how Homeschool students should proceed through his course (with our own suggestions added):

(1) Read the sections in the text which correspond with that day's video lesson. Peruse the exercises, but do not do them yet.

(2) Watch the video lesson and take notes.

(3) Do the exercises in the text, correct them, then review any parts which you missed.

(4) Do the tests as they come due. Review any problems which you miss on the test until you understand why you missed them. Do not proceed to the next video lesson until you score at least ninety percent correct on the test.

(5) Take the final test.

In Logos School, Mr. Nance's Logic class takes three months of one hour classes, five days a week, in order to finish this course. We expect Homeschoolers may take somewhat longer to finish the same course, spending thirty minutes to an hour each day. Your previous experience in *Critical Thinking Books 1 and 2* will be good preparation. Because there is no teacher's guide, we have briefly outlined the *Introductory Logic* course for you. Each video lesson should be done as follows:

Video Lesson 1: Introduction – text pages 1-2 (no exercises). Mr. Nance gives a good introduction to the Christian philosophy of logic in Lesson 1, but it is one of the hardest lessons to understand. It may discourage you at first. When you are done with the last video lesson in this course, then go back and watch the first lesson again. You will then understand better some of the fundamental ideas which Mr. Nance is teaching.

Video Lesson 2: Statements and the Laws of Thought – text pages 3-7.

Video Lesson 3: Types of Statements – text pages 8-12.

Video Lesson 4: Relationships Between Statements – text pages 13-20. Test 1.

Video Lesson 5: Statements in Categorical Form – text pages 21-26.

Video Lesson 6: The Square of Opposition – text pages 27-44. Test 2.

Video Lesson 7: Arguments – text pages 45-52. The definitions of validity and truth are often difficult for students when they first encounter them.

Video Lesson 8: The Syllogism – text pages 53-56. Students often resist accepting as true the rules for syllogisms.

Video Lesson 9: Mood and Figure of Syllogisms – text pages 57-60. Test 3.

Video Lesson 10: Testing Syllogisms by Counter-example – text pages 61-64.

Video Lesson 11: Distributed Terms and Testing Syllogisms by Rules – text pages 65-72. Mr. Nance is often too abstract in explaining these concepts. Find some real-life examples on your own.

Video Lesson 12: Immediate Inferences – text pages 73-79. We found Lesson 12 on immediate inferences to be the most difficult of all the lessons. It took us a week to complete it.

Video Lesson 13: Extra Lesson: Venn Diagrams and The Existential Presupposition – This lesson is not in the text. Test 4.

Video Lesson 14: Translating Ordinary Statements – text pages 80-82. Mr. Nance told us that Lessons 14 through 18 are the most difficult for his students to understand. But they were the easiest for us.

Video Lesson 15: Parameters and Exclusives – text pages 83-87.

Video Lesson 16: Enthymemes – text pages 88-92. Test 5.

Video Lesson 17: Hypothetical Syllogisms – text pages 93-100.

Video Lesson 18: Extra Lesson: Hypotheticals to Syllogisms – This lesson is not in the text.

Video Lesson 19: Informal Fallacies – text pages 101-118. Test 6.

Video Lesson 20: Extra Lesson: Overview and Further Study – This lesson is not in the text. Final Comprehensive Test.

Introductory Logic by Wilson and Nance is often sold separately from the video course. Our advice is: buy the videos. The explanations in the text are inadequate without Mr. Nance's video lectures.

8. Mathematics

The usual sequence for studying mathematics in the Wisdom Level is:

Age sixteen: Advanced Math (Algebra 3, Trigonometry, Pre-Calculus)

Age seventeen: Elective — Calculus, Computer Science, Accounting, or Engineering (depending upon future goals).

Age eighteen: Elective — Calculus, Computer Science, Accounting, or Engineering (depending upon future goals).

You may choose to drop math at age seventeen to make room for other important studies. One of our children went on to study Calculus. There are many fine mathematics curricula available to Homeschooling families today. Although we used the Saxon Math textbook series, we substituted Harold Jacobs' *Geometry* at age fifteen, and skipped the Geometry sections in Advanced Math at age sixteen.

9. Science

The study of science will take the most diverse directions during the Wisdom Level. It is in various aspects of science where many students find their interests and livelihood. This does not mean that everybody should become astrophysicists or bio-technicians! Farming is a Science. Electricians are scientists, as are carpenters and brick masons. Even housekeeping involves an incredible amount of science if one is to actually become a master of that wonderfully feminine art. This is why, along with the more structured subjects of Biology, Chemistry, and Physics, students in the Wisdom Level may wish to pursue some of their own individual interests in science.

Age sixteen: Biology course and Science Fair or Contest
Age seventeen: Chemistry course and Science Fair or Contest
Age eighteen: Physics course and Science Fair or Contest

There are several ways to study the subjects of Biology, Chemistry, and Physics. In past years, we have used video courses and correspondence courses, but we were not quite satisfied. We much prefer the *Exploring Creation* series by Jay Wile (Apologia Educational Ministries). Science Fair Projects or Science Contests are very useful supplements to textbooks. They put what you have learned to creative and practical use – which is what the Wisdom Level is all about.

OTHER IDEAS FOR STUDYING SCIENCE

Here are some ideas for studying science on the Wisdom Level:

1. Do an in-depth study of the subject of origins and find another student with whom to debate. Students should be able to argue both sides of the question. The books, tapes, and videos from Institute for Creation Research, Answers in Genesis, and Ken Hovind will be indispensable resources for you.
2. Artistic students may compose a notebook with nature or scientific drawings accompanied by descriptions.
3. Produce a newsletter or a web page on some specific topic of scientific interest – gems, origins, birds, or tropical fish.
4. If you have a student who is not theoretically oriented, then give him more practical projects – automobile repair, construction, gardening – and incorporate the science at appropriate places.
5. One year, not too long ago, we bought a dissecting kit. Though the equipment included in the kit was excellent, we have yet

to find a dissecting book which we like. The preserved specimens in most kits are mushy and very difficult to dissect. It is best to dissect fresh specimens if you can find them.
6. If you continue a nature study notebook, then expect a higher and more complex level of work. For example, after researching the subject at the library, the student could draw a sketch of a hand on the top half of a page, then write about the anatomy of the hand on the bottom half of the page. Or the student could draw different kinds of cells and label all of their parts, then describe the function of each type of cell.
7. Regularly View Creation Science videos from Midwest Creation Fellowship.

10. Art and Music

The student should follow his interests here. Art and music appreciation could be studied, or formal lessons could be pursued if desired. As in the science fields, many students find their interests and livelihood in some form of art and music. It will always be to the student's advantage to learn a musical instrument while he is young. It will give him enjoyment throughout his life, and it will teach him self-discipline and attention to finer details.

The Norton Programmed Texts in Music Theory: *Scales, Intervals, Keys, Triads, Rhythm, and Meter*, by John Clough and Joyce Conley, is a self-instruction curriculum for ages sixteen and up. It is an excellent resource for beginning your study of music theory.

BEYOND ACADEMICS

During the Early Knowledge Level, parents are molding their children. During the later Knowledge and Understanding Levels, parents are developing their children's fundamental skills – giving them the basic tools. But in the Wisdom Level, though skills are still being developed, the child begins to pursue a particular course for life, based upon his abilities, talents, and interests. Parents should assess their children's abilities and talents, help them to explore their peculiar interests, and encourage them in certain directions. We may encourage hobbies (HAM radio, carpentry, coin collecting, knitting, or crochet), special activities (livestock shows, fair exhibits, debate), or special instruction (computer programming, first aid instruction, flight lessons). Our role in their education will slowly change from instructor to counselor, as the Lord begins to call them forward and lead them in other directions, and eventually to marry and to establish a new household.

Though boys and girls may study the same subjects, boys will use the information to pursue different goals than will girls. A boy may study math and science to prepare for making a livelihood, while a girl may study math and science to use in managing a household. These are not only traditional and customary roles, they are also Biblically defined roles, the legitimate exceptions to which should be most rare. God does not endorse uni-sex careerism. A mother's place is in the home, to hold and love those from her womb.

Preparation for Marriage

Marriage is not a minor part of life. Rather, it is the primary earthly relationship for all of life. Almost everyone marries. Then why do we not prepare our offspring for marriage? Well, in the past, they did. But several generations of humanism intruding into our culture have driven out the principles of Christian culture to the point that most people do not even recognize Christian culture – they classify courtship and betrothal, large families, work-at-home fathers, and stay-at-home mothers as part of the lunatic fringe. (Never mind that it has been the norm for six millennia.)

The first step in preparing your progeny for marriage is to model a good marriage for them. In your home, establish Biblical roles and relationships for husbands and fathers, wives and mothers, offspring and siblings. Do not just do what comes natural, or what you saw your parents or others do. Do what God teaches. A good modeling of marriage is also a good preparation for church – Christ is the Head, and the church is His bride.

What are the important relationships in life? Relationship to God, to the family, to the household of God, and to our neighbors. At different moments and periods in our life, the priority of these relationships will change. But our relationship to the world, to business, and to civil government should be dependent upon family and church, not vice versa. The family should be the center of our earthly lives.

Gaining a Livelihood and Managing a Home

We need to prepare our children for their calling in life, which includes their calling in marriage as well as their calling in making a living and keeping a home for the spouses and sprouts in the marriage. Boys must prepare to support a family and to be spiritual leaders. Girls must prepare to manage a household, to train and teach children, and to be a help to their husbands. If girls neglect their academic education, they will be less helpful to their husbands and less able to educate their children.

We believe the ideal scenario is for the father to make a family-friendly livelihood from out of his own home, and his sons to learn skills while helping him at his work. If the sons desire to go on to something else, they will still have these basic skills learned at home as a foundation to build upon and to fall back upon. Obviously, we all cannot drop everything and follow this ideal "classical" scenario, but we can begin to move in this direction. This does go against the grain of latter twentieth century living, but so do plenty of other good classical Christian cultural norms.

Daughters will learn creative homemaking from their mothers: how to plan and prepare meals, how to grow and store food, how to entertain guests, how to attend to a family's clothing, how to care for younger children, how to educate the next generation.

To be well academically prepared, but to have skipped the practical skills for boys and girls, is to have missed the mark by a large margin. If you spend your time only teaching for the academic tests of life, you will miss the real tests of life. For some parents, this may all seem like a "no-brainer," while other parents have not the first clue. Most of us are somewhere in between, but we all need to teach these things. If children cannot do the practical things, then there will be huge gaps in their real education. Inversely, if we slight the academics and focus only on the practical, our children will be ill prepared to serve God in the world and against the world. If we accomplish our goal of a good classical liberal arts education balanced with a good classical Hebrew education, then we will have produced some straight and sharp arrows for God's use.

We will discuss this topic in more detail in Chapter Fifteen.

Ten Things To Do From Ages Sixteen Through Eighteen

1 Family Worship	Family Bible Study morning and evening; Wisdom Level Questions; memorization.
2 Reading Aloud	Continue to read aloud; Oral Narration.
3 History & Literature	Combine these two subjects; read classics; Written Narration; memorization; History Notebook; study history chronologically if possible; use primary sources.
4 Rhetoric	Reading; Composition; Oral Interpretation; Speech; Debate.
5 Government, Economics & Law	Age sixteen: American Government; Age seventeen: Economics; Age eighteen: Constitutional and Practical Law.
6 Languages	Greek Grammar; Greek Language Notebook. (Could begin Hebrew Grammar.)
7 Logic	Age sixteen: With Good Reason; Rulebook for Arguments; Introductory Logic audio (Sproul); Age seventeen: Introductory Logic video series (Wilson and Nance); Age eighteen: The Art of Reasoning (Kelley).
8 Mathematics	Age sixteen: Advanced Math; Age seventeen: Calculus (if desired); Age Eighteen: Elective (if desired).
9 Science	Age sixteen: Biology; Age seventeen: Chemistry; Age eighteen: Physics (if desired). Study Scientific method; Science Fairs, Projects, and Contests.
10 Art & Music	Could pursue formal Music lessons; interest directed.

Figure 14A

For books and curriculum materials mentioned in this Chapter, and other resources, see our Resource List at the very end of this book.

A SUGGESTED DAILY SCHEDULE FOR FAMILIES WITH AT LEAST ONE CHILD IN THE WISDOM LEVEL

The following is only a suggested outline.

Principles to consider: The children should be doing much of the housework, which will free the parents to give attention to personal or administrative tasks. "Early to bed, early to rise" is generally a good policy, though a father's work schedule or other considerations may not allow for this.

5:00-6:30 Parents rise, children rise, showers, dressing, early morning chores, personal devotions.

7:00 Breakfast. Morning Family worship.

8:00 Daily chores (predetermined schedule).

8:30-9:30 General School Meeting:
1. Recite memory work: All children recite memory work.
2. Practice reading: Each child who is able will read aloud a portion of something while all others listen.
3. Practice narration: All children practice narration (if there are several children, then break it up – half in the morning, half in the afternoon).

9:30-10:15 Mother reads aloud to all children (narration could be included). Children can work on arts and crafts while Mother reads.

10:15-11:30 1. Phonics instruction for younger children (or in the afternoon, when infants are sleeping).
2. Mother helps children ages ten and up (as necessary) with academics.
3. Independent academics for ages ten and up.
4. Copywork, history notebook, and timeline.

11:30 Prepare lunch. Straighten house.

12:00 Lunch. Midday chores.

1:00 Naps. Independent academic work for ages ten and up.

2:00-2:45 Mother reads aloud and finishes narration (children can work on arts and crafts).

2:45-4:30	Independent academic work for ages ten and up. Same as 10:15 period; play outside; go for walks; once a week volunteer work (nursing home, etc.); field trips; library.
4:30-5:00	Prepare supper. Straighten house.
5:00	Supper. Evening chores.
6:30	Evening Family worship.
7:00-7:45	Father reads aloud to family.
8:00-8:30	Family activities.
8:30-9:00	Prepare for bed.
9:00	Lights out.

Chapter Fifteen

The Finishing Level: Ages Nineteen and Onward

And that from a child thou hast known the holy scriptures, which are able to make thee wise unto salvation through faith which is in Christ Jesus. All scripture *is* given by inspiration of God, and *is* profitable for doctrine, for reproof, for correction, for instruction in righteousness: That the man of God may be perfect, throughly furnished unto all good works. — 2 Timothy 3:15

SORRY, SCHOOL NEVER ENDS

THE TRIVIUM IS MORE than a curriculum, it is a way of life. And Homeschooling is more than a renaissance in education, it is becoming a subculture in America. The full implications of Homeschooling work their way out into family renewal, church renewal, and eventually into all facets of life in all corners of society.

As homeschooled children grow into Christian adults, they will take their place in a society which has, in many ways, been headed in the opposite direction. We want to discuss some of the choices which homeschooled adults will need to make. As we move out of the home and into the world, we don't want to deny the vision which has guided us all the way through school.

KNOWLEDGE LEVEL: HOW WE CAME TO WHERE WE ARE

When our own children were young, we assumed that when they reached the age of eighteen they would leave home and go to college, and that would be the end of our responsibilities. In our mind, success in life equaled going to a good college (with a generous scholarship, of course). So, in order to go to a good college, most of our goals were academically oriented, not spiritually oriented.

We wrote away for dozens of college catalogs and asked about requirements for homeschooled students. Nathaniel, our oldest, took the ACT and SAT tests in 1992. The day came in May of 1993 when we received back some of those scores, and we thought "why are we in such a hurry to get rid of this boy?" Yes, with these scores, he could probably go to any college he wanted. Yes, we had accomplished the academic goals we had set for ourselves. But where are we headed? Nathaniel didn't want to go to college. So why were we pushing him?

God used personality conflict in our family to straighten out our thinking. As our children grew older we began to see the need to focus more on character than on academics. We also came to understand the different roles God has for boys and girls. We had never realized that the most important goal was to prepare our children for marriage.

In this Chapter, we are describing our own experiences and opinions. This is not a "you must do like we do" command, but simply suggestions and ideas from our family to yours. You may disagree with us, and that's fine. But let us open the dialogue about these issues.

UNDERSTANDING LEVEL: PRINCIPLES FOR MAKING DECISIONS AND SETTING GOALS

Wisdom is *not* bound up in the heart of a child. Parents need to teach their children how to make decisions about their life, because children will not naturally learn how to set wise goals and how to be persistent in those goals. Here are some principles for making decisions and setting goals:

1. *Instill in your children the desire to listen to advice from their elders.* Parents can show their children how to listen to other's advice by exemplifying good listening habits themselves. A father or mother who does not show respect for the counsel of others, especially elders, will communicate that attitude to their children. God will probably show children what choices to make in life through the advice of others. A spirit of listening can go a long way towards learning wisdom.

2. *Make wisdom-based decisions about your future.* Easy-in-easy-out decisions result in an unstable life – one which hops from place to place, from job to job. This comes from making decisions based upon hunches. Even in moral decisions, which must be based upon moral principles regardless of the circumstances, there is often more than one right way to respond to a situation. Don't make a decision to do something because you *hope* it will turn out well. Gather the facts, understand the theory, then put into practice what you have good reason to believe will work. Decisions based purely upon hopes or desires for the future, or upon feelings or hunches, are unreliable.

3. *Accumulate multigenerational wisdom.* Different families have different standards for making decisions. This affects the stability of the family life – how long a family remains focused upon a single vision without shifting to a new direction. The goal is for a family to accumulate wisdom for making decisions, and to pass that wisdom on to each succeeding generation. Even if a family never becomes wealthy in a material way, the community will recognize that family as a source of wisdom and multigenerational vision.

4. *Don't work without clear goals.* If you don't know what to do, then your goal is to move in the direction of finding out what to do. If you don't know where you want to go, then at least spend time learning to read a map. When your inspiration comes, you'll be better prepared to act. If you don't have the information you need for making a decision, then at least you know one thing: you need to find that information. There's always something you can do.

5. *Learn to sort the necessities from the niceties.* Can you tell the difference between a good idea and the idea you should pursue? If you find yourself dropping what you are doing every time you meet another good idea on the street, then you will never find stability. Learn to sort the *must-dos* and the *should-dos* from the *might-be-a-nice-idea-to-dos*. There are many good ideas out there – be a missionary to China, open an orphanage, run for congress – but what is the thing which God put you on this earth to do?

6. *God will use talents, interests, and unique opportunities to give you direction.* If God has given you a special talent, then He may wish you to minister to others through that talent. If you have a special interest, then maybe God wants you to pursue that further. If you make your living from your hobby, then you should live a very contented life. If your neighbor wants to hire you to make mahogany bases for the ceramic toadstools he molds in his basement, that may be a unique opportunity.

7. *Limitations may be your greatest opportunities.* Sometimes it is the moral restriction which God puts upon us, or the restrictions of our upbringing, or of our physical disabilities, which force us to do what others will not do, and thereby we become successful where others failed. Joseph learned how to be an administrator in prison so that God could later give him the care of all Egypt. After growing up in the opulent circumstances of Pharaoh's court, Moses needed to learn humility at the back of the desert before God would give him a great commission. If you chafe under the moral burdens which God has put on your heart, then maybe God wants you to overcome your frustration in order to pursue a great and remarkable job in His service.

8. *God may make you wait for a vision.* If you don't know what to do, then maybe God wants to show you a process by which to discern what to do. Maybe you should continue what you are already doing, and wait for better judgment. God may have you do a repetitive task which seems to you to be going nowhere, but which He will use to teach you something which you could learn no other way. Life has many little lessons which we resist learning, but which are the keys to success for God's vision in our lives.

9. *A boy's goal is to develop a livelihood.* Parents should assume their sons will marry. So, whether their son intends to grow the crops to feed a family, or work for money to buy the food, a son will need to learn a livelihood.

The difference between a "career" and a "livelihood" is found in how a man views his profit-making activities. A career makes a man's activities the source of his fulfillment in life. By contrast, a livelihood is a man's source for whatever he needs to pursue his goals for his family. Which takes first place – profit-making activities, or family relationships and multigenerational vision? Even if a man makes a living by being a missionary to China, his family should come first.

Many homeschooled young men want to find a livelihood which will nourish a Biblical family culture. That should be their first consideration. A son will normally learn his fathers livelihood. Jesus was a carpenter because Joseph was a carpenter. A son may follow the livelihood of his father, or if father and son decide something else would be better, the father should be intimately involved with his son in building that other occupation . . . even to the point of possibly changing his own livelihood to help his son.

10. *If you can, be an entrepreneur.* There is a difference between the "I'm eighteen, so I need to go out and get a job," mentality, and the "I'm sixteen, and I wonder if I can make some money with this hobby of mine." The first makes little worker bees in a factory, the second makes little entrepreneurs. A profit-making enterprise is probably staring you in the face, but you'll never see it until you escape from the "get a job" mentality.

We are not saying that there is anything necessarily wrong with working for someone else. A good start, and many valuable lessons can be learned from working for someone else. Indeed, children have already been working for Mom and Dad for years. But the Bible says that if we can, then we should seek to be free (First Corinthians 7:21,22). Servanthood, or a stewardship, is not to be contemned. But it will limit the choices a father can make in building his family culture. His employer will make many of his decisions for him.

An entrepreneurial spirit is often handed down from generation to generation. If Grandpa made his money working for himself, then the grandson will be more likely to do the same. If the father worked for a company all his life, then the son will be more likely to seek security in the arms of a corporation. Entrepreneurial parents steer their sons away from just "getting a job." Everybody can be an entrepreneur to some extent – even if it is a part-time entrepreneur.

11. *The purpose of life goes beyond earning a livelihood.* God gives every person a mission – or several missions throughout their life. God may give you an interest which you will develop over many years. Then, someday, God will call you with an opportunity to use what you have developed to help others.

12. *A girl's goal is to be a homemaker.* Parents should assume that their daughters will marry and raise children. The home is a dominion with challenge, with creativity, and with a significance which will last for many generations – for good or for evil. Therefore parents should guide their daughters toward learning skills for keeping a happy, organized, educated, productive house. Girls will need to prepare to help their husband, by stimulating him spiritually, and providing knowledge and skills which will help him in his livelihood.

This is especially true if the family makes its living from a home business. A wife, and children can be an integral part of the family livelihood. Instead of family members being economic parasites living off the father's livelihood, a father can fashion his family culture so that each member of the family contributes to the livelihood of the family. The father is not the family breadwinner, the whole family should work together to win the bread.

There are plenty of things to keep a young girl busy learning while she waits for a spouse. Practical medical skills is an example, as well as teaching, music, accounting, research, gardening, cooking, and innumerable other skills forgotten by our culture. A young girl can serve her family and perform many good works while she waits for God to bring to her the mate whom He has chosen for her.

Objection: Shouldn't we prepare our daughters for the possibility that God wants them to remain single?

Response: No. We cannot prepare for all future possibilities. There is only so much time in the day. How is a young woman's time best spent? Should we spend much time preparing for the possibility that she will die in an automobile accident? Obviously not.

Education carries with it an element of predestination.

> Train up a child in the way he should go: and when he is old, he will not depart from it. — Proverbs 22:6

If we train up our daughters to live independently, then guess what? That's how they're likely to live. If they enter a marriage with an independent spirit, and without the skills of motherhood and homemaking, then guess what? It is likely that their home will lack peace and harmony. Just whose vision are we following, anyway? The independent career woman should neither be the ideal nor the norm. Emergencies may require that a woman take on tasks which should ordinarily be considered a man's calling, but a good education and training in all of the skills of a normal family life will prepare a woman for almost any emergency.

On the other hand, if we prepare our daughters to marry – to have a submissive spirit, to care for others, and to rule their homes – then will we be surprised if they become loving wives and mothers with orderly and peaceful homes?

> The aged women . . . teach the young women to be sober, to love their husbands, to love their children, *To be* discreet, chaste, keepers at home, good, obedient to their own husbands, that the word of God be not blasphemed. — Titus 2:3-5

Should our daughters never marry, what harm will come from their having learned to have a submissive spirit, to care for others, and to rule their homes. Rather, how much more good would come!

What about College

Either go to college and become successful in life, or don't go to college and work as a gas station attendant. This is the attitude which has been driven into our minds by a culture which has been created by the educational establishment. Educators think so much of what they do that they want you to keep coming to them for more all through your life. The odd thing is, once you're hooked on their system, it's much less likely that you'll be able to break from it. As we explained in Chapter Four, it's a system which creates dependency.

The purpose of the Liberal Arts is to free us from those things which the educational system – of which college has become an integral part – enslaves us.

Our culture looks down upon those who do not attend college – unless, of course, they became a big success without it. Our culture also looks down upon children who are homeschooled – unless, of course, they become a big success despite it. Huh! What's the parallel here? Let's think this thing through a little deeper.

Ten Reasons to Go to College

1. *College teaches discipline*. Many people attend college because they know they would never get around to teaching themselves what they need to know. College classes force students to learn self-discipline, to study, and to be organized. But most homeschooled students have already learned these things, are self-motivated, and are focused on their goals.

2. *College furthers your education*. If there were subjects you missed in high school, then college gives you an opportunity to go back and learn them better. College provides the opportunity to round out your education, and go deeper into your studies. But most homeschooled students – especially those taught the Trivium – know how to learn just about any subject on their own.

3. *College will get you a good job*. A college degree will give you an advantage when applying for a job. And while you're at college, you may find the contacts which will secure you that job. College is often the shortest route to a successful career. But many corporations would welcome innovative hard-working homeschooled students. And corporations want to see experience on a resume, more so than a college de-

gree. Besides, many men never use their college degree in their work – they find a better job in a different – often unrelated – field.

4. *College offers the best teachers*. Colleges hire the best thinkers in a field to teach their students. You can learn at the feet of big names. And your fellow students will become the movers-and-shakers of tomorrow. But you might do better to read your great professor's textbook, and learn his ideas that way – comparing his ideas with those of other great professors. You may end up knowing more than him. And then there's the question of how much some big name professors really know anyway, and how much personal access you may have to his personal knowledge. Sometimes there are better ways to learn.

5. *College gives you respect*. People will respect your work if you have a degree after your name. For instance, if you wish to write and you have a Ph.D. after your name, then people will listen to what you say. But many people don't even notice the Ph.D. anymore. In some fields of learning, a Ph.D. degree is almost a guarantee that you are thoroughly confused. People should respect you if you have the reputation for knowing what you're talking about and for doing wise and meaningful things. A Ph.D. guarantees no such thing.

6. *College is the only way into the licensed professions*. You must obtain a degree from an accredited institution of higher learning in order to enter the medical profession, the legal profession, become a CPA, etc. These professions lobbied the government to license and regulate their professions ostensibly to maintain the uniform quality. But we know of two home-study courses for law which are accepted by two state bar associations, and the trend is to devise alternative means for other professions as well.

7. *College provides socialization*. Continually interacting with classmates and roommates will teach you how to get along. You will let go of your mother's apron strings and learn to make independent decisions. You will now meet people every day, and that interaction will widen your perspective of society. But college is an artificial environment of young people unnaturally segregated from the rest of society. So how does that teach you how to get along in society? It may teach you how to get along with people in the same situation as yourself, but that's no tough lesson to learn, and it can be learned at much less bother and expense. College-level socialization does not prepare you for real life – unless you are perpetually going to college!

8. *College provides an escape from a bad home environment*. If there is anger in your home, or too much busy activity, then college will provide a getaway. Didn't God tell Abraham to leave his pagan homeland in order

to bless him? But, you may be jumping from the frying pan into the fire. The college environment may be different, but that does not necessarily suggest that it is better. What we've seen on many college campuses suggests the opposite.

9. *College will find you a wife or a husband.* We met at the University of Iowa in an introductory Greek class. Our children wouldn't be here if it weren't for that. College provides an opportunity to meet many intelligent men or women – an opportunity which you may never have in your local community. But God is merciful and gracious, and overrules our mistakes by turning them into blessings. Tell Joseph that his brothers did the right thing. God often blesses us in our stupidity, but that is no argument for stupidity. God is able to bring to you your partner for life, despite all of your wanderings. When you are ready, your partner will arrive.

10. *College will give you direction in life.* If you don't know what God wants you to do with your life, then He might show you while you are at college. Many people go to college not knowing specifically what they want to do, but by exploring different interests, and taking different courses, they eventually find it. But God is already showing you what He wants you to do with your life, and college may be a detour to a dead end which you are arranging for yourself. If you don't know what to do, then college can be a very expensive, time consuming, and potentially dangerous place to waste time until you find out. Shouldn't the decision to go to college itself be part of the calling and leading of God? The fact that some people received some direction while in college is no evidence that they received the right direction, or received it in the right way, or that they could not have received it somewhere else. God overrules our actions to serve His purposes, but that's no excuse for our actions.

It seems that a good homeschool education combined with an accurate view of reality renders college less useful. College may still be important in the realm of credentials and specialized learning, but those barriers are being broken down even as we speak.

Seven Reasons Not to Go to College

1. *College culture is corrupt.* Have you ever noticed how college towns are different from others towns? They support an abnormal culture. The college campus is often a rarified atmosphere which is out of this world, separated from reality by a great distance. We wish we could report that Christian colleges were exceptions, but instead it seems that they have a different strain of the same disease. Just because a child is

grown does not make it any less true that

> He that walketh with wise *men* shall be wise: but a companion of fools shall be destroyed. — Proverbs 13:20

nor does it make it any less true that we should

> Be not misled, *for* bad companionships corrupt good character. Awake to righteousness, and do not sin; for there are some who have no knowledge of God: I say *this* to your shame. — First Corinthians 15:33 (v.l.t.)

The culture of many colleges may differ to some degree with Sodom, but only by degree, not by kind. Lot was mistaken to move his family there, and Lot was brought to shame and his family was ruined because he dwelt in a place which required bad companionships with those who had no knowledge of God – companionships which corrupted his family's otherwise good character. If you wouldn't raise a family there, then why would you send your offspring there to learn its ways? We're not claiming that no one ever survives college without scars. God is gracious. But there is a big difference between falling off a cliff and being saved by the hand of God, and jumping off that same cliff and expecting God to save you. Lot was barely saved.

2. *Colleges do not teach from a Biblical worldview.* In secular colleges most of the professors are atheists and socialists. Even many Christian colleges have compromised with the world's philosophy and watered down the distinctively Christian nature of each subject they teach. They frequently teach without reference to God – which Paul called "this ignorance."

3. *College is not a good place to discover vision for your life.* If you don't have a good vision before you go to college, then you may catch the wrong vision at college, and spend years following the wrong path. College may be more of a diversion than a vision – and an expensive, time-consuming, and dangerous one at that.

Going to college can give you a false sense of direction – it looks like you are going somewhere because you are so busy. You are confusing the blur of a merry-go-round life, with the sensation of movement you have when you are driving somewhere in a car. When you don't know where you're headed, you at least like to feel that you're moving.

If you want to discover the livelihood which God would have you pursue, then you might try looking in places where other people are pursuing godly, useful, contented livelihoods. College may not be the place to look for this.

4. *College is not the classical way to learn a livelihood*. What is now called alternative education used to be the common road towards a profession. Most young men learned their livelihood from their father, or in an apprenticeship. If they needed book learning, such as mathematics in order to pilot a ship, or theological training and biblical languages in order to be a minister, then they studied under a private tutor in their community, or from a special teacher in city nearby. Early colleges, such as Cambridge in England or Harvard in New England, were only for a select few. Over the years, as college became more popular, college did not raise the standards of education. College used to be more useful. But college today is what high school was a century ago – or less, in some ways. We're not speaking against more education. That's exactly what we're for. But college may not be the way to get it – at least not necessarily.

5. *College costs money*. It forces many people into debt, and those debts will force them to make decisions about where you get a job after school. When you actually run out the numbers, colleges often cost more than their eventual material benefits will justify. There may be a better investment of your time and money. Run some numbers and see if it might be better to work in a field of interest as an apprentice, or even as a volunteer, and gain experience while living at home.

6. *College degrees don't mean much anymore*. A college degree used to mean that a person had a competent level of education in a particular field. They don't necessarily mean that anymore. They just mean that you spent plenty of money, and had plenty of ideas pumped into your head. They often mean you have had little practical experience. Many corporations expect to spend much time and effort retraining these sparkling new college graduates in how the real world works. When they discover someone who actually knows what he's talking about, understands what he's doing, and can apply it in the real world (that's the Trivium again), they hire them – degree or no degree. Indeed, the people with the degrees often are not those people. The whole system of college education is beginning to collapse. Institutionalized education cannot keep up with the changes. The death of school was inevitable with the birth of the Internet. Be on the cutting edge – teach yourself. Homeschooling may now be found among a small segment of culture and applied to children, but within a generation – barring socialist oppression – it will grow and blossom while the subsidized institutions of learning will fade and wither.

7. *College has many alternatives.* Why pay a college professor $4,000 to teach you what you can read in his $40 book? Of course this may not

apply to skills which you can't learn from a book – "learn brain surgery in ten easy lessons." That is where apprenticeships come into play. Professionals in many fields have told us that a bright, self-motivated homeschool student could learn their profession either from reading books, or in an apprenticeship. This includes carpenters, cabinet makers, electricians, engineers, publishers, computer programmers, editors, graphic designers, farmers, car mechanics, landscapers, architects, politicians, and lawyers. Find someone who does what you want to do, and ask him how you can get into it. Most of the problem is knowing what work you want to get into, and being self-motivated and organized about pursuing it.

Correspondence courses will teach what you can't learn from an apprenticeship or tutor. The number of accredited correspondence courses from colleges and universities is booming. The Internet is a growing medium for this.

We must warn you though: if you choose an alternative education, it may influence you into an alternative livelihood. People who learn to think along nontraditional lines will be the innovators of tomorrow. You are living out the alternative mindset.

Objection: *I don't assume that I should go to college, but I know what I want to be (pastor, nurse, etc.) and I think college is the best path in that direction.*

Response: What are the hurdles before your chosen livelihood? (1) Learn the important facts about your profession: vocabulary, established theories, industry standards and conventions, history of the profession, influential associations, governing laws. (2) Learn the practice of the profession: use of tools, client relationships, profit margins, experience. (3) Get over the doorstep: get people to look at your job application, get hired, get starting capital, open an office, print business cards.

Is college the only way to get these? If it is, then that may be the route you must travel. Maybe there are other more difficult routes, but ones which will give you greater freedom. Have you talked with several independent-minded professionals in the field? What are their opinions? Do they know of ways you could get around college if you are serious about reaching your goal?

College is not always the wrong choice. College is itself a tool which you must use correctly to your own advantage. If you understand the danger of college, the costs, and the alternatives, but you know how to handle all of these things within God's rules, and you are sure this is the way He is leading you to go, then college may be the best choice for you. But often the bad out weighs the good. We believe college should be the exception, not the rule. Self-education and apprenticeships should be the norm. We want to put college where it belongs, at the bottom of the list.

Things to Remember when Preparing for College

1. Have faith in God's Word, and be skeptical of what your professors say. Ferret out the presuppositions of your college professors. This will give you the key to understanding how their teaching is philosophically biased.
2. Keep in close contact with your family, and have less contact with your college peers. Find a spiritual counselor in the area to whom you can maintain accountability regarding your spiritual growth and personal devotions.
3. Don't make large philosophical shifts while at college. You will have a much more realistic perspective on what you have learned when you are back home than when you are in the atmosphere of the college.

College and a Classical Liberal Arts Education

Classically, a liberal arts education was to give a man the tools to teach himself. If we took a snapshot of the ideal product of this education, what would he look like? What would he be able to do? If he were on a desert island, with the Library of Congress as his only resource, he should be able to reconstruct western society. He knows how to learn from books. He knows how to train his hands to perform a skill, and to train his mind to think. Classical education should make further college education superfluous.

Objection: What if the student did not receive a good classical education in high school?

Response: Education does not need to happen from before age eighteen. If you haven't received an education, even if you are ninety years old, then you need to give yourself one.

To catch up, the student should study the basic skills of the liberal arts: (1) how to research a subject, (2) how to discern good reasoning from bad reasoning, (3) the basic facts of world history, classical literature, economics, law, mathematics, science, etc. (4) Biblical languages, theology, hermeneutics, Apologetics, (5) how to translate abstract principles from books into practical skills, (6) how to communicate effectively in writing and speaking. Do you already know these things? Can you teach them to yourself?

WISDOM LEVEL: HOMESCHOOLING IS FOR LIFE

Be aggressive in teaching yourself about all of your interests, hobbies, and business pursuits. Accumulate a bank of knowledge and interests which you can pass on to the next generation. This means that you must be a well read person. A classical education is an education which never ends.

Take dominion over segments of our culture by studying diverse interests, determining the Christian principles involved, and applying them.

If you are interested in pet gecko lizards, study how God's word applies to the care of geckoes, what relationship humans should have toward geckoes, what use geckoes are in furthering God's kingdom, what place geckoes should have in Christian Homeschooling culture, write a book about it, become a national speaker on "The Christian Gecko," and move on to something else. This applies to rock collecting and stamp collecting, to horseback riding and dog obedience, to Lego building and computer programming, to crocheting and cross stitching, to bread making and table manners, to home decorating and gardening, to child training and personal hygiene, to file drawer organization and support group leadership, to business relationships and house maintenance, to geriatrics and changing diapers, to community volunteering and picking up trash.

THE NEXT STEP IN HOMESCHOOLING

We believe that what we've said in this book expresses some of the logical implications of Homeschooling. They seem to be conclusions which follow inescapably from the premise that God rules the world, establishes its order, and that the place of the Christian Homeschooling family is fundamental to that order.

As homeschooled children begin the transition into adulthood, this will mark a second step in the Christian Homeschooling movement. This will force changes in the family further back toward Biblical norms. The pioneers in Homeschooling faced the seemingly insurmountable task of teaching their own children in the face of opposition from their friends and relatives – and often, the government. Now we who have grown sons and daughters must watch the same process begin as we take the second step in Homeschooling. "What will the relatives think now! You began by Homeschooling them, and now you aren't letting them date, and you aren't sending them to college. The poor children. They just won't fit into this world." Are we unrealistic? Do we really understand the limitations within which a homeschooler must work? We believe the limitations will not stand against the pressures of the calling of God to be faithful and to follow. If God is pleased to allow us liberty, then Homeschooling may prove to be an important agent of a movement from God to restore order to our culture and bring glory to His name.

Those Christians who have resisted Homeschooling look at it as a short-lived aberration in history. They smirk, and wait for homeschoolers to wake up and join the real world. They will be waiting until the end of the world. Homeschooling is an even more fundamental philosophical culture-shift than what took place when the parochial Christian school movement began in the 1960s. Homeschooling is here to stay, because it answers questions Christians have been asking ever since God began to put the desire in the hearts of parents to pass on their faith to their children.

THE THIRD STEP IN HOMESCHOOLING

The first is the worst. We began Homeschooling without any examples to follow. We made many mistakes as we stumbled along. Thank God for His mercies. But now we have set an example for our children to improve upon. They now have our lowered shoulders to stand upon. They now have a Homeschooling literature to access. These homeschooled children will be making choices regarding how to raise their own children and how to fashion their own family lifestyle after a Biblical model. They will advance the cause further than we can envision. They will develop the homeschool philosophy. May God bless them and prosper them in the way.

CONCLUSION

The Homeschooling movement began when Eve bore children to Adam. It was carried on by Abraham who commanded his children to keep the way of the Lord. It was in the heart of God's greatest commandment when He commanded parents to teach their children diligently. It was Paul's passion to tell fathers to bring up their children in the nurture and admonition of the Lord. This is our heritage. Where will Homeschooling end? It has only one logical end: the transformation of all of culture to bring it into conformity to God's order and under the rule of

His law. Transformation works from the inside out.

FOR FURTHER STUDY

To learn more about the college question, we suggest *Making Wise Decisions about College and Life after Home School* an audio tape series by Doug Phillips, published by Vision Forum.

There are numerous books to tell you how to do college at home. The most well known guide to nontraditional education and reputable correspondence courses is *Bears' Guide to Earning Degrees by Distance Learning*, by John Bear. Searching the Internet will lead you to many other guides to correspondence courses.

For schools Online, the key word is e-learning. Online schools are evolving so fast that it is best that we do not mention any specifically.

College Level Examination Program (CLEP) allows you to obtain college credit without attending classes. Information on how to obtain college credit by examinations can be obtained from the College Board (CLEP web site www.collegeboard.org/clep).

Chapter Sixteen

Conclusion: Life's Goals Begin at Home

Say ye to the righteous, that *it shall be* well *with him*:
for they shall eat the fruit of their doings. — Isaiah 3:10

And let us not be weary in well doing: for in due season we shall reap,
if we faint not. — Galatians 6:9

Therefore, my beloved brethren, be ye stedfast, unmoveable,
always abounding in the work of the Lord, forasmuch as ye know
that your labour is not in vain in the Lord. — First Corinthians 15:58

A DEFINITION FOR EDUCATION

> EDUCATION, The bringing up, as of a child; instruction; formation of manners. Education comprehends all that series of instruction and discipline which is intended to enlighten the understanding, correct the temper, and form the manners and habits of youth, and fit them for usefulness in their future stations. To give children a good education in manners, arts and science, is important; to give them a religious education is indispensable; and an immense responsibility rests on parents and guardians who neglect these duties. — Noah Webster, *American Dictionary of the English Language*, 1828.

Noah Webster did more than define *education* here. He gave direction to it. With this definition in mind, we offer a few questions to help parents evaluate their Homeschooling:

1. Are we building a proper foundation for our children's future education?
2. Are we providing our children with the tools which they will need in order to continue their learning on their own?
3. Have we instilled in our children a love for learning?
4. Do our children respect, honor, and obey us?
5. Is there peace in our home?
6. Are we preparing our children for a life of devotion and service to the Lord?
7. Are our children being prepared to marry and establish their own family?

Of course, this list doesn't cover everything. Every family must add their own questions. Our point is that we need to focus on where we want to go – our final destination. If we don't, then we'll never know where we're going until we get there. You will find that your children grow up much too fast. You aren't going to ruin your children with a few mistakes and oversights. The children belong to the Lord, and He doesn't give them over to your safe custody with the idea that you know everything. He will use them to humble you, and to teach you how you must depend upon Him for everything, and to sanctify you in His ways. Ultimately, the children are in His hands, and so are you.

OUR MISTAKES

We've made many mistakes in our homeschool. Perhaps you can learn from this short list of things we have learned:

1. Children must have character discipline developed within them before they can develop the outward academic disciplines.
2. Discipline of others will be a disaster, if first yourself you do not master.
3. Children's socialization should be under adult control at all times.
4. Boys and girls do not necessarily need to study all of the same things.
5. Communication is the key to family harmony.
6. Family worship is more than just a nice thing to add on at your convenience.
7. Fathers should be more than figuratively the head of your Homeschool.

SOME QUESTIONS

Too Little or Too Much?

Question: Can you give any advice on how to make sure I'm covering the right things and yet not go overboard with having too many things?

Answer: Of course, there are some fundamental things which everyone needs to know, but there is no possible way that you can know all of the things which you child will need to know. Your child could study a dozen subjects which he may never use, and he may end up continuously using something which you never made him study. You need to give him the skills of learning – which is what teaching by the Trivium is all about. You practice with the Trivium on these many subjects, and though the subjects themselves may prove less profitable, the skill of learning – developed through these subjects – will always prove profitable.

Christian classical education is not driven by curriculum. Some mothers try to find the perfect Latin (or history, or logic, or grammar) program, switching from one to another, and at the same time they tell us they try to limit their child's time with computer games and television to two hours per day – and then they wonder why their children are not excited about learning. The particular type of curriculum you choose is not as important as the need to develop your child's mind with that curriculum. Christian teaching by the Trivium is more than Latin and Logic. It's a way of life. It's about developing proper appetites. It's developing the imagination and creativity. It's having time to play and explore in the old fashioned way. It's encouraging a love for learning. It's building a firm foundation in the child's mind with memorization and narration. And it's about learning to obey and serve our heavenly Father.

Is it Too Late to Begin the Trivium?

Question: My child is a teenager. Is it too late for me to begin with the classical approach?

Answer: It is never too late, though in some cases it may be very difficult. If you have a fifteen-year-old who has been raised by the government school, fed a diet of television programs for four hours a day, never been read to, nor read much for himself, and is not trained how to think, then Homeschooling with the Trivium will be a challenge. But much can be accomplished with the right motivation and a willing attitude. Self-discipline and obedience are the first obstacles to overcome.

A FINAL PRAYER

Our Father in heaven,

As a nation, and as a people, we have sinned grievously in Thy sight, for we have turned aside from Thy great and holy commandment to teach our children Thy ways. We have abandoned our own children to be raised by the Philistines. And what we have sown, we have reaped.

We beseech Thee, O God: Cause us to plow up the fallow ground of our own proud and blind hearts. Grant unto us repentance. Turn Thou the hearts of the fathers of this land back to their own children, in order that we may remove this curse from our land.

We know that Thou wilt test us, in order to purify us. Grant us strength, Lord, to stand in the evil day.

Richly bless those families of our land who have entered the battle to bring our culture back to reality and to restore the foundations of Christian order.

For the glory of Thy Kingdom and for Thy righteousness we pray these things. And may our prayer be heard in the Name of Thy Son.

Amen.

SINGING THE PRAISES OF HOMESCHOOLING

Psalm 127

Except the LORD build the house,
they labour in vain that build it:
except the LORD keep the city,
the watchman waketh *but* in vain.
It is vain for you to rise up early,
to sit up late,
to eat the bread of sorrows:
for so he giveth his beloved sleep.
Lo, children *are* an heritage of the LORD:
and the fruit of the womb *is his* reward.
As arrows *are* in the hand of a mighty man;
so *are* children of the youth.
Happy *is* the man that hath his quiver full of them:
they shall not be ashamed,
but they shall speak with the enemies in the gate.

Appendix One

Articles on Education

Article One

The Lost Tools of Learning, by Dorothy Leigh Sayers, was originally read at a Vacation Course in Education, in 1947, at Oxford University; and was published in the Hibbert Journal in 1948.

Dorothy Leigh Sayers was born on June 13, 1893, the only child of the Rev. Henry Sayers. She became a scholar who specialized in the Middle Ages. Among her many accomplishments were the translation of Dante's *Divine Comedy*, a series of detective novels, radio plays, and a defense of Christianity. She numbered among her friends T.S. Eliot, Charles Williams, C.S. Lewis, J.R.R. Tolkein, and Owen Barfield. She died unexpectedly from heart failure on December 17, 1957 while engaged in translating Dante's third volume, *Paradiso*.

Every effort has been made to reproduce the original text in its entirety – including original British spellings (*s* for *z*, words ending in *-our* instead of *-or*, past tense in *-t* instead of *-ed*, hyphenations, etc.). The divisions of the text and section titles are our own editorial addition. We have drawn the substance of the titles directly from the text. We have added sixteen commas, one semicolon, one period, one apostrophe; replaced one semicolon with a colon; and we have divided five lengthy paragraphs. We have otherwise retained all the peculiarities of British expression. All other editorial additions to the text are clearly marked by enclosure in brackets [ ]. Explanations of terms and expressions are preceded by a slash [/] . In order to allow readers to read without interruption, we have supplied definitions for some of the uncommon words and expressions. We have also freely added our own comments where we thought appropriate. You are welcome to ignore them all, if you so choose.

The Lost Tools of Learning

by Dorothy Sayers

TOO MUCH SPECIALIZATION IS NOT A GOOD THING

THAT I, WHOSE EXPERIENCE of teaching is extremely limited, and whose life of recent years has been almost wholly out of touch with educational circles, should presume to discuss education is a matter, surely, that calls for no apology. It is a kind of behaviour to which the present climate of opinion is wholly favourable. Bishops air their opinions about economics; biologists, about metaphysics; celibates, about matrimony; inorganic chemists, about theology; the most irrelevant people are appointed to highly-technical ministries; and plain, blunt men write to the papers to say that Epstein and Picasso do not know how to draw. Up to a certain point, and provided that the criticisms are made with a reasonable modesty, these activities are commendable. Too much specialisation is not a good thing. There is also one excellent reason why the veriest [/ truest] amateur may feel entitled to have an opinion about education. For if we are not all professional teachers, we have all, at some time or another, been taught. Even if we learnt nothing – perhaps in particular if we learnt nothing – our contribution to the discussion may have a potential value.

Without apology, then, I will begin. But since much that I have to say is highly controversial, it will be pleasant to start with a proposition with which, I feel confident, all teachers will cordially agree; and that is, that they all work much too hard and have far too many things to do. One has only to look at any school or examination syllabus to see that it is cluttered up with a great variety of exhausting subjects which they are called upon to teach, and the teaching of which sadly interferes with what every thoughtful mind will allow to be their proper duties, such as distributing milk, supervising meals, taking cloak-room duty, weighing and measuring pupils, keeping their eyes open for incipient mumps, measles and chicken-pox, making out lists, escorting parties round the Victoria and Albert Museum, filling up forms, interviewing parents, and devising end-of-term reports which shall combine a deep veneration for truth with a tender respect for the feelings of all concerned.

Upon these really important duties I will not enlarge. I propose only to deal with the subject of teaching, properly so-called. I want to inquire whether, amid all the multitudinous subjects which figure in the syllabuses, we are really teaching the right things in the right way; and whether, by teaching fewer things, differently, we might not succeed in "shedding the load" (as the fashionable phrase goes) and, at the same time, producing a better result.

This prospect need arouse neither hope nor alarm. It is in the highest degree improbable that the reforms I propose will ever be carried into effect. Neither the parents, nor the training colleges, nor the examination boards, nor the boards of governors, nor the Ministry of Education would countenance them for a moment. For they amount to this: that if we are to produce a society of educated people, fitted to preserve their intellectual freedom amid the complex pressures of our modern society, we must turn back the wheel of progress some four or five hundred years, to the point at which education began to lose sight of its true object, towards the end of the Middle Ages.

Before you dismiss me with the appropriate phrase – reactionary, romantic, mediaevalist, *laudator temporis acti* [/praiser of times past], or whatever tag comes first to hand – I will ask you to consider one or two miscellaneous questions that hang about at the back, perhaps, of all our minds, and occasionally pop out to worry us.

THE RESULTS OF MODERN EDUCATIONAL METHODS

When we think about the remarkably early age at which the young men went up to the University in, let us say, Tudor times [Sixteenth Century England], and thereafter were held fit to assume responsibility for the conduct of their own affairs, are we altogether comfortable about that artificial prolongation of intellectual childhood and adolescence into the years of physical maturity which is so marked in our own day? To postpone the acceptance of responsibility to a late date brings with it a number of psychological complications which, while they may interest the psychiatrist, are scarcely beneficial either to the individual or to society. The stock argument in favour of postponing the school leaving-age and prolonging the period of education generally is that there is now so much more to learn than there was in the Middle Ages. This is partly true, but not wholly. The modern boy and girl are certainly taught more subjects – but does that always mean that they are actually more learned and know more? That is the very point which we are going to consider.

Has it ever struck you as odd, or unfortunate, that to-day, when the proportion of literacy throughout Western Europe is higher than it has ever been, people should have become susceptible to the influence of advertisement and mass-propaganda to an extent hitherto unheard-of and unimagined? Do you put this down to the mere mechanical fact that the press and the radio and so on have made propaganda much easier to distribute over a wide area? Or do you sometimes have an uneasy suspicion that the product of modern educational methods is less good than he or she might be at disentangling fact from opinion and the proven from the plausible?

Have you ever, in listening to a debate among adult and presumably responsible people, been fretted by the extraordinary inability of the average debater to speak to the question, or to meet and refute the arguments of speakers on the other side? Or have you ever pondered upon the extremely high incidence of irrelevant matter which crops up at committee-meetings, and upon the very great rarity of persons capable of acting as chairmen of committees? And when you think of this, and think that most of our public affairs are settled by debates and committees, have you ever felt a certain sinking of the heart?

Have you ever followed a discussion in the newspapers or elsewhere and noticed how frequently writers fail to define the terms they use? Or how often, if one man does define his terms, another will assume in his reply that he was using the terms in precisely the opposite sense to that in which he has already defined them?

Have you ever been faintly troubled by the amount of slipshod syntax going about? And, if so, are you troubled because it is inelegant or because it may lead to dangerous misunderstanding?

Do you ever find that young people, when they have left school, not only forget most of what they have learnt (that is only to be expected), but forget also, or betray that they have never really [/actually] known, how to tackle a new subject for themselves? Are you often bothered by coming across grown-up men and women who seem unable to distinguish between a book that is sound, scholarly, and properly documented, and one that is, to any trained eye, very conspicuously none of these things? Or who cannot handle a library catalogue? Or who, when faced with a book of reference, betray a curious inability to extract from it the passages relevant to the particular question which interests them?

Do you often come across people for whom, all their lives, a "subject" remains a "subject," divided by water-tight bulkheads from all other "subjects," so that they experience very great difficulty in making an immediate mental connection between, let us say, algebra and detective fiction, sewage disposal and the price of salmon, cellulose and the distribution of rainfall – or, more generally, between such spheres of knowledge as philosophy and economics, or chemistry and art?

Are you occasionally perturbed by the things written by adult men and women for adult men and women to read? Here, for instance, is a quotation from an evening paper. It refers to the visit of an Indian girl to this country: –

> Miss Bhosle has a perfect command of English ("Oh, gosh," she said once), and a marked enthusiasm for London.

Well, we may all talk nonsense in a moment of inattention. It is more alarming when we find a well-known biologist writing in a weekly paper to the effect that: "It is an argument against the existence of a Creator" (I think he put it more strongly; but since I have, most unfortunately, mislaid the reference, I will put his claim at its lowest) – "an argument against the existence of a Creator that the same kind of variations which are produced by natural selection can be produced at will by stock-breeders." One might feel tempted to say that it is rather an argument *for* the existence of a Creator. Actually, of course, it is neither; all it proves is that the same material causes (re-combination of the chromosomes by crossbreeding, and so forth) are sufficient to account for all observed variations – just as the various combinations of the same 13 semitones are materially sufficient to account for Beethoven's Moonlight Sonata and the noise the cat makes by walking on the keys. But the cat's performance neither proves nor disproves the existence of Beethoven; and all that is proved by the biologist's argument is that he was unable to distinguish between a material and a final cause.

Here is a sentence from no less academic a source than a front-page article in the [*London*] *Times Literary Supplement*: –

> The Frenchman, Alfred Epinas, pointed out that certain species (e.g., ants and wasps) can only face the horrors of life and death in association.

I do not know what the Frenchman actually did say; what the Englishman says he said is patently meaningless. We cannot know whether life holds any horror for the ant, nor in what sense the isolated wasp which you kill upon the window-pane can be said to "face" or not to "face" the horrors of death. The subject of the article is mass-behaviour in *man*;

and the human motives have been unobtrusively transferred from the main proposition to the supporting instance. Thus the argument, in effect, assumes what it sets out to prove – a fact which would become immediately apparent if it were presented in a formal syllogism. This is only a small and haphazard example of a vice which pervades whole books – particularly books written by men of science on metaphysical subjects.

Another quotation from the same issue of the T.L.S. [/*The London Times Literary Supplement*] comes in fittingly here to wind up this random collection of disquieting thoughts – this time from a review of Sir Richard Livingstone's *Some Tasks for Education*: –

> More than once the reader is reminded of the value of an intensive study of at least one subject, so as to learn "the meaning of knowledge" and what precision and persistence is needed to attain it. Yet there is elsewhere full recognition of the distressing fact that a man may be master in one field and show no better judgement than his neighbour anywhere else; he remembers what he has learnt, but forgets altogether how he learned it.

I would draw your attention particularly to that last sentence, which offers an explanation of what the writer rightly calls the "distressing fact" that the intellectual skills bestowed upon us by our education are not readily transferable to subjects other than those in which we acquired them: "he remembers what he has learnt, but forgets altogether how he learned it."

Is not the great defect of our education to-day – a defect traceable through all the disquieting symptoms of trouble that I have mentioned – that although we often succeed in teaching our pupils "subjects," we fail lamentably on the whole in teaching them how to think? They learn everything, except the art of learning. It is as though we had taught a child, mechanically and by rule of thumb, to play *The Harmonious Blacksmith* upon the piano, but had never taught him the scale or how to read music; so that, having memorised *The Harmonious Blacksmith*, he still had not the faintest notion how to proceed from that to tackle *The Last Rose of Summer*. Why do I say, "as though"? In certain of the arts and crafts, we sometimes do precisely this – requiring a child to "express himself" in paint before we teach him how to handle the colours and the brush. There is a school of thought which believes this to be the right way to set about the job. [This remarkably resembles Outcome-Based Education.] But observe – it is not the way in which a trained craftsman will go about to teach himself a new medium. *He*, having learned by experience the best way to economise labour and take the thing by the right end, will start off by doodling about on an odd piece of material, in order to "give himself the feel of the tool."

THE TRIVIUM SYLLABUS

Let us now look at the mediaeval scheme of education – the syllabus of the Schools. It does not matter, for the moment, whether it was devised for small children or for older students; or how long people were supposed to take over it. What matters is the light it throws upon what the men of the Middle Ages supposed to be the object and the right order of the educative process.

The syllabus was divided into two parts; the Trivium and Quadrivium. The second part – the Quadrivium – consisted of "subjects," [Arithmetic, Geometry, Astronomy and Music,] and need not for the moment concern us. The interesting thing for us is the composition of the Trivium, which preceded the Quadrivium and was the preliminary discipline for it. It consisted of three parts: Grammar, Dialectic [/Logic], and Rhetoric, in that order.

Now the first thing we notice is that two, at any rate, of these "subjects" are not what we should call "subjects" at all: they are only methods of dealing with subjects. Grammar, indeed, is a "subject" in the sense that it does mean definitely learning a language – at that period it meant learning Latin. But language itself is simply the medium in which thought is expressed. The whole of the Trivium was, in fact, intended to teach the pupil the proper use of the tools of learning, before he began to apply them to "subjects" at all. First, [in "Grammar"] he learned a language; not just how to order a meal in a foreign language, but the structure of language – *a* language, and hence of language itself – what it was, how it was put together, and how it worked. Secondly, [in "Logic"] he learned how to use language: how to define his terms and make accurate statements; how to construct an argument; and how to detect fallacies in argument (his own arguments and other people's). Dialectic, that is to say, embraced Logic and Disputation. Thirdly, [in "Rhetoric"] he learned to express himself in language; how to say what he had to say elegantly and persuasively. At this point, any tendency to express himself windily or to use his eloquence so as to make the worse appear the better reason would, no doubt, be restrained by his previous teaching in Dialectic [/Logic]. If not, his teacher and his fellow-pupils, trained along the same lines, would be quick to point out where he was wrong; for it was they whom he had to seek to persuade.

At the end of his course, he was required to compose a thesis upon some theme set by his masters or chosen by himself, and afterwards to defend his thesis against the criticism of the faculty. By this time, he would have learned – or woe betide [/befall] him – not merely to write an essay on paper, but to speak audibly and intelligibly from a platform, and to use his wits quickly when heckled. The heckling, moreover, would not consist solely of offensive personalities or of irrelevant queries about what Julius Caesar said in 55 B.C. – though no doubt mediaeval dialectic [/logic] was enlivened in practice by plenty of such primitive repartee [/ replies]. But there would also be questions, cogent and shrewd, from those who had already run the gauntlet [/taken up the thrown glove of challenge] of debate, or were making ready to run it.

It is, of course, quite true that bits and pieces of the mediaeval tradition still linger, or have been revived, in the ordinary school syllabus of to-day. Some knowledge of grammar is still required when learning a foreign language – perhaps I should say, "is again required"; for during my own lifetime, we passed through a phase when the teaching of declensions and conjugations was considered rather reprehensible, and it was considered better to pick these things up as we went along. School debating societies flourish; essays are written; the necessity for "self-expression" is stressed, and perhaps even over-stressed. But these activities are cultivated more or less in detachment, as belonging to the special subjects in which they are pigeon-holed rather than as forming one coherent scheme of mental training to which all "subjects" stand in a subordinate relation. "Grammar" belongs especially to the "subject" of foreign languages, and essay-writing to the "subject" called "English"; while Dialectic [/Logic] has become almost entirely divorced from the rest of the curriculum, and is frequently practiced unsystematically and out of school-hours as a separate exercise, only very loosely related to the main business of learning. Taken by and large, the great difference of emphasis between the two conceptions holds good: modern education concentrates on *teaching subjects*, leaving the method of thinking, arguing, and expressing one's conclusions to be picked up by the scholar as he goes along; mediaeval education concentrated on first *forging and learning to handle the tools of learning*, using whatever subject came handy as a piece of material on which to doodle until the use of the tool became second nature.

THE PROPER AND IMPROPER USE OF SUBJECTS

"Subjects" of some kind there must be, of course. One cannot learn the use of a tool by merely waving it in the air; neither can one learn the theory of grammar without learning an actual language, or learn to argue and orate without speaking about something in particular. The debating subjects of the Middle Ages were drawn largely from theology, or from the Ethics and History of Antiquity. Often, indeed, they became stereotyped, especially towards the end of the period, and the far-fetched and wire-drawn absurdities of scholastic argument fretted Milton and provide food for merriment even to this day. Whether they were in themselves any more hackneyed and trivial than the usual subjects set nowadays for "essay writing". I should not like to say: we may ourselves grow a little weary of "A Day in My Holidays," "What I should like to Do when I Leave School," and all the rest of it. But most of the merriment is misplaced, because the aim and object of the debating thesis has by now been lost sight of.

A glib speaker in the Brains Trust once entertained his audience (and reduced the late Charles Williams to helpless rage) by asserting that in the Middle Ages it was a matter of faith to know how many archangels could dance on the point of a needle. I need not say, I hope, that it never was a "matter of faith"; it was simply a debating exercise, whose set subject was the nature of angelic substance: were angels material, and if so, did they occupy space? The answer usually adjudged correct is, I believe, that angels are pure intelligences; not material, but limited, so that they may have location in space, but not extension. An analogy might be drawn from human thought, which is similarly non-material and similarly limited. Thus, if your thought is concentrated upon one thing – say, the point of a needle – it is located there in the sense that it is not elsewhere; but although it is "there," it occupies no space there, and there is nothing to prevent an infinite number of different people's thoughts being concentrated upon the same needle-point at the same time. The proper *subject* of the argument is thus seen to be the distinction between location and extension in space; the *matter* on which the argument is exercised happens to be the nature of angels (although, as we have seen, it might equally well have been something else); the practical lesson to be drawn from the argument is not to use words like "there" in a loose and unscientific way, without specifying whether you mean "located there" or "occupying space there." Scorn in plenty has been poured out upon the mediaeval passion for hair-splitting: but when we look at the shameless abuse made, in print and on the platform, of controversial expressions with shifting and ambiguous connotations, we may feel it in our hearts to wish that every reader and hearer had been so defensively armoured by his education as to be able to cry: *Distinguo*. [/Distinguish (your meaning).]

For we let our young men and women go out unarmed, in a day when armour was never so necessary. By teaching them all to read, we have left them at the mercy of the printed word. By the invention of the film and the radio, we have made certain that no aversion to reading shall secure [/protect] them from the incessant battery of words, words, words. They do not know what the words mean; they do not know how to ward them off or blunt their edge or fling them back; they are a prey to words in their emotions instead of being the masters of them in their intellects. We who were scandalised in 1940 when men were sent to fight armoured tanks with rifles, are not scandalised when young men and women are sent into the world to fight massed propaganda with a smattering of "subjects"; and when whole classes and whole nations become hypnotised by the arts of the spell-binder, we have the impudence to be astonished. We dole out lip-service to the importance of education – lip-service and, just occasionally, a little grant of money; we postpone the school leaving-age, and plan to build bigger and better schools; the teachers slave conscientiously in and out of school-hours; till responsibility becomes a burden and a nightmare; and yet, as I believe, all this devoted effort is largely frustrated, because we have lost the tools of learning, and in their absence can only make a botched and piecemeal job of it.

PROGRESSIVE RETROGRESSION

What, then, are we to do? We cannot go back to the Middle Ages. That is a cry to which we have become accustomed. We cannot go back – or can we? *Distinguo*. [/Distinguish (your meaning).] I should like every term in that proposition defined. Does "Go back" mean a retrogression in time, or the revision of an error? The first is clearly impossible *per se* [/by itself]; the second is a thing which wise men do every day. "Cannot" – does this mean that our behaviour is determined by some irreversible cosmic mechanism, or merely that such an action would be very difficult in view of the opposition it would provoke? "The Middle Ages" – obviously the 20th century is not and cannot be the 14th; but if "the Middle Ages" is, in this context, simply a picturesque phrase denoting a particular educational theory, there seems to be no *a priori* [/deductive] reason why we should not "go back" to it – with modifications – as we have already "gone back," with modifications, to, let us say, the idea of playing Shakespeare's plays as he wrote them, and not in the "modernised" versions of Cibber and Garrick, which once seemed to be the latest thing in theatrical progress.

Let us amuse ourselves by imagining that such progressive retrogression is possible. Let us make a clean sweep of all educational authorities, and furnish ourselves with a nice little school of boys and girls whom we may experimentally equip for the intellectual conflict along lines chosen by ourselves. We will endow them with exceptionally docile parents; we will staff our school with teachers who are themselves perfectly familiar with the aims and methods of the Trivium; we will have our buildings and staff large enough to allow our classes to be small enough for adequate handling; and we will postulate a Board of Examiners willing and qualified to test the products we turn out. Thus prepared, we will attempt to sketch out a syllabus – a modern Trivium "with modifications"; and we will see where we get to.

THE THREE STAGES OF LEARNING

But first: what age shall the children be? Well, if one is to educate them on novel lines, it will be better that they should have nothing to unlearn; besides, one cannot begin a good thing too early, and the Trivium is by its nature not learning, but a preparation for learning. We will, therefore, "catch 'em young," requiring of our pupils only that they shall be able to read, write, and cipher. [Classically, this was accomplished between ten and twelve years of age.]

My views about child-psychology are, I admit, neither orthodox nor enlightened. Looking back upon myself (since I am the child I know best and the only child I can pretend to know from inside) I recognise in myself three stages of development. These, in a rough-and-ready fashion, I will call the Poll-Parrot, the Pert, and the Poetic – the latter coinciding, approximately, with the onset of puberty.

The Poll-Parrot stage is the one in which learning by heart is easy and, on the whole, pleasurable; whereas reasoning is difficult and, on the whole, little relished. At this age, one readily memorises the shapes and appearances of things; one likes to recite the number-plates of cars; one rejoices in the chanting of rhymes and rumble and thunder of unintelligible polysyllables; one enjoys the mere accumulation of things.

The Pert age, which follows upon this (and, naturally, overlaps it to some extent), is only too familiar to all who have to do with children: it is characterised by contradicting, answering-back, liking to "catch people out" (especially one's elders); and in the propounding of conundrums (especially the kind with a nasty verbal catch in them). Its nuisance-value is extremely high. It usually sets in about the Lower Fourth [/ about Eighth Grade].

The Poetic age is popularly known as the "difficult" age. It is self-centered; it yearns to express itself; it rather specialises in being misunderstood; it is restless and tries to achieve independence; and, with good luck and good guidance, it should show the beginnings of creativeness, a reaching-out towards a synthesis of what it already knows, and a deliberate eagerness to know and do some one thing in preference to all others.

Now it seems to me that the lay-out of the Trivium adapts itself with a singular appropriateness to these three ages: Grammar to the Poll-Parrot, Dialectic [/Logic] to the Pert, and Rhetoric to the Poetic age.

The Grammar Stage

Let us begin, then, with Grammar. This, in practice, means the grammar of some language in particular; and it must be an inflected language. The grammatical structure of an uninflected language is far too analytical to be tackled by any one without previous practice in Dialectic [/ Logic]. Moreover, the inflected languages interpret the uninflected, whereas the uninflected are of little use in interpreting the inflected. I will say at once, quite firmly, that the best grounding for education is the Latin grammar. I say this, not because Latin is traditional and mediaeval, but simply because even a rudimentary knowledge of Latin cuts down the labour and pains of learning almost any other subject by at least fifty per cent. It is the key to the vocabulary and structure of all the Romance languages and to the structure of all the Teutonic languages, as well as to the technical vocabulary of all the sciences and to the literature of the entire Mediterranean civilisation, together with all its historical documents.

Those whose pedantic preference for a living language persuades them to deprive their pupils of all these advantages might substitute Russian, whose grammar is still more primitive. (The verb is complicated by a number of "aspects" – and I rather fancy that it enjoys three complete voices and a couple of extra aorists – but I may be thinking of Basque or Sanskrit.) Russian is, of course, helpful with the other Slav dialects. There is something also to be said for Classical Greek. But my own choice is Latin. Having thus pleased the Classicists among you, I will proceed to horrify them by adding that I do not think it either wise or necessary to cramp [/to pain with spasms] the ordinary pupil upon the Procrustean bed of the Augustan Age, with its highly elaborate and artificial verse-forms and oratory. The post-classical and mediaeval Latin, which was a living language down to the end of the Renaissance, is easier and in some ways livelier, both in syntax and rhythm; and a study of it helps to dispel the widespread notion that learning and literature came to a full-stop when Christ was born, and only woke up again at the Dissolution of the Monasteries.

However, I am running ahead too fast. We are still in the grammatical stage. Latin should be begun as early as possible – at a time when inflected speech seems no more astonishing than any other phenomenon in an astonishing world; and when the chanting of "*Amo, amas, amat*" is as ritually agreeable to the feelings as the chanting of "eeny, meeny, miney, moe." [We suggest that memorizing understandable passages which include a variety of inflections would be more profitable than merely memorizing bald paradigms.]

During this age we must, of course, exercise the mind on other things besides Latin grammar. Observation and memory are the faculties most lively at this period; and if we are to learn a contemporary foreign language we should begin now, before the facial and mental muscles become rebellious to strange intonations. Spoken French or German can be practiced alongside the grammatical discipline of the Latin.

In *English*, verse and prose can be learned by heart, and the pupil's memory should be stored with stories of every kind – classical myth, European legend, and so forth. I do not think that the classical stories and masterpieces of ancient literature should be made the vile bodies on which to practice the techniques of Grammar – that was a fault of mediaeval education which we need not perpetuate. The stories can be enjoyed and remembered in English, and related to their origin at a subsequent stage. Recitation aloud should be practiced, individually or in chorus; for we must not forget that we are laying the groundwork for Disputation and Rhetoric. [We dissent from Sayers' preference for the classical myth and legend. These myths include material inappropriate for youths. The Scriptures supply far superior material.]

The grammar of *History* should consist, I think, of dates, events, anecdotes, and personalities. A set of dates to which one can peg all later historical knowledge is of enormous help later on in establishing the perspective of history. It does not greatly matter *which* dates: those of the Kings of England will do very nicely, provided that they are accompanied by pictures of costumes, architecture, and other "every-day things," so that the mere mention of a date calls up a strong visual presentment of the whole period.

Geography will similarly be presented in its factual aspect, with maps, natural features, and visual presentment of customs, costumes, flora, fauna, and so on; and I believe myself that the discredited and old-fashioned memorising of a few capital cities, rivers, mountain ranges, etc., does no harm. Stamp-collecting may be encouraged.

Science, in the Poll-Parrot period, arranges itself naturally and easily 'round collections – the identifying and naming of specimens and, in general, the kind of thing that used to be called "natural history," or, still more charmingly, "natural philosophy." To know the names and properties of things is, at this age, a satisfaction in itself; to recognise a devil's coach-horse [a variety of large harmless beetle] at sight, and assure one's foolish elders that, in spite of its appearance, it does not sting; to be able to pick out Cassiopeia and the Pleiades [star constellations of the northern hemisphere], and possibly even to know who Cassiopeia [wife of Cepheus, fabled king of Ethiopia] and the Pleiades [Greek myth: the seven daughters of Atlas] were; to be aware that a whale is not a fish, and a bat not a bird – all these things give a pleasant sensation of superiority; while to know a ring-snake from an adder or a poisonous from an edible toadstool is a kind of knowledge that has also a practical value. [Instead of "a pleasant sensation of superiority," we would rather hope for a sense of personal accomplishment for the glory of God and self-confidence in our God-given abilities.]

The grammar of *Mathematics* begins, of course, with the multiplication table, which, if not learnt now, will never be learnt with pleasure; and with the recognition of geometrical shapes and the grouping of numbers. These exercises lead naturally to the doing of simple sums in arithmetic; and if the pupil shows a bent that way, a facility acquired at this stage is all to the good. More complicated mathematical processes may, and perhaps should, be postponed, for the reasons which will presently appear.

So far (except, of course, for the Latin), our curriculum contains nothing that departs very far from common practice. The difference will be felt rather in the attitude of the teachers, who must look upon all these activities less as "subjects" in themselves than as a gathering-together of *material* for use in the next part of the Trivium. What that material actually is, is only of secondary importance; but it is as well that anything and everything which can usefully be committed to memory should be memorised at this period, whether it is immediately intelligible or not. The modern tendency is to try and force rational explanations on a child's mind at too early an age. Intelligent questions, spontaneously asked, should, of course, receive an immediate and rational answer; but it is a great mistake to suppose that a child cannot readily enjoy and remember things that are beyond its power to analyse – particularly if those things have a strong imaginative appeal (as, for example, *Kubla Khan*), an attractive jingle (like some of the memory-rhymes for Latin genders), or an abundance of rich, resounding polysyllables (like the *Quicunque Vult*).

[Young children often benefit from learning and memorizing many things which they do not fully understand or appreciate. "...[T]he minds of children may well be employed in learning to spell and pronounce words whose signification is not within the reach of their capacities; for what they do not clearly comprehend at first, they will understand as their capacities are enlarged." (Noah Webster, The Elementary Spelling Book, 1829, p. 6) However, the value of memorizing large amounts of material which is, at an early age, entirely unintelligible, takes on the qualities of drudgery.]

This reminds me of the Grammar of *Theology*. I shall add it to the curriculum, because Theology is the mistress-science, without which the whole educational structure will necessarily lack its final synthesis. Those who disagree about this will remain content to leave their pupils' education still full of loose ends. This will matter rather less than it might, since by the time that the tools of learning have been forged, the student will be able to tackle Theology for himself, and will probably insist upon doing so, and making sense of it. Still, it is as well to have this matter also handy and ready for the reason to work upon. At the grammatical age, therefore, we should become acquainted with the story of God and Man in outline – i.e., the Old and New Testament presented as parts of a single narrative of Creation, Rebellion, and Redemption – and also with "the Creed, the Lord's Prayer, and the Ten Commandments." At this stage, it does not matter nearly so much that these things should be fully understood as that they should be known and remembered. Remember, it is material that we are collecting.

The Logic Stage

It is difficult to say at what age, precisely, we should pass from the first to the second part of the Trivium. Generally speaking, the answer is: so soon as the pupil shows himself disposed to Pertness and interminable argument (or, as a schoolmaster correspondent of mine more elegantly puts it: "When the capacity for abstract thought begins to manifest itself"). For as, in the first part, the master-faculties are Observation and Memory, so, in the second, the master faculty is the Discursive Reason.

In the first, the exercise to which the rest of the material was, as it were, keyed, was the Latin Grammar; in the second, the key-exercise will be Formal Logic. It is here that our curriculum shows its first sharp divergence from modern standards. The disrepute into which Formal Logic has fallen is entirely unjustified; and its neglect is the root cause of nearly all those disquieting symptoms which we have noted in the modern intellectual constitution. Logic has been discredited, partly because we have fallen into a habit of supposing that we are conditioned almost entirely by the intuitive and the unconscious. There is no time now to argue whether this is true; I will content myself with observing that to neglect the proper training of the reason is the best possible way to make it true, and to ensure the supremacy of the intuitive, irrational and unconscious elements in our make-up. A secondary cause for the disfavour into which Formal Logic has fallen is the belief that it is entirely based upon universal assumptions that are either unprovable or tautological. This is not true. Not all universal propositions are of this kind. But even if they were, it would make no difference, since every syllogism whose major premise is in the form "All A is B" can be recast in hypothetical form. Logic is the art of arguing correctly: "If A, then B"; the method is not invalidated by the hypothetical character of A. Indeed, the practical utility of Formal Logic to-day lies not so much in the establishment of positive conclusions as in the prompt detection and exposure of invalid inference.

Let us now quickly review our material and see how it is to be related to Dialectic [/Logic]. On the *Language* side, we shall now have our Vocabulary and Morphology at our finger-tips; henceforward we can concentrate more particularly on Syntax and Analysis (i.e., the logical construction of speech) and the history of Language (i.e., how we came to arrange our speech as we do in order to convey our thoughts).

Our Reading will proceed from narrative and lyric to essays, argument and criticism, and the pupil will learn to try his own hand at writing this kind of thing. Many lessons – on whatever subject – will take the form of debates; and the place of individual or choral recitation will be taken by dramatic performances, with special attention to plays in which an argument is stated in dramatic form.

Mathematics – Algebra, Geometry, and the more advanced kinds of Arithmetic – will now enter into the syllabus and take its place as what it really [/actually] is: not a separate "subject" but a sub-department of Logic. It is neither more nor less than the rule of the syllogism in its particular application to number and measurement, and should be taught as such, instead of being, for some, a dark mystery, and, for others, a special revelation, neither illuminating nor illuminated by any other part of knowledge.

History, aided by a simple system of ethics derived from the Grammar of Theology, will provide much suitable material for discussion: Was the behaviour of this statesman justified? What was the effect of such an enactment? What are the arguments for and against this or that form of government? We shall thus get an introduction to [British] Constitutional History – a subject meaningless to the young child, but of absorbing interest to those who are prepared to argue and debate.

Theology itself will furnish material for argument about conduct and morals; and should have its scope extended by a simplified course of dogmatic theology (i.e., the rational structure of Christian thought), clarifying the relations between the dogma and the ethics, and lending itself to that application of ethical principles in particular instances which is properly called casuistry [/the resolving of issues of conscience].

Geography and the *Sciences* will likewise provide material for dialectic [/logic].

But above all, we must not neglect the material which is so abundant in the pupils' own daily life. There is a delightful passage in Leslie Paul's *The Living Hedge* which tells how a number of small boys enjoyed themselves for days arguing about an extraordinary shower of rain which had fallen in their town – a shower so localised that it left one half of the main street wet and the other dry. Could one, they argued, properly say that it had rained that day *on* or *over* the town or only *in* the town? How many drops of water were required to constitute rain? and so on. Argument about this led on to a host of similar problems about rest and motion, sleep and waking, *est* and *non est* [/being and non-being], and the infinitesimal division of time. The whole passage is an admirable example of the spontaneous development of the ratiocinative faculty and the natural and proper thirst of the awakening reason for definition of terms and exactness of statement. All events are food for such an appetite. An umpire's decision; the degree to which one may transgress the spirit of a regulation without being trapped by the letter; on such questions as these, children are born casuists [/those who resolve issues of conscience], and their natural propensity only needs to be developed and trained – and, especially, brought into an intelligible relationship with events in the grown-up world. The newspapers are full of good material for such exercises: legal decisions, on the one hand, in cases where the cause at issue is not too abstruse [/remote from comprehension]; on the other, fallacious reasoning and muddleheaded argument, with which the correspondence columns of certain papers one could name, are abundantly stocked.

Wherever the matter for Dialectic [/Logic] is found, it is, of course, highly important that attention should be focused upon the beauty and economy of a fine demonstration or a well-turned argument, lest veneration should wholly die. Criticism must not be merely destructive; though at the same time both teacher and pupils must be ready to detect fallacy, slipshod reasoning, ambiguity, irrelevance, and redundancy, and to pounce upon them like rats. [Rather, they should develop responses appropriate to the situation: sometimes graciously instructive; other times pointed and lethal.]

This is the moment when precis-writing [/concise summary] may be usefully undertaken; together with such exercises as the writing of an essay, and the reduction of it, when written, by 25 or 50 percent.

It will, doubtless, be objected that to encourage young persons at the Pert Age to browbeat [/arrogantly assert], correct, and argue with their elders will render them perfectly intolerable. My answer is that children of that age are intolerable anyhow; and that their natural argumentativeness may just as well be canalised [/channeled] to good purpose, as [be] allowed to run away into the sands. It may, indeed, be rather less obtrusive [/brash] at home if it is disciplined in school; and, anyhow, elders who have abandoned the wholesome principle that children should be seen and not heard have no one to blame but themselves. The teachers, to be sure, will have to mind their step, or they may get more than they bargained for. All children sit in judgment on their masters; and if the Chaplain's sermon or the Headmistress's annual Speech-day address should by any chance afford an opening for the point of the critical wedge, that wedge will go home the more forcibly under the weight of the Dialectical [/Logical] hammer, wielded by a practised hand. That is why I said that the teachers themselves would need to undergo the discipline of the Trivium before they set out to impose it on their charges. [We dissent regarding the intolerableness of youth. That is largely a matter of training in respect for authority – or the lack thereof.]

Once again: the contents of the syllabus at this stage may be anything you like. The "subjects" supply material; but they are all to be regarded as mere grist [/grain to be ground] for the mental mill to work upon. The pupils should be encouraged to go and forage [/search everywhere for food] for their own information, and so guided towards the proper use of libraries and books of reference, and shown how to tell which sources are authoritative and which are not.

The Rhetoric Stage

Towards the close of this stage, the pupils will probably be beginning to discover for themselves that their knowledge and experience are insufficient, and that their trained intelligences [intellectual faculties] need a great deal more material to chew upon. The imagination – usually dormant during the Pert age – will re-awaken, and prompt them to suspect the limitations of logic and reason. This means that they are passing into the Poetic age and are ready to embark on the study of Rhetoric. The doors of the storehouse of knowledge should now be thrown open for them to browse about as they will. The things once learned by rote will be seen in new contexts; the things once coldly analysed can now be brought together to form a new synthesis; here and there a sudden insight will bring about that most exciting of all discoveries: the realisation that a truism is true.

It is difficult to map out any general syllabus for the study of Rhetoric: a certain freedom is demanded. In literature, appreciation should be again allowed to take the lead over destructive criticism; and self-expression in writing can go forward, with its tools now sharpened to cut clean and observe proportion. Any child that already shows a disposition to specialise should be given his head: for, when the use of the tools has been well and truly learned, it is available for any study whatever. It would be well, I think, that each pupil should learn to do one, or two, subjects really [/very] well, while taking a few classes in subsidiary subjects so as to keep his mind open to the inter-relations of all knowledge. Indeed, at this stage, our difficulty will be to keep "subjects" apart; for as Dialectic [/Logic] will have shown all branches of learning to be inter-related, so Rhetoric will tend to show that all knowledge is one. To show this, and show why it is so, is pre-eminently the task of the Mistress-science. But whether Theology is studied or not, we should at least insist that children who seem inclined to specialise on the mathematical and scientific side should be obliged to attend some lessons in the Humanities and *vice versa*. At this stage, also, the Latin Grammar, having done its work, may be dropped for those who prefer to carry on their language studies on the modern side; while those who are likely never to have any great use or aptitude for mathematics might also be allowed to rest, more or less, upon their oars. Generally speaking, whatsoever is *mere* apparatus may now be allowed to fall into the background, while the trained mind is gradually prepared for specialisation in the "subjects" which, when the Trivium is completed, it should be perfectly well equipped to tackle on its own. The final synthesis of the Trivium –

the presentation and public defense of the thesis – should be restored in some form; perhaps as a kind of "leaving examination" during the last term at school.

The Ages of the Stages

The scope of Rhetoric depends also on whether the pupil is to be turned out into the world at the age of 16 or whether he is to proceed to public [=private] school and/or university. Since, really [/actually], Rhetoric should be taken at about 14, the first category of pupil should study Grammar from about 9 to 11, and Dialectic [/Logic] from 12 to 14; his last two school years would then be devoted to Rhetoric, which, in his case, would be of a fairly specialised and vocational kind, suiting him to enter immediately upon some practical career. A pupil of the second category would finish his Dialectical [/Logic] course in his Preparatory [=High] School, and take Rhetoric during his arst [/erst = first] two years at his Public [=Private] School. At 16, he would be ready to start upon those "subjects" which are proposed for his later study at the university: and this part of his education will correspond to the mediaeval Quadrivium [= arithmetic, geometry, astronomy and music]. What this amounts to is that the ordinary pupil, whose formal education ends at 16, will take the Trivium only; whereas scholars will take both the Trivium and the Quadrivium.

[We would add one year to Dorothy Sayers' ages: Grammar from 10 to 12; Logic from 13 to 15; Rhetoric from 16 to 18. These age spans are not inflexibly determined. Each child develops differently. These are only guidelines which apply in most cases.]

THE TRIVIUM IS SUFFICIENT

Is the Trivium, then, a sufficient education for life? Properly taught, I believe that it should be. At the end of the Dialectic [/Logic], the children will probably seem to be far behind their coaevals [/age-equals] brought up on old-fashioned "modern" methods, so far as detailed knowledge of specific subjects is concerned. But after the age of 14 they should be able to overhaul [/pass beyond] the others hand over first [/ fist] [i.e. rapidly]. Indeed, I am not at all sure that a pupil thoroughly proficient in the Trivium would not be fit to proceed immediately to the university at the age of 16, thus proving himself the equal of his mediaeval counterpart, whose precocity [/unusually early fruits] astonished us at the beginning of this discussion. This, to be sure, would make hay of [i.e. throw into confusion] the [English] public[=private]-

school system, and disconcert the universities very much – it would, for example, make quite a different thing of the Oxford and Cambridge Boat-race. But I am not here to consider the feelings of academic bodies: I am concerned only with the proper training of the mind to encounter and deal with the formidable mass of undigested problems presented to it by the modern world. For the tools of learning are the same, in any and every subject; and the person who knows how to use them will, at any age, get the mastery of a new subject in half the time and with a quarter of the effort expended by the person who has not the tools at his command. To learn six subjects without remembering how they were learnt does nothing to ease the approach to a seventh; to have learnt and remembered the art of learning makes the approach to every subject an open door.

It is clear that the successful teaching of this neo-mediaeval curriculum will depend even more than usual upon the working together of the whole teaching staff towards a common purpose. Since no subject is considered as an end in itself, any kind of rivalry in the staff-room will be sadly out of place. The fact that a pupil is, unfortunately, obliged, for some reason, to miss the History period on Fridays, or the Shakespeare class on Tuesdays, or even to omit a whole subject in favour of some other subject, must not be allowed to cause any heart-burnings – the essential is that he should acquire the method of learning in whatever medium suits him best. If human nature suffers under this blow to one's professional pride in one's own subject, there is comfort in the thought that the end-of-term examination results will not be affected; for the papers will be so arranged as to be an examination in method, by whatever means.

I will add that it is highly important that every teacher should, for his or her own sake, be qualified and required to teach in all three parts of the Trivium; otherwise the Masters of Dialectic [/Logic], especially, might find their minds hardening into a permanent adolescence. For this reason, teachers in Preparatory [=High] Schools should also take Rhetoric classes in the Public [=Private] Schools to which they are attached; or, if they are not so attached, then by arrangement in other schools in the same neighbourhood. Alternatively, a few preliminary classes in Rhetoric might be taken in Preparatory Schools from the age of 13 onwards. [One can easily see how this whole method of instruction adapts better and more easily to parental Homeschooling than to professional classroom schooling.]

EDUCATIONAL CAPITAL NOW SPENT

Before concluding these necessarily very sketchy suggestions, I ought to say why I think it necessary, in these days, to go back to a discipline which we had discarded. The truth is that for the last 300 years or so we have been living upon our educational capital. The post-Renaissance world, bewildered and excited by the profusion [/extravagance] of new "subjects" offered to it, broke away from the old discipline (which had, indeed, become sadly dull and stereotyped in its practical application) and imagined that henceforward it could, as it were, disport [/amuse] itself happily in its new and extended Quadrivium without passing through the Trivium. But the scholastic tradition, though broken and maimed, still lingered in the public [=private] schools and universities: Milton, however much he protested against it, was formed by it – the debate of the Fallen Angels, and the disputation of Abdiel with Satan, have the tool-marks of the Schools upon them, and might, incidentally, profitably figure as set passages for our Dialectical [/Logic] studies. Right down to the 19th century, our public affairs were mostly managed, and our books and journals were for the most part written, by people brought up in homes, and trained in places, where that tradition was still alive in the memory and almost in the blood. Just so, many people to-day who are atheist or agnostic in religion, are governed in their conduct by a code of Christian ethics which is so rooted in their unconscious assumptions that it never occurs to them to question it. [That is the advantage of culture.]

But one cannot live on capital forever. A tradition, however firmly rooted, if it is never watered, though it dies hard, yet in the end it dies. And to-day a great number – perhaps the majority – of the men and women who handle our affairs, write our books and our newspapers, carry out our research, present our plays and our films, speak from our platforms and pulpits – yes, and who educate our young people – have never, even in a lingering traditional memory, undergone the scholastic discipline. Less and less do the children who come to be educated bring any of that tradition with them. We have lost the tools of learning – the axe and the wedge, the hammer and the saw, the chisel and the plane – that were so adaptable to all tasks. Instead of them, we have merely a set of complicated jigs, each of which will do but one task and no more, and in using which eye and hand receive no training, so that no man ever sees the work as a whole or "looks to the end of the work." [Sayers' description of "jigs" describes well our modern Outcome-Based Education.]

THE TRUE GOAL OF EDUCATION

What use is it to pile task on task, and prolong the days of labour, if at the close the chief object is left unattained? It is not the fault of the teachers – they work only too hard already. The combined folly of a civilisation that has forgotten its own roots is forcing them to shore up the tottering weight of an educational structure that is built upon sand. They are doing for their pupils the work which the pupils themselves ought to do. For the sole true end of education is simply this: to teach men how to learn for themselves; and whatever instruction fails to do this is effort spent in vain.

Article Two

The Trivium in Scripture

THIS IS AN EXPANSION upon the remarks made in Chapter Four. The amount of material which could be covered here could easily fill an entire book. We must be content to restrict ourselves to a brief summary which touches on the principal topics.

THE TRIVIUM OF FACULTIES

The English words *Knowledge*, *Understanding*, and *Wisdom* correspond to Scriptural expressions which largely cover the range of mental faculties or capacities for learning. These expressions are not used in Scripture to describe three distinct and separate compartments with no interchange or overlap between them. Rather, they describe three complementary faculties which work and develop together.

THE BASIC VOCABULARY

Though there are many Hebrew and Greek words and expressions which may convey the concepts of Knowledge, Understanding, and Wisdom, there is a basic vocabulary which covers these three concepts rather regularly.

Hebrew Vocabulary

Below is the basic Hebrew vocabulary. For those unfamiliar with Hebrew, we have placed in brackets a transliteration of the Hebrew, and listed in parentheses the numbers from *Strong's Exhaustive Concordance* followed by the numbers from the *Theological Wordbook of the Old Testament*.

KNOWLEDGE

דַּעַת [DAH‘-ahth] (1847; 848c)
= knowledge gained by the senses.

יָדַע [yahw-DAH‘] (3045; 848)
= to know, to cause to know, perceive, recognize.

יְדַע [yehd-AH‘ (Aramaic)] (3046; 2765)
= to know, to cause to know.

מַדָּע [mahd-DAHW‘] (4093; 848g)
= knowledge, thought, the storeplace of knowledge (= mind).

מַנְדַּע [mahn-DAH‘ (Aramaic)] (4486; 2765a)
= knowledge, power of knowing (equivalent to Greek gnîsij).

UNDERSTANDING

בִּין [biyn] (995; 239)
= to discern between, distinguish, to understand, consider.

בִּינָה [biy-NAHW] (998; 239b)
= understanding, insight, discernment – a power of judgement beyond the mere gathering of information.

בִּינָה [biy-NAHW (Aramaic)] (999; 2627)
= understanding, discernment.

שָׂכַל [sahw-KHAHL] (7919; 2263, 2264)
= to be prudent, to ponder, to be or to act circumspect, to have insight, to comprehend – nearly synonymous with biyn, but while biyn discerns between things, sahwkhahl sorts out more complex arrangements.

שְׂכַל [sehkh-AHL (Aramaic)] (7920; 3009)
= to consider, to contemplate.

שֵׂכֶל [SEHY-kehl] (7922; 2263a)
= prudence, insight, understanding.

שָׂכְלְתָנוּ [sohkheh-lehth-ahw-NOOW (Aramaic)] (7924; 3009a)
= insight, understanding.

תְּבוּנָה [tehb-oohw-NAHWH] (8394; 239c)
= the act or faculty of understanding, insight, discretion.

WISDOM

חַכִּים [hhah-KHIYM (Aramaic)] (2445; 2729a)
= wise, wise one.

חָכַם [hhahw-KAHM] (2449; 647)
= to be wise, to make wise, to teach wisdom, to show wisdom – with its derivatives, it is the most frequently used term to describe intelligence, it is often used as a comprehensive term to include under it both knowledge and understanding, extending to the idea of proficient skill, seasoned craftsmanship, expert counsel, experienced practical advice.

חָכָם [hhahw-KHAHWM] (2450; 647b)
= wise, intelligent, skillful, shrewd, clever, learned.

חָכְמָה [hhohkheh-MAHWH] (2451; 647a)
= ethical or religious wisdom, practical or technical skill.

חָכְמָה [hhahwkheh-MAHWH (Aramaic)] (2452; 2729b)
= wisdom.

חָכְמָה [hhohkheh-MAHWH] (2454; 647a)
= wisdom.

Greek Vocabulary

Below is the basic Greek vocabulary. For those unfamiliar with Greek, we have placed in brackets a transliteration of the Greek, and listed in parentheses the numbers from *Strong's Exhaustive Concordance*.

KNOWLEDGE

ἀναγνωρίζομαι [ahn-ahg-nohw-RIH-zoh-maiy] (319)
= to make (oneself) known, to recognize.

γινώσκω [gih-NOHW-skohw] (1097)
= to take in knowledge, to come to know, to become acquainted with, to perceive.

γνωρίζω [gnohw-RIH-zohw] (1107)
= to make (something) known, passive: to become known, to be recognized (Earlier Greek: to gain a thorough knowledge of).

γνῶσις [GNOHW-sihs] (1108)
= the act of knowing, general knowledge, or special knowledge – enlarged, advanced, mature knowledge.

γνώστης [GNOHW-stehys] (1109)
= a knower, one who is knowledgable.

γνωστός [gnohw-STOHS] (1110)
= (well) known, notable.

διαγινώσκω [diy-ah-gih-NOHW-skohw] (1231)
= to know thoroughly, to learn accurately, to ascertain

exactly; legal: to examine for purposes of deciding.

διαγνωρίζω [diy-ah-gnohw-RIH-zohw] (1232)
= to thoroughly make known, to tell throughout (a territory), to publish.

ἐπιγινώσκω [eh-pih-gih-NOHW-skohw] (1921)
= to know upon (some particular mark), to recognize the identity; to become fully acquainted with; to acknowledge (upon recognition).

ἐπίγνωσις [eh-PIH-gnohw-sihs] (1922)
= full – correct – knowledge (of a particular thing), recognition, discernment, acknowledgment (upon recognition).

ἐπίσταμαι [eh-PIH-stah-maiy] (1987)
= to put (the mind) upon, to fix the attention to, to comprehend; to be acquainted with (to the point of recognition), to know.

ἐπιστη'μων [eh-pih-STEHY-mohwn] (1990)
= possessed of the knowledge of an expert, personally experienced, intelligent.

ἴσημι [IH-sehy-miy] (2467)
= to know.

UNDERSTANDING

ἀσύνετος [ah-SOOH-neh-tohs] (801)
= without understanding, not ignorant – but stupid, unable to reason, undiscerning.

διάνοια [diy-AH-noi-ah] (1271)
= deep thought, the mind, the use of the mind to understand, the process of reasoning, understanding.

δυσνόητος [doohs-NOH-ehy-tohs] (1425)
= hard to understand.

νοιέω [noi-EH-owh] (3539)
= to use the mind, understand, consider, ponder.

νοῦς [NOUS] (3563)
= the mind, the faculty for reasoning, understanding; meaning.

σύνεσις [SOOH-neh-sihs] (4907)
= a (mental) putting together, intellect, understanding.

συνετός [sooh-neh-TOHS] (4908)
= (mentally) put together, prudent, intelligent.

συνίημι [sooh-NIH-ehy-miy] (4920)
= to (mentally) put together, to comprehend, to under-

stand.

φρη'ν [FREHYN] (5424)
= (the midriff, the heart, the feelings, the sensitive nature), the mind, the understanding.

φρονέω [froh-NEH-owh] (5426)
= to use the mind, to have a thoughtful opinion, to be mentally disposed toward a thing, to be interested, to care.

φρόνησις [FROH-nehy-sihs] (5428)
= mental activity, insight, prudence, wisdom.

φρόνιμος [FROH-nih-mohs] (5429)
= prudent, mindful of one's owns interests, discreet.

φρονίμως [froh-NIH-mohws] (5430)
= prudently, wisely.

WISDOM

σοφία [soh-FIY-ah] (4678)
= comprehensive insight, practical wisdom.

σοφίζω [soh-FIH-zohw] (4679)
= to render wise; to form (plausible) sophisms.

σοφός [soh-FOHWS] (4680)
= wise, skilled.

PASSAGES WHERE THE BASIC TRIVIUM VOCABULARY APPEARS TOGETHER

Below, we list every passage, within a range of three verses, where are used at least one Hebrew or Greek term for each of the three categories: Knowledge, Understanding, and Wisdom. The Strong's number is inserted in brackets after each term, followed by a letter to identify it as:

K for Knowledge.
U for Understanding.
W for Wisdom.

Though not every passage we have found is necessarily instructive, we have nevertheless been exhaustive. We have included parts of the context as might seem relevant. We did edited out several passages which happened to include the Trivium, but with no apparent connection between the verses. We have placed short comments after selected passages.

Please note: we have limited our search for passages with all three categories. If we were to make a search for only two terms together – Knowledge and Understanding, Understanding and Wisdom, or Knowledge and Wisdom – there would be multiples more passages to consider.

> Now therefore let Pharaoh look out a man discreet [995-U] and wise [2450-W], and set him over the land of Egypt. . . . And Pharaoh said unto Joseph, Forasmuch as God hath shewed [3045-K] thee all this [/made all this known to thee], *there is* none so discreet [995-U] and wise [2450-W] as thou *art*: — Genesis 41:33,39

> And I have filled him [Bezaleel] with the spirit of God, in wisdom [2451-W], and in understanding [8394-U], and in knowledge [1847-K], and in all manner of workmanship, — Exodus 31:3

> And he hath filled him with the spirit of God, in wisdom [2451-W], in understanding [8394-U], and in knowledge [1847-K], and in all manner of workmanship; — Exodus 35:31

> Then wrought Bezaleel and Aholiab, and every wise [2450-W] hearted man, in whom the LORD put wisdom [2451-W] and understanding [8394-U] to know [3045-K] how to work all manner of work for the service of the sanctuary, according to all that the LORD had commanded. — Exodus 36:1

Comment: The fully capable workman must have wisdom, understanding, and knowledge. Compare First Corinthians 12:7,8; Second Timothy 3:16,17.

> Take [\Give] you wise [2450-W] men, and understanding [995-U], and known [\knowledgeable] [3045-K] [from] among your tribes, and I will make them rulers over you. . . . So I took the chief of your tribes, wise [2450-W] men, and known [\knowledgeable] [3045-K], and made [\gave] them heads over you, captains over thousands, and captains over hundreds, and captains over fifties, and captains over tens, and officers among your tribes. — Deuteronomy 1:13,15

Comment: Men must have a full intellectual capacity for leadership.

> He *was* a widow's son of the tribe of Naphtali, and his father *was* a man of Tyre, a worker in brass: and he was filled with wisdom [2451-W], and understanding [8394-U], and cunning [1847-K] to work all works in brass. And he came to king Solomon, and wrought all his work. — First Kings 7:14

Huram said moreover, Blessed *be* the LORD God of Israel, that made heaven and earth, who hath given to David the king a wise [2450-W] son, endued with [3045-K] prudence [7922-U] and understanding [998-U], that might build an house for the LORD, and an house for his kingdom. And now I have sent a cunning [2450-W] man, endued [3045-K] with understanding [998-U], of Huram my father's, The son of a woman of the daughters of Dan, and his father *was* a man of Tyre, skilful [3045-K] to work in gold, and in silver, in brass, in iron, in stone, and in timber, in purple, in blue, and in fine linen, and in crimson; also to grave any manner of graving, and to find out every device which shall be put to him, with thy cunning men [2450-W], and with the cunning men [2450-W] of my lord David thy father. — Second Chronicles 2:12-14

Comment: Good workmen have a fully developed intelligence.

Hast thou heard the secret of God? and dost thou restrain wisdom [2451-W] to thyself? What knowest [3045-K] thou, that we know [3045-K] not? *what* understandest [995-U] thou, which *is* not in us? —Job 15:8-9

But where shall wisdom [2451-W] be found? and where *is* the place of understanding [998-U]? Man knoweth [3045-K] not the price thereof; neither is it found in the land of the living. —Job 28:12-13

I said, Days should speak, and multitude of years should teach [\make known] [3045-K] wisdom [2451-W]. But *there is* a spirit in man: and the inspiration [\breath] of the Almighty giveth them understanding [995-U]. Great men are not *always* wise [2449-W]: neither do the aged understand [995-U] judgment. —Job 32:7-9

Should it be according to thy mind ?[\from with thee?] he will recompense it, whether thou refuse, or whether thou choose; and not I: therefore speak what thou knowest [3045-K]. Let men of understanding [\of heart] tell me, and let a wise [2450-W] man hearken unto me. Job hath spoken without knowledge [1847-K], and his words *were* without wisdom [\understanding] [7919-U]. — Job 34:33-35

To know [3045-K] wisdom [2451-W] and instruction; to perceive [995-U] the words of understanding [998-U]; To receive the instruction of wisdom [7919-U], justice, and judgment, and equity [\equities]; To give subtilty [/ subtle understanding] to the simple, to the young man knowledge [1847-K] and discretion. A wise [2450-W] *man* will hear, and will increase learning; and a man of understanding [995-U] shall attain unto wise counsels: To understand [995-U] a proverb, and the interpretation [/an eloquent speech]; the words of the wise [2450-W], and their dark sayings. The fear of the LORD *is* the beginning [/the principal part] of knowledge [1847-K]: *but* fools despise wisdom [2451-W] and instruction. My son, hear the instruction of thy father, and forsake not the law of thy mother: For they *shall be* an ornament [\adding] of grace unto thy head, and chains about thy neck. — Proverbs 1:2-9

Comment: From these examples, it is plain that the Trivium is obviously very closely connected and intertwined.

My son, if thou wilt receive my words, and hide my commandments with thee; So that thou incline thine ear unto wisdom [2451-W], *and* apply thine heart to understanding [8394-U]; Yea, if thou criest after knowledge [998-U], *and* liftest up [\givest] thy voice for understanding [8394-U]; If thou seekest her as silver, and searchest for her as *for* hid treasures; Then shalt thou understand [995-U] the fear of the LORD, and find the knowledge [1847-K] of God. For the LORD giveth wisdom [2451-W]: out of his mouth *cometh* knowledge [1847-K] and understanding. He layeth up sound wisdom for the righteous: *he is* a buckler to them that walk uprightly. He keepeth the paths of judgment, and preserveth the way of his saints. Then shalt thou understand [995-U] righteousness, and judgment, and equity; *yea*, every good path. When wisdom [2451-W] entereth into thine heart, and knowledge [1847-K] is pleasant unto thy soul; Discretion shall preserve thee, understanding [8394-U] shall keep thee: Proverbs 2:1-11

Trust in the LORD with all thine heart; and lean not unto thine own understanding [998-U]. In all thy ways acknowledge [3045-K] him, and he shall direct [\make straight] thy paths. Be not wise [2450-W] in thine own eyes: fear the LORD, and depart from evil. — Proverbs 3:5-7

The LORD by wisdom [2451-W] hath founded the earth; by understanding [8394-U] hath he established the heavens. By his knowledge [1847-K] the depths are broken up, and the clouds drop down the dew. — Proverbs 3:19,20

The wise [2450-W] shall inherit glory: but shame shall be the promotion of fools [\exalteth the fools]. Hear, ye children, the instruction of a father, and attend to know [3045-K] understanding [998-U]. — Proverbs 3:35-4:1

My son, attend unto my wisdom [2451-W], *and* bow thine ear to my understanding [8394-U]: That thou mayest regard discretion, and *that* thy lips may keep knowledge [1847-K]. — Proverbs 5:1,2

Doth not wisdom [2451-W] cry? and understanding [8394-U] put forth her voice? She standeth in the top of high places, by the way in the places of the paths. She crieth at the gates, at the entry of the city, at the coming in at the doors. Unto you, O men, I call; and my voice *is* to the sons of man. O ye simple, understand [995-U] wisdom: and, ye fools, be ye of an understanding [995-U] heart. Hear; for I will speak of excellent things; and the opening of my lips *shall be* right things. For my mouth shall speak truth; and wickedness *is* an abomination to my lips. All the words of my mouth *are* in righteousness; *there is* nothing froward or perverse in them. They *are* all plain to him that understandeth [995-U], and right to them that find knowledge [1847-K]. Receive my instruction, and not silver; and knowledge [1847-K] rather than choice gold. For wisdom [2451-W] *is* better than rubies; and all the things that may be desired are not to be compared to it. I wisdom [2451-W] dwell with prudence [/subtle understanding], and find out knowledge [1847-K] of witty inventions. — Proverbs 8:1-12

Comment: Instruction is sometimes associated with Knowledge, and at other times with Understanding. Here it is associated with both. In the last verse, each member of the Trivium is clearly distinguished.

Reprove not a scorner, lest he hate thee: rebuke a wise man [2450-W], and he will love thee. Give *instruction* to a wise [2450-W] *man*, and he will be yet wiser [2449-W]: teach [3045-K] a just *man*, and he will increase in learning. The fear of the LORD *is* the beginning of wisdom [2451-W]: and the knowledge [1847-K] of the holy *is* understanding [998-U]. For by me thy days shall be multiplied, and the years of thy life shall be increased. If thou be wise [2449-W], thou shalt be wise [2449-W] for thyself: but *if* thou scornest, thou alone shalt bear *it*. — Proverbs 9:8-12

In the lips of him that hath understanding [995-U] wisdom [2451-W] is found: but a rod *is* for the back of him that is void of understanding [\of heart]. Wise [2450-W] *men* lay up knowledge [1847-K]: but the mouth of the foolish *is* near destruction. — Proverbs 10:13,14

Comment: Notice the intertwining: Understanding leads to Wisdom in speaking. Wisdom stores up Knowledge.

The law of the wise [2450-W] *is* a fountain of life, to depart from the snares of death. Good understanding [7922-U] giveth favour: but the way of transgressors *is* hard. Every prudent *man* dealeth with knowledge [1847-K]: but a fool layeth [\spreadeth] open *his* folly. — Proverbs 13:14-16

A scorner seeketh wisdom [2451-W], and *findeth it* not: but knowledge [1847-K] *is* easy unto him that understandeth [/the intelligent] [995-U]. Go from the presence of a foolish man, when thou perceivest [3045-K] not *in him* the lips of knowledge [1847-K]. The wisdom [2451-W] of the prudent *is* to understand [995-U] his way: but the folly of fools *is* deceit. — Proverbs 14:6-8

Comment: Knowledge is easy to the one who Understands. The wisdom of the prudent is to Understand.

> Wisdom [2451-W] resteth in the heart of him that hath understanding [995-U]: but *that which is* in the midst of fools is made known [3045-K]. — Proverbs 14:33

Comment: Because Wisdom is the ultimate goal, Wisdom is at the heart of Understanding.

> A scorner loveth not one that reproveth him: neither will he go unto the wise [2450-W]. The heart of him that hath understanding [995-U] seeketh knowledge [1847-K]: but the mouth of fools feedeth on foolishness. — Proverbs 15:12,14

Comment: Because Knowledge is essential, Knowledge is also at the heart of Understanding.

> He that hath [3045-K] knowledge [1847-K] spareth his words: *and* a man of understanding [8394-U] is of an excellent [\a cool] spirit. Even a fool, when he holdeth his peace, is counted wise [2450-W]: *and* he that shutteth his lips *is esteemed* a man of understanding [995-U]. — Proverbs 17:27,28

Comment: He who has Wisdom always has a full measure of Understanding and Knowledge, so, from the Hebrew point of view, they are almost synonymous.

> The heart of the prudent [995-U] getteth knowledge [1847-K]; and the ear of the wise [2450-W] seeketh knowledge [1847-K]. — Proverbs 18:15

> When the scorner is punished, the simple is made wise [2449-W]: and when the wise [2450-W] is instructed [/made to understand] [7919-U], he receiveth knowledge [1847-K]. The righteous *man* wisely considereth [7919-U] the house of the wicked: *but God* overthroweth the wicked for *their* wickedness. — Proverbs 21:11,12

> Through wisdom [2451-W] is an house builded; and by understanding [8394-U] it is established: And by knowledge [1847-K] shall the chambers be filled with all precious and pleasant riches. — Proverbs 24:3,4

> If thou sayest, Behold, we knew [3045-K] it not; doth not he that pondereth the heart consider [995-U] *it*? and he that keepeth thy soul, doth *not* he know [3045-K] *it*? and shall *not* he render to *every* man according to his works? My son, eat thou honey, because *it is* good; and the honeycomb, *which is* sweet to thy taste [\upon thy palate]: So *shall* the knowledge [3045-K] of wisdom [2451-W] *be* unto thy soul [/Know this: such is wisdom for your soul]: when thou

hast found *it*, then there shall be a reward, and thy expectation shall not be cut off. — Proverbs 24:12-14

Surely I *am* more brutish than *any* man, and have not the understanding [998-U] of a man. I neither learned wisdom [2451-W], nor have [\know] [3045-K] the knowledge [1847-K] of the holy. Who hath ascended up into heaven, or descended? who hath gathered the wind in his fists? who hath bound the waters in a garment? who hath established all the ends of the earth? what *is* his name, and what *is* his son's name, if thou canst tell [3045-K]? — Proverbs 30:2-4

Comment: Learning Wisdom and knowing Knowledge are distinguished.

Whatsoever thy hand findeth to do, do *it* with thy might; for *there is* no work, nor device, nor knowledge [1847-K], nor wisdom [2451-W], in the grave [\Sheol], whither thou goest. I returned, and saw under the sun, that the race *is* not to the swift, nor the battle to the strong, neither yet bread to the wise [2450-W], nor yet riches to men of understanding [995-U], nor yet favour to men of skill [3045-K]; but time and chance happeneth [\occurrence occurreth] to them all. For man also knoweth [3045-K] not his time: as the fishes that are taken in an evil net, and as the birds that are caught in the snare; so *are* the sons of men snared in an evil time, when it falleth suddenly upon them. — Ecclesiastes 9:10-12

Comment: There is no device [reasoning-Understanding], nor Knowledge, nor Wisdom in the grave.

That say, Let him make speed, *and* hasten his work, that we may see *it*: and let the counsel of the Holy One of Israel draw nigh and come, that we may know [3045-K] *it*! . . . Woe unto *them that are* wise [2450-W] in their own eyes, and prudent [995-U] in their own sight! [\before their face!] — Isaiah 5:19,21

And there shall come forth a rod out of the stem of Jesse, and a Branch shall grow out of his roots: And the spirit of the LORD shall rest upon him, the spirit of wisdom [2451-W] and understanding [998-U], the spirit of counsel and might, the spirit of knowledge [1847-K] and of the fear of the LORD; — Isaiah 11:1,2

And the book is delivered to him that is not learned [\knowledgeable] [3045-K], saying, Read this, I pray thee: and he saith, I am not learned [\knowledgeable] [3045-K]. Wherefore the Lord said, Forasmuch as this people draw near *me* with their mouth, and with their lips do honour me, but have removed their heart far from me, and their fear toward me is taught by the precept of men: Therefore, behold, I will proceed [\add] to do a marvellous work among

> this people, *even* a marvellous work and a wonder: for the wisdom [2451-W] of their wise [2450-W] *men* shall perish, and the understanding [998-U] of their prudent [995-U] *men* shall be hid. Woe unto them that seek deep to hide their counsel from the LORD, and their works are in the dark, and they say, Who seeth us? and who knoweth [3045-K] us? Surely your turning of things upside down shall be esteemed as the potter's clay: for shall the work say of him that made it, He made me not? or shall the thing framed say of him that framed it, He had no understanding [995-U]? — Isaiah 29:12-15

Comment: In judgement, God causes the leaders of a nation to lose all intelligence – Wisdom, Understanding, and Knowledge.

> For my people *is* foolish, they have not known [3045-K] me; they *are* sottish children, and they have none understanding [995-U]: they *are* wise [2450-W] to do evil, but to do good they have no knowledge [3045-K]. —Jeremiah 4:22

> I will scatter them also among the heathen, whom neither they nor their fathers have known [3045-K]: and I will send a sword after them, till I have consumed them. Thus saith the LORD of hosts, Consider [\understand] [995-U] ye, and call for the mourning women, that they may come; and send for cunning [2450-W] *women*, that they may come: —Jeremiah 9:16,17

> Thus saith the LORD, Let not the wise [2450-W] *man* glory in his wisdom [2451-W], neither let the mighty *man* glory in his might, let not the rich *man* glory in his riches: But let him that glorieth glory in this, that he understandeth [7919-U] and knoweth [3045-K] me, that I *am* the LORD which exercise lovingkindness, judgment, and righteousness, in the earth: for in these *things* I delight, saith the LORD. — Jeremiah 9:23,24

Comment: The wise man understands and knows.

> Children in whom *was* no blemish, but well favoured, and skilful [\understanding] [7919-U] in all wisdom [2451-W], and cunning [\knowledgeable] [3045-K] in knowledge [1847-K], and understanding [995-U] science [4093-K], and such as *had* ability in them to stand in the king's palace, and whom they might teach the learning and the tongue of the Chaldeans. — Daniel 1:4

Comment: Notice the intertwining: Understanding in Wisdom; Knowledgeable in Knowledge and Understanding.

> As for these four children, God gave them knowledge [4093-K] and skill [\understanding] [7919-U] in all [book] learning and wisdom [2451-W]: and Daniel had understanding [/he made Daniel understand] [995-U] in all visions and dreams. — Daniel 1:17

Comment: Knowledge is distinguished from Understanding and from Wisdom.

> Daniel answered and said, Blessed be the name of God for ever and ever: for wisdom [2452-W] and might are his: And he changeth the times and the seasons: he removeth kings, and setteth up kings: he giveth wisdom [2452-W] unto the wise [2445-W], and knowledge [4486-K] to them that know [3046-K] understanding [999-U]: He revealeth the deep and secret things: he knoweth [3046-K] what *is* in the darkness, and the light dwelleth with him. I thank thee, and praise thee, O thou God of my fathers, who hast given me wisdom [2452-W] and might, and hast made known [3046-K] unto me now what we desired of thee: for thou hast *now* made known [3046-K] unto us the king's matter. — Daniel 2:20-23

> There is a man in thy kingdom, in whom *is* the spirit of the holy gods; and in the days of thy father [/grandfather] light and understanding [7924-U] and wisdom [2452-W], like the wisdom [2452-W] of the gods, was found in him; whom the king Nebuchadnezzar thy father, the king, *I say*, thy father, made master of the magicians, astrologers, Chaldeans, *and* soothsayers; Forasmuch as an excellent spirit, and knowledge [4486-K], and understanding [7924-U], interpreting [/of an interpreter] of dreams, and shewing of hard sentences, and dissolving [/of a dissolver] of doubts [\knots], were found in the same Daniel, whom the king named Belteshazzar: now let Daniel be called, and he will shew the interpretation. Then was Daniel brought in before the king. *And* the king spake and said unto Daniel, *Art* thou that Daniel, which *art* of the children of the captivity of Judah, whom the king my father [/grandfather] brought out of Jewry? I have even heard of thee, that the spirit of the gods *is* in thee, and *that* light and understanding [7924-U] and excellent wisdom [2452-W] is found in thee. And now the wise [2445-W] *men*, the astrologers, have been brought in before me, that they should read this writing, and make known [3046-K] unto me the interpretation thereof: but they could not shew the interpretation of the thing: And I have heard of thee, that thou canst make interpretations [\interpret], and dissolve doubts: now if thou canst read the writing, and make known [3046-K] to me the interpretation thereof, thou shalt be clothed with scarlet, and *have* a chain of gold about thy neck, and shalt be the third ruler in the kingdom. — Daniel 5:11-16

Comment: Light represents spiritual Knowledge. Understanding is interpreting. Wisdom is dissolving of knots.

> Who *is* wise [2450-W], and he shall understand [995-U] these *things*? prudent [\understanding] [995-U], and he shall know [3045-K] them? for the ways of the LORD *are* right, and the just shall walk in them: but the transgressors shall

> fall therein. — Hosea 14:9

Comment: Notice the gradation: The wise will Understand; Understanding will know.

> At that time Jesus answered and said, I thank thee, O Father, Lord of heaven and earth, because thou hast hid these things from the wise [4680-W] and prudent [4908-U], and hast revealed them unto babes. . . . All things are delivered unto me of my Father: and no man knoweth [1921-K] the Son, but the Father; neither knoweth [1921-K] any man the Father, save the Son, and *he* to whomsoever the Son will reveal *him*. — Matthew 11:25,27

> In that hour Jesus rejoiced in spirit, and said, I thank thee, O Father, Lord of heaven and earth, that thou hast hid these things from the wise [4680-W] and prudent [4908-U], and hast revealed them unto babes: even so, Father; for so it seemed good in thy sight. All things are delivered to me of my Father: and no man knoweth [1097-K] who the Son is, but the Father; and who the Father is, but the Son, and *he* to whom the Son will reveal *him*. — Luke 10:21,22

> Because that which may be known [1110-K] of God is manifest in [/to] them; for God hath shewed *it* unto them. For the invisible things of him from the creation of the world are clearly seen, being understood [3539-U] by the things that are made, *even* his eternal power and Godhead; so that they are [/may be] without excuse: Because that, when they knew [1097-K] God, they glorified *him* not as God, neither were thankful; but became vain in their imaginations, and their foolish [801-U] heart was darkened. Professing themselves to be wise [4680-W], they became fools, And changed the glory of the uncorruptible God into an image made like to corruptible man, and to birds, and fourfooted beasts, and creeping things. — Romans 1:19-23

Comment: The heathen first lose Knowledge of the facts of God, then their Understanding of the nature of God, and finally they turn their Wisdom into folly and worship the creature.

> O the depth of the riches both of the wisdom [4678-W] and knowledge [1108-K] of God! how unsearchable *are* his judgments, and his ways past finding out! For who hath known [1097-K] the mind [3563-U] of the Lord? or who hath been his counsellor? — Romans 11:33,34

Comment: "Both the Wisdom and Knowledge" means they can be distinguished.

> For it is written, I will destroy the wisdom [4678-W] of the wise [4680-W], and will bring to nothing the understanding [4907-U] of the prudent [4908-U]. Where *is* the wise [4680-W]? where *is* the scribe? where *is* the disputer of

> this world? hath not God made foolish the wisdom [4678-W] of this world? For after that in the wisdom [4678-W] of God the world by wisdom [4678-W] knew [1097-K] not God, it pleased God by the foolishness of preaching to save them that believe. — First Corinthians 1:19-21

Comment: Wisdom and Understanding are clearly distinguished.

> Wherein he hath abounded toward us in all wisdom [4678-W] and prudence [/understanding] [5428-U]; Having made known [1107-K] unto us the mystery of his will . . . . — Ephesians 1:8,9

> That the God of our Lord Jesus Christ, the Father of glory, may give unto you the spirit of wisdom [4678-W] and revelation in the knowledge [1922-K] of him: The eyes of your understanding [1271-U] being enlightened; that ye may know what is the hope of his calling, and what the riches of the glory of his inheritance in the saints, — Ephesians 1:17,18

> For this cause we also, since the day we heard *it*, do not cease to pray for you, and to desire that ye might be filled with the knowledge [1922-K] of his will in all wisdom [4678-W] and spiritual understanding [4907-U]; That ye might walk worthy of the Lord unto all pleasing, being fruitful in every good work, and increasing in the knowledge [1922-K] of God; — Colossians 1:9,10

Comment: All three faculties are clearly distinguished.

> That their hearts might be comforted, being knit together in love, and unto all riches of the full assurance of understanding [4907-U], to the acknowledgement [1922-K] of the mystery of God, and of the Father, and of Christ; In whom are hid all the treasures of wisdom [4678-W] and knowledge [1108-K]. — Colossians 2:2,3

Comment: Being knit together in the spiritual Trivium brings comfort.

PASSAGES WHERE THE IDEA OF THE TRIVIUM APPEARS

The quotations above consisted of passages where the Trivium is patent (open to view). There are many more where the Trivium is latent (lying below the surface). There are many passages where the idea of the Trivium appears, but the precise vocabulary does not. Searching for such passages is not as simple. Below, we list many passages where we have found the idea of Knowledge, Understanding, and Wisdom, though not the precise vocabulary. We have inserted a K, U, or W in brackets after the place where we find the idea of each. We have placed short comments in brackets after selected passages. Consider the following examples.

> Buy the truth, and sell it not; also wisdom [W], and instruction [K], and understanding [U]. — Proverbs 23:23

> Who hath directed the spirit of the Lord, or being his counsellor [W] hath taught [K] him? With whom took he counsel [W], and who instructed him [U], and taught him in the path of judgement [U], and taught [K] him knowledge [K], and shewed [K] to him the way of understanding [U]? — Isaiah 40:13,14

Comment: Compare this with the Romans 11:33,34 above.

> . . . they found him [Jesus] in the temple, sitting in the midst of the doctors, both hearing them [K], and asking them questions [U]. And all that heard him were astonished at his understanding and answers [U]. . . . And Jesus increased in wisdom [W] and stature, and in favour with God and man. — Luke 2:46,47,52

Comment: The three levels of child development are here mentioned. Jesus was "hearing" the doctors. That involves the Knowledge Level of gathering information. But he was also "asking them questions," which is the Understanding Level, for he had "understanding and answers." Having Knowledge and Understanding, "Jesus increased in wisdom" which is the Wisdom Level where he made practical application, which caused him to find favor "with God and man."

> . . . that ye henceforth walk not as other Gentiles walk, in the vanity of their mind [W], Having the understanding darkened [U], being alienated from the life of God through the ignorance that is in them [K], because of the blindness of their heart [K]: . . . And be renewed in the spirit of your mind; And that ye put on the new man, which after God is created in righteousness [W] and true [K] holiness [U] — Ephesians 4:17,18,23,24

> And have put on the new man, which is renewed in knowledge after the image of him that created him. — Colossians 3:10

Comment: The Gentiles walk in foolish "vanity," which is the lack of Wisdom, "darkened understanding," which is the lack of Understanding, and "ignorance" with "blindness of heart," which is the lack of Knowledge. Christians are to be renewed in Knowledge (Colossians), and renewed in the image of their Creator, in truth, holiness, and righteousness (Ephesians). We suggest that this corresponds to the Trivium: Knowledge of the truth, Understanding to walk in holiness, and Wisdom to do righteousness. Truth is correct knowledge, to overcome ignorance. Holiness is correct understanding, to depart from evil. Righteousness is correct wisdom, to act in the fear of the Lord.

> Let the word of Christ dwell in you richly in all wisdom [W]; teaching [K] and admonishing [U] one another in psalms and hymns and spiritual songs, singing with grace in your hearts to the Lord. — Colossians 3:16

Comment: The church practices the Trivium in its service of song: teaching in Knowledge, admonishing for Understanding, causing Wisdom of Christ to dwell in it richly.

> And that from a child thou hast known the holy scriptures [K], which are able to make thee wise [W] unto salvation through faith which is in Christ Jesus. All scripture *is* given by inspiration of God [K], and *is* profitable for doctrine, for reproof, for correction, for instruction in righteousness [U]: That the man of God may be perfect, throughly furnished unto all good works [W]. — Second Timothy 3:15-17

Comment: The training of Christian children is to follow the Trivium: Begin with inspired Scripture at the Knowledge Level; move on to doctrine, reproof, correction, and instruction at the Understanding Level; finish with a thorough furnishing for all good works at the Wisdom Level.

A FEW BRIEF OBSERVATIONS

Both in the Old and the New Testaments, there is a threefold description of the faculties of the mind – Knowledge, Understanding, and Wisdom. Like the Persons of the Trinity – Father, Son, and Holy Spirit – they are closely intermeshed, and rarely appear in a 1-2-3 order. The definitions and relationships of the three faculties can be discerned.

1. *Knowledge* is the acquisition or gathering of information, the recognition or perception of things. Knowledge is best when it is thorough, accurate, and complete, becoming fully acquainted with the facts.
2. *Understanding* goes beyond the mere gathering of information. Understanding uses Knowledge to distinguish between things, to consider and ponder the nature of things, to reason and discern the order of things, to sort out and arrange things, to have insight into things.
3. *Wisdom* goes beyond the mere distinguishing of things. Wisdom uses the Knowledge and the Understanding to discern

> the true, the best, or the most valuable use of things. Wisdom is experienced, skillful, shrewd, clever toward the practical use of things. Wisdom is a comprehensive insight which gives sound counsel or advice.

The term *God* is sometimes used to refer only to God the Father, but it is also used as a generic term for all three Persons of the Godhead: the Father, the Son, and the Spirit. Wisdom is manifold, multicolored, or variegated.

> To the intent that now unto the principalities and powers in heavenly *places* might be known by the church the **manifold wisdom of God**, — Ephesians 3:10

Wisdom is also used as a generic term for all three faculties: Knowledge, Understanding, and Wisdom. Wisdom is the first or highest of the faculties and Understanding is the second, but neither of them can be gotten without Knowledge.

> Yea, if thou criest after knowledge, *and* liftest up thy voice for understanding; If thou seekest her as silver, and searchest for her as *for* hid treasures; Then shalt thou understand the fear of the LORD, and find the knowledge of God. . . . Wisdom *is* the principal thing; *therefore* get wisdom: and with all thy getting get understanding. — Proverbs 2:3-5; 4:7

Certainly, Wisdom can never operate without the other two faculties.

> For the LORD giveth wisdom: out of his mouth *cometh* knowledge and understanding. — Proverbs 2:6

When God imparts His Wisdom to man, it comes first as the Knowledge of Wisdom, then the Understanding of Wisdom, finally the Wisdom of Wisdom.

> So *shall* the knowledge of wisdom *be* unto thy soul . . . . — Proverbs 24:14

> The fear of the LORD *is* the beginning of knowledge: *but* fools despise wisdom and instruction. — Proverbs 1:7

> The fear of the LORD *is* the beginning of wisdom: and the knowledge of the holy *is* understanding. — Proverbs 9:10

A child has childish wisdom – all of his wisdom is actually his father's as he obeys his father's instructions. A mature man has his own wisdom, because he has developed all of the faculties of wisdom.

First, there is the initial training, where all of the child's systems are booting up. There is an initial capacity for Knowledge, Understanding, and Wisdom in the child, but they develop in successive order. So the initial Knowledge is very lineal.

The second Knowledge stage is more complex. The child's Knowledge develops first under the Knowledge, Understanding, and Wisdom of the parents. The child learns the Knowledge – the facts and the rules – but the Knowledge is selected and taught in a wise and understanding way from his parents. The child depends upon the Wisdom and Understanding of his parents, while gradually learning to rely upon his own accumulating Knowledge.

Then, while the child's Knowledge continues to develop, his Understanding begins to develop under the Understanding and Wisdom of the parents. The child learns the Understanding – the patterns and connections – but the Understanding is selected and taught in a wise and understanding way from his parents. The child depends upon the Wisdom of his parents, while gradually learning to rely upon his own accumulating Knowledge and Understanding.

Then, while the child's Knowledge and Understanding continue to develop, his Wisdom begins to develop under the guidance of His parents.

Finally, the child – now approaching adult, with all three capacities developed, caps off his full development by filling in Wisdom for his future life. He matures in his ability to make responsible decisions for which he will be held accountable. His conscience is matured.

A child becomes dysfunctional when essential parts are not properly developed. Until they are remediated – if ever – the child will continue to develop in dysfunctional ways.

Man cannot deny the essence of his own nature without eventually destroying himself. The Greek and Roman models for education agreed, in form, with the basic constitution of man's faculties. They either developed the Trivium from ancient forms which survived the flood through Noah, or else they were forced by the very nature of things to conform to the form. However, when they filled this form with their own highly corrupted and perverted contents, they became evermore dangerous, because they became more effective in propagating their corruptions. As Christians, we must take back the form, clean it up, and fill it with reality.

Article Three

Ancient Education: Hebrew, Greek, and Roman

MUCH OF THIS SECTION is gleaned from the book *Educational Ideals in the Ancient World*, by William Barclay, Grand Rapids: Baker Book House, 1974.

1. HEBREW EDUCATION: TRAINING FOR SERVICE TO GOD

Jewish education was entirely religious education. In pre-exilic times (before Ezra and Nehemiah), the Scripture was the only text book, the home was the only school, and the parents were the only teachers. Israel had the highest literacy of all ancient history. In post-exilic times (Ezra, Nehemiah and after), schools were attached to the synagogues, and teaching was oral recitation and repetition. Their basic texts included: The Shema (Deuteronomy 6:4-9; 11:13-21; Nehemiah 15:37-41); The Hallel (Psalms 113-118); The Creation (Genesis 1-5); and Levitical Law (Leviticus 1-8). Teachers had a trade and taught for nothing as a privilege.

2. GREEK EDUCATION: TRAINING FOR SERVICE TO THE CULTURE

In Sparta, individuality was erased through the service to the State. "In no country in the world was education ever so deliberately planned, controlled, and designed by the state as in Sparta, until the rise of the modern totalitarian state." Education consisted of a bare minimum of reading and writing, music (moral, not aesthetic), military dancing, and athletics. The goals of education were a courageous and modest character, and universal endurance of the body and mind. In Athens the individual was trained for service to the culture. Greek boys went to three teachers who taught the three basic subjects:

1) the γραμματιστή΄ς [grammatistEs: "teacher of rudiments"] taught reading, writing and arithmetic;
2) the κιθαριστή΄ς [kitharistEs: "harp or lyre player"] taught the lyre and songs;
3) the παιδοτρίβης [paidotribEs: "child trainer"] taught wrestling, boxing, running, jumping, javelin and discus.

3. ROMAN EDUCATION: TRAINING FOR SERVICE TO THE STATE

In early years, Roman education was directed toward the production of character, to fit a man for his duty to the gods, the state and the family. Roman education centered around the home, and therefore was never standardized. The first seven years the child was under his mother's influence. Thereafter, his association was with his father, who was his constant companion and often his only teacher. The education of his children was the father's life work. Plutarch wrote of the great general and statesman Aemilius Paulus, ". . . he. . . devoted himself. . . to the education of his children. . . . To this purpose he. . . procured masters to teach them grammar, logic and rhetoric. . . and, if he was not hindered by public affairs, he himself would be with them at their studies, and see them perform their exercises. . . ." At the age the child became a citizen, usually sixteen, the father would, for a year or longer, put his son under the charge of a distinguished friend rich in years, experience and honor. When Rome became an empire, the father was claimed for service in the armies and to the state, and could no longer preside over his children's education. Hence a school system arose. This education proved to be a failure. It undermined morals, mishandled bodies and taught useless information. It finally sunk to the point where young army recruits could not be assumed literate enough to keep books for the corps. Cartoons were used to communicate simple tasks. [The modern American army, because of the extensive illiteracy, uses comic books to teach the use of military hardware.] There were three stages to Roman education:

1) Litterator taught the elements of knowledge, the three "R's" (ages 7-12).
2) Grammaticus taught Greek grammar (there was no Latin), logic and rhetoric.
a. recte loquendi scientia = knowledge of right speaking including history of the letters and vowels, changes in inflection, parts of speech, correct clear and elegant diction.
b. poetarum enarration = the explanation of the poets including reading the correct text, hearing the lecture on the passage.
c. music
d. geometry
e. gymnastics
3) Rhetor

Article Four

Mediaeval Education: The Seven Liberal Arts

THE SEVEN MEDIAEVAL Liberal Arts consisted of the Elementary Trivium and the Advanced Quadrivium. These were formally established by Martianus Capella in his *Marriage of Philology and Mercury* (early fifth Century), and became widely accepted by the ninth Century.

1. THE TRIVIUM

The actual term "Trivium" does not appear until the ninth Century, but its catalog (Grammar, Logic and Rhetoric) may be found in ancient Roman, Greek and Hebrew education. The natural and Biblical triplet of Knowledge, Understanding and Wisdom is its ultimate foundation. The Trivium of Isocrates (fourth Century B. C.) was preparatory to studying philosophy. Christians believed that without the Trivium, one could not study the higher philosophy of theology. Hence Christians viewed the Trivium as comprising philosophy itself, serving as the "handmaidens of theology."

a. Grammar consisted of the practical study of Latin language and classic literature. Where the curricula was limited, this was the one subject which was never cut (hence the "grammar school").

b. Logic (also known as Dialectic) was the art of logical argument. It was essentially the study of formal logic, mostly Porphyry and Aristotle.

c. Rhetoric was the art of speaking. It included the study of composition of prose and poetry, writing letters, and the study of law.

2. THE QUADRIVIUM

The term Quadrivium was invented by Boethius in his "De Institutione Arithmetica" (early sixth Century). The Quadrivium was a fourfold division of mathematics which, to Beoethius, represented the pathway whereby the student of philosophy passed from material concerns to pure knowledge. All four members of the Quadrivium are mathematical disciplines founded upon the Pythagorean concept of "quantity."

a. Arithmetic is the study of "discrete quantity in number" (square numbers, perfect numbers, etc.). Plato divided this into logistic (numbered objects) and arithmetic (numbers).
b. Music (that is, Greek harmonic Music) is the study of "discrete quantity in numerical ratios."
c. Geometry (including Geography) is the study of "continuous quantity in fixed lines." Plato included stereometry, which is measuring volume.
d. Astronomy (or sphaeric) is the study of "continuous quantity in moving forms," the speed of the stars, and their rising and falling.

It was thought that the manipulation of such abstract truths through these four disciplines prepared the mind to contemplate higher truths of philosophy. The development of the memory was considered essential, as possession or even access to books was minimal at best and nonexistent at worst.

Article Five

Education of the Clergy

The following are selections from *Education of the Clergy* (819 A. D.) by Rhabanus Maurus, Scholasticus (Teacher of Rhetoric) of the monastery at Fulda. He lists Rhetoric before Logic, while we prefer to list Rhetoric after Logic.

THE FIRST OF THE LIBERAL arts is Grammar, the second Rhetoric, the third Dialectic [Logic]. . . .

. . . Grammar is the source and foundation of the liberal arts. It should be taught in every Christian school, since the art of writing and speaking correctly is attained through it. . . . How should one learn to know the articulation of discourse, the advantages of figurative language, the laws of word formation, and the correct forms of words, if one had not familiarized himself with the art of grammar?

. . . Through rhetoric anything is proved true or false. Who would have the courage to maintain that the defenders of truth should stand weaponless in the presence of a falsehood, so that those, who dare to show false arguments, should know how by their discourse to win the favor and sympathy of the hearers, and that, on the other hand, the friends of truth should not be able to do this; that those should know how to present a falsehood briefly, clearly, and with the semblance of truth, and that the latter, on the contrary, should clothe the truth in such an exposition, that listening would become a burden, apprehension of the truth a weariness, and faith in the truth an impossibility?

. . . Dialectic [Logic] is the science of the understanding, which fits us for investigations and definitions, for explanations, and for distinguishing the true from the false. It is the science of sciences. It teaches how to teach others; it teaches learning itself; in it the reason marks and manifests itself according to its nature, efforts, and activities; it alone is capable of knowing; it not only will, but can lead others to knowledge; its conclusions lead us to an apprehension of our being and of our origin;

through it we apprehend the origin and activity of the good, of Creator and creature; it teaches us to discover the truth and to unmask falsehood; it teaches us to draw conclusions; it shows us what is valid in argument and what is not; it teaches us to recognize what is contrary to the nature of things; it teaches us to distinguish in controversy the true, the probable, and the wholly false; by means of this science we are able to investigate everything with penetration, to determine its nature with certainty, and to discuss it with circumspection. Therefore [Christians] must understand this excellent art and constantly reflect upon its laws, in order that they may be able keenly to pierce the craftiness of errorists, and to refute their fatal fallacies.

. . . When those, who are called philosophers, have in their expositions or in their writings, uttered perchance some truth, which agrees with our faith, we should not handle it timidly, but rather take it as from its unlawful possessors and apply it to our own use.

Article Six

The Metalogicon of John of Salisbury: A Twelfth Century Defense of the Trivium

This is a Latin work completed in 1159. The title, Metalogicon, is a contrived compound from the Greek words meta (= on behalf of) and logikon (= reasoning), here taken in the broad sense of the science of verbal expression encompassing the arts of the Trivium: Grammar, Dialectic (or Logic) and Rhetoric. The work is an able summary of and convincing argument for the educational method known as the Trivium.

WHAT IS ELOQUENCE but the faculty of fittingly saying what our mind wants to express? As such, it brings to light and in a way publishes what would otherwise be hidden in the inner recesses of man's consciousness. Not everyone who speaks, nor even one who says what he wants to in some fashion, is eloquent. He alone is eloquent who fittingly and efficaciously expresses himself as he intends. . . . One who can with facility and adequacy verbally express his mental perceptions is eloquent. . . . For myself, I am at a loss to see how anything could be more generally useful: more helpful in acquiring wealth, more reliable for winning favor, more suited for gaining fame, than is eloquence. Nothing, or at least hardly anything, is to be preferred to this gift of nature and grace. The liberal arts are said to have become so efficacious among our ancestors, who studied them diligently, that they enabled them to comprehend everything they read, elevated their understanding to all things, and empowered them to cut through the knots of all problems possible of solution. Those to whom the system of the Trivium has disclosed the significance of all words, or the rules of the Quadrivium have unveiled the secrets of all nature, do not need the help of a teacher in order to understand the meaning of books and to find the solutions of questions. . . . Grammar is the science of speaking and writing correctly, the starting point of all liberal studies.

Grammar is the cradle of all philosophy, and in a manner of speaking, the first nurse of the whole study of letters. . . . [T]his branch, which teaches language, is the first of the arts to assist those who are aspiring to increase in wisdom. . . . [I]t is clear that grammar is not narrowly confined to one subject. Rather, grammar prepares the mind to understand everything that can be taught in words. Consequently, everyone can appreciate how much all other studies depend on grammar. . . . For grammar equips us both to receive and to impart knowledge. . . . [W]ho will exclude it from the threshold of philosophy, save one who thinks that philosophizing does not require an understanding of what has been said or written? Accordingly, those who would banish or condemn grammar are in effect trying to pretend that the blind and deaf are more fit for philosophical studies than those who, by nature's gift, have received and still enjoy the vigor of all their senses. . . . Seneca always has something to say. Thus he feels that liberal studies do not make a person good. I agree with him, but I think that the same also holds true of other studies. Knowledge puffeth up; it is charity alone that makes one good. . . . [T]hose who are merely philosophers are not good men. . . . [A]s Quintilian observes, these studies harm, not those who pass through them, but only those who become bogged down in them." The chief aids to philosophical inquiry and the practice of virtue are reading, learning, contemplation and constant application. . . the performance of good works, lest the Lord become angry and take away what he seems to possess.

In its narrower sense, logic is the science of argumentative reasoning, which provides a solid foundation for the whole activity of prudence. . . . Logic is exercised in inquiry into the truth. . . . Prudence consists entirely in insight into the truth. . . . [P]rudence is the root of all the virtues. If this root is severed, then the other virtues will wither and die of thirst. . . . One who comprehends truth is wise, one who loves it is good, one who orders his life in accordance with it is happy [Proverbs 3:18]. . . . [I]t is impossible that one who seeks and embraces the truth with his whole heart should remain a suitor and servant of vanity. Just as grammar. . . is concerned with ways of saying things, dialectic [=Logic] is concerned with what is said. While grammar chiefly examines the words that express meanings, dialectic investigates the meanings expressed by words. . . . A word's force consists in its meaning. Without the latter it is empty, useless, and (so to speak) dead. Just as the soul animates the body, so (in a way) meaning breathes life into a word. Those whose words lack sense are "beating the air," [First Corinthians 9:26] rather than speaking.

Article Seven

A Sixteenth Century Course of Study

THE FOLLOWING IS A TYPICAL formal grammar school course of study, compiled from several selections of the Sixteenth century (Lutheran and Reformed). What is listed below (under ages six to eight) most students learned either privately at home or in a formal grammar school at age nine. (The more fully developed mental faculties of a nine year old can comprehend the material more rapidly.) During the middle ages, the English had a chantry song school until formal grammar school began at age twelve. We do not recommend nearly so rigorous a schedule. Our purpose here is only to show what was typically expected of students in the past. They began Latin grammar by age nine, and Greek grammar by age twelve. We might add a year to these ages. They began formal Logic and Rhetoric about age fourteen. We might subtract a year. They began Arithmetic about age fourteen. We would begin at age ten and extend it over a longer period of time. Formal Science was taught at age sixteen. One could begin Physics, Chemistry, or Biology at age fourteen. School hours were typically five hours a day: 8 a.m. to 10 a.m., 12 p.m. to 1 p.m., 3 p.m. to 5 p.m., six days per week, eleven months of the year, with August off.

AGES 6-8: Latin Alphabet, Reading, Pronunciation, Writing and Spelling. Latin Declensions and Conjugations. Memorize the Catechism, Lord's Prayer, Seven Penitential Psalms.

AGE 8/9: Oral drill in Latin Declensions and Conjugations. Latin Vocabulary, memorization of Latin phrases.

AGE 9/10: Mastery of all Latin Declensions and Conjugations. Eight Parts of Speech. Latin reading, with constant reference to Syntax. Emphasis on composition and style in Latin.

AGE 10/11: Extensive reading in Latin with explanations of Syntax. Memorization of Latin for form, written exercises in style. Translate Catechism into Latin. Musical Notation.

AGE 11/12: (Grammar School Level) Latin Grammar and Syntax finished. Full Latin Vocabulary, Rules of Latin poetry. Extensive Latin reading, written exercises for style. Greek Grammar begun. Musical timing.

AGE 12/13: (Grammar School Level) Extensive Latin Reading, written exercises for style and poetry. Write an encyclopedia of Latin words. Greek Vocabulary expanded, Greek Grammar largely finished. Simple reading of Gospels in Greek and Latin.

AGE 13/14: (Grammar School Level) Extensive Latin Reading and Writing. Latin Composition in prose and verse for style. Greek Grammar and Syntax Completed. Reading of Paul's Epistles in Greek. Eloquence and Diction.

AGE 14/15: (Preparatory Level) Extensive Reading and memorization in Greek and Latin. Translation from Greek to Latin and vice versa. Reading of Paul's Epistles in Greek. Readings in Logic and Rhetoric. Drama, Roman history, Arithmetic.

AGE 15/16: (Preparatory Level) Daily exercises in style and composition in prose and verse. Interpretation of Greek. Memorize the Epistle to the Romans in Greek. Disputations in Grammar, Logic and Rhetoric applied to readings. Elegance of Diction, Drama, History. Mathematics Square and Cube root.

AGE 16/17: (University Level) Formal Logic and Rhetoric applied to readings. Natural philosophy (Science). Translation back and forth between Latin and Greek. Exposition of Pauline Epistles. Mathematics, Geometry. Hebrew, Theology.

AGE 17/18: (University Level) Moral and Practical Philosophy (Ethics, Politics, Economics). Greek, Hebrew, Theology. Mathematics, Astronomy. Mutual Questioning and Disputation.

Article Eight

A Comparison of Ancient Alphabets

THE PURPOSE OF THIS APPENDIX is to provide useful information for those who study the classical languages: Latin, Greek, and Hebrew. This is no substitute for specific materials to teach each ancient alphabet, but it is a supplement which gathers into one place much useful information for comparing the alphabets. Specific materials treating of each alphabet will reach deeper into the phonetics of each language.

GENERAL OBSERVATIONS

Hebrew is written from right to left (backwards from our English perspective). "English" would be *hsilgnE*. Well, actually, the Hebrew letters are pointed backwards (from our perspective). So "English" would actually be:

dsilgnƎ

Greek was originally written *boustrophedon*, which means *as the ox plows*. It plowed one row left to right, then turned around and plowed the next row right to left, then turned and plowed left to right again. And the letters were turned backwards and forwards to point the direction in which the row was being plowed. Sometimes we wonder if the real reason behind the dyslexia which confuses b and d, p and q, is simply a reversion to this bidirectional writing. ?kniht uoy od tahW The Greeks eventually decided to write from left to right, and we're glad.

Originally, Hebrew, Greek, and Latin were written only in capital letters with no spaces or punctuation between the words.

THATCANMAKEREADINGDIFFICULTIFYOURENOTUSEDTOIT

Bless the Lord for editors of classical texts.

In the alphabetical tables below, we have listed the letter forms as they appear in modern editions – both smalls and capitals (a, A), shorts and longs (a, A; ā, Ā), and consonant forms of vowels (I-J, U-V).

Some Hebrew letters have special forms, called *final forms*, which are used when they appear at the end of a word. (That would help the ancients to divide words.) Greek also had one final form. Hebrew and Greek letters also had a numerical value. Hebrew letters also appear to have had a symbolic meaning. We have listed their symbolic meaning, with some proposed alternatives.

We have listed and numbered the letters according to their ancient alphabetical order. Some Greek letters (ϝ, ϙ) were really obsolete by classical times, so we have listed them, but have not included them in the enumeration. Some Latin letters (G,J,V) were invented after classical times, one (K) became virtually obsolete, and some (X,Y,Z) were used only for Greek transliteration. We have nevertheless included them all in the enumeration. A few alphabetical letters are repeated, once to show their alphabetical order, then again to show their relation to another letter.

Hebrew originally had no vowel letters. The vowels were interpolated. Later editors added vowel points to the letters. Also, many Greek and Latin vowel letters had more than one value. A separate study of the vowels appears after the full alphabet chart.

The names for Hebrew and Greek letters in their respective languages are well known. We have transliterated them into English. The names for Latin letters are less known. Even English has experienced some alteration in how we name our letters. It appears that the names of the English alphabetic letters are handed down only by tradition because, though everyone knows how to pronounce them, nobody knows how to spell them. We are ordinarily content simply to write the letter alone and let it stand by itself, then pronounce its name as if the letter were a word. We have here invented spellings for English letters which we hope serve some purpose.

Transliteration Scheme

While short and long English vowels often differ in *quality*, ancient vowels differed only in quantity.

English Vowels *Differ in Quality*				**Ancient Vowels** *Differ in Quantity*			
short A	*bat*	long A	*bait*	short A	*yacht*	long A	*yawn*
short E	*bet*	long E	*beet*	short E	*bet*	long E	*bait*
short I	*bit*	long I	*bite*	short I	*bit*	long I	*beet*
short O	*bought*	long O	*boat*	short O	*boat*	long O	*bowl*
short U	*butt*	long U	*butte*	short U	*put*	long U	*pool*

We further explain ancient vowels at the end of this article.

We have devised the following scheme for spelling in English the ancient vowel sounds. It may seem odd at first sight, but there is system to it, and it is usable. (It is no more difficult that using various diacritical marks over and under the vowels.) In this system, every short vowel is followed by the letter H, and every long vowel is followed by the letters HW or HY.

Short Vowel		**Long Vowel**	
AH	= *yacht, taught, cot*	AHW	= *yawn, hurrah*
EH	= *bed*	EHY	= *bay, obey*
IH	= *chin*	IHY	= *bean, machine*
OOH	= *foot, put*	OOHW	= *blue, blew, boo, pool*
OH	= *oh, moat*	OHW	= *owe, moan, ohm*

The following two diphthongs have no H in them.

auw = the diphthong sound of au as in sauerkraut, how, towel

aey = the diphthong sound of ai as in aisle, aye aye sir

k<h p<h t<h represent explosive consonants, as the initial k p t in *kicker, popper, totter*: k<hicker p<hopper, t<hotter. The k p t in the middle of these words are not explosive. (Put your hand in front of your mouth, and you will feel a puff with the initial letter, but not with the middle letter.)

FOUR ALPHABETS COMPARED LETTER BY LETTER

*	Language	Symbol (Name)	Pronunciation	Numerical Value - Picture = Meaning
* Numerical Order according to the Modern form of the Alphabet.				

1	Hebrew	א (אָלֶף) (Aleph = AH-lehf)	co-ed (a slight glottal sound of breath escaping)	1- Ox Head = Power /Lead
1	Greek	α,Α (ἄλφα) (Alpha = AHL-fah)	short: yacht long: yawn	1
1	Latin	a,A ā,Ā (Ā = ahw)	short: yacht long: yawn	
1	English	a,A (Ay)	cat, crate, yacht, yawn	

2	Hebrew	בּ (בֵּית) (Beth = behyth) ב (בֵית) (Bheth = bvehyth)	bob (hard B) obvious (breathy B, like a V)	2- House /Tent = Family /Within
2	Greek	β,Β (βῆτα) (Beta = BEHY-tah)	bob	2
2	Latin	b,B (Bē = behy)	bob, but pronounced as p before letters t and s: apt, laps	
2	English	b,B (Bee)	bob, debt	

3	Hebrew	ג (גִּימֶל) (Gimel = GIHY-mehl) ג (גִימֶל) (Ghimel = GHIHY-mehl)	gag (hard G) gila monster (breathy G, almost an H, but with sound)	3- Camel [/Foot] = Carry /Lift /Burden
3	Greek	γ,Γ (γάμμα) (Gamma = GAHM-mah)	gag	3
3	Latin	c,C (Cē = kehy)	cocoa	
3	English	c,C (Cee = See)	cat, city, ocean, indict	

Latin C originally sounded like G and came from a slanting form of the Greek Gamma Γ which was then rounded into a C. Later, C took on the K sound as well. But since C had both G and K sounds, someone decided to put a line through the C to represent the G sound – thereby inventing G. Originally C stood before I and E, K stood before consonants and A, and Q (another K sound) stood before O and U. But that introduced so many consonantal variations in inflections that the K and Q were dropped and only C was used. Latin K is retained only in abbreviations, and Q is used only before consonantal U (QU = KW). If that's all seems quite confusing, then wait until you come to U.

4	Hebrew	ד (דָּלֶת) (Daleth = DAH-lehth) ד (דָלֶת) (Dhaleth = DTHAH-lehth)	dad (hard D) that (breathy D)	4- Tent Door = Hang Down /In and Out
4	Greek	δ,Δ (δέλτα) (Delta = DEHL-tah)	dad	4
4	Latin	d,D (Dē = dehy)	dad	
4	English	d,D (Dee)	dad, educate, handkerchief	

5	Hebrew	ה (הֵא) (He = hehy)	hair	5- Window = Look /Behold!
5	Greek	ϵ,E (ἒ ψιλόν) (Epsilon = EH-psih-LOHN)	whet	5
5	Latin	e,E ē,E (ē = ehy)	Short: whet Long: whey	
5	English	e,E (Ee)	whet, debate, cafe, whey, face	

The Hebrew He, and the Greek Epsilon, Eta, and the Hard Breather (ʽ) are all related to the Latin/English letters E and H. Originally, Greek ϵ,E was named ϵἶ = ehy, but second century grammarians altered the name to ἒ ψιλόν (bare or plain e). Modern Latin script in grammars places a Macron over long vowels to distinguish them from short vowels. See vowel charts after this alphabetic chart.

6	Hebrew	ו (וָו) (Waw = wahw, later, pronounced as vahv)	wow (later: valve)	6- Hook / Nail / Peg = And / Add / Attach
—	Greek	ϝ,F (ϝαῦ / δίγαμμα) (Wau or Bvau /Digamma = wahw or vahw /DIHY-gahm-mah)	wow (later: valve)	6 Obsolete letter, functions only as a number
6	Latin	f,F (Ef = ehf)	fluff	
6	English	f,F (Eff)	fluff	

Greek Wau/Bvau/Digamma was no longer enumerated with the alphabet, but still served as a number according to its old position. It is related to the consonantal use of the Greek letter Upsilon, which appears later in the alphabet. The name Digamma came from the fact that it looks like one capital gamma on top of another.

Stigma ϛ also is used to represent the number 6, as well as the final form of Sigma ς which you will encounter below.

7	Hebrew	ז (זַיִן) (Zayin = ZAH-yihyn)	zuzim	7- Plow /Weapon = Harvest / Food / /Armor
6	Greek	ζ,Z (ζῆτα) (Zeta or Dzeta or Zdeta = DZEHY-tah or ZDEHY-tah)	adze or mazda	7
7	Latin	g,G (Gē = gehy)	gag	
7	English	g,G (Gee = jee)	gag, cage, beige, cough, sing, sign	

For Latin G see Latin C.

There is a relationship between Greek Zeta and Latin G.

There is some difference of opinion as to the correct pronunciation of Greek Dzeta. Some say it should be as our Z, and others say it should be ZD as in mazda, not DZ as in adze. Probably all three pronunciations are correct for certain words at certain times in certain places.

8	Hebrew	ח (חֵית) (Hheth = hhehyth)	loch (breathy H, almost a K)	8- Hedge /Tent Wall /Barrier = Outside /Divided
7	Greek	η,H (ἦτα) (Eta = EHY-tah) ῾ (πνεῦμα δασύ = NEW-mah dah-SOOHW) (Rough Breather) ᾿ (πνεῦμα ψιλόν = NEW-mah psih-LOHN) (Smooth Breather)	whey hey, hair heir (silent H)	8
8	Latin	h,H (Hā = hahw)	hair	
8	English	h,H (Aytch)	hair, heir	

The Greek vowel Eta, the Greek Rough breather (πνεῦμα δασύ) and Smooth Breather (πνεῦμα ψιλόν) are related to the Latin consonant H, but the story is too long to tell. [See our *Greek Alphabetarion*.] Not all Latins considered H a separate letter, but more as a rough breather like the Greek ῾. Otherwise, H was treated as a vowel, not as a consonant, and its quality was connected to the following consonant letter, K (Kā =

Kahw). The English name for this letter, Ehytch, which sounds like a sneeze, may come from a later Latin name for this letter, ahha, then accha.

9	Hebrew	ט (טֵית) (Teth = t<hehyth)	totter (initial T, explosive T, as in bit+hard)	9- Basket [/Ball /Serpent] = Contain /Around
8	Greek	θ,Θ (θῆτα) (Theta = T<HEHY-tah)	totter (Modern Greek: as in thin)	9
—	Latin	th (a trans-literation)	Beethoven, explosive T, as when combining bit+hard	
—	English	hard th soft th transliterated th	then (silent: clothes) thin Thomas	

Greek Theta was originally pronounced as an explosive T. Modern Greek pronounces it as a soft English TH, and modern grammars of ancient Greek use this pronunciation as an accommodation to the English ear.

English once had separate letters for hard th, ð,Ð (Edth), and soft th, þ,Þ (Thorn).

10	Hebrew	י (יוֹד) (Yodh = yohwdth)	yoyo, savior	10- Hand /Arm = Work /Make
9	Greek	ι,Ι (ἰῶτα) (Iota = ihy-YOHW-tah)	Short: chin Long: machine Glide: savior	10
9 10	Latin	i,I ī,Ī (Ī= ihy) j,J [[Jā = yahw]]	Short: chin Long: machine Glide: savior, yoyo	
9 10	English	i,I (Aye) j,J (Jay)	chin, chime, machine, savior jelly [foreign words, "H" Juanita]	

Originally, Latin had only I. Latin literature has since been edited to write the consonantal use of I as J. So Latin J is really a later amendment – an orthographic anachronism. We completely made up the name for J,

Jā pronounced Yahw, basing it on an analogy to the Latin names for H and K. That's why we placed the name within double brackets. Since the fifteenth century, Latinists have moved back and forth over whether to keep the J or go back to I only.

English J has a soft G sound, which is actually a sonant TCH sound, which, if you removed the fricative action, would approximate the English consonantal Y sound.

11	Hebrew	כ ך (כַּף) (Kaph =kahf) כ ך (כַף) Khaph = k hahf)	kicker (middle or ending hard short K) kicker (initial explosive K as in back+hand)	20- Palm of Hand /Sole of Foot = Open /Curved /Subdue
10	Greek	κ,Κ (κάππα) (Kappa = KAHP-pah)	kicker (middle or ending hard short K)	20
11	Latin	k,K (Cē = kahw)	kicker (middle or ending hard short implosive K sound) (ch = explosive K)	
11	English	k,K (Kay)	kicker, know	

Hebrew final forms ך ך are called סוֹפִית sophith, and appear only at the end of a word. Because Hebrew reads "backwards," final Hebrew forms appear on the left side.

Latin K was basically an obsolete letter, and appeared only in a few abbreviations.

12	Hebrew	ל (לָמֶד) (Lamedh = LAHW-mehdth)	lull	30- Shepherd Staff /Rod /Ox Goad = Walk /Lean on /Take hold
11	Greek	λ,Λ (λάμβδα) (Lambda = LAHM-dah)	lull	30
12	Latin	l,L (El = ehll)	lull	
12	English	l,L (Ell)	lull, talk	

Greek Lambda was originally spelled *λάβδα*, with out the Mu *μ*.

13	Hebrew	מ ם (מֵם) (Mem = mehym)	mom	40- Water /Stain = Unknown /Mighty /Blood
12	Greek	μ,M (μῦ) (Mu = myoohw)	mom	40
13	Latin	m,M (Em = ehm)	mom	
13	English	m,M (Emm)	mom, mnemonic	

14	Hebrew	נ ן (נוּן) (Nun = noohwn)	noon	50- Fish [/Seed Sprout] = Continue /Life
13	Greek	ν,N (νῦ) (Nu = nyoohw)	noon (gg = anger, gk = link, gx = lynx, gc = anchor)	50
14	Latin	n,N (En = Ehn)	noon; rancor, anchor, anger, link, conquer, lynx	
14	English	n,N (Enn)	noon, longer, link, lynx	

15	Hebrew	ס (סָמֶךְ) (Samekh = SAHW-mehk h)	salsa (brief middle S)	60- Hand on Staff = Walk /Support /Uphold
14	Greek	ξ,Ξ (ξῖ) (Ksi or Xi = ksihy)	box	60
—	Latin	—	—	
—	English	—	—	

Greek Ksi was originally spelled ξεῖ, pronounced ksehy.

16	Hebrew	ע (עַיִן) (`Ayin = AH-yihyn)	Bo`az (the sound of the throat tightening and exploding breath)	70- Eye [/Well] = See /Perceive /Pay attention
15	Greek	*o*,O (*ὂ μικρόν*) (Omicron = OH-mih-KROHN)	Short: oh	70
15	Latin	o,O ō,Ō (Ō = ohw)	Short: oh Long: own	
15	English	o,O (Owe)	oh, own, on, food, foot	

The original name of Greek Omicron was *οὖ*. The name was altered in order to distinguish the Greek Short O (Omicron) from the Greek Long O (Omega), which appears at the end of the Greek Alphabet.

17	Hebrew	פּ ף (פֵּא) פ ף (פֵא) (Pe = p<hehy or pehy) (Phe = fehy)	popper (probably both explosive and implosive P) phosphor (frictional P, like F)	80- Mouth = Speak /Open /Edge
16	Greek	π,Π (*πῖ*) (Pi = pihy)	popper (implosive middle P)	80
16	Latin	p,P (Pē = pehy)	popper (implosive middle P) (ph = explosive initial P, not as an F)	
16	English	p,P (Pee)	popper, pneumonia	

Greek Pi was originally spelled *πεῖ*, pronounced pehy.

18	Hebrew	צ ץ (צָדֵי) (Tsadhe = TSAHW- thehy)	cents (sharp, explosive S)	90- Man on Side [/Step /Scythe] = Side /Hunt /Adversity
—	Greek	ϡ (ϡᾶν/σαμπῖ) (Tsan /Sampi = tsahn /sahm-PIHY, see below)	cents	
—	Latin	—	—	
—	English	—	—	

19	Hebrew	ק (קוֹף) (Qoph = kohwf)	plaque (brief K)	100- Sun on Horizon [/Axe Head /Ape] = Circle /Contract
—	Greek	ϙ (ϙόππα /κόππα) (Qoppa /Koppa = KOHP-pah)	plaque	90
17	Latin	q,Q (Cū = koohw)	plaque, lacquer	
17	English	q,Q (Que = kyoohw)	plaque, lacquer	

20	Hebrew	ר (רֵישׁ) (Resh = rehysh)	roar, rhetoric	200- Head of a Man = Top /First /Begin
17	Greek	ρ,Ρ (ῥῶ) (Rho = hr-rohw)	roar, rhetoric	100
18	Latin	r,R (Er = ehrr)	roar, rhetoric, a Scottish rolled R	
18	English	r,R (Ahr)	roar, rhetoric	

Greek Rho and Latin R were probably rolled, as in Spanish, Italian, and theatrical English.

21	Hebrew	שׂ (שִׂין) (Sin = sihyn) שׁ (שִׁין) (Shin = shihyn)	sun, mess (plain S) shun, mesh (frictional S, SH)	300- Tooth /Teeth = Eat /Press /Double
18	Greek	σ,ς,Σ (σίγμα) (Sigma = SIHYG-mah)	hiss, his	200
19	Latin	s,S (Es = ehss)	hiss (never a buzzing Z sound, as in roses)	
19	English	s,S (Ess)	hiss, his, sure, vision, chassis	

Final Sigma ς appears only at the end of words. Its numerical value is six.

22	Hebrew	תּ (תָּו) (Taw = tahw) ת (תָו) (Thaw = thahw)	totter (plain hard T) thin (frictional T, as a soft TH)	400- Crossed Sticks = Mark /Sign /Write
19	Greek	τ,T (ταῦ) (Tau = tauw)	totter	300
20	Latin	t,T (Tē = tehy)	totter (implosive middle T)	
20	English	t,T (Tee)	totter, ratio, nature, ballet	

—	Hebrew	—	—	—
20	Greek	υ,Υ (ὖ ψιλόν) (Upsilon = OOHW-psih-LOHN)	put rule	400
21 22	Latin	u,U u, (u= oohw) v,V [[Va = wahw]]	put rule, glue wow	
21 22 23	English	u,U (Yoo) v,V (Vee) w,W (Double-Yoo)	put, putt, repute, ruby, suave,tongue vine wine, whine, answer, whole	

Greek Upsilon was originally named ῦ, hoohw, and came originally from the obsolete consonant letter Bau/Digamma, which sounded like our W, but later like our V, and came from the Phoenetian/Hebrew letter Waw, also called Vau or Vav. The Latin vowel U came from a form of Greek Upsilon. Actually, it looked like a V. Someone switched the U and V around and made the V a consonant which sounded like our English W. The Latins called it *consonans U* or *u digammon*. As with Latin J above, so here, we have invented a name and placed it in double brackets. The English later added the W to stand for double V – that is, double U. Confused yet? As you can see, there's a lot of history around this letter. We think the Greeks were on to something with *Bvau*, after the Hebrew *Waw*, and should have stuck with it, but it's too late now to change. Anyway, English changed Latin V (Vā-Wahw) into Vee, originally pronounce Ev, after the analogy of F (Ef). English V is a sonant version of English F, which happens to look like the Greek Bvau (F,ϝ). What goes around comes around.

—	Hebrew	—	—	—
21	Greek	ϕ,Φ (ϕῖ) (Phi = p<hihy; Modern: fihy)	popper (initial explosive P, as in top+hat) (Modern: as in phosphor)	500
—	Latin	ph (a trans-literation)	popper (initial explosive P, as in top+hat)	
—	English	ph (a trans-literation)	phosphor	

Greek Phi was originally spelled *ϕεῖ (p<hehy)*, pronounced as an explosive P. Modern Greek pronounces it as an English F, and modern Grammars of ancient Greek use this pronunciation as an accommodation to the English ear.

—	Hebrew	—	—	—
22	Greek	χ,Χ (χῖ) (Khi or Chi = k<hihy ; Modern: kchihy)	kicker (initial explosive K, as in back+hand) (Modern: as in Scottish loch)	600
—	Latin	ch (a trans-literation)	chrome (initial explosive K, as in back+hand)	
—	English	ch (a trans-literation)	child, chrome, chateau	

Greek Khi was originally spelled *χεῖ (k<hehy)*, pronounced as an explosive K. Modern Greek pronounces it as a Scottish CH, and modern Grammars of ancient Greek use this pronunciation as an accommodation to the English ear.

—	Hebrew	—	—	—
23	Greek	ψ,Ψ (ψῖ) (Psi = psihy)	lips	700
—	Latin	ps (a trans-literation)	lips	
—	English	ps (a trans-literation)	lips, psalm, corps	

Greek Psi was originally spelled ψεῖ, pronounced *psehy*.

—	Hebrew	—	—	—
24	Greek	ω,Ω (ὦ μέγα) (Omega = OHW-MEH-gah)	owe	800
	Latin	o	owe	
	English	o		

Greek Omega was originally named ὦ, ohw. It is a double-O, made from putting two o's together. Compare the Greek Digamma or double gamma ϝ, which looks like two gammas Γ put together, and our English double-U (W) which looks like two U's (which originally looked like V's) put together.

—	Hebrew	ץ צ (Tsadhe)		
—	Greek	ϡ (ϡᾶν /σαμπῖ) (Tsan /Sampi = tsahn /sahm-PIHY)		900
—	Latin	—		
—	English	—		

Greek Tsan or Sampi was long obsolete, but served well as a numeral. Because Tsan look like a Pi leaning on one side, it was called Sampi "as a Pi."

—	Hebrew	ס (Samekh)	balsa	
—	Greek	ξ,Ξ (ξῖ) (Ksi or Xi = ksihy)	box	
23	Latin	x,X (Ex or Ix = ehks or ihyks)	box	
24	English	x,X (Eks)	box, exact, xerox	

Latin X was alternately named Ix, pronounced Ihyks, after the analogy of the Greek letter from which it is derived: Ξ, spelled Ξι and pronounced Ksihy.

—	Hebrew			
20	Greek	υ,Υ (ὖ ψιλόν) (Upsilon = OOHW-psih-LOHN)	put rule	
24	Latin	y,Y (Hu = hihyoohw or heeooh)	Pronounce bee while articulating boo	
25	English	y,Y (Wye)	yarn, why, hymn, baby	

To accommodate words borrowed from Greek, Latin added Y at the end of the alphabet. Its early name was probably Hū, pronounced Hoohw, which is its original name in Greek. It was also referred to as Y graeca, that is, Ī graeca (*Ihy graey-kah*). Who knows where the English name for Y came from, and how we should spell it? *Ye* was a pronoun in older English, which may have prevented the letter Y from being named Yihy. Since English Y shares the sounds of English I, and since Y is the Greek symbol for Latin U, perhaps the idea suggested itself that the consonantal U sound, which is the English W, should combine with the name for English I. We're just guessing. We think the best name for it would have been Yahw, which is the name we made up for Latin J. If you reverse the articulation of Yahw, you get the name for English Y, Why.

—	Hebrew	ז (Zayin)	zuzim	
—	Greek	ζ,Ζ (ζῆτα) (Zeta or Dzeta or Zdeta = dzehy-tah or zdehy-tah)	adze or mazda	
25	Latin	z,Z (Zeta = zehytah)	zuzim	
26	English	z,Z (Zee)	zuzim, quartz, azure	

To accommodate words borrowed from Greek, Latins also added Z at the end of the alphabet, and called it after the name of the Greek letter. The British sometimes call this letter zed, while we Americans have renamed it Zee after the pattern of other letters.

Latin X, Y, and Z were used for transliterations of Greek words.

Further Comments on the Alphabet

The Hebrew and Greek Letter-names are all acrophonic – that is, the first letter says the phonetic value. The Latin and English Letter-names either begin or end with the phonetic value, with a couple of exceptions.

All but three of the Greek names (Epsilon, Omicron, Upsilon) end in a vowel, but these three are actually compound names: (E-psilon, O-micron, U-psilon).

The last letter of the Hebrew alphabet, Tau ת, has the numerical value of 400. But the Hebrew numbers do not end there. The five final forms of consonants, ך ם ן ף ץ, or else a little addition with some other letters, supplies the deficiency:

500 = ך or 400+100 = תק
600 = ם or 400+200 = תר
700 = ן or 400+300 = תשׁ or 400+200+100 = תרק
800 = ף or 400+400 = תת
900 = ץ or 400+400+100 = תתק

Classical Vowel Letters and Sounds

Because English has a very irregular system of vowel pronunciation, English speaking persons often find other languages confusing.

Vowel pronunciations for the Classical Languages are very regular. There are five Classical vowels, each vowel has a short and a long, and two vowels have a Consonantal pronunciation, called a Glide.

	"A"	"E"	"I"	"O"	"U"
Short	yacht	bed	chin	oh	put
Long	yawn	hey	machine	owe	vacuum or rule
Glide			savior (Y sound.)		Suave (W sound.)

Classical Latin originally had one symbol for each vowel, whether Long, Short or Glide. In modern Latin grammars and elsewhere, *Modern Latin script* places a Macron (a line above the letter, ¯) over a vowel in order to indicate that it is Long (ā, Ā; ē, Ē; ī, Ī; ō, Ō; ū, Ū). Less frequently, *Modern Latin script* also adds two symbols to represent the two Glides (j,J for Glide "I", and v,V for Glide "U").

Ancient Greek originally had one symbol for each vowel, whether Long, Short or Glide. *Later Classical Greek* added two symbols to represent Long E (η) and Long O (ω).

Original Hebrew had no separate vowel symbols at all. Vowels were interpolated between the Consonants – which is a fancy way of saying that they guessed what the word was from the consonants alone. If we saw HBRWSND we might guess it stood for H*e*BR*e*W S*ou*ND. Of course, it could stand for HeBReWS NoD, or H*u*B R*ay* W*a*S N*ee*D*y* – which might make sense in some context. Adding the vowels would certainly provide greater accuracy. So in *Later Hebrew*, separate Vowel Points were added in order to represent each Long Vowel, each Short Vowel, and each Consonant Glide; and another Vowel Point was added to represent a Very Short or *Half-Length (Hateph)* Vowel for A, E, and O, and an Extra Short or *Quarter-Length (Shewa)* Vowel for E.

The Five Classic Vowels

Hebrew Vowel Points usually appear below the Hebrew consonantal letter. In the examples below, we have used the consonant Aleph (א). The names of the Hebrew Vowel Points are in parentheses. (*Hateph* = short; *Hatuph* = swift)

Various English spellings of the classical vowel sounds appear below each chart.

"A"	Half	Short	Long
Hebrew	(Hateph Pathah) אֲ alone, ago	(Pathah) אַ yacht	(Qamets Gadol) אָ yawn
Greek	—	α,A (Alpha) yacht	α,A (Alpha) yawn
Latin	—	a,A yacht	ā,Ā yawn
English	—	a,A yacht	a,A yawn

English Spellings for Classical "A" Sound:
Short A: watch, hawk, taught, talk, yacht, ah, got, cough, thought (not cat).
Long A: father, yawn, sauce, calm, awe, hurrah, aah, bomb, knowledge, heart, (never sounds like A in kate).

"E"	Quarter & Half	Short	Long
Hebrew	(Shewa) אְ derive (Hateph Seghol) אֱ enemy	(Seghol) אֶ bed	(Tsere) אֵ hey (Tsere Yodh) אֵי hey
Greek	—	ϵ,E (Epsilon) bed	h,H (Eta) hey
Latin	—	e,E bed	ē,E hey
English	—	e,E bed	e,E hey

English Spellings for Classical "E" Sound:
Short E: bed, been, bread, friend, heifer, many, said, says, foederal, aesthetic.
Long E: crepe, hey, great, veil, feign, freight, table, date, hay, bait, valet, gauge, (never sounds like E in me, met, meet).

"I"	Short	Long	Glide
Hebrew	(Hireq Qatan) אִ chin	(Hireq Yodh) אִי machine	(Yodh) י savior
Greek	ι,I (Iota) chin	ι,I (Iota) machine	ι,I (Iota) savior
Latin	i,I chin	ī,Ī machine	j,J savior
English	i,I chin	i,I machine	i,I savior

English Spellings for Classical "I" Sound:

Short I: chin, myth, forfeit, sieve, mountain, pretty, women, business, England.

Long I: farina, machine, fatigue, ceiling, field, me, meet, mete, meat, key, city, amoeba, Caesar, people, radii, (never sounds like I in kite).

Glide I: savior, brilliant, spaniel, yoyo, tortilla, hallelujah, unity, vacuum, ewe.

"O"	Half	Short	Long
Hebrew	(Hateph Qamets) אֳ collision	(Qamets Hatuph) אָ oh	(Holem) אֹ owe (Holem Waw) וֹ owe
Greek		ο,Ο (Omicron) oh	ω,Ω (Omega) owe
Latin		o,O oh	ō,Ō owe
English		o,O oh	o,O owe

English Spellings for Classical "O" Sound:
Short O: odor, oh, note, goat, (never sounds like O in not, to).
Long O: over, low, owe, ohm, floor, loan, lone, toe, soul, though, bureau, sew.

"U"	Short	Long	Glide
Hebrew	(Qibbuts) אֻ put	(Shureq) וּ rule	(Waw) ו suave
Greek	υ,Υ (Upsilon) put	υ,Υ (Upsilon) vacuum	υ,Υ (Upsilon) suave
Latin	u,U put	ū,Ū rule	v,V suave
English	u,U put	u,U vacuum	u,U suave

English Spellings for Classical "U" Sound:

Short U: put, look, would, woman, wolf, (never sounds like U in putt).

Long U: unit, vacuum, you, cue, feud, beauty, few, ewe, cute, impugn, pugh OR truly, fruit, sue, to, too, two, group, through, grew, move, shoe.

Glide U: suave, quire, choir, wow, what, one.

BOOKS ON CLASSICAL PRONUNCIATION

Vox Graeca, A Guide to the Pronunciation of Classical Greek, by William Sidney Allen, Cambridge: Cambridge University Press, Third Edition, 1987.

Vox Latina, A Guide to the Pronunciation of Classical Latin, by William Sidney Allen, Cambridge: Cambridge University Press, Second Edition, 1978.

Outlines of Latin Phonetics, by Max Niedermann, edited by H.A. Strong and H. Stewart, London: George Routledge & Sons, Limited, 1910.

Pronunciation of Ancient Greek, by Wilhelm Friederich Blass, translated by W.J. Purton, Cambridge: Cambridge University Press, 1890.

The Sounds of Latin, by Roland G. Kent, Baltimore Maryland: Linquistic Society of America, 1940.

The Pronunciation of Greek and Latin, by Edgar H. Surtevant, Philadelphia: Linquistic Society of America, Second Edition, 1940.

Article Nine

On Christian Doctrine by Augustine

A large part of St. Augustine's Treatise "On Christian Doctrine" is a defense of Christian instruction in Grammar, Logic and Rhetoric. Especially Book II, paragraph 23 on Grammar, paragraphs 48 -53 on Logic, paragraphs 54, 55 and most of Book IV on Rhetoric. Here are some excerpts.

"THE SCIENCE OF REASONING is of very great service in searching into and unraveling all sorts of questions that come up in Scripture, only in the use of it we must guard against the love of wrangling and the childish vanity of entrapping an adversary." (II, 48)

Augustine discusses the argument of Paul in First Corinthians 15:12-20 that if there is no resurrection of the dead, then Christ is not risen, then our preaching is in vain, then we are false witnesses, then your faith is in vain, then you are yet in your sins, then those who have fallen asleep in Christ have perished. "But all these false inferences followed legitimately from the opinion of those who said that there is no resurrection of the dead. These inferences, then, being repudiated as false, it follows that since they would be true if the dead rise not, there will be a resurrection of the dead. As then valid conclusions may be drawn not only from true but from false propositions, the laws of valid reasoning may easily be learnt in the schools . . . . But the truth of propositions must be inquired into in the sacred books. . . ." (II, 49)

". . . [T]he validity of logical sequences is not a thing devised by men, but is observed and noted by them. . . . [I]t exists eternally in the reason of things, and has its origin with God. For as the man who narrates the order of events does not himself create that order; . . . and as he who points out the stars and their movements does not point out anything that he himself or any other man has ordained; in the same way, he who says, 'When the consequent is false, the antecedent must also be false,' says what is most true; but he does not himself make it so, he only points out that it is so. And it is upon this rule that the reasoning . . . from the Apostle Paul proceeds. For the antecedent is, 'There is no resurrection of the dead. . . .' . . . the necessary consequence is 'Then Christ is not risen.' But this consequence is false, for Christ has risen; therefore the antecedent is also false. . . . We conclude therefore that there is a resurrection of the dead. . . . This rule, then, that when the consequent is removed, the antecedent must also be removed, is not made by man, but only pointed out by him. And this rule has reference to the validity of the reasoning, not to the truth of the statement." (II, 50)

Article Ten

The Christian Use of Logic

YOU WILL NOT FIND the word "logic" in your Bible concordance. You will, however, find such words as "think, consider, reason." There is good reasoning, poor reasoning and evil reasoning. What does the Bible say about "logic."

We will begin with a little word study. From the Greek word for reasoning [*διαλέγω*: dialegO] we derive the word dialectic, which is that branch of logic which teaches the rules and modes of reasoning. The word is used thirteen times in the New Testament, always in the sense of "reasoning." Here are some selected instances from the book of Acts:

> Now according to custom, Paul went in to them [in the synagogue] and for three sabbaths **reasoned** with them from the Scriptures, **fully opening and presenting** that it was necessary for Christ to have suffered and to have risen from among those dead, and that "Jesus is this Christ Whom I announce to you." And some of them were **persuaded** . . . . — Acts 17:2-4 Very literal translation (v.l.t.)

> Therefore, first of all, he [Paul] **was reasoning** – both in the synagogue, with the Jews and with those *Gentiles who* were devout, and in the market place each and every day, with those *who* were happening by. — Acts 17:17 (v.l.t.)

> And he [Paul] **reasoned** in the synagogue every sabbath, and persuaded Jews and Greeks. — Acts 18:4 (v.l.t.)

> . . . But he [Paul] himself, having entered into the synagogue, **reasoned** with the Jews. — Acts 18:19 (v.l.t.)

> And having entered into the synagogue, he [Paul] spoke boldly, **reasoning** and **persuading** the things concerning the kingdom of God for three months. . . . he separated the disciples, **reasoning** each day in the school of a certain Tyrannus, and this was for two years, so that all those inhabiting Asia heard the

word of the Lord Jesus, both Jews and Greeks. — Acts 19:8-10 (v.l.t.)

Now on the first *day* of the week, the disciples having been assembled to break bread, Paul **reasoned** with them, . . . as Paul **was reasoning** on longer . . . — Acts 20:7,9 (v.l.t.)

. . . [Felix] heard him [Paul] concerning faith in Christ. And as he [Paul] **reasoned** concerning righteousness and self-control and the judgement about to happen . . . — Acts 24:24,25 (v.l.t.)

From these texts we make the following observations:

1. It was the custom among the Jews to reason from the Scriptures in their synagogues.
2. Reasoning included "fully opening" and "presenting," and "persuading."
3. Paul reasoned from the Scriptures wherever he went: Jewish synagogue, Gentile marketplace, Gentile school, Christian assembly, and even before Gentile governors.
4. The Christian faith is presented by reasoning, and is spread by continuous daily reasoning.

From all of this, we can conclude that logic is very important to the Christian faith. Just how important is it?

. . . **having girded up the loins of your mind** . . . As newborn babes, earnestly desire **the unadulterated milk of reasoning** [λογικόν: *logikon*] in order that by it you may grow. . . . Now sanctify the Lord God in your hearts [=minds]; and always be prepared for (presenting) **a logical defense** to everyone who requests **reason** from you concerning the hope which is among you, (doing so) with meekness and fear . . . .— First Peter 1:13; 2:2; 3:15 (v.l.t.) [The Greek word *logikon* is translated "of the word" in the KJV, NASV, NKJV, YOUNG'S, etc.; "spiritual" in the RSV, NIV, etc.; but *logikon* means "what belongs to the sphere of reason."]

12:1 Therefore, I exhort you, brethren, by the compassions of God, to present your bodies *as a consecrated* sacrifice: living, holy, acceptable to God, which is your **logical** [λογικὴν: *logikEn*] priestly-ministry; And do not conform yourselves to this age, but be transformed by **the renewing of your mind**, in order for you to **prove** what *is* the will of God: what is good and acceptable and mature. — Romans 12:1,2 (v.l.t.) [*logikEn* is the same Greek word as in First Peter 2:2 above.]

Brethren, do not become children **in *your* minds**, rather, be infants in malice, but **in *your* minds become mature**. — First Corinthians 14:20 (v.l.t.)

For the weapons of our warfare *are* not fleshly. Rather *they are* powerful in God for *the* pulling down of strong defensive *barriers*: *for* pulling down **reasonings [/logical arguments],** and every high *barrier which* lifts itself up against the **knowledge** of God, and *for* capturing **every thought** [/all intellect] to the obedience of Christ. — Second Corinthians 10:4,5 (v.l.t.)

. . . I am appointed for the **logical defense** of the Gospel. — Philippians 1:17 (v.l.t.)

We are to earnestly desire logic, always be prepared to give a logical defense to those who request reason from us, and be transformed by God through the renewing of our minds to prove God's will through logical service. Logic is central to Christian faith and practice. What are we to do with this logic?

. . . **proving** what is acceptable to the Lord . . . . do not become mindless, rather, *be ye always* understanding what the will of the Lord is. — Ephesians 5:10,17 (v.l.t.)

And this I pray, in order that your love may abound more and more in **knowledge** and all **understanding** in order for you to **prove** the things that (make a) difference . . . — Philippians 1:10 (v.l.t.)

Test and prove all things; retain what is good [i.e. true]. — First Thessalonians 5:21 (v.l.t.)

Beloved, do not believe every *prophetic* spirit, but **test and prove the spirits,** whether they are from God; because many false prophets have gone out into the world. — First John 4:1 (v.l.t.)

But Saul [/Paul] was becoming more powerful [in reasoning], and confounded the Jews who dwelt in Damascus, **proving** that This One is the Christ. — Acts 9:22 (v.l.t.)

Therefore, knowing the fear of the Lord, we **persuade** men. — Second Corinthians 5:11 (v.l.t.)

But not all reasoning is good reasoning.

For **corrupt reasonings** come out of the heart . . . — Matthew 15:19 (v.l.t.)

For **evil reasonings** go out from within the heart of men . . . — Mark 7:21 (v.l.t.)

. . . they became **empty** in their **own reasonings** . . . For the **mind of the flesh** *is* death; but the mind of the spirit *is* life and peace. On account of this, the **mind of the flesh** *is* enmity toward God, for it is not in submission to the law of God, for neither *is it* able *to be in submission*. So those *who* are *walking* in *their* flesh, they are not able to please God. — Romans 1:21; 8:6-8 (v.l.t.)

We must be careful of those who are irrational, and sneak within the fold of the assembly.

But there came also false prophets among the people [of Israel], as also there will be false teachers among you, who will stealthily introduce destructive heresies . . . and many will follow their destructive ways, through whom the way of truth will be blasphemed. And with avarice they will exploit you with well-formed words . . . But these – **as naturally irrational animals** who have been born for capture and spoil, *while* blaspheming regarding those things of which they are ignorant, – shall utterly perish in their corruption. . . . the untaught and unsteady distort . . . the . . . Scriptures [force a false confession by torture] to their very own destruction. — Second Peter 2:1-3,12; 3:16 (v.l.t.)

But these [dreamers] speak evil of whatever things they indeed do not know, but **whatever things they do understand,** ***they understand*** **naturally, as irrational animals**, *and* in these things they corrupt themselves. — Jude 10 (v.l.t.)

Always learning, and never able to come to *the* **knowledge** of *the* truth. — Second Timothy 3:7 (v.l.t.)

FUNDAMENTAL LAWS OF LOGIC

There are three fundamental laws of logic, and all three can be found expressed in the language of the Bible.

1. The *Law of Identity* says that if any statement is true, then it is true – truth does not change.

For I am the LORD, I change not . . . — Malachi 3:6.

. . . with [God] is no variableness, neither shadow of turning. — James 1:17.

But He is in one mind, and who can turn him? . . . –Job 23:13.

A double minded man is unstable in all his ways. –James 1:8.

2. The *Law of Non-Contradiction* says that no statement can be both true and false at the same time and in the same respect.

. . . and the scripture cannot be broken; — John 10:35

. . . no lie is of the truth. — First John 2:21

> . . . God, that cannot lie . . . — Titus 1:2.

> . . . *it was* impossible for God to lie . . . — Hebrews 6:18.

> . . . He [God] cannot deny himself. — Second Timothy 2:13

3. The *Law of the Excluded Middle* says that any statement is either true or false, there is no other possibility.

> So likewise, whosoever he be of you that forsaketh not all that he hath, he cannot be my disciple. — Luke 14:33

> And if by grace, then *is it* no more of works: otherwise grace is no more grace. But if *it be* of works, then is it no more grace: otherwise work is no more work. — Romans 11:6

> Ye cannot drink the cup of the Lord, and the cup of devils: ye cannot be partakers of the Lord's table, and of the table of devils. — First Corinthians 10:21

All other principles and operations of logic are derived from these three laws. If these laws are found in the language of the Bible, and if the Bible is the absolute truth, and the source of only true propositions, then the science of logic is an absolute science – when properly performed.

Article Eleven

History and Research on the Teaching of Math

FORMAL ARITHMETIC AT AGE TEN, HURRIED OR DELAYED?

Provincialism is the word which we use to describe an opinion which is narrow and self-centered in perspective. Because the common practice in our culture in our day is to begin formal instruction in arithmetic as early as age four or five, many have questioned the suggestion that one may wait until age ten before beginning formal instruction in arithmetic. Waiting until age ten for formal instruction in arithmetic is often misnomered "late start" or "delayed academics."

A broader perspective would examine more than what is simply the prevailing practice of a particular culture at a particular time – especially if that practice is a policy largely imposed by the government. We don't claim to have the last word on the subject, but we have examined the matter more broadly, and in this article we will present some of the things which we have discovered. We will quote only a small selection from authorities we have found, and we will allow you to form your own opinion before we comment.

THE HISTORICAL PERSPECTIVE

What the Ancients Did

> Strange though it may seem at first, it is nevertheless quite clear that addition, subtraction, multiplication and division – comparatively simple operations, which we inflict on our children while they are still quite young – were, in antiquity, far beyond the horizon of any primary school. The widespread use

of calculating-tables and counting-machines [abacus] shows that not many people could add up – and this goes on being true to a much later date, even in educated circles. — *A History of Education in Antiquity*, by Henri I. Marrou, translated by George Lamb, Sheed and Ward, London, 1956, page 158.

What the Mediaevals and Later Did

[page 204] Before the Reformation there was little or nothing accomplished in the way of public education in England. In the monasteries some instruction was given by monks, but we have no evidence that any branch of mathematics was taught to the youth (some idea of the state of arithmetical knowledge may be gathered from an ancient custom at Shrewsbury, where a person was deemed of age when he knew how to count up to twelve pence. See Tylor's Primitive Culture, New York, 1889, Vol. I., p. 242.) . . . In the sixteenth century, on the suppression of the monasteries, schools were founded in considerable numbers . . . and for centuries have served for the education of the sons mainly of the nobility and gentry. In these schools the ancient classics were the almost exclusive subjects of study; mathematical teaching was unknown there. Perhaps the demands of every-day life forced upon the boys a knowledge of counting and of the very simplest computations, but we are safe in saying that, before the close of the last century, the ordinary boy of England's famous public schools [page 205] could not divide 2021 by 43, though such problems had been performed centuries before according to the teaching of Brahmagupta and Bhaskara by boys brought up on the far-off banks of the Ganges . . . . All the information we could find respecting the education of the upper classes points to the conclusion that arithmetic was neglected, and that De Morgan was right in his statement that as late as the 18th century there could have been no such thing as a teacher of arithmetic in schools like Eton. In 1750, Warren Hastings, [page 206] who had been attending Westminster, was put into a commercial school, that he might study arithmetic and book-keeping before sailing for Bengal.

At the universities little was done in mathematics before the middle of the 17th century . . . . During the reign of Queen Elizabeth, fresh statutes were given, excluding all mathematics from the course of undergraduates, presumably because this study pertained to practical life, and could, therefore, have no claim to attention in a university . . . .

[page 207] This scorn and ignorance of the art of computation by all but commercial classes is seen in Germany as well as England.

It was not before the present century that arithmetic and other branches of mathematics found admission into England's public schools. At Harrow "vulgar fractions, Euclid, geography, and modern history were first studied" in 1829. At the Merchant Taylors' School "mathematics, writing, and arithmetic were added in 1829." At Eton mathematics was not compulsory till 1851.

Since the art of calculation was no more considered a part of a liberal education than was the art of shoe-making, it is natural to find the study of arithmetic relegated to the commercial schools. The poor boy sometimes studied it; the rich boy did not need it. In the Latin schools it was unknown, but in schools for the poor it was sometimes taught . . .

[page 217] The first arithmetics used in the American colonies were English works . . . . The earliest arithmetic written and printed in America appeared anonymously in Boston in 1729. Though a work of considerable merit, it seems to have been used very little . . . . In 1788 appeared at Newburyport the *New and Complete System of Arithmetic* by Nicholas Pike . . . . It was intended for advanced schools . . . . [page 218] Reform in arithmetical teaching in the United States did not begin until the publication of Warren Colburn, in 1821, [page 219] of the *Intellectual Arithmetic*. This was the first fruit of Pestalozzian ideas on American soil . . . . The success of this little book was extraordinary. But American teachers in Colburn's time, and long after, never quite succeeded in successfully engrafting Pestalozzian principles on written arithmetic . . . .

—*A History of Elementary Mathematics with Hints on Methods of Teaching*, by Florian Cajori, Ph. D., London: Macmillan Company, 1917, pages 204-207, 217-219.

. . . *The American Calculator,* first published in 1828 . . . is reasonably typical of the colonial period. This text was used with older students (beginning at about the age of eleven). It was complete in itself, not one book of a series such as the texts that evolved in later years. — *Readings in the History of Mathematics Education*, edited by James K. Bidwell and Robert G. Clason, National Council of Teachers of Mathematics, Washington, D. C., n. d., page 2.

. . . The study of it [arithmetic] used to be put off to a very late period. Scholars under twelve or thirteen years of age were not considered capable of learning it, and generally they were not capable. Many persons were obliged to leave school before they were old enough to commence the study of it. — *Readings in the History of Mathematics Education*, page 25, taken from "Teaching of Arithmetic," text of an address delivered by Warren Colburn before the American Institute of Instruction in Boston, August, 1830, reprinted from the *Elementary School Teacher* 12 (June 1912): 463-480.

[In the early seventeenth century, the grammar school curriculum was] almost certainly confined to Latin grammar, the Catechism and Bible study . . . . [P]upils arriving at Oxford and Cambridge frequently did not have any knowledge of Arabic numerals, to say nothing of the elementary arithmetical operations. —*A History of Mathematics Education in England*, by Goeffrey Howson, Cambridge University Press, Cambridge, 1981, page 30.

When It Changed

. . . Pestalozzi. It is to the latter (1803) that we owe the greatest impetus in the rational teaching of arithmetic to young children. The essential features of his reform are as follows: (1) He taught arithmetic to children as soon as they entered school, basing his work on perception. (2) He insisted upon a knowledge of numbers and the simplest operations, using objects, before the figures were taught. (3) He approached the subject of fractions in the same way. (4) He made arithmetic the most prominent subject in the school, and it is to his influence that its present prominence is due. (5) He emphasized oral arithmetic, a movement that led to the great success of Warren Colburn in the United States . . . . Tuerk (1816) did not wish arithmetic in what we call the first grade, nor before the child reached the age of 10 years, and of this idea there is just at present a temporary revival as if it were a new discovery, although it was practically universal before Pestalozzi . . . . — *A Cyclopedia of Education*, Edited by Paul Monroe, New York: The Macmillan Co., 1919, Volume I, Article on *The History of Teaching Arithmetic*, by David Eugene Smith, Ph D., LL.D., Professor of Mathematics, Teachers College, Columbia University, New York City, page 206.

Summary of the Historical Evidence

The material which we have read indicates that the formally teaching of arithmetic to young children was not practiced by the ancients, the mediaevals, nor up to modern times. In fact, it was common to withhold formal instruction in arithmetic until somewhere between the ages of fifteen and eighteen.

It was not until the sixteenth century that arithmetic began to be taught to children as young as age twelve, or even ten.

It was Pestalozzi, at the beginning of the nineteenth century, who began to teach arithmetic to children as young as age six or seven, though the practice of waiting until age ten persisted well into the twentieth century.

So to wait until age ten to teach arithmetic is actually, from an historical perspective, to advocate an "early start." It is only from a decidedly modern perspective – a provincial perspective – that waiting until age ten would appear to be a "late start." We have not discovered any material which might indicate the contrary.

THE RESEARCH PERSPECTIVE

The research is quoted here to demonstrate the point at hand. We recognize that studies are open to various interpretations.

Inefficient, Period

> . . . early childhood may simply be an inefficient period in which to try to teach skills that can be relatively quickly learned in adolescence. — *Prime Time for Education: Early Childhood or Adolescence*? by William D. Rohwer, Jr., Harvard Educational Review, Vol. 41, No. 3, August 1971, page 316, from the summary.

Children Don't Do Better in Math, But They Do Learn to Hate School

> In a cross-national study of mathematics achievement (Husen, 1967), stratified samples were drawn from the total population of all students enrolled in the modal grade for thirteen-year-olds in twelve different nations: Finland, Germany, Japan, Sweden, Belgium, France, Israel, Netherlands, Australia, England, Scotland, and the United States. Among other observations, a score was obtained for each student on a standardized test of mathematics achievement and, in an attitude inventory, on a scale designed to reflect the degree of positive attitude toward school. For each national sample, information was also obtained yielding the median age of school entry. Thus it is possible to rank the samples in terms of age of school entry and to obtain rank correlation coefficients between this variable and those of ranked mean mathematics test scores and ranked mean attitude-toward-school scores. The results reveal a negligible negative correlation between age of school entry and mathematics achievement (rho = -. 06, p>. 05) and a strong negative correlation between entry age and attitude toward school (rho = -. 72, p<. 01). The average performance of students on the mathematics test did not improve significantly as a function of additional years of schooling despite the fact that the extremes of the nations sampled were separated by nearly two years of formal academic work. More alarming is the suggestion inherent in the high negative correlation between entry age and attitudes toward school that the longer the student

was enrolled prior to testing the more negative his attitudes toward school itself. Clearly, there is no indication in these results that revising the mandatory age of school entry to younger levels would improve the student's chances of subsequent school success.

Of course it might be argued that these results do not confront the issue directly since the argument in favor of earlier school entry is most persuasive for low-income children. The Husen (1967) report, however, speaks directly to this point as well. For all of the students tested, information was obtained to permit a categorization of father's occupation. Accordingly, correlation coefficients can be computed separately for two large groupings within each national sample, that is, for those occupations falling in the higher-SES categories (clerical through professional) and for those falling in lower-SES categories (skilled through unskilled manual). The correlations between entry age and mathematics achievement test scores are not significantly different from zero in either case but it is interesting to note that the coefficient for the higher-SES categories is positive (rho = +. 19, p>. 05) while that for the lower-SES categories is negative (rho = -. 39, p>. 05). Thus, even in its qualified version, the presumption that early school entry promotes school success in children from lower income families finds no support in the results of the Husen (1967) study; indeed, these data appear to contradict the presumption. In these examples, support can be found for the assertion that legitimizing curricular demands in terms of later extra-school success is vulnerable with respect to the typically rigid timing of those demands. — *Prime Time for Education: Early Childhood or Adolescence*? page 322.

Fractional Reserve

Research in grade placement and readiness has had two effects on the arithmetic curriculum. They are commonly known as the "stepped-up" curriculum and the "stretched-out" curriculum. The stepped-up curriculum is largely due to the study of the Committee of Seven . . . . Over a period of a few years and in hundreds of cities, the committee sought to determine the mental age level at which various topics could be taught to "completion." Typically, they found that addition of like fractions required a mental age of 10 to 11 years, and unlike fractions, 14 to 15 years. Two-figure division required a mental age of 12 to 13 years. As a result, many courses of study and textbooks moved selected topics to higher grade levels. Hence, the name "stepped-up" curriculum . . . .

. . . Benezet in Manchester, N H, carried out a study from which he concluded "If I had my way, I would omit arithmetic from the first six grades . . .

. The whole subject could be postponed until the seventh year . . . and mastered in two years' study." This led many people to conclude erroneously that all arithmetic could be deferred until the seventh grade. However, closer observation showed that there was much arithmetic taught in grades I to VI. Thiele visited the Manchester, N. H., schools and said: "Firsthand observation leads me to conclude that Benezet did not prove that arithmetic can be taught incidentally . . . . Instead, he provided conclusive evidence that children profit greatly from an organized arithmetic program which stresses number concepts, relations, and meaning. Buswell found that Benezet had only deferred "formal" arithmetic, and that all other aspects of a desirable arithmetic curriculum were present. Of the formal arithmetic, Buswell said, "I should like to eliminate it altogether." On the same topic, "deferred arithmetic," Brueckner says, "From these studies the conclusion should be drawn not that arithmetic should be postponed, [page 18] but that the introduction of social arithmetic in the first few grades does not result in any loss in efficiency when the formal computational aspect of the work is introduced later on, say in grade three."

— *What does Research say about Arithmetic?* By Vincent J. Glennon and C.W. Hunnicutt, National Education Association, Washington D. C., 1952, page 17.

Drive Them to Abstraction

Harris has pointed out that in the first stages of the development of the mind, the mathematical process is decidedly more complex than the other mental processes which are taking place at that time.

"The reason why it requires a higher activity of thought to think quantity [abstract number] and understand mathematics than it does to perceive quality (or things and environments) [physical objects] lies right in this point. The thought of quantity is a double thought. It first thinks quality [object] and then negates it, or thinks it away. In other words, it abstracts from quality. It first thinks thing and environment (quality), and then thinks both as the same in kind or as repetitions of the same. A thing becomes a unit [number] when it is repeated so that it is within an environment of duplicates itself [number among numbers]."

Several very important consequences for the practical teaching of mathematics can be drawn from the fact formulated.

The mathematical process may not be introduced before [page 50] there is a considerable stock of qualitative facts in the child's mind on which to work, and not until the child's mental powers are sufficiently developed to take the steps implied in even the simplest mathematical concept. It is a question whether we are not tending to introduce the abstractions of mathematics too early. The German boy who enters the gymnasium at the age of nine is expected to know only the four fundamental operations on integers, and in his first year (corresponding to our fourth grade) he learns further only the German weights and measures (decimal system) and the simplest operation with decimals; by this time our children are introduced to the complexities of fractions, common and decimal, to our system of weights and measures, far more complicated than the international (decimal) system used in Germany, and even sometimes to percentage and some use of generalized (literal) numbers. And yet the German boy does not come out behind at the end of the race ten years later.

[page 100] It has even been urged that no formal study of mathematics is needed at all, but that pre-collegiate mathematics at least could be developed incidentally in the study of natural phenomena. Though this proposal is extreme, it contains much good; yet the time must come when the child sees that he will save himself much trouble if he makes a mathematical tool; and practices with it enough to have a fair amount of skill in its use. The concrete application gives zest to the work, but there must be occasions when the mathematical process itself is a centre of interest.

— *The Teaching of Mathematics in the Elementary and the Secondary School,* by J.W.A. Young, Longmans, Green and Co. New York, 1919, page 49, 50, 100.

Math Class Postponed

[page 288] Several groups of important investigations on the teaching of arithmetic have contributed findings that have led schools to make changes in the organization of the curriculum. One group of studies dealt with the effect of postponing or deferring the teaching of arithmetic in the primary grades. Included in this group are the studies by Ballard in 1912, Taylor in 1916, Wilson in 1930, and Benezet in 1935-36. In these studies formal arithmetic instruction was withheld in one group and administered as usual in another group. At the end of the experimental period, the comparative achievements of the two groups were measured. In each case the experimenter recommended the postponement of "formal" arithmetic – Ballard for two years or the age of seven, Taylor for one year, Wilson for two years, and Benezet until grade 5.

On the basis of these and other studies the plan of eliminating formal arithmetic instruction from grades one and two, sometimes also grade three, has been adopted by a considerable number of school systems. In some systems there is not even an approved plan of informal or incidental arithmetic. Such a procedure fails to recognize certain very important facts about the studies referred to above. A careful reading of the reports of these four experiments shows that while formal practice on computational processes was postponed in the experimental groups, there was a great deal of use made in these classes of various kinds of activities, games, projects, and social situations through which the child was brought into contact with numbers and given the opportunity to use them informally in meaningful ways. It is especially clear in the studies by Wilson and Benezet that arithmetic was not in fact postponed at all. It is evident that what happened in these two studies was that computational arithmetic was replaced by what I called earlier in this paper, social arithmetic. In each study the plan was to emphasize number meanings, to develop an understanding of the ways in which number functions in the daily lives of children both in and out of school, and to develop what is called number "readiness" for the more formal work to follow . . . .

— *Mathematics Teacher*, Volume 31, October, 1938, pages 287-292, article "Deferred Arithmetic" by Leo J. Brueckner, from a paper read at the annual meeting of the National Council of Teachers of Mathematics in Atlantic City, J. J., Feb. 26, 1938.

Two Years Before the Math

[page 195] Preliminary to any useful discussion of the topic it is wise to clarify the issue. Although the proposal to defer parts of arithmetic has been made periodically for a number of decades, the present rather widespread interest was no doubt stimulated very directly by the series of three articles written by Superintendent Benezet and published in the *Journal of the National Education Association* in 1935 and 1936. In the first of these articles Mr. Benezet expresses his belief as follow: "If I had my way, I would omit arithmetic from the first six grades . . . . The whole subject of arithmetic could be postponed until the seventh year of school and it could be mastered in two years' study by any normal child." — *The Mathematics Teacher*, Volume 31, Number 5, May 1938, article "Deferred Arithmetic" by G.T. Buswell, pages 195-200.

The Chorean War

. . . The exaggerated ideas of the efficacy of arithmetic in the cultivation of the mind and the resulting over-pressure and premature training are strongly condemned by [studies in mental] hygiene . . . .

. . . An English physician, Dr. Sturgis, has studied chorea in children, and many of these cases he has found due, as he thinks, to causes connected with the school work, and arithmetic he deems an especial factor in producing the disorder. In the case of a nervous child he maintains that working sums is liable to cause chorea. [page 643, Chorea is an irregular nervous twitching of a muscle or group of muscles, accompanied by irritability, forgetfulness, sleep disturbance, visual difficulties. The majority of cases begin between ages five and ten, and usually go away after the child is removed from classroom and schoolwork for three months.] In the case of some children, as pointed out by General Walker, work in arithmetic is a frequent cause of worry and interference with sleep. When children do sums in their dreams, this is a danger signal . . . . Certain habits of interference of association, certain arrests, as they have been called by Dr. Triplett, illustrate very well these secondary effects of certain methods and processes of learning.

Number forms sometimes illustrate the secondary effects of instruction. Such habits represent not only so much mental ballast, but usually also interference of association and often the germs of pathological neuroses. They are probably pretty common. The counting habit, arithmomania, so-called, is likely to have several representatives in each class, according to Triplett's investigations. This is a real handicap, filling the mind with quantitative ideas to the exclusion of causal relations.

Hygiene is especially concerned with the problem of the age when work in arithmetic should be begun. In order to answer this question it is necessary to consider briefly the mental operations involved in arithmetical work. In the simpler study of number and number relations, in addition, subtraction, and the rest, the process of learning is chiefly one of acquiring habitual associations. What hygiene demands here is that these should be formed naturally and that interference of association or mental confusion shall be avoided.

Again, in teaching arithmetic to very young children all sorts of objective methods and devices have been developed, and these are deemed necessary in such instruction. Still further, it appears that the number forms and the like which are common in adults are developed in the early years of instruction. From these are likely to develop artificial and grotesque habits of thought, as illustrated by Dr. Triplett's so-called arrests and by some of the number forms.

The problem of the proper age for beginning arithmetic is then something like this. At what age can a child be drilled in arithmetical processes without the aid of artificial devices and the like which are likely to persist as arrests or habits of interference of association; and at what age should the study of logic be begun; at what age does the child have a nascent interest for arithmetical work? We have at present no adequate data for answering these questions, but until further investigations have been made the verdict of hygiene is that ordinarily formal instruction in arithmetic should be postponed until at least the age of 8 or 10. The Italian physiologist, Mosso, President G. Stanley Hall, Professor Patrick, and others agree in condemning formal instruction in this subject before this age. "Mathematics in every form," writes Professor Patrick, "is a subject conspicuously ill-fitted to the child mind. It deals not with real things, but with abstractions. When referred to concrete objects, it concerns not the objects themselves, but their relations to each other. It involves comparison, analysis, abstraction . . . . The grotesque number forms which so many children have, and which originate in this period, are evidence of the necessity which the child feels of giving some kind of bodily shape to these abstractions which he is compelled to study."

The practical teachings of the hygiene of instruction as regards arithmetic may be summed up in the light of our present knowledge somewhat as follows: the formal instruction in this subject should not be begun before the age of 8 or 10. Arithmetical work before this should be spontaneous activity on the part of the child. By postponing arithmetic until this age, it is possible to do away for the most part with artificial devices and methods which may lead to arrests or interference of association later on. The work in arithmetic should be simple, and the complex examples in logic and the like should be eliminated. In the case of nervous children special care should be taken to avoid worry and the development of neuroses like chorea. And, in general, special attention should be given in this subject to the secondary effects which are important from the point of view of mental hygiene.

— *Cyclopedia of Education*, p. 208, article by William H. Burnham, Ph.D., Professor of Pedagogy and School Hygiene, Clark University, Worcester, Mass.

Moore Says Less

[Page 10] In 1972 under the auspices of the Hewitt Research Foundation we conducted a broad investigation of approximately 3,000 sources in early childhood education research and other literature . . . . The Hewitt investigation . . . traces the single idea of school readiness . . . . We then carefully checked the bibliographies of relevant items for further sources . . . These various sources yielded more than 7,000 studies and papers . . . . About 1,000 items were closely analyzed and categorized, of which 700 or so have been included here.

[Page 11] Scott cautions wisely that much "research" in education fails to produce new information that can be used beyond the situation in which it is acquired . . . . But when the findings of such studies, in concert with the findings of many other studies, all point in the same direction, the implications deserve examination.

. . . It is obviously unscholarly, unethical, and unwise to wave aside a possible truth because it does not agree with presently accepted knowledge or conventional practice. Some of the trends here identified in early childhood literature are provocative in this respect.

. . . Here is a challenge to early childhood scholars to reexamine the early childhood dilemma.

[page 140] . . . [Rohwer] showed that the effects [of early instruction in mathematics] noted by Austin were not statistically significant. What was significant was a strong negative correlation between school-entry age and attitude toward school. Additional years in school did not contribute significantly to average performance in mathematics; but the earlier children had started school, the more negative their attitudes toward school.

[page 141] . . . Developmental readiness, however, was still the most important factor for doing arithmetic and understanding paragraph meaning.

. . . A number of studies verify . . . the younger a child is when he starts to school, the more chronological age appears to affect this progress throughout his school life . . . . Cumulative records over a period of six years revealed a continued disadvantage, even though as a group they had a slightly higher IQ than those who entered school from six to nine months later. Children in the younger group were also more likely to repeat a grade.

. . . Feyberg's results showed that successful school achievement in areas requiring use of concepts – such as numbers, classes, and spatial and causal relationships – correlated highly with mental age. Developing these concepts was especially associated with success in arithmetic, problem solving, and spelling.

[page 142] . . . Strom observed that the excessive value attached to academic achievement and the pressures to grow up and achieve earlier could be damaging to personal development . . . .

[page 228] If, as neurophysiologists suggest, brain structure and function move along together, requiring a child to undertake tasks for which he is not fully prepared is risking damage to the central nervous system. It may also risk potential difficulties in the affective and motivational aspects of learning due to frustration, because the learning "tools" simply are not yet ready. [Our emphasis] Recent findings . . . confirm this.

. . . If we expect reading and arithmetic based on understanding rather than on rote learning, delay of formal training in these areas appears wise – although informal education through warm parental responses is desirable. Some scholars and clinicians conclude that formal education should wait until ages ten to fourteen . . . . Strong clinical and research evidence indicates that early exposure to the so-called stimulation of school often destroys childhood motivation for learning. By grade three or four many children become stranded on a motivational plateau, never recovering their early excitement for learning. Most primary teachers agree.

— *School Can Wait*, by Raymond S. and Dorothy N. Moore et. al., Brigham Young University Press, Provo, Utah, Hewitt Research Foundation, Berrien Springs, Michigan, 1982.

The Brain, It's Plain, Is Sprained if It Is Strained

[Page 66] [T]he axons, or output parts of [brain] neurons, gradually develop a coating of a waxy substance called myelin, which insulates the wiring and facilitates rapid and clear transmission. At birth, only the most primitive systems, such as those needed for sucking, have been [page 67] coated with myelin . . . . The process of myelination in human brains is not completed at least until most of us are in our twenties. While animal studies have shown that total myelin may reflect levels of stimulation, scientists believe its order of development is mainly predetermined by a genetic program.

While the system, overall, is remarkably responsive to stimulation from the environment, the schedule of myelination appears to put some boundaries around "appropriate" forms of learning at any given age . . . . [W]e should stop for a moment to discuss some potential hazards in trying too hard to "make" intelligence or learning happen. Some of the skill deficits of today's schoolchildren, in fact, may have resulted from academic demands that were wrong – either in content or in mode of presentation – for their level of development.

The same mentality that attempts to engineer stimulation for baby brains also tries to push learning into schoolchildren much like stuffing sausages. For example, some parents now wonder if their schools are any good if they don't start formal reading instruction, complete with worksheets, in preschool . . . .

Before brain regions are myelinated, they do not operate efficiently. For this reason, trying to "make" children master academic skills for which they do not have the requisite maturation may result in mixed-up patterns of learning. As we have seen, the essence of functional plasticity is that any kind of learning – reading, math, spelling, handwriting, etc. – may be accomplished by any of several [brain] systems. Naturally, we want children to plug each piece of learning into the best system for that particular job. If the right one isn't yet available or working smoothly, however, forcing may create a functional organization in which less adaptive, "lower" systems are trained to do the work.

[page 68] . . . As an example, let's take the kind of reasoning needed for understanding (not just memorizing one's way through) higher-level math. Perhaps some readers of this book shared a common experience when they took algebra: many of us functioned adequately until we reached Chicago, where two planes insisted on passing each other every day in class. When it wasn't planes, it was trains or people digging wells or other situations that did not seem in any way related to graphs and [page 69] equations of X, Y, and Z. Personally, I found that the more I struggled, the more confused I became, until soon I was learning more confusion than algebra. Moreover, I began to believe I was pretty dumb. Was I developing what Herman Epstein calls "negative neural networks" (resistant circuitry) toward this worthy subject?

Having fled from math courses at the first available opportunity, I have since talked to other adults who confided that, after a similar experience, they also avoided math until forced years later to take a required course in graduate school. At this point, their grownup brains discovered they actually liked this sort of reasoning . . . .

In this personal example, it is very possible that the necessary neural equipment for algebra – taught in this particular manner – may not yet have been automatically available in my early-adolescent brain. The areas to receive the last dose of myelin are the association areas responsible for manipulating highly abstract concepts – such as symbols (X, Y, Z; graphs) that stand for other symbols (numerical relationships) that stand for real things (planes, trains, wells). Such learning is highly experience-dependent, and thus there are many potential neural routes by which it can be performed. Trying to drill higher-level learning into immature brains may force them to perform with lower-level systems and thus impair the skill in question . . . .

I would contend that much of today's school failure results from academic expectations for which students' brains were not prepared – but which were bulldozed into them anyway . . . .

The brain grows best when it is challenged, so high standards for children's learning are important. Nevertheless, curriculum needs to be considered in terms of brain-appropriate challenge. Reorganizing synapses is much more difficult than having the patience to help them get arranged properly the first time around!

[page 289] Abstract rule systems for grammar and usage should be taught when most students are in high school. Then, if previously prepared, they may even enjoy the challenges of this kind of abstract, logical reasoning. Only, however, if the circuits are not already too cluttered up by bungled rule-teaching.

One ninth-grade student who came to me last year for help with grammar was hopelessly confused about the simplest parts of speech. Although she was intelligent and could, at her current age, have mastered this material in a week, she had been a victim of meaningless "grammar" drills since second grade. As Michelle and I struggled on the simple difference between adjectives and adverbs, I often wished I could take a neurological vacuum cleaner and just suck out all those mixed-up synapses that kept getting in our way. It took us six months . . . But finally one day the light dawned. "This is easy!" she exclaimed. It is, when brains are primed for the learning and the student has a reason to use it with real literary models.

[page 290] Immersing children in good language from books and tapes, modeling patterns for their own speech and writing, and letting them enjoy their proficiency in using words to manipulate ideas are valid ways to embed "grammar" in growing brains . . . . No amount of worksheets or rule learning will ever make up for deficits resulting from lack of experience with the structure of real, meaningful sentences.

It is folly to ignore the importance of oral storytelling, oral history, and public speaking in a world that will communicate increasingly without the mediation of print. These skills build language competence in grammar, memory, attention, and visualization, among many other abilities.

. . . I personally believe . . . that helping students at all grade levels memorize some pieces of good writing – narrative, expository, and poetic – on a regular basis would provide good practice for language, listening, and attention. I do not mean reverting to a rote-level curriculum, but simply taking a little time each week to celebrate the sounds of literate thought . . . .

At the same time, schools must get into the business of teaching children to listen effectively because no one else seems to be doing it.

— *Endangered Minds, Why Children Don't Think and What We Can Do About It*, by Jane M. Healy, Simon and Schuster, New York, 1990.

WHAT SHOULD WE THEN DO?

Historically, the age for instruction in arithmetic and mathematics seems to have slowly shifted from age fifteen or later down to age ten. Then, about a century ago, this was shifted again to about age seven, or six. In very recent times it has shifted again to age five or four. But recorded history may not be the place to go in order to find substantive support for the practice of beginning formal instruction in arithmetic at any age – five, ten, or fifteen.

There is more material in arithmetic and mathematics to learn and to use today than the ancients studied. Some may argue that starting earlier allows more time to learn more material. It seems obvious to them that if a child learns to do multiplication and division at age ten, then he is five years ahead of the child who learns to do multiplication and division at age fifteen. Right? Perhaps. So if we teach him to multiply and divide at age five he would be ten years ahead. At birth, fifteen years ahead. Get the point? This is more than merely an issue of enough time. This is an issue of development.

How much math there is to learn, and how early children may have been forced to "learn" some math – these considerations do not give us data to define the time when it is most effective and most efficient to begin teaching arithmetic and mathematics. Most obviously, there is a time when it is too early. Those who advocate formal arithmetic at age five appear to have ignored this developmental issue, and when the results are not like they want, they patch them up with experimental classroom methods which try to emulate informal experiences in arithmetic – a tacit witness to informal instruction before age ten.

In our culture, we erroneously perceive that the only way anyone anywhere at any time can learn arithmetic is from early formal instruction – usually in a classroom school. But young children have learned the basic concepts of number in every culture without any formal instruction. Games, measurements, and commercial activity have been the primary childhood instructors. They are still the best instructors of young children. Withholding formal instruction until age ten will by no means guarantee failure. Depending on what arithmetic activities are done, it may actually guarantee the child's success.

What we suggest is:

1) Formal textbook or workbook instruction in arithmetic may begin at age ten. It is about age ten that the developmental light bulb goes on, and the child becomes capable of a great deal more mental and physical skill. (Of course that's not an absolute rule. With a few children, it is as early as eight. We call them "bright" children because the developmental light bulb goes on early.) Waiting until the child is developmentally prepared to handle the concepts makes instruction in arithmetic very easy, because the child learns very quickly.
2) There is no necessity for formal teaching in arithmetic before age ten. Once all of the developmental parts are there, most children can learn – in a few weeks – everything which they might have spent six years learning (kindergarten through fifth grade), that is, if they haven't already learned it through questions and experiences and working things out on their own — which is generally the case.
3) Depending upon the child, upon the method, and upon the subject matter covered, there exists the potential for developmental harm from the formal teaching of arithmetic before age ten. Small children cannot understand many arithmetic concepts at an early age. We can teach them to perform the process, but we cannot make them understand the concepts. The child "learns" to hate "learning." The child's understanding develops along the wrong lines. He may actually develop mental "blocks" to arithmetic – actual physiological blocks in the brain. (This may give new meaning for the term "blockhead.")
4) Not formally teaching arithmetic before age ten frees up a lot of time for other activities which will build the vocabulary of the child. Vocabulary is the number one index of intelligence. Developing vocabulary was one of the deliberate foci of ancient education. We waste valuable time for developing vocabulary and verbal language skills if we instead spend those hours teaching a five year old to count by fives. (He'll know it intuitively by age ten anyway, without ever being taught.) Instead, we ought to spend those hours reading to him. We only have so much time in the day. Do we want to spend it trying to force math skills into a child who developmentally is not optimally prepared, or spend it doing what is

> developmentally natural to a young child – learning new words and associating them with new ideas and experiences. Stretch the child's vocabulary during the formative years, and when he's developmentally ready to do some deeper thinking, he'll have a mind prepared to take on the task, and he'll take off like a rocket.

Please note: We are not saying that no child should ever utter the name of a number before age ten. Not at all. About age four, most children discover money, and there is no hiding numbers from them after that. They encounter numbers all of the time. If we encourage learning, then they'll be asking lots of questions, and we'll be full of opportunities to teach numbers and measurement. But we would not encourage using a formal workbook before age ten, unless the child has a genuine desire to do so, he shows that he is competent to handle the work, and it does not take away time from other valuable activities. We are not going to ruin the child if we wait until age ten before beginning the formal teaching of arithmetic.

Article Twelve

Outcome-Based Education Versus Trivium-Based Education

ANCIENT PERSECUTION OF THE TRIVIUM

ON DECEMBER 11, 361, Julian became Emperor of Rome. He immediately set out to restore the worship of the ancient gods. On February 4, 362, he proclaimed religious "toleration," and moved to reopen the pagan temples. He had learned that a direct attack upon Christianity would only increase its following. So he publicly disclaimed any desire to injure the Christians. Instead, Julian mounted an administrative persecution to humiliate Christians without directly attacking them. He effectively closed the courts to Christians by requiring everyone to burn incense before speaking in court. Anyone who refused to burn incense was declared "godless" and deprived of citizenship. He ordained that Christians thereafter were to be referred to only as "Galileans." His final attack on Christianity was in three stages:

1. May 12, 362, he confirmed upon school teachers all special privileges which were formerly granted to Christians – right to travel by the public post, exemption from municipal service, etc.
2. June 17, he decreed all schoolteachers in the empire must be examined, endorsed, and sanctioned by the emperor. His purpose was to use the educational system as a propaganda weapon for the formation of public opinion.
3. Immediately thereafter he declared Christians to be insane and demented because of their contradictory views and prac-

> tices; and he refused to allow them to be teachers. His aim was to turn all schools into centers of pagan religion. The effect was to "forbid masters of rhetoric and grammar to instruct Christians." Julian "considered such studies conducive to the acquisition of argumentative and persuasive power." Augustine wrote, "Was he [Julian] not a persecutor that forbade the Christians to be taught the liberal arts [Grammar, Logic, and Rhetoric]?" (City of God 18:52)

Julian died on June 26, 363. His successor, Valentinian, rescinded his edicts.

Julianus Redivivus

The parallels between Julian's actions and modern socialized education are startling. The teaching of pagan practices such as perverted-sexuality and aborticide are protected in socialized schools under a cloak of "toleration." Socialized schools require teachers to be certified by the state, effectively closing the schools to Christians who cannot "burn incense" to the methods, principles, values and goals required for certification. Christians are now referred to disparagingly as "right-wing fundamentalist fanatics." They have been subjected to a humiliating administrative persecution for many years – though never directly attacked.

We may now be entering on the final attack. Federal legislation essentially requires that all school teachers in the socialized schools be examined, endorsed and sanctioned by the Federal Department of Education. Holding to moral absolutes is declared by some to be insane and demented, and absolutes are not allowed to be taught. Socialized schools are thereby effectively turned into centers of amoral pagan religion. Outcome-Based Education (O.B.E.) is mandated in some form in all socialized schools. Federal legislation was formulated to forbid the teaching of the Trivium, declaring it to be a "disproven theory."

> The Congress declares it to be the policy of the United States that . . . this title builds upon what has been learned: . . .The disproven theory that children must first learn basic skills [Grammar and Logic] before engaging in more complex tasks [Rhetoric] continues to dominate strategies for classroom instruction, resulting in emphasis on repetitive drill and practice. . . . A schoolwide program shall include the following components: . . . help provide an enriched and accelerated curriculum [Rhetoric only, or Outcome-Based] rather than remedial drill and practice [Grammar and Logic Based]."

Such things as learning phonics and the math facts would be federally outlawed. The Trivium, which has worked for millennia, is now considered a "disproven theory" while O.B.E., which has not worked anywhere it has ever been tried, is now the officially sanctioned method.

O.B.E. is "outcome-skills based." It teaches "rhetoric" level skills without teaching the basic "grammar" and "logic" level skills. (An illustration of this appears in Chapter Four.)

O.B.E. proponents have now declared mathematics to be a group sport. Students solve their math problems as a group. We call this "conversational math." But if you solve math problems as a group, then you will foster dependency upon others, and you won't learn to do math on your own. Math is an individual sport.

The Federal government has decided it knows more about us than our Creator. We will now be recreated into the image invented by Politically Correct Outcome Based Government Socialist Educators.

Under O.B.E., the academic levels of public education will rapidly deteriorate. Modern education has been failing on many fronts, but we seem now to be on the threshold of its complete collapse – along with the collapse of our culture – because fundamental language skills are no longer being mastered. Failure to master fundamental language skills will cripple a student in every other subject of study.

Where are you, Valentinian, when we need you?

Outcome Based Education is not a revolution in education. It is a great climactic and confrontational battle in a revolution which has been going on for decades. We have had wave after wave of educational experiments in government schools, followed by wave after wave of academic decline. But instead of going back to the traditional Trivium method of classical education which has worked for six millennia, the government introduces a new and bolder experiment ostensibly to resolve the problems its earlier experiments have created – without ever admitting their experiments have actually created the problems. But the results of each new cure always turn out to be worse than the results of the last cure.

A CONTRAST OF OPPOSITES

Opposita juxta se posita magis elucescunt.

Opposites placed by one another are more apparent.

We will not attempt to duplicate the many excellent literature exposing O.B.E. Instead, we wish to present an analysis of O.B.E. in contrast with the Trivium, examining first its principles, then its values, and finally its goals.

Principles

A principle is a cause, source or origin of anything, or the foundation or basis upon which a thing is supported. If a thing is built upon a solid foundation, or comes from a reliable source, then it may be expected to stand. If not, then it will fall.

The principle upon which Trivium-Based Education is based is the simple progression: first comes Knowledge, then comes Understanding, and last comes Wisdom. The Scriptures teach this progression, and nature, of course, agrees. Indeed the principle is so entwined in the warp and woof of things that the three-step pattern continually appears. The ancients taught the formal academics of 1) Grammar 2) Logic and 3) Rhetoric. Music is composed of 1) notes 2) arranged 3) to be performed. The computer must have 1) input 2) processing and 3) output. The study of a subject begins with the 1) facts, then 2) the theory, then 3) the practical uses and applications. Our offspring develop in three stages: 1) childhood, spent absorbing facts and rules, 2) youth and early teens, spent investigating the reasons for things, and 3) older teens through adult, spent expressing and applying the things they have learned and are learning.

The driving principle of O.B.E. is the "outcomes." O.B.E. planners have designed the process to determine the product. (Psychosocial predestination.) Technically speaking, this would not necessarily exclude using the Trivium. It is only when you realize that O.B.E. outcomes are largely nonacademic, and that they do not want the population to truly know the facts, honestly analyze the theory, and effectively apply the results – only when you realize these things do you understand that the Trivium is in fact anathema to O.B.E. advocates. They speak of "the disproven theory that children must first learn basic skills before engaging in more complex tasks." They are, in fact, correct – from their perspective. People can learn to play Beethoven's "Moonlight Sonata" without learning to read music or to finger the piano keys properly. And there are a few who can figure out on their own the musical notation and the fingering after learning to play the "Moonlight Sonata." Our society has been getting along fine for nearly a century manipulating accounting units and calling them dollars without understanding even the first principles of modern money mechanics. For decades children have been learning to read by "look-say" instead of phonics. The O.B.E advocates are quite right, children do not need to first learn basic skills before engaging in more complex tasks. But children ought to! A population which does not know the basics, and has no true thinking skills, but only knows how to perform practical tasks – such a population is more easily manipulated. They become slaves to their trainers. They lack the basic tools to free themselves.

According to O.B.E. advocates, there is too much emphasis upon traditional academic skills. They want to reduce the amount of time spent on such things as reading, writing and arithmetic by 40% to 50%. The sad fact is this: they might be able to teach students these skills in less time, if only they would adopt effective teaching methods. Unfortunately they intend to go the opposite direction, moving from "look-say" reading to the next level of incompetence: "whole language."

Values

A value is what you consider of positive worth, importance or significance. Education cannot be neutral. Whatever an educator values to teach, he teaches as having value. Whatever he does not value to teach, he teaches as having no value. To deny that you have an agenda of values in education is to deny that you educate.

Trivium-Based Education places value on Knowledge, Understanding and Wisdom. It values teaching the student the skills necessary to learn on his own. It values making a person intellectually independent and self-reliant.

O.B.E. disdains the teaching of basic skills such as phonics and math facts. O.B.E. does, however, teach what it calls "critical thinking skills." This should not be confused with legitimate "critical thinking" or "logic." The O.B.E. program teaches children to make subjective choices from among options which the program presents. The program systematically omits Christian choices. The child is programmed in an amoral mode of thinking – a mode of thinking which recognizes no absolute standards. The child determines for himself what is right and wrong. (O.B.E constructs a tree of knowledge of good and evil, and invites the children to choose from its fruits.) What they call "critical thinking skills" is actually "selected thinking profiles." O.B.E. does not value making a person intellectually independent and self-reliant.

Here is an assessment question actually in use.

> There is a secret club at school called the Midnight Artists. They go out late at night and paint funny sayings and pictures on buildings. A student is asked to join the club. In this situation, I would join the club when I knew:
>
> (a) my best friend asked me to join

(b) the most popular students were in the club

(c) my parents would ground me if they found out I joined.

The student must agree with the "correct" answers, which are (a) and (b), and disagree with he "incorrect" answer, which is (c). In other words, the student is to yield to pressures of friendship and popularity, and is not to consider the values of his parents important, but only to consider their punishment. There should be a fourth answer: (d) "I would never join the club, because graffiti destroys the property of others, which is stealing, which is contrary to God's law, which should be reflected in every man's conscience." And a fifth answer (e) "I would inform competent authorities of the names of the vandals." The assessment does not allow the student the choice of not joining the club.

O.B.E. does not focus upon academic achievement. Instead, it focuses upon "affective" learning. Out of 415 items which a typical O.B.E. program assesses, only 30 are academic. That's only 7%. The rest of the assessment is for things like "locus of control" and "thresholds of behavior" and "scale of adjustment." Your "locus of control" measures how easily you agree with your peers and go with the flow. "Thresholds of behavior" measures what it takes to get you to avoid punishment and go with the group. "Scale of adjustment" measures how rapidly you can adjust to change without protest. O.B.E. is not merely designed to assess and correct academic skills on a micro-scale. The goal is a "minimum positive attitude" as defined by the outcomes.

O.B.E. squashes the individual personality. The O.B.E. program becomes the parent, the character model, and all children are (as much as possible) formed after the image of O.B.E. The program does not merely create a "learning loop" to make sure students achieve goals, but it introduces "behavioral modification" techniques which reduce the student to a manipulated animal.

O.B.E. discourages academic excellence. A student who is a high achiever is allowed to go ahead just so far, then he is kept busy or employed as a change agent upon peers to bring them up to his level. Achievers soon learn not to achieve so quickly.

In sum, O.B.E. wants to appear as if it is built upon a foundation of educational reform to encourage educational achievement. In fact, it is built upon a foundation of psycho-sociological methods designed to achieve a collectivist mindset in all students. It values personalities which are easily manipulated and which depend upon the government.

Goals

A goal is the point or mark toward which one aims, the end or final purpose which one seeks to reach or accomplish.

The goal of Trivium-Based Education is to create an intellectually independent and self-reliant person – a person who can think for himself and act for himself.

What is the goal of O.B.E.? Every O.B.E. program, without exception, promotes a political, not an academic agenda. The political agenda of O.B.E. is always an amoral, one-world collectivist mentality. Here are some examples (from Oklahoma and Pennsylvania State Guidelines).

> First Grade Outcome:
>
> "The student will identify different types of family structures, so that no single type is seen as the only possible one."
>
> Ninth through Twelfth Grade Outcome:
>
> "The student will develop communication skills, including being able to talk with one's actual or potential partner about sexual behavior."
>
> All grades:
>
> "All students understand and appreciate their worth as unique and capable individuals, and exhibit self esteem."

The emphasis is upon attitudes. The child must have "correct" positive attitudes toward issues such as multiculturalism, non-sexism, environmental extremism, global citizenship, collectivism, and of course, government control of all areas of life.

A facade is created that parent-teacher cooperative committees determine the outcomes for each state. By means of careful selection of committee members, public town-meetings, and secret revisions, the consensus engineers produce virtually identical results – sometimes word-for-word identical results – from state to state. (Can parents from 38 different states coincidentally arrive independently at over 400 identical outcomes? But can graduates of government education ever calculate the probability of this happening?)

Can individuals opt out of O.B.E. through private education? The government is presently organizing society to require O.B.E.. If you don't have it, then you won't be able to participate in society – hold a job, have medical care, own property, buy and sell. Even if you could participate, you still must deal with a society with uniform O.B.E. values.

Despite all of their talk about "multicultural diversity" and "tolerance," O.B.E. imposes an intolerant monolithic philosophy upon society. Children are shifted away from recognizing God and parents as authorities, and toward recognizing collective authorities – public opinion (determined by the government), peer groups (determined by the government) and the government itself (collectivist). The school is called the "new family" and the "real family" in O.B.E. literature.

If there are no absolutes, the government must become the maker of absolutes, determining the limits, not on the basis of God's law, but on the basis of its own agenda. A government which thinks it is god will become totalitarian, and everyone becomes its slave. Everything is restrained by the government except the government. When the notion of accountability to God is removed, all outward restraint is removed, and the state deifies itself. The state is accountable to no one. The state is god. To fail to acknowledge the almighty power of the state is equivalent to atheism.

CONCLUSION

The Trivium model for education conforms to the reality of human nature, it values developing those skills necessary for self-learning, and it strives toward the goal of making the individual intellectually independent and self-reliant.

The O.B.E. model for education attempts to mold human nature into a new form, it seeks to instill individuals with a subject/slave mentality, and it has a goal of creating the ideal collectivist society.

COMPARISON OF O.B.E. & T.B.E.

Trivium-Based Education	Outcome-Based Education
T.B.E tests academic achievement	O.B.E. tests value systems
T.B.E. teaches moral absolutes.	O.B.E. teaches moral relativism.
T.B.E. teaches moral absolutes.	O.B.E. teaches moral relativism.
T.B.E. teaches the logical deduction of values from absolutes.	O.B.E. teaches self-clarification of values from a limited offering of politically correct options.
T.B.E. teaches academic skills, while seeking the highest individual achievement.	O.B.E. teaches "social" skills, while reducing academics to the lowest common denominator.
T.B.E. educates for the individual and the family.	O.B.E. educates for the state.

FIGURE 17-12A

But be careful. When government education finally collapses, beware of what is proposed in its place.

Contra negantem principia non est disputandum.

Against one that denies principles, we must not dispute.

Article Thirteen

Contests in Your Curriculum

CONTESTS ARE AN EDUCATIONAL experience especially suited for homeschooled students. Contests let the student bring together and apply the skills he learns at home in his everyday schooling. What can contests do for our child academically? Consider:

CONTESTS ARE GREAT MOTIVATORS

Envision a typical Homeschool assignment: Mom asks Henry to write a composition on "What Valentine's Day Means to Me." Henry isn't particularly interested in Valentine's Day and he knows his finished composition will go no further than in front of Mom's eyes and then into the three-ring binder on the schoolroom bookshelf. As a consequence, his motivation level is mediocre and his effort is halfhearted. Now suppose that Mom tells Henry she wants him to draw a scene from intergalactic space and to write a scientific narrative of that scene. Henry, who is the local expert on space exploration, lights up at this idea. When she tells him they will enter his drawing and narrative in the Intergalactic Art Competition (part of the Space Science Student Involvement Program), and he might win an all-expenses paid trip to the National Space Science Symposium in Washington, D. C. . . well, the fire is lit and look out world, because Henry has a lot to say on that subject. It was a combination of good topic, competition, and reward that did the trick.

CONTEST PARTICIPATION DEVELOPS RESEARCH SKILLS

Writing a scientific narrative on space exploration will take more than our 1952 Encyclopedia Britannica, so off to the library we must go. Here is the perfect opportunity to teach the lad how to do research. Along with our own local library, we will want to utilize a good college or university library. Arrange for personal interviews. Don't forget to tap into the Internet. The Great Online Research Challenge is an interesting new contest for eleventh and twelfth grade students. Students are given a time limit to solve problems by researching Lexis/Nexis, which is a database of databases which includes massive full-text libraries. What is attractive about this contest is the prize: two years of Lexis/Nexis for your family. Now, that's what I call a prize. Go, kids, go!

CONTESTS CAN BRING IT ALL TOGETHER

A contest can bring together into one exciting finale all the skills we've taught our children. To write this paper on space exploration, numerous subjects will be covered: grammar, spelling, punctuation, science, penmanship or typing skills, logic (construction of arguments), and rhetoric (expressing a point in an eloquent manner). This one essay contest is actually not just "another composition" to write, but a whole unit study in itself, with the final product bringing, as Jessica Hulsey says, "closure."

CONTESTS DEVELOP CHARACTER QUALITIES

Many of these contests take a long time to complete. A Science and Engineering Fair science project may take an entire school year. Longer term projects develop perseverance and diligence. Contests can seem overwhelming and unmanageable if looked at as a whole, but the process can be broken down into bite sized pieces by planning and organizing. The student strives toward his goal, doing his best job, and in the end can obtain the "satisfaction and pride of a job well done" (as Ranger Bill would say). Some contests require teamwork. The National Written & Illustrated By . . . Awards Contest provided an opportunity for Johannah, our oldest daughter, to teach watercolor techniques to Helena, her younger sister.

ADVANTAGES OF TIME

Time wise, Homeschooled students are at an advantage in contest participation. The first contest we ever entered was a local science fair. I learned about this competition only two weeks before it was held, so we devoted those two weeks full time to the contest. What an exciting experience! That was back in 1989, but all the kids remember the fun of those days. Two weeks of pure science, not to be distracted by Latin declensions.

WHICH CONTESTS TO PICK

Which contest should we pick for our child? If the child is extra good at math, then any of the numerous math competitions will stretch his skills. There are plenty of art contests for the artistically inclined. To integrate contests into the curriculum, we suggest this plan: For the first year, pick one of the fun contests which goes along with the child's interest (Make It Yourself With Wool Contest; chess competitions; Scripps Howard National Spelling Bee; Rocky Mountain Philatelic Exhibition; National Association of Rocketry contests; American Morgan Horse Association contests). Check out the deadline for the contest and make out a rough schedule for progress. Break the process down into bite size pieces. Example: by October have the project topic decided, have outlines finished by November, rough drafts by December, etc.

The next year, have the student enter one of the project contests (National History Day, science fairs, or invention projects). By the third year we will be considered a contest pro. We may make contests a major part of our curriculum. Each year, to make a well rounded curriculum, the student can enter a writing contest, a speech contest, and a project contest. We can also use contests to help our student work on areas in which he is weak.

A FEW WARNINGS

Here are a few warnings about contests: Avoid politically correct contests. If the registration form requires us to list our race, then it is possible that winners will be chosen on the basis of race, not merit. Some contests require us to travel long distances or cost large sums of money. MathCounts, a very popular math competition, recently started charging $40 per school. Avoid contests that just want to sell or promote a product or build a mailing list (some of the poetry contests do this). Some of the Internet "contests" are really sweepstakes, not contests.

TRIVIUM PURSUIT'S LIST OF NATIONAL CONTESTS AND EXAMS OPEN TO HOMESCHOOLERS

(Originally compiled in 1986, updated yearly, last updated April, 2001)

Ford/AAA Student Auto Skills
American Automobile Association
1000 AAA Drive, Box 75, Heathrow, FL 32746
407-444-8378; www.autoskills.com
automotive technician competition; 12th grade

Academy of Applied Science, Jr Science and Humanities Symposium
Box 2934, Concord, NH 03302
603-228-4520; www.jshs.org
original research project in science, engineering or math; grades 9-12

All-American Soap Box Derby
Box 7225, Akron, OH 44306
330-733-8723; www.aasbd.org
soap box racing; ages 9-16

American Association of Teachers of French, National French Contest
AATF-Mailcode 4510, Southern Illinois University, Carbondale, IL 62901
618-453-5731; aatf.utsa.edu
French contest; all grades

American Association of Teachers of German
112 Haddontowne Court, No.104, Cherry Hill, NJ 08034
609-795-5553; www.aatg.org
National German Examination; high school

American Classical League, National Latin Examination
Box 95, Mount Vernon, Virginia 22121
800-459-9847; www.vroma.org/~nle
National Latin exam; all grades

American Classical League, National Greek Examination
Miami University, Oxford, OH 45056
513-529-7741; www.vroma.org/~nle/grkex.html
National Greek exam; high school

American College Testing
2201 North Dodge Street, Box 168, Iowa City, Iowa 52243
319-337-1000; www.act.org
ACT tests; high school
The American Legion
Box 1055, Indianapolis, IN 46206
www.legion.org/orator.htm
national oratorical contest; 9th through 12th grade
American Mathematics Competitions
University of Nebraska, Box 880658, Lincoln, NE 68588
402-472-6566; www.unl.edu/amc
math exams; all grades
The American Morgan Horse Association
122 Bostwick Road, Box 960, Shelburne, VT 05482
802-985-4944; www.morganhorse.com/yp-creative.html
literary and photo contests; all ages
American Statistical Association
1429 Duke Street, Alexandria, VA 22314
888-231-3473; www.amstat.org
statistical research project or poster; all grades
AMVETS Contests
Program National Headquarters, 4647 Forbes Boulevard, Lanham, MD 20706
301-459-9600
poster and essay contests; grades 3-12
Arbor Day National Poster Contest
P.O. Box 85784, Lincoln, NE 68501
www.arborday.org/
poster contest; grade 5
Ayn Rand Essay Contest
Box 6004, Inglewood, CA 90312
800-365-6552 x 209; www.aynrand.org
essay contests; grades 9-12
BMI Student Composer Awards
Ralph N. Jackson, 320 West 57th Street, New York, NY 10019
repertoire.bmi.com/bmifoundation/student.asp
music composition contest; all grades
Center for the American Founding
1401 Chain Bridge Road, Suite 100, McLean, VA 22101
703-556-6595; www.founding.org/tour/html/compass.html

essay competition; high school grades

Children's Creative Writing Campaign
Box 999, Cooper Station, New York, NY 10276
212-228-3041
creative writing contest; through age 14

The College Board
45 Columbus Avenue, New York City, NY 10023
212-713-8077; www.collegeboard.org
Advance Placement Program; PSAT/NMSQT tests; SAT tests; high school

Columbia Scholastic Press Assoc.
Columbia University, 2960 Broadway, New York City, NY 10027
212-854-1754; www.columbia.edu
newspaper, yearbook, & magazine contest; all grades

Computer Learning Foundation
Box 60400, Palo Alto, CA 94306
408-720-8898; www.computerlearning.org
numerous computer related contests; all grades

Craftsman/NSTA Young Inventors Awards Program
National Science Teachers Assoc., 1840 Wilson Blvd, Arlington, VA 22201
888-494-4994; www.nsta.org/programs/craftsman.htm
invent or modify a tool; grades 2-8

Daughters of the Am. Revolution
1776 D Street, NW, Washington DC 20006
202-628-1776; contact local chapter through www.dar.org
American history essay contests; grades 5-10
Junior Am. Citizens contest (art, creative writing, photography, video, and other special projects); all ages

Dick Blick Linoleum Block Print Contest
Box 1267, Galesburg, IL 61402
800-447-8192; www.dickblick.com
art contest; grades 4-12

Dupont Challenge Science Essay Awards
Gen. Learning Comm., 900 Skokie Blvd, #200, Northbrook, IL 60062
847-205-3000; www.glcomm.com/dupont
science essay awards program; grades 7-12

Earth and Sky Young Illustrators and Producers Contests
Box 2203, Austin, TX 78768

www.earthsky.com
art contest; radio science presentations; grades K-12

Eldred World War II Essay Contest
201 Main Street, Box 273, Eldred, PA 16731
814-225-2200; www.eldredwwiimuseum.org
essay contest; grades 9-12

Energy Smart Schools Invention Kids Contest
c/o Owens Corning, 1 Owens Corning Parkway, Toledo, OH 43659
800-363-3732; www.eren.doe.gov/energysmartschools
invention contest; grades 4-6

Health Occupations Students of America
6021 Morriss Rd., Suite 111, Flower Mound, TX 75028
800-321-HOSA; www.hosa.org
numerous competitive events; high school

International Aviation Art Contest
8401 Colesville Road, Suite 505, Silver Spring, MD 20910
301-588-0587; www.nasao.org/
art contest; ages 6-12

International Bridge Building Contest
3101 S. Dearborn Street, Chicago, IL 60616
312-567-3498; www.iit.edu/~hsbridge
design and build a bridge that holds the most weight

International Jugglers Association
P.O. Box 218, Montague, MA 01351
800-367-0160; www.juggle.org
juggling competitions; all ages

International Whistlers Convention
Box 758, Louisburg, NC 27549
919-496-1191
whistling contests; all ages

Invent America!
Box 26065, Alexandria, VA 22313
703-684-1836; www.inventamerica.org
student invention contest; grades K-8

Junior Engineering Technical Society
1420 King Street, Suit 405, Alexandria, VA 22314
703-548-5387; www.jets.org
engineering examination and other engineering competitions; grades 9-12

Letters About Literature
Weekly Reader Corporation, 200 First Stamford Place, Bok 120023, Stamford CT 06912
203-705-3500; www.weeklyreader.com/features/privacy.html
essay contest; grades 4-7

Make It Yourself With Wool Contest
Marie Lehfeldt, Box 175, Lavina, MT 59046
406-636-2731; www.sheepusa.org
sew with wool contest; all ages

The Mandelbrot Competition
Greater Testing Concepts, Box 380789, Cambridge, MA 02238
www.mandelbrot.org
math competitions; high school grades

Mandelbrot Midlevels
Greater Testing Concepts, Box 382805, Cambridge, MA 02238
www.midlevels.org
math competitions; middle school grades

MathCounts Foundation
1420 King Street, Alexandria, VA 22314
703-684-2828; www.mathcounts.org
math competition; grades 7-8

Mathemat. Olympiads for Elem. & Middle Sch.
2154 Bellmore Avenue, Bellmore, NY 11710
516-781-2400; www.moems.org
math contests; grades 4-7

Midwest Creation Fellowship Essay Contest
Box 952, Wheaton, IL 60189
essay on selected creation science topics; ages 11-18

Mississippi Valley Poetry Contest
Box 3188, Rock Island, IL 61204
319-359-1057
poetry contest; all ages

Modern Woodmen of America
1701 1st Avenue, Rock Island, IL 61204
309-786-6481; www.modern-woodman.org
civic oration contest; grades 5-8
essay contest; grades 5-8

Mothers Against Drunk Driving Essay Contest
800-GET-MADD; www.madd.org/under21
Essay contest; grades 4-12
National Assoc. of Rocketry
Box 177, Altoona, WI 54720
www.nar.org
model rocketry contests; all grades
NASA Student Involvement Competitions
2067 Massachusetts Avenue, Suite 2, Cambridge, MA 02140
800-848-8429; www.nsip.net
several space science competitions; grades 3-12
The National Cursive Handwriting Contest
Peterson Directed Handwriting, Box 249, Greensburg, PA 15601
800-541-6328; www.peterson-handwriting.com
cursive handwriting contest; grades 3-8
National Forensic League
Box 38, Ripon, WI 54971
920-748-6206; debate.uvm.edu/nfl
numerous speech & debate contests; high school students
National Geographic Society
1145 17th Street, NW, Washington, D.C. 20036
202-828-6659; www.nationalgeographic.com/geobee
national geography bee; grades 4-8
The National Handwriting Contest
Zaner-Bloser, Box 16764, Columbus, OH 43216
800-924-9233
handwriting contest; grades 1-6
National History Day
University of MD, 0119 Cecil Hall, College Park, MD 20742
301-314-9767; www.thehistorynet.com
history project competitions; grades 6-12
National Junior Horticultural Assoc.
15 Railroad Avenue, Homer City, PA 15748
724-479-3254; www.njha.org/
numerous horticultural contests; all grades
National Mythology Exam
Elementary Teachers of Classics, The American Classical League

Miami University, Oxford, OH 45056
513-529-7741; www.mythologyexam.org
mythology exam; grades 3-9

National Scholastic Press Assoc.
2221 University Ave. SE, Suite 121, Minneapolis, MN 55414
612-625-8335; www.studentpress.org/nspa
photography contest; story of the year contest; all grades

National Social Studies Olympiad
Box 2196, St. James, NY 11780
516-584-2016; members.xoom.com/quartararo
social studies contests; grades 2-12

Newscurrents Student Editorial Cartoon Contest
Box 52, Madison, WI 53701
800-356-2303; www.newscurrents.com
political cartoon contest; all grades

Ocean Pals
495 New Rochelle Road, Bronxville, NY 10708
914-664-4310; www.beneaththesea.org/opals
marine environment poster contest; all grades

Odyssey of the Mind
c/o Creative Competitions Inc., 1325 Route 130 S. Suite F, Gloucester City, NJ 08030
856-456-7776; www.odysseyofthemind.org
problem solving contests; grades K-college

Optimist International
4494 Lindell Blvd., St. Louis, MO 63108
314-371-6000; www.optimist.org/
essay contest; 10th through 12th grade
oratorical contest; up to age 16

Origami By Children Exhibition
15 West 77th Street, New York, NY 10024
212-769-5635; www.origami-usa.org
origami competition; all ages

Pentel of America
2805 Columbia Street, Torrance, CA 90509
310-320-3831; www.pentel.com/
art and essay contests; K-12

Plymouth Rock Foundation
1120 Long Pond Rd., Plymouth, MA 02360
800-210-1620; www.plymrock.org

America's Christian Heritage Essay Contest; grades 9-12

Quill and Scroll Society
School of Journalism and Mass Communication, The University of Iowa
Iowa City, IA 52242
319-335-5795; uiowa.edu/~quill-sc/
international newspaper writing and photo contest; high school

Right to Life
contact a local or state chapter www.nrlc.org/
speech contest; grades 11-12

Rocky Mountain Philatelic Exhibitions
Box 2044, Englewood, CO 80150
stamp collecting; all grades

Scholastic Art & Writing Awards
555 Broadway, New York, NY 10012
212-343-6493; www.scholastic.com/artandwriting/
writing and art contests; grades 7-12

Science Olympiad
5955 Little Pine Lane, Rochester Hills, MI 48306
248-651-4013; www.soinc.org
science competitions; all grades

Science Service
1719 N Street, NW, Washington, DC 20036
202-785-2255; www.sciserv.org
report of an independent research project; 12th grade
International Science & Engineering Fairs; 9-12th grade

Scripps Howard National Spelling Bee
www.spellingbee.com
spelling bee; up through grade 8

Sons of the American Revolution
NSSAR Headquarters, 1000 South Fourth Street, Louisville, KY 40203
www.sar.org
essay and oration contests; grades 10-12

Space Settlement Design Contest, NASA Ames Research Center
MS 236-7, Moffett Field, CA 94035
lifesci3.arc.nasa.gov/spacesettlement
students design a space colony; grades 6-12

Technology Student Association
1914 Association Dr, Reston, VA 20191
703-860-9000; www.tsawww.org/
many different competitions; all ages

Think Quest
Advanced Network & Services, 200 Business Park Dr., Armonk, NY 10504
914-965-1100; www.thinkquest.org
a web building contest; ages 9-19

Toshiba/NSTA ExploraVision Awards Program
1840 Wilson Blvd., Arlington, VA 22201
800-EXPLOR-9; www.toshiba.com/tai/exploravision
science competition; grades K-12

Toshiba/NSTA Laptop Learning Challenge
1840 Wilson Blvd, Arlington, VA 22201
877-LAP-1-TOP; www.nsta.org/programs/laptop
innovative uses of laptop computers; grades K-12

USA Math Talent Search
COMAP, 57 Bedford Street, Suite 210, Lexington, MA 02420
781-862-7878, ext. 37; www.comap.com/highschool/contests
math competition; highschool grades

USA Today
1000 Wilson Boulevard, Arlington, VA 22229
703-276-5890
academic competition; high school

USA Weekend Student Fiction Contest
Box 4087, Blair, NE 68009
www.usaweekend.com/classroom
writing contest; grades 9-12

United States Chess Federation
054 NYS Route 9W, New Windsor, NY 12553
914-562-8350; www.uschess.org
chess competitions; all grades

United States Holocaust Memorial Museum, May Family National Art and Writing Contest
100 Raoul Wallenberg Place, SW, Washington, DC 20024
202-488-2661; www.ushmm.org
art and writing contests; grades 7-12

United States Institute of Peace
1200 17th St. NW, Suite 200, Washington, DC 20036
202-457-1700; www.usip.org
National Peace Essay Contest; grades 9-12

VFW, Voice of Democracy Audio Essay Competition
contact a local VFW Post
www.vfw.org/vod/index.shtml
audio essay competition; grades 9-12

Young Naturalist Awards
c/o Alliance for Young Artists and Writers, Inc.
555 Broadway, 4th Floor, New York, NY 10012
212-343-6493; www.amnh.org/youngnaturalistawards
science essays; grades 7-12

Article Fourteen

Family Bible Study by the Trivium

Could the Christians of the first century have had family Bible Studies? They may not have had individual copies of the Scriptures in their homes, but they memorized the Scriptures, and read and sang them aloud when they gathered for worship. Sometimes we think they had it better without copies of the Bible than we do with multiple translations of the Bible. We may quote a verse from a version, where they could quote its entire context in the original language. But they did not have the leisure hours which we have.

CHOOSING A BIBLE TRANSLATION

Everyone in the family should use the same translation of the Bible during Bible study. Reading from various translations is confusing, and defeats the memory mechanism. The choice of a Bible is very important. There is no perfect English translation of the Bible, but some are clearly better than others. Here are three things you should consider:

1) The Greek Text Underlying the Translation (Knowledge Level: the facts, the raw data.)

The modern critical Greek text is largely a patchwork quilt constructed from a handful of recently discovered portions and fragments of often contradictory manuscripts dating from the time of the theological controversies of the third and fourth centuries. By contrast, the traditional Greek text represents an immense textual tradition which amounts to a whole cloth, with perhaps a few tattered edges, but which can be traced down a continuous stream into the first and second centuries. The traditional text has many readings which are not found in the supposed "oldest manuscripts," but which appear in quotations from the first two centuries. Translations which are based on the traditional text include the more popular King James Version and New King James Version and the less popular Young's Literal Translation and the Modern King James Version. (For more on this subject, see our Trivium Loop Archives, www.triviumpursuit.com.)

2) The Method of Translation (Understanding Level: the theory underlying the words.)

Word-for-word translations are based upon the theory that the primary unit of meaning is in and between words (vocabulary and syntax). Such translations tend to be very literal, and leave most interpretation to the notes and commentaries. Thought-for-thought translations are based upon the theory that the primary unit of meaning is in and between sentences. Such translations tend to introduce a great deal of interpretation into the translation – adding things which are not actually said, and omitting things which are actually said. The King James Version, New King James Version, and Young's Literal Version, Modern King James Version, and New American Standard Version all fall more or less within the word-for-word translations. The New International Version, Today's English Version, and just about every other modern version are closer to thought-for-thought interpretations.

3) The Literary Quality (Wisdom Level: the effectiveness of expression).

Look-say reading programs in our institutions of socialized education (public schools) have created a need for a new literature with simplified look-say vocabulary and grammar. Readers who read by the look-say method cannot read the King James Version. But the King James Version has proven to be the most memorizable. This is because it is a literary masterpiece – it was not written in everyday modern language. It wasn't even written in everyday Elizabethan language. The higher the literary quality, the more memorizable the translation. The more "everyday" the language, the less memorizable. The New International Version, Today's English Version, and all the modern paraphrases such as the "Living Bible" are not good examples of literary quality.

There is no perfect English translation. Though the King James has a good textual base and an excellent literary style, it does lack some accuracy and consistency in vocabulary, and it is abundant with archaisms. Though the New King James has a good textual base and a fair degree of accuracy, it suffers from a dumbed down vocabulary and poor English grammar. The New American Standard Version has a poor textual base. The New International Version fails on many counts – textual base, translation method, and literary style. But it has much company, for almost all of the other modern translations fail on the same accounts. Unless you have a compelling reason to use another translation, we recommend the King James, New King James, Modern King James, or the Twenty-first century King James, and we recommend that you avoid the NIV and other such translations.

BIBLE READING

Choose a regular time for Bible Study, such as 7:00 a.m. every week day. Everyone in the family should know the time and be ready at that time. (No announcement should need to be made that it's time for Bible Study, unless circumstances rule that the time needs to be changed.) Read through one book of Scripture at a time. How do you choose what book to read? The father must determine what the family needs to study. Historical sections such as Genesis and Exodus, Joshua through Esther, or the Gospels and Acts are good studies. You can usually read a chapter at a time in the Old Testament, but in the New Testament you may have to slow down to as little as a paragraph at a time. The Legal and Ceremonial sections (Exodus 21 through Deuteronomy) are important, but some parts can be difficult to handle in a family study, especially when you have very small children. You may choose to skip some of the rotes, repetitions, and redundancies such as the genealogies, and avoid a few sections inappropriate for younger ears. The Poetic and Prophetic sections (Job through Malachi), by their nature, require more preparation by the father. The Doctrinal and Practical sections of the New Testament Epistles may require you to slow down to only a few verses per day, or even to reread the same verses for more than one day.

Everyone has his part in the Bible Study. It is customary to begin with prayer, which includes a request for God's enlightenment upon His word. You could have just the father read, or allow a different person to read every day in rotation, or the verses could be divided up for each person to read a portion each day. If there is a child just learning to read, give him a Bible. You may have him identify some letters, or spell out and sound out a few selected words. This way everyone practices reading the Scriptures out loud.

IMPLEMENTING THE TRIVIUM

When the children are all very small, Dad may just be satisfied with reading the Bible, asking a few questions, and making a few comments. By the time you have teenagers, you can implement the full Trivium in your study.

First is the Knowledge Level. Test yourselves on the facts. You might require someone to narrate out loud the facts of the passage. This might be done in great detail, or it may be prompted by questions from the father. In historical passages, you may assign one child to retell the story in his own words. (You may assign him before the reading in order to give him fair warning of what's coming and he'll pay more attention. Then again, maybe not.) After the narration, others can fill in any omitted details. Mom and Dad should narrate once in a while in order to prove how poor their memories are becoming.

After this, the study moves to the Understanding Level. Require each teenager and above (that includes the parents) to ask a question which explores the meaning or implications of the passage. Don't let them get away with answering "I can't think of any." If they try this too often, then take them through the passage verse by verse and ask a question for each verse in order to show them that their problem isn't that it's impossible to think of any, but only that they are not applying their minds. Discuss the question. Invite everyone to participate in thinking up all of the possible answers. You can allow some of those teenager specialties – those ridiculous or hilarious possibilities – but don't let it get out of hand. Then try to logically narrow down the possibilities. You should keep some Bible study resources on hand in order to look things up when necessary.

Finally, we reach the Wisdom Level. Sometimes applications flow right out of the Understanding Level discussion. At other times you may need to prompt everyone with a question which draws out an application. You might try a "what if" hypothetical question. How would one obey what is taught in this passage? How should it determine our behavior, or the behavior of others? How do the teachings or examples of the text help us in our decisions, actions, discernments, etc. Look for principles, values, and goals. Again, don't let them get away with answering "I don't know." Of course, the older the age, the more prone one will be toward applications, but don't ignore the younger children here. Sometimes they come up with the good applications.

STUDY BIBLES

The market is now being saturated with study Bibles. Don't let them dominate you. Think for yourself. Use them as an aid, not as the primary instructor. If, during your family study, you need to research a matter a little deeper, use the cross-references or the maps or the concordance, before you resort to those notes. If you use the notes too often, you can become enslaved to them. Oh yes, and your kids will soon discover that they can use them as cheat sheets to avoid thinking.

AFTER THE STUDY

At some point the father calls the study to a close. Twenty minutes to a half-hour is a good length, but sometimes you may need or want to go longer. Dad can ask for a discussion of what he should pray about, then close with prayer.

If you follow this method, you will grow in Knowledge, Understanding, and Wisdom as a family.

> But grow in grace, and *in* the knowledge of our Lord and Saviour Jesus Christ. To him *be* glory both now and for ever. Amen. — Second Peter 3:18

(For more information about Family Worship, and other approaches to Bible Study, see our booklet *On Family Worship*.)

Article Fifteen

Beginning A Homeschool Speech and Debate Club

GOALS

I. To teach students how to speak in front of an audience.

II. To learn the mechanics of speaking.

- A. Quality of voice.
- B. Articulation.
- C. Loudness.
- D. Expressiveness.
- E. Breathing techniques.

III. To give students practical experience in a variety of speech forms.

- A. Interpretive Reading (student reads non-original material)
    1. Prose.
    2. Poetry.
    3. Duet.
    4. Non-original oratory.
- B. Speech (original).
    1. Informational.
    2. Extemporaneous.
    3. Oratory (persuasive speech).
    4. Humorous.
- C. Debate.
    1. Lincoln-Douglas.
    2. Cross-Examination Policy.

IV. To expose students to a variety of types of prose and poetry.

V. To develop effective public speaking techniques through contest participation and special programs.
VI. To learn the proper way to write and deliver an original speech.
VII. To learn how to debate.
VIII. To form a speech and debate team and compete with other homeschool speech and debate teams.

SUGGESTIONS FOR LEADERS

1. Hold meetings twice a month, each meeting lasting two or three hours.
2. Charge a fee to students who wish to participate ($5 to $20). If you charge a fee students will attend more regularly, students will be more serious about completing assignments, and parents will be diligent about getting students to meetings on time. The money collected can help with the cost of copying handouts.
3. Each student should keep a notebook (three-ring binder) to hold all handouts, notes, readings, speeches, and assignments.
4. So that parents can enter schedule of meetings on their calendars, hand out a schedule of meetings by the beginning of September.
5. Students must be thirteen years or older to attend meetings. If younger students wish to participate, form a separate group for them.
6. Leaders should keep a file (and be continually adding to this file) of readings (prose, poetry, duet, and non-original oratory) for students to select from. Dewey Decimal numbers 808.5 through 900 are a good place to begin your file.
7. In order to accommodate nervous students, start the year off with the students doing only interpretive readings. Interpretive readings are easy to perform, and this will give students time to adjust to the situation. Move on to speech and debate later in the year.
8. Have students study logic before moving into debate.
9. Combine Speech and Debate Club with Drama Club.
10. Encourage students to enter contests.
11. Plan a final program to be held in May. Invite relatives to this program.

12. Organize speech and debate competitions with other homeschool speech and debate clubs.
13. All students should obtain a good quality blank cassette tape and bring it to each meeting. All readings, speeches, and debates at all meetings will be recorded for later analysis by the group or by the individual.

SUGGESTED SCHEDULE FOR MEETINGS

1. Students perform readings or speeches (nervous students like to get this over with right away).
2. Analyze and critique each reading or speech (encourage students to participate in this – perhaps by means of directed questions).
3. Give assignment for next meeting.
4. As a group, go through some articulation or inflection exercises.

Article Sixteen

Pointers for Public Speaking

FIVE POINTS TO WATCH FOR WHEN GIVING AN INTERPRETIVE READING OR SPEECH

1. Quality of your voice (not breathy, strident, harsh, nasal, throaty, or hoarse; is the voice pleasant): Your throat and mouth passageways must be open, relaxed, and free of unnecessary tension. Your lips, jaw, and tongue must be agile and flexible. Tone must be projected to the front of the mouth.
2. Articulation (not mumbling; is the voice easily understood).
3. Loudness (volume, projection, intensity; is the voice clear, distinct, and accurate).
4. Expressiveness (is the voice animated, expressive and varied, and well pitched).
5. Appropriateness (are the speech sounds and the pronunciation natural and generally acceptable; a good voice doesn't attract undue attention to itself).

PROPER BREATHING AND RELAXATION WHEN SPEAKING AND DEBATING

Experienced teachers of speech and debate agree that it is advisable to breathe from the diaphragm for good voice production. You should achieve the necessary enlargement of the chest cavity chiefly by diaphragmatic action (accompanied both by expansion at the waistline and by a slight raising of the lower ribs) and minimum action in the upper chest.

This is how to breathe from the diaphragm: as you take in air, only allow your stomach and lower ribs to extend (do not allow your shoulders or upper chest to move).

Whenever you get up in front of a group to do interpretive readings, give speeches, or to debate you should be breathing from the diaphragm. There is less effort involved in diaphragmatic as opposed to chest breathing. Diaphragm breathing will help with voice projection and tone production. It will give to the voice firmness, body, variety, and staying power. Diaphragm breathing will also help avoid tenseness in the throat and mouth area.

The beginning speaker can develop diaphragm breathing only by conscious and persistent experimentation and exercise. When you are practicing your piece at home (at least once a day), remember to:

1. Relax mouth, neck and throat area.
2. Breathe from the diaphragm.

Practice until it becomes natural. Continue to practice your readings and speeches with the tape recorder on, listen to yourself on the tape and evaluate yourself.

ARTICULATION, ENUNCIATION, DICTION

(The following is from *McGuffey's New Sixth Eclectic Reader*, 1867.)

The most common faults of articulation are the following:

1. Dropping an unaccented vowel.

CORRECT	INCORRECT
mock er y	mock ry
im mor tal	im mor t'l
lam en ta tion	lam'n ta tion
har mo ny	harm ny
fel o ny	fel'ny
reg u lar	reg'lar
cul ti vate	cult'vate
cir cu la tion	cir cl'a sh'n

2. Sounding incorrectly an unaccented vowel.

CORRECT	INCORRECT
lam en ta tion	lam un ta tion
ob sti nate	ob stun it
sys tem	sys tum or sys tim
e vent	uv ent
ter ri ble	ter rub ble

cir cu lar	cir ky ler
sen si ble	sen sub ble

PRACTICE:

This is my particular request.
She is universally esteemed.
His fears were justified by the event.
He was delighted with the exhibition.
The whole nation lamented him.

3. Suppressing the final consonants.

EXAMPLES:

John an' James are frien's o' my father.
Gi' me some bread.
We seldom fine' men o' principle to ac' thus.
Thrus' thy sickle into the harves'.
The want o' men is occasioned by the want o' money.

PRACTICE:

He learned to write.
Did you find any birds' nests?
I regard not the world's opinion.
The masts of the ship were cast down.
Such were his commands.

4. Omitting or mispronouncing whole syllables.

CORRECT	INCORRECT
ex tem po ra ry	ex tem po ry
tol er a ble	tol rer ble
mis er a ble	mis rer ble
lit er a ry	lit rer ry
nec es sa ry	ne ces ry

PRACTICE:

He devoted his attention chiefly to literary pursuits.
He is a venerable man.
His faults were owing to the degeneracy of the times.
The manuscript was undecipherable.
The confederacy continued for many years.

5. Blending the end of one word with the beginning of the next.

EXAMPLES:

I court thy gif sno more.
Bag sof gold.
Han d'me the slate.
The grove swere God sfir stemples.
My hear twas a mirror, that show' devery treasure.

PRACTICE:

The magistrates ought to arrest the rogues speedily.
Life flutters convulsed in his quivering limbs.
He went over the mountains.
What awful sounds assail my ears?
Old age has on their temples shed her silver frost.

INFLECTIONS

(The following is from *McGuffey's Sixth Eclectic Reader.*)

Inflection is a bending or sliding of the voice either upward or downward. The upward (rising inflection) is marked by the acute accent (/); and in this case the voice is to slide upward.

Example: Did you call / ? Is he sick / ?

The downward (falling inflection) is marked by the grave accent (\ ); and indicates that the voice is to slide downward.

Example: Where is London \ ? Where have you been \ ?

Sometimes both the rising and falling inflections are given to the same sound. Such sounds are designated by the circumflex (V) or (Λ). The former is called the rising circumflex; the latter the falling circumflex.

When several successive syllables are uttered without either the upward or downward slide, they are said to be uttered in a monotone, which is marked thus (—).

EXAMPLES:

1) Does he read correctly / or incorrectly \ ?
In reading this sentence the voice should slide somewhat as
represented in the following diagram:

Does he read cor-/-rectly or in-\-correctly?

2) What / ! Did he say no / ?
To be read thus:

Wh-/-at! Did he say n-/-o?

3) He did \ : he said no \
To be read thus:

He d-\-id: he said n-\-o

4) Did he do it voluntarily / , or involuntarily \ ?
To be read thus:

Did he do it vol-/-untarily, or in-\-voluntarily?

EXERCISES:

1. Are they at home / , or abroad \ ?
2. Is he willing / , or unwilling \ ?
3. You should walk \ , not ride \
4. My father / , must I stay / ?
5. Oh! But he pau-/\-sed upon the brink.
6. Is he rich / , or poor \ ?
7. It shall go hard with me, but I shall u-/\-se the weapon.
8. Where are your gibes \ now? your gambols \ ? your songs \ ? your flashes of merriment, that were wont to set the table in a roar \ ?

RULES FOR INFLECTIONS

RULE 1: Sentences and clauses which make complete sense in themselves require the falling inflection.

By virtue we secure happiness \ .
One deed of shame is succeeded by years of penitence \ .
This proposition was, however, rejected \ , and not merely rejected, but rejected with insult \ .

RULE 2: The language of emphasis generally requires the falling inflection.

Charge \ , Chester, charge \ , on \ , Stanley, on \ .
I insist \ upon this point \ : I urge \ you to it; I press \ it, demand \ it.
To arms \ ! They come \ ! The Greek \ ! The Greek \!

RULE 3: Interrogative sentences and members of sentences which can not be answered by yes or no generally require the falling inflection.

How many books did he purchase \ ?
Why reason ye these things in your hearts \ ?
Whence this pleasing hope \ , this fond desire \ , this longing after immortality \ ?

RULE 4: In the introductory part of a sentence, where the sense is dependent or incomplete, the rising inflection is generally used.

As the whirlwind passeth / , so the wicked are no more.
Ye crags / and peaks / , I'm with you once again.
Brother / , give me thy hand; and, gentle Warwick / , let me embrace thee in my weary arms.

RULE 5: Negative sentences and members of sentences usually require the rising inflection.

My Lord, we could not have had such designs / .
They are not fighting / : do not disturb / them.

RULE 6: When a sentence closes with the falling inflection, the rising inflection, for the sake of harmony, often precedes it.

He fought the Scythian in his cave / , and the unconquered Arab fled before \ him.
Be perfect \ , be of good comfort \ , be of one mind / , live in peace \ .

RULE 7: Interrogative sentences and members of sentences which can be answered by yes or no, generally require the rising inflection.

Do we mean to submit / ?
Are fleets and armies necessary to a work of love and reconciliation / ?
If it be admitted that strict integrity is not the shortest way to success, is it not the surest / , the happiest / , the best / ?

RULE 8: Interrogative exclamations, and words repeated as a kind of echo to the thought, require the rising inflection.

What / ! Might Rome have been taken / ? Rome taken when I was consul / ?
And this man is called a statesman. A statesman / ? Why, he never invented a decent humbug.
And this fellow calls himself a painter. A painter / ! He is not fit to daub the sign of a paltry ale-house.

RULE 9: Words and members of a sentence expressing antithesis or contrast require opposite inflections.

It is sown in corruption / ; it is raised in incorruption \ .
What they know by reading / , I know by experience \ .
Shall we advance / , or retreat \ ?

RULE 10: All the members of a commencing series usually require the falling inflection, except the last, which receives the rising inflection.

War \ , famine \ , pestilence \ , storm \ , and fire / besiege mankind. The knowledge \ , the power \ , the wisdom \ , the goodness / of God must all be unbounded.

RULE 11: All the members of a concluding series usually require the falling inflection, except the last but one, which has the rising inflection.

It is our duty to pity \ , to support \ , to defend / , and to relieve \ the oppressed.
I protest against this measure as cruel \ , oppressive \ , tyrannous / , and vindictive \ .

RULE 12: A clause included in a parenthesis should be read more rapidly and in a lower tone than the rest of the sentence and should terminate with the same inflection that next precedes it. If, however, it is complicated or emphatic or disconnected with the main subject, the inflections must be governed by the same rules as in other cases.

God is my witness / , (whom I serve with my spirit, in the gospel of his Son / ,) that, without ceasing, I make mention of you always in my prayers, making request / , (if, by any means, now at length, I might have a prosperous journey by the will of God / ,) to come unto you.

RULE 13: The circumflex is used to express irony, sarcasm, hypothesis, or contrast.

RULE 14: The use of the monotone is confined chiefly to grave and solemn subjects. When carefully and properly employed, it gives great dignity to delivery.

The unbeliever! One who can ga -- ze upon the su -- n and mo -- on and st -- ars and upon the unfa -- ding and imp - - erishable sky spread out so magnificently ab -- ove him and s -- ay, "All this is the w -- ork of cha -- nce!"

Appendix Two

Resource List

Resource List

INTRODUCTION

This is by no means an exhaustive curriculum guide and resource list. We are not trying to replace other lists. We have not limited our list to books and curricula currently in print. If we did, it would be a dull list indeed. Therefore, many of the books and some of the curricula will be found only at a large library, through interlibrary loan, or through a used book store.

We have included many things which we have used ourselves, but there are some things with which we may not be thoroughly familiar, and we are by no means experts in evaluating all curricula. Do not interpret an omission as a disapproval. We have omitted many things which we would have included if we were writing a whole book, not just an appendix. Also, there are some materials we may not know about it, or we may have somehow overlooked. We recommend that you obtain more than one opinion, and, if possible, have one of those opinions be from someone who has actually used the material.

Fair Warning

This is our blanket warning covering all books. Properly used, we believe that the materials which we mention in this Resource List should be satisfactory for most discerning Christian Homeschoolers. But just because we mention a book does not mean it necessarily will not require any special discernment. Technically, we could raise some objection to almost every book. But you don't want to wade through our picayune and idiosyncratic objections, so we've kept our comments few and short.

How To Use This Guide

Look up the category which you want to examine in the General Index which appears below, then follow the numbers and look it up in the Resource List which follows. What you want may appear in more than one place.

Each division of the Guide is cross-referenced back to a chapter in the book, constituting a rough topical index of the book.

We sometimes add notes with information about the materials, such as where to obtain them.

GENERAL INDEX

1. CLASSICAL EDUCATION

(Chapter 4)

Abelson, Paul. *The Seven Liberal Arts: A Study in Medieval Culture*. New York: Columbia University, 1906.

Adler, Mortimer J. *The Paideia Proposal*, New York: Macmillan Publishing Co., Inc., 1982. A very disturbed socialist philosophy of education, but not without some profitable observations which can inform the Trivium model.

Barclay, William. *Educational Ideals in the Ancient World*. Grand Rapids: Baker Book House, 1974. An excellent resource of historical observations on education.

Berquist, Laura M. *Designing Your Own Classical Curriculum: A Guide to Catholic Home Education*. Warsaw, ND: Bethlehem Books, 1994.

Blake, William N. "A Christian Philosophy of Method in Education: An Application of The Lost Tools of Learning." *The Teaching Home*, August/Sept, 1985, Box 20219, Portland, OR 97294, (503-253-9633), www.teachinghome.com.

Bluedorn, Harvey. *Teaching the Trivium Seminar Tapes*. Trivium Pursuit, PMB 168, 139 Colorado Street, Muscatine, IA 52761, (309-537-3641), www.triviumpursuit.com. Classical education seminar tapes.

Covenant Home Curriculum, N63 W23421 Main St., Sussex, WI 53089 (800-578-2421), www.covenanthome.com. Complete classical approach, K-12 curriculum for home educators with a Reformed Christian world view.

Escondido Tutorial Service, 2634 Bernardo Avenue, Escondido, CA 92029, (760-746-0980), www.gbt.org. Great Books Online tutorial.

Farris, Michael P. *The Future of Homeschooling*. Hamilton, VA: Michael Farris, 1997.

Hicks, David V. *Norms & Nobility*. New York: Praeger Publishers, 1981. An idealistic and compromised approach to a classical humanist education as applied to the classroom school.

Marrou, H. I. *A History of Education in Antiquity*. Trans. George Lamb. New York: Skeed and Ward, 1965.

The Metalogicon of John of Salisbury. Latin text completed in 1159. Translated by Daniel D. McGarry. University of California at Berkley.

Meyer, Adolph E. *An Educational History of the Ancient World*. New York: McGraw Hill, 1972.

"The Principles of Classical Education," *The Teaching Home*, Sept/Oct 1997, Box 20219, Portland, OR 97294 (503-253-9633).

Quine, David. *Worldviews of the Western World*. Cornerstone Curriculum, 2006 Flat Creek Place, Richardson, TX 75080.

Sayers, Dorothy. "The Lost Tools of Learning." *Teaching the Trivium: Christian Homeschooling in a Classical Style*. Trivium Pursuit, PMB 168, 139 Colorado Street, Muscatine, IA 52761.

Trivium Pursuit's Homeschooling with the Trivium Email Discussion Loop. Contact trivium@muscanet.com for more information.

Veith, Gene Edward. *Philanthropy, Culture and Society*. "Pursuing the Trivium: The Assoc. of Classical and Christian Schools." Capital Research Institute, Apr., 1995.

Veith, Gene Edward and Andrew Kern. *Classical Education: Towards the Revival of American Schooling*. Washington DC: Capital Research Center, 1997.

Veritas Press, 1250 Belle Meade Dr., Lancaster, PA 17601 (800 922 5082). Catalog with a large selection of materials useful to homeschoolers using the classical approach.

Wagner, David L. *The Seven Liberal Arts in the Middle Ages*. Bloomington, IN: Indiana University Press, 1983.

Wilson, Douglas. *Recovering the Lost Tools of Learning*. Wheaton, Illinois: Crossway Books, 1991. A Christian philosophy for a classical style of education applied to the classroom school model.

Wilson, Douglas, editor. *Repairing the Ruins*. Moscow, Idaho: Canon Press, 1996. Canon Press, Box 8729, Moscow, ID 83843. Christian philosophy for a classical style of education applied to the classroom school model.

Wilson, Douglas. *The Paideia of God*. Moscow, Idaho: Canon Press, 1999. Canon Press, Box 8729, Moscow, ID 83843. Christian philosophy for a classical style of education applied to the classroom school model.

Wilson, Douglas, Wesley Callihan, and Douglas Jones. *Classical Education & The Home School*. Moscow, Idaho: Canon Press, 1995. Canon Press, Box 8729, Moscow, ID 83843. Application of the classical classroom school model to Homeschooling.

Wise, Jessie and Susan Wise Bauer. *The Well Trained Mind*. New York: W.W. Norton & Company, 1999. The classical style of education applied to Homeschooling. A good overall resource with lots of practical particulars and lists of reliable resources.

2. GENERAL HOMESCHOOLING

2A. General Preparation (Chapters 2, 11)

The Always Incomplete Catalog, 3900 Chalet Suzanne Drive, Lake Wales, FL 33853. Catalog filled with great articles on Homeschooling and Homeschooling books and curricula.

Beechick, Ruth. *You Can Teach Your Child Successfully: Grades 4-8*. Golden, CO: Arrow Press, 1999. Best all-round introduction to Homeschooling ever published.

Beechick, Ruth. *The Three R's: K-3*. Golden, CO: Arrow Press (2000). All Homeschooling parents should read these three little booklets on teaching math and reading: A Strong Start in Language; A Home Start in Reading; An Easy Start in Arithmetic.

Bluedorn, Harvey. *Seven Undeniable Truths of Homeschooling* seminar audio tape. Trivium Pursuit, PMB 168, 139 Colorado Street, Muscatine, Iowa 52761, (309-537-3641), www.triviumpursuit.com.

Blumenfeld, Samuel L. *How to Tutor*. New Rochelle, NY: Arlington House, 1973.

Blumenfeld, Samuel L. *The New Illiterates*. New Rochelle, NY: Arlington House, 1973.

Blumenfeld, Samuel L. *NEA-Trojan Horse in American Education*. Boise, ID: Paradigm Co., 1984.

Blumenfeld, Samuel L. *Is Public Education Necessary?* Old Greenwich, CT: Devin-Adair, 1981.

Bloom, Allan. *The Closing of the American Mind*. New York: Simon and Schuster, 1987.

Boyer, Rick. *The Socialization Trap*. Rustburg, VA: The Learning Parent, 1994.

Boyer, Rick. *Home Education with Confidence*. Rustburg, VA: The Learning Parent, 1995.

Cannon, Ron and Inge. Education PLUS, Taylors, SC, (864-609-5411), www.edplus.com. Lots of excellent materials for the new and veteran homeschooler.

Clarkson, Clay. *Whole Hearted Child: Home Education Handbook*. Walnut Springs, TX: Whole Heart Ministries, 1994.

Colfax, David & Micki. *Homeschooling for Excellence*. New York: Warner Books, 1988.

Duffy, Cathy. *Christian Home Educators Curriculum Manual: Elementary Grades* and *Christian Home Educators Curriculum Manual: Jr/Sr High*. Grove Publishing, 16172 Huxley Circle, Westminster, CA 92683, (714-841-1220), www.grovepublishing.com.

Duffy, Cathy. *Government Nannies: From the Cradle to the Grave*. Gresham, OR: Noble Publishing, 1995.

The Elijah Company catalog, 1053 Eldridge Loop, Crossville, TN 38558, (888-2 ELIJAH). Valuable Homeschooling articles and Homeschooling books and curricula.

Gatto, John. *Dumbing Us Down*. Philadelphia: New Society Publishers, 1992.

Granger, Lori and Bill. *The Magic Feather-The Truth About Special Education*. New York: E.P. Dutton, 1986.

Grover, Alan. *Ohio's Trojan Horse-A Warning to Christian Schools Everywhere*. Greenville, SC: BJU Press, 1977.

Healy, Jane. *Endangered Minds: Why Our Children Don't Think and What We Can Do About It.* New York: Touchstone, 1990.

Healy, Jane. *Failure to Connect: How Computers Affect Our Children's Minds for Better and Worse*. New York: Simon and Schuster, 1998.

Home School Digest. Wisdom's Gate, PO Box 374, Covert, MI 49043, www.homeschooldigest.com.

Home School Researcher. Brian Ray. National Home Education Research Institute, Box 13939, Salem, OR 97309, (503-364-1490), www.nheri.org. This quarterly, refereed, scholarly journal presents basic research on home-based and family-based education in areas such as socialization, academic achievement, history, and law. This unique periodical keeps home educators, researchers, and others abreast of the most current factual and theoretical research information available on home education.

Homeschooling Today, Box 1608, Fort Collins, CO 80522, (970-493-2716), www.homeschooltoday.com.

Home Education Network Radio, Box 3338, Idaho Springs, CO 80452, (303 567 4092), wwwhomeschoolingusa.com..

Home School Legal Defense Association, Box 3000 Purcellville, VA 20134, (540-338-5600), www.hslda.org.

Klicka, Christopher J. *Home Schooling in the United States: A Legal Analysis.* Paeonian Springs, VA: *HSLDA, 1995.*

Klicka, Christopher J. *The Right Choice.* Gresham, OR: Nobel Publishers, 1992.

Howshall, Marilyn. *Wisdom's Way of Learning*. Howshall Home Publications, Box 1750, Eatonville, WA 98328, (360-832-8845).

MacCauley, Susan Schaefer. *For the Children's Sake*. Westchester, IL: Crossway Books, 1984.

Mander, Jerry. *Four Arguments for the Elimination of Television*. New York: Quill, 1978.

Montgomery, Zach. *Poison Drops in the Federal Senate*. Washington DC: Gibson Brothers, 1886.

Moore, Raymond & Dorothy. *Better Late Than Early*. Readers Digest Press, 1975.

Moore, Raymond & Dorothy. *Home Grown Kids.* Dallas, TX: Word Publishers, 1981.

Moore, Raymond & Dorothy. *School Can Wait.* Provo, UT: BYU Press, 1982.

Moore, Raymond & Dorothy. *The Successful Homeschool Family Handbook.* Nashville, TN: Thomas Nelson., 1994.

Moore, Raymond & Dorothy. *Minding Your Own Business.* Brentwood, TN: Wolgemuth Hyatt, Publishers, Inc., 1990.

Moore Report International Magazine, Box 1, Camas, WA 98607, (360-835-2736).

Morris, Barbara M. *Change Agents in the Schools*. Upland, CA: The Barbara M. Morris Report, 1979.

NATHHAN News, Box 39, Porthill, ID 83853, (208-267-6246), www.nathhan.com. National Challenged Homeschoolers Associated Network. NATHHAN is a Christian, nonprofit organization dedicated to providing encouragement to families with special needs children who are Homeschooling. This is one of my favorite magazines.

The Nebraska Civic Digest, 312 Brentwood, Norfolk, NE 68701, www.familiesthatflourish.com. A monthly pro-family, Christian newspaper. Not just for Nebraska residents.

Patrick, James, ed. *America 2000/Goals 2000: Research Manual*. Moline, IL: Citizens for Academic Excellence, 1994. East Moline Christian School, 900 46th Avenue, East Moline, IL 61244, (309-796-1485).

Practical Homeschooling Magazine, Mary Pride, Box 1250, Fenton, MO 63026, www.home-school.com.

Pride, Mary. *The Big Books of Home Learning* (3 volumes). Home Life, Inc., 1999.

Quit You Like Men Magazine: A Call to True Christian Manliness, 152 Maple Lane, Harriman, TN 37748. Robert Green, editor and publisher. This magazine "is for men who want to lead simple, godly lives, close to home, close to their wives and children, close to God."

Ray, Brian D., Ph.D. *Home Schooling on the Threshold: A Survey of Research at the Dawn of the New Millennium*. NHERI, PO Box 13939, Salem, OR 97309, (503-364-1490), www.nheri.org. This is the most current review of research on a variety of topics related to home schooling.

Ray, Brian D., Ph.D. *Strengths of Their Own – Home Schoolers Across America: Academic Achievement, Family Characteristics, and Longitudinal Traits.* NHERI, PO Box 13939, Salem, OR 97309, (503-364-1490), www.nheri.org. This unique book is an engaging comprehensive report, on Dr. Ray's largest-ever nationwide and longitudinal study, that includes statistics, analyses, and an evaluation of home education's benefits to children, families, and society. This book presents a summary of many researchers' studies on home schooling, explains the methods used in this nationwide study, presents many pages and graphs of data and statistics, summarizes the findings, and concludes with a chapter on the strengths of home schooling.

Reed, Karl. *The Bible, Homeschooling and the Law*. Christian Home Ministries, 1991.

Sacks, Peter. *Standardized Minds, The High Price of America's Testing Culture and What We Can Do to Change It.* Cambridge, MA: Perseus Books, 1999.

Stout, Maureen. *The Feel-Good Curriculum, The Dumbing-Down of America's Kids in the Name of Self-Esteem*. Cambridge, MA: Perseus Books, 2000.

The Teaching Home Magazine, Box 20219, Portland, OR 97294, (503-253-9633), www.teachinghome.com.

Vitz, Paul C. *Censorship-Evidence of Bias in Our Children's Textbooks*. Ann Arbor, MI: Servant Books, 1986.

Whitehead, John W. *Home Education and Constitutional Liberties*. Westchester, IL: Crossway, 1986.

Winn, Marie. *The Plug-In Drug: Television, Children and the Family*. New York: Penguin Books, 1985.

2B. Discipline (Chapter 11)

Abbott, John S. C. *The Mother At Home.* GAM Publications, 1998. Originally published in 1833. Can purchase from Grace and Truth Books, 3406 Summit Boulevard, Sand Springs, Oklahoma, 74063, (918-245-1500) www.graceandtruthbooks.com.

Barth, Jeff & Marge. *Child Training and the Home School*. Charlotte, VT: Parable, 1991.

Davis, S.M. *Changing the Heart of a Rebel* (booklet and video). Park Meadows Baptist Church, 800 Memorial Park Road, Lincoln, IL 62656 (1-800-500-8853).

Witherspoon, John. *Letters on the Education of Children*, published in *Foundations of Liberty – John Witherspoon*, East Moline, Illinois: MacArthur Institute, 2001. MacArthur Institute, 900 46th Avenue, East Moline, Illinois, 61244, (309-796-1485).

2C. Unit Studies (Chapter 10)

Beautiful Feet Books, 139 Main Street, Sandwich, MA 02563 (800-889-1978), www.bfbooks.com. History Through Literature Series.

Bendt, Valerie. *How to Create Your Own Unit Study*. Tampa, FL: Common Sense Press/Bendt Family Ministries, 1994.

Hulsey, Jessica. *Konos,* Box 250, Anna, TX 75409, (972-924-2712), www.konos.com.

Lambert, Jane Claire and Becky Jane Lambert. *Five in a Row*, Box 707, Grandview, MO 64030, (816-246-9252), www.fiveinarow.com.

Stout, Kathryn. *Guides to History Plus*. History, geography, government and economics are incorporated into an easy-to-use guide for the study of any period or culture in grades K-12. Design-A-Study, 408 Victoria Avenue, Wilmington, DE 19804, (302-998-3889), www.designastudy.com

2D. Principle Approach (Chapter 10)

Foundation for American Christian Education, Box 9588, Chesapeake, VA 23321, (800-352-3223), www.face.net. Principle Approach materials including the "Big, Red Books" and The NOAH Plan.

Rose, James. *A Guide to American Christian Education for Home & School: Principle Approach*. American Christian History Institute, Box 648, Palo Cedro, CA 96073, (530 547 3535). Principle Approach materials.

Slater, Rosalie. *Teaching and Learning America's Christian History: The Principle Approach*. Foundation for American Christian Education, Box 9588, Chesapeake, VA 23321, (800-352-3223), www.face.net.

3. LANGUAGE ARTS & ENGLISH

3A. Phonics (Chapter 11)

Blumenfeld, Samuel. *Alpha-Phonics: A Primer for Beginning Readers.* Paradigm Company, 3500 Mountain View Drive, Boise, Idaho, 83704, (208-322-4440), www.howtotutor. Excellent, inexpensive intensive phonics curriculum.

Dettmer, Bonnie. *Phonics for Reading and Spelling.* Small Ventures, 1618 Kendolph, Denton, TX 76205, (940-566-6123). Teaches intensive phonics in the same style as *The Writing Road to Reading*. Ages 4-13.

Diehl, Kathryn. *Johnny Still Can't Read But You Can Teach Him at Home.* New York: Cal Industries, 1976.

Flesch, Rudolf, *Why Johnny Can't Read*. New York: Harper and Row, 1966.

PhonicsTutor, 4:20 Communications, Box 421027, Minneapolis, Minnesota, 55442, (888-420-7323), www.phonicstutor.com. Phonics, reading, and spelling curriculum for the computer based upon *Alpha-Phonics*.

Rogers, Frank. *The Great Saltmine and Hifwip Direct Phonics Reading Program*. Tatras, PO Box 44093, Tacoma, WA 98444, (253-531-0312), wwwtatrasaverticalphonics.com. Inexpensive, thorough, phonogram-based reading curriculum. This is the one I would use with my kids if I was starting over.

Spalding, Romalda Bishop and Walter T. Spalding. *The Writing Road to Reading: A modern method of phonics for teaching children to read*. New York: Quill, 1969.

3B. Readers (Chapters 11, 12)

Christian Liberty Press, 502 West Euclid Avenue, Arlington Heights, IL 60004, (800-348-0899), www.homeschools.org. Reprints of old nature study, literature, and history readers.

McGuffey's Readers. Fairfax, VA: Christian School Edition, 1974.

3C. Copywork (Chapter 11)

Beechick, Ruth, *The Three R's: K-3,* Golden, CO: Arrow Press *(*2000*)*. Three little booklets including A Strong Start in Language.

Rushton, Cindy. *Language Arts...The Easy Way*, 1225 Christy Lane, Tuscumbia, AL 35674, (256-381-2529), www.utmost-way/bookfair/bftime4tea.htm..

3D. Spelling (Chapter 12)

Adams-Gordon, Beverly L. *Spelling Power*. Castlemoyle Books, PO Box 520, Pomeroy, WA 99347, (888-SPELL-86), www.castlemoyle.com.

Bluedorn, Harvey. *Handy English Encoder and Decoder*. Trivium Pursuit, PMB 168, 139 Colorado Street, Muscatine, IA 52761. All the spelling and phonics rules.

Christian Technologies, Inc., Box 2201, Independence, MO 64055 (800-366-8320), www.christiantech.com. Webster's 1828 Dictionary on CD ROM.

Noah Webster's 1828 Dictionary. San Francisco, CA: Foundation for American Christian Education, 1980. Reprint of Webster's dictionary.

Reader's Digest Family Word Finder: A New Thesaurus of Synonyms and Antonyms in Dictionary Form, The Reader's Digest Association, Inc., Pleasantville, NY, 1986.

Stout, Kathryn. *Natural Speller*. Design-A-Study, 408 Victoria Avenue, Wilmington, DE 19804, (302-998-3889), www.designastudy.com

Webster, Noah. *The Elementary Spellingbook*. Republished by Trivium Pursuit, PMB 168, 139 Colorado Street, Muscatine, IA 52761, (309-537-3641), www.triviumpursuit.com.

3E. English Grammar (Chapter 12)

Phillips, Wanda C. *Easy Grammar*. ISHA Enterprises, Box 12520, Scottsdale, AZ 85267, (480-502-9456), www.easygrammar.com. This is a good, thorough grammar curriculum.

3F. Sentence Diagramming (Chapter 12)

Daly, Mary. *The Complete Book of Diagrams.* The Riggs Institute, 4185 S.W. 102nd Avenue, Beaverton, OR 97005, (503-646-9459), www.riggsinst.org.

Hajek, Ellen. *Diagramming: The Key to Understanding Grammar*. Purchase from Builder Books, PO Box 5789, Lynnwood, WA 98046, (425-778-4526), www.bbhomeschoolcatalog.com.

3G. Outlining (Chapters 12, 13, 14)

Bradrick, Susan, *Understanding Writing*. Bradrick Family Enterprises, 25 Geissler Road, Montesano, WA 98563, (360-249-2472). Teaches outlining skills.

3H. Composition (Chapters 12, 13, 14)

Bradrick, Susan. *Understanding Writing*. Bradrick Family Enterprises, 25 Geissler Road, Montesano, WA 98563, (360-249-2472). Complete and thorough Christ centered writing curriculum. Covers all aspects of writing. All ages.

Flesch, Rudolf and Abraham H. Lass. *The Classic Guide to Better Writing*. New York: Harper Perennial, 1996. Each chapter is about ten pages long, including a brief summary and extensive exercises at the end. It is not extensive, but gives essential information. The second half of the book is an English grammar review focusing on common mistakes in grammar. This is a good book to remediate students coming out of the government school system, including adults. Ages 13 and up.

Thaxton, Carole. *Learn to Write the Novel Way*. Konos Connection, 111 Bethea Road, Fayetteville, GA 30214, (800-780-6827), www.konos.org. Writing curriculum for producing your own novel, grades 5-12.

Wiener, Harvey S. *Any Child Can Write: How to Improve Your Child's Writing Skills from Preschool to High School*. New York: Bantam Books, 1990. Motivational book for the parent to read to help him teach his child how to write. Read this book when your child is still young.

The Writing In Narrative Series. The Elijah Company, 1053 Eldridge Loop, Crossville, TN 38558, (888-2 ELIJAH). All ages.

Zinsser, William. *On Writing Well: An informal guide to writing nonfiction*. New York: Harper and Row, 1980. For rhetoric level students to brush up on writing skills.

3I. Research (Chapters 13, 14)

Barzun, Jacques and Henry F. Graff. *The Modern Researcher*. Orlando, FL: Harcourt, Brace, Jovanovich Publishers, 1985. This book is for anyone who is or will be engaged in research and report-writing, regardless of his field of interest. Includes learning to use aids to research (indexes, bibliographies, dictionaries, etc.); verifying and assembling data; evaluating sources; writing clearly; taking notes; and much more.

Bluedorn, Nathaniel. *How to Use the Internet to Do Research* seminar audio tape. Trivium Pursuit, PMB 168, 139 Colorado Street, Muscatine, Iowa 52761, (309-537-3641), www.triviumpursuit.com.

Lamm, Kathryn. *10,000 Ideas for Term Papers, Projects, Reports, and Speeches*. New York: MacMillan, 1998. Full of interesting topics suitable for almost any research assignment from ages 10 and up.

Roth, Audrey J. *The Research Paper: Process, Form, and Content* (6th ed). Belmont, CA: Wadsworth Publishing, 1989. Best book we have found on writing a research paper.

3J. Oral Narration (Chapters 11, 12, 13)

Andreola, Karen. *A Charlotte Mason Companion*. Charlotte Mason Research and Supply, 1998.

Macaulay, Susan Schaeffer. *For the Children's Sake*. Westchester, IL: Crossway Books, 1984.

4. RHETORIC

4A. Textbooks (Chapters 7, 14)

Adler, Mortimer J., and Charles Van Doren. *How to Read a Book*. New York: Simon and Schuster, 1972.

Aristotle. *Rhetoric*. Trans. Rhys Roberts.

Corbett, Edward P. J. *Classical Rhetoric for the Modern Student*. 4th ed. Oxford: Oxford University Press, 1998. An attempt to bring rhetoric into the classroom. Standard rhetoric textbook. Large bibliography of primary and secondary texts.

Dabney, Robert L. *Lectures in Sacred Rhetoric*.

Dixon, Peter. *Rhetoric*. London: Methuen and Company, 1971. A history of rhetoric, the rules of rhetoric, and a large bibliography.

Horner, Winifred. *Rhetoric in the Classical Tradition*.

Howes, Raymond F., ed. *Historical Studies of Rhetoric and Rhetoricians*. Ithaca, NY: Cornell University Press, 1961.

Murphy, James J. "The Origins and Early Development of Rhetoric." *A Synoptic History of Rhetoric*. Davis, CA: Hermagoras, 1983.

Newborn, Maryalice B. *Study Guide for How to Read a Book*, 2371 Adams Court, Export, PA 15632.

Quintilian. *Institutio Oratoria*. Trans. H. E. Butler.

Vickers, Brian. *In Defense of Rhetoric*. Oxford: Clarendon Press, 1988. Contains large rhetoric bibliography and definitions of rhetorical figures and tropes.

4B. Composition (Chapter 14)

Flesch, Rudolf and Abraham H. Lass. *The Classic Guide to Better Writing*. New York: Harper Perennial, 1996. Each Chapter is about ten pages long, including a brief summary and extensive exercises at the end. It is not extensive, but gives essential information. The second half of the book is an English Grammar review focusing on common mistakes in grammar. This is a good book to remediate students coming out of the government school system, including adults.

Zinsser, William. *On Writing Well: An informal guide to writing nonfiction*. New York: Harper and Row, 1980. For rhetoric level students to brush up on writing skills.

4C. English Handbooks and Style Manuals (Chapter 14)

The Chicago Manual of Style: For authors, editors, and copywriters. Chicago: The University of Chicago Press, 1982.

Collins, Grace C. *English Handbook for Christian Schools*. Bob Jones University Press, Greenville, SC 29614.

Fowler, H.W. *The King's English*, numerous publishers and editions. The standard guide to grammar and diction. A half-century old, it is still reprinted. Not as subject to the corruptions which creep into modern treatments of grammar. Covers well, and interestingly: Vocabulary, Syntax, Airs and Graces (Subtleties of Expression), Punctuation, and a miscellaneous collection of much more. Could be used as Wisdom Level review of grammar focusing on mistakes easily made and subtleties of expression.

Lunsford, Andrea and Robert Conners. *The St. Martin's Handbook*. New York: St. Martens Press, 1995.

Skillin, Marjorie E. and Robert M. Gay *Words into Type*. Englewood Cliffs, NJ: Prentice-Hall, Inc., 1974.

Strunk, William Jr. and E.B. White. *The Elements of Style*. New York: MacMillan Publishing Company, 1979.

4D. Oral Interpretation. (Chapters 7, 11, 12, 13, 14)

Bahn, Eugene, and Margaret L. Bahn. *A History of Oral Interpretation*. Minneapolis, MN: Burgess Publishing Company, 1970. From the classical Greek period to the twentieth century.

Bob, Son of Battle by Alfred Ollivant or other books of fiction that are written in a foreign dialog.

Deplitch, Edith Martha. *Poems of Fun and Fancy for the Little Folks—Arranged for Group Speaking*. Boston: Expression Company, 1942.

Fairbanks, Grant. *Voice and Articulation Drillbook*. New York: Harper and Brothers, 1940. Includes articulation, pronunciation, breathing, time, pitch, loudness, and voice quality with lots of exercises.

Farma, William J., ed. *Prose, Poetry and Drama for Oral Interpretation*. New York: Harper and Brothers Publishers, 1936.

Granger, Edith, ed. *An Index to Poetry and Recitations: Being a Practical Reference Manual for the Librarian, Teacher, Bookseller, Elocutionist, etc.* Chicago: A. C. McClurg and Co., 1904, 1918, 1929, 1940. These books index the contents of hundreds of volumes, comprising standard and popular collections of poetry, recitations (both prose and verse), orations, drills, dialogues, selections from dramas, etc. all in print at the time of compilation.

Gray, Margie, ed. *Anne's Anthology: Following the Footnote Trail, Poetry Popular in the Victorian Era.* Silver City, NM: Cadron Creek Christian Curriculum, 2000.

Hanschke, Roy. *Voice Personality: Dress Your Voice with Personality*. Voice Personality, PO Box 3099, Littleton, CO 80161, (800-604-8843), www.voicepersonality.com. Speaking voice training with booklet and tapes.

Hendry, Jim and Shelley. Helps for interpretive reading, drama, and speech (audio and video tapes). Christian Homeschooling family. Write for their catalog: His Image Ministries, Box 1715, Clarksville, VA 23927 (804-372-5565). Email hisimag@kerrlake.com

Johnson, Gertrude E. *Dialects for Oral Interpretation: Selections and Discussion*. New York: The Century Company, 1926. A usable text and source of material in dialect form—suitable both for study for the sake of the dialect, and also to use as good program numbers (Scotch, Italian, Negro, French, Scandinavian, Irish, misc., one act plays in dialect).

Kidd, Robert. Voice Culture and Elocution—with numerous exercises in reading and speaking. Wilson, Hinkle and Company, 1857.

Lee, Charlotte I. *Oral Interpretation*. Boston: Houghton Mifflin Company, 1952, 1959. Table of contents includes: Basic Principles of Oral Interpretation; The Interpretation of Prose; The Interpretation of Drama; The Interpretation of Poetry; A Brief History of Theories of Interpretation; Suggested Material for Oral Interpretation.

McGuffey's Readers. Fairfax, VA: Christian School Edition, 1974.

McHale, Frank. *Pieces That Have Won Prizes*. Freeport, New York: Books for Libraries Press, 1930, 1972.

Parrish, Wayland Maxfield. *Reading Aloud*. New York: The Ronald Press Company, 1932. Includes objectives in the study of oral reading, method in the study of reading, interpretation of attitude, vividness of expression, the reading of verse, voice improvement, pronunciation, the emotional quality in poetry, the imaginative quality in poetry, impersonation and the art of interpretation.

Procter, Leslie C. and Gladys Trueblood Stroop, eds. *Selections for Public Speaking*. New York: Charles Scribner's Sons, 1930.

Reeves, James and Norman Culpan. *Dialogue and Drama*. Boston: Plays, Inc., 1950. A book of passages to read aloud.

Shoemaker, Charles C., ed. *Choice Dialect and Other Characterizations: Containing Readings and Recitations in Irish, German, Scotch, French, Negro, and other Dialects*. Philadelphia: The Penn Publishing Company, 1924.

Shoemaker, Mrs. J. W., ed. *Shoemaker's Best Selections for Readings and Recitations Series*. Philadelphia: The Penn Publishing Company, 1911.

Woods, Ralph L., ed. *A Treasury of the Familiar Series*. New York: MacMillan Company, 1942. A collection of readings for recitation.

One of the best sources for interpretive readings will be your local old book store. Here you will find numerous collections of recitations and readings from the best authors. Choose books published before 1950.

Another good source for interpretive readings will be the 808 (Dewey Decimal, literature) section of the library. We recommend books published before 1950.

Using the Library of Congress System, oral interpretation is found at PN4145 to PN4180; selections for oral interpretation (including choral readings) start at PN4199; and voice and articulation books start at PN4193.

4E. Speech (Chapters 7, 12, 13, 14)

Aslett, Don. *Is There a Speech Inside You?* Cincinnati, OH: Writer's Digest Books, 1989. Humorous.

Buys, William E., ed. *Creative Speaking*. Lincolnwood, IL: National Textbook Co., 1981. Provides comprehensive guidance for students preparing for speech events (oratory, oral interpretation of prose and poetry, extemporaneous speaking, serious dramatic interpretation, humorous dramatic interpretation, etc.).

Buehler, E. C., and Richard L. Johannesen. *Building the Contest Oration*. New York: The H. W. Wilson Company, 1965. For high school age students.

Cicero, Marcus Tullius. "The Making of an Orator." Trans. E. W. Sutton. Harvard University Press, Cambridge, MA, 1942.

Duerr, Edwin. *Radio and Television Acting—Criticism, Theory and Practice*. New York: Rinehart and Company, 1959.

Ewbank, Henry L. and Sherman P. Lawton. *Projects for Radio Speech: A Manual for the Student*. New York: Harper and Brothers Publishers.

Faris, Jerri. Audio tapes on how to start a homeschool speech and debate club (RR3, Box 49, Delphi, IN 46923, 219-686-2908).

Gondin, William R. and Edward W. Mammen. *The Art of Speaking Made Simple: A Comprehensive Course for Self-Study and Review*. Garden City, NY: Doubleday and Co., 1981.

Holm, James Noble. *How to Judge Speech Contests*. Portland, Maine: Platform News Publishing Company, 1938.

Jeub, Chris. *Jeub's Complete Guide to speech and Debate*. Training Minds Ministry, 16315 Rickenbacker Avenue, Monument CO 80132, (719-487-7621)

Litfin, Duane. *Public Speaking: A Handbook for Christians*. Grand Rapids, Michigan: Baker Book House, 1992. Textbook on public speaking.

Monroe, Alan H. and Douglas Ehninger. *Principles and Types of Speech*. Glenview, Illinois: Scott, Foresman and Company, 1967. Speech textbook.

Moon, Teresa M. *Beginning Public Speaking*. The simple, user friendly, no experience needed, easy to follow program of introducing and building public speaking skills for the Christian student (and teacher). Training Minds Ministry, 16315 Rickenbacker Avenue, Monument CO 80132, (719-487-7621)

Mulgrave, Dorothy I., Clark S. Marlor, and Elmer E. Baker, Jr. *Bibliography of Speech and Allied Areas—1950-1960*. New York: Chilton Company, 1962. Bibliography of doctoral dissertations and books that relate to speech and allied areas.

Oliver, Robert T. *Effective Speech*. New York: Holt, Rinehart and Winston, 1939. Speech textbook.

Platz, Mabel. *The History of Public Speaking—A Comparative Study of World Oratory*. New York: Noble and Noble, 1935. The ancient Greek period through the World War period.

Raubicheck, Letitia. *How to Teach Good Speech in the Elementary Schools*. New York: Noble and Noble,1937. Techniques and procedures in teaching the speech arts. Includes a bibliography of choral speaking materials.

The Teaching Home Magazine, Box 20219, Portland, OR 97220. "Communication Skills" Feb/March 1993 issue. "Debate" Oct/Nov 1985 issue.

Thonssen, Lester, Elizabeth Fatherson, and Dorthea Thonssen. *Bibliography of Speech Education*. New York: The H. W. Wilson Company, 1939. A bibliographical index of literature on speech education. Includes rhetoric, interpretation, and dramatics.

Thonssen, Lester, Mary Margaret Robb, and Dorthea Thonssen. *Bibliography of Speech Education—Supplement: 1939-1948*. New York: The H. W. Wilson Company, 1950.

Toastmasters (check with your library for address).

Trivium Pursuit's List of National Contests Open to Homeschoolers. Trivium Pursuit, PMB 168, 139 Colorado Street, Muscatine, Iowa 52761.

You will find speech textbooks starting at about PN4000 (using the Library of Congress System) in your library.

4F. Debate (Chapters 7, 13, 14)

Bluedorn, Laurie. *The Bare Bones Basics of Debate* seminar audio tape. Trivium Pursuit, PMB 168, 139 Colorado Street, Muscatine, Iowa 52761, (309-537-3641), www.triviumpursuit.com.

Chandler, Robert A. "Selected Bibliography on Argumentation and Debate." in *Advanced Debate: Readings in Theory, Practice and Teaching*. 3rd edition. Edited by David A. Thomas and Jack Hart. Lincolnwood, IL: National Textbook, 1987.

Colburn, Frank E. "The Art of Debate." Old Greenwich, Connecticut: Listening Library. Recorded message by a debate coach.

Courtney, Luther W. and Glenn R. Capp. *Practical Debating*. Chicago: J. B. Lippincott Company, 1949. College debate textbook. Contains an example of a formal debate and a radio debate.

Crocker, Lionel. *Argumentation and Debate*. New York: American Book Company, 1944. Debate textbook. Bibliography of collections of speeches, list of argumentative speeches, resolutions for debate, topics for argumentative speeches, example of a debate brief, and several famous speeches are analyzed for study.

Farris, Christy. *An Introduction to Argumentation and Debate*. HSLDA, Box 3000, Purcellville, VA 20134. Published 1997. A basic, easy-to-understand debate textbook written from a Christian, homeschool perspective. If you've never studied debate, here is where to begin. This 83-page text covers all the fundamentals of formal debate, including logic, research, stock issues, affirmative case construction, negative strategies, evidence, and more.

Foster, William Trufant. *Argumentation and Debating*. Boston: Houghton Mifflin Company, 1908. Chapters on: phrasing the proposition, analyzing the proposition, proving the proposition, refuting opposing arguments, constructing the brief, developing the argument from the brief, arousing the emotions, and debating. Also contains exercises for each chapter, specimen brief, specimen forensic, specimen debate, instructions to judges, and a list of propositions.

Fryar, Maridell and David A. Thomas. *Basic Debate*. Skokie, IL: National Textbook Company, 1979. A basic textbook for beginning-level debate students.

Hensley, Dana and Diana Prentice. *Mastering Competitive Debate*. Caldwell, ID: Clark Publishing, 1982.

Holzer, Harold, ed. *The Lincoln-Douglas Debates: The First Complete Text.*

Home School Heartbeat radio broadcasts with Michael P. Farris. Debate Week, Shows 1546-1550. HSLDA, Box 3000, Purcellville, VA 20134.

An Introduction to Argumentation and Debate Video Tape Set with Deborah Haffey, Cedarville College Debate Team Coach. HSLDA, Box 3000, Purcellville, VA 20134. The first video in this two-video set features a 45-minute lecture on the principles of debate theory; the second tape features an actual debate with comments between speakers.

Jeub, Chris. *Jeub's Complete Guide to Speech and Debate*. Training Minds Ministry, 16315 Rickenbacker Avenue, Monument CO 80132, (719-487-7621). An educational guidebook that shows how to train children and teens in the skills of public speaking and debating. Specifically designed for Homeschooling families.

Kay, Jack and Walter Ulrich. *Bibliography on Debate Theory and Individual Events*. Kansas City: National Fed. of State High School Associations, 1990.

Kruger, Arthur N. *Modern Debate—Its Logic and Strategy*. New York: McGraw-Hill Book Company, 1960. Textbook with exercises and sample debate.

Lahman, Carroll Pollock. *Debate Coaching: A Handbook for Teachers and Coaches*. New York: The H. W. Wilson, 1930. Judging the debate, speech and debate bibliography, topics for debate.

Miller, Marion Mills, ed. *Great Debates in American History*. New York: Current Literature Publishing Company, 1913.

Moulton, Eugene R. *The Dynamics of Debate*. New York: Harcourt, Brace & World, Inc., 1966. Textbook with exercises and questions.

Musgrave, George McCoy. *Competitive Debate: Rules and Techniques*. New York: The H. W. Wilson Company, 1957.

National Christian Forensics and Communications Association (NCFCA), Box 500208, San Diego, CA 92150, (858) 774-2291, www.ncfca.org. Organization which offers resources on debate and speech and sponsors the annual national homeschool speech and debate tournament.

Nichols, Egbert Ray. *Intercollegiate Debate—The Year Book of College Debating—Affirmative and Negative*. New York: Noble and Noble. These annuals were published from around 1920 till after WWII. Dozens of debates on numerous topics.

O'Neill, James Milton, Craven Laycock, and Robert Leighton Scales. *Argumentation and Debate*. New York: The Macmillan Company, 1917. Lists the rules for writing a brief.

Pattee, George K. *Practical Argumentation*. New York: The Century Company, 1909. "Argumentation is the art of presenting truth so that others will accept it and act in accordance with it. Debate is a special form of argumentation: it is oral argumentation carried on by opposing sides."

Phelps, Edith M., ed. *Debaters' Manual*. New York: The H. W. Wilson Company, 1924. How to prepare a debate, how to form and manage a debating society, and a large bibliography on public speaking, argumentation, and debate.

Phelps, Edith M. *University Debaters Annual—Constructive and Rebuttal Speeches Delivered in Debates of American Colleges and Universities*. New York: The H. W. Wilson Company. These annuals were published starting around 1914 till sometime after WWII. Dozens of debates on numerous topics.

Sandford, William Phillips and William Hayes Yeager. *Problems for Debate Practice*. New York: T. Nelson and Sons, 1933.

Summers, Harrison Boyd. *How to Debate: A Textbook for Beginners*. New York: The H. W. Wilson Company, 1940, 1950, 1963.

Training Minds Ministry, 16315 Rickenbacker Avenue, Monument, CO 80132, (719) 487-7621. Speech and debate coach Chris Jeub distributes top-quality resources for students and families who wish to start academic debate and individual speech events. Mr. Jeub also writes a yearly book discussing the debate topic and providing basic research to jump-start the novice debator. Immigration Reform: Debating the 2000-2001 Home School Resolution, study guide for this year's debate; e-mail loop by e-mailing jeub@earthlink.net; free sample of The Christian Debater magazine.

Trivium Pursuit Web Page. Information on homeschool speech and debate www.triviumpursuit.com.

Wiese, Jeffrey. *Lincoln-Douglas Debate: Values in Conflict*. Topeka, Kansas: Clark Publishing.

Winkler, Carol, William Newnam and David Birdsell. *Lines of Argument for Policy Debate*. Madison, WI: Brown and Benchmark Publishers, 1993. College level text.

Wood, Roy V. and Lynn Goodnight. *Strategic Debate*. Lincolnwood, IL: National Textbook Company, 1968. A book designed specifically for the academic debater. Easy to understand.

Using the Library of Congress System, debate books are found starting at PN4180 in your library.

5. LITERATURE

5A. Reading Aloud (Chapters 11, 12, 13, 14)

Bethlehem Books, 15605 County Road Fifteen, Mento, North Dakota, 58261, (800-757-6831). Reprints of classic children's literature. Excellent historical fiction.

Grace and Truth Books, 3406 Summit Boulevard, Sand Springs, Oklahoma, 74063, (918-245-1500) www.graceandtruthbooks.com. This catalog carries numerous reprints of old literature, especially children's literature. Highly recommended.

McGuffey's Readers. Fairfax, VA: Christian School Edition, 1974.

Preston Speed Publications, 51 Ridge Road, Mill Hall, Pennsylvania, 17751, (570-726-7844), www.prestonspeed.com. Publishers of the G.A. Henty series. Paperback and hardback.

Robinson Books G.A. Henty Collection, 99 Books (the complete works) and 53 Short Stories by G. A. Henty with 216 additional Henty era Short Stories on 6 CD-ROMs. Oregon Institute of Science and Medicine, 2251 Dick George Road, Cave Junction, Oregon 97523.

Vision Forum, 32326 Sterling Browning, San Antonio, TX 78232, (800-440-0022), www.visionforum.com. Catalog that offers valuable books for family reading aloud time.

5B. Booklists (Chapters 11, 12, 13, 14)

Bluedorn, Nathaniel. *Hand That Rocks the Cradle: A List of Good Books to Read Aloud to Children*. Trivium Pursuit, PMB 168, 139 Colorado Street, Muscatine, IA 52761. List of classics which our family has read.

Bluedorn, Ava. *Lives in Print: Biographies and Autobiographies*. Trivium Pursuit, PMB 168, 139 Colorado Street, Muscatine, IA 52761. List of biographies and autobiographies.

Hatcher, Carolyn. *Let the Authors Speak*. Joelton, TN: Old Pinnacle Publishing, 1992. A guide to worthy books based on historical setting.

Masterplots, 15-Volume combined edition, 1510 Plot-Stories and Essay-Reviews from the World's Fine Literature, edited by Frank N. Magill, story editor Dayton Kohler, Salem

Press, Inc., New York, 1964. Other editions would be just fine also. Master Plots is a set of books that can be found in most any library's reference section. This set of books is very useful if you want to find out what a book is about – its plot and characters. There is a one page description of most all the classics from all time periods.

McFarlane, Patricia Anne. *Authors, Authors: A Chronological Annotated Bibliography of Authors and Literary Works of Western Literature from Ancient Times Through 1798.* A Word in Season, 17114 Barcelona Drive, Friendswood, TX 77546.

Miller, Christine. *All Through the Ages: A Guide to Experiencing History Through Literature.* Nothing New Press, 1015-M South Taft Hill Road #263, Fort Collins, CO 80521. Extensive compilation of books arranged chronologically and geographically. All ages.

Who Should We Then Read? BooksBloom, Box 877, Cokato, MN 55321, (320-286-5676), www.abebooks.com. This 250 page reference guide contains 140 biographies of authors of great books for children and young adults and alphabetical lists of quality series like Landmarks, "We Were There," Vision Biographies, and Childhood of Famous Americans.

5C. Classics (Chapters 8, 9, 13, 14)

WHERE TO FIND THE ENGLISH TRANSLATIONS OF CLASSICAL GREEK AND LATIN LITERATURE:

1. Large public libraries and college and university libraries carry English translations of the Greek and Latin classics.

The Loeb Classical Library founded by James Loeb, with numerous editors. Cambridge, MA: Harvard University Press, numerous dates. This is a huge set of Greek and Latin classics which has the Greek or Latin on one side of the page and the English on the other side. Greek Volumes, Library of Congress: PA3622-5340. Latin Volumes, Library of Congress: PA6121-6801.

2. Purchase English translations from catalogs:

Greenleaf Press, 3761 Hwy. 109 North, Unit D, Lebanon, TN 37087 (800-311-1508), www.greenleafpress.com. This catalog carries several of the Greek and Latin classics.

Veritas Press, 1250 Belle Meade Dr., Lancaster, PA 17601 (800-922-5082). This catalog carries several of the Greek and Latin classics.

3. There are hundreds of on-line sources for the English translations. Listed below are our favorites:

http://classics.mit.edu The Internet Classics Archive by Daniel C. Stevens–Select from a list of 441 works of classical literature by 59 different authors. Mainly Greco-Roman works (some Chinese and Persian), all in English translation.

http://www.history.mcs.st-and.ac.uk/history The MacTutor History of Mathematics Archive–an integrated collection of over 1000 biographies and historical articles of a mathematical nature.

http://www.fordham.edu/halsall The Internet History Sourcebooks Project by Paul Halsall–collections of public domain and copy-permitted historical texts presented cleanly for educational use. Includes ancient, medieval, and modern history

www.perseus.tufts.edu The Perseus Digital Library

www.ipl.org The Internet Public Library – numerous online texts

www.digital.library.upenn.edu/books The On-Line books Page – search their 12,000+ listings

www.eserver.org Eserver.org – publishes online quality works (30, 180 of them) in arts and humanities

www.ukans.edu/history/VL History Central Catalog

www.ccel.org Classic Christian books in electronic format

www.gutenberg.net Fine literature digitally republished

http://un2sg4.unige.ch/athena/html/athome.html Athena: nearly 10,000 links to books on all subjects.

GREEK AND LATIN CLASSICS MENTIONED IN CHAPTERS 8 AND 9

The History by Herodotus
The History of the Peloponnesian War by Thucydides
Ancient Geography by Strabo
Parallel Lives by Plutarch
Antiquities of the Jews by Josephus
The Roman Antiquities by Dionysius of Halicarnassus
Lives of the Philosophers by Diogenes Laertius
The Constitution of Athens by Aristotle
Aesop's Fables
Select Fragments of poetry by Solon
The Education of Cyrus the Great by Xenophon
The Behistan Inscription of King Darius
The Histories by Polybius
First and Second Tetralogies and selected speeches by Antiphon
Historical Library by Diodorus Siculus
The Persian by Aeschylus
Selected works by Hippocrates (The Oath; On the Sacred Disease; On Airs, Waters, and Places; On Ancient Medicine)
Helenica by Xenophon
The Anabasis by Xenophon
Crito by Plato
Phaedo by Plato
Apology of Socrates by Plato
The Republic by Plato

The Laws by Plato
The Panegyricus by Isocrates
On the Areopagiticus by Isocrates
First Philippic by Demosthenes
To Philip by Isocrates
Letter to Herodotus and Letter to Menoeceus by Epicurus
Third Philippic by Demosthenes
Anabasis of Alexander by Arrian
On the Crown by Demosthenes
selected works by Aristotle
The Early History of Rome by Livy
Republic by Cicero
Natural History by Pliny the Elder

5D. Books Recorded on Tape (Chapter 11)

Audio Book Club, Box 6375, Indianapolis, IN 46206, www.audiobookclub.com

Audio Bookshelf, 174 Prescott Hill Rd., Northport, ME 04849 (800-234-1713), www.audiobookshelf.com.

Blackstone Audio Books, Box 969, Ashland, OR 97520 (800-729-2665), www.blackstoneaudio.com.

Books in Motion, 9922 East Montgomery, Suite 31, Spokane, WA 99206 (800-752-3199), www.booksinmotion.com.

Books on Tape, Box 7900, Newport Beach, CA 92658 (800-88-BOOKS), www.booksontape.com.

Cargo Company, Box 272, Rapid City, SD 57709 (877-744-2565) www.classicsontape.com

Children's Classics Library, Newport Publishers, 912 E. Union St., Pasadena, CA 91106 (800-579-5532).

Jim Hodges Productions, 20601 S.E. 74th Street, Newalla, OK 74857, (405-391-5762). Henty books on tape.

Knowledge Products, The Audio Classics Series, 722 Rundle Avenue, Nashville, TN 37210. (800-876-4332), www.knowledgeproducts.net

Listening Library, One Park Avenue, Old Greenwich, CT 06870 (800-243-4504), www.listeninglib.com/audio.

Orion's Gate, Box 430, Dobbins, CA 95935 (530-692-1124) www.orionsgate.org.

Recorded Books, Inc., 270 Skipjack Road, Prince Frederick, MD 20678 (800-638-1304), www.recordedbooks.com.

Spoken Word Audio Books, 350 Bay Street, Toronto, Ontario M5H 2S6 (888-spo-ken2), www.spoken-word.com.

Vision Forum Audio, 326 Sterling Browning, San Antonio, TX 78232, (800-440-0022), www.visionforum.com.

6. HISTORY

6A. Histories and Textbooks (Chapters 11, 12, 13, 14)

Carson, Clarence B. *A Basic History of the U.S.* (5 volumes). Also available on audio tape. American Textbook Committee, 1720 Mayfair Lane, Alexander City, AL 35010.

D'Aubigne, J.H. Merle. *The History of the Reformation in Europe in the Time of Calvin.*

D'Aubigne, J.H. Merle. *History of the Reformation in the Sixteenth Century.*

Schaff, Philip. *The History of the Christian Church.*

Stanaton, Mary and Albert Hyma. *Streams of Civilization, Volumes One and Two.* Arlington Heights, Illinois: Christian Liberty Press, 1992. Christian Liberty Press, 502 West Euclid Avenue, Arlington Heights, IL 60004.

6B. Reprints of Old History books (Chapters 11, 12, 13, 14)

Christian Liberty Press, 1992. Christian Liberty Press, 502 West Euclid Avenue, Arlington Heights, IL 60004. Reprints of old history readers for children.

Mantle Ministries, 228 Still Ridge, Bulverde, TX 78163, (830-438-3777), www.mantlemin.com. Catalog of reprints of old books, videotapes, and American Heritage Historical Cassettes.

Vision Forum, 326 Sterling Browning, San Antonio, TX 78232, (800-440-0022), www.visionforum.com.

6C. Catalogs (Chapters 11, 12, 13, 14)

Bluestocking Press, Box 2030, Shingle Springs, CA 95682 (800-959-8586). Catalog containing any book about American History you might want.

Dover Publications, 31 East 2nd Street, Mineola, NY 11501 (516-294-7000). Huge catalog including numerous hard-to-find history books.

The Elijah Company, 1053 Eldridge Loop, Crossville, TN 38558 (888-2 ELIJAH). Everything you need in the way of history, from ancient to modern, including lots of historical fiction.

Greenleaf Press, 3761 Hwy. 109 North, Unit D, Lebanon, TN 37087 (800-311-1508), www.greenleafpress.com. Catalog of history resources from ancient to modern.

Mayflower Institute, 201 South Street, Rice Lake, WI 54868, (888-222-2001), www.mayflowerinstitute.org. Books, films, and audio seminars on American History.

Mount Vernon, Mount Vernon, VA 22121. Catalog of materials to make George Washington and the early history of America exciting and meaningful.

WallBuilders, Box 397, Aledo, TX 76008, (817-441-6044), www.wallbuilders.com. Books and videos with non-censored views of America's Christian History.

6D. Primary Sources (Chapters 12, 13, 14)

Bailyn, Bernard, ed. *The Debate on the Constitution: Federalist and Antifederalist Speeches, Articles, and Letters During the Struggle Over Ratification* 2 Volume Set. The Library of America, Literary Classics of the United States, 14 East 60th Street, New York, NY 10022. Primary sources.

Bluedorn, Hans, editor. *That For Which Our Fathers Fought*. Muscatine, IA: Trivium Pursuit, 1994. American history primary sources.

Bluedorn, Hans, editor. *That of Which Our Fathers Spoke*. Muscatine, IA: Trivium Pursuit, 1994. American history primary sources.

Commager, Henry Steele, ed. *Documents of American History*. New York: Appleton-Century-Crofts, Inc., 1948.

Commager, Henry Steele and Richard B. Morris, eds. *The Spirit of 'Seventy-Six: The Story of the American Revolution as told by Participants*. Da Capo Press, Inc., 233 Spring Street New York, NY 10013. This is a large volume of 1352 pages composed almost entirely of primary source material concerning the American Revolution. There are numerous illustrations and maps to accompany the texts. First published in 1958.

Hart, Albert Bushnell. *The Source-Readers in American History*. Includes Colonial Children and Camps, Firesides of the Revolution, How Our Grandfathers Lived, and The Romance of the Civil War. Firsthand narratives, diary entries, personal letters, and patriotic songs and poems. Originally published at the turn of the century and now back in print. For ages 10 to adult. Easy to use with any American history curriculum, the excerpts appear in chronological order by subject. 1331 pages.

Hyneman, Charles S. and Donald S. Lutz, eds. *American Political Writing during the Founding Era1760-1805* – 2 Volumes. Liberty Fund, Inc., 7440 North Shadeland Avenue, Indianapolis, IN 46250. Primary sources.

O'Reilly, Kenin. *Critical Thinking in U.S. History Series*. Trivium Pursuit, PMB 168, 139 Colorodo Street, Muscatine, IA 52761 (309-537-3641). Teaches students how to evaluate primary sources.

Sandoz, Ellis, ed. *Political Sermons of the American Founding Era: 1730-1805*. Liberty Fund, Inc., 7440 North Shadeland Avenue, Indianapolis, IN 46250. "Professor Sandoz has provided a superb collection of sermons bearing on the politics of the era of the American Revolution and the early Republic. He has chosen these sermons carefully and avoided, for the most part, sermons available in modern editions in other collections. He has also provided short, crisp introductions to each sermon and important biographical information about their authors." Robert Middlekauff, The Huntington Library

6E. Timeline Materials (Chapters 9, 11, 12, 13, 14)

Grun, Bernard. *The Timetables of History: A Horizontal Linkage of People and Events* – The world-famous reference that tells who did what when from 4500 B.C. to the present now updated for the 1990's. Based upon Werner Stein's Kulturfahrplan. Simon and

Schuster/Touchstone, Simon and Schuster Building, Rockefeller Center, 1230 Avenue of the Americas, New York, NY 10020. First published in 1946. This is a book you will want to have in your library. It lists what happened for every year in politics, literature, theater, religion, philosophy, learning, visual arts, music, science, technology, growth, and daily life. It is especially useful if you want to use primary sources in your study of history or science. You will find listed the titles of works written by all well known (and lesser known) scientists, historians, and fiction and nonfiction writers.

Hedgerow House Ltd., 36 Tennis Crescent, Toronto, Ontario, Canada M4K 1J3 (800-910-5556). History of the world civilization timeline wall chart.

Hull, Edward. *The Wall Chart of World History*. London: Dorset Press, 1988. This is my favorite timeline.

Reese, Edward. *The Reese Chronological Bible*. Minneapolis, MN: Bethany Fellowship, 1980.

Walton, John H. *Chronological and Background Charts of the Old Testament*. Grand Rapids, MI: Zondervan Publishing, 1994. A book of charts that assembles a wide range of material from the Old Testament.

6F. Geography (Chapters 11, 12, 13, 14)

Guy, Arnold. *Physical Geography*. Palo Cedro, CA: American Christian History Institute, 1988. A reprint of the 1873 edition, grades 7-12.

6G. Miscellaneous

America, the First 350 Years. Steve Wilkins. Covenant Publications, 224 Auburn Avenue, Monroe, LA 71201, (318-323-3061). Audiotape course on American history.

The Famous Monarchs of England Card Game, ages 7+, Published by Trioview Ltd., Heritage Toy and Game Company, made in Belgium. Write to Heritage Games, Box 17, Eastwood, Nottingham, NG16 2XU, UK. A colorful, fun way to learn, in order, the monarchs of England.

Foxe, John. *The Complete Book of Martyrs*.

7. GOVERNMENT, LAW, AND ECONOMICS

(Chapter 14)

Bizzoco, Dennis, editor. *The Exhaustive Concordance to the United States Constitution with Topical Index and Rapid Reference Constitution*, Hardback, 186 pages. Firm Foundation Press, 104 John Arnold Street, Chattanooga, TN 37412, (800-571-7244), www.firmfoundation.com.

Black's Law Dictionary containing definitions of the terms and phrases of American and English jurisprudence, ancient and modern and including the principal terms of international, constitutional, ecclesiastical and commercial law, and medical jurisprudence, with a collection of legal maxims, numerous select titles from the Roman, modern civil,

Scotch, French, Spanish, and Mexican law, and other foreign systems, and a table of abbreviations, by Henry Campbell Black, first published in 1891. Several editions available.

Bluestocking Press, Box 2030, Shingle Springs, CA 95682 (800 959 8586). Catalog containing any book about American history and government you might want.

Carson, Clarence B. *Basic Economics*. American Textbook Committee, 1720 Mayfair Lane, Alexander City, AL 35010.

Carson, Clarence B. *Basic American Government*. American Textbook Committee, 1720 Mayfair Lane, Alexander City, AL 35010.

Cushman, Robert Eugene. *Leading Constitutional Decisions*. New York: F.S. Crofts, 1946.

Equipping a Generation of Christian Statesmen, American Heritage Party, Box 241, Leavenworth, WA 98826 (888 396 6247), ahp@americanheritageparty/org. A comprehensive video library curriculum designed to train individuals and families in the principles and practice of Christian statesmanship. Video teachers R.C. Sproul Jr., Dr. Herb Titus, Daniel Eby, Gary DeMar, James Rose, Dr. Chalres Hull Wolfe, Stephen McDowell. Presents Biblical principles such as sovereignty, authority, stewardship, providence, accountability.

Foundations of Liberty, James R. Patrick, Editor, East Moline Christian School, 900 46th Avenue, East Moline, IL 61244 (309-796-1485). These booklets, covering numerous topics concerning American History and freedom issues, are sent out six times a year.

Haar, Charles M., ed. *The Golden Age of American Law*. New York: George Braziller, 1965.

Hazlitt, Henry. *Economics in One Lesson*. Can purchase from Bluestocking Press, Box 2030, Shingle Springs, CA 95682, (800-959-8586).

Ideas on Liberty. The Foundation for Economic Education, 30 South Broadway, Irvington-on-Hudson, NY 10533 (914-591-7230), www.fee.org. A monthly study journal of free market, private property, limited government ideas and ideals.

Jehle, Paul. *An Overview of Constitutional Law* tape series. Plymouth Rock Foundation, 1120 Long Pond Road, Plymouth, MA 02360, (800-210-1620), www.plymrock.org.

Jehle, Paul. *American Civics and Constitutional Law Course*. Plymouth Rock Foundation, 1120 Long Pond Road, Plymouth, MA 02360, (800-210-1620), www.plymrock.org

Klotter, John C. and Jacqueline R. Kanovitz. *Constitutional Law*. Cincinnati, OH: Anderson Publishing, 1991.

Legal Research. Nolo Press, 950 Parker Street, Berkeley, CA 94710, (800-728-3555), www.nolo.com.

Liberty Tree, 100 Swan Way, Oakland, CA, 94621 (800-927-8733). Catalogue of books, games, audio tapes, video tapes, collectibles dealing with American liberty.

Maybury, Richard. *Uncle Eric's Model of How the World Works* series. Bluestocking Press, Box 2030, Shingle Springs, CA 95682, (800-959-8586).

Nolo's Encyclopedia of Everyday Law. Nolo Press, 950 Parker Street, Berkeley, CA 94710, (800-728-3555), www.nolo.com.

Oak Brook College of Law and Government Policy, Box 26870, Fresno, CA 93729 (559-650-7755), www.obcl.edu. Correspondence law school.

Parsons, Geoffrey. *The Land of Fair Play: A Text-Book of American Civics*. Christian Liberty Press, 502 West Euclid Avenue, Arlington Heights, IL 60004. Ages 10 and up.

Plymouth Rock Foundation, 1120 Long Pond Road, Plymouth, MA 02360, (800-210-1620), www.plymrock.org. Periodicals, special reports, study courses, books, and audio and video cassettes dedicated to a total Christian world and life view and to the rebuilding of the American Republic.

Rutherford, Samuel. *Lex, Rex, or the Law and the Prince*. Harrisonburg: Sprinkle Publications, 1982. Sprinkle Publications, PO Box 355, Bridgewater, VA 22812, www.sprinklepub.com.

Skousen, Cleon. *The Making of America*. Plymouth Rock Foundation, 1120 Long Pond Road, Plymouth, MA 02360, (800-210-1620), www.plymrock.org.

Smith, R.J., editor. *The Factual Guide to the Constitution for the United States of America*. The Eureka Group, 7672 Montgomery Road, Cincinnati, Ohio state, Non Domestic 45356. Table of Contents: Quotations, Outline of the Constitution, Outline of the Articles of Amendment, The Constitution, The Articles of Amendment, Delegates to the 1787 Convention, Ratification Tables, Failed Amendments, Declaration of Independence, Presidential Data, Star-Spangled Banner, Pledge of Allegiance, Anatomy of the Flag, Maps, Glossary.

Sprinkle Publications, PO Box 355, Bridgewater, VA 22812, www.sprinklepub.com. Valuable catalog for history resources. Reprints of old history books.

Stansbury, Arthur J. *Elementary Catechism on the Constitution of the United States*. Ed. William H. Huff. Westminster: Huff, 1993. Purchase from William H. Huff, 12 Carroll Street, #119, Westminster, MD 21157, (410-374-4255), www.lexrex.com. First published in 1828.

The Story of the Constitution. Christian Liberty Press, 502 West Euclid Avenue, Arlington Heights, IL 60004. Ages 10 and up.

Story, Joseph. *A Familiar Exposition of the Constitution of the United States*. Lake Bluff: Regnery Gateway, Inc., 1986.

Titus, Herbert W. *God, Man, and Law: The Biblical Principles*. Oak Brook, IL: Institute for Basic Life Principles, 1994. Introductory course in law. Ages 16 and up.

Upshur, Abel P. and C. Chauncey Burr, eds. *The Federal Government: Its True Nature and Character: Being a Review of Judge Story's Commentaries on the Constitution of the United States*. Houston: St. Thomas Press, 1977.

8. LANGUAGES

8A. Vocabulary Studies Curricula (Chapter 5)

American Classical League, Miami University, Oxford, Ohio 45056, (513-529-7741). Source of numerous Latin/Greek vocabulary studies.

English From the Roots Up by Joejil Lundquist. Literacy Unlimited, PO Box 278, Medina, WA 98039, (425-454-5830), www.literacyunlimited.com. Grades 3-12.

Greek and Latin in English Today by Richard M. Krill. Bolchazy-Carducci Pub, 1000 Brown St., Unit 101, Wauconda, IL 60084.

Rummy Roots (Latin/Greek card game). Eternal Hearts, Box 107 Colville, WA 99114, (507-732-4147).

Spelling Keys to 1001 Words From 10 Latin/Greek Roots by Raymond E. Laurita. Leonardo Press, Box 1326, Camden, ME 04843, (207- 236- 8649)

Vocabulary Bridges From English to Latin and Greek by Harvey Bluedorn. Trivium Pursuit, PMB 168, 139 Colorado Street, Muscatine, Iowa 52761. Ages 10 and up.

Vocabulary From Classical Roots (3 volumes) by Norma Fifer and Nancy Flowers. Educators Publishing Service, Inc., 31 Smith Place, Cambridge, MA 02138, (800-435-7728)

8B. Selected Latin Bibliography (Chapter 5, 11, 12, 13, 14)

Artes Latinae by Waldo Sweet. Bolchazy-Carducci Publishers. Purchase through Trivium Pursuit, PMB 168, 139 Colorado St., Muscatine, IA 52761. Consists of student text, teacher's manual, cassettes, reader, tests; also available on CD ROM. Classical pronunciation. Programmed interactive. This is the Latin curriculum we recommend.

Ecce Romani by Gilbert Lawall and David Tafe. New York: Longman, 1990. Textbooks, student activity books, teacher's handbooks, cassettes. Inductive.

First Year Latin by Charles Jenney Jr. Prentice Hall, 4350 Equity Drive, PO Box 2649, Columbus, OH 43216, (800-848-9500). Consists of student text, teacher's resource book with cassettes, and workbook. Also available 2nd, 3rd, 4th year Latin. Classical Pronunciation. Deductive.

Latin Primer, Books 1, 2, and 3, by Martha Wilson and *Latin Grammar* Book 1, by Douglas Wilson. Canon Press, P.O. Box 8741, Moscow, ID 83843, (800-488-2034), www.canonpress.org. Workbooks plus teacher's manual. Classical pronunciation. Deductive.

The Latin Road to English Grammar by Barbara Beers. Schola Publications, PMB 162, 1698 Market Street, Redding, CA 96001, (530-275-2064), www.thelatinroad.com. Ecclesiastical pronunciation. Deductive.

Latina Christiana I and II, by Cheryl Lowe. Memoria Press, 4103 Bishop Lane, Louisville, KY 40218, (877-862-1097), www.memoriapress.com. Ecclesiastical Pronunciation. Deductive.

Latin's Not So Tough, by Karen Mohs. Greek n' Stuff, PO Box 882, Moline, IL 61266, (309-796-2707), www.greeknstuff.com. Classical pronunciation. Deductive.

Wheelock's Latin, 5th edition by Frederic M. Wheelock. Richard A. LaFleur, Revision Editor. New York: Harper Collins Publishers, Inc. Uses V and macrons, but does not use J. Designed to be used in classrooms with an experienced teacher. At the back of the book it does include Self-Tutorial Exercises with an answer key. Deductive.

8C. Selected Greek Bibliography (Chapters 5, 11, 12, 13, 14)

The Alphabet for Biblical Greek written and illustrated by Johannah Bluedorn. Trivium Pursuit, PMB 168, 139 Colorado Street, Muscatine, Iowa 52761, (309-537-3641), www.triviumpursuit.com. Elementary Greek Alphabet primer; for young children.

Basic Greek in 30 Minutes a Day by Jim Found. Bethany House Publishers, 11400 Hampshire Avenue South, Minneapolis, MN 55438, (800-328-6109), www.bethanyhouse.com. Teaches Greek Vocabulary from English cognates, uses fill-in-with-Greek Scripture quotes. Does not go deeply into Grammar. Deductive, Workbook.

Essentials of New Testament Greek by Ray Summers. Nashville, TN: Broadman Press, 1950. Cloth, 171pp. Good Introductory Grammar. Uses 8 Case System. Deductive.

Greek Alphabetarion by Harvey Bluedorn. Trivium Pursuit, PMB 168, 139 Colorado Street, Muscatine, Iowa 52761, (309-537-3641), www.triviumpursuit.com. Workbook, Audio Tape, Computer Disk, Flash Cards, Banner. Teaches Greek Alphabet and Pronunciation; for all ages. Deductive.

Greek: A Programed Primer by John R. Werner. Presbyterian & Reformed Pub. Co. Binder, 3 Vol., 1236 pages. Teaches BOTH Classical and Biblical Greek. Programmed interactive.

Greek 1. Alpha Omega, 300 North McKerny Ave., Chandler, AZ 85226. Deductive workbook.

Greek I (same as above) by Arthur L. Farstad & Rudolph Moor. Christian Light Education, PO Box 1212-N, Harrisonburg, VA 22801, (540-434-0750), www.christianlightbookstore.com. Paper: 10 Lifepac / Lightunit Booklets; 2 Answer Keys; 1 Test Key; 1 Greek Manual.

Hey, Andrew, Teach Me Some Greek by Karen Mohs. Greek n' Stuff, PO Box 882, Moline, IL 61266, (309-796-2707), www.greeknstuff.com.

Homeschool Greek Vol. I by Harvey Bluedorn. Trivium Pursuit, PMB 168, 139 Colorado Street, Muscatine, Iowa 52761, (309-537-3641), www.triviumpursuit.com. Teaches Greek grammar; for ages 13 and up. Deductive and programmed interactive.

It's Greek to Me! Volume I by Dr. John F. Hart. Hart & Home Publishers, PO Box 807, Chesterton, IN 46304, (219-926-2551). Similar to Found, not as extensive.

New Testament Greek: A Beginning and Intermediate Grammar by James Allen Hewett. Peabody, MA: Hendrickson Publishers, 1986. Cloth, 234 pages. Deductive.

New Testament Greek: Key to Exercises. Paper, 1987, 25 pages. Excellent, thorough grammar.

A Reading Course in Homeric Greek, Book I & II by Raymond V. Schoder & Vincent C. Horrigan. Chicago: Loyola University Press, 1985. Paper, 2 Vol., 340 pages; 312 pages. Teacher's Manual and Key available. Excellent Homeric Greek Grammar. Well illustrated, interesting quotations, word studies. Feeds the mind. Deductive.

Teach Yourself (Classical) Greek by F. Kinchin Smith & T.W. Melluish. Deductive.

Teach Yourself New Testament Greek by R.K. Harrison. Westminster MD: Random House Inc. Paper. Brief but good, economical. Deductive.

8D. Selected Hebrew Bibliography

The Alphabet for Biblical Hebrew written and illustrated by Johannah Bluedorn. Trivium Pursuit, PMB 168, 139 Colorado Street, Muscatine, IA 52761. Elementary Hebrew Alphabet primer for young children.

Behrman House, 11 Edison Place, Springfield, NJ 07081, (800-221-2755), www.behrmanhouse.com. Easy to use Hebrew materials, programmed interactive. These are the materials we would recommend using first.

Biblical Hebrew Step by Step by Menahem Mansoor. Grand Rapids: Baker Book House, 1978. Paperback, 258 pp. Good Introductory Grammar —Simplified. Tapes and Answer Keys available. Deductive.

Classical Hebrew Learning Materials. EKS Publishing Company, 1029A Solano Avenue, Albany, CA 94706, (510-558-9200), www.ekspublishing.com. Simplified materials, Modern Hebrew pronunciation. Publishes numerous Hebrew materials.

Handbook of Biblical Hebrew by William Sanford LaSor. Grand Rapids: Wm B. Eerdman's, 1978. Paper, 3 Vol. in one, 530 pages. Technical, with 80 Two-Page lessons. Extensive Reference Grammar. Inductive.

Hebrew Exercises: A Programmed Approach by Robert I. Vasholz. Grand Rapids: Baker Book House, 1981. Paper, 277 pages. Good supplement to any grammar.

The Learnables. International Linquistics Corporation, 3505 East Red Bridge, Kansas City, MO 64137, (800-237-1830). Hebrew Level I (Book I & 5 tapes). Level II (Book II & 6 tapes). Basic Structures (book & 5 tapes). Conversational Modern Hebrew using pictures and tapes. Inductive.

A Practical Grammar for Classical Hebrew by J. Weingreen. Oxford University Press, 1939. Cloth, 316. Considered a Scholarly Standard. Deductive.

Teach Yourself Biblical Hebrew by R.K. Harrison. Westminster, MD: Random House Inc., 1955. Paperback, 217 pp. Good introductory grammar. Condensed, economical. Deductive.

8E. Other Resources

American Bible Society, 1865 Broadway, NY, NY 10023, (800-32-bible). Publishes a "Scholarly Resources" Catalog includes Greek, Hebrew and Latin, Old & New Testaments.

Audio Forum, 96 Broad Street, Guilford, CT 06437, (800-243-1234), www.audioforum.com. Offers Modern Hebrew and Greek learning tapes. Ancient Greek and Latin pronunciation tapes.

Hebrew is Greek by Joseph Yahuda. Oxford: Becket Publications, 1982. An interesting book which shows the relationship between the Hebrew and the Greek languages.

Home Schooler's Latin Network. Bolchazy-Carducci Publishers, 1000 Brown Street, Unit 101, Wauconda, IL 60084. Homeschool Latin Newsletter.

Moody Bible Institute, 820 North La Salle Drive, Chicago, IL 60610, (800-DL-MOODY), www.moody.edu. Offers Correspondence Courses in Hebrew and Greek.

Trinitarian Bible Society, TBS Canada, 39 Caldwell Cres., Brampton, Ontario L6W 1A2, Canada, (905-454-4688), www.trinitarian.com. Publishes the Greek New Testament text which underlies the King James Version.

Vis-Ed, 581 W. Leffel Ln, Springfield, OH 45501, (800-243-7070), www.vis-ed.com. Offers 1 1/2 X 3 1/2 vocabulary cards for Classical Latin and Greek and Biblical Greek and Hebrew.

8F. Interlinear, Interleaf and Intercolumnar Texts (Chapter 5)

Berry, George Ricker. *The Interlinear Literal Translation of the Hebrew Old Testament: Genesis and Exodus*. Hinds and Noble, 1897; reprint Grand Rapids, Michigan: Kregel, 1970.

Green, Jay P., ed. *Interlinear Greek-English New Testament*. Lafayette, IN: Sovereign Grace Publishers, 1996. Trivium Pursuit, PMB 168, 139 Colorado Street, Muscatine, Iowa 52761, (309-537-3641), www.triviumpursuit.com.

The Loeb Classical Library, founded by James Loeb, with numerous editors, Cambridge, Massachusetts: Harvard University Press, numerous dates (20th century). Earlier editions: London: William Heinemann; New York: B. P. Putnam's Sons. Greek Volumes, Library of Congress: PA3622-5340. Latin Volumes: Library of Congress: PA6121-6801.

JPS Hebrew-English Tanakh, The Traditional Hebrew Text and the New JPS Translation, Philadelphia: The Jewish Publication Society, 2000. This is an intercolumnar text using the Biblia Hebraica Stuttgartensia and the most recent Jewish translation into English.

The Septuagint Version, Greek and English. Grand Rapids: Zondervan Publishing House, n.d. This is a Greek version of the Old Testament, with an accompanying English translation.

8G. Selected Latin texts

LATIN BIBLES:

Biblia Sacra, Londini: Sumptibus Samuelis Bagster et ff., n.d.

Novum Testamentum Latine, Stuttgart: Deutsche Bibelgesellschaft, 1984.

LATIN VERSIONS OF PROTESTANT CONFESSIONS:

Many of these may be found in Philip Schaff's *Creeds of Christendom*. Others are available on the internet. For some, you will need to look in large libraries or interlibrary loans.

Lutheran

1. *Confessio Augustana*, The Augsburg Confession, 1530.
2. *Formula Concordiae*, The Formula of Concord, 1584, German original, 1576.

Reformed

1. *Articuli Sive Conclusiones LXVII Huldrici Zwinglii*, The Sixty-seven Articles or Conclusions of Ulrich Zwingli, 1523, German original, no date.
2. *Theses Bernenses*, The Ten Conclusions of Berne, 1528.

3. *Confessio Helvetica Prior*, The First Helvetic (Swiss) Confession, 1535.
4. *Confessio Helvetica Posterior*, The Second Helvetic (Swiss) Confession, 1566.
5. *Confessio Belgica*, The Belgic Confession, Latin edition revised by the Synod of Dordt, 1619, French original, 1561.
6. *Confessio Fidei Scoticana* I, The First Scotch Confession, 1572, English original 1560, & *Confessio Fidei Scoticana II*, The Second Scotch Confession, no date, English original, 1580.
7. *Articuli XXXIX. Ecclesiae Anglicanae*, The Thirty-nine Articles of Religion of the Church of England, 1563, English edition, 1571, & *Articuli Lambethani*, The Lambeth Articles, 1595.
8. *Canones Synodi Dordrechtanae*, The Canons of the Synod of Dordt, 1618/1619.
9. *Confessio Fidei Westmonasteriensis*, The Westminster Confession of Faith, unofficial Latin version 1656, English original 1647, & *Catechismus Westmonasteriensis Major / Minor*, The Westminster Larger / Shorter Catechism, unofficial Latin version 1656, English original 1647.
10. *Confessio nuper edita Independentium seu Congregationalium in Anglia*, A Declaration of the Faith and Order Owned and Practiced in the Congregational Churches in England, unofficial Latin version 1662, English original, 1658.

A few Latin texts are available on the Internet.

8H. Selected Greek texts

Lightfoot, J.B. and J.R. Harmer, eds. *The Apostolic Fathers*. Grand Rapids: Baker Book House, 1987. The Greek texts and English translations of selected writings of the apostolic fathers.

9. MATHEMATICS

(Chapters 12, 13, 14)

Jacobs, Harold R. *Geometry*. New York: W. H. Freeman and Company, 1987. Comes with answer key and tests. Best geometry text. Self-teaching.

Saxon Publishers, 2450 John Saxon Blvd, Norman, OK 73071, (800-284-7019), www.saxonpub.com. Math textbooks. All grades through Calculus. Self-teaching.

10. LOGIC

10A. Pre-Logic Curricula – Knowledge Level (Chapter 12)

Building Thinking Skills by Sandra Parks and Howard Black. Pacific Grove, CA: Critica Thinking Books and Software, 2000. Can be purchased through Trivium Pursuit PME 168, 139 Colorado Street, Muscatine, Iowa 52761, (309-537-3641) www.triviumpursuit.com.

10B. Logic Curricula – Understanding and Wisdom Levels (Chapters 13, 14)

The Art of Reasoning by David Kelley. W.W. Norton & Company, 500 5th Avenue, New York, New York 10110. Lots of exercises, teacher manual available.

Critical Thinking, Books 1 and 2 by Anita Harnadek. Pacific Grove, CA: Critical Thinking Books and Software, 1998. Can be purchased through Trivium Pursuit PMB 168, 139 Colorado Street, Muscatine, Iowa 52761, (309-537-3641), www.triviumpursuit.com.

Critical Thinking in U. S. History, Volumes 1-4 by Kevin O'Reilly. Pacific Grove, CA: Critical Thinking Books and Software, 1991. Can be purchased through Trivium Pursuit, PMB 168, 139 Colorado Street, Muscatine, Iowa 52761, (309-537-3641), www.triviumpursuit.com.

Introductory Logic by R.C. Sproul (6-60 minute audio tapes). Ligonier Ministries, Box 547500, Orlando, Florida 32854 (800-435-4343).

Introductory Logic video series by Douglas Wilson and James Nance. Canon Press, Box 8729, Moscow, ID 83843 (800-488-2034).

A Rulebook for Arguments by Weston Anthony. Hacker Publishing, Box 44937, Indianapolis, IN 46244.

With Good Reason by Morris S. Engel. St. Martins Press, 345 Park Avenue South, New York, NY 10010.

10C. Other Resources (Chapter 6)

Come Let Us Reason by Norman Geisler and Ronald Brooks. Baker Books, Box 6287, Grand Rapids, MI 49516.

Intermediate Logic by James Nance. Canon Press, Box 8729, Moscow, ID 83843 (800-488-2034).

Introduction to Logic by Leonard Copi. Prentice Hall, Upper Saddle River, NJ 07458.

Introduction to Logic (9 audio tape course) by John W. Robbins. The Trinity Foundation, Box 68, Unicoi, TN 37692 (423-743-0199).

Learning Logic at Home by Nathaniel Bluedorn. Trivium Pursuit, PMB 168, 139 Colorado Street, Muscatine, IA. Reasons to study logic, self-teaching logic books recommended, suggested course of study, suggestions for children and adults, FAQs.

Logic: The Right Use of Reason by Isaac Watts. Soli Deo Gloria Publishers, Box 451, Morgan, PA 15064.

Logic by Gordon H. Clark. The Trinity Foundation, Box 68, Unicoi, TN 37692, (423-743-0199).

Traditional Logic Books 1 and 2 by Martin Cothran. Memoria Press, 4103 Bishop Lane, Louisville, Kentucky, 40218.

WFF in PROOF Games for Thinkers, 1490 South Boulevard, Ann Arbor, MI 48104, (734-665-2269).

11. BIBLE AND THEOLOGY

11A. Bible Study Helps (Chapter 14)

Guideposts Family Topical Concordance to the Bible. New York: Thomas Nelson Publishers, 1982.

Hendricksen, William. *A Survey of the Bible*.

Nelson's Illustrated Bible Dictionary. Herbert Lockyer, Sr., general editor. New York: Thomas Nelson Publishers, 1986. An authoritative one-volume reference work on the Bible, with full-color illustrations.

Smith, Jerome H., ed. *Treasury of Scripture Knowledge*. Nashville, TN: Thomas Nelson Publishers, 1992. Use this book to find a cross-reference for any verse in the Bible.

Strong's Concordance. A concordance is an alphabetical list of words that appear in the Bible, together with the citation for each appearance, and information about the Greek and Hebrew originals.

Wycliffe Bible Encyclopedia (2 volume).

Young's Concordance

Zondervan Pictorial Encyclopedia of the Bible (5 volume).

11B. Family Worship (Chapters 11, 12, 13, 14)

Bluedorn, Harvey, *On Family Worship* pamphlet and audio tape, Trivium Pursuit, PMB 168, 139 Colorado Street, Muscatine, IA 52761 (309) 537-3641, www.triviumpursuit.com.

Gundersen, Dennis. *Your Child's Profession of Faith*. Grace and Truth Books, 3406 Summit Boulevard, Sand Springs, OK 74063, (918-245-1500), www.graceandtruthbooks.com. Catalog containing numerous tapes and books on children and family.

Ptacek, Kerry. *Family Worship*.

Wakefield, Norm. Elijah Ministries, 30063 U.S. Hwy 281 N., PMB 801, Bulverde, TX 78163, (803-980-5606). Audio tapes on all aspects of marriage and family living.

11C. Theology (Chapter 14)

Archer, Gleason. *Encyclopedia of Bible Difficulties*.

Bluedorn, Harvey. *The Biblical Evidence for House Assemblies*. Trivium Pursuit, PMB 168, 139 Colorado Street, Muscatine, Iowa 52761, (309-537-3641), www.triviumpursuit.com.

Bluedorn, Harvey. *Observations on the Order of the Assembly*. Trivium Pursuit, PMB 168, 139 Colorado Street, Muscatine, Iowa 52761, (309-537-3641), www.triviumpursuit.com.

Bluedorn, Harvey. *The Covenantal Allegory*. Trivium Pursuit, PMB 168, 139 Colorado Street, Muscatine, Iowa 52761, (309-537-3641), www.triviumpursuit.com.

Bonar, Horatius. *The Everlasting Righteousness*.

Bridges, Jerry. *The Pursuit of Holiness*.

Bruner, Frederick Dale. *A Theology of the Holy Spirit*.

Buchanan, James. *The Doctrine of Justification*.

Calvin, John. *The Institutes of the Christian Religion*. A systematic theology.

Calvin, John. *Calvin's Commentaries.*

Calvin, John. *Calvin's Calvinism.*

Charnock, Steven. *The Existence and Attributes of God.*

Clark, Gordon H. *The Atonement*. The Trinity Foundation, Box 68, Unicoi, TN 37692 (423-743-0199).

Clark, Gordon H. *Sanctification*. The Trinity Foundation, Box 68, Unicoi, TN 37692 (423-743-0199).

Clark, Gordon H. *The Biblical Doctrine of Man*. The Trinity Foundation, Box 68, Unicoi, TN 37692 (423-743-0199).

Clark, Gordon H. *The Incarnation.* The Trinity Foundation, Box 68, Unicoi, TN 37692 (423-743-0199).

Clark, Gordon H. *God's Hammer: The Bible and Its Critics.* The Trinity Foundation, Box 68, Unicoi, TN 37692 (423-743-0199).

Clark, Gordon H. *Logical Criticisms of Textual Criticism*. The Trinity Foundation, Box 68, Unicoi, TN 37692 (423-743-0199).

Clark, Gordon H. *Predestination*. The Trinity Foundation, Box 68, Unicoi, TN 37692 (423-743-0199).

Clark, Gordon H. *Faith and Saving Faith*. The Trinity Foundation, Box 68, Unicoi, TN 37692 (423-743-0199).

Cunningham, William. *Historical Theology*, Two Volumes.

Cunningham, William. *The Reformers and the Theology of the Reformation.*

Dabney, Robert L. *Discussions*, Five Volumes. Republished by Sprinkle Publications, Harrisonburg, Virginia.

Dabney, Robert L. *Lectures in Systematic Theology.*

Gill, John. *Exposition of the Old Testament and New Testament*. Streamwood, IL: Primitive Baptist Library, 1976. First published in 1810.

Gill, John. *The Cause of God and Truth.*

Gaussen, Louis. *The Divine Inspiration of Scripture.*

Halley, John. *Alleged Discrepancies of the Bible.*

Harris, R. Laird, Gleason L. Archer and Bruce K. Waltke, eds. *Theological Wordbook of the Old Testament,* Volume 1. Chicago: Moody, 1981.

Luther, Martin. *The Bondage of the Will.*

Pickering, Wilbur. *The Identity of the New Testament Text.*

Pink, A.W. *The Sovereignty of God*. Grand Rapids: Baker Book House, 1973. This edition is much better than the Banner of Truth edition.

Pink, A.W. *Profiting From the Word*. London: The Banner of Truth, 1970.

Seeberg, Reinhold. *Textbook of the History of Doctrines*. Grand Rapids: Baker Book House, 1952.

Smeaton, George. *The Doctrine of the Atonement According to the Apostles.*

Smeaton, George. *The Doctrine of the Atonement According to Christ.*

Terry, Milton S. *Biblical Hermeneutics, A Treatise on the Interpretation of the Old and New Testaments.*

Van Bruggen, Jakob. *The Future of the Bible.*

Wallace, Eric. *Uniting Church and Home: A Blueprint for Rebuilding Church Community*. Lorton, VA: Solutions for Integrating Church and Home, 1999.

Warfield, Benjamin. *The Inspiration and Authority of the Bible.*

Warfield, Benjamin. *The Person and Work of Christ.*

Warfield, Benjamin. *Counterfeit Miracles.*

11D. Devotional (Chapter 14)

Henry, Matthew. *The Secret of Communion with God*. London: Marshall, Morgan and Scott, 1964.

Philpot, J.C. *Ears From Harvested Sheaves; or, Daily Portions*. England: Gospel Standard Trust Publications, 1990. First published in 1884. Purchase from Gospel Mission, Inc., PO Box 318, Choteau, MT 59422, (406) 466-2311. Our favorite.

Philpot, J.C. *Through Baca's Vale; or, Daily Words for Zion's Wayfarers*. England: Gospel Standard Trust Publications, 1992. First published in 1893. Purchase from Gospel Mission, Inc., PO Box 318, Choteau, MT 59422, (406) 466-2311. Our favorite.

Steele, Richard. *The Religious Tradesman; or Plain and Serious Hints of Advice for the Tradesman's Prudent and Pious Conduct; From His Entrance into Business, to His Leaving It Off.* Harrisonburg, VA: Sprinkle, 1989. First published in 1747.

11E. Confessions and Catechisms

The Westminster Confession of Faith (Presbyterian). The Trinity Foundation, Box 68, Unicoi, TN 37692 (423-743-0199).

The Westminster Larger and Shorter Catechisms. Free Presbyterian Publications, 1983.

The Savoy Declaration of Faith (Independent). The First Congregational Church, 19 Bridge Street, Millers Falls, MA 01349.

The First London Confession (Baptist). Backus Book Publishers, Box 8274, Rochester, NY 14617.

The Second London Confession (Baptist)

The Baptist Catechism

The Belgic Confession (Reformed)

The Heidelberg Catechism

Beeke, Joel B. and Sinclair B. Ferguson. *Reformed Confessions Harmonized With an Annotated Bibliography of Reformed Doctrinal Works*. Grand Rapids: Baker Books, 1999.

Leith, John H., ed. *Creeds of the Churches: A Reader in Christian Doctrine From the Bible to the Present*. Garden City, NY: Anchor Books, 1963.

Lumpkin, William L. *Baptist Confessions of Faith*. Valley Forge: Judson Press, 1974.

Spurgeon, C.H. *A Catechism with Proofs*. Pilgrim Publications, Box 66, Pasadena, TX 77501.

The Tract Primer. Originally published by the American Tract Society. Christian Communicators Worldwide, 7104 Comanche, North Little Rock, AR 72116.

11F. Catalogs

Christian Literature World (Jay P. Green), Box 4998, Lafayette, IN 47903, (765-429-4122).

Gospel Mission, Inc., PO Box 318, Choteau, MT 59422, (406) 466-2311. Catalog with books by J.C. Philpot, John Bunyan, John Gill, John Owen, and many others.

The Trinity Foundation, Box 68, Unicoi, TN 37692 (423-743-0199).

11G. Bible Versions

King James

New King James

Literal Translation, edited by Jay P. Green. Christian Literature World, Box 4998, Lafayette, IN 47903, (765-429-4122).

Young's Literal Translation

12. PHILOSOPHY

Clark, Gordon H. *William James and John Dewey*. The Trinity Foundation, Box 68, Unicoi, TN 37692 (423-743-0199).

Clark, Gordon H. *Thales to Dewey: A History of Philosophy*. The Trinity Foundation, Box 68, Unicoi, TN 37692 (423-743-0199).

Clark, Gordon H. *Essays on Ethics and Politics*. The Trinity Foundation, Box 68, Unicoi, TN 37692 (423-743-0199).

Clark, Gordon H. *An Introduction to Christian Philosophy*. The Trinity Foundation, Box 68, Unicoi, TN 37692 (423-743-0199).

Clark, Gordon H. *Religion, Reason and Revelation*. The Trinity Foundation, Box 68, Unicoi, TN 37692 (423-743-0199).

Clark, Gordon H. *A Christian View of Men and Things*. The Trinity Foundation, Box 68, Unicoi, TN 37692 (423-743-0199).

Clark, Gordon H. *A Christian Philosophy of Education*. The Trinity Foundation, Box 68, Unicoi, TN 37692 (423-743-0199).

Clark, Gordon H. *Ancient Philosophy*. The Trinity Foundation, Box 68, Unicoi, TN 37692 (423-743-0199).

Clark, Gordon H. *The Philosophy of Science and Belief in God*. The Trinity Foundation, Box 68, Unicoi, TN 37692 (423-743-0199).

Clark, Gordon H. *Three Types of Religious Philosophy*. The Trinity Foundation, Box 68, Unicoi, TN 37692 (423-743-0199).

Gospel Films, Box 455, Muskegon, MI 49443 (231-773-3361). "How Should We Then Live?" 3-video series; "Whatever Happened to the Human Race" 3-video series.

Machen, J. Gresham. *Education, Christianity, and the State*. The Trinity Foundation, Box 68, Unicoi, TN 37692 (423-743-0199).

Noebel, David A. *Understanding the Times*. Summit Ministries, Box 207, Manitou Springs, CO 80829 (719-685-9103), www.summit.org.

Rushdoony, Rousas John. *The Philosophy of the Christian Curriculum*. Valecito, CA: Ross House Books, 1981.

Rushdoony, Rousas John. *The Messianic Character of American Education: Studies in the Philosophy of Education*. Nutley, NJ: The Craig Press, 1972.

Rushdoony, Rousas John. *Intellectual Schizophrenia*. Philadelphia: Presbyterian and Reformed, 1973.

13. SCIENCE

13A. Textbooks (Chapters 13, 14)

Exploring Creation series by Jay Wile. Apologia Educational Ministries, 1106 Meridian Plaza, Suite 220, Anderson, IN 46016 (888-524-4724) www.highschoolscience.com. Best courses in physical science, biology, chemistry, physics, and advanced sciences.

Gray's Anatomy by Henry Gray. There are many editions of this book.

13B. Microscopes and Other Science Equipment

Carolina Catalog of Science and Math (800-334-5551), www.carolina.com. This is a huge catalog (1356 pages) that carries all the equipment you will need to teach science. I purchased several of their live algae and protozoa specimens and was very happy with the service and product.

Home Training Tools, 2827 Buffalo Horn Drive, Laurel, MT 59044, (800-860-6272), www.hometrainingtools.com.

13C. Nature Study (Chapters 11, 12, 13)

Christian Liberty Press, 502 West Euclid Avenue, Arlington Heights, IL 60004. Reprints of old science and nature readers.

Comstock, Anna Botsford. *Handbook of Nature Study*. Ithaca, NY: Comstock Publishing Associates, first published in 1911, numerous reprintings.

The Elijah Company catalog, 1053 Eldridge Loop, Crossville, TN 38558, (888-2 ELIJAH), www.elijahco.com. Valuable articles on studying science and nature.

Holden, Edith. *The Country Diary of An Edwardian Lady*. New York: Holt Rinehart and Winston, 1977. Originally published 1906.

The Peterson Field Guide Series, edited by Roger Tory Peterson. Boston: Houghton Mifflin Company. Field guides on all nature subjects.

Reader's Digest North American Wildlife. Pleasantville, NY: Reader's Digest Association, 1982.

13D. Creation Science (Chapters 11, 12, 13, 14)

Answers in Genesis, PO Box 6330, Florence, KY 41022, (800-778-3390), www.answersingenesis.org. Numerous creation science resources including the magazine *Creation*.

Ken Hovind, 29 Cummings Road, Pensacola, FL 32503, (850-479-DINO), www.drdino.com. Best creation science videos we have seen.

Institute for Creation Research, 10946 Woodside Ave. North, Santee, CA 92071, (800-628-7640), www.icr.org. Numerous creation science resources.

Midwest Creation Fellowship Library-By-Mail, Box 479, Gurnee, IL 60031. Library source for hundreds of science videos.

Unlocking the Mysteries of Creation by Dennis Petersen. Creation Resource Foundation, PO Box 570, El Dorado, CA 95623, (530-626-4447), www.awesomeworks.com. Excellent creation science book. Videos also available.

14. ART AND MUSIC

14A. Art (Chapters 11, 12, 13, 14)

Dover Publications, 31 East 2nd Street, Mineola, NY 11501 (516-294-7000). Huge catalog including numerous hard-to-find history books.

ART CURRICULA

Harter, Jim, ed. *Animals: 1,419 Copyright-Free Illustrations of Mammals, Birds, Fish, Insects, etc., A Pictorial Archive from Nineteenth-Century Sources*. Dover Publications, 31 East 2nd Street, Mineola, NY 11501 (516-294-7000).

14B. Art Appreciation (Chapters 11, 12, 13, 14)

Casey, William C. *Masterpieces in Art*. Christian Liberty Press, 502 West Euclid Avenue, Arlington Heights, IL 60004, (847-259-4444), www.homeschools.org. Art appreciation for children written from a Christian perspective.

Chutter, Frances Elizabeth. *The Art-Literature Readers* (Books 1-3). Our Lady of Victory, 103 East 10th Avenue, Post Falls, ID 83854, (208-773-7265), www.olvs.org. Art-literature readers for grammar stage children.

Gallery: An Art Card Game

Lester, Katherine Morris. *Great Pictures and Their Stories* (9 volumes). New York: Mentzer Bush and Company, 1930. Old art-literature readers for all ages. Beautiful.

Quine, David. *Adventures in Art*. The Cornerstone Curriculum Project, 2006 Flat Creek, Richardson, TX 75080, (972-235-5149), www.cornerstonecurriculum.com. Art appreciation curriculum for all ages.

University Prints, 21 East Street, Winchester, MA 01890, (781-729-8006), www.universityprints.net. The University Prints is a visual archive of some 7,500 art historical subjects. Edited & reviewed by various scholars, this collection surveys virtually every area of western and non-western art history, arts, and architecture spanning prehistoric times to the present. Create your own visual textbook from their catalogue of 300 color and 7,200 black & white, inexpensive illustrations or choose from hundreds of pre-made scholarly sets that illuminate aesthetic and historic topics.

14C. Art Curricula (Chapters 11, 12, 13, 14)

How Great Thou Art Publications, Box 48, McFarlan, NC 28102, (800-982-3729), www.howgreatthouart.com. A wide variety of art curricula.

Visual Manna, PO Box 553, Salem, MO 65560, (888-275-7309), www.rollanet.org/~arthis. Rich and Sharon Jeffus have produced numerous valuable art materials including *Visual Manna's Complete Art Curriculum.*

14D. Music Appreciation (Chapters 11, 12, 13, 14)

Kinscella, Hazel Gertrude. *Kinscella Music Appreciation Readers*. New York: The University Publishing Company, 1928. Old music readers for grammar stage students. Illustrated.

14E. Music Theory (Chapters 13, 14)

Clough, John and Joyce Conley. *Scales, Intervals, Keys, Triads, Rhythm, and Meter: A Self-Instruction Program*. New York: W.W. Norton, 1983. In this text, the procedures of programed instruction are applied to the entire spectrum of basic theory elements so that the beginner can prepare for more advanced work, and the advanced student can review the fundamentals of music theory. Ages 14 and up. Highly recommended.

Clough, John and Joyce Conley. *Basic Harmonic Progressions: A Self-Instruction Program*. New York: W.W. Norton, 1984. In this text, designed to follow *Scales, Intervals, Keys, Triads, Rhythm, and Meter* by the same authors, the procedures of programed instruction are utilized to promote the student's mastery of part-writing fundamentals and understanding of the basic concepts of harmonic progression. Ages 15 and up.

15. MISCELLANEOUS RESOURCES

(Chapter 15)

Adams, Jay E. *Competent to Counsel*.

Adams, Jay E. *Christian Living in the Home*.

Amazon Drygoods and Pickling Works, (800-798-7979). This catalog carries authentic patterns from the past.

Barth, Jeff and Marge Barth. *Old-Fashioned Courtship and How it Works Today*. Middleburg, VT: Parable Publishing, 1998.

Bear, John. *Bear's Guide to Earning Degrees by Distance Learning*. www.degree.net.

College Board CLEP. www.collegeboard.org/clep.

Jehle, Paul. *Dating Vs. Courtship*. Plymouth, MA: The Plymouth Rock Foundation, 1997.

Lazarus Ministries Press, VIP, Box 463, Owensville, Ohio 45160 (513-641-2221). This publishing company specializes in reprinting books and bibles that have been lost to the modern generation. The publisher sees the value in maintaining correct versions of American history and providing exact replica versions of Bibles over 400 years old.

Miller, Natali. *The Pattern of Courtship*. Moscow, ID: Canon Press, 1996.

The Moneychanger, Franklin Sanders, Box 178, Westpoint, TN 38486, (888-218-9226), www.the-moneychanger.com

Phillips, Doug. *Making Wise Decisions About College and Life After Homeschool* audio tape series. Vision Forum, 326 Sterling Browning, San Antonio, TX 78232, (800-440-0022), www.visionforum.com.

The Phyllis Schlafly Report, Box 618, Alton, IL 62002, (618-462-5415), www.eagleforum.org.

PsychoHeresy Awareness Newsletter, 4137 Primavera Rd, Santa Barbara, CA 93110, www.psychoheresy-aware.org.

Schlect, Christopher. *Critique of Modern Youth Ministry*. Moscow, ID: Canon Press, 1995.

Colophon

The scene in oils on the cover
and the chapter title illustrations
are by Johannah Bluedorn.

The illustrations in Chapter One
are by Helena Bluedorn.

The book was designgd
by Nathaniel Bluedorn.

The font used is Bembo (Aldine 401 BT).
The book was printed and bound
by Plus Communications,
St Louis, Missouri.